AC·CESS®
MEXICO

S0-AXU-028

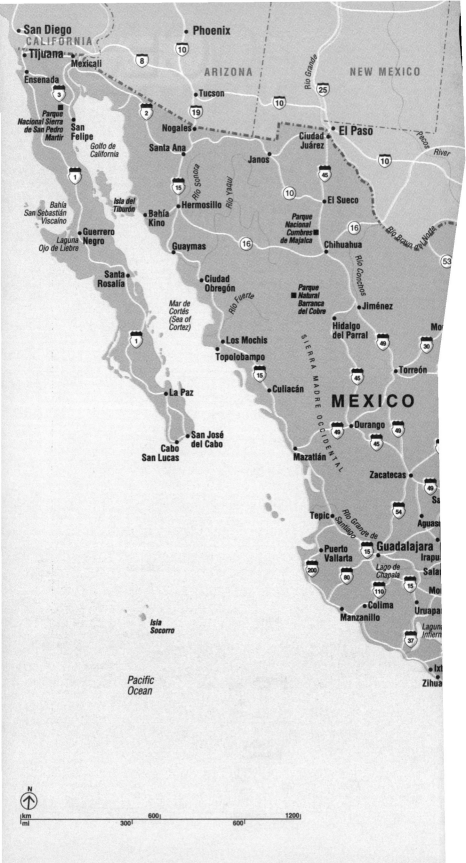

Orientation

Ancient mysteries, magic, and myths shroud the character of Mexico like the soft clouds settling over her volcanoes or the deadly smog smothering her cities. Travelers who try to understand her in a short stay will only scratch the surface—but such visits lure many visitors back to deepen their acquaintance. The country caricatured by some outsiders as the land of mariachis and palms is actually an intriguingly complex blend of old and new, of indigenous and imported cultures, of light-hearted celebrations and serious political issues.

Mexico encompasses 31 states bisected by the **Sierra Madre** mountains, which run from the US border to Guatemala. To the east, the languid **Caribbean Sea** rims the white sands of the **Yucatán Peninsula**, while 1,500 miles west the **Pacific Ocean** pounds the cliffs of the **Baja California Peninsula**. Most Mexicans carry the blood of the Spanish *conquistadores*, live in modern cities and towns, and speak Spanish. But more than 60 indigenous languages are spoken in remote villages where Maya, Aztec, Zapotec, and Mixtec traditions endure.

Such contrasts of nature and culture attract millions of visitors to Mexico each year, much to the federal government's delight. The growth of tourism has been high on the agenda of most presidential administrations since 1974, when an agency dubbed **FONATUR** (National Foundation for Tourism Development) took on the task of transforming huge swaths of jungle and sand into megaresorts. The government focused on the country's most desirable areas along the shores of the Pacific Ocean and the Caribbean Sea. This guidebook follows that lead by offering an in-depth tour of Mexico's most popular coastal resorts, starting at the southern tip of the Baja California Peninsula in **Los Cabos** and moving across the **Gulf of California** to the mainland Pacific coastal destinations of **Mazatlán, Puerto Vallarta, Manzanillo, Ixtapa, Zihuatanejo,** and **Acapulco.** At the far southern section of the Pacific lies the **Oaxacan Coast** and the tropical resorts of **Puerto Escondido** and **Huatulco.**

On the northern side of the **Sierra Madre del Sur** mountains, the city and state of **Veracruz** attract travelers to the **Gulf of Mexico,** bordering the western shores of the Yucatán Peninsula. Like the Pacific Coast, the Yucatán Peninsula contains several distinct destinations. **Mérida,** the capital of the state of Yucatán, is the center of the Maya world, while the resorts of **Cancún, Isla Mujeres, Cozumel,** and the **Quintana Roo Coast** are Caribbean in style and mood, with jungles enveloping Maya ruins.

The country's capital, **Mexico City,** is a destination unto itself. The second-largest city in the world, the capital is a metropolis of some 23 million residents representing the cultures of the country. Built upon the Aztec city of **Tenochtitlán,** Mexico City is filled with world-class museums, restaurants, hotels, and attractions and is a popular stopover on the way to the resorts.

Throughout the 20th century Mexico has raced toward modernity while clinging to her history, with the rights of disparate cultures complicating the struggle for unity. The 1990s have been especially turbulent. The 1993 signing of the North American Free Trade Agreement (NAFTA) between Mexico, the United States, and Canada brought worldwide attention, and when the Zapatista Liberation Force took over the historic city of **San Cristóbal de las Casas** on New Year's Day 1994, Mexicans and the international community saw a different side of the country's indigenous peoples. Since then, unrest has simmered—sometimes boiled—in the ongoing battle to balance the rights of the people with the privileges of the powerful. The assassination of presidential candidate Luis Donaldo Colosio in 1994 further evidenced Mexicans' growing dissatisfaction with the Partido Revolucionario Institucional (PRI), which has ruled the country since 1940. The election of President Ernesto Zedillo Ponce de León later that year ensured the party's rule for another six-year term, but the PRI's standing is shaky at best, especially since the peso devaluation in early 1995. Demonstrations throughout the country have become commonplace, and crime is on the rise. Candidates from opposition political parties have become state governors and federal representatives, and the PRI is beginning to lose its power.

Combined with great natural beauty and visible remains of past cultures, the contrasts and even the conflicts make Mexico an exciting, attractive, and pleasurable destination for travelers from all over the world. Some bask in the Acapulco sun, sipping piña coladas by sapphire-blue pools, while others clamber about the temples of **Tulum,** puzzling over Maya mysteries and gazing at the sea. Naturalists gather sea-turtle eggs under midnight skies, guarding endangered leatherbacks from extinction during annual migrations to Quintana Roo's shores, and snorkelers and divers cruise silently along Cozumel's coral reefs, captivated by eels, groupers, and schools of neon-bright fish. The beaches are no longer the refuge of reclusive travelers: Four-lane highways have replaced dusty dirt roads, and rustic beach huts are dwarfed by big-name hotels. But hideaways do exist on Mexico's soft sand beaches and rugged clifftops. You can still stretch a hammock between two palms at the end of an unmarked trail and watch the sunset. You have to work at avoiding the ever-expanding sybaritic zones of commerce and lavish consumption, but it is still possible to find simplicity, solitude, and a sense of undeveloped space in this vast country. After all, variety is one of Mexico's greatest appeals.

How To Read This Guide

ACCESS® MEXICO is arranged by city so you can see at a glance where you are and what is around you. The numbers next to the entries in the chapters correspond to the numbers on the maps. The text is color-coded according to the kind of place described:

Restaurants/Clubs: Red   **Hotels:** Blue

Shops/ 🍷 **Outdoors:** Green   **Sights/Culture:** Black

Rating the Restaurants and Hotels

The restaurant star rating takes into account the quality of the food, service, atmosphere, and uniqueness of the restaurant. An expensive restaurant doesn't necessarily ensure an enjoyable evening; while a small, relatively unknown spot could have good food, friendly service, and an interesting or scenic setting. Therefore, on a purely subjective basis, stars are used to judge the overall dining value (see star ratings at right). Keep in mind that chefs and owners often change, which can drastically affect the quality of a restaurant. The ratings in this guidebook are based on information available at press time.

The price ratings, categorized at right, apply to restaurants and hotels. These figures describe general price-range relationships among other restaurants and hotels in this book, although readers should keep in mind that prices can vary significantly from one region of Mexico to another. In areas such as Cancún and Los Cabos, very expensive hotels charge $250 and more per night. Other areas, such as Puerto Escondido or Mérida, offer an abundance of rooms in the $30-per-night range. The restaurant price ratings are based on the average cost of an entrée for one person,

excluding tax and tip. Hotel price ratings reflect the base price of a standard room for two people for one night during the peak season.

Restaurants

★	Good
★★	Very Good
★★★	Excellent
★★★★	An Extraordinary Experience
$	The Price Is Right (less than $6)
$$	Reasonable ($6-$12)
$$$	Expensive ($12-$15)
$$$$	Big Bucks ($15 and up)

Hotels

$	The Price Is Right (less than $50)
$$	Reasonable ($50-$100)
$$$	Expensive ($100-$150)
$$$$	Big Bucks ($150 and up)

Map Key

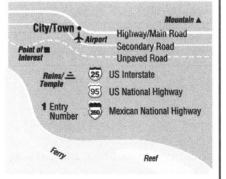

City/Town •	Mountain ▲
✈ Airport	Highway/Main Road
Point of ■ Interest	Secondary Road
	Unpaved Road
Ruins/ ⚲ Temple	25 US Interstate
	95 US National Highway
1 Entry Number	260 Mexican National Highway
Ferry	Reef

To call Mexico from the US, dial 011-52-area code-number.

Getting to Mexico

Airports

Mexico City's **Aeropuerto Internacional de Benito Juárez** (Benito Juárez International Airport) is Mexico's hub, with connections made by numerous international and regional carriers. Connections can also be made in the capital cities of most states and at major coastal resorts. Airports at the coastal resorts are typically single-terminal operations with snack bars, gift shops, and car-rental desks. The airline and car-rental counters may be open only before flights depart and just after they arrive, and airport management offices are virtually nonexistent. Always call airline or car-rental counters before heading to the airport.

For information on other Mexican airports and local telephone numbers for airlines, see the orientation sections of the individual chapters.

Airlines Mexico is served by international and regional airlines. Charter flights have become very common and often are offered in conjunction with reduced rates at hotels. Package deals including airfare and accommodations are also common, especially in Cancún, Los Cabos, Mazatlán, and Puerto Vallarta. Check the ads in newspaper travel sections and talk with your travel agent; the savings can be considerable with such deals. Regional airlines with offices only in Mexico serve some of the country's more out-of-the-way destinations. Mexico's regional airports typically have only one terminal with airline and car-rental counters, currency exchange booths, and snack shops. The airport services are usually open only when flights are arriving and departing. For more information on regional airlines and airports, see the orientation sections of the individual city chapters. Always confirm your flight reservations at least 24 hours before departing from Mexico.

AeroCalifornia	800/237.6225
Aeroméxico	800/237.6639
Alaska Airlines	800/426.0333
American Airlines	800/443.7300
America West	800/235.9292
Aviateca	800/327.9832
Continental	800/525.0280
Delta	800/221.1212
Lacsa	800/225.2272
Mexicana	800/531.7921
Northwest	800/225.2525
Taesa	800/328.2372
United	800/241.6522

Getting to and from Mexican Airports

Airport transportation is controlled by the taxi drivers' union in Mexico. In most places, transportation is provided by *colectivos* (multipassenger vans that stop at hotels along a given route) or private taxis. Taxis typically charge one-third to one-half more than the *colectivos*, but the difference may be worth it because *colectivos* may stop at several hotels before reaching yours. Taxi counters are located near the baggage claim areas; tell the clerk your destination and whether you want to travel by taxi or *colectivo*. After you pay the fare and receive a ticket, give it to the person supervising transportation, who will assign you to a vehicle. When the demand slows down, the taxis disappear, headed to more profitable territory. In most places you must rely on private taxis to return to the airport.

By Car

Drivers bringing cars from the US into Mexico must carry a Temporary Car Importation Permit, available at US border area **AAA** offices or at Mexican Customs offices just inside the border. To receive the permit you must present the following documents: The car's ownership papers, original vehicle registration or car-rental agreement; a notarized letter from the bank or finance company (if the car is leased or financed) stating that you have permission to take the car into Mexico; an insurance policy from a Mexican insurance company to cover the length of your stay (US insurance is not valid in Mexico); a credit card in the same name as the car registration, to be used to cover the processing fee (without a credit card, you may have to pay a bond equal to the value of the car); a valid driver's license; proof of nationality such as a passport or original birth certificate (Hispanic-Americans in particular should carry documentation proving their US residency to avoid trouble leaving Mexico—a passport is best); and a valid Mexican Tourist Card (see "Customs and Immigration" on page 9). US, Canadian, and international drivers' licenses are valid in Mexico.

Mexican auto insurance must be purchased at the border or before crossing it. For more information, contact **Sanborn's Mexico Insurance** (PO Box 310, Department FR, 2009 S 10th St, McAllen, TX 78502, 210/686.0711, 800/222.0158; fax 210/686.0732) or your local **AAA**, both of which provide good road maps of Mexico.

By Bus

Greyhound/Trailways (800/231.2222) has bus service to US border cities; passengers may then walk across the border and continue their travel with Mexican bus companies (see "Buses," page 7).

By Train

Amtrak (800/872.7245) has train service to some US border cities, but only in the border city of **Mexicali** can you shift directly to the Mexican rail system.

Getting Around Mexico

Buses Traveling by bus is one of the best ways to fully experience Mexico, and it's becoming a far more pleasant mode of transportation. Granted, if you're determined to ride with the chickens and pigs, you can do so for a pittance on the agonizingly slow second-class lines that travel to every hamlet and pueblo between two major points. But first-class service is a bargain as well. For a few pesos more you can travel in air-conditioned comfort in an assigned seat with a window. (No matter what class you travel, be sure to carry toilet paper, bottled water, and snacks.) Most major routes are also serviced by luxury motorcoaches with reclining seats, air-conditioning, refreshments, and even music videos or movies on television screens.

In major cities the various bus lines are based either in a central terminal, in separate first- and second-class terminals, or in terminals offering service to and from specific destinations. Schedules are normally posted on the wall, and tickets for the more popular routes are often sold in advance.

Though it's tempting to travel long distances by bus at night, it can be more dangerous than day travel. Mexican highways are usually poorly lighted (if they're lighted at all), and bus drivers, intolerant of slower vehicles in front of them, can be more daring than they should be in passing.

Driving For the most part, driving is a great way to see the countryside and small towns of Mexico, but keep some caveats in mind. First, do not drive in Mexico City if you can avoid it; traffic is horrendous, and most Mexican drivers do not hesitate to assert what they view as their right to be wherever they need to be on the road. Public transportation (buses and a clean if often very crowded subway system) is a much better alternative, although it's also popular with pickpockets and other petty thieves. Avoid driving at night anywhere in the country; in many places the roads are not in good condition, are poorly lighted or unlighted, and are shared with pedestrians, cattle, horses, and dogs. In addition, robbers in remote areas prey on rental cars filled with gringos (don't stop or open your door if someone flags you down in such an area). Talk to the locals before heading off into the hinterlands and take their advice as to the safety of your route. If there has been a recent rash of robberies, consider heading in another direction or driving in a caravan with other vehicles.

If you do drive in Mexico City, keep in mind that sooner or later, you'll have to park the car. Parking is a challenge best avoided by using guarded lots; on-street parking is scarce, and if you do find a place, you're likely to be penned in by double-parked cars. Resort areas normally have plenty of spaces at attractions, hotels, restaurants, and shopping centers. Look for signs designating *No Estacionamiento* (No Parking) zones that list hours when parking is allowed. If you disobey the rules in some places, the police remove the car's license plates, and you must go to the police station to pay a fine before you can get your plates back. Always lock valuables in the trunk of your car whether in a city or at an isolated beach.

Renting a Car Car-rental agencies are located at all tourist centers, but car availability is unreliable. The most common rental car is a manual-transmission VW Beetle; open-air, four-wheel drive, Jeep-type vehicles are also available at many coastal resorts. It is best to reserve your car with a US agency well before your arrival date, especially if you want air-conditioning or a full-size sedan. You can usually get a better rental rate by paying in advance through one of the following companies:

Avis	800/331.1212
Budget	800/527.0700
Dollar	800/800.4000
Hertz	800/654.3131
National	800/328.4567

Note: Most US auto insurance policies do *not* cover rental cars in Mexico. For information on Mexican car insurance and the myriad requirements one must satisfy before driving into Mexico, see "Getting to Mexico By Car," above. For information on road signs and conditions, see "In the Driver's Seat" (page 8).

Ferries Passenger and car ferries travel between Cancún and Isla Mujeres, and between **Playa del Carmen, Puerto Morelos,** and Cozumel on the Caribbean side of Mexico. The ferries, run by private companies, usually are well equipped with life jackets, seats, and safety equipment. See the "Isla Mujeres" and "Cozumel" chapters for additional details.

Taxis The first and most important rule for using Mexican taxis is to confirm the price of your ride *before* the cab starts moving. If language is a problem, have the driver write the amount on a piece of paper in new pesos or dollars. Rates are regulated in many tourist areas, and hotels post the prices for the most common destinations. Mexico City cabs have meters, which simplifies matters unless the driver insists the meter is broken. Even if the driver says the meter is working, it's usually prudent, before getting in the cab, to ask the driver how much the trip will cost. Hotel bellmen may also be able to tell you in advance about what the fare should be. In addition to being inexpensive and convenient for travel within a given city, taxis are ideal for getting to and from sights such as ruins and isolated beaches, especially if you can converse with the driver. Some will charge an hourly rate to transport travelers from one attraction to the next and are sure to offer unusual observations and tidbits of gossip (some of which may even be true) that you wouldn't get on a more "official" tour.

It is considered rude for residents of the United States to refer to themselves as Americans when talking with Mexicans. *Estadounidense* ("from the United States") is the proper, albeit unwieldy, term.

In the Driver's Seat

If you want to rent a car for a journey into the hinterlands, drive during the daylight hours, lest you wind up hitting a stray cow or horse or a truck driver whose headlights have burned out (a more common occurence than you might think). Always fill up the gas tank whenever you see a station; although modern facilities are popping up all over the country, you can't always be guaranteed there will be anything in those gleaming new tanks. And do your best to avoid driving in overly congested **Mexico City**—it could end up creating the biggest headache of your trip.

NO PARKING

As for the rules of the road, forget nearly everything you practice at home. Cars, buses, and trucks will pass you on the right or left, whichever is easiest. Bus drivers are particularly fond of passing three or four cars in a row while rounding a blind curve on a mountain pass; it adds a certain machismo to their style. Don't try to match their bravado.

Signals from other drivers' headlights and taillights can be quite confounding at first. If the left blinker starts flashing on the slow-moving truck ahead of you, the driver may be signaling that it's safe for you to pass him on the left. Or he may be passing an even slower truck ahead of him, turning onto a well-hidden side road, or just greeting a fellow trucker headed toward you.

NO REBASE

NO PASSING

The increased number of tourists driving on country roads has created a rash of accidents, most involving confusion over the use of the left blinker. If turning left off a country road, use your right blinker, pull onto the right shoulder, watch for traffic, and cross both lanes when clear. If you use your left signal, the drivers behind you may assume they are clear to pass you, and would broadside your car as you turn.

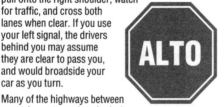

STOP

Many of the highways between coastal resorts, archaeological sites, and other tourist attractions pass through small towns and villages where children, roosters, pigs, and dogs often roam the streets. To discourage speeding, most towns have *topes* (speed bumps) or *vibradores* (a series of bumps in the road) designed to obliterate the suspension system of any vehicle traveling faster than three miles per hour. Highway *topes* generally are paved ridges or bumps in the road, but in remote areas you may run into a row of large rocks or a

length of thick rope lying in the sand. Keep an eye out for signs that say *"Disminuya su velocidad"* (Lower your speed), or those with drawings of a row of bumps. And remember, not all *topes* come with warning signs.

The highways are patrolled by the *Angeles Verdes* (Green Angels), a fleet of vehicle-assistance trucks bearing gasoline, tools, and uniformed drivers who usually speak some English and greet each new breakdown as a challenge to their resourcefulness. In small towns, people are extremely helpful and resourceful in at least temporarily remedying your problem.

If you have any spirit of adventure, you will eventually turn down a rutted dirt road that just might lead to a spectacular hidden cove or buried temple. Since the temptation to do so is irresistible, always carry a bottle of drinking water, mosquito repellent, a dependable spare tire, and an infinite measure of patience. If you break down, someone is bound to come along eventually and help, unless you're on the proverbial road to nowhere. Use common sense about going down these alluring back roads, especially in the rainy season.

TRAFFIC CIRCLE

In the cities, the *glorietas* (traffic circles) are the driver's greatest challenge. Your best bet is to

CONSERVE SU DERECHA

USE RIGHT LANE

wrangle your way between two cars headed in roughly the same direction as you, and move when they do. Don't fret about which way to go; just stay on the circle until you figure your way out. Nearly everyone you ask will give you directions, regardless of whether they know the way. They're simply being polite. Ask two or three people and maybe you'll get a logical consensus and a vague sense of direction. In many areas directional signs and street names are rare and wondrous surprises. Again, just keep going around in circles or squares, asking *"¿dónde está. . . ?"* (where is. . . ?)

Signs with international symbols for common road conditions and warnings are starting to appear along major thoroughfares, but it helps to know a few Spanish words such as *alto* (stop), *peligroso* (dangerous), *cuidado* (watch out), and *despacio* (slow). A *derrumbe* is a rockslide or earthquake zone; a *vado* is a gully or arroyo; a *puente* is a bridge. Most rental-car companies will give you a list of road sign translations and maps for the areas you plan to visit.

LIMITE

PARKING LIMIT

Tours Tour operators tend to specialize in certain areas of Mexico or in particular types of activities. Most package tours go to beach resorts, colonial cities, or archaeological sites. The Mexico City–based **Mexican Association of Adventure Travel and Ecotourism** (5/661.9121; fax 5/662.7354) publishes a booklet on adventure tour operators within Mexico. The following US-based companies offer specialized tours to Mexico:

Armadillo Tours 800/284.5678

Backroads 800/537.4025

Friendly Holidays 800/221.9748

Mexico Trails 800/487.4783

Sanborn Tours 800/315.8482

Solar Tours 800/338.7652

Tauck Tours 800/468.2825

Trains Although trains travel throughout much of Mexico, they vary considerably in comfort and safety. Major routes from Mexico City usually offer a first-class section, where attendants keep the car relatively clean and serve refreshments. But in other parts of the country first class can range from fairly comfortable to totally horrid, depending on the condition of the train and the number of passengers. On long trips the train may be clean at the beginning of your journey, but conditions can rapidly deteriorate as you proceed; the rest rooms are particularly dreadful after a few hours—carry your own toilet paper and practice holding your breath. And unless you are an absolute masochist, forget about second class. The ultimate in comfort are the private sleeping compartments—definitely worth the extra cost on long trips.

For more information on schedules and fares, contact **Ferrocarriles Nacionales de Mexico** (National Railways of Mexico; Terminal Buenavista, Mexico City, DF 06358, 5/547.8972).

Walking Walking is the best way to explore most Mexican cities and coastal areas. People stroll everywhere and rarely rush from place to place. When trying to make your way through a crowd, say *"Con permiso"* (with permission; excuse me).

FYI

Accommodations Tourism is highest at Mexico's coastal resorts during US and Mexican holiday times, especially Christmas and Easter (*Semana Santa* or Holy Week). Tourism peaks again in August, when Mexican nationals and Europeans fill the resort areas. Advance reservations are essential at those times. Major hotel chains with US toll-free reservation numbers have properties in the major cities and coastal resorts, with predictable rooms and services. For information, contact:

Mexico Resorts International 800/262.2656

UTELL International 800/44U.TELL

One of Mexico's greatest pleasures is its abundance of one-of-a-kind hotels, from beach bungalows to historic haciendas turned into luxurious inns. In the past, guests had to call Mexico to make reservations, an often frustrating and expensive task. Many of the smaller properties now have fax numbers and accept credit card deposits for reservations. The fax line, however, may be the same as the phone number, and you must ask the clerk to turn on the fax *("Darme el tono por fax, por favor")*. Several travel agencies in the US specialize in Mexico's smaller properties; for information, contact:

Alexander and Associates 800/221.6509

Jarvenin and Associates 800/876.5278

Robert Reid and Associates 800/228.6510

Climate Mexico's Pacific and Caribbean coasts are both ideal winter getaways, with little or no rain, air temperatures hovering in the 70s to 90s, and water temperatures in the 60s or above. Both the air and water become warmer the farther south you travel along the Pacific coast; it can be downright chilly in Mazatlán in January, yet hot enough for a sunburn in Acapulco. Los Cabos, at the tip of the Baja California Peninsula, is best in the fall and spring, as it gets windy and cold in January and February and unbearably hot from July through September. The Caribbean is at its best from November through May; the rains and subsequent humidity build through the summer months, and September and October are hurricane season. The air in Veracruz tends to be more humid than in the other coastal resorts, and high winds are common in the winter. The high altitude makes Mexico City cool from December through February and rainy from June through September. The best time to visit the capital city is in the autumn or spring, when it's warm and dry, although the rain does clear some pollution from the air.

Customs and Immigration Visitors to Mexico are issued a Mexican Tourist Card upon entering the country. You must have a passport or an original birth certificate as well as a photo ID to prove your nationality—a driver's license alone will not suffice. The customs official gives you one copy of the tourist card (actually a flimsy piece of paper); guard it carefully, since replacing it can be an absolute nightmare. Your copy will be collected when you leave Mexico, and you'll need a passport or birth certificate to pass through US Customs on the way home. You are allowed to bring $400 in purchases, one liter of alcohol, and one carton of cigarettes from Mexico into the US every 30 days. Some products may not be brought into the US at all, such as Cuban cigars and black-coral items.

Travelers under the age of 18 unaccompanied by parents or guardians must have a notarized affidavit signed by both parents or their legal guardian granting permission for them to travel in Mexico. This law is occasionally enforced by the customs guards in border towns frequented by teenagers in search of a good time.

Dress Shorts, T-shirts, and bathing suit coverups are acceptable at the coastal resorts, but this kind of attire is generally frowned upon in Mexico City and in small, conservative towns. Respect local customs and don't wear shorts, tank tops, or halter tops in churches. Men rarely need a full suit and tie unless attending a very formal event.

Drinking Tequila and beer are to Mexico what wine is to France—national beverages that accompany nearly every meal or social occasion. Tequila can be as rough as firewater or as smooth as sherry; drink cheap tequila and you'll regret it for days. Be wary of free margaritas served at Happy Hours or on boat tours. They're normally made with the cheapest tequila around—if you feel a stabbing pain in your temples after a few sips, switch to mineral water or beer.

Several great beers are brewed in different regions of the country; in the Yucatán try Negro Modelo, León Negra, or Montejo. Wineries in Baja California produce respectable table wines that are much cheaper than imported wines. Imported liquors such as scotch, whiskey, and gin are extremely expensive.

The legal drinking age in Mexico is 18.

Embassies The following English-speaking countries maintain embassies in Mexico City:

Australia 5/531.5225
Canada 5/724.7900
New Zealand 5/281.5486
UK..5/207.2449
US..5/211.0042

For information on foreign embassies and consulates elsewhere in Mexico, see the orientation sections of the individual city chapters.

Health and Medical Care Nothing destroys a vacation more effectively than a bout of *turista;* the diarrhea, nausea, vomiting, and chills can pass in a few hours or linger for days, causing serious health problems. To avoid this dreaded malady, as well as intestinal bacteria and cholera, be careful about what you eat and drink.

Water is the number one culprit. To be completely safe, drink only bottled water sold in sealed containers. In most of the tourist resorts, the hotels have water purification systems and post signs in bathrooms stating that the water is safe to drink *(aqua potable)*. Some hotels provide complimentary bottled drinking water. In restaurants, order *agua purificada* (purified water) or *agua mineral* (mineral water), both *sin hielo* (without ice, which may not be made with purified water) and outside of tourist hotels and restaurants, stay away from salads, uncooked vegetables, and uncooked meats and fish (such as ceviche or sushi). Don't be tempted by the aroma of food sold by street vendors.

If *turista* attacks, drink lots of purified water, eat bland foods, and rest until the symptoms pass. Use medications cautiously; some stop diarrhea so effectively they seal harmful germs in your system, which can cause serious complications. If diarrhea lasts longer than 24 hours, consult a doctor.

Before traveling to Mexico, it's a good idea to get a tetanus booster shot if you haven't had one in the past 10 years. Other inoculations are not required. However, consider the hepatitis vaccine now available, especially if visiting during the hurricane season, when water can get polluted.

Most of the hotels in tourist regions have English-speaking doctors on call for emergencies, and embassies usually have lists of doctors and dentists who are accustomed to assisting travelers. Pharmacists in Mexico are also a valuable resource for minor medical problems and can dispense many drugs without a prescription. Be cautious when taking any drugs, and use only the prescribed dosage; stop taking the medication if you notice any side effects. In the event of a serious accident or illness, you can get emergency air transport from Mexico to the US through **Aeromedical Group** (see "Phone Book," on page 12).

Hours Opening and closing times for shops and attractions in this book are listed only by day(s) if they open between 8 and 11AM and close between 5 and 9PM. Many shops, especially in small towns, close from 1 or 2PM until 4 or 5PM. In all other cases, specific hours will be given (e.g., 6AM-2PM, daily 24 hours, noon-5PM).

Language Though Spanish is Mexico's native tongue, in resorts most Mexicans speak "Spanglish," a mix of Spanish and English that facilitates communication on both sides. Many educated Mexicans speak reasonable English. In smaller towns and around the archaeological sites, residents may speak one of 50 or more Indian dialects, but if they deal with tourists frequently they'll know a smattering of Spanish as well. Also see "¿Habla Español?" on page 224.

Money Mexico's currency is the new peso, or NP, written "N$" on price tags and signs. New peso coins come in denominations of 10, 20, and 50 centavos, and 1, 2, 5, and 10 new pesos. The coins are a bit confusing at first, and it's easy to forget their value. Save those in the lower denominations for tips to children who bag your groceries. Bills come in denominations of 10, 20, 50, and 100 new pesos. Always keep a stash of small bills and coins, as change is often hard to come by. US dollars are used as commonly as new pesos in many resort areas. Be sure to check whether a price marked with a $ is in new pesos or dollars.

Traveler's checks usually can be exchanged for new pesos at bank branches in major airports and at large banks in the cities. However, most banks have limited hours for exchanging money, usually between 10AM and noon on weekdays. Some banks will ask to see your passport or tourist card. Hotels will usually exchange traveler's checks, though the rate of exchange may be worse than at the banks. *Casas de cambio* (exchange houses) are common in tourist zones, and their rates may differ from each other and be slightly better or worse than a bank's. Always change traveler's checks on weekdays, and don't expect to be able to do so in small towns or at archaeological sites. Carry traveler's checks in denominations no larger than $50, and keep a few $20 checks on hand for times when change is scarce.

MasterCard and Visa cards are accepted at many first-class hotels and restaurants; American Express cards are less frequently accepted. You may be charged an additional fee for using your credit card in some Mexican shops. Cash machines using international systems (such as Star or Cirrus) are available in large resort areas and in Mexico City; check with your bank or credit card company for a list of machines and instructions on how to use them.

Personal Safety Though crime has increased since the devaluation of the peso in 1994, Mexico is no more dangerous for the average traveler than the US. Take the same safety precautions in Mexico City that you would in Manhattan: Don't walk alone at night except in heavily trafficked areas such as the **Zona Rosa;** only use licensed taxis and stay alert in the metro and on buses; and lock your valuables and passport in your hotel safe or keep them with you in a protected place, such as a money belt. Most coastal resorts are very safe; you're in more danger of being hustled than being robbed outright. Be cautious with street vendors and impromptu tour guides. The easiest way to get in trouble is to overindulge in alcohol and stumble around bars, discos, and streets in a stupor. And stay far, far away from illegal drugs—this is a country that takes drug abuse and transportation of drugs extremely seriously, and you don't want to spend the night, or the rest of your life, in a Mexican jail.

Travel to remote areas has become more dangerous since the devaluation; small gangs of robbers sometimes set up roadblocks on remote highways and back roads. Try to caravan with other drivers so you're not stranded if something happens, and absolutely do not drive at night in unpopulated areas.

Publications English-language newspapers (including the *Miami Herald, The New York Times,* and *USA Today*) are available in hotel gift shops in large resort areas, as are magazines such as *Newsweek, Time,* and *People. The News,* an English-language daily paper published in Mexico City, is also commonly available at resorts and carries international news stories, editorials, comics, and columns from US sources.

The bilingual monthly magazine *Mexico Desconocidos* (Unknown Mexico) is published in Mexico City and is a valuable resource for travelers in search of off-the-beaten-path adventures. *Artes de Mexico* is a handsome quarterly magazine with articles in Spanish and English and gorgeous photographs. The Mexican edition of *Vogue* is worth a look, even if you can't read a word of Spanish.

Rest Rooms Public bathrooms can be difficult to find in cities and towns. When touring, you're best off using the facilities in hotels and restaurants. Rest rooms in airports, bus stations, and gas stations run the gamut from marble stalls with doors, toilet-paper dispensers, and flush toilets with seats to simple outhouses. Plumbing is primitive in some places, and a wastebasket is often set next to the toilet for toilet paper, which would clog the pipes if disposed of in the usual way. Signs are usually posted in the stalls asking you to use either the bucket or the bowl. Toilet paper is sometimes nonexistent or coarse; get in the habit of carrying a packet of tissues (or a roll of toilet paper) wherever you go.

Restaurants Dress is casual in most coastal resort restaurants; men are only required to wear suits in the most formal Mexico City restaurants. Reservations are rarely required or even accepted in the tourist areas. See "Beyond Your Basic Bean Burrito" (page 189) for a glossary of common Mexican dishes.

Shopping Closing shop for the afternoon siesta is still an honored tradition throughout much of rural Mexico, but it's a waning practice in the cities and resorts. Many large stores and businesses now stay open from 9AM to 7PM. Smaller shops and galleries and stores in small towns are usually open from 8 or 9AM to 2PM, and 4PM to 7 or 8PM, give or take an hour or two in either direction.

Smoking Cigarette smoke permeates the air in most restaurants and bars, but smoking has largely been banned from buses and trains. Tourist restaurants at the resorts sometimes have no-smoking sections, though these are the exception rather than the rule.

Street Signs Street signs are still a novelty in many parts of Mexico, which can greatly hamper tourists accustomed to clear directions. The actual street address in some area may not be used very much; it's not uncommon to ask a business owner for the street address of his business only to receive a blank stare in response. Most Mexicans want to be helpful and have been known to give encouraging directions even if they don't know how to get to where you want to go ("Keep going on this road, you can't miss it.") rather than appear discourteous by failing to help. Always ask for landmarks when getting directions, and always ask more than one person. Streets often have lengthy names based on historical events or figures, which are abbreviated for everyday use.

Taxes A 15-percent value-added tax called *Impuesto de valor agregado (IVA)* is added to all goods and services, including hotel rooms and rental cars. In some resort areas, a 2-percent hotel tax is also charged. Be sure to ask if the tax is included in the quoted price or added to the final bill; in restaurants the tax is usually included in the price on the menu.

Telephones Phone calls to, within, and from Mexico are inordinately expensive, and long-distance operators can be difficult to contact. The least expensive way to make international calls from

Mexico is to call collect. Credit card calls cost a bit more, and direct calls are the most expensive. Many hotels tack an additional service charge onto both your local and long-distance calls; ask about the fee before you begin dialing. Some hotels now have direct access to international operators from their guest rooms, yet still add a service charge.

Public pay phones take a 10-centavo coin, as do the new LADATEL phones that have made long-distance calling less expensive. To dial direct from a LADATEL phone, insert a 10-centavo coin and punch the country code and area code for the city (for example, 001/619 for the US and San Diego). The charge per minute will flash on the LCD window. You'll need a walletful of coins to make your call, and you may still have to wait a while for a long-distance operator, but at least you'll bypass the hotel's service fee. You can purchase prepaid phone cards, available in several denominations, at many pharmacies and small markets. AT&T Direct service allows you to contact a US long-distance operator for collect and credit card calls; to reach the operator from a push-button phone push **01; no coins are necessary.

☎ To call Mexico from the US, dial 011–52–area code–number.

☎ To call the US from Mexico, dial 001–area code–number.

☎ To call long distance within Mexico, dial 01–area code–number.

In recent years telephone area codes have been changing in Mexico, often without notice. Local numbers change frequently as well. In some places, three-digit area codes have been changed to two digits, with the third digit added to the local number. For example, the area code in Cancún used to be 988, followed by a five-digit local number. The area code is now 98, followed by a six-digit local number beginning with 8. Hotel operators are invaluable when the numbers are in transition; telephone company operators are virtually useless. Telephone directories are not always helpful either, particularly if you're trying to reach an individual; the names under which the telephone is listed don't change necessarily when the occupants of the house do.

Time Zones Most of Mexico is on Central Standard Time, although some western states are on Mountain Standard Time; consult individual chapters for details.

Daylight Saving Time was instituted in 1996, and the time changes correspond with those in the US.

Tipping Traditionally, Mexican taxi drivers have not expected tips, but in the busy tourist areas these days, they'll give you a scornful look if they don't get one. If the driver has been particularly helpful or has lugged your bags around, add 10 percent to the fare. Bell captains get the equivalent of 50¢ per bag—more if the service warrants it. Housekeepers (who are normally paid abysmally) get 50¢ per day; waiters expect a 10-percent tip but welcome 15 percent.

Closely related to the tip is the *mordida* (bribe), which can greatly facilitate negotiations with Mexican officials in various capacities. Federal, state, and local governments try to limit the use of *mordidas* in tourist areas and caution police officers, in particular, to refrain from soliciting bribes from tourists. A note of caution: Although common, this practice is illegal and requires some familiarity with the culture and the language to carry out. You may conceivably offer a sum of money and find yourself confronted with an indignant and honest official who doesn't take kindly to the implication that he can be bribed. If you think you're in a situation that warrants a furtive exchange of cash, and your Spanish is good enough, ask diplomatically how much the fine or fee is for your infraction, then negotiate a sum with the official. Authorities in many areas are now asking tourists to please insist upon going to the police station to pay fines in an attempt to decrease *mordida* scams.

Visitors' Information The **Mexican Tourist Office**'s toll-free number in the US (800/482.9832) will connect you to their Mexico City branch. The helpful bilingual staff there can provide information on Mexico City and other areas of the country.

Phone Book

Aeromedical Group
.................619/278.3822 in San Diego, California,
..............954/772.0003 in Fort Lauderdale, Florida,
....800/010.0986 in Mexico.

Tourist Help Line (24 hours)
..................................5/250.0150 in Mexico City,
......5/525.9380 or 5/525.9384 for legal assistance

US State Department Citizens' Emergency Center Hotline
....202/647.5225

Mexico's Famous Feasts and Festivals ✦

Holidays are celebrated with extreme fervor and passion in Mexico, where any occasion is an excuse for parties, parades, and fireworks. In addition to the national religious and political holidays, all towns celebrate the feast of their patron saint. Most celebrations occur at night, starting with a parade past the main plaza and followed by parties and dances that last until dawn. Foods traditional to the area are sold from carts and stands around the plaza. Banks, post offices, businesses, and stores are closed on national holidays, though in resort areas some shops and tourist-oriented businesses stay open or have abbreviated hours.

January

Año Nuevo (New Year's Day, 1 January) is a national holiday.

Día de los Reyes (Feast of the Epiphany, 6 January) is the day Mexican children receive gifts from the Three Kings who visited the Christ child.

Fiesta de San Antonio (Feast of St. Anthony, 17 January) is observed with the blessing of livestock and pets.

February

Día de la Constitución (5 February), a national holiday, commemorates the signing of Mexico's Constitution on this day in 1917.

Día de la Bandera (24 February) is Mexico's Flag Day.

Carnival is celebrated throughout Mexico during February or March, most notably in **Veracruz, Mérida, Cozumel,** and **Mazatlán.**

March

Fiesta de Benito Juárez (21 March), the birthday of President Benito Juárez, Mexico's first Indian head of state, is a national holiday.

March/April

Semana Santa (Holy Week), which leads up to **Easter Sunday**, is observed throughout the country with special Passion Plays reenacting Christ's last days. **Good Friday** and **Holy Saturday** are national holidays.

May

Día de Trabajo (Labor Day, 1 May) is a national holiday. Workers, many of whom are union members, take the day off and participate in parades and fiestas.

Cinco de Mayo (5 May) is commonly thought of by foreigners as Mexico's Independence Day. Actually, it marks the anniversary of Mexico's defeat of the French in **Puebla** in 1862 and is a national holiday.

Día de las Madres (Mother's Day, 10 May) is celebrated with long, leisurely family lunches and dinners and is essentially a national holiday.

June

Día de Naval (Navy Day, 1 June) is celebrated in most port cities, including **Acapulco** and **Manzanillo.**

Fiesta de Corpus Christi (Feast of Corpus Christi, 66 days after Easter) is marked throughout Mexico with parades and fiestas. In **Mexico City** children are blessed at the **Catedral Metropolitana** (Metropolitan Cathedral).

Fiesta de San Juan el Bautista (Feast of St. John the Baptist, 24 June) is a national holiday. It's celebrated with parades and fiestas throughout the country, especially in towns where the parish church is named after the saint.

July

Fiesta del Virgen de la Carmen (Feast of the Virgin of Carmen, 16 July) is marked by fireworks, fairs, bullfights, and fishing competitions.

Fiesta de Santiago (Feast of St. James, late July) is a national holiday celebrated with *charreadas* (Mexican-style rodeos).

August

Fiesta de Asunción de la Virgen María (Feast of the Assumption of the Virgin Mary, 15 August) is observed with various religious processions.

September

Informe Presidencial (1 September) is the day the president gives his annual address to Congress; it's also a national holiday.

Día de la Independencia (Independence Day) is riotously celebrated on two days (15-16 September) with fireworks and parades. In Mexico City, buildings around the **Zócalo** (town square) are strung with red, green, and white lights, and huge portraits of national heroes are made from hundreds of lightbulbs in a wire frame. Thousands of people jam the Zócalo on the night of the 15th for the president's annual *grito* (shout) from the **Palacio Nacional** (National Palace). The *grito* replicates the cry of Father Miguel Hidalgo, who, in 1810, encouraged the war for independence from Spain by calling for freedom from the pulpit of his church in **Dolores Hidalgo, Guanajuato.** On the 16th, a national holiday, a military parade draws thousands of onlookers to **Monumento de la Independencia** (Independence Monument).

October

Día de la Raza (Day of the Race, 12 October) is a national holiday commemorating Columbus's arrival in the Americas and the blending of races within Mexico.

November

Días de los Muertos (Days of the Dead, 1-2 November)—known in the US as **All Saints'** and **All Souls' Days**—are national holidays in Mexico. Deceased children are honored on the first, adults on the second. Altars to the dead are set up in homes and cemeteries; photographs of the departed are surrounded with flowers (especially marigolds), candles, and their favorite foods and beverages. The smell of copal incense fills the air, and candies and breads shaped like skulls and skeletons abound.

Aniversario de la Revolución (20 November), the anniversary of the Mexican revolution of 1910, is honored with a national holiday.

December

Fiesta de Nuestra Señora de Guadalupe (Feast of Our Lady of Guadalupe, 12 December), a national holiday, is celebrated days and even weeks in advance at the **Basílica de Guadalupe** outside Mexico City. Pilgrims from throughout the country arrive by the carload and on foot, and approach the Virgin's shrine on their knees. Vendors hawk her likeness on statues, plates, and even gearshift knobs, and the scene is one of nearly garish revelry. Smaller celebrations are held throughout the country, particularly in towns where Our Lady of Guadalupe is the patron saint.

Noche Buena (Christmas Eve, 24 December) and **Navidad** (Christmas, 25 December) are important religious and family holidays throughout Mexico. The 12 days before Christmas are marked by processions *(posadas)* that recall Mary and Joseph's search for an inn. Families come together on the 25th to attend church, exchange gifts, break open piñatas, and share a lavish feast. *Feliz Navidad* is Spanish for "Merry Christmas."

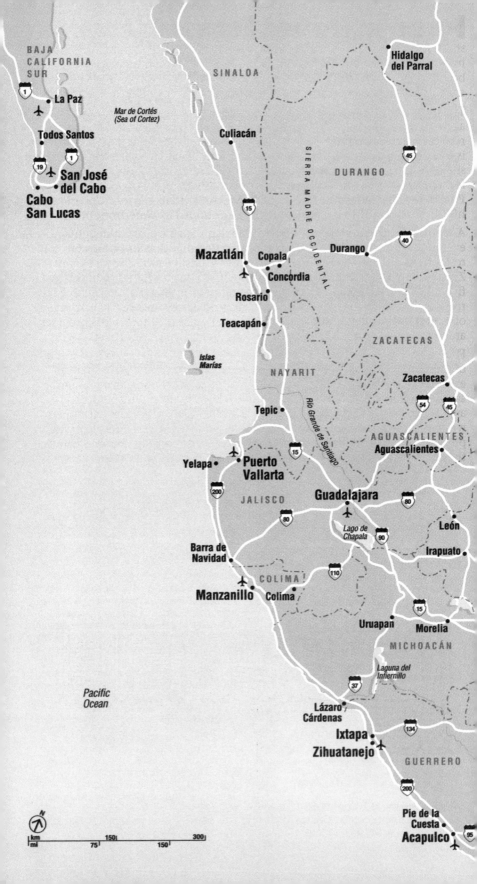

Pacific Coast Resorts

Mexico's Pacific coast is a land of stark beauty and wide contrasts, from deserts dotted with blossoming cacti to lush, thick jungles and high mountain passes that drop hundreds of feet to beaches and coves. The power of nature here is overwhelming and visually stunning, and much of the Pacific coastline remains secluded and untouched.

The most protected bays provided safe harbor for seafarers hundreds of years ago and have since developed into modern resorts. These bustling holiday retreats continue to grow, drawing thousands of visitors every year. **Mazatlán** is one of the best sportfishing destinations in Mexico, as well as the annual site of some of the most spectacular Carnival festivities. It's also one of the few coastal cities with visible remains of its early European immigrant era. **Puerto Vallarta** offers the flavor of Old Mexico with its tile rooftops and steep hillsides. **Manzanillo** is a busy port city surrounded by waterfront hotels.

Acapulco is the entertainment hub of Mexico's Pacific coast. It delights everyone who comes here with its sophisticated nightlife and gourmet restaurants and also boasts one of the world's most beautiful bays. Quaint **Zihuatanejo** is a tranquil Mexican town with low-key, charming hotels just five miles down the coast from the more modern **Ixtapa**, with its glitzy high-rise hotels, golf courses, and tennis courts. And across the **Mar de Cortés** (Sea of Cortez), at the end of the **Baja California Peninsula, Los Cabos** provides an ideal destination for fishing enthusiasts, golfers, and sun-seekers.

First-time visitors to Mexico's coastal resorts will discover the juxtaposition of modern and colonial-style architecture (footprints of the early Spanish explorers). Bits and pieces of pre-Columbian history are scattered about in small museums, a reminder of the people who lived here long before the arrival of the first European explorers, much less the tourists. As developers work to accommodate the influx of visitors, concerned residents are trying to preserve both the balance of nature and remnants of earlier cultures, which they now realize must be handled prudently if they are to survive.

Acapulco

North Market Street Graphics

Los Cabos

Baja California offers its visitors a blend of the novel and the familiar, part Mexican, part pseudo-Southern Californian. Nowhere is this juxtaposition more apparent than in Los Cabos, the southernmost tip of the 1,059-milelong **Baja California Peninsula**, a destination that is a hybrid created out of two small, traditional towns and the stretch between them. Over the past 10 years, with intensive effort by developers, Los Cabos has hit the big time and is now the most expensive seaside resort in Mexico. Golf courses designed by Jack Nicklaus and Tom Weiskopf receive Pebble Beach–level greens fees. Exclusive hotel properties charge from $250 upwards a night for a room. Especially in winter, more and more air routes go to this lonely place stuck at the end of desert mountains.

Los Cabos was spawned by Mexican bankers and politicians in the early 1970s and nourished by international investors in the 1980s and 1990s. The resort was formed from **San José del Cabo**, the municipal headquarters, and **Cabo San Lucas**, the center of the commercial and sportfishing industries—with an 18-mile road between them called the **Corridor**. All this is unconnected to mainland Mexico, and only a highway links it to the United States border at San Diego, California.

The visionaries who dreamed of Mexico as a tourist haven dubbed the area *Los Cabos* (The Capes) and declared that it would someday become a megaresort with golf courses, marinas, lavish hotels, and an endless stream of tourists and their money. They were right—Los Cabos is now becoming known as an elite destination.

The area has always had a certain cachet. Long before the developers discovered the place, wealthy adventurers were flying or yachting to Los Cabos, then known as "Marlin Alley," for sportfishing. World War II pilots sighted schools of billfish leaping from the waters around Baja's tip; later, astronauts studied the convergence of the **Pacific Ocean** and the **Mar de Cortés** (Sea of Cortez) and knew it would make for a fine fish trap. Legendary outdoorsmen of the John Wayne era roughed it at rustic lodges set in the desert on sandstone cliffs above the sea. Today those early outposts are treasured landmarks that have adapted to keep pace with the luxurious competition. Nevertheless, they still attract the hardy vacationer.

San José del Cabo is the northernmost town in Los Cabos, and also the most Mexican. The offices of **FONATUR** (the National Foundation for Tourism Development) are located here, as is the area's first golf course, several condo and housing projects, and a hotel zone along the shores of the Mar de Cortés. If only the beaches were safe for swimmers, it would be the ideal destination. If you can live without actually diving into these waves, though, their sound as they crash into the shore is the best tranquilizer of all, and San José's sleepy serenity may make this your perfect retreat.

The **Parroquia de San José** (Parish Church of San José) is the social center of this community with a population of nearly 25,000 full-time residents. Like most of the town's 18th- and 19th-century buildings, the church is simple in style, with none of the grandeur of those in mainland Mexico. Earth-toned brick-and-stucco boutiques, cafes, and shops line **Boulevard Mijares**, the main avenue, while local residents go about their business a few blocks away in the central market, at the *tortillerías* (small stands where tortillas are made), and in the rutted dirt streets of the neighborhoods. Along Mijares, locals and travelers conduct official business at the **Palacio Municipal** (City Hall), dine by candlelight under boughs of fuchsia bougainvillea at **Damiana**, and catch up on televised sports at **Tropicana Bar**, all at a leisurely, amicable pace.

Despite its uninspired name, the Corridor is actually the most gorgeous and valuable stretch of real estate in Los Cabos. The winding, two-lane road between the two towns has been replaced with a smooth four-lane highway that cuts through sandstone cliffs over a series of dramatic bays. One-of-a-kind hotels and resorts claim the most scenic clifftops, sequestering guests in luxurious sanctuaries dedicated to privacy, peace, and pleasure. One of the most enjoyable ways to pass a day in Los Cabos is to embark on a leisurely tour of a half dozen or so hotels in the Corridor. A late breakfast on the **Palmilla**'s sun-dappled balcony is a good way to start, followed by drinks, snacks, and hikes to lone beaches and summit trails at the **Twin Dolphin**. Plan for a snorkeling break at **Bahía Chileno**, splurge on lunch at the pricey **Las Ventanas**, and relax over a sunset cocktail at either branch of **Da Giorgio**.

Cabo San Lucas is where the action is. Vestiges remain of its origins as the fishing and canning capital of Baja California Sur, despite the endless campaign to transform the small, dusty settlement into a tourist mecca. But next to these reminders of the town's past, trendy boutiques and bars are jammed together in a jumble of styles. Too many tourists behave as though Cabo San Lucas was a playground for narcissists, where those who over-imbibe tequila and beer can get away with whatever rowdy behavior they'd never dare to try at home. They refer to the town simply as "Cabo," and call the Baja California Peninsula "the Baja."

To appreciate Cabo San Lucas proper, walk through the town early in the morning, while the revelers are still nursing their hangovers, and stay away when a cruise ship drops anchor in the bay. Start at the main plaza, where the shops carry a tasteful selection of folk art, clothing, and souvenirs, and the restaurants cater to locals, not tourists. A miniature maze of short blocks without street signs leads to the waterfront, and it is on these side streets that you'll find tasteful interior-design galleries adjacent to sleazy nightclubs and a hodgepodge of restaurants, bars, taco stands, and shopping arcades.

Boulevard Marina, along the curve of Bahía San Lucas, is the no-holds-barred tourist strip. The watering holes have cutesy names and blaring music, the restaurants have sidewalk grills offering sizzling treats, and the congested street is filled with mopeds, taxis, and Jeep-style vehicles. Attractive young women and men loiter on just about every street corner in so-called tourist information stands, trying desperately to entice you to visit a timeshare presentation (they're paid by commission). Unless you're fond of the free breakfasts, tours, and gifts that come with the spiel, you'll quickly learn to bolt past these sidewalk hustlers and their friendly repartee.

Parroquia de San José

ANTHONY QUARTUCCIO

Area code 114 unless otherwise noted.

Getting to Los Cabos

Airport

The **Aeropuerto Internacional de Los Cabos** (Los Cabos International Airport) is 11 kilometers (7 miles) north of San José del Cabo and 40 kilometers (25 miles) north of Cabo San Lucas. The airport is a small, single-terminal facility that handles both national and international flights. Services such as airline and car-rental counters are open only when flights are arriving and departing.

Airport Services
Information..20341

Airlines
AeroCalifornia 33700, 30848, 800/237.6225

Aeroméxico.................20397, 20398, 800/237.6639

Alaska Airlines 21015, 800/426.0333

America West 22882, 22880, 800/235.9292

Continental 23880, 20959, 800/525.0280

Mexicana 20230, 22722, 800/531.7921

United 22880, 800/241.6522

Getting to and from Aeropuerto Internacional de Los Cabos

By Bus Airport vans called *colectivos* shuttle passengers from the airport to hotels and are the least expensive choice (unless four people share a taxi). The vans do not operate from hotels to the airport so you must rely on taxis for your return trip. *Colectivo* fares are about $3 to San José del Cabo, $4 to $10 to the Corridor, and over $10 to Cabo San Lucas.

By Car Highway 1 runs south from the airport to San José del Cabo (10 minutes), the Corridor (15-30 minutes), and Cabo San Lucas (30-45 minutes).

The following car-rental agencies have counters at **Aeropuerto Internacional de Los Cabos** and are open only when flights are arriving and departing.

Amca 32515, 21314

Avis.................34607, 20680, 21080, 800/331.1212

Budget 34190, 30241, 800/527.0700

Dollar 20100, 31250, 800/800.4000

Hertz.......................................20375, 800/654.3131

National 22422, 31414, 800/328.4567

By Taxi Taxis wait in front of the airport and are relatively expensive; they cost about $6 to San José del Cabo, $8 to $16 to the Corridor, and $16 to $20 to Cabo San Lucas. Since you must take a taxi for your return to the airport, many hotels have a sign-up sheet at the front desk where you can solicit fellow passengers to share the fare.

> A popular saying appropriate to the Baja terrain is *"Es tan Mexicano como el nopal"* (He is as Mexican as a cactus).

Getting Around Los Cabos

Los Cabos has no public transportation, so rental cars come in handy, especially if you want to tour the whole region. Highway 1, the Corridor, connects San José del Cabo and Cabo San Lucas.

Buses No local bus service operates within Los Cabos, but long-distance buses traveling between Los Cabos and towns to the north stop in both Cabo San Lucas and San José del Cabo.

The bus station in San José del Cabo is located at **Valerio Gonzáles Canseco** and Boulevard Mijares. Call 21100 for schedule information.

The bus station in Cabo San Lucas is located at **Niños Héroes** and **José María Morelos**. Call 30400 for schedule information.

Driving Traffic in downtown San José del Cabo can be very congested during the day, especially along Boulevard Mijares. Some of the side streets in town are unpaved and very rough; drive with caution. Traffic is also extremely heavy along Boulevard Marina in Cabo San Lucas—park on a side street and walk around town. Both towns have a few marked one-way streets. Still, it's hard to get lost since both are so small. Many tourists rent a car for just one day to explore the area. Car-rental desks can be found at most hotels.

Taxis Taxis wait for passengers at the hotels and can be flagged on the street in the two towns. In the Corridor it's best to take a taxi from your hotel rather than trying to flag one down on the highway.

FYI

Accommodations Los Cabos has some of the highest hotel room rates in Mexico, and budget hotels are nearly nonexistent. Prices are highest at the resort hotels along the Corridor, where it's not uncommon to pay $250 and up per night. The least expensive hotels are in the downtown areas of both towns. Reservations are essential around Thanksgiving, Christmas, Easter, spring break, and during US holiday weekends. Some hotels lower their room rates in the summer months (June through August). Many properties offer package deals that include airfare, hotel, golf, fishing, and other activities.

Publications Several free English-language, tourist-oriented newspapers and magazines, including the *Baja Sun,* the *Gringo Gazette,* and *Cabo Life,* are distributed in hotels, restaurants, and shops.

Shopping Los Cabos has become an excellent shopping area in the last few years, especially for interior-design items. Galleries in both towns display gorgeous hand-carved armoires, terra-cotta fountains and birdbaths, hand-painted dishes, and hand-blown glassware. The folk art selection has improved as well, and some shops are selling beaded masks and belts by Huichol artists.

The best bargains for standard souvenirs are at the artisans' stands at the marina in Cabo San Lucas and in San José del Cabo. Cabo San Lucas is the place for sportswear—boutiques line the streets and offer a good selection of sundresses, T-shirts, and shorts at prices comparable to those in the US.

Telephones Though San José del Cabo and Cabo San Lucas are linked under the Los Cabos name and share the same area code, they have different telephone exchanges. All local numbers that begin with a 3 are in the Cabo San Lucas exchange; those that begin with a 2 are in the San José exchange. Calls between the two are long distance, and to make the connection you must dial 91 and the area code (114) before the number.

Time Zone Los Cabos is on Mountain Time, one hour ahead of California and two hours behind New York.

Tours The following tour operators will show you Los Cabos from various perspectives: **Baja Expeditions** (2625 Garnet Ave, San Diego, CA 92109, 619/581.3311, 800/843.6967; fax 619/581.6542) has specialized in adventure travel in Baja for nearly two decades, with hiking, biking, kayaking, whale watching, and diving trips to all of Baja's natural wonders, including the Pacific and the Mar de Cortés. **Cabo's Moto Rent** (30808) offers several guided tours on all-terrain vehicles to outlying spots; the ATVS are also a popular transport to the old lighthouse and sand dunes on the Pacific Coast. **Discover Baja** (32181) offers a daylong bus tour of the Los Cabos region. **Los Lobos del Mar** (22983), at the Brisas del Mar RV park in San José, has kayak tours and rentals. **Tio Sports** (32986) offers tours and rents water sports equipment; they have offices in several hotels. **Tour Cabos** (Plaza Los Cabos, Local B-2, San José del Cabo, 20982) is the main tour operator in Los Cabos, with scuba and snorkeling trips, sunset cruises, city tours, and other excursions.

The best way to truly capture the magnitude of the Baja California Peninsula is to drive its length from San Diego to Cabo San Lucas. **M&M Jeeps** (Presidente Inter-Continental Los Cabos, Paseo Malecón, east of Blvd Mijares, San José del Cabo, 21181; or 2200 El Cajon Blvd, San Diego, CA 92104, 619/297.1615; fax 619/297.1617) rents four-wheel-drive vehicles and can arrange itineraries with hotels and maps.

Visitors' Information Center The visitors' information office in Cabo San Lucas dispenses brochures and information on the region; it's located on Madero (between Vicente Guerrero and Miguel Hidalgo, 34180; fax 32211). In San José the tourist office is located on Ignacio Zaragoza (between Blvd Mijares and Miguel Hidalgo, 22960 ext 148).

"The very air here is miraculous, and outlines of reality change with the moments. A dream hangs over the entire region."

John Steinbeck,
Log from the Sea of Cortez

Phone Book

Hospital Raul A. Carillo Manuel Doblado and Muñoz, San José del Cabo 20316

Hospital IMSS Hwy 19 (north of Lázaro Cárdenas), Cabo San Lucas 30102

Police San José del Cabo 20361

Police Cabo San Lucas 33977

Red Cross Cabo San Lucas...........................33300

Red Cross San Jose Del Cabo 20316

San José del Cabo

San José del Cabo is a small, traditional Mexican town with a central plaza, a public market, and a local social life that revolves around the church and children. Visitors stay in modest hotels, stroll through the town streets shaded with leafy jacaranda trees, and hang out with friends at small cafes. Although the beaches are beautiful, the surf is extremely rough, so swimming is not advisable. Parking is tight—San José is also the municipal headquarters, and locals joust with tourists for limited parking spaces.

1 Huerta Verde $$ This eight-room bed-and-breakfast is nestled among century-old mango trees at the edge of the San José River, outside San José. The least expensive rooms are located in the main house. All rooms have private baths, patios, domed ceilings, and brick archways, and are gorgeously decorated with hand-painted armoires and porcelain sinks. Situated by itself at the side of the property, the **Palo Verde** master suite also has a living room, and the master bedroom boasts a hot tub. The other four suites are in adjoining buildings. Breakfast is included in the rate; lunch and dinner are available on request and well worth sampling. The heated swimming pool is surrounded by flowering shrubs. Hikers enjoy the mountainous terrain nearby; one particularly strenuous hike takes you to a peak with views of both the ocean and sea. If you plan to stay at the hotel, call for directions before striking out on dirt streets. It's on the south side of the small community of Santa Rosa, between San José and the airport.
◆ Credit cards accepted only with advance reservations made in the US. Las Animas Altas (east of Hwy 1). 80511; fax 80511. For reservations: 7674 Reed St, Arvada, CO 80003. 303/431.5162; fax 303/431.4455

2 Pescaderia El Mercado del Mar ★★$ This tiny seafood place on the main highway is worth a trip from the beach. Readily identifiable by an archway painted with a picture of a crab, the restaurant has a half-dozen tables under a *palapa* (palm-thatch hut) with a bar at one end. Start with *toritos*, small yellow Caribe chilies roasted and stuffed with smoked marlin, or a giant shrimp cocktail; entrée choices include oysters, clams, scallops, octopus, calamari, or fish fillet with oyster sauce, all expertly prepared. You can also buy smoked fish, cured on the premises, or cooked seafood to go. ♦ Seafood ♦ Daily lunch and dinner. Ignacio Zaragoza (between Muñoz and Hwy 1). 23266

3 Parroquia de San José (Parish Church of San José) Two simple, cream-colored wooden steeples (illustrated on page 17) poke humbly above the skyline, marking the town's religious, social, and historical hub. Be sure to examine the tile mural above the front door, depicting the martyred priest Nicolás Tamaral being dragged to the fire by Pericúe Indians. Not a pleasant fate, but the indigenous residents of this sacred land did not benefit from the missionary invasion of the 1700s, either. Along with their doctrine, the padres brought smallpox and syphilis. By the turn of the century, the local population had been virtually eradicated. Though not the first of the California missions, the church, built in 1734, was an early addition to the chain that eventually spread north to what is now Sonoma, California. ♦ Ignacio Zaragoza (between Miguel Hidalgo and José María Morelos)

4 Plaza and Kiosko The church sits above the town plaza, where taxi drivers congregate with their cabs, and children jump off the stairs to the white wrought-iron *kiosko* (gazebo). The small-town, community feeling is strongest on late Sunday afternoon and evening, and the plaza is a good spot for a rest in the shade. ♦ Ignacio Zaragoza (between Blvd Mijares and Miguel Hidalgo)

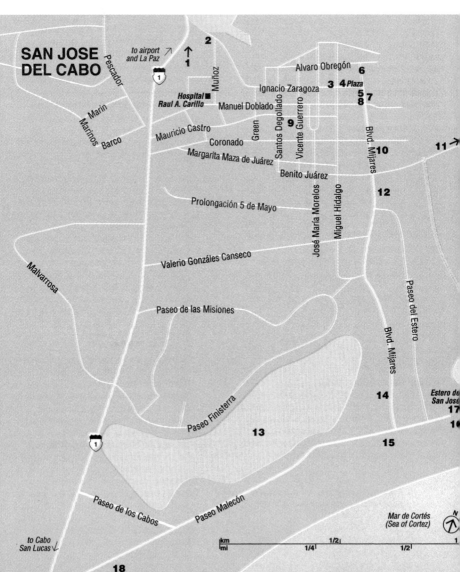

Anglers Alley

No matter how chic **Los Cabos** becomes, it will remain first and foremost a fisher's paradise. Your chances of hooking a trophy-sized marlin or sailfish are quite good here, plus there's no shortage of smaller game fish. By dawn, the sea around Cabo San Lucas is filled with everything from state-of-the-art yachts sporting electronic fish-finders to classic Baja *pangas* captained by fishermen raised on these seas. Fishing is such a big draw here that the annual **Bisbee Black and Blue Marlin Jackpot Tournament,** held at the end of October, carries a prize of more than a half-million dollars. Several smaller tournaments have recently been organized, too.

All of this fishing activity has taken its toll on the supply of the really big ones. To help preserve these fish, investors in the sportfishing industry have established a successful and popular catch-and-release program that encourages people who hook the giant game fish to commemorate their catch with a photograph and certificate (rather than a mounted specimen) and then return the fish to the sea.

With a combined fleet of more than 125 cabin cruisers and countless *pangas,* the sportfishing operators usually can accommodate all potential customers. However, the really great boats are often booked far in advance during the high season (October to Easter) and even in the late summer months, when certain species are most plentiful. Most hotels can arrange fishing charters in advance, and several specialized companies advertise in US sportfishing magazines. Some of the top-notch companies include:

Hacienda 30122, 800/733.2226

Juanita's Fleet 30522, 800/421.8925

Los Cabos Sportfishing Charters 800/814.3487

Palmilla 20582, 800/637.2226

Pices....................................30588, 800/521.2281

Solmar 30022, 800/344.3349

---

5 ADD The shop lives up to its name (which stands for art, design, and decoration) by offering a wealth of items large and small to beautify any home. The selection of pottery from Guanajuato is particularly fine, and you'll wish you could cart home the carved dressers and tables from Michoacán. If you can't resist buying things you can't carry, the shop will ship your purchase. ♦ M-Sa. Ignacio Zaragoza and Blvd Mijares. 32055

5 Huichol Collection The beadwork of the mainland Huichol Indians is one of Mexico's finest indigenous art forms. This orderly, well-lighted gallery presents beaded masks, dolls, and belts artfully arranged around a diorama of a Huichol hut. Masks covered with thousands of tiny blue, yellow, and red beads fetch prices in the hundreds, but the belts are within souvenir budgets. You may be approached by a smooth-talking time-share salesperson here; don't let the rap keep you from admiring the wares. ♦ Daily. Blvd Mijares and Ignacio Zaragoza. 24170. Also at: Blvd Marina and Lázaro Cárdenas, Cabo San Lucas. 34055

6 Plaza Mijares Wrought-iron benches and narrow pathways are nearly hidden by trees covered with orange blossoms, making this tiny plaza a pretty place to rest and regroup. Tour buses often pick up their passengers here, while solo travelers and locals sip coffee at outdoor cafes. During high season, many local artists, sculptors, and photographers display their works on the lawn on Sunday morning. ♦ Off Alvaro Obregón

At Plaza Mijares:

Damiana ★★★$$ Husband-and-wife team Luis and Leticia Klein have transformed a crumbling 18th-century hacienda into a serene patio where you feel as if you're dining among friends in a secret hideaway. The restaurant is tucked away off Plaza Mijares beside similar houses. Dining tables sit in the courtyard under a canopy of fuchsia bougainvillea, accompanied by the soothing sound of a gurgling fountain. The pièce de résistance is the imperial shrimp steak, made of chopped fresh shrimp pressed into a patty and grilled. Purists may prefer their gigantic prawns au naturel, sprinkled with bits of toasted garlic. The chateaubriand is sufficient for two hungry carnivores, and the Mexican dishes, especially the *chiles rellenos,* are very good. ◆ Seafood/Mexican ◆ Daily lunch and dinner. 20499

COPAL

Copal The selection remains impressive at San José's long-standing, outstanding folk art gallery, which moved to a new location in 1997. Look for silk hammocks from the Yucatán, wool rugs from Oaxaca, and an irresistible selection of hand-crafted silver jewelry. ◆ Daily. No. 10. 23070

El Café Fiesta ★★$ Tables set under the plaza's shade trees are the perfect spot to enjoy a cappuccino, salad, or sandwich while watching others shop. The cafe also delivers pizzas to hotels. ◆ Mexican/American ◆ Daily breakfast, lunch, and dinner. 22808

7 Almacenes Goncanseco This one-stop, multipurpose market sells batteries, postcards, cold drinks, snacks, and groceries. ◆ M-Sa; closed at midday. Blvd Mijares (between Manuel Doblado and Plaza Mijares). No phone

8 Palacio Municipal (City Hall) The name is far grander than the building itself—a pale, sand-colored plaster edifice with a peaked clock tower and a simple inner courtyard. Within are the municipal offices for Los Cabos, where official business for both towns is conducted. A plaque at the entrance commemorates the founding of San José (and the building's construction) in 1730. Another plaque observes San José's designation as the municipal headquarters of Los Cabos in 1981, when the original building was renovated, and two stories of offices were added around the courtyard. A silent guard stands under the front archway directing visitors with a nod of his head. ◆ Blvd Mijares (between Manuel Doblado and Ignacio Zaragoza)

9 Mercado Municipal Though not as spectacular as those on mainland Mexico, San José's enclosed public market has a good enough selection to satisfy your needs for chilies, oranges, mangoes, and avocados, amidst a heady aroma of spices and humanity. ◆ Daily. Mauricio Castro (between Vicente Guerrero and Santos Degollado). No phone

10 Tropicana Inn $$ The nicest place to stay in downtown San José is this peaceful and pretty inn with 40 air-conditioned rooms. A tile reproduction of a calla lily painting by Diego Rivera decorates the reception area, and the tile theme continues throughout the complex, including in the spacious showers.

All rooms have two double beds, satellite TV, and telephone and are decorated with cotton spreads and curtains in pastel colors and oil paintings of colonial village scenes. A giant *palapa* covers the pool bar, which is a great place to have a piña colada. The beach is eight blocks away, but all of San José's attractions are within walking distance. ◆ Blvd Mijares 30 (between Benito Juárez and Coronado). 20907, 21580; fax 21590, 510/939.2725 in the US

Within the Tropicana Inn:

Tropicana Bar & Grill ★★$$ An enduring favorite in an area where restaurants struggle to survive, this eatery is alternately romantic and rowdy, depending on the crowd. The air-conditioned bar is a popular spot for watching televised sporting events and music videos, while the back garden remains serene and picturesque. Machines that emit a light mist cool the air at sidewalk tables. The menu includes seafood, barbecued ribs, *chiles rellenos* with a fish filling, and tacos, all decently prepared. Low-priced breakfast and lunch specials are available, too. ◆ Seafood/Continental ◆ Daily breakfast, lunch, and dinner. 21580, 20927

11 Pueblo la Playa For a truly out-of-the-way experience, drive two kilometers (one mile) down the rutted dirt road east of downtown San José to this tiny settlement where the town's original crumbling lighthouse still stands, along with a newer concrete one. There's a popular surfing beach, too, though you're likely to be alone as you walk on the long beach toward the San José estuary, since few tourists spend much time here. The *pangas* (small skiffs) on the beach are available for sportfishing trips; for information, contact **La Playa Sportfishing** at 21195. ◆ Northeast of Blvd Mijares (look for the La Playita sign)

Within Pueblo la Playa:

La Playita $$ Much to the delight of escapists, this 24-room inn sits just a few yards from the peaceful and often deserted beach. The clean, white, air-conditioned

rooms have large, tile showers, two queen-size beds, a built-in table, ceiling fans, and plenty of closet space. The two penthouse suites have separate bedrooms and kitchenettes. The pool is long enough for swimming laps, and the restaurant is a two-minute walk away. ♦ 24166; fax 24166

Within La Playita:

Restaurant La Playita ★★$ The menu features the catch of the day, which arrives each morning on the fishing fleet at the nearby beach. The fish is prepared in the traditional *mojo de ajo*–style (grilled with oil and garlic), with mango sauce or fresh basil. Burgers, chicken, and beef are also available, but it's the fish and the scenery that keep diners coming in by the carload from San José. ♦ Seafood/American ♦ Tu-Su breakfast, lunch, and early dinner. 23774

Gordo Banks Sportfishing San Jose lacks a marina, so large fishing boats can't depart from here. But there is a fleet of *pangas* headquartered at the beach in Pueblo la Playa. The *pangeros* (*panga* captains) are experts at fishing the Mar de Cortés, and they specialize in catching wahoo, a particularly feisty game fish. Visit the beach when the *pangas* are coming in with their catch. ♦ 21147, 800/408.1199

La Playita Sportfishing It's worth checking out all fishing operations on this beach, especially if using their gear. This operation is one of the better ones in terms of the condition of their equipment (at some, the reels and fishing line may be barely usable). ♦ 21195

12 Mercado de Artesanías Vendors display typical crafts at open-air stands shaded with bright blue plastic tarps along Mijares on the southern edge of downtown. Bartering for cotton serapes, ironwood fish carvings, and silver baubles is expected, and prices are somewhat lower than at the shops in town. ♦ Daily. Blvd Mijares and Paseo del Estero. No phone

13 Los Cabos Campo de Golf Los Cabos's original golf course now has some mighty competition from newer courses along the Corridor and in Cabo San Lucas. Designed by Mario Schjetnan and built by **FONATUR,** it has nine well-established and challenging holes (par 35, 3,000 yards). Private homes and condos surround the country club, which sits on a hillside with coastal views. The club also has six lighted tennis courts and a clubhouse and is open to nonmembers. ♦ Paseo Finisterra (between Blvd Mijares and Hwy 1). 20900/1, 20905

14 Panteón San José (San José Cemetery) The entrance to this 19th-century cemetery is hard to find, but it's worth the effort for those interested in local culture. Tombs marked by headstones shaped like small churches are half hidden behind tall, dry grass, and colorful plastic flowers are tucked all around plaster angels and crosses. One tomb has 17 brick sides. ♦ Daily. Blvd Mijares (between Paseos Malecón and Finisterra)

15 Plaza Comercial Part of **FONATUR's** master plan, this isolated commercial center has been less than successful for shops and restaurants and now houses business offices, travel agencies, a video-rental shop, and a few small restaurants. ♦ Daily. Paseo Malecón and Blvd Mijares

16 Presidente Inter-Continental Los Cabos $$$$ An overwhelming impression of cactus and sand prevails at the oldest of the San José hotel zone's occupants, which rests on a solitary piece of land between the sea and the junglelike estuary. Low-rise tan buildings surround a long pool that's great for water volleyball and swimming laps. The best of the 250 rooms are on the first floor toward the beach and estuary, with shaded patios near the sand. Rooms are furnished in earth tones with heavy drapes to block the sun. Mornings, when the estuary's birds are in full chorus, are especially lovely here. The hotel now operates on an all-inclusive basis, with all meals covered in the room rate. ♦ Paseo Malecón (east of Blvd Mijares). 20211, 800/327.0200; fax 20232

17 Estero de San José The Río San José snakes toward the sea through the acres of nearly impenetrable twisting vines and trees that run along the dry and dusty shoreline. Thus far, the estuary's damp and dense terrain has protected it (and its 200 species of birds) from civilization's slow crawl up the coast. Plans to build a marina here have been nixed, and all boats are banned from the estuary, which is now an ecological preserve. ♦ Daily. Paseo Malecón (east of Paseo del Estero). No phone

Within the Estero de San José:

LOS CABOS
CENTRO CULTURAL

Los Cabos Centro Cultural Volunteers have set up a small museum and cultural center at the edge of the estuary and are working to create an indoor/outdoor education facility. The building houses exhibits on sea fossils and Los Cabos history, along with gorgeous photos and paintings of Baja's petroglyphs. A replica of a Pericúe Indian home constructed of tree limbs and palm fronds sits along a walking trail by the water. ◆ Admission. Tu-Su mornings. 21504

18 Fiesta Inn $$ Moderate prices and frequent package deals (including airfare) make this 152-room hotel a reasonable option, especially as the simply furnished rooms have carpeting, satellite TV, balconies, and bathtubs—a rarity in this price range. The white stucco buildings sit right on San José's beach, where the sound of pounding waves is enough to deter you from tackling the surf. Smart swimmers stick to the large pool, saving the beach for long walks and horseback riding. Tour groups congregate at the lobby bar; the restaurant serves fairly good Mexican and American dishes. ◆ Paseo Malecón (between Paseo de los Cabos and Hwy 1). 20701, 800/343.7821; fax 20480

The Corridor

Lavish state-of-the art resorts line the Corridor, an 18-mile stretch of road between **San José del Cabo** and **Cabo San Lucas** that winds along the clifftops that rise above hidden bays, where tropical fish entertain snorkelers. As more resorts go up beside the fairways and greens, championship golf courses have become one of the Corridor's biggest attractions, second only to the hotels.

19 Costa Azul One of the most popular surfing beaches in the area sits in an *arroyo* (dip) in the highway just south of San José. Die-hard surfers stay in a few weathered cabanas or camp by the beach and spend their time in the waves. The annual October Cabo Classic Reggae Surf-Splash contest fills nearby hotels with revelers and attracts thousands to the park. Just southwest of the beach is a hilltop lookout on the southeast side of the highway, where you can watch the surfers in action. ◆ Hwy 1 (southwest of Paseo Malecón)

20 Palmilla $$$$ Gorgeous, luxurious, and classically Mexican, this romantic place never fails to evoke purrs of pleasure from its guests and murmurs of envy from outsiders. Set atop Punta Palmilla, overlooking one of the most beautiful bays along the coast, the hotel's property spreads across 900 acres in a gentle rise between the highway and the sea. A $12-million renovation restored or replaced the original 72 rooms and added 62 suites. All are furnished simply, using traditional Mexican crafts—hand-carved furniture, piles of cushy pillows covered in handwoven fabrics on the king-size beds, and pottery jars of candies on the nightstands. Framed embroideries and carved wooden masks hang on the walls; hand-painted tiles add another nice detail. Some suites have red-tile patios, low walls shaped in lacy, layered arches, white wrought-iron tables and chairs, and padded lounges. The renovation added modern amenities to the rooms—televisions and VCRs hidden in armoires and telephones that can be transferred to voice-mail pickup. Wake-up calls are personally delivered by a waiter bearing fresh coffee, orange juice, and pastries. The new swimming pool is a joy, with fountains, waterfalls, a bar hidden behind boulders and plants, and very shallow areas where you can lie in the cool water while reading or daydreaming. The beach club just north of the hotel has all the water toys you need to play in the calm waters of the small bay. The wedding chapel on a low hill overlooking the property seems to always be in use. Wedding, honeymoon, and golf packages are available. ◆ Hwy 1 (southwest of Paseo Malecón). 45000, 800/637.2226; fax 45100

Within the Palmilla:

La Paloma ★★★★$$$ Even if you're staying elsewhere, be sure to have a meal here on the second-story patio overlooking the pool and the sea. This has always been one of Los Cabos's best restaurants, offering substantial filet mignon, lamb chops, and lobster, along with an innovative duck dish prepared with maple-and-soy marinade, and venison with a mango sauce. A poolside cafe expands dining options with its outstanding salads, burgers, and dorado sandwiches. For a total gourmet experience, spend an indulgent Sunday afternoon in the dining room, making your way through a brunch that will linger in your memory for years. ◆ Mexican/Nouvelle ◆ Daily breakfast, lunch, and dinner. 45000

 Palmilla Golf Club Located across the highway from the hotel, the **Palmilla**'s golf course (72 par, 18 holes—9 more being added at press time) was designed by Jack Nicklaus to take full advantage of the dramatic terrain and coastal views. Ancient cacti loom over emerald greens, and deep *arroyos* present natural challenges for golfers of all levels. It's a shame the course can't double as a park for nongolfers; don't pass up a chance to tour the grounds. The hotel offers golf packages; those staying in other hotels pay higher greens fees. ◆ 45250, 800/386.2465

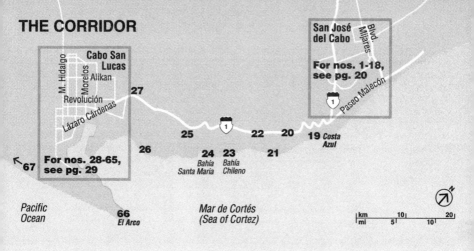

THE CORRIDOR

San José del Cabo

For nos. 1-18, see pg. 20

Cabo San Lucas
Alikan
27

M. Hidalgo
Morelos
Revolución
Lázaro Cárdenas

For nos. 28-65, see pg. 29
67

25   22   20   19 Costa Azul

26   24 23   21
      Bahía Bahía
      Santa Maria Chileno

Pacific Ocean

66
El Arco

Mar de Cortés
(Sea of Cortez)

km   10   20
mi   5   10

---

21 Westin Regina $$$$ Dramatic architecture and bold pink-and-yellow walls in the lobby never fail to evoke gasps of surprise from first-time visitors. Stairs and walkways lead down from the lobby atop a cliff overlooking the Mar de Cortés to the 305 rooms and suites in terra-cotta–colored buildings right by the beach. The rooms have both air-conditioning and ceiling fans, private balconies with ocean views, sitting areas, and enormous bathrooms with separate bathtubs and showers. It was one of the first hotels in the area with a full fitness center that provides exercise equipment, sauna, steam room, and whirlpool. Three outdoor swimming pools and four restaurants and bars complete the picture. ◆ Hwy 1 (Km 22.5). 29000, 800/228.3000; fax 29010

22 Cabo Real Several luxury hotels are operating in this expanding development, which already includes one completed 18-hole golf course and has a second 18 holes in the works. Residential villas and condos are filling in the background slopes, and the beachfront is now dotted with swimming pools, lounge chairs, and golf tees and fairways. ◆ Hwy 1 (Km 19.5)

Within Cabo Real:

Meliá Cabo Real $$$$ This terra-cotta sprawl of cubes and angles looks a bit forbidding, but it's much more welcoming—and impressive—inside. The grounds are astounding, with rock pathways winding past cactus gardens toward white tents billowing in the breeze. Waterfalls, fountains, ponds, and swimming pools appear to blend into a crystal-blue mirage that goes clear to the horizon. A stairway leads down to an immaculate artificial beach and a rock jetty that creates a peaceful miniature bay for swimming and snorkeling. Large and expensive by current Los Cabos standards, the hotel houses 296 rooms and suites in long

five-story buildings that encircle the inner grounds. The thoroughly modern rooms have TVs, bathtubs, mini-bars, and dependable air-conditioning. On-site attractions include an 18-hole golf course, horseback riding, a water sports center, and a health and fitness center. All the amenities, including bars, restaurants, shops, and a health club, keep guests happy right there on the premises. Golf, fishing, and diving packages are available. Meliá has a second Cabo Real project called **Meliá Los Cabos** ($$$$), which opened in April 1998. With 150 suites, two pools, and a full spa and gym, this hotel rivals other deluxe properties along the Corridor. ◆ 40000, 800/336.3542; fax 40101

Casa Del Mar $$$$ A secret hideaway tucked between the golf course and the sea, this luxurious hotel with 25 rooms and 31 suites offers seclusion and pampering. Fountains gurgling under archways that frame sea vistas, along with an abundance of antique furnishings and oil paintings, make you feel as if you're in a colonial-era hacienda. But the white-on-white rooms are totally modern, with whirlpools, in-room safes, satellite TV, seaview balconies, and both ceiling fans and air-conditioning. A waterfall flows beside the stairway leading to the free-form pool. An Avanti spa includes a fitness center and offers tempting aromatherapy massages and treatments using algae, seaweed, mud, and salt concoctions to soothe the skin. An in-house restaurant and room service provide additional convenience, and a small store sells snacks. Golfers appreciate the proximity of the excellent golf course, and those seeking

solitude have no need to leave the grounds.
♦ 40030, 800/221.8808; fax 40034

Cabo Real Golf Course Designed by Robert Trent Jones Jr., the 18-hole course (par 72, 7,000 yards) is a challenge for all levels of golfers and claims the most difficult hole in Los Cabos—number five. Numerous *arroyos*, sand traps, and hillsides confront players, along with pleasantly distracting views of the Mar de Cortés. A second 18-hole course is scheduled for completion in 1999. Guests at Cabo Real hotels receive a discount on greens fees. ♦ 40040, 40155

LAS VENTANAS
· AL PARAISO ·
LOS CABOS, MEXICO

Las Ventanas $$$$ In-room telescopes for stargazing, fireplaces, and private terraces with hot tubs are luxuries enough to keep guests from opening their hand-carved cedar doors to the outside world. Part of Rosewood Hotels & Resorts, the 61-suite hotel is filled with original art; even the wrought-iron door latches and hinges are made by hand. Hand-laid pebble pathways in intricate designs lead past bronze sculptures and murals by Mexican artist Rodrigo Pimental to a series of low-slung sand-colored buildings. Treatments at the world-class spa attract guests from nearby hotels for lavender-scented salt scrubs, soothing algae wraps, and other forms of pampering. Spa gels and lotions are placed in each room, luring guests to the enormous bathtubs. A blissfully air-conditioned workout room is equipped with top-of-the-line fitness machines. Guests may also use the several lap pools and the adjacent golf course. The library is stocked with books and magazines as well as current videos for use in guest rooms. ♦ 40257, 888/525.0483; fax 40255

Todos Santos

Visitors who never stray beyond **Los Cabos** miss the best of **Baja**'s natural beauty and potential, which are most evident in the coastal community of Todos Santos, some 63 kilometers (39 miles) north. Rent a car for a day and drive up the **Pacific** coastline on **Highway 19,** along the base of the **Sierra de San Lázaro.** Take time to stop along the way at solitary beaches to gather driftwood and shells usually found near giant cacti. The scenery grows greener as you enter the town of Todos Santos, home of the nurseries and organic gardens that provide plants and produce for the tourist enclaves farther south.

Though the town may not look luxurious to an outsider, Todos Santos is becoming an artists' colony and an exclusive enclave for Mexicans and expatriates who can afford its rapidly spiraling real estate costs. The crumbling 19th-century brick homes along the main plaza may look unimpressive now, but artists and entrepreneurs are investing in renovations, with promises of galleries, restaurants, and charming inns in the future. Small galleries and cafes open and close as dreamers cope with the reality of tourism's whims.

The steady survivor is the **Cafe Santa Fe** (★★★★$$; Centenario, between Marques de Leon and Topete, 40340) owned by Paula and Ezio Colombo. Diners travel south from La Paz and north from Los Cabos just to visit this tiny cafe nestled in a refurbished stucco house. Taking advantage of the locally grown organic produce and herbs grown beside the outdoor dining tables, the menu includes superb salads and herb garnishes for the freshest fish imaginable. Ezio prepares homemade pastas, pizzas, and calzones that draw rave reviews. Be sure not to dawdle too long, though; you absolutely *do not* want to drive back to Los Cabos after dark.

If you decide you like small-town life, spend a night or two at the biggest establishment in town, the 15-room **Hotel California** ($; Juárez, between Morelos and Marques de Leon, 50002; fax 50002).

Within Las Ventanas:

The Sea Grill ★★★$$$ A chef stands beside an open grill at this waterfront cafe, where guests choose from simple but expertly prepared dishes such as fresh-grilled shrimp skewers, mahimahi with mango sauce, or thick burgers on sourdough bread. Shaded tables are set between the pool and the sand. ◆ Seafood/Nouvelle ◆ Daily lunch and early dinner. 40257

The Restaurant ★★★$$$$ The bread alone is worth a meal here—few can resist the baskets of focaccia and different kinds of rolls—beer, potato, and sourdough. The entrées pair local seafood with unusual sauces and side dishes—start with a shrimp cocktail with mango puree served in an oversized martini glass, followed by *chiles rellenos* with shellfish filling and covered with goat-cheese sauce, or filet mignon with *guajillo* chilies and almonds. Desserts are equally memorable. The patio tables are ideal for dining on starry nights, though the air-conditioning in the enclosed dining room can be a welcome relief from the heat. ◆ Seafood/Nouvelle ◆ Daily breakfast, lunch, and early dinner. 40257

La Concha
RESTAURANTE
CLUB DE PLAYA

Club la Concha A man-made cove with boulders protects swimmers from open sea waves, the water is clear and calm, and schools of tropical fish hang out near the rocks. Created because the Corridor lacks safe swimming beaches, this niche also houses a beach club with a swimming pool, playground equipment, lounge chairs, and hammocks under awnings and umbrellas. Towels and snorkeling gear may be rented. There's a fine Mexican restaurant, too. At press time, the management was considering initiating an admission fee. ◆ 40102

22 Cuadra San Francisco Hidden surprises in the wilderness make the desert terrain perfect for horseback riding. Tours offered at this horse ranch include the back country and the beach; riding lessons are also available. ◆ Hwy 1 (Km 19.5). 40160

23 Bahía Chileno A dirt road off the highway leads to this secluded, clear cove, one of the best along this coastline for snorkeling, scuba diving, and swimming. During high season, a small stand rents snorkeling and dive equipment. ◆ Hwy 1 (Km 15)

On Bahía Chileno:

Hotel Cabo San Lucas $$$ Looking more like a northwestern hunting and fishing lodge than a tropical oasis, this is one of the Corridor's original hotels, as well as one of its most legendary. This is where weathered, die-hard fisherfolk return for their yearly hunt. The hotel had lost much of its glory over the years, but the renovation of its 89 rooms has helped restore its charm. The grounds have grown spectacularly with age, and mature palms, scheffleras, and hibiscus seem to envelop the complex in shade. The impressive dining room/bar has rock-and-wood walls with large windows facing the water. The huge fireplace is welcome on chilly nights, and entertainment is provided by one of the best mariachi groups around. The hotel has villas for rent as well. ◆ Hwy 1 (Km 14). 40014, 800/733.2226; fax 40015, 213/655.3243 in the US

24 Bahía Santa Maria  Another lovely bay where locals and travelers escape the crowds and snorkel among angel and parrot fish. A stall with equipment rentals is open in high season. ◆ Hwy 1 (Km 12.5)

24 Twin Dolphin $$$$ Stark, austere, exclusive, and dramatic, this small inn has a dedicated upscale clientele—80 percent of the guests are satisfied returnees. Rather than trying to mimic a tropical paradise, owner David Halliburton Sr. took full advantage of Baja's sparse beauty and set the low, long, white buildings amid landscaping of rolling hills and stately cacti. Square, white, patio umbrellas poke up beside boulders, and the light-blue pool shimmers in the sun. Paco, the resident parrot, squawks in his cage in the hotel's entryway. The 44 rooms and six suites reflect the minimalist theme, with low platform beds, small refrigerators, enormous showers, and a state-of-the-art air-conditioning system. Public spaces are decorated with reproductions of the peninsula's famed cave paintings, discovered in remote caves deep in some of Baja's most deserted regions. Artist Ristine Crosby Decker projected slides of the drawings onto the hotel's walls, then sketched over the forms and painted exact copies of the originals. The hotel's restaurant is open for all three meals; packages including meals are available. The **Twin Dolphin** fishing fleet, anchored in the Cabo San Lucas marina, is excellent; anglers can also book fishing trips in small *pangas* that depart from the shore near the hotel. ◆ Hwy 1 (Km 12). 30256, 800/421.8925; fax 30496

25 Cabo del Sol Like a city unto itself, this 1,800-acre resort is emerging along two miles of the Mar de Cortés coastline, forever changing the landscape of the Corridor. By the turn of the century, the development is scheduled to include four deluxe hotels, 3,000 custom homes and residential units, and a replica of a Mexican village with restaurants and boutiques. One of the three planned championship 18-hole golf courses is open, and a second course designed by Tom Weiskopf is under construction. A gourmet restaurant, **Pitahahayas** (see below), is already open for business. Underway is a 600-room resort that Fiesta Americana is building within the compound, with the first phase scheduled for completion as we went to press. Ritz-Carlton is also slated to finish a 350-room oceanfront property by late 1999. ◆ Hwy 1 (Km 10). 33149, 800/637.2226

Within Cabo del Sol:

Pitahayas ★★★$$$$ It's amazing how few Los Cabos restaurants take advantage of the scenery. At this establishment (named for a tropical fruit), the sea plays a feature role, especially when shimmering under the light of the rising moon. The best tables sit along a curving wall just above the sand, with the sound of the waves in the background. The menu is ambitious, and the unusual blends of flavors aren't always completely successful, but when they are, you're in for a treat. The appetizer of goat cheese marinated in a vinaigrette of peppers, ginger, and cilantro is superb and can easily be shared by two; the Caesar salad is less satisfying. The spiced duckling with mushroom risotto and

tangerine-plum sauce is crisp and not the least bit greasy, and the sautéed sea bass comes with a rich lobster hash. The restaurant is located down a long road through the golf course and can be difficult to find. Get there at sunset for a great view. ◆ Pacific Rim ◆ Daily lunch and dinner. 32157, 32158

 Cabo del Sol Golf Club Jack Nicklaus himself called Cabo del Sol "the best golf property I've ever seen," and golf writers from throughout the world echo his sentiments. The 18-hole course (par 72, 7,051 yards) stretches for more than a mile along the Mar de Cortés coastline, with cardon cacti and natural piles of sandstone boulders framing the greens. ◆ 58200, 800/386.2465

26 Da Giorgio ★★★$$ The location is the main attraction of this restaurant, which sits right above the sea with an unrivaled view of the rock arches at land's end. There isn't a better seat in Los Cabos for a sunset drink than at these private tables, dotted along small terraces on the oceanside cliffs. The views and atmosphere are so enchanting that it can be hard to move on to more solid fare. The spell continues by starlight, as you dine on dishes as simple as a shared pizza or as elaborate as butterflied shrimp in white wine. The ample salad bar is a definite plus, and the pasta dishes are satisfying if unexciting. The sunset, however, is not to be missed. ◆ Italian ◆ Daily breakfast, lunch, and dinner. Misiones del Cabo, Hwy 1 (Km 5). 32988. Also at: Hwy 1 (Km 25). 21988

27 Cabo San Lucas Country Club Though situated in a private residential community, this 18-hole golf course (par 72, 7,000 yards) is open to the public. Designed by Roy Dye, the course includes a large lake, several changes in elevation, and enough hazards to challenge experienced golfers. ◆ Hwy 1 (Km 2). 34653

Cabo San Lucas

Trendy, casual restaurants, bars, and shops attract travelers to Cabo San Lucas, "action central" for the Los Cabos region. The town frames a large bay and marina where cruise ships, fishing boats, private yachts, and small skiffs rock in the water. No matter where visitors are staying, they always make at least one trip into "Cabo" (as the town is commonly called) to quaff a few cold ones, try out the newest eateries, and pick up some souvenirs.

Nearly 30 million people made up the indigenous population of Mexico when the Spaniards arrived in 1519 and introduced smallpox, measles, syphilis, and other diseases to the country. Fifty years later, these diseases had wiped out most of the population—fewer than 3 million Indians were left in Mexico.

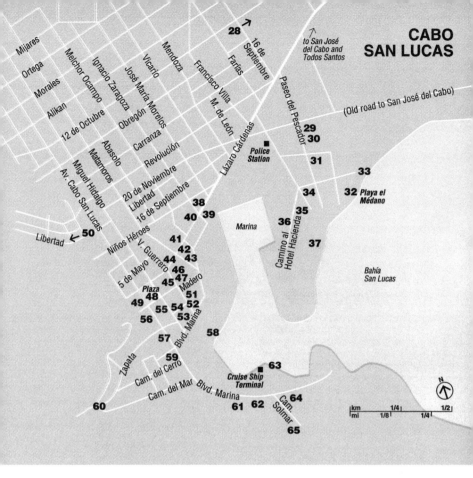

28 Glass Factory Don't even think of trying to find this place on your own. It's hidden in a maze of dusty no-name streets, boatyards, and homes near the highway to Todos Santos (see "Todos Santos," on page 26), and even locals who've been here frequently get lost. The factory is run by a master glassblower from Guadalajara who oversees a dozen or so workers in a very hot room where fire roars in huge gas furnaces. The craftsmen stick long tubes into the fire and scoop up globs of molten glass, then blow first forcefully and then gently as they twirl the globs into goblets. Others shape plates and bowls, then color them with streaks of green and blue. Guests are invited to blow their own glass, which is much harder than it looks. Shelves at the front of the workroom display distinctive mugs, beer steins, shot glasses, and dishes, many unlike what you'll find in town. The prices are said to be wholesale, though they seem a bit high. It's considered polite to purchase something after the show; the little blue shot glasses adorned with emerald green cacti are a lightweight and inexpensive choice. ♦ M-Sa. Southwest of Hwy 19. 30255, 30120

29 La Golondrina ★$$$ The official, unwieldy name is **The Trailer Park Restaurant at La Golondrina,** reflecting the ties between this pretty dining room and the longtime gringo hangout at the **Faro Viejo** trailer park a few blocks inland. This restaurant is housed in the oldest building in Cabo San Lucas. During the warm months dinner is served in the courtyard in front; in the winter tables are set up in a cozy dining room with an arched brick ceiling. The menu emphasizes bountiful feasts of barbecued chicken, platters of stir-fried chicken, beef, scallops, or shrimp (prepared as spicy as you wish), lobsters cooked five ways, and at least four types of fresh fish. Breakfasts are equally enormous. The place is popular with tourists who can count on hefty portions (at high prices) and friendly banter. ♦ Mexican/American ♦ Tu-Su breakfast, lunch, and dinner, November through April; Tu-Su dinner, May through October. Paseo del Pescador (just south of the old road to San José del Cabo). 30542

30 Peacocks ★★★$$$ Thick tree trunks support finely woven A-frame *palapas* covering two large rooms of this classy restaurant, where diners are seated on comfortable bent-willow chairs around bright white tables. Candles glowing in hurricane lamps and flames from the grills in the open kitchen illuminate the space. The menu changes every few days, but always includes the ever-popular fettuccine

29

Alfredo with shrimp and scallops. If they're available, try the chicken liver mousse or baked feta cheese for an appetizer, and the blackened cabrilla with capers as an entrée. The wine list boasts several California labels (including Champagne). Chef Bernard Voll's talents soar with his desserts, especially the swan-shaped puff-pastry profiteroles filled with vanilla ice cream and chocolate sauce. Brewed decaffeinated coffee is another rare treat. ◆ Nouvelle ◆ Daily dinner. Paseo del Pescador (south of the old road to San José del Cabo). 31558

31 El Rey Sol ★★$$
Seeing several generations of a Mexican family gathered here for their weekly feast is a good sign that the chefs know their way around a tortilla. This place has been here for years, serving authentic home-style Mexican meals. Bring your fresh-caught dorado—one of Cabos's most popular catches—and have it fried, breaded, or sautéed, and be prepared for a savory repast. Decorated with snapshots and business cards from dedicated clientele, the enclosed brick dining room is always cool and shady. Breakfast is especially good and is capable of *levantando los muertos*—raising the dead, or at least those sad souls suffering from murderous hangovers. ◆ Mexican ◆ Daily breakfast, lunch, and dinner. Paseo del Pescador (south of the old road to San José del Cabo). No phone

32 Playa el Médano Easily the most popular in San Lucas, this beach (its name means sand dune) is filled from sunup to sundown with *panga* captains picking up fishing clients, water taxis shuttling passengers to other hotels on Bahía San Lucas, windsurfers, jetskiers, vendors hawking straw hats, and beachcombers. Several small *palapa* restaurants dot the sand: **The Office** restaurant is immensely popular among vacationers, who snap souvenir shots of each other lounging in front of the sign. Areas of the water are sectioned off for swimmers to protect them from the various watercraft roaring about. ◆ Bahía San Lucas

32 Meliá San Lucas $$$$ The enduring headquarters for the local fun set is the swim-up pool bar, *palapa* restaurant, and beach at the more casual of the two Meliá hotels in Los Cabos. The view of **El Arco** (the granite arch where the Pacific meets the Mar de Cortés; see page 39) is outstanding, and the buildings form a staggered horseshoe of tile roofs, arches, and patios that changes in color from sand pale to sunset glow throughout the day. The 150 cool pastel rooms and suites are perfect for escaping the blazing sun, especially if there's a good movie showing on satellite TV. As neither the cuisine nor the camaraderie is spectacular in the restaurants and bars, the beachside *palapa* is probably your best choice. Downtown Cabo San Lucas is within walking distance, and the hotel also offers a shuttle service to the **Meliá Cabo Real** for a change of scenery. Various golf, fishing, and diving packages also are available. ◆ East of Paseo del Pescador. 34444, 34408, 800/336.3542; fax 30418, 30420

33 Pueblo Bonito $$$$ A stark white exterior with arches and domes gives a Mediterranean look to this resort on the Playa el Médano. The 148 suites, which are also available as time-shares, have kitchenettes, dining areas, oceanfront balconies, and a pleasing blue-and-white decor. Beveled glass doors, chandeliers, and mosaic marble floors give the public spaces a sense of elegance typical of the Pueblo Bonito resorts, which take the time-share concept to new heights. The adjacent **Pueblo Bonito Rosé**, which opened in 1997, is painted a pale pink and topped with white-tile domes. The hotel has 255 lush suites, a health club, and spa. The popular beach area fronting the hotels is filled with parasailors, windsurfers, and jetskiers. Five restaurants are located within the two hotels, and several more are within walking distance. ◆ East of Paseo del Pescador. 32900, 800/937.9567, 800/442.5300; fax 31995

34 Casa Rafael's $$ This bright pink boutique hotel above Playa el Médano has only 12 rooms, each individually and comfortably decorated with an eclectic array of antiques, folk art, and modern furnishings. All rooms are air-conditioned and have private baths; the rate depends on the size of the room and the quality of the view. A lap pool is situated in a private, secluded area behind the house. There's also a fully equipped exercise room, a hot tub, and massage services. For those who wish to remove themselves completely from the crowd, this is the perfect spot. ◆ Between Paseo del Pescador and Camino al Hotel Hacienda. 30739; fax 30739

Within Casa Rafael's:

Casa Rafael's Restaurant ★★★$$$
If you're looking for romance, courteous and attentive service, and fine cuisine, be sure to spend a special evening in this enchanting dining room. Two live toucans pose behind glass next to one of the best tables in the interior candlelit dining room, while cooling breezes rustle the vines in the garden room. Diners are expected to settle in for the evening's full dining experience, which can easily last for three hours. Memorable appetizers include a smoky dorado pâté and seared ahi wrapped in romaine lettuce leaves with a ginger dipping sauce. Chef Willie Mitchell prepares a sublime dish of lobster medaillons with black bean sauce; the USDA steaks make you think you're in Kansas. The wine list is probably the largest in town, and there's an impressive selection of brandies and liqueurs. ◆ Continental/Nouvelle ◆ Daily dinner. Reservations recommended. 30739

35 Galeria Gattamelata A true paradise for connoisseurs of Mexican folk art and antiques, this large gallery is filled with collectibles. Garish masks hang on the walls over heavy, carved desks covered with pewter frames, wooden statues, and lamps made from Oaxacan pottery. A glass case holds a selection of hard-to-resist antique jewelry. ◆ Daily; closed Sunday July through October. Camino al Hotel Hacienda (south of the old road to San José del Cabo). 31166

36 Marina Fiesta Resort $$$ Visitors who stay for a week or more and enjoy having a kitchen will be happy in this 144-suite hotel, where even the smallest studios are equipped with kitchenettes, and the one- and two-bedroom suites offer full kitchens and dining areas. The hotel's location, facing town across a private marina, is ideal. All that's lacking is a swimming beach, but the free-form pool is large and inviting. The restaurant, **El Shrimp Bucket,** which is part of Carlos Andersen's chain, serves up dependable Mexican and American dishes. ◆ Camino al Hotel Hacienda (south of the old road to San José del Cabo). 31998, 32689; fax 32688

37 Hotel Hacienda $$$ It's easy to see why this hostelry has remained popular for nearly two decades. Set on a spit of land jutting into Bahía San Lucas, the hotel looks like a whitewashed mission with a bell in its arched tower. Stone carvings of Aztec and Maya gods overlook walkways, town houses, and cabanas, and each turn brings another surprise, such as pastel paper flowers tucked into a bougainvillea arch. The hotel has 114 rooms, with the more expensive accommodations offering seaside balconies, separate living rooms, and marble baths. The beach is just a few steps away and has a great view of **El Arco** and the marina. The **Hacienda** is owned by Budd Parr, a Los Cabos pioneer (who also opened the **Hotel Cabo San Lucas** in the Corridor). His son Mitch oversees the hotel and visits with guests and their families, some of whom he's known since he was a child. The restaurant offers decent Mexican dishes and seafood. ◆ Camino al Hotel Hacienda (south of the old road to San José del Cabo). 32062, 30122, 213/655.2323, 800/733.2226; fax 30666

Within the Hotel Hacienda:

Operador Pez Gato If you're going out on the water to sightsee rather than dive or fish, consider a sunset catamaran cruise with this operator. The Pacific glows gold as the boat sails along the shore, and if you're lucky, you might see a baby whale off the bow. There are also snorkeling and sailing tours. The boats depart from the dock by the **Hacienda**'s water sports center. ◆ Daily. 33797

Cabo Acuadeportes All the equipment you could need to play on or in the water is available at this water sports center. Boats depart from the hotel's dock for snorkeling, diving, whale watching, and sightseeing trips, and the equipment available for rent includes canoes, kayaks, wave runners, Windsurfers, and snorkeling gear. ◆ Daily. 30117. Also at: Bahía Chileno, Hwy 1 (Km 15). No phone

38 Squid Roe ★★$ Part of Carlos Andersen's chain of fun, unbeatably popular tourist hangouts found in most Mexican resort towns. The menus are standardized and dependable, with barbecued ribs (under the "Oink-Oink" column), chicken ("Peep-Peep"), and steaks (yes, "Moo-Moo"). Portions are bountiful, beer comes in silver buckets with six frosty bottles, and waiters do everything they can to convince patrons to try at least one tequila shooter. The decor is junkyard carnival, with objects of amusement dangling from the ceiling and walls. Don't expect a quiet meal, as the noise level is always deafening, even when the place is empty. Other members of the chain are **Carlos 'n' Charlie's** (Blvd Marina, 30973) and **El Shrimp Bucket** (Marina Fiesta Resort, Camino al Hotel Hacienda, south of the old road to San José del Cabo, 32498). ◆ American/Mexican ◆ Daily lunch and dinner. Lázaro Cárdenas (between José María Morelos and Ignacio Zaragoza). 30655

39 Plaza Bonita There's little chance you'll overlook this bulky, burnt-orange shopping and dining complex that's situated where the main road curves to Boulevard Marina and the waterfront at Cabo San Lucas's only traffic light. Part of a grouping with offices, condos, and a private marina, the plaza has an Old Mexico feeling with fountains, arches, inner courtyards, and tile domes. Various businesses come and go here, but some have found their niche and held firm. The plaza is within easy walking distance of the **Meliá** and **Hacienda** hotels, along a dirt pathway leading to the marina and town. ◆ Daily. Lázaro Cárdenas and Blvd Marina

Within Plaza Bonita:

Francisco's Cafes del Mundo ★$
Visiting java junkies needn't do without their cappuccino and bran muffins; here they can get their coffee fix, nibble on a pastry, peruse a pile of free tourist pamphlets, and watch boats cruise through the marina. There are tables both inside and out and English-speaking clerks at the counter. ◆ Coffeehouse ◆ Daily. No credit cards accepted. 32366

Dos Lunas Of the many sportswear boutiques in Cabo San Lucas, this one stands out for its high-quality selection of shorts, T-shirts, and pants, all done in vibrant tropical patterns. The prices are as high as you would pay for similar merchandise in the US, but being in the vacation mode may make you feel like splurging. ◆ M-Sa. 31969

Restaurants/Clubs: Red   Hotels: Blue
Shops/🍴 **Outdoors:** Green   **Sights/Culture:** Black

CARTES

Cartes This shop's selection of gorgeous china, pewter platters, antiques, and handwoven fabrics will make you wish you had a home nearby to furnish. Fortunately, there are plenty of small items to pack in your bags, including picture frames painted with sunflowers and calla lilies, plates and bowls with various fish scenes, and heavy blown-glass vases. ◆ Daily. 31770

Libros If you want to get to the literary heart of Mexico, this small bookstore has a good selection of English- and Spanish-language novels and magazines and some excellent hardcover books on Baja. The *Los Angeles Times* and *USA Today* both arrive by mid-afternoon. ◆ Daily. 33171

Hard Rock Cafe ★★$$ You know Cabo has hit the big time when a branch of this chain comes to town. Like all its restaurants, this one specializes in clean, wholesome fun. It's the kind of place you can take the kids and know they'll be entranced with the rock 'n' roll memorabilia hanging from walls and ceiling. They'll dig into the decent burgers, too. The music tends to be loud and the restaurant crowded. ◆ American ◆ Daily breakfast, lunch, and dinner. 33806

40 Supermercado Plaza No matter where you're staying, it's a good idea to stock up on some groceries at the beginning of your visit. The selection at this supermarket is downright astounding, especially for those who remember the dark ages (several years past) when pickings were slim here. The frozen food cases are stocked with luxuries you thought you'd left behind—gourmet ice creams, frozen pastries, microwave dinners—and there's a wide selection of produce, fresh meats, and sundries. ◆ Daily. Plaza Aramburo, Lázaro Cárdenas (between Ignacio Zaragoza and Melchor Ocampo). 31450

41 Zen-Mar Though undistinguished from the outside, this small shop carries a good selection of painted wooden figurines, picture frames, and masks, all from Oaxaca. ◆ Daily; closed at midday. Lázaro Cárdenas (between Melchor Ocampo and Matamoros). 30661

42 Cabo Gourmet $ Though most fishing boats and tours supply box lunches, they're often uninspired and unappetizing. Bring your own by stopping here to pick up a thick roast beef or avocado-and-cheese sandwich, potato or pasta salad, and bottled iced tea. The deli opens before dawn so that fishermen can drop by for their orders. Breakfast options include bagels or English muffins and cheese sandwiches and strong coffee. A few tables sit beside the self-serve counter (there's air-conditioning). ◆ Deli/Takeout ◆ Daily. No credit cards accepted. Lázaro Cárdenas (between Melchor Ocampo and Matamoros). 34555

42 Temptations The flowing, loose-fitting styles and light-as-air fabrics displayed at this resortwear boutique are perfect for warm climates, and the designs are quite stylish and chic. You can also find the María of Guadalajara line of cotton gauze clothing in vivid purples, aquas, and pinks. ♦ M-Sa. Lázaro Cárdenas and Matamoros. 31015

43 Giggling Marlin $$ Some anything-goes types think this spot is the ultimate for frivolity and food. The wildly whimsical decor certainly makes it seem that way. From the signs at the front door claiming "Broken English Spoken Here" to the ceiling-high fish scale where inebriated patrons dangle by their heels, this place screams fun. Tacos, burgers, and the like are mediocre at best, and the noise is downright deafening, but the patrons seem quite content. ♦ American/Mexican ♦ Daily breakfast, lunch, and dinner. Blvd Marina and Matamoros. 31182

44 Mar de Cortez $ A longtime favorite with those who spend more time on the sea than in their rooms, this hotel is surprisingly quiet and cool although located in the midst of the action. The 72 rooms are housed in two sections, the oldest of which has brick ceilings, colonial-style hardwood furnishings, and tile floors. The newer rooms are less traditional. All rooms have air-conditioning, and some have small patios facing the swimming pool. Fishing and diving packages are available. A streetside facade constructed in 1996 includes several shops and travel agencies, and the sportfishing desk in the hotel can help plan outings. **Spencer's Garden Court** restaurant inside the hotel's grounds specializes in shrimp dishes and bountiful American and Mexican breakfasts. ♦ Lázaro Cárdenas (between Matamoros and Vicente Guerrero). 30032; fax 30232. For reservations: 17561 Vierra Canyon Rd 99, Salinas, CA 93907. 408/663.5803, 800/347.8821; fax 408/663.1904

El Callejón
GALERIA•MUEBLES•DECORACION

45 El Callejón This classy showroom/gallery/ shop seems anomalous among the block's showgirl clubs and rock 'n' roll bars. Interior designer Claudia Reyes has shaped the style of many a home and business in Los Cabos, and her multiroom shop and courtyard contain an enviable collection of vases, lamps, tiles, and armoires. Take time to wander the rooms and the kitchen, bath, and dining displays. Shipping and interior-design consultation are available. ♦ M-Sa. Vicente Guerrero (between Madero and Lázaro Cárdenas). 31139; fax 31139

45 El Rancho Finally, a local entrepreneur has tapped into regional crafts and created a small shop that houses a fascinating collection. Most of the space is dedicated to pitchers, bowls, and plates that ranching families from outlying towns fashioned from local clay. Also notable are the knives with handles carved from cow bones. ♦ M-Sa. Vicente Guerrero (between Madero and Lázaro Cárdenas). 30593

46 Cabo Wabo Bar & Grill ★$ Members of the rock group Van Halen opened this cavernous club a few years ago with major fanfare and appearances by several LA groups. Rumors abound every weekend as to what stars in town may appear on stage. Most of the time, however, the music is canned. An open-air cantina outside the dance hall serves decent tacos, nachos, and sandwiches, and there's even **Waboutique**, where you can buy your very own **Cabo Wabo** T-shirt. ♦ Admission. Daily. Vicente Guerrero (between Madero and Lázaro Cárdenas). 31198

47 Minerva's Baja Tackle and Sportfishing Local anglers say this shop has the widest selection of tackle and gear in Los Cabos. Try a Mexican flag—a vivid red, white, and green feather—to lure a dorado. **Minerva's** also has one of the best fishing fleets around. ♦ M-Sa; closed at midday. Madero (between Blvd Marina and Vicente Guerrero). 32766, 31282; fax 30440

Addresses in Mexico often consist of nothing more than "Domicilio Conocido," meaning the residence is known, at least by the person delivering the mail.

Cabo San Lucas Kiosko

J. DEL GAIZO

48 Cabo San Lucas Kiosko and Plaza
Cabo San Lucas's true downtown is several blocks north of here, but the main plaza is in the tourist zone near the waterfront. Unlike in the plazas found in most Mexican towns, you won't find many families gathered for an evening stroll here, but it is a pretty spot to rest and regroup, and there are several shops and restaurants located around the square. ♦ Bounded by Miguel Hidalgo and Av Cabo San Lucas, and Madero and Lázaro Cárdenas

49 Mi Casa ★★★$$ The search for good Mexican food in Los Cabos was made easier a few years ago when this small cafe opened in an ancient cobalt-blue house facing the plaza. The restaurant quickly outgrew its original dining room (which turned into a folk art shop) and became an enchanting outdoor eating spot, with tables set on several levels in a courtyard behind the building. The walls surrounding the property are painted in an elaborate mural of village scenes by artist Rafa Nafa. Spanish is the language of choice, and the menu includes nary a burrito, tostada, or fajita. Instead, those longing for tastes from the mainland enjoy chicken with mole (a dark, rich sauce of spices and chocolate), fish with a sauce of *guajillo* chilies, and poblano chilies stuffed with seafood. Even if the names of some of the dishes baffle you, give one a try; you won't find more authentic Mexican cuisine anywhere in town. ♦ Mexican ♦ M-Sa lunch and dinner. Av Cabo San Lucas (between Madero and Lázaro Cárdenas). 31933

50 The Bungalows $$ Tucked away in a new residential area is this delightful small inn with 16 units of various sizes, from single rooms to two-bedroom bungalows. All have carved wooden headboards, terra-cotta and painted tiles, air-conditioning, and ceiling fans. Breakfast (included in the rate) is served in an open-air dining room, and the deep swimming pool is shaded by mature palms. Smoking is not allowed on the property. ♦ Libertad (west of Av Cabo San Lucas). 30585, fax 35035. For reservations: 9051-C Siempre Viva Rd, Suite 40-497, San Diego, CA 92173

51 The Fish Company ★★$ Owner Miguel Olvera has developed a cadre of fans at his small restaurant, which holds only 11 tables, prettily covered in blue or white cloths. His success comes from providing simple, tasty, reasonably priced food in a welcoming setting. Try the chorizo-and-cheese omelette at breakfast, or the fish prepared with garlic and oil for dinner. You're sure to meet locals here who shun the rowdier places in favor of Olvera's peaceful dining room. ♦ Mexican/Seafood ♦ Daily. Vicente Guerrero (between Blvd Marina and Madero). 31405

"Cruising" Los Cabos

Cabo San Lucas is a port of call for several ships sailing the **Pacific** coast of **Baja** and the west coast of mainland Mexico. The vessels anchor east of **El Arco** in the **Mar de Cortés;** passengers are ferried to the **Bahía San Lucas** marina and sportfishing dock, less than a 10-minute walk from downtown. And that's when the fun begins.

Sportfishing enthusiasts can hire a *panga* (a type of skiff) at the dock for a quick troll out to sea, but don't count on hauling in a big catch; the best action seems to occur at dawn, before the cruise ships have docked. Golfers have better luck, especially if they arrange tee times in advance for the **Palmilla** (Hwy 1, southwest of San José del Cabo, 45250, 800/386.2465), **Cabo del Sol** (Hwy 1, Km 10, 58200, 800/386.2465), or **Cabo Real** (Hwy 1, Km 19.5, 40040, 40155) golf courses. Many people take a glass-bottom boat ride, but if you're short on time, skip it and move swiftly through the open-air artisans' market, unless you're a die-hard treasure hunter (there are some good finds in silver jewelry, if you can tell real from fake). If your aim is to shop, eat, and drink, you'll be satisfied by the various establishments located along **Boulevard Marina** and the side streets.

Energetic hikers will appreciate Baja's natural beauty by walking east across Boulevard Marina and past the **Solmar Suites'** (Camino Solmar, 33535; fax 30410) pool bar to the craggy peak of Baja's southernmost tip, where the Mar de Cortés and the Pacific meet. Walk west along the windswept beach, but don't attempt a swim here; the waves are brutal, and even surfers stay clear of these treacherous waters. The stunning **Hotel Finisterra** (Blvd Marina, between Caminos Solmar and del Mar, 30000; fax 30590) sits high above the west end of the beach, built into the foothills of the **Sierra de San Lázaro.** Hike up the steep rock stairs from the beach and then collapse into a deck chair at the **Whale Watcher Bar** and enjoy the breathtaking view. The walk back to the dock via the hotel's driveway is downhill.

To see equally spectacular scenery with less physical exertion, you can hire a taxi for a tour between Cabo San Lucas and **San José del Cabo.** Make as many stops as time allows at the stark bays and dramatic resort hideaways, especially the **Westin Regina** (Hwy 1, Km 22.5, 29000, 800/228.3000; fax 29010), **Meliá Cabo Real** (Cabo Real, 40040), and **Palmilla** hotels, which may change your mind about cruising and prompt you to remain settled onshore.

Cruise lines docking in Los Cabos include:

Carnival 800/327.9501

Princess 800/421.0522

Royal..800/227.4534

52 Galería El Dorado This large gallery and souvenir shop displays rotating shows of paintings and sculptures by Mexican and international artists. It also offers fanciful papier-mâché animals and one-of-a-kind silver and gold jewelry. The backroom has knickknacks, onyx items, and inexpensive trinkets from throughout Mexico. ◆ Daily. Blvd Marina 81 (at Vicente Guerrero). 30817

53 Hotel Marina $ Surprisingly quiet and calm in the midst of the waterfront frenzy, the 27-room hotel sits above a peaceful courtyard with a small pool and hot tub. All rooms have tile baths; the most expensive rooms have small refrigerators and TVs. There's a small parking lot on the property, and a decent restaurant called **La Placita**. ◆ No credit cards accepted. Blvd Marina and Vicente Guerrero. 31499, 30030; fax 32484

53 Restaurant Cafe Europa ★$ An oasis amid the Boulevard Marina bustle, this small cafe serves *caffè latte,* cappuccino, bagels, quiche, and pastries at outdoor tables. It's a nice place to hang out while waiting for shopping friends to exhaust themselves. ◆ Cafe ◆ Daily breakfast, lunch, and dinner. No credit cards accepted. Blvd Marina 75B (between Vicente Guerrero and Miguel Hidalgo). 33699

53 Magic of the Moon Local seamstresses create the one-of-a-kind bustiers, halter tops, lacy lingerie, and ruffed cha-cha blouses displayed in this flourishing shop. Also stocked are plenty of loose-fitting sundresses, skirts, and shorts perfect for the steamy Cabo climate. ◆ Daily. Miguel Hidalgo (between Blvd Marina and Zapata). 33161

Siesta Suites
• HOTEL •

54 Siesta Suites $ These apartmentlike units are among the best deals to be found in Cabo. The immaculate 20 suites have air-conditioning, kitchenettes, and seating areas. Special rates are available for stays of a week or more. ◆ No credit cards accepted. Zapata (between Vicente Guerrero and Miguel Hidalgo). 32773; fax 32773. For reservations: 909/945.5940

"All the vegetation visible to the eye seems to conspire against the intrusion of man. Every shrub is armed with thorns. The cactus tortures the travelers with piercing needles and remorseless fangs. Burrs with barbed thorns cover the ground. The very grass, wherever it grows, resents the touch with wasplike stings that fester in the flesh. . . A land accursed of God!"

> J. Ross Browne on Baja California,
> *Harper's Magazine,* 1863

RESTAURANT
PANCHO'S

54 Pancho's ★★★$$ Bright yellow, green, orange, and blue tablecloths and mats cover the wooden tables where some of the best Mexican food in town is served. No mind that the owners are gringos; they've put together a place where you can sample over 100 varieties of tequila, Oaxacan mole, shrimp tacos, pozole, pickled nopales cactus pads, and other regional specialties. ◆ Mexican ◆ Daily breakfast, lunch, and dinner. Miguel Hidalgo (between Zapata and Madero). 30973

54 Mama's Royal Cafe ★★★$ Mama's has moved a few times, but it's always worth seeking out for breakfast. You can go all the way and have French toast stuffed with cream cheese and covered with fruit, or stick with the more healthful spinach or asparagus omelettes. Over 20 varieties of omelettes are available, as well as eggs benedict with novel combinations of ingredients. Expect a wait in high season, when lines form outside the dining room. ◆ Cafe ◆ Daily breakfast. Miguel Hidalgo (between Zapata and Madero). 34290

55 Restaurant/Taquería San Lucas ★$ Also known as the "Broken Surfboard," this streetside *taquería* is a longtime favorite among San Lucas regulars. The tacos, enchiladas, burgers, and *huevos Mexicanos* (scrambled eggs with onions, tomatoes, and chilies) are cheap, filling, and reasonably tasty. ◆ Mexican ◆ Daily breakfast, lunch, and dinner. No credit cards accepted. Miguel Hidalgo (between Zapata and Madero). 30454

56 Mamma Eli's A mind-boggling, wallet-draining array of Mexican folk art, clothing, jewelry, and glassware is temptingly arranged throughout three stories of display rooms, giving the browser a great overview of mainland Mexico's artistic wealth. This store is a refreshing discovery after you've gone through the silver baubles, cotton blankets, pottery, and tawdry trinkets at most of the other gift shops. Stop here first for a view of the best, then compare with the rest. ◆ Daily; closed at midday. Av Cabo San Lucas (between Zapata and Madero). 31616

57 Parroquia de San Lucas (Parish Church of San Lucas) You might easily overlook this simple Catholic church (illustrated at right), as it's situated on a small side street, but it's worth the search. Atop a wall near its driveway is a large stone book engraved with a description of the church's origins. It explains, in Spanish, that the area was inhabited by the Pericúe Indians, who called their settlement Anikan. Spanish explorers renamed it Cabo San Lucas in the early 1700s, and the church was established in 1730 by Spanish missionary and priest Nicolás Tamaral (later killed by the Pericúe). A stone archway, which holds a bell sent to San Lucas by the Spaniards in 1750, is inscribed "St. Ignacium, 1746." Fuchsia bougainvillea splashes color along the outer stone walls, but the only fancy touch within is the splattering of glitter in the ceiling plaster. Simple signs near the altar quote the Bible: *"Yo soy el pan de la vida"* (I am the bread of life). The faithful, who love their parish church, are ministered to by padres from Italy. ◆ Av Cabo San Lucas (between Blvd Marina and Zapata)

58 Plaza Las Glorias $$$ Few locals have kind words for this six-story, four-blocklong mass of earth-toned buildings, which houses a 287-room hotel and several restaurants and bars. The complex effectively blocks the water view and cooling sea breezes from the neighborhood's long-established businesses and residences. The hotel seems cavernously bare, with dark hallways leading to nowhere, but it often offers discounted room rates and packages including reduced airfare. It's certainly the most convenient place to stay if you lack a car and want to be in the midst of the action. Several small restaurants are located at the back of the property facing the water, and the hotel offers a shuttle service to the beach. ◆ Blvd Marina (south of Lázaro Cárdenas). 31220, 800/342.AMIGO; fax 31238

59 Romeo y Julieta ★★$$ The area's Italian restaurant craze was launched here, and even in the low season patrons find themselves crowded elbow to elbow in the bar. Offerings include pizzas (the best in town, some locals claim) and crusty bread from brick, wood-burning ovens, and homemade pastas. Newcomers often leap to their feet to snap photos of liquid flames as the waiter prepares a sinfully sweet *café Mexicana flambeau* with Kahlúa and ice cream. The refreshingly cool dining room is both romantic and informal, with candlelight and flowers decorating the tables where fishermen gather in T-shirts and shorts. ◆ Italian ◆ Daily dinner. Camino del Cerro and Blvd Marina. 30225

60 El Pedregal If your rental car has a cooperative transmission and reliable brakes, take a drive up the narrow twisting roads past dump trucks and construction crews to the gorgeous homes where wealthy Cabo devotees take up residence on their extended vacations. Roofs are covered with terra-cotta or hand-painted sunflower-yellow tiles, white archways frame cobbled stairways, and most windows face west to a stunning view above the Pacific. ◆ West of Blvd Marina

Parroquia de San Lucas

ANTHONY QUARTUCCIO

61 Hotel Finisterra $$$ One of Cabo's original hotels, the **Finisterra** (which means land's end in Latin) has undergone a complete transformation. Together, the two towers on the beach and the original clifftop hotel offer a total of 220 rooms. The tower rooms have oceanfront balconies, satellite TV, phones, coffeemakers, and hair dryers. The **Palapa Beach Club** is an oasis of palms and gigantic swimming pools; an elevator carries passengers from the beach up to a bridge leading to the original buildings (in the past, only the hardiest of souls braved the steep climb up and down the cliffs from the hotel to the beach). ♦ Blvd Marina (between Caminos Solmar and del Mar). 33333, 32460, 800/347.2252; fax 30590. For reservations: 6 Jenner, Suite 120, Irvine, CA 92618

Within the Hotel Finisterra:

The Whale Watcher Bar There isn't a better place in Los Cabos for viewing great gray whales than this spot. It's easy to while away an entire afternoon in this open-air bar, sipping margaritas, scanning the horizon, and waiting for the sun to set in a blaze of color. ♦ Daily. 30000

62 El Galeón ★★★$$$ The view of the marina at sunset from the second-story balcony is reason enough to dine here. This restaurant is more sedate and refined than most Cabo San Lucas eateries, with courtly waiters, subdued lighting, and satisfying Italian cuisine. Definitely splurge on the giant lobsters if they're available. Caesar salad and flaming coffees are prepared tableside, and several veal dishes appear on the menu. You can keep the tab low by ordering pizza or pasta and antipasto. Argentinean pianist Ronald Valentino is a big draw with couples who shun the blaring rock 'n' roll of many in-town restaurants, preferring a repertoire from Gershwin to Chopin. ♦ Italian ♦ Daily dinner. Blvd Marina (between Caminos Solmar and del Mar). 30443

63 Bahía San Lucas and Marina The busiest waters in the Mar de Cortés have to be along the Cabo San Lucas waterfront, from the sportfishing docks to **El Arco** nearly a mile from shore. Cruise ships anchor nearby and passengers are shuttled to shore by the score. Sportfishing and sightseeing *pangas* clog the wooden docks, while luxury yachts and sailing ships line up in marinas removed from the mobs. Nearly every tourism service has a booth here, with barkers on commission enticing you to go fishing, scuba diving, sailing, and more. Prospective anglers cluster around the southern edge of the marina where fishing boats bring in their haul. If you don't mind flies and the strong smell of fish, visit the sportfishing docks between 1 and 3PM, when the boats come in, and see proud anglers posing beside their catches at the weighing station.

Cruise passengers have a waiting lounge with bathrooms and snack shops to the north. Between the docks and the cruise area is an open-air artisans' market, designed to capture the tourist dollar before it gets to town. The entire marina is a good place to shop and compare prices. Check out any boat before you board—are there seats, lifejackets, and canopies to shade you from the sun? Does the engine at least look like it will run smoothly? Does the operator provide *cold* drinks and purified water? A trip out to sea is imperative in Los Cabos, and much nicer if you sail in comfort.

Within Bahía Cabo San Lucas and Marina:

Artisans' Market You'll find a good selection of handicraft-style souvenirs by browsing among the tables and stands at this market on the water's edge. The most unusual and indigenous items are the ironwood carvings of marlin, sailfish, turtles, and whales. The best bargains can be found in silver jewelry, if you can tell the difference between real silver and alloys. Real silver should be stamped "925," while alpaca (known in the US as German silver or nickel silver), the most common silver imitation, is a mix of nickel and tin and is lighter in color and weight than sterling. ♦ Daily

64 Amigos Del Mar One of the oldest and most reputable scuba companies in Los Cabos, this outfit has dive trips to the underwater sandfalls (similar to waterfalls, but made of sand) near **El Arco,** as well as to the coral reef northeast of Los Cabos at Cabo Pulmo. ♦ Daily. Blvd Marina (just east of Camino Solmar). 30505, 800/344.3349; fax 30887

65 Solmar Suites $$$ These low, white-stucco buildings look like space colony pods against the sandstone foothills of the Sierra de San Lázaro. The rocky ridge extends into the sea at the peninsula's tip, cupping the hotel in stark seclusion. The Pacific pounds onto a dramatic stretch of pristine beach, crowded only in the winter months, when people gather to watch the whales swimming a few yards offshore. This resort has by far the most striking setting of any of the local hotels, and does a great job of enhancing, rather than intruding upon, the scenery. Town is just a 10-minute walk away, yet you feel completely removed from the action. An enormous brick-domed ceiling covers the lobby, where the tour desk does a brisk business. The 90 rooms are designed as suites with sitting areas, balconies, telephones, mini-bars, air-conditioning, and satellite TV (a blessing on hot afternoons when a cool room and a good movie are requisites). The pool has a shallow area with pulsing jets of water and submersed stools at the *palapa*-shaded bar. A second pool and hot tub, available to hotel guests, are located in the center of the adjacent **Solmar Beach Club** time-share condos. The property's stark beauty and sense of isolation make it the ideal destination for those seeking soothing solitude. ◆ Camino Solmar (south of Blvd Marina). 33535; fax 30410. For reservations: Box 383, Pacific Palisades, CA 90272. 310/459.9861, 800/344.3349; fax 310/454.1686

Within the Solmar Suites:

La Roca ★★$$ The outdoor patio seats at this restaurant command a peerless view of a pretty palm garden and the sea, and the food is good enough to keep guests from going into town for a meal. Dinner is particularly pleasant as mariachis serenade the diners, backed by the pounding of the surf. The chef goes all out for the Saturday night Mexican fiesta, with a buffet of regional dishes, including great tamales, *chiles rellenos,* chicken mole, and various marinated salads. Staff members present an impressive folk dance show, and all guests get a kick out of swinging a bat at a giant piñata. ◆ Mexican/American ◆ Daily breakfast, lunch, and dinner. 33535

Solmar Fishing Fleet This is the largest sportfishing fleet in Los Cabos, with at least 21 cruisers and *pangas.* There are full- and half-day fishing trips from the marina and ships for group charters. Take a gander at the marlin, dorado, and sailfish mounted on walls and hanging from ceilings all over the hotel for an idea of what the fishing enthusiasts are so wild about. The custom-built 112-foot *Solmar V* is a stunning ship with interiors of gleaming mahogany, brass, and etched glass. There are 12 cabins with private baths and VCRs and a luxurious dining room and salon. The live-aboard ship travels to nearby dive sites, but its specialty is long-range diving trips to the Socorro Islands some 300 miles offshore. The weeklong trips give divers a chance to swim with manta rays, hammerhead sharks, whale sharks, and other pelagic giants. When not at sea the ship is docked in the marina; look for its distinctive green-and-yellow trim. ◆ 33535; fax 30410. For reservations: Box 383, Pacific Palisades, CA 90272. 310/459.9861, 800/344.3349; fax 310/454.1686

66 El Arco The granite arch at land's end where the Pacific meets the Mar de Cortés is Baja's trademark. Equally dramatic are the gray-brown granite boulders rising from under the sea south of the arch. Note the skinny tall one that looks like the Baja Peninsula turned upside-down. A cruise past the arch is imperative for any first-timer; chances are good you'll see sea lions sunbathing and cavorting on the rocks, and you'll use up at least one full roll of film trying to capture the arch's natural majesty. ◆ East of Cabo San Lucas, accessible only by boat

67 El Faro de Cabo Falso (The Lighthouse) A small crook of land pokes into the Pacific about five miles west of San Lucas, forming a miniature tip that looks like land's end from the sea—the *capo falso,* or false cape. The lighthouse was built here in 1890 and served as the peninsula's beacon until it was destroyed by a *chubasco* (hurricane) in 1957; today it still stands, but in a state of ruin. Since no paved road leads to it, you'll need a four-wheel-drive or off-road vehicle to take you there. When motorcycle groups aren't racing by, it's a secluded and stunning spot that gives a sense of Baja's wild majesty. The lighthouse is also visible from boats on the Pacific. ◆ 8 km (5 miles) northwest of Cabo San Lucas

El Arco

M. KOHNKE

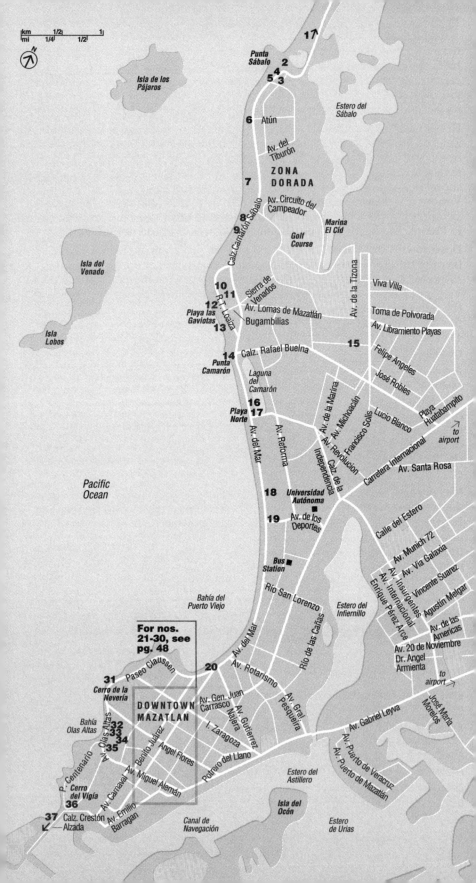

km |____|____|____| **1/2** |____| **1**
mi |____| **1/4** |____| **1/2** |____|

Isla de los
Pájaros

17

Punta
Sábalo **2**
5 **4**
3

6 Atún

Av. del Tiburón

Estero del
Sábalo

**Z O N A
D O R A D A**

7

Av. Circuito del
Campeador

Isla del
Venado

8
9

Golf
Course

Marina
El Cid

Calz. Camarón Sábalo

Av. de la Tizona

Viva Villa

Isla
Lobos

10
11

Sierra de
Venados

Toma de Polvorada

12
Playa las
Gaviotas **13**

Av. Lomas de Mazatlán
Bugambilias

Av. Libramiento Playas

Av. R.T. Loaiza

Felipe Angeles

José Robles

15

14
Punta
Camarón

Calz. Rafael Buelna

Lucio Blanco

Laguna
del
Camarón

Francisco Solís

Playa
Huatabampito

16
Playa **17**
Norte

Av. de la Marina

Av. Michoacán

Av. Revolución

Av. de la Independencia

Calz. de la Independencia

Carretera Internacional

→
to
airport

Av. del Mar

Av. Reforma

Av. Santa Rosa

Pacific
Ocean

18 Universidad
Autónoma

19 Av. de los
Deportes

Calle del Estero

Av. Munich 72

Av. Vía Galaxia

Bus
Station

Av. Insurgentes

Vincente Suárez

Río San Lorenzo

Av. Internacional

Agustín Melgar

Enrique Pérez Arce

Av. de las
Américas

Bahía del
Puerto Viejo

Estero del
Infiernillo

Río de las Cañas

Av. 20 de Noviembre
Dr. Angel
Armienta

**For nos.
21-30, see
pg. 48**

→
to
airport

Av. del Mar

José María Morelos

31
Cerro de la
Nevería

Paseo Claussen

20

Av. Rotarismo

Av. Gral. Pesqueira

Av. Gabriel Leyva

**DOWNTOWN
MAZATLAN**

Av. Gen. Juan
Carrasco

Av. Gutiérrez
Nájera

Bahía
Olas Altas

32
33
34
35

Av. Olas Altas

I. Zaragoza

Av. Puerto de Veracruz

Av. Benito Juárez

Angel Flores

Potrero del Llano

Av. Puerto de Mazatlán

P. Centenario
Cerro
del Vigía
36

Av. Camaral

Av. Miguel Alemán

Estero del
Astillero

37 Calz. Crestón
←— Alzada

Av. Emilio
Barragán

Isla del
Ocón

Estero
de Urías

Canal de
Navegación

Mazatlán

The traditional Mexican port city of Mazatlán, with its stunning coastline, marks the beginning of the **Mexican Riviera** along the **Pacific** coast. Inhabited today by almost half a million people, Mazatlán was one of Mexico's earliest coastal tourist centers and has some of the best sportfishing around. Nearly one million visitors pass through here each year to enjoy the area's comfortable climate, reasonable prices, and renowned hospitality.

Hotels, restaurants, and shops can be found along the **Zona Dorada** (Golden Zone), a popular congregating area that includes a 14-milelong stretch of beach and bustling streets. The zone edges slightly farther north each year as developers clear the way for new resorts and marinas along acres of prime shoreline. Still, isolated, beautiful beaches remain that can be easily explored. Various travel agencies and hotels offer day trips that include snorkeling, swimming, and picnicking to such uninhabited offshore islands as **Isla de la Piedra**, **Isla de los Chivos**, **Isla de los Pájaros**, and **Isla del Venado**.

Downtown Mazatlán, with its central market, plaza, and cathedral, is the heart of the city's activities and has kept its traditional atmosphere despite the development that surrounds it. On the edges of downtown is **Mazatlán Viejo**, where historians, architects, and entrepreneurs are working to restore the noble old buildings, many dating from the late 1800s and early 1900s, that were once the city's treasures. The **Teatro Angela Peralta** (Angela Peralta Theater), centerpiece of Mazatlán Viejo, reopened in 1992 after decades of neglect, and many buildings in neighboring streets have undergone renewal.

A primary port since the arrival of the Spaniards, Mazatlán has one of Mexico's biggest harbors and is home to a thriving commercial fishing fleet and a large fish-packing and export business. The surrounding sea offers anglers the opportunity to land giant marlin and sailfish, and excellent charter boats are available in a range of sizes and prices. (A growing number of sportfishers here are practicing the catch-and-release method; they enjoy the thrill of the fight and capture, then return the graceful fish to the sea to ensure the survival of the species.)

Mazatlán's reputation as a party town dates back almost a century—mainly due to its magnificent Carnival celebration (held for a week before Lent in late February or early March). Costumed night and day, residents and visitors dance in the streets and party in cafes until the wee hours. (Visitors who return for the celebration annually make their hotel reservations at least six months in advance.) Canadian and American snowbirds flock to the Zona Dorada in winter; during Easter Week, the place is taken over by students on spring break.

Area code 69 unless otherwise noted.

Getting to Mazatlán

Airport

Aeropuerto Nacional Rafael Buelna (Rafael Buelna National Airport) is located 16 kilometers (10 miles) east of town. There is one terminal handling both national and international flights daily.

Airlines Be sure to reconfirm flight reservations at least 24 hours before your departure.

Aero California 132042, 162190, 800/237.6225

Aeroméxico 131111, 131621, 800/237.6639

Alaska Airlines 852730, 800/426.0333

Delta 132709, 800/221.1212

Mexicana 827722, 800/531.7921

Getting to and from Aeropuerto Nacional Rafael Buelna

By Bus Look for the *colectivo* (van) ticket counter at the airport. The *colectivo* fare is $5 to $8, depending on the location of your hotel. When you return to the airport, you must take a taxi; there are generally plenty waiting at the hotels.

By Car Mazatlán's airport is a 30-minute drive from downtown. Drive west on **Avenida Gabriel Leyva** to downtown, or southwest on **Carretera Internacional**, west on **Calzada Rafael Buelna**, and north on **Calzada Camarón Sábalo** to reach the Zona Dorada.

The following car-rental agencies have counters at the airport but are open only when flights are arriving and departing.

Budget...............................826363, 800/527.0700

Hertz 850845, 800/654.3131

National.............................824000, 800/328.4567

By Taxi Taxis wait in front of the baggage claim area; the fare to town is $5 to $10, depending on the location of your hotel.

Getting Around Mazatlán

Buses Public buses travel the length of Calzada Camarón Sábalo, which becomes Avenida del Mar as it goes south to downtown. Buses marked *Sábalo Centro* go from the Zona Dorada to the downtown plaza and market area. The main bus station is on **Río Chachalacas** (between Av General Juan Carrasco and Rio Fuerte). Call 817625 or 813684 for information.

Driving Bus transportation is quite good, so unless you'll be going to out-of-the-way places you don't need a car here. Traffic is congested and parking difficult to find in both the Zona Dorada and downtown. If you do wish to drive, the following car-rental agencies have offices downtown:

Avis Calzada Camarón Sábalo 314 ....140040, ...140050, 800/331.1212

Budget Calzada Camarón Sábalo 402 ....132000, ...800/527.0700

Hertz Av del Mar 1111 ....136060, 800/654.3131

National Calzada Camarón Sábalo
(at Plaza el Camarón) 136000, 800/227.7368

Taxis Cabs are easily flagged down on the street. *Pulmonías* are open-air jitneys that cost almost the same as taxis. To hire a taxi, call 816129 or 823189.

FYI

Accommodations Mazatlán's hotels run from very low-end budget to very expensive deluxe. The least expensive places are downtown in the **Olas Altas** area, while moderate and expensive hotels are located in the **Playa Norte** (North Beach) and Zona Dorada sections. Mazatlán doesn't have many truly luxurious, full-scale resorts like those in Cancún; most are informal, low-key affairs regardless of their size.

Consulates

US Consulate..165589

Canadian Consulate Hotel Playa Mazatlán,
Av Rodolfo T. Loaiza 202 (at Playa las Gaviotas) 837320

Publications The free English-language *Pacific Pearl* newspaper is published monthly and contains news and information for tourists. It's available at most hotels and tour desks.

Shopping Shopping is a major tourist activity in Mazatlán, though the quality of the merchandise is unexceptional. The Zona Dorada has many shops selling sportswear and a few good ones offering folk art. Most travelers browse through the selection at the **Centro de Artesanías** (Mazatlán Arts & Crafts Center) at least once. Best buys there include wooden fish painted with elaborate, colorful designs, wood carvings, and knickknacks made from seashells.

Sportfishing Both commercial and recreational deep-sea fishing are big business in Mazatlán, where world records are often broken. Local captains encourage sportfishers to release their big catches— after a commemorative snapshot—particularly the large marlin and sailfish for which the area is known. An estimated 12,000 billfish are caught in these waters annually. Several sportfishing fleets operate out of the pier on **Boulevard Joel Montes Camarena** on the Pacific side of **Cerro del Crestón**. Stop by the pier in mid-afternoon to see how the anglers are faring and to talk to the captains before choosing a charter. The **Star Fleet** (Blvd Joel Montes Camarena, 822665, 823878; fax 825155, 210/377.0451) is the largest sportfishing operation in Mazatlán. The **Aries Fleet** (El Cid Marina, 800/633.3085) departs from the marina in the hotel zone.

Time Zone Mazatlán is on Central Time, two hours ahead of California and one hour behind New York.

Tours The following tours are available through several agencies.

In the **City Tour** a bus cruises along Mazatlán's oceanside drive, providing you with a view of divers leaping from cliffs, as well as a visit to the **Mercado Romero Rubio** (Romero Rubio Market), the **Catedral de la Inmaculada Concepción** (Cathedral of the Immaculate Conception), **Mazatlán Viejo**, and **Cerro del Vigía** (Lookout Hill). Some companies offer this tour in the evening and include dinner at a downtown restaurant.

The **Fiesta Cruise** (852237) is a three-hour boat tour of Mazatlán's bay and sheltered harbor.

The **Mountain Tour** consists of a daylong exploration of the nearby colonial towns of **Copala** and **Concordia,** home of popular hardwood furniture factories (see "Off the Tourist Track" on page 48).

For information and reservations contact:

Marlin Tours ....135301; fax 164616

Tropical Tours ....165076; fax 165077

Viajes Playa Sol ....137777; fax 137212

Tour Guide Association...............................827534

Visitors' Information Center The **Coordinacion General de Turismo de Sinaloa** is open daily. It is located in the **Banctural Building** at Calzada Camarón Sábalo and Avenida del Tiburón, 165160/1/2, fax 165166, 165167.

Phone Book

Hospital/24-hour Medical Clinic Carretera
Internacional..863343

Police...148444

Red Cross...816355

Mazatlán

Most visitors to Mazatlán flock to the elegant hotels, shops, and restaurants of the Zona Dorada, to the north of downtown. Beyond these attractions, though, the area offers miles of lovely, isolated beaches and several offshore islands that are perfect for day trips.

1 Marina Mazatlán A work in progress, this megaresort project sprawls over more than 1,000 acres north of the Zona Dorada. A marina for 1,200 vessels is partially open, and some private homes have been built. Slated for completion after the turn of the century, the complex will include private vacation homes and condos and an 18-hole golf course. ♦ Av del Delfin (north of Punta Sábalo). 164188

2 Hotel Camino Real $$$ An aristocrat among local hotels, this one commands an exclusive setting on a hillside overlooking the sea. The location between the marina and the Zona Dorada makes it one of the most isolated properties, blessedly free of the varied decibels of noise that surround other hotels. Half of the 169 rooms have private balconies. Those on the west look out on the Pacific and miles of beaches, while those on the east take in a lagoon and the distant Sierra Madre. Accommodations are spacious, air-conditioned, and decorated in pinks and purples. Rocks jut into the sea on both sides of the beach, breaking the waves and keeping the water calm. The small pool is heated, and there is one tennis court. You can count on quality meals at several restaurants. ♦ Calzada Camarón Sábalo (at Punta Sábalo). 132111, 800/722.6466; fax 140311

3 Sr. Pepper ★★★★$$ Ask anyone in Mazatlán to recommend a high-quality steak house, and you'll probably end up here, savoring tender Sonora beef barbecued over mesquite coals. Choose between the rib eye, porterhouse, or filet mignon. (These are enormous steaks; if you tell them you want to share, they will cut it in half and bring two plates with all the trimmings.) Start with a huge margarita and move on to the fried zucchini appetizer. There's also succulent lobster, jumbo shrimp, and Cajun blackened fish. After your meal, order *brewed* decaffeinated coffee—this is one of the few places in Mazatlán that offers it. An intimate candlelit atmosphere, a piano bar, crystal and silver settings, and attentive waiters make each visit a special occasion. Service is excellent, right down to the crumb sweeper after your meal. ♦ International ♦ Daily dinner. Calzada Camarón Sábalo (north of Blvd del Marlin). 140120

4 La Costa Marinera ★★★$$ Decorated with fishing nets, seashells, and buoys, this beachfront restaurant specializes in seafood.

For an all-out feast, order the seafood *parrillada*—a clay hibachi loaded with shrimp, frogs' legs, oysters, and delicate fish fillets stuffed with seafood, all garnished with onions, peppers, tomatoes, and limes. ♦ Mexican/Seafood ♦ Daily lunch and dinner. Privada Camarón and Calzada Camarón Sábalo. 141928

5 Pueblo Bonito $$$ An opulent chandelier crowns the beautiful lobby, and antique art tastefully fills the public rooms of this all-suite hotel and time-share resort, one of the most elegant places to stay in town. Its 247 rooms, most done in pink, all have domed ceilings, king-size beds, tile baths, kitchenettes, and ocean views. Adding a tropical touch, the gorgeously landscaped grounds resound with the cries of the resident peacocks, parrots, and flamingos. Amenities include two swimming pools, restaurants, bars, and satellite TV. ♦ Calzada Camarón Sábalo 2121 (at Blvd del Marlin). 143700, 800/442.5300; fax 143723

6 DoubleTree Club Resort $$$ A recent addition to the hotel zone, this seven-story hotel has only 118 rooms, which gives it a more intimate atmosphere than other nearby properties. With cool tile floors and a simple decor, rooms have private balconies facing the sea, pool, or gardens, two double beds, shower, and in-room safe. The water sports center rents equipment, and the pool is large enough for impromptu water volleyball games among strangers. The hotel's two restaurants are supplemented by a weekly beach barbecue in high season. ♦ Calzada Camarón Sábalo and Atún. 130200, 800/222.TREE; fax 166261

7 Fiesta Inn $$ Popular with Mexican families and small tour groups, this high-rise hotel has 117 rooms, all with oceanfront balconies. Ample and pleasantly decorated in soft pastels, the rooms have satellite TV with movie channels, small table and chairs, and both tubs and showers. The restaurant features Mexican specialties and offers a good buffet breakfast every morning. You can swim laps in the large pool and find water sports equipment on the beach. The fitness center is a big plus, with aerobics classes offered daily. ♦ Calzada Camarón Sábalo 1927 (between Avs Rodolfo T. Loaiza and del Tiburón). 890100, 800/343.7821; fax 890130

Restaurants/Clubs: Red	**Hotels:** Blue
Shops/♥ Outdoors: Green	**Sights/Culture:** Black

8 El Cid Mega Resort $$$ This city-within-a-city hotel and residential resort sprawls over 720 acres and consists of three beachfront hotel buildings, private villas, and a 27-hole golf course. Its thousand rooms are spread out among the **Castilla,** a 17-story tower that is the hotel's main building; the 25-story **El Moro Tower,** an all-suite facility with penthouses; and the less expensive **Granada,** featuring rooms in low-rise buildings by the swimming pools. The resort's lush grounds are connected by walkways and bridges, as well as shuttles. Guests may use the golf course and the 17 lighted tennis courts (clay and all-weather); also here are 5 restaurants, 11 bars, 5 swimming pools, a health and fitness club, a fishing fleet, children's activities, shops, and a disco. Not surprisingly, the resort staff actively pursue potential time-share buyers a bit more aggressively than you'd like. ♦ Calzada Camarón Sábalo (between Avs Rodolfo T. Loaiza and del Tiburón). 133333, 800/525.1925; fax 141311

Within the El Cid Mega Resort:

La Concha ★★★$$$ Located right on the beach, this flamboyant restaurant boasts an elaborate *palapa* (thatch-roofed hut) illuminated with hanging spotlights. Some guests eat all three meals here, starting with the bountiful brunch buffet, followed by a mid-afternoon snack and a late dinner accompanied by live music. For a total seafood extravaganza, order the *parrillada de mariscos,* one of the more spectacular presentations of the ubiquitous Mazatlán dish. This version includes lobster, shrimp, oysters, and octopus on a bed of lettuce and rice. Dine inside or out, with a view of the ocean either way. ♦ International ♦ Daily breakfast, lunch, and dinner. 133333

Marina El Cid Hotel $$$ Though not on the beach, the fanciest parts of this megaresort are clustered around the marina and yacht club. The 210-room hotel, whose several Mediterranean-style buildings frame the marina, includes both one- and two-bedroom suites, all with balconies and kitchenettes. There's both a saltwater and a freshwater pool, a restaurant, and a fitness center. One of the area's best fishing fleets is based at the 90-berth marina, and guests have access to the resort's golf course. ♦ 133333, 800/525.1925; fax 141311

9 Hotel Costa de Oro $$ The three complexes that make up this 293-room resort sit on both sides of the street. The beach complex is the most popular, with one pool and two restaurants. The newer tower is made up entirely of suites with kitchenettes and has its own pool. The third section is adjacent to three tennis courts. Guests may opt for the all-inclusive package with meals, domestic wine, beer, soft drinks, and tax. There are two restaurants and three bars. Time-shares are available. ♦ Calzada Camarón Sábalo (between Avs Rodolfo T. Loaiza and del Tiburón). 135444, 132005, 800/342.2431; fax 144209

10 Centro de Artesanías (Arts & Crafts Center) If the hotel zone had a public market, it would be this sprawling center. Shoppers should allow plenty of time to explore Mexican crafts in the labyrinth of shops and workshops inside this two-story, thatch-roofed structure. Potters create original ceramics, and carvers work wood into traditional or modern creations. Rug weavers, tinsmiths, and jewelers will fill your personal requests, and orders are taken for custom-made clothing. ♦ Daily. Av Rodolfo T. Loaiza (between Garzas and del Mar). 135243

Within the Centro de Artesanías:

No Name Cafe ★★$ A totally north-of-the-border cafe right down to a menu that lists prices in US currency, this spot is favored by a young crowd that goes for the televised sports. Cold Pacífico beer is the drink of choice; burgers and fries are the favorites on the menu. The patio is a good spot to wait while your friends finish their shopping. ♦ American ♦ Daily breakfast, lunch, and dinner. 132031

10 Sea Shell City Always wanted a lampshade covered in scallop shells or a sea horse night-light? This is the place—a two-story monument to the many uses, be they elegant, decorative, or tawdry, for some of the sea's debris. Serious collectors can drop a few clams here on corals and sea fans. ♦ Daily. Av Rodolfo T. Loaiza (between Garzas and del Mar). 131301

11 Baby Tacos ★$ Taco stands abound throughout Mazatlán and are by far the least expensive places to eat. This one is a step above the street-vendor variety, with a clean food-preparation area and outdoor seating. You'll pay less here than at the fast-food franchises and eat like a Mexican. ◆ Mexican ◆ Daily lunch and dinner. Garzas (between Calzada Camarón Sábalo and Av Rodolfo T. Loaiza). No phone

11 Pura Vida ★★$$ Tucked away in a back street, surrounded by bushes and trees, this health-food cafe is a welcome sight for those craving salads and grains. Soy burgers and veggie-and-cheese sandwiches come on whole-wheat buns, or try the imaginative versions of classic Mexican dishes made with meat substitutes. The selection of juices and smoothies is enough to keep you coming back for more. ◆ Vegetarian/Health food ◆ M-Sa breakfast, lunch, and dinner. Laguna and Garzas. 165815

12 El Paraíso Tres Islas ★★★$$ Families gather for Sunday afternoon feasts at this *palapa* on the beach, with sizzling seafood cooked on clay hibachis usually on the menu. At night, couples take over the candlelit tables for seafood dinners accompanied by live music. The restaurant is named for the three islands it faces—Isla Lobos, Isla del Venado, and Isla de los Pájaros. The bustle of the tourist zone seems far away here, though it's just up the street from the beach. ◆ Seafood ◆ Daily breakfast, lunch, and dinner. Av Rodolfo T. Loaiza 404 (at Playa las Gaviotas). 142812

12 Hotel Playa Mazatlán $$ The first hotel built along the Zona Dorada remains one of the most popular. Though not as glitzy as some of the newcomers, this 420-room establishment has a carefree atmosphere that pleases the many guests who return annually and stay for weeks on end. Tour groups are often booked here, and the pool and beach can get very busy and crowded. If you want an ocean view and a balcony, make reservations in advance and request one of the 54 deluxe units. The most peaceful rooms, including several two-bedroom suites, are those around the garden and second pool. Gear needed for every kind of water activity is available for rent, and there are fast-food stands near the lobby. ◆ Av Rodolfo T. Loaiza 202 (at Playa las Gaviotas). 134444, 800/762.5816; fax 140366

Within the Hotel Playa Mazatlán:

Fiesta Mexicana Home to the city's best Mexican fiesta for over 25 years, this place is so good even locals attend. The fiesta is held on Sunday and other days as well in high season. The admission fee covers the enormous Mexican buffet and all the tequila and beer you can consume. An excellent folkloric dance show, relatively tame cockfights, ranchero and mariachi performances, and a spectacular fireworks display make up the entertainment. Tickets are available at travel agencies and hotel tour desks. ◆ Admission. Su; more often in tourist season (mid-November through mid-April). 134444, 134455

Terraza Playa ★★★$$ A *palapa* shades the tables on this patio, an ideal perch to enjoy a meal and watch the beach action. This is really a place for a soup-to-nuts dinner— shrimp cocktail, Creole soup (with bits of tortillas, green peppers, and cheese), and *churrasco Argentine* (a tender, marinated beef fillet). The chef's salad served in a tortilla shell is a nice change from heavy meals.

Vendors strolling along the beach will whistle to catch your attention, then show you their blankets, straw hats, purses, silver jewelry, and more. If you're not interested, just avoid eye contact. Many vendors are friends with the hotel's regular guests, and their banter is amusing and amiable. Sometimes you can get good buys, especially if you're skilled at bargaining. At night the restaurant sparkles, with a backdrop of stars and music for dancing. On Sunday night the patio tables are good for watching the 8PM fireworks show. ◆ International ◆ Daily breakfast, lunch, and dinner. 134444, 134455

Mexico Mexico Women who discover this tiny clothing shop early in their stay will be tempted to invest in a whole new wardrobe. The brightly colored gauze clothing is perfect for tropical climates, especially when personalized with the one-of-a-kind accessories. ◆ Daily; closed at midday. No phone

La Carreta Owner Julieta Fuentevilla Alvarez travels throughout Mexico selecting the best folk art and furnishings for her shop. Among the treasures are pillowcases showing scenes of village life, made from *molas*, a reverse-appliqué technique. True collectors will want to browse thoroughly through her merchandise. ◆ Daily; closed at midday. 165045

Many shops in resort towns give cabdrivers a 10-percent commission on purchases made by the tourists they drop off at their stores. So make sure your driver takes you where you really want to go.

los sabalos

13 Hotel Los Sabalos $$$ One of Mazatlán's better high-rise hotels where athletic types can enjoy the two lighted tennis courts, pool, sauna, and whirlpool. Many of the 74 small standard rooms have windows that don't open; the 111 suites and junior suites cost more, but have balconies where you can get fresh air. ♦ Av Rodolfo T. Loaiza 100 (between Calzada Camarón Sábalo and Playa las Gaviotas). 835333, 800/528.8760; fax 838156

Within the Hotel Los Sabalos:

Joe's Oyster Bar and Grill ★★$
There's no better place to view the beach scene than from this immensely popular seaside cafe, where scantily clad diners quaff cold beers and lemonade after long sessions of sunbathing. The ambience is far more exciting than the food; stick with simple tacos and seafood cocktails. Patrons get rowdy when the band blares rock 'n' roll favorites nightly after dark. ♦ Seafood/Mexican ♦ Daily lunch and dinner. 135333

14 Valentino's Complex You can't miss the white turrets and domed Arabesque rooftops perched atop Punta Camarón on the south end of the Zona Dorada. Overlooking the sea, this complex enjoys one of the most breathtaking views in Mazatlán. At one time the only tenant was **Valentino's** lively disco, but the distinctive structure continues to grow and now houses a cluster of businesses geared for nighttime dining and entertainment. ♦ Punta Camarón (just west of Calzada Camarón Sábalo). 836212

Within Valentino's Complex:

Valentino Discotheque No expense was spared in creating this extraordinary dance club. The sound system and laser lights are straight out of Hollywood, and revelers dance up a storm. For those who prefer less noise, there's another dance floor next door with a quiet, intimate atmosphere, soft music, and the chance to enjoy slow dancing. A gameroom is available with tables set up for checkers, backgammon, and chess. It's not "in" to arrive before midnight, and customers are expected to dress up. ♦ Cover. Daily. 841666

Enchanting Refuge

Hacienda Las Moras, a neglected tequila ranch in the countryside outside **Mazatlán,** has become the area's most innovative and deluxe resort ($$$$). Guests stay in private cabanas filled with folk art and antiques, dine in a restored hacienda, and sunbathe by the pool in ultimate tranquility. Horseback riding through the mountains to isolated pueblos is the main recreational activity, along with tennis, hiking, and hayrides. Owner Michael Ruíz has also turned the 3,000-acre ranch into a refuge for animals by importing miniature horses and all sorts of birds. Peacocks stroll the grounds beside guinea hens, while wild falcons and hawks soar in the sky. Chickens of every imaginable strain have full run of the property, laying their eggs in window boxes and pottery planters. A white wedding chapel overlooks the property; the original stable is now a glassed-in lounge.

To protect its patrons' privacy, drop-in visits to the ranch are not allowed. You can, however, make reservations in advance to dine at its restaurant (★★★★$$$$), an experience not to be missed: Tables covered with embroidered mantillas, and set with painted pottery and blown glass (all made by hand) overlook the grounds and pool, and the chef bakes all the bread in an outdoor wood-burning oven and specializes in outstanding regional Mexican cuisine. Settle in for a leisurely lunch and you may never want to leave.

For resort reservations, contact Camarón Sábalo 204, Suite 17, Mazatlán, 165044; fax 165045. In the US, write to 9051-C Siempre Viva Rd, Suite 15-203, San Diego, CA 92173.

El Sheik ★★$$$ The bubbling waterfall and intimate banquettes scattered about the room provide a cozy setting, and dress is more formal than at most local restaurants (no shorts, please). Seafood is your best bet here, especially the giant Sheik-style shrimp; for the purist, the shrimp brochette is sweet and fresh. Don't order the steak—it's simply not their forte. The waiters put on a great show with the flaming coffees and desserts. Even if you're not hungry, consider visiting the restaurant for the spectacular views. Call early and request a table on the balcony where the breeze is balmy and you can see the stars. ♦ Seafood ♦ Daily dinner. Reservations recommended in winter. 141616

15 Plaza de Toros la Monumental (Bullring) Bullfights are presented here every Sunday from Christmas through Easter and are taken very seriously by aficionados, especially when superstar matadors are in town. Seats in the *sombra* (shady) side of the arena are the most expensive, but you'll appreciate them as the temperature rises. If you haven't been to a bullfight before, be prepared for a gory finale. Tickets are available at travel agents and hotel tour desks. Rodeos (called *charreadas*) are also held at the ring sporadically throughout the year. The bullring becomes a baseball field where Mazatlán's excellent team, Los Venados, plays from October through January. ♦ Admission. Calzada Rafael Buelna (just east of Av de la Marina). 841666

Hotel Posada de Don Pelayo
Las Sirenas Suites

16 Hotel Posada de Don Pelayo $ Some of the most reasonably priced accommodations can be found at Playa Norte (North Beach), between downtown and the Zona Dorada. Among them, this old favorite has been completely refurbished; the 96 rooms and 72 junior suites have central air-conditioning (but no in-room controls) and satellite TV. Suites come with kitchenettes, and the rooms facing the main street and beach have balconies. The hotel is popular with families for its two pools, tennis court, and inexpensive coffee shop. ♦ Av del Mar 1111 (between Av Revolución and Calzada Rafael Buelna). 831888; fax 840799

17 Olas Altas Inn $ Despite its name (high waves), this inn is actually across the street from Playa Norte. The ultramodern mauve-and-gray decor sets this place apart from the older hotels in the neighborhood, and though the 50 rooms are small, they're spotless and comfortable. The pool is small as well and sits just back from the sidewalk beside the inn's coffee shop. ♦ Av del Mar 719 (between Av Revolución and Calzada Rafael Buelna). 813192; fax 853720

18 Señor Frog's ★★★$$ If you can handle the unbelievably high level of music and revelry (the place is known throughout Mexico as a rowdy hangout where drinking, dancing, and flirting are the norm), this restaurant is well worth at least one dinner, since the food is very good. Try the *molcajete* (strips of chicken or pork served on a heated clay tray with grilled green onions and melted cheese). Steaks and barbecued chicken and ribs are among the most popular meals, and all the Mexican specialties are exceptionally well prepared. A line forms at the front door on weekend nights, so it's best to arrive early if you're more interested in the food than the fun. The shop by the entrance carries the ever-popular T-shirts with the restaurant's logo. ♦ Mexican/American ♦ Daily lunch and dinner. Av del Mar (between Avs de los Deportes and Revolución). 821925

19 Acuario de Mazatlán (Mazatlán Aquarium) The dozens of tanks at this aquarium are filled with colorful sea horses, eels, lobster, and Day-Glo tropical fish—at least 300 species of fresh- and saltwater fish are on display. Other highlights include the show put on several times a day by California sea lions and singing birds and the educational films on the marine world shown in the auditorium. Schoolchildren on field trips visit the adjacent playground and botanical garden; amid the trees in the garden is a small zoo—be sure not to miss the sinister-looking crocodiles. ♦ Admission. Daily. Av de los Deportes 111 (between Avs Reforma and del Mar). 817815; fax 817816

Off the Tourist Track

Just over an hour's drive from **Mazatlán,** through low hills covered with rugged bushes and green mango groves, lies the **Pueblo Concordia,** which was founded in the 1500s and inhabited by Spanish settlers and Jesuit missionaries who profited from the success of nearby gold and silver mines. Today the town is a craft center known for its hand-carved hardwood furniture and pottery. There are more than 60 resident cabinetmakers here, most with workshops attached to their homes. Also worth seeing is the town's large plaza, which dates back to the colonial era, and the **Catedral de San Sebastián** (Cathedral of St. Sebastian); the oldest Baroque church in the state, it was built between 1706 and 1785.

A few miles away is the village of **Copala,** a tranquil retreat into the gold-mining epoch of the late 1800s and early 1900s. This former boomtown is now a well-preserved Mexican pueblo of some 600 and a growing population of US expatriates and retirees. **Daniel's Restaurant** (★★$$; no phone) at the entrance to town, is a requisite stop for lunch and a piece of banana-cream coconut pie. Owner Daniel Garrison, whose grandmother is buried in the town cemetery, hails from California. A local hangout, the serene eatery offers a calming view of the countryside. If you want to spend the night (well worth it), try the large, comfortable rooms in **Daniel's** small hotel ($).

After the tour groups leave, the town settles into bucolic serenity, with the silence broken only by crowing roosters and barking dogs. The cobblestone and dirt streets are lined with century-old white stucco homes, their tile roofs smothered in fuchsia bougainvillea. Neighbors gather at the small central plaza in early evening and stop by the **Catedral de San José** (Cathedral of San José) built in 1641. If it weren't for the electric lights (installed in 1979) and the occasional car, you'd think you had wandered into the past. You can get there by rental car or through arrangements with tour companies, who will drop you off one day and take you back to the city the next.

20 **Monumento al Pescador** Constructed in 1958, this bronze sculpture is a tribute to the hardworking fishermen who built the industry that still beats tourism as the leader of Mazatlán's economy. The rather bizarre design of a reclining nude woman extending her hand to a burly, naked fisherman is sure to catch your eye. ♦ Avs del Mar and Gutierrez Najera

21 **Cerro de la Nevería (Ice Box Hill)** In the 1800s tall-masted ships from San Francisco sailed into Mazatlán's port carrying all types of cargo. One of the most important was ice. A ship would barely be docked before the precious load was rushed up to this hill and placed in tunnels and caves packed carefully with gunnysacks and sawdust. The ice preserved fresh-caught shrimp for the fledgling industry and pampered those who could afford this extravagance. Before it became an ice locker, the hill served as a lookout station for the Spanish. Soldiers on patrol searched the horizon for the masts of pirate ships commanded by such evildoers as Captains Cavendish and Drake, who brought trouble and tragedy to Mexico's coastal cities in their search for Spanish galleons laden with gold and silver. Mazatlán's port was the main shipping point for the neighboring mining communities Rosario, Copala, and Pánuco. Years later, during the Mexican Revolution, the hill was used as a repository for munitions. ♦ Paseo Vistahermosa (south of Jacarandas)

DOWNTOWN
MAZATLAN

22 Mercado Romero Rubio In the heart of downtown, the enclosed, cast-iron market bustles with residents on their daily errands. Built in the 1890s, it was renovated for its hundredth birthday. Chickens hang in the open air in the meat section (which can be particularly odiferous); piles of shrimp and fresh fish lie atop ice. Papayas, mangoes, pineapples, and other fruits are stacked beside each other in colorful arrays—bring your camera for memorable shots. One section specializes in herbs, incense, and magical potions, another in religious statues and prayer cards. Leather goods, straw baskets and hats, and souvenirs are priced far lower than at shops in the Zona Dorada, especially if you're good at bartering. Visit early in the morning, before the crowds, heat, and aromas become overwhelming. ♦ Daily. Bounded by Av Aquiles Serdan and Benito Juárez, and Leandro Valle and Melchor Ocampo

23 Pasteleria Panamá ★★★$$ You'll be lucky to get a table here at lunchtime, when it seems that all the downtown offices and shops empty out into the restaurant's three dining rooms. Try to snag a seat by the windows looking out onto the cathedral, and be sure to survey the goodies at the bakery counter before placing your order. On display are lavish French pastries, sweet rolls packed with raisins or nuts, multilayer cakes filled with whipped cream, and cookies. This eatery is most famous for its desserts, but the sandwiches, soups, and enchiladas are quite good as well. The Zona Dorada branch is equally popular and a great place for breakfast or an afternoon coffee break. ♦ Bakery/Mexican ♦ Daily breakfast, lunch, and dinner. Benito Juárez and José María Canizales. 851853. Also at: Calzada Camarón Sábalo and Garzas. 132941

24 Centro de Idiomas (Spanish-Language School) More and more visitors to Mazatlán are combining their vacations with intensive Spanish study at this small school. Owner Dixie Davis, a US native, has made her establishment an informal meeting place for travelers and locals, offering Spanish and English conversation groups on Friday evenings and walking tours of Mazatlán Viejo once a month. Spanish classes begin on Monday (the minimum course is for one week). For those who want individual instruction, Davis matches students with teachers of like interests. She also arranges homestays. ♦ Belisario Domínguez 1908 (between 21 de Marzo and José María Canizales). 822053; fax 855606

25 Catedral de la Inmaculada Concepción (Cathedral of the Immaculate Conception) The two yellow-tiled spires poking into the sky over downtown Mazatlán are relatively new additions to this cathedral of many architectural styles. Construction of the church began in 1855 under the orders of Bishop Pedro Lozay Pardave and was completed 20 years later. The facade and central altar are Gothic, while the two side altars are Neo-Classical. The many chandeliers, ethereal frescoes, gilded arches, marble pillars, and formal balconies give the interior a decidedly Baroque effect. The two peaked belfries were added in the early 1900s, and the cathedral was designated a basilica in 1935. ♦ 21 de Marzo and Benito Juárez

26 Plaza Revolución Sometimes referred to as "Plaza República," the town's main square bustles with shoeshine boys looking for business, people chatting on park benches, and children playing. On Friday evenings families socialize, and vendors sell *elota* (hot ears of corn), balloons, cotton candy, and cold drinks. At the center of the park is a two-story wrought-iron gazebo with an interior cafe that looks like a 1950s diner. In 1913 the plaza's gazebo was the site of the first radio telegraph station in Mazatlán. Cables serving as antennae were stretched to the dome of the cathedral across the street. During the 1920s and 1930s, it was the stage for Carnival dance bands, and bands still appear here often, especially on Friday, Saturday, and Sunday evening. A ceremonial color guard lowers the flag near the plaza daily at dusk. ♦ Bounded by Benito Juárez and Guillermo Nelson, and Angel Flores and 21 de Marzo

Mazatlán Viejo

In the late 1800s, when it was the major port for the Pacific coast of Mexico, Mazatlán was quite a wealthy city. Immigrants from Germany, Spain, and the Philippines made their fortunes in silver and gold from mines in the nearby mountains and from the country's most profitable foundry. Wealthy mine owners and shipping magnates built palatial mansions befitting their social standing just a short carriage ride from the central plaza. As the mines were depleted and other ports thrived along the coast, Mazatlán's boom dwindled, and the old homes fell into decline.

In the late 1980s, the people of Mazatlán began to pay attention to the old neighborhoods and their history and tradition. A group of architects and preservationists persuaded the government to delineate a historic center and protect the older buildings from neglect and destruction. The neighborhood now called Mazatlán Viejo radiates inland from a promenade along a particularly gorgeous stretch of sand and sea known as **Olas Altas** (High Waves), at the foot of **Cerro del Vigía** (Lookout Hill). Buildings are gradually being restored as cafes, theaters, and schools, and the area is thriving as a result of its revival. Wander these back streets for a view of the true Mazatlán, filled with architectural surprises and a sense of cultural renewal.

27 Doney ★★★★$$ A mansion built more than 125 years ago was cleverly converted into this charming restaurant where locals come to enjoy a fiery *asada al carbón* (Mexican-style barbecued meat) or spicy sausage and fried *plátanos* (plantains). Run by the same family for years, the establishment provides consistently outstanding home-style Mexican cooking. On Sunday afternoons it's filled with families enjoying the *comida corrida,* an entire meal that includes soup, entrée, and dessert. If it's offered, try the sensational *cochinita pibil* (pork cooked in banana leaves). On most tables you'll see a pitcher of fresh *naranjada* (orangeade), a sweet and cold treat. Check out the photos of Mazatlán Viejo and don't leave without having a piece of apple or lemon-meringue pie. ◆ Mexican ◆ Daily breakfast, lunch, and dinner. Mariano Escobedo 610 (between Benito Juárez and Av Carnaval). 812651

28 Cafe Pacífico ★★$$
The structure that houses this unpretentious cafe was built in 1875; the bar has the original old-style bricks and scorched timbers. The full-length, open-air windows with iron bars (wooden shutters close it up at night) make the place feel like a small Spanish tapas bar. Don't expect fancy fare, just a few seafood dishes, sandwiches, drinks. It's a great vantage point for watching activities across the street at Plaza Machado, especially from the umbrella-shaded sidewalk tables. ◆ Mexican ◆ Daily breakfast, lunch, and dinner. Constitución (between Benito Juárez and Av Carnaval). No phone

29 Plaza Machado The centerpiece of Mazatlán Viejo, this square has a new Moorish-style gazebo surrounded by flowering trees and iron benches. Some of the buildings facing the plaza have been rescued from decline and obscurity and now house cafes and private businesses. ◆ Constitución and Av Carnaval

30 Teatro Angela Peralta Mazatlán Viejo's future was guaranteed with the opening of this restored theater a few years ago. In 1869 the theater's original benefactor, Filipino merchant Manuel Rubio, felt Mazatlán needed a cultural center and studied pictures of the grand opera houses of Europe for inspiration. Construction progressed slowly on the **Teatro Rubio,** lapsing for a time after Rubio was lost at sea while on a fund-raising journey. In 1883, the theater was finally ready for its inaugural concert by Mexican diva Angela Peralta. But tragedy struck once again: The star arrived by ship from San Francisco but succumbed to bubonic plague before her performance. Appropriately, the theater was renamed in her honor.

For much of the next century the building served as a cultural, political, and entertainment center for the city, though its grandeur was often ignored. It was the venue for spirited rallies during the revolution of 1910, and for boxing matches and vaudeville shows. The roof blew away during Hurricane Olivia in 1975, but even after that occasional concerts were still held under the starlit sky. Finally, in 1986, the Friends of the Teatro Angela Peralta was formed to spearhead the theater's reconstruction.

Architect **Juan José León Loya,** who bears a strong resemblance to the theater's original master carpenter, his great-grandfather Santiago León Astengo, oversaw the reconstruction. The original tropical Neo-Classical facade was restored and painted a soft rose; the ornate Baroque interior was rebuilt to resemble the original as closely as possible. Performances are held in the concert hall, which is open for public viewing during the day. ◆ Daily. Av Carnaval (between Libertad and Constitución). 824447

31 El Mirador The pounding surf and rocky shoreline are a spectacular setting for the cliff divers, who display their bravery by diving from a platform into the sea. (The platform is about two stories high.) The show is usually performed when tour buses are around; the divers emerge from the water, mingle with spectators, and request donations. ◆ Av Olas Altas (between Angel Flores and Ignacio Zaragoza)

32 La Siesta $ Favored by travelers who prefer downtown, this hotel sits across the street from the crashing waves of Olas Altas. It has the advantage of being close to Mazatlán Viejo's historical sites; guests feel as if they're staying in a Mexican town rather than a homogenized tourist district. Rooms are on two levels of a well-maintained old wooden structure; those with balconies at the front of the hotel have a view of the sea, and the background sound of pounding waves drowns out the music from the courtyard restaurant below. All 56 rooms and bathrooms are large and clean, perfectly serviceable, if unexciting. ◆ Av Olas Altas 11 (between Mariano Escobedo and Angel Flores). 134655

Within La Siesta:

WORLDS FAMOSO

El Shrimp Bucket

RESTAURANT BAR

El Shrimp Bucket ★★★$$ This landmark restaurant, the first of the enormously successful Carlos Andersen chain, has been completely remodeled. The bright dining room now has street-level windows that open to let in the ocean breezes, while the courtyard feels like a private garden. Popular among groups, the courtyard is also the setting for live marimba music; if you want to observe the festivities, you can eat in the courtyard even if you're not part of the group. The menu features shrimp—fried or grilled and, if you wish, topped with garlic and butter—along with a wide selection of Mexican dishes. ♦ Mexican/Seafood ♦ Daily breakfast, lunch, and dinner. Reservations recommended during winter. 816350, 828019

33 Hotel Belmar $ One of the oldest hotels in downtown Mazatlán, this would be a real gem if it were better maintained. The main five-story building, with rocking chairs in the lobby, faces Olas Altas, but other buildings in the back have a drab view of the parking lot. Still, the 150 rooms and apartments with kitchens all have air-conditioning and cable TV; there's a swimming pool in the garden and restaurants within easy walking distance. Considering the amenities, this is a great deal. ♦ Olas Altas 166 (between Osuna and Mariano Escobedo). 811111; fax 813428

34 El Museo de Arqueología (Archaeology Museum) The city's small archaeological museum contains artifacts from the state of Sinaloa, as well as changing exhibits of paintings, sculpture, and other works by local artists. ♦ Donations. Tu-Su; closed at midday. Osuna (between Belisario Domínguez and Av Olas Altas). 853502

35 Copa de Leche ★★★$$ A wonderful spot for a meal or snack any time of day, this old favorite faces the sea at Playa Olas Altas. In the morning elderly gentlemen linger over their coffee and newspapers at the sidewalk tables. Office workers fill the dining room at lunch, feasting on beef cooked with onion, peppers, and mushrooms, or a fragrant, filling seafood soup. At sunset, travelers and locals meet at the handsome bar, and dinner is a leisurely affair. ♦ Mexican ♦ Daily breakfast, lunch, and dinner. Av Olas Altas 33 Sur (between Av Miguel Alemán and Osuna). 825753

36 Cerro del Vigía (Lookout Hill) Some of Mazatlán Viejo's finest buildings are at the bottom of this hill. On the way up you'll pass the **Universidad de Mazatlán**, housed in a 19th-century mansion, and the gray **Casa de Aduanas** (Customs House) constructed in 1828. Near the top is a lookout point and the **Observatorio** (Observatory), a bunker with gun slits built in 1872. The view encompasses the sportfishing, commercial, and naval piers on the east side of downtown, and the lighthouse atop Cerro del Crestón (Creston Hill). ♦ Paseo Centenario (south of Av Miguel Alemán)

37 El Faro (The Lighthouse) Perched on the top of Cerro del Crestón, this is the world's second-highest lighthouse after the one in Gibraltar. About 505 feet above sea level, its light is visible offshore for 36 nautical miles. It was built during the 1930s, part of a project ordered by President Porfirio Díaz, linking what was then an offshore island to the mainland by the construction of a complex breakwater. The hike to the top takes about 30 minutes. Carry along some water and snacks; cold sodas are available from the lighthouse keeper. ♦ Cerro del Crestón (south of Calzada Crestón Alzada)

Retreat in the Wild

Although the coastline south of **Mazatlán** is dotted with small fishing villages that are largely ignored by the outside world, **Teacapán** has attracted more attention than most, thanks to its natural attributes. Two hours and 131 kilometers (81 miles) south of the city, the town sits at the end of an 18-milelong peninsula bordered by the **Pacific** and a series of canals and mangrove lagoons. At the **Boca de Teacapán**, the mouth of **Río Teacapán**, local fishermen beach their boats after netting shrimp. They are always willing to take passengers on bird-watching cruises through the lagoons, to which herons, flamingos, ducks from Canada, and many more species of birds migrate. On land, mango orchards and palm groves are interspersed with cattle ranches and clusters of vacation homes along the peninsula, where much of the land is wild enough to harbor ocelots, wild boar, and deer. Some residents and ecologists would like the peninsula protected as an ecological preserve; others see the coastline and river as the perfect spot for resorts and marinas. For now, there are few tourist services.

The best place to stay is **Rancho Los Angeles** ($; Km 25, Carretera Escuinapa-Teacapán; 695/32550; fax 695/32550. Reservations: Palmas 1-B, Colonia Los Pinos, Mazatlán, 69/817867; fax in Mazatlán 69/817867). This 14-room hotel, between the beach and a large coconut grove, is run by Dr. Ernest Rivera Gúzman and his sons. The complex includes a hacienda-style building on the beach with a pool, dining room, and a half-dozen rooms, some with terraces facing the sea. The other rooms are in a motel-like structure by the peninsula's main road. Boat tours and horseback riding are available. In all, these secluded surroundings afford yet another view of Mexico's varied landscape.

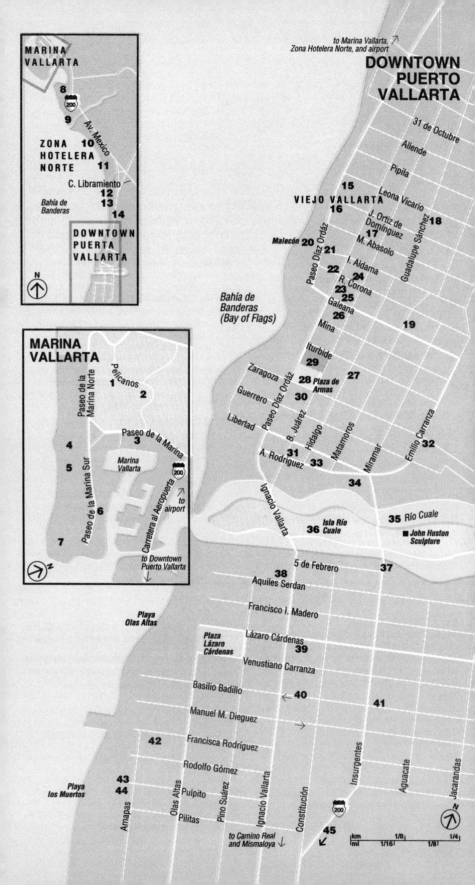

Puerto Vallarta

Nestled alongside the broad **Bahía de Banderas** (Bay of Flags), Puerto Vallarta is documented in ships' logs from the early 1500s, but it didn't develop into a city until centuries later. The first village on the site, **Las Peñas**, began with just a lean-to used to shelter workers unloading salt for the neighboring mining towns of Cuale and San Sebastián. By 1880 the population had grown to 1,500, and six years later the village was given official political standing. In 1918 the name Las Peñas was changed to Puerto Vallarta, after **Jalisco**'s governor Ignacio L. Vallarta.

It wasn't until the early 1930s that tourists started trickling into town. But by 1963, when Richard Burton and Ava Gardner starred in the film *The Night of the Iguana,* shot in Puerto Vallarta, international publicity attracted droves of curious people. That prompted a building frenzy that almost got out of hand. Hotels, restaurants, shops, and roads sprouted up without much forethought, both downtown and along the northern coastline. Fortunately, civic leaders realized that the city was in danger of being destroyed by progress, and they undertook a development project that has restored at least some of Puerto Vallarta's original beauty.

On the northern outskirts of town, the **Marina Vallarta** project has become a full-scale resort. The road from the marina and airport to downtown has been widened, and downtown traffic congestion has been slightly eased with the construction of a new road leading to the coastal highway that bypasses the city. **Viejo Vallarta** streets have been paved with cement and cobblestones, and the web of telephone and electrical wires that marred the landscape is now buried. The old town still has many one-of-a-kind galleries and restaurants, but, perhaps inevitably, it is now also home to a flock of chain hangouts, including **Planet Hollywood**, the **Hard Rock Cafe**, and **McDonald's**.

On the southern coast of Puerto Vallarta, the area's natural beauty remains intact. Lush green jungle grows to the edge of the sea, and the road cut out of the mountainside twists and climbs through spectacular scenery. The lavish homes gracing this coast are owned by North Americans and out-of-town Mexicans, who make up a large part-time community. Puerto Vallarta has its faithful followers who wouldn't dream of missing their annual journeys to this charming colonial city by the sea.

Area code 322 unless otherwise noted.

Getting to Puerto Vallarta

Airport

The **Gustavo Díaz Ordáz Aeropuerto Internacional** (Gustavo Díaz Ordáz International Airport) is located approximately 6.5 kilometers (4 miles) north of downtown Puerto Vallarta. The single terminal handles both national and international flights. Note that airport services such as car rentals and shops are open only when flights are arriving and departing.

Airport Services
Information 11325

Airlines
AeroCalifornia 41499, 800/237.6225

Aeroméxico 42777, 800/237.6639

Alaska Airlines 11252, 800/426.0333

American 11799, 800/443.7300

Continental.............................11025, 800/525.0280

Mexicana 11266, 800/531.7921

Getting to and from Gustavo Díaz Ordáz Aeropuerto Internacional

By Bus Transportation is provided from the airport by *colectivo* (van) direct to your hotel; rates are set by the zone and range from $3 to $10. No public buses run to the airport.

By Car **Carretera al Aeropuerto** runs south from the airport to most hotels; the road's name changes to **Avenida de las Palmas** and **Avenida Medina** along the way. **Marina Vallarta** is 5 minutes south of the airport; downtown Puerto Vallarta is a 20-minute drive south.

The following car-rental agencies have counters at the airport, open only when flights are arriving and departing. Most agencies also have offices along road to town or in the major hotels.

Avis	11112, 800/331.1212
Budget	22980, 800/527.0700
Hertz	11473, 800/654.3131
National	11226, 800/328.4567

By Taxi Taxis await passengers in front of the airport. The fare to downtown is about $10.

Getting Around Puerto Vallarta

Buses Transports marked *Marina* run north from town to Marina Vallarta; those with a *Mismaloya* sign run south to **Camino Real** and **Mismaloya**. Buses designated *Hoteles* travel between town and the north **Zona Hotelera Norte** (Northern Hotel Zone); those marked *Centro* go from the hotel zone to downtown.

The buses can be hot and crowded, but the nominal price (under 50¢) makes them a great way to get around. Stops are indicated by a blue-and-white sign with a drawing of a bus. Buses traveling north begin and end routes at **Plaza de Armas** near the **Palacio Municipal;** those headed south begin and end at **Plaza Lázaro Cárdenas** near **Playa Olas Altas.**

Driving A car isn't really necessary in town, where the traffic gets terribly congested and other means of transport are available, but it comes in handy for side trips to the jungle and isolated beaches. Tours also go to these spots; signing up for one may be a better idea if you want to make sure you don't miss any of the sights.

Taxis Cabs are abundant and easy to flag down. Most hotels have signs posting the fares to points around town. Confirm the fare with the driver before taking off.

FYI

Accommodations Hotels run from inexpensive, bare-bones hostelries to full-scale, lavish resorts. The most expensive hotels are located in Marina Vallarta and along the coast south of town, while the Zona Hotelera is filled with moderate-to-expensive places. Most of the less expensive hotels are downtown and along **Playa los Muertos.** Puerto Vallarta is a popular destination for Mexican nationals, so book ahead for Christmas, Easter, and Mexican holidays.

Consulates

Canadian Consulate Zaragoza 160 (between Benito Juárez and Paseo Díaz Ordáz) 25398

US Consulate Zaragoza 160 (between Benito Juárez and Paseo Díaz Ordáz)...............20069; fax 30074

Cruises and Water Sports The view from the sea to the mountains is one of Puerto Vallarta's greatest attributes; several companies offer day trips to the secluded beaches at **Yelapa** and **Las Animas** and sunset cruises with dinner served aboard ship or on a beach. Snorkeling and scuba diving excursions to **Las Tres Marietas,** an underwater reserve, are especially rewarding, as are winter cruises to spot migrating humpback whales. Kayaking in the bay has become very popular, and a few ecologically oriented companies offer instruction and tours. Most hotels have water sports centers that rent wave runners, kayaks, and other water toys. Boat tours generally leave from the Marina dock just south of Marina Vallarta, next to the **Maritime Terminal** where cruise ships dock, or south of downtown at the dock between Playa los Muertos and Playa Olas Altas.

The following companies have proven track records:

Chico's Dive Shop	21895
Open Air Expeditions	23310
Princesa Cruises	44777
Vallarta Adventure	10657

Dining Puerto Vallarta is an exceptional dining town, with Mexican, US, and European chefs all doing their utmost to lure visitors. New restaurants come and go, but several excellent establishments have remained in business for years, adjusting their menus to reflect Asian, Californian, and even Swiss influences. Unfortunately, some of the best restaurants close down during slow seasons and the humid, rainy months of August and September. To be sure an establishment's open, call ahead or check in advance with your hotel's concierge.

Publications English-language tourist publications come and go here; among those usually available are the magazine *Puerto Vallarta Lifestyles* and the daily newspaper *Vallarta Today.*

Shopping Shopping is one of the major attractions here and for good reason: The downtown area is filled with excellent art galleries and folk art boutiques carrying top-quality hand-crafted items from all over the country. Don't overlook the deluxe hotels; many have shopping arcades with very fine jewelry and sportswear shops. Most shops in town are closed on Sunday.

Street Plan Puerto Vallarta is actually several destinations in one, running down the long sweep of **Bahía de Banderas.** Marina Vallarta is at the north end of the bay, followed by the Zona Hotelera Norte. Downtown Puerto Vallarta is divided by the **Río Cuale;** most of the best galleries and shops are on the northern side, while the southern side has many great restaurants and most of the budget hotels.

Time Zone Puerto Vallarta is on Central Time, two hours ahead of California, one hour behind New York.

Tours Most hotels have a travel agency or information desk with information on city tours and driving tours to rivers and restaurants in the jungle. For a completely different perspective, try signing up for mountain biking, bird watching, or hiking trips in the **Sierra Madre.** The following companies have proven reliable:

American Express	32955
BikeMex	31680
Harris Bus Tours	32972
Open Air Expeditions	23310
Intermar Vallarta	10777

Visitors' Information Center The **Oficina de Turismo** (Tourism Office) is open Monday through Saturday and is located in the **Palacio Municipal** (Benito Juárez, between Plaza de Armas and Iturbide, 12242; fax 12243). The helpful staff here can solve most problems.

Phone Book

Fire	47701
Hospital Carretera Libramiento	Km 1.5. 44000
Police	20123
Red Cross	21533

Marina Vallarta

This expanding megadevelopment lies at the north end of town, conveniently close to the airport, but a 15-minute taxi ride to downtown Puerto Vallarta. The property sprawls along the west side of the airport road with an 18-hole golf course at the northern end. Time-shares, condos, private homes, and hotels surround the 350-slip marina in the center of the development, while elegant hotels line the beachfront. The area is confusing to newcomers, and distances between various attractions are significant. The best ways to get around are on the shuttle bus that runs between the hotels, by bicycle (available for rent at your hotel), or by one of the many taxis available. A water taxi service also transports guests to various locales around the marina. Public buses marked *Marina* run from downtown to some of the marina hotels.

1 Bel-Air Hotel $$$$ Mexican architects **Roberto** and **Ricardo Elias** created their hotel in a California-Mexican style, with striking archways, dramatic domes, and a soft pink facade. The whimsical masks and pastel fish of the famous Mexican artist Sergio Bustamante hang above the beds in the hotel's 75 suites and villas, many of which have small blue-tile pools and hot tubs on private terraces. Guests lounge in billowing, Moroccan-style tents by the pool amid a landscape of fountains and fish ponds. Privacy is guaranteed, since the hotel is surrounded by the marina's golf course—the 18th hole and clubhouse are just a short walk away. ◆ Pelicanos 311 (between Paseos de la Marina and de la Marina Norte). 10800, 800/457.7676; fax 10801

2 Marina Vallarta Club de Golf Joe Finger designed this 18-hole course that sprawls over the north end of the marina development. Obstacles and distractions include waterfalls and a natural lagoon that attracts herons and alligators. It has a pro shop and several clubhouses; membership is available to marina residents. Hotel guests can arrange tee times through their concierges. ◆ Paseos de la Marina and de la Marina Norte. 10545; fax 10171

3 Marina Business Center The promenade around the north shore of the marina is gradually filling up with small cafes, delicatessens, shops, and offices, though some of the 120 commercial spaces are still vacant. **El Faro,** the white lighthouse, stands as a beacon for boats at the harbor entrance. Slips accommodate vessels of up to a hundred feet long, and water taxis transport boaters to their hotels. ◆ Paseo de la Marina (between Hwy 200 and Paseo de la Marina Sur)

Within the Marina Business Center:

El Faro Lighthouse Bar With a 360° view of the marina and the sea, this glass-enclosed cocktail lounge atop the lighthouse is the most romantic setting for watching the sunset. It is open only in the evenings, when drinks are served to the accompaniment of romantic ballads. ◆ Daily. Royal Pacific Yacht Club. 10541, 10542

Porto Bello ★★★$$$$ A dark-green awning stretches over the patio, which faces the boats at this marina-front trattoria. The inside dining room is more intimate, with heavy white linen tablecloths and subdued lighting. Locals come here for the veal scallopini with shrimp (veal is hard to come by in these parts). The fusilli with artichokes and black olives is fragrant with basil. A trio plays Italian ballads during dinner. ◆ Italian ◆ Daily lunch and dinner. 10003

Las Palomas Doradas ★$$ While this may not be the fanciest-looking restaurant from the outside, it offers excellent local dishes. The small *tampiqueño*-style beef steak (marinated and grilled) is butter-tender, and the tasty trimmings include chicken enchiladas, beef *taquitos*, spicy *chiles rellenos*, beans, rice, and great guacamole and chips. For a delightful meal, try dining outside at the wrought-iron tables. ◆ Mexican/Seafood ◆ Daily breakfast, lunch, and dinner. 10470

Puerto Vallarta's popular park, Jardín del Arte, used to be the local graveyard.

Restaurants/Clubs: Red	**Hotels:** Blue
Shops/ ⑧ Outdoors: Green	**Sights/Culture:** Black

4 Marriott Casa Magna $$$$ A desire to immerse guests in supreme luxury is evident throughout this Mexican-style Taj Mahal. Hotel staff greet guests at the airport and provide complimentary transportation to the hotel. Most of the 433 rooms have private safes, lovely toiletries, mini-bars, and iron and ironing boards in the closets. You need a map to navigate around multileveled interior stone waterfalls, fountains, and long hallways with polished marble and glittering chandeliers. Outside, immense artificial lakes blend gently into the swimming pool. A bar under a waterfall is an unusual and cooling place to sip a margarita. The three restaurants serve breakfast, lunch, and dinner. After a good workout in the sophisticated health center, spoil yourself with an expert massage. The hotel occasionally offers golf packages. ♦ Paseo de la Marina 5 (at Paseo de la Marina Sur). 10004, 800/223.6388; fax 10760

5 Paradisus Puerto Vallarta Resort $$$$ Palatial is the word for this completely renovated, all-inclusive hotel, operated by the Spanish-owned Meliá chain. Everything here is spacious, from the 365 large bedrooms with gleaming marble floors to the two-story lobby and bar, the huge swimming pool (designed in the shape of Picasso's peace dove) to the 400-seat theater that offers nightly entertainment. All three meals are served in three restaurants. Amenities that are part of the rate include the use of two tennis courts, a children's program, land and water sports, Spanish lessons, and nightly entertainment. ♦ Paseo de la Marina Sur (south of Paseo de la Marina). 10200, 800/336.3542; fax 10118

6 Mayan Palace Water Park You can't miss the tall, twisting water slides rising atop this children's amusement park, where parents can relax poolside while lifeguards monitor the children. The five-story slides thrill the older kids, who don't seem to mind climbing several steep stairways to the top. Smaller children ride floats along a lazy river, past waterfalls and giant mushroom-shaped fountains surrounding a play area. Parents can also escape to a smaller pool hidden by bushes and trees. Tired tots can rest in a nursery/first-aid station; the snack bar offers energy-replenishing hot dogs and milk shakes. ♦ Admission. Daily. Paseo de la Marina Sur (south of Paseo de la Marina). 11500

7 Westin Regina Vallarta $$$$ Easily the most architecturally striking hotel in this area, the property was designed by **José Iturbe** in the modern Mexican style originated by **Luis Barragan.** Recessed squares and windows are painted vivid orange and pink against the hotel's cool white facade, and lemon-yellow domes and ceilings brighten the long corridors and spacious rooms. The designers deserve kudos for the extra details that make the 280 guest rooms delightful: Ceiling fans and huge windows allow those who enjoy sea breezes to remain cool and comfortable. The floors are covered with soft, woven, straw mats, and solid tropical colors sooth the eye—no fussy florals here. Islands of blossoms and palm trees break the meandering pool into four private areas, lending an air of seclusion from other guests. The lounges and walkways resemble galleries; don't miss the display of oversize fanciful animals by some of Oaxaca's most noted wood carvers. Guests who don't feel like leaving the hotel may take advantage of the several restaurants on the premises. The hotel is also a favorite of honeymooners, who enjoy the special pampering offered in romance packages. ♦ Paseo de la Marina Sur 205 (south of Paseo de la Marina). 11100, 800/228.3000; fax 11141

Jungle Oasis

Those who dream of adventure in the jungle and a tropical-island lifestyle should hop on the shuttle boat from **Puerto Vallarta** to **Yelapa** and **Las Animas,** two fishing villages where life moves slowly. This is where you can get away from it all—there are no paved roads, telephones, or even swimming pools. Instead, you'll find US and Canadian expatriates enjoying a laid-back way of life.

As soon as you arrive onshore, representatives from the towns' restaurants will approach you and offer umbrellas and lounge chairs for rent. The small cafes serve simple meals (often featuring seafood) and cold drinks.

Probably the biggest draw in Yelapa is the beautiful waterfall with its inviting swimming hole, well worth the 15-minute hike, some of it through jungle terrain. (If you're not feeling hardy enough that day, for a few dollars you can rent a horse to make the trek.) It's everything a remote jungle pool should be, although you *can* buy sodas and beer and relax at the few simple tables and chairs close by. *Raicilla* (local moonshine) is available if you ask for it. Yelapa offers fishing, swimming, and, for bird watchers, a multitude of winged creatures that stop at the waters of nearby **Río Tuito.** Las Animas is less crowded than Yelapa and offers the same sense of a jungle getaway.

Boats leave Puerto Vallarta's commercial boat docks daily; a water taxi service in small *pangas* (fishing skiffs) departs from **Playa los Muertos.**

Zona Hotelera Norte (Northern Hotel Zone)

Puerto Vallarta's original hotel zone draws a large number of visitors who want long beaches, plenty of water toys, and easy access to downtown by public bus or taxi. The wide boulevard running from the marina to downtown is divided by islands of palms. (Note: This thoroughfare is referred to by three names—"Avenida las Palmas," "Carretera al Aeropuerto," and "Avenida Medina"—which can cause some confusion.) Lined with shopping centers and hotel entrances, the road is not particularly conducive to walking. You're better off strolling down the long **Playa Norte** (also called "Playa de Oro") on the waterfront side of the hotels.

8 Terminal Marítima (Maritime Terminal)
Cruise ships dock here and deposit their passengers for a fun-filled day in Puerto Vallarta. Some excursion boats also depart from a separate dock here sometimes called the Marina dock. ♦ Hwy 200 (south of Paseo de la Marina)

9 Krystal Vallarta Hotel $$$ This resort is like a small village where streets are open only to pedestrians and the silent electric golf carts that transport arriving guests to their rooms. *Palapas* (palm-thatched huts) line the beach, and colonial-style stone water fountains bubble everywhere. The 450 rooms come in a variety of sizes and styles—from standards and suites to three-bedroom villas with private pools. Boutiques, travel agents, bars, coffee shops, specialty restaurants, dozens of swimming pools, fiesta grounds, and convention facilities are spread about on the 37 acres, with plenty of space for privacy and seclusion. ♦ Av de las Garzas (west of Hwy 200). 40202, 800/231.9860; fax 40150

Within the Krystal Vallarta Hotel:

Bogart's Restaurant ★★
$$$ As much a stage set as a restaurant, this place is beloved for extravagant, romantic, dress-up dinners. Waiters in red fezzes disappear behind white Arabesque arches and walls and return to deliver an elaborate meal—maybe the *reina del mar Marraquech* (juicy lobster medaillons with Cognac sauce) or the *scherezada* (crispy lettuce, fresh mushrooms, provolone, and Italian dressing). Whatever entrée you choose, be sure to save room for the crepes suzette—a delicate combination of fresh oranges, limes, brandy, and Cointreau. ♦ International ♦ Daily dinner. Reservations recommended. 21459

10 Fiesta Americana Puerto Vallarta $$$$ A gigantic *palapa* marks the entryway to this classically Mexican hotel, whose nine-story, sand-colored building holds 291 spacious, airy rooms and suites. Decorated with light woods and floral linens, all have small balconies facing the pool and beach. The pool flows through the grounds beside small palm groves and casual cafes, and the hotel's beach and water sports center attract parasailors, snorkelers, and swimmers. A buffet breakfast is served in the poolside restaurant, while more formal meals are featured in the restaurant, **La Hacienda.** The hotel participates in a sea turtle conservation project, roping off part of the beach when turtles are nesting in the summer. ♦ Hwy 200 (north of Carretera Libramiento). 42010, 800/343.7821; fax 42108

11 Plaza las Glorias $$$ The hacienda-style architecture gives a nice Mexican feel to this 237-room property. White stucco buildings with red-tile roofs face the pool, palms, and gardens; most rooms have terra-cotta–tile floors, white walls with decorations molded into the plaster, and arched doorways leading to small balconies with wooden railings. The **Pérgola** restaurant offers decent, if unexciting, meals. Across the street from the beach, the hotel has 152 villas with kitchenettes and living and dining areas that are available both as time-shares and nightly rentals. The same company operates the **Continental Plaza** hotel next door, and guests at either hotel have the use of the other's facilities. ♦ Av de las Garzas and Hwy 200. 44444, 800/342.2644; fax 46559

12 Sheraton Buganvilias $$$ Location, service, and the friendly clientele make this a longtime favorite of Puerto Vallarta regulars. Downtown is just a 15-minute walk south, and the beach is one of the best for swimming and water sports. The 501 guest rooms in the main tower overlook the pool and beach and have powerful shower massages in the baths, firm king-size beds, huge closets, and windows that open to let in the sea breezes. The all-suite time-share vacation club has its own pool, though everyone seems to congregate at the enormous main pool where there's plenty of shallow space for the kids and a swim-up bar for the grownups. Thick groves of coconut and fan palms wrapped in hardy vines give the grounds a tropical feel and provide welcome shade during the midday heat. Daily brunch in the coffee shop is quite popular; there are also several restaurants. ♦ Av de las Palmas 999 (between Atlatenco and Carretera Libramiento). 30404, 800/325.3535; fax 20500

Within the Sheraton Buganvilias:

Mexican Fiesta The longest-running and most spectacular fiesta in Puerto Vallarta draws an especially large crowd of revelers in the high season, though it continues in less grand style all year round. The weekly fiesta includes an endless flow of tequila, a bountiful Mexican buffet, and performances by an outstanding 12-piece mariachi band and folkloric dancers. In the high season the fiesta is held on the beach and culminates with a grand fireworks finale. ◆ Admission. Thursday evenings. 30404

13 Buenaventura $$ Facing the sea on the edge of Viejo Vallarta, this establishment is an enduring favorite of families and budget travelers. The five-story atrium lobby is a popular gathering place. Rooms on the fifth floor have balconies overlooking the pool; all 210 guest rooms have pale wooden furnishings and a cool yellow-and-white decor. Despite an enforced rule against noise after 11PM, some might find the place a bit loud. If you don't want to venture out, the hotel's restaurants are good. ◆ Av México 1301 (between Nicaragua and San Salvador). 32737, 800/878.4484; fax 23546

14 Alfareria Tlaquepaque A large selection of baskets, blown glass, ceramic vases, and ornately patterned bowls and plates fill the shelves here. Prices are lower than at shops along the *malecón*. ◆ M-Sa. Av México 1100 (between Honduras and Nicaragua). 32121

Viejo Vallarta

Red-tile roofs, brick trim, tile floors, and white stucco are the hallmarks of the buildings in Viejo Vallarta (Old Vallarta), which lies within the boundaries of the original village. In Mexican design circles, this architecture is referred to as Puerto Vallarta style. Civic leaders recognized the value of maintaining the colonial look and passed a regulation requiring all new buildings to be constructed in this manner. Businesses are also encouraged to use old-fashioned signs and to avoid neon and ultramodern designs.

In fact, Viejo Vallarta has been modernized in ways that greatly enhance its charm. Downtown's bumpy, dusty cobblestone streets have been ripped up and improved. Telephone wires are buried underground, no longer marring the view from the hills above town. The streets running inland from the seaside *malecón* are filled with one-of-a-kind galleries, shops, and restaurants, all well worth visiting.

15 Cenaduria Doña Raquel ★★$ Ask anyone where to go for Mexican home-style cooking, and they'll mention this cafe. It's a small, no-frills place, but the *pozole* (a hominy-and-pork stew) is legendary, and the demand is so high that it is now served nightly instead of only as a traditional Thursday special. The tostadas are made with beef tongue, *lomo* (pork loin), and *cuerito* (pickled pork skin), though the less adventurous may prefer shredded chicken or beef or the more predictable enchiladas and *taquitos*. ◆ Mexican ◆ Tu-Su dinner. No credit cards accepted. Leona Vicario 131 (between Morelos and Paseo Díaz Ordáz). 10618

16 La Dolce Vita ★★★$$ Possibly the least expensive restaurant across from the *malecón* (except for **McDonald's**), this pizzeria serves respectable individual-size pizzas and nutmeg-scented spinach-and-cheese canneloni. Pastas are loaded with meat and seafood sauces, and decent national wines and a few imported Chiantis are served by the bottle or glass. The dinng room is dark and cozy, with recorded divas singing in the background. ◆ Italian ◆ M-Sa lunch and dinner; Su dinner. Paseo Díaz Ordáz 674 (between Mariano Abasolo and Josefa Ortiz de Domínguez). 23852

17 Papaya 3 ★★$ The plants that fill this restaurant lend it the ambience of a beautiful garden, and the food makes it a great find for those seeking respite from spicy sauces and fried foods. Fresh vegetables are the restaurant's forte, and the salads are exceptional. Try the mixed salad of shredded carrots and cabbage, lettuce, tomatoes, and onion, topped with fresh tuna. Soft jazz playing in the background enhances the experience. ◆ Health food ◆ M-Sa breakfast, lunch, and dinner; Su breakfast and lunch. Mariano Abasolo 169 (between Benito Juárez and Morelos). 20303

18 Cafe des Artistes ★★★★$$$$ In a town with many excellent restaurants, this one stands out for its superb cuisine and sophisticated decor. Chef Thierry Blouet has reached star status among locals and frequent visitors, and travelers have been known to dine here several times during their stays. His prawn-and-pumpkin soup, served in a gourd bowl, is legendary, and any fresh fish preparation is memorable—try the crab stuffed with shredded grilled tuna. The roasted duck glazed in lime-and-ginger sauce is equally remarkable. The desserts are exceptional as well, especially the raspberry sorbet atop crisp chocolate "fettuccine." The soft gray ceiling, mauve tablecloths, and sparkling votive candles add an air of subdued elegance, enhanced by the pianist's eclectic repertoire. ♦ Nouvelle Mexican ♦ Daily brunch and dinner. Reservations recommended. Guadalupe Sánchez 740 (at Leona Vicario). 23228

Hotel Los Cuatro Vientos

19 Los Cuatro Vientos $ Make reservations far in advance for one of the 13 rooms in this enchanting hostelry overlooking downtown Puerto Vallarta and the bay. The hotel fills quickly with guests who return annually—and for good reason. Pink bougainvillea and the brilliant yellow blossoms of the *copa de oro* (cup of gold) vine are draped over the building and balconies, which frame a small courtyard and pool. Pretty flowers and birds are painted over doorways and arches; rooms are decorated with folk art and antiques. Massage and facials are available. Downtown is within walking distance, and the climb back up the hill to your room will earn you a well-deserved siesta. The rooftop sundeck is the perfect spot for sunset cocktails, and the restaurant, **Chez Elena,** serves international cuisine at dinner. ♦ Mariano Matamoros 520 (between Galeana and Ramon Corona). 20161; fax 22831. For reservations: Hotel Los Cuatro Vientos, Apdo 83, Puerto Vallarta, Jalisco 48350, Mexico

20 Malecón This wide sidewalk along Puerto Vallarta's oceanfront plays an important part in city life. By day, tourists stroll along the promenade enjoying the smell of the sea and the panoramic views. Charming bronze sculptures are scattered about, including the city's symbol: a boy riding a sea horse. On Sunday evenings, families walk together, buying balloons and cotton candy from vendors, and local musicians perform at the small stage and amphitheater at the walkway's south end. Though many downtown shops and restaurants traditionally close on Sunday, some along here open Sunday evening. ♦ Paseo Díaz Ordáz (between Rodríguez and 31 de Octubre)

21 Las Palomas ★★$$ As soon as guests are seated for breakfast, the waiter pours a mug of steaming Mexican coffee, a good strong brew with a touch of cinnamon. Most customers here are high-powered local businesspeople. It's not unusual to see the mayor, a local publisher, or a Puerto Vallarta Rotarian committee discussing a regional issue. For an authentic breakfast, the *chilaquiles* (fried corn tortilla pieces in a tomato sauce served with fried eggs or shredded chicken) are the best in town, and the *pan dulce* (sweet bread) tastes great with coffee. Check out a local specialty, *divorciados*—two eggs, one with green sauce, one with red, separated by a bed of beans. For lunch, pick a favorite Mexican dish, such as the *chiles rellenos,* which are fresh, rich, and spicy. A fixed-price *comida* (full meal) is offered daily. ♦ Mexican/Seafood ♦ Daily breakfast, lunch, and dinner. Paseo Díaz Ordáz and Ignacio Aldama. 23675

22 Galería Uno The city's premier gallery remains a success because of the artists it represents and the hospitality of owners Janice Lavender and Martina Goldberg, who treat their clients like friends. Works by such Mexican legends as Rufino Tamayo and Mañuel Lepe, as well as pieces by contemporary artists, hang in rooms that give the feeling of an inside courtyard. One show included paintings by Vladimir Cora and sculptures by Diego Martínez, who has created larger pieces for plazas in Guadalajara. This is a required stop for anyone interested in the local art scene. ♦ M-Sa. Morelos 561 (at Ramon Corona). 20908

23 Tutifruti ★$ Take a break from shopping and gallery hopping at this tiny lunch counter, where fresh juice—orange, papaya, watermelon, pineapple, or a mixture of your choice—is prepared to order. Cheese or chicken sandwiches are served on *bolillos* (crusty rolls), and the yogurt is homemade. ♦ Juices/Sandwiches ♦ M-Sa breakfast, lunch, and dinner. Morelos 552 (at Ramon Corona). 21068

24 Arte Mágico Huichol Huichol Indians from northern Jalisco bring their finest work to owners Magua and Mahomedalid, whose entire gallery is dedicated to Huichol yarn and bead art. Huichol art is closely tied to the ancient beliefs of these people, which include the traditional ritualistic use of peyote (a cactus known for its hallucinogenic properties). The unique, complex wall hangings portray nature, gods, and events in vibrant, multicolored tableaux; ritual masks are beaded in intricate designs. These are one-of-a-kind pieces that take hours of labor and are priced accordingly. José Benitez, who has successfully exhibited his work in New York, San Francisco, and Chicago, is just one of the fine artists represented. ♦ M-Sa. Ramon Corona 164 (between Benito Juárez and Morelos). 23077

25 Rosas Blancas This shop/gallery/cafe complex is built around an old mango tree in the courtyard of a former home. One section is devoted to art supplies and books, while other small rooms house high-quality handmade lace, tin-framed mirrors, and regional folk art. The brick courtyard holds cafe tables and is a pleasant spot to regroup over espresso and cake. ♦ M-Sa. Benito Juárez 523 (between Galeana and Ramon Corona). 21168

25 Querubines Angel collectors are in heaven as they stroll through the many rooms in this folk art shop filled with figures of cherubs. The angels are made from a variety of materials, including terra-cotta, and the store also offers swaths of Guatemalan cloth, Oaxacan rugs and shawls, hand-painted tiles and light switch plates, and a host of other gift ideas. ♦ M-Sa. Benito Juárez 501 (at Galeana). 22988

26 Panadería Munguia Early-morning aromas of fresh bread lead visitors right to the door of one of the best bakeries in town. It was opened in the late 19th century by the grandfather of the present town historian, Carlos Munguia. Check out the cookies, flaky pastries, and typical Mexican *pan dulce*. ♦ Daily. Benito Juárez 467 (at Galeana). 22090

27 La Iglesia de Nuestra Señora de Guadalupe (The Church of Our Lady of Guadalupe) History says the first Catholic service in Puerto Vallarta was held by Father Ayala under a tree very close to the present church. Ayala began building this masonry structure in 1892 and finished 10 years later. Engineered by Guerrero de Alba, the actual construction was done by the grandparents and great-grandparents of today's Puerto Vallarta residents. On Sunday mornings, parishioners on their way to mass picked up as many stones as they could carry to add to the growing edifice.

Two different stories circulate about the origin of the ornate crown replica on top of the building. The first version says it was copied from the one worn by Carlota, Empress of Mexico, from 1864 to 1867. Others hold that the crown is the same as the one seen throughout Mexico in many paintings of the Virgin of Guadalupe. Don't wear shorts or T-shirts when visiting this church—or any other in Mexico. ♦ Hidalgo 370 (at Iturbide)

28 Plaza de Armas Puerta Vallarta's main square is next to the **Palacio Municipal** (City Hall) in the middle of town. It's always a busy place, filled with locals and strolling tourists. ♦ Benito Juárez and Zaragoza

29 Palacio Municipal (City Hall) Set right next to the central plaza, this building houses the state tourism office, a good source of information and maps on the area. Be sure to look at the mural on the second-floor stairwell; it was painted by the late Mañuel Lepe, noted artist from Puerto Vallarta. ♦ Tourism office: M-Sa. Benito Juárez (between Plaza de Armas and Iturbide). 20242, 30844; fax 20243

30 Galería Sergio Bustamante Prepare to see some wild flights of imagination by this well-known artist. Pottery, wood, and papier-mâché have been transformed into many different creatures, including life-size humans in unlikely poses and shapes. Bustamante caused a stir in the Mexican art world with his original designs, which have since been imitated by many artists. ♦ M-Sa. Benito Juárez 275 (at Zaragoza). 21129

31 La Tienda de Maria This closet-size shop specializing in miniatures is a delight for those enamored of Mexico's skull and skeleton art, a national fixation. The shelves are filled with tiny three-dimensional household and village scenes, armies of soldiers, and animals smaller than a fingernail. ♦ Daily; closed at midday. Benito Juárez 182 (between Rodríguez and Libertad). 22116

32 Gringo Gulch Lovely homes line this hilly neighborhood's steep cobblestone streets, which are often better suited to donkeys than autos. Richard Burton lived in one during the filming of *The Night of the Iguana*. Long before that, it was an enclave of thousands of expatriates from the US, hence the name. It's still a popular hangout for North American celebrities. ♦ Zaragoza (east of Emilio Carranza)

33 Chef Roger ★★★★$$$
A native of Switzerland with much of his accent still intact, chef Roger Dreier receives rave reviews from locals and travelers alike, who consider dining in his small restaurant's candlelit courtyard a sublime event. The eclectic menu includes some of Roger's Swiss favorites—cheese fondue seasoned with kirsch, *boeuf bourguignon* (beef cooked in Burgundy wine), and hearty bratwurst with German mustards—as well as an outstanding Mexican delicacy combining fresh shrimp, *huitlacoche* (a mushroomlike fungus cultivated in corn husks), and squash-blossom sauce. Save room for the chocolate marquis, a dense, fudgey cake with a mint sauce. The ambience is tropical, casual, and unpretentious. ◆ Nouvelle Continental ◆ M-Sa dinner; closed August through September. Reservations recommended. Rodríguez 267 (between Mariano Matamoros and Hidalgo). 25900

34 Mercado Municipal Artisans' stands line the outskirts of Puerto Vallarta's public market, displaying a wide range of T-shirts, leather items, straw hats, and souvenirs. Housewares and produce fill the market's interior. You won't find many treasures here (the merchandise hardly compares with what can be found in the city's fine folk art galleries), but if you're looking for inexpensive gifts for everybody back home, this may be the place. Bargaining is encouraged. ◆ Daily. Rodriguez (just west of Insurgentes). No phone

35 Río Cuale The river's source lies in the mountains above Puerto Vallarta. During the summer rainy season, it sends voluminous amounts of water rushing through a river canyon in the middle of town, then dries to little more than a trickle in the winter. Old-timers remember when cars were driven right through the low water across the rocky, potholed riverbed before Puente Viejo (Old Bridge) was built. If they had to cross when the water was high, they pulled themselves over the river on a chain. On the other side, they would trade car keys with a friend and go on about their business.

36 Isla Río Cuale (Río Cuale Island) Just below Puerto Vallarta's busy downtown streets lies a small island in the middle of the Río Cuale. Also known as "Isla de los Niños," it's a lovely park with wide cement-and-stone walkways, antique wrought-iron benches, flora, and white stucco buildings housing an assortment of shops and restaurants. There are two ways to reach this island—by steps at the beginning of Puente Viejo on Ignacio Vallarta or from Insurgentes on the east end

of downtown. Two antiquated, suspended wooden swing bridges (for foot-traffic only) lead from the island to the south side of town. Plan on some thrills and chills on the swing bridge—a few slats are missing, and kids enjoy jumping on and shaking the bridge when tourists are crossing. It's definitely a rail-clutcher, but apparently no one's been knocked yet into the river rushing below. Many shops and artisans' stands on the island are open on Sunday, unlike those in town.

On Isla Río Cuale:

John Huston Sculpture In many parks across Mexico, visitors see statues of Benito Juárez, the father of the revolution who freed the poor and broke up the holdings of the rich. Not so on Isla Río Cuale, where a fine, larger-than-life sculpture of John Huston stands below the Insurgentes bridge. The late film director earned the respect of Puerto Vallartans when he chose their sleepy village, of which he was very fond, as the location for *The Night of the Iguana*. Many feel he was ultimately responsible for drawing attention to the tropical paradise and turning it into one of Mexico's top tourist destinations. ◆ Just east of the Insurgentes bridge

Le Bistro ★★★★$$$ All you need to bring to this popular cafe is an appreciation of good food and jazz. Since 1979, it's been a hangout for well-known (and not-so-well-known) musicians. There's a feel-good atmosphere here, with tall trees creeping over glass roofs on the patio, lush plants, linen tablecloths, a risqué statue of a mermaid, and a great sound system. The decor is a study in black and white, trendy and traditional art, and touches of brass. The day begins with recorded classical music for breakfast, switches to smooth jazz for lunch, and moves into lively jazz for evening. Dining on the deck overlooking the river, you'll hear the sounds of splashing water along with the syncopated rhythms of Dave Brubeck. And the food here is great, with dishes such as creamy spinach-and-lime soup and coconut-tempura shrimp. Dessert lovers should save room for one of the famous double-fudge crepes. During the high season, expect to wait for a table. ◆ Mexican ◆ M-Sa breakfast, lunch, and dinner. Just east of the Insurgentes bridge. 20283

The popular beach south of the Río Cuale is traditionally called Playa los Muertos (Beach of the Dead), a name civic leaders find unappealing. Several attempts have failed to change the name to Playa del Sol (Beach of the Sun) or Olas Altas (High Waves); locals and travelers alike refuse to kill off Los Muertos.

Restaurants/Clubs: Red   **Hotels:** Blue

Shops/ 🎋 **Outdoors:** Green   **Sights/Culture:** Black

Tabu Fabric artist Patti Gallardo creates one-of-a-kind hand-painted jackets, shirts, and dresses splashed with paints and glitter. She's been commissioned to create everything from wall murals to upholstery and is swamped with orders from faithful customers returning for more on their annual vacations. ♦ M-Su; closed September. Across the walkway from Le Bistro. 23528

Centro Cultural (Cultural Center) Now a work space and meeting ground for artists and art lovers alike, this place was restored by the artists themselves. Almost every day, easels are scattered about the white stucco building with painters doing what they love most. Well-known local names such as Rodrigo Lepe and Marta Gilbert are the backbone of the association, and all artists are invited to join. On any day the work

of such local artists as Raymundo Gonzalez, Javier Fernandez, Ruben Leyva, or Ramiz Barquet could be on exhibit. Many US artists also enjoy the pleasures of living and creating art in Puerto Vallarta; some, such as Russel Davis, have been part of the scene here for years. ♦ East of the Insurgentes bridge. No phone

37 **Galería Pacífico** Specializing in contemporary Mexican works, this gallery showcases paintings and sculptures, including some unique pieces in bronze and wood. Private showings of art that's not on display are offered frequently (ask when the next showing is scheduled if you're interested). A gift shop sells posters, photographs, and other graphics and art with prices ranging from $5 to $15,000. ♦ M-Sa. Insurgentes 109 (between 5 de Febrero and Emilio Carranza). 21982

Child's Play

When you travel with children in Mexico, the country opens its arms to you. Children are treasured, revered, and doted upon by Mexicans of all ages. Visit the central plaza in any Mexican town on a Sunday evening, and you'll find scores of children dressed in their finest chasing pigeons and each other past beneficent grownups doling out pesos for plastic toys and balloons. Every Mexican tourism destination has its special children's attractions. Here are a few the whole family will enjoy.

Ride a *triciclo* (three-wheeled bicycle) around **Mérida**'s **Plaza Mayor** on a Sunday afternoon.

Swoosh down the water slide at the **Water Park** in **Puerto Vallarta** or the **Mágico Mundo** aquarium in **Acapulco**.

Laugh at the antics of the sea lions at the **Acuario de Mazatlán** (Mazatlán Aquarium), where schoolkids on field trips scamper through the adjacent playground.

Swim with schools of neon-colored tropical fish at **Cozumel**'s **Parque Nacional Chankanab** or **El Garrafón** on **Isla Mujeres**.

Be awed by the cliff divers at **La Quebrada** in Acapulco or **El Mirador** in Mazatlán.

Thrill to the ancient chants of Maya warriors and watch colored lights highlight spooky carvings on the ruins of **Chichén Itzá** and **Uxmal** during the nightly sound and light shows.

Float along an underground river at **Xcaret** on the **Quintana Roo Coast.**

Ride a kayak through **Laguna de Nichupté** in **Cancún.**

Crawl through tunnels and mazes at **Mexico City**'s **Papalote Museo del Niño (Papalote Museum of the Child)** in **Bosque de Chapultepec (Chapultepec Park),** then move on to the panda exhibit at the park's zoo.

Climb to the top of the **Nohuch Mul** pyramid at **Cobá** on the Quintana Roo Coast, and keep an eye out for wild parrots squawking in the trees.

38 Hotel Molina de Agua $$ A favorite among those who enjoy staying right in town, this tranquil, 65-room hotel is beautifully landscaped with cobblestone paths, fruit trees, and tropical plants. The bungalow rooms are typically Mexican and a bit worn, with red-tile floors and colorful flowers painted above the bed; some rooms have etched-glass windows. Newer rooms in the two-story building have air-conditioning, sitting areas, and spectacular views. The restaurant, with its two-for-one margaritas, is a cool, comfy spot by the pool and hot tub. ♦ Ignacio Vallarta 130 (at Aquiles Serdan). 21957, 21907; fax 26056

39 Olinala Gallery Mexico's many indigenous cultures are represented in this enchanting gallery filled with an intriguing selection of masks, carvings, sculptures, and wooden skeletons. Collectors beware—you won't leave here empty-handed. ♦ M-Sa. Lázaro Cárdenas 274 (between Constitución and Ignacio Vallarta). 11985

40 Memo's La Casa de Pancakes (Memo's Pancake House) ★★★$ The food is great, prices are low, and the general camaraderie among the diners makes this the best place in town to start your day. Pancakes and waffles are filled with nuts or fruit as a main course or can be ordered on the side with a full American-style breakfast that includes delicious hash browns. Try a breakfast burrito filled with eggs and potatoes and drenched in salsa, or a big plate of sliced fresh fruit covered with yogurt and granola. Late risers enjoy ordering breakfast until early afternoon. ♦ American/Mexican ♦ Daily breakfast. No credit cards accepted. Basilio Badillo 289 (between Constitución and Vallarta). 26272

41 Balam ★★★$$$ The owner was one of Vallarta's leading commercial fishermen before opening this restaurant, which is quite possibly the best in town for fresh seafood. The ubiquitous red snapper gets a new preparation in the *huachinango globo* (a foil-encased, fragrant blend of snapper, shrimp, tomatoes, onions, green peppers, and cilantro in a savory broth). Ceviche tostadas served as an appetizer are loaded with fresh shredded fish marinated in lime juice; one or two as a

side dish with a bowl of *sopa albondigas camarones* (seafood broth with ground shrimp balls) makes a satisfying meal. The eatery is housed in a renovated typical Vallarta home, with wood-beam ceilings, brick arches, and a small altar in a recessed bookshelf. ♦ Seafood ♦ Daily lunch and dinner. Basilio Badillo 425 (between Aguacate and Insurgentes). 23451

42 Archie's Wok ★★★$$ Archie and Cindy Alpenia graciously greet their guests at this Asian restaurant, where the best seats are in a small Japanese-style garden. The menu features ingredients from Thailand and the Philippines; try the egg rolls with mushrooms, the Thai coconut fish, or the spicy glazed ribs. Though a cold beer goes well with the spicier dishes, you may find the iced herbal tea more refreshing. ♦ Asian ♦ M-Sa lunch and dinner. Francisca Rodríguez 130 (between Olas Altas and Amapas). 20411

43 La Palapa ★★★★$$$ Elegant and casual both, this restaurant uses simple ingredients, adds some distinctive touches, and ends up with cuisine that goes beyond the typical beach restaurant fare. Located on Playa de los Muertos, the *palapa* dining room is furnished with wooden tables covered with floral cloths. Candles flicker as a guitarist plays romantic *boleros* in the background. The menu emphasizes seafood, but what seafood it is—red snapper in a spicy *pibil* marinade or shrimp with *guajilo* chilis. You can also get more standard fare such as chicken fajitas. Finish with Mexican coffee, mixed with liqueurs and topped with fresh whipped cream. ♦ Seafood ♦ Daily breakfast, lunch, and dinner. Pulpito 103 (just west of Amapas). 25225

44 El Dorado ★$$ Americans and Canadians who have taken up residence in Vallarta consider this *palapa* on Playa los Muertos a neighborhood hangout. It's the ideal laid-back spot to have an icy beer and maybe some fresh red snapper with garlic, while scoping out the beach. Stop by for *huevos rancheros* in the morning or a margarita at sunset. ♦ Seafood/Mexican ♦ Daily breakfast, lunch, and dinner. Pulpito 110 (just west of Amapas). 21511

Get a Horse

Puerto Vallarta is perfect horseback riding country, with long stretches of isolated beach, jungle, and mountain foothills; equestrians get a view of the area that most tourists never see. A late-afternoon sunset ride can be particularly nice (but be sure to bring along bug repellent).

For those interested in exploring astride, several ranches offer guided horseback riding tours,

including transportation to and from your hotel, for all levels of ability:

Cuatro Milpas 47211

El Charro 40114

El Ojo de Agua 48240

Rancho Palma Real 12120

The South Coast

The coastal highway south of the city twists and turns up hillsides into a jungle landscape that threatens to cover the asphalt. The road is lined with million-dollar private villas, exclusive hotels, and cliff-top restaurants. Rivers and waterfalls rush down the hills, tempting travelers to explore the jungle. Most tour operators offer jungle trips that include a stop at riverside restaurants or beaches along southern **Banderas Bay;** taxis and public buses transport passengers between town and the southern neighborhoods.

45 Hotel Playa Conchas Chinas $$ You'll find the lobby at the top of the hill just off the coastal highway, with floors dropping down the face of the cliff to the beach below. All 39 rooms have views, air-conditioning, and simple decor. Some suites come with Jacuzzis. No restaurant, but at the **El Set** next door (see below), guests celebrate the sunset daily, accompanied by guitar music. ♦ Hwy 200 (Km 2.5). 20156

45 El Set ★★$$$ The name is simply a tribute to the films shot in Puerto Vallarta and to the artists who come to this hilltop restaurant. Here celebrities and regular folks spend hours watching the ever-changing sunset, followed by long, enjoyable evenings sampling Mexican fare. One great dish is the steaming bowl of tortilla soup with chunks of avocado and crispy tortillas served with a cold Pacífico beer. The casual restaurant's festive decor is splashed with vivid Mexican colors in the red, green, and purple plaid tablecloths and other touches. This is an ideal place to have some good food and drink or to wait out a passing rainstorm and watch flashes of lightning on the horizon. ♦ Mexican ♦ Daily

lunch and dinner. Reservations recommended. Hwy 200 (Km 2.5). 15342

45 Quinta Maria Cortez $$$ This sophisticated small inn with only six suites is a favorite of reclusive film stars and others in the know. The Mediterranean vine-shrouded villa sits above a secluded beach; most units have a kitchenette and balcony. A common sitting room with fireplace and a dining room are located mid-level in the terraced building, while the swimming pool beckons guests to mingle in the sun. The charming interior features an abundance of tiles, paintings, colorful fabrics, and folk art. ♦ Sagitario 132 (west of Hwy 200). 15371, 888/640.8100; fax in the US 801/531.1633

45 Hotel Camino Real $$$$ For many frequent visitors, this isn't just a great hotel, it's the only hotel. Located a 10-minute drive south of town, the two buildings sit on an exquisite bay with a crescent-shaped sandy beach, below the highway. Walkways are lined with lush tropical plants and trees. In the lobbies and hallways, cobalt-blue walls that echo the shades of the sky and sea are open to the cooling breezes. It was here that Arnold Schwarzenegger watched magenta sunsets after long, sweaty days filming in the nearby jungle. Other stars are frequently sighted, though those with unlimited funds hide out in luxurious suites with private pools and hot tubs. The **Royal Beach Club** is the newest section of the hotel, with 81 mini-suites and several larger suites, some with private hot tubs. The 245 rooms in the original building have views of the sea from private balconies. The grounds sprawl along the beach, with several pools and restaurants tucked under towering palm trees. **La Perla,**

the gourmet Italian restaurant, attracts local diners as well as hotel guests. Those seeking peace and quiet stake out one of the 80 shady *palapas* along the beach, raising the flag atop the *palapa* when they want a waiter's attention; more gregarious types hang out at the main pool's swim-up bar. ♦ Hwy 200 (at Playa las Estacas). 15000, 800/722.6466; fax 16000

45 Presidente Inter-Continental $$$$ Considered small by some standards, with 120 suites (some with Jacuzzis), this hotel has retained the intimacy of a small inn while still providing the luxuries of a large all-inclusive resort. The suites have a separate seating area with a fold-out couch; deluxe and master suites come with whirlpools. The hotel's narrow beach faces a small cove with exceptionally clear water that's perfect for snorkeling. The all-inclusive rates cover room service, tennis and water sports, and all meals in any of the several restaurants. ♦ Hwy 200 (Km 8.5). 80507, 800/327.0200; fax 80116

45 El Eden ★★★$$$ Follow a dirt road into the jungle, and you'll find this hideaway restaurant, where *The Predator* was filmed. Diners select their meal from a refrigerated case displaying frogs' legs, crayfish from the river, shrimp, and chicken kabobs. A burned-out helicopter sits beside the *palapa* restaurant, a reminder that the place was rebuilt after the owners graciously consented to its complete destruction in a spectacular fire scene in the film. The best tables are beside the river, where swimmers slide down slippery rocks, swing from ropes to drop into deep pools, and wade across the river to hike along jungle trails. ♦ Seafood ♦ Daily lunch. Hwy 200, Mismaloya. No phone

45 La Jolla de Mismaloya Resort $$$$ This hotel has its own beach surrounded by jungle, and the vines and trees dotting the

hillsides grow down the cliff almost to the water's edge. The two towers that frame three large free-form pools hold the 303 one- or two-bedroom suites, some with kitchens. Amenities include a fitness center with steam rooms, a sports bar with video games and pool tables, a water sports center with boat tours and equipment, several restaurants, organized children's activites, several shops, and a mini-market. The village of Mismaloya sits beside the hotel, blending into the jungle backdrop. *Night of the Iguana* was filmed on this beach, and parts of the movie set have crumbled into ruins on the rocks above the sand. ♦ Hwy 200 (at Playa Mismaloya), Mismaloya. 80660, 800/322.2344; fax 80500

45 Le Kliff ★★★★$$$ A series of *palapa* dining rooms descend a hillside facing the bay, offering the perfect setting for an equally excellent sunset dinner. Start with the fresh tuna marinated in olive oil and salsa and served with fresh tortillas, followed by fresh dorado or snapper in coriander sauce, then finish with pistachio flan. Nightfall brings a distinctly junglelike atmosphere as strange creatures rustle in the trees. ♦ Seafood ♦ Daily dinner. Hwy 200 (southwest of Mismaloya). 40975

45 Chico's Paradise ★★★$$ Set in the mountains, just 19 kilometers (12 miles) south of town, this is the perfect daylong getaway. The restaurant is located back from the road beside a river, and if you stick with the Mexican dishes, you'll find the food surprisingly good for what might be considered a tourist trap. Plan to spend a full afternoon playing in the river and eating, and don't forget your bug spray. ♦ Mexican ♦ Daily lunch. No credit cards accepted. Hwy 200 (Km 20). 80747

Bests

Katharine A. Diaz
Writer, Mexico City, Federal District

Puerto Vallarta, Jalisco

Sun worship on the area's beautiful beaches, even the ones that can only be reached by boat. But don't leave without exploring the town's cobblestone streets.

Because of the resident and semiresident artist community in PV, the art galleries are a must-see.

Mexico, General

Mass Transit Take public mass transit. It's cheaper and real. Try buses, *colectivos*, and, when in Mexico City, the subway. It's clean and user-friendly.

Public Markets The heart of any town is the public market, where buying fresh is still the name of the game. Take the time to notice the variety of herbs, chilies, beans, fruits, vegetables, and cuts of meats.

A true cultural experience. You also may find souvenirs cheaper here than in shops.

Jan Lavender
Owner/Director of Fine Art and Folk Art Galleries

Marina Vallarta

Have sunset cocktails at **El Faro Lighthouse Bar** at the new marina overlooking the private yacht harbor. The view is panoramic and really lovely. After this (or before), stroll along the waterfront looking in the shops and watching the action on the boats and in the bars.

Viejo Vallarta

Sunday night is the night to go down to the old town and stroll along the *malecón* (waterfront), have an ice cream, and listen to the band concert in the square.

The Coastal Highway and Manzanillo

South of Puerto Vallarta, **Highway 200** leads to Manzanillo, running between the ocean and the **Sierra Madre** mountains. Thanks to its rugged terrain, this area has seen very little development. Rivers flow into isolated coves, and dirt roads lead to pristine beaches. A few exclusive, spectacular resorts, including the luxurious **Las Alamandas** and **Hotel Costa Careyes**, lie along this coastline in private, self-contained compounds where the rich and famous hide out. Most of these places are difficult to reach, requiring flights into either Puerto Vallarta or Manzanillo and then long trips in rental cars or hired taxis.

Manzanillo, 256 kilometers (159 miles) south of Puerto Vallarta, is a port city with one of Mexico's most glamorous hotels, the opulent **Las Hadas**. The Spaniards first settled in the region in 1522, choosing Manzanillo as a port and beachhead for Spain's conquest of Mexico. Cortés is said to have established Mexico's first shipyard here in 1531, using hardwoods from the nearby mountains for his galleons. Spaniard Miguel López Legaspi led his troops from Manzanillo on an expedition to conquer the Philippines in 1564, while other troops headed across the Pacific to what's now called **Baja California**. Manzanillo's twin bays—**Santiago** and **Manzanillo**—have sheltered sailing ships ever since, and its port is one of the busiest in the country.

Manzanillo and the surrounding countryside suffered a major earthquake in 1995. Though one hotel in the city was destroyed and others along the coast suffered damage, most of the resorts in the area were back in full operation within a few weeks.

The Coastal Highway

Although the coastline from Puerto Vallarta to Manzanillo is largely undeveloped and has only a few luxurious resorts tucked into the jungle near secluded bays, a new megaresort, **Isla de Navidad**, is slated for completion in 1999. Situated between the town of **Barra de Navidad** and Manzanillo, it will have 36 holes of golf, a 500-slip marina, and several hotels and condominium complexes.

The drive south along Highway 200 starts near the coast at Puerto Vallarta, then follows a steep, winding route through jungles and mountain foothills. A few small roads lead toward the coast and remote hideaway hotels.

> "Poor Mexico! So far from God and so close to the United States."
>
> Porfirio Díaz

Map labels:

- Río Ameca
- Bahía de Banderas
- **Puerto Vallarta** (200)
- **Yelapa**
- **El Tecuan**
- **El Tuito**
- Río Tomatlán
- **Tomatlán**
- **Campo Acosta**
- Río San Nicolás
- 1
- (200)
- **Bahía Chamela**
- **Chamela** (80)
- 2
- **Bahía Tenacatita**
- **Barra de Navidad** 3
- Río Chacala
- 4
- Aeropuerto Internacional Playa de Oro
- **Pacific Ocean**
- Bahía Manzanillo
- **Manzanillo**
- For nos. 5-14, see pg. 68
- N
- km / mi — 20 / 40 / 40 / 80

Area code 333 unless otherwise noted.

1 Las Alamandas $$$$
Set within a 1,500-acre private reserve, this exclusive hostelry has room for only 22 guests. Four gorgeous villas (some divided into suites) rest above a white sand beach surrounded by fruit trees, jungle, and bird-filled lagoons. The resort is owned by Isabel Goldsmith, daughter of the Bolivian tin magnate Don Antenor Patiño, who developed nearby **Las Hadas.** Advance reservations are absolutely necessary, since the hotel is sometimes closed for high-powered gatherings. Activities include horseback riding, boat rides, hiking, exercise in the fitness center, and, of course, lounging by the pool. The restaurant specializes in healthful cuisine, with fruits and vegetables grown on the premises and seafood caught just offshore. The villas have fully equipped kitchens; the suites have mini-bars; and all accommodations are decorated with one-of-a-kind folk art, handwoven fabrics, and hand-crafted furnishings. ♦ Hwy 200 (between Chamela and Campo Acosta). 70259; fax 70161. For reservations: Paseo de las Palmas 755, Lomas de Chapultepec, 11000 Mexico D.F., Mexico. 5/5407657; fax 5/5407658

2 Hotel Bel-Air Costa Careyes $$$$ One of the most exclusive resort communities in Mexico is nestled in the Sierra Madre foothills over a crescent-shaped beach far from any signs of civilization. In fact, the mountain-edged beach area of Costa Careyes lies approximately 154 kilometers (95 miles) south of Puerto Vallarta and 96 kilometers (60 miles) north of Manzanillo. Transportation is available from the Manzanillo airport. The resort was originally designed by Italian architect **Gian Franco Brignone** in an Italian-Mexican village style, with sweeping palm-frond roofs over pastel-washed terraces that offer stunning views of the sea. Private homes within the resort have been featured in architectural magazines and books as examples of the finest tropical design, complementing the area's natural beauty. The hotel has always attracted a fascinating clientele; in fact, writer Alice Walker credits it in her book *Possessing the Secret of Joy.* The 51 guest rooms in the main U-shaped hotel complex were renovated a couple of years ago; they have private terraces and soft Mediterranean pastel color schemes. Satellite television and direct-dial telephones, long banned from the rooms, have been added to meet the changing needs of patrons unwilling

or unable to endure total isolation. Guests lounge by swimming pools set in lush courtyards and submit to delicious pampering in **The Spa,** a state-of-the-art health and beauty facility. The broad beach is ideal for sunbathing and swimming, and snorkeling is good around the rocky islands offshore. A restaurant, horses, and yachts are also available. Sea turtles nest on the beaches near here in the summer, and migratory birds arrive in great flocks in the winter. ♦ Off Hwy 200 (south of Chamela). 335/10000, 800/457.7676, 800/525.4800; fax 335/10100

2 Club Med Playa Blanca $$$$ Located near the **Costa Careyes,** this hotel has 590 basic, bright rooms in adobe brick buildings spread around landscaped grounds. Most activities take place around the large pool and along the palm-lined beach. Children over 12 are welcome, but there are no special facilities or activities for them.

An intensive English horseback-riding program, scuba diving lessons, circus workshops, and rock-climbing lessons on an artificial wall are all available. Equipment for nearly every water sport is provided, and for those with energy left over, there's a high-tech disco. This is an all-inclusive hotel, with meals and many activities part of the deal. Package prices include airfare, but not airport transfers, which can be very expensive. ♦ Off Hwy 200 (south of Chamela). 335/10001, 800/258.2633; fax 70733

3 Melaque Also known as "San Patricio," this small beach town sits in the middle of Bahía de Navidad near the town of Barra de Navidad. It is only a few blocks square, with simple accommodations. Along the beach, small, low-key hotels lure those on a budget. Open-air cafes serve strong coffee and simple but good meals. On Saint Patrick's Day the sea is the scene of a festive *flotilla* during which the boats are blessed and everyone parties. ♦ Hwy 200 (south of Hwy 80)

3 Barra de Navidad On another beautiful out-of-the-way beach, this tranquil resort town has a variety of casual cafes and shops. Rumor has it that the area will soon explode with heavy tourism as the Isla de Navidad development progresses. But for now, you can enjoy long walks on the sand, small hotels, and fresh-caught seafood prepared in various ways. ♦ Hwy 200 (east of Melaque)

4 Grand Bay Hotel Puerto de la Navidad $$$$ At present this hacienda-style hotel remains an island unto itself, though the area is slated for other exclusive properties. The 191 large rooms and suites all have balconies with sea views, hand-carved wooden furnishings, hair dryers, irons, safes, and bidets. The hotel has three pools, three tennis courts, and several restaurants; guests also have access to the development's golf course and marina. A full-service spa was scheduled to be opened as we went to press. ♦ Isla de Navidad (8 km/5 miles southwest of Hwy 200). 335/55050, 888/80GRAND; fax 335/56071

MANZANILLO

Santiago
8
7
6

Salagua
200

Av. de la Audiencia

Av. del Tesoro

Laguna
Peñitas

Playa
Olas Altas

Playa
Santiago

Playa
Salagua

Costera Madrid

5

Playa
Miramar

200

← to airport

Bahía de
Santiago

Playa
Audiencia

Playa
Las Hadas

Rincón de
las Hadas

Península
de Santiago
9

Península
de Juluapan

Pacific Ocean

N

| km | 1/2 | 1 |
| mi | 1/4 | 1/2 |

Manzanillo

The small coastal city of Manzanillo in the state of **Colima** is south of Puerto Vallarta in the middle of lush jungle. Once a railhead where cargo was transferred between ships and trains, it remains one of the most important ports on the **Pacific** and a center for iron mining and smelting. Fishing was the main tourist attraction until 1974, when Bolivian Don Antenor Patiño completed **Las Hadas,** his fairyland getaway resort. Soon after, the hotel and adjacent **Mantarraya Golf Course** began to attract international attention. The area now has some 7,000 hotel rooms, and the population has reached 150,000.

Although it's not a major tourist mecca, Manzanillo will please those who enjoy fishing, bird watching, clean beaches, clear water, and a low-key, friendly ambience. It's also inexpensive, with many resorts providing accommodations, meals, and activities at reasonable, all-inclusive rates. Airlines are beginning to offer direct flights from gateway cities in the US, and a cruise-ship pier is in the planning stages. During national holidays, Mexican families flock here, so rooms are booked well in advance, traffic increases, and the beaches become quite crowded.

Traveling southeast from the airport on **Highway 200,** also called "Costera Madrid," you first reach **Bahía de Santiago,** the site of all-inclusive hotels, the area's best beaches, and the town of **Santiago.** Next comes **Península de Santiago,** separating the two main bays. **Las Hadas,** an 18-hole golf course, and other hotels are located here. To the east is **Bahía de Manzanillo** and the **Las Brisas** neighborhood, where the beaches are lined with moderately priced hotels and restaurants. The city of Manzanillo is located at the far edge of the bay, its large port facing the open sea. Downtown Manzanillo, though not especially geared toward tourism, is worth visiting, especially in the early evening when locals gather around the main plaza beside the waterfront.

Getting to Manzanillo

Airport

Aeropuerto Internacional Playa de Oro (Playa de Oro International Airport) is located about 46 kilometers (29 miles) northwest of Manzanillo. The airport is small but handles both national and international flights. Such airport services as snack stands, gift shops, and car-rental desks are open only when flights are arriving and departing.

On the map: Laguna de Las Garzas; Costera Madrid; 200; 10; 11; 12; 13; Playa Azul; Carretera Las Brisas; Punto Interior; Playa Las Brisas; Bahía de Manzanillo; Av. Morelos; 14; Manzanillo

Airport Services
Information...41555

Airlines
AeroCalifornia 41414, 800/237.6225

Aeroméxico..............................32424, 800/237.6639

America West 800/235.9292

Mexicana 32323, 800/531.7921

Getting to and from Aeropuerto Internacional Playa de Oro

By Bus Transportation is provided from the airport by *colectivo* (van) direct to your hotel; rates are set by the zone and range from $5 to $8. No public buses run to the airport.

By Car The drive to Manzanillo from the airport takes about 45 minutes on Highway 200. The following car-rental agencies have counters at the airport but are open only when flights are arriving and departing.

Avis 31590, 800/331.1212

Budget 31445, 800/527.0700

National 30611, 800/328.4567

The Coastal Highway and Manzanillo

By Taxi Taxis await passengers in front of the airport. The fare to downtown is about $20.

Getting Around Manzanillo

Few numerical street addresses are used in Manzanillo. People designate their location by neighborhood or street, so don't waste your time looking for numbers.

Buses City buses run along the waterfront to all the main beaches and hotels.

Driving Rental cars are expensive and unnecessary if you plan on staying within the confines of the resorts. They are handy for visiting out-of-the-way beaches and small towns in the countryside. Many visitors rent a car for one day at the rental desks in the hotels and use taxis for transport within town.

Taxis Cabs are plentiful and are usually parked in front of the hotels, plazas, and beaches.

FYI

Accommodations Room rates in Manzanillo are low except at the most lavish hotels. Reservations are essential during Carnival, Easter Week, and Mexican national holidays.

Publications The tourist publication *Costa Azul* is sometimes available at hotels and travel agencies, though it's hard to find a copy in English.

Shopping Few shops carry quality folk art in Manzanillo; souvenirs consist of T-shirts, beach towels, seashells, and carved wooden fish.

Street Plan Manzanillo's layout can be confusing. Some of the main beaches face southeast rather than west, so it's disconcerting if you think you're facing the Pacific Ocean but see the sun rise.

Time Zone Manzanillo is on Central Time, two hours ahead of California and one hour behind New York.

Tours City tours and trips to Colima are available through local agencies, including **Viajes Bahías Gemelas** (Costera Madrid 1556, 31000, 31053; fax 30649), **Viajes Tlaloc** (Hwy 200, Km 14, 41180; fax 41181), and **Viajes Hecturs** (Camino Real Las Hadas, Rincón de las Hadas, south of Av del Tesoro, 31707), which also has a branch at Costero Madrid 3147 (between Carretera Las Brisas and Salagua, 31707).

Visitors' Information Center The **Oficina de Turismo** (Tourism Office) is located at Costero Madrid 4960, between Carretera Las Brisas and Salagua. Its hours are erratic. For information, call 32277, 32264; fax 31426.

Phone Book

Fire...25238

Hospital Civil Hwy 200 (between Carretera Las Brisas and Salagua) 21903

Police..21004

Red Cross...25169

Club MAEVA
All Inclusive Resort

5 Club Maeva $$$ Families with children love this all-inclusive place. There are playgrounds and pools just for kids and a dance club and 12 tennis courts to keep the adults happy. The little ones especially like the pool with its long, curving water slide, and the video-game room; daytime nursery care is available for toddlers. There are 514 rooms; some bungalows have kitchenettes. You can take a bridge across the highway to the beach on the other side, which is lined with umbrellas, a small artisans' market, and snack stands. ♦ Hwy 200 (west of Santiago). 36878, 800/466.2382; fax 30395

6 Vista Club Playa de Oro $$$ Another all-inclusive hotel popular with Mexican families, it has 300 rooms in several white buildings on a hillside overlooking the sea. Facilities include two pools, two restaurants, a miniature-golf course, and two tennis courts. The beach is across the street, and the town of Santiago is within walking distance. ♦ Hwy 200 (west of Santiago). 36133, 800/882.8215; fax 32840

7 Hamburguesas Juanito's ★★$ A longtime institution, this spot is beloved by locals and tourists alike for first-rate burgers, fries, milk shakes, and American-style breakfasts. Talk to knowledgeable local residents here to pick up inside information. ♦ American ♦ Daily breakfast, lunch, and dinner. No credit cards accepted. Hwy 200 (just west of Santiago). 32019, 31388

8 Santiago The small settlement sprawls up dusty streets north of Costera Madrid. The municipal market is worth visiting for its displays of local produce and tropical fruits, and the neighborhood has several good taco stands and small family-operated restaurants. For a taste of village life, observe the locals gathering in early evening in the tree-lined plaza facing the highway and beach.

Within Santiago:

Centro Artesanal Las Primaveras The best folk art shop in the Manzanillo area is in a back street across from the market. Papier-mâché figurines, pewter picture frames, clay masks, and holiday decorations fill the main showroom, while pottery and furniture occupy a side yard and upstairs gallery. Most taxi drivers know how to get here; coming from the highway, turn north on Avenida Juárez by **Julio's Tacos.** ♦ Daily. Av Juárez 40 (at Reforma). 31699

9 Península de Santiago When **Las Hadas** was constructed in the early 1970s, this hilly peninsula was virtually uninhabited. Now it's filled with hotels and private residences, including the handsome, luxurious villas of the exclusive La Punta community. Travelers staying here are a bit isolated from businesses outside the hotels; though a bus does run up the peninsula, it's a long walk from the bus stops to many hotels. The small shopping area on the road to the hotels has a bank, two restaurants, and some shops. ♦ South of Hwy 200 (between Salagua and Santiago)

On Península de Santiago:

Plaza Las Glorias Hotel $$ Painted a deep ocher, this hotel looks like a tiny pueblo on the side of the hill. A cable car carries guests and luggage to the hotel entrance at the top. All 86 rooms and 15 suites are comfortable and pleasantly furnished, although those by the pool can be noisy. Some suites have Jacuzzis in the bedrooms, and furnished kitchenettes are available on request; ask to see your room before you sign on the dotted line, to be sure you get what you want. The hotel is a little run-down, and the housekeeping could be improved, but the dining room has both a great view of the **Mantarraya Golf Course** and good Mexican food. An all-inclusive plan covering meals and some activities is available. ♦ Av del Tesoro (between Rincón de las Hadas and Hwy 200). 30440, 41054, 800/342.2644; fax 31395

Hotel Sierra Manzanillo $$ This 19-story tower looms above the Playa Audencia, where Cortés is said to have met with Indian kings. A common sight today are tour buses with charter groups from the US and Canada. The 309 rooms are serviceable but not luxurious; some have balconies or terraces. Under the all-inclusive program, there's a choice of restaurants. The beach frames a peaceful cove with calm water and good snorkeling. ♦ Av de la Audencia 1 (between Rincón de las Hadas and Hwy 200). 32000; fax 32272

LAS HADAS

Camino Real Las Hadas $$$ This became the best-known hotel in Manzanillo after Dudley Moore and Bo Derek romped here in the movie *10*. One of a kind, it was built by Bolivian millionaire Antenor Patiño as a playground for his family and friends. Spanish architect **José Luis Ezquerra** spent a decade (1964-74) supervising construction of Patiño's fantasy village, which seems straight out of the *Arabian Nights*. The 224 rooms and four suites are all white, spacious, and spotlessly clean with elegant decor. Most have balconies with breathtaking views. Topiaries line walkways, and fuchsia bougainvillea tumbles over white turrets, domes, and walls. On the beach and around the pool, white awnings protect delicate skin from the sun; the calm waters by the beach are perfect for swimming and snorkeling. Three restaurants offer a choice of seafood and international and Mexican fare, and there are outstanding shops and boutiques. Since some rooms and the golf and tennis clubhouse are far from the lobby, golf carts are used for transportation. Dive, snorkeling, and sunset cruises leave from the hotel's marina; a daily cruise goes to downtown Manzanillo and allows time for shopping and sightseeing. There are 12 tennis courts and an 18-hole golf course. ♦ Rincón de las Hadas (south of Av del Tesoro). 40000, 42000, 800/722.6466; fax 41950

Within the Las Hadas Hotel:

Legazpi ★★$$$ For a gastronomic treat, have dinner here, where candlelight sparkles on crystal and silver and the atmosphere is full of romance. Gourmet food is beautifully presented with special touches: tender filet mignon, cooked vegetables served in pastry boxes, and fresh-baked pastries. ♦ International ♦ Daily dinner December through April. Reservations recommended. 40000

 Mantarraya Golf Course This 18-hole course challenges golfers to loft balls over sea-filled gorges. Designed by Pete and Roy Dye, it is considered as one of the top courses in Mexico, as well as one of the hundred best in the world. A lush 5,994-yard par-71 course, it meanders past lagoons, canals, palm trees, and wildlife. A full 18-hole game will take you down to the beach. During tournaments, there's a traveling cart filled with cold soda, beer, and any other desired liquid refreshment. ♦ Daily. 30246

Indigeno's Here you'll find fantastic and expensive folk art and an impressive selection of silver jewelry. ♦ M-Sa. Shopping arcade. 40000

10 Hotel Fiesta Mexicana $$ Though not overly luxurious, this hotel has a wonderful location on the beach. It's always crowded with Mexican tourists, and the 200 rooms and public places are attractively decorated with handicrafts. The restaurant serves good Mexican and international food. This is a festive place, filled with families and the music of mariachi bands. ♦ Hwy 200 (between Carretera Las Brisas and Salagua). 31100; fax 32180

11 Carlos 'n' Charlie's ★★$ Can anything go wrong in one of Carlos Andersen's chain of well-known restaurants? It's fun times, cluttered decor, and good food for all. Mexican specialties are a sure thing here, as are the ribs. ♦ Mexican ♦ Daily lunch and dinner. Hwy 200 (between Carretera Las Brisas and Salagua). 31150

12 Suites las Palmas $ The 48 apartment-style units in this complex are a great value, each with a kitchenette, two bedrooms, and a living room. The units are immaculate, with blue-tile floors, glass-top tables, and pastel linens. Though not on the beach, the hotel has a small pool and is across the street from Manzanillo Bay. There are good restaurants in the neighborhood (but none at the hotel), and the public bus runs right by the front door. ♦ Hwy 200 (Km 7). 31010; fax 32349

13 Osteria Bugatti ★★$$ Those who know what well-prepared Italian-style seafood is return year after year. Try the oysters, the lobster diablo, or a rich pasta-and-shrimp dish. ♦ Italian ♦ Daily lunch and dinner; closed the last two weeks of September. Carretera Las Brisas and Hwy 200. 32999

13 Willy's ★★★$$ Many locals maintain that this is the best restaurant in town. Owner/chef Michel and his wife, Jeanne Françoise, serve French specialties and seafood to please the gourmet palate. The barbecue sizzles with lobster and shrimp kabobs grilling over a mesquite fire. Guests can dine and watch the sunset at a table reserved for the evening; many return nightly until they've sampled the entire menu. ♦ Seafood/French ♦ Daily dinner. Reservations recommended. Carretera Las Brisas (just southeast of Hwy 200). 31794

14 Downtown Manzanillo Many travelers who stay put on the beaches miss the true Manzanillo, a classic port city with considerable character. Although the road into town passes along the edge of the port, with its freighters, loading docks, and railroad cars, a beautification project is under way. With any luck, the colorful central plaza will remain as it has been for decades—pigeons perching on the green roof of the white iron bandstand, water spurting from stone swans in the fountains. Hibiscus bushes shaped into topiaries of baskets bloom with red and pink flowers in season, and on weekend evenings navy bands entertain.

Within downtown Manzanillo:

Hotel Colonial $ The name befits this aged building with its heavy, dark furnishings, stained-glass windows, and wrought-iron chandeliers. The hotel has seen better days, but it's a fun place to stay if you want to soak in the downtown atmosphere. The 38 rooms have fans, leaky plumbing, and sagging beds, but they're clean. The restaurant is a popular lunch spot for business leaders. ♦ No credit cards accepted. Bocanegra 28 (at Av Mexico). 21080, 21134

Roca del Mar ★$ If you're looking for a pleasurable way to spend the early evening, grab a sidewalk table at this cafe. The dishes, including seafood cocktails, grilled fish, and enchiladas, are inexpensive. Bring your postcards or a book, or watch the promenade of families passing through the plaza. ♦ Mexican/Seafood ♦ Daily breakfast, lunch, and dinner. 21 de Marzo 204 (between Benito Juárez and Av Morelos). 20302

Ixtapa/Zihuatanejo

Combine a modern hotel zone with a traditional fishing community and you have the two-in-one destination of Ixtapa (pronounced Ees-*ta*-pa) and Zihuatanejo (pronounced See-wah-ta-*neh*-ho), in the state of **Guerrero**. Only six kilometers (four miles) apart, each town has its own gorgeous bay and beaches, and both are favorite hideaways for experienced travelers. Those seeking luxurious creature comforts head to Ixtapa, which opened as a resort area in 1975. Zihuatanejo, a fishing town with ancient roots, attracts those in search of the true Mexico, without glamour and glitz.

Wherever they unpack their bags, most travelers shuttle back and forth between the two, sampling the best of each place. Ixta/Zihua (a nickname that saves a lot of syllables) is well worth a vacation of a week or more, allowing a couple of days for visiting isolated beaches, another for scuba diving or fishing, a day for shopping in both towns, and, of course, as much time as possible for simply relaxing on the beach or by the pool.

Ixtapa is small, fashionable, and blissfully free of the overdevelopment so common in planned resorts—the town's movers and shakers seem intent on keeping the resort under control. The two-milelong hotel zone along **Playa del Palmar** and **Paseo Ixtapa** contains fewer than a dozen hotels. The **Marina Ixtapa** complex is low-key and spacious, and the two 18-hole golf courses at opposite ends of the tourist zone offer unbroken stretches of green.

Zihuatanejo was something of a cult destination long before the jungle and palm groves were cleared from Ixtapa's shores. Artifacts found over the years during various building projects support the belief that Zihuatanejo dates back to the pre-Columbian matriarchal Cuitlateca society. The **Museo Arqueológico de la Costa Grande** (Archaeology Museum) on the shores of the town's main beach contains displays of figurines with a decidedly feminine theme.

Changes to Zihuatanejo have enhanced its charm without destroying its character—roads and businesses now exist where small planes once landed, and there is an international airport 15 minutes from town. Revitalization projects continue—dirt streets are paved with decorative brick, and the **Paseo del Pescador** (Fisherman's Walkway) runs along the bay. Locals congregate around the beachside basketball court, which doubles as an amphitheater for weekend entertainment. The public market is still the main place to buy food, as well as the shorefront where fisherfolk sell their day's catch.

The thick coconut palms along the coast were imported from the Philippines by the treasure-seeking Spaniards. While many people think of Zihuatanejo as a sleepy fishing village, the area's real economic backbone was once the millions of coconuts harvested here yearly.

Getting to Ixtapa/Zihuatanejo

Airport

The **Ixtapa/Zihuatanejo Airport** is 16 kilometers (10 miles) east of Zihuatanejo. The airport handles international and national flights, though international travelers often have to change planes in Mexico City to get here.

Airport businesses such as car-rental agencies and shops are typically open only when planes are arriving and departing.

Airport Services
Information 42070

Airlines
Aeroméxico 42022, 42237, 800/237.6639

Alaska Airlines 800/426.0333

Continental 42579, 800/525.0280

Mexicana 42208, 800/531.7921

Getting to and from Ixtapa/Zihuatanejo Airport

By Bus *Colectivos* (vans) run to hotels in both towns and cost far less than private taxis. The fare to Ixtapa is about $10; the fare to Zihuatanejo is about $8.

By Car The drive to Zihuatanejo from the airport takes about 15 minutes, to Ixtapa about 25 minutes. The following car-rental agencies have counters at the airport but are open only when flights are arriving and departing.

Avis 42248, 800/331.1212

Budget 43060, 800/527.0700

Dollar 42314, 800/800.4000

Hertz.......................................42952, 800/654.3131

By Taxi Taxis await passengers in front of the airport. The fare to Ixtapa is about $20, to Zihuatanejo about $15.

Getting Around Ixtapa/Zihuatanejo

Ixtapa's main drag, called **Paseo Ixtapa,** runs east from **Marina Ixtapa** just inland from **Playa del Palmar.** It intersects **Highway 200,** also called **Carretera Costera,** east of the Ixtapa hotel zone; the highway travels from here to Zihuatanejo. The main waterfront street in downtown Zihuatanejo is **Juan Alvarez,** which runs parallel to the pedestrian-only **Paseo del Pescador.** From Zihua, **Paseo Costera** runs along the hills east of town to the hotels above **Playa Madera** and **Playa la Ropa.** A car comes in handy, especially if you plan to go back and forth between the two towns frequently.

Buses Buses run regularly between the two towns, and less frequently into Marina Ixtapa and out to **Playa Quieta.** Daily buses leave from the terminal on Highway 200 to most cities in Mexico. About eight trips a day are made to Acapulco. The main bus lines are:

Estrella Blanca 43477

Estrella del Oro 42175

Driving Driving in Ixtapa is easy, since there's only one road through the hotel zone. There are large parking lots at the hotels and shopping centers. In

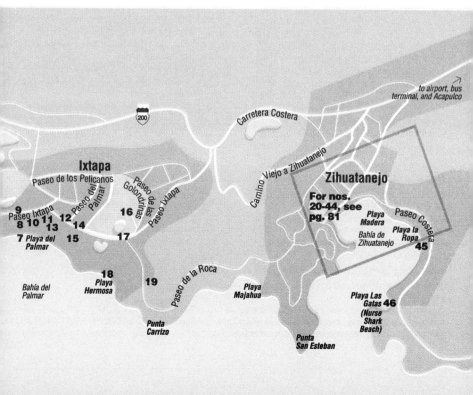

Zihuatanejo, the streets are narrow and street signs rare. There is a free public parking lot by the **Municipal Pier,** and downtown businesses are within walking distance.

Taxis Cabs are plentiful and are usually parked in front of the hotels, plazas, and beaches. Fares are fixed; most hotels post a list of fares in the lobby.

FYI

Accommodations Ixtapa's hotels are primarily chain-operated properties, with rates in the moderate-to-expensive range. Zihuatanejo has some of the best small luxury hotels in Mexico, with rates commensurate with their exclusivity. Zihua also has some of the least expensive casual beachfront hotels in the country. Reservations are essential during Christmas, Easter Week, and Mexican national holidays. Villas and apartments can be booked through **JOB Representaciones** (44374; fax 44374).

Publications Precious few English-language tourist publications are available, but the tourist information office sometimes has copies of "What to Do, Where to Go," a small pamphlet with hotel and restaurant listings.

Shopping Shops carrying high-quality folk art are scattered throughout Ixtapa's several small shopping plazas. Zihuatanejo has a great municipal market, and the neighborhood streets around it are filled with small artisans' stands. The best buys are leather sandals and huaraches. Both towns have artisans' markets selling seashell knickknacks, T-shirts, and serapes.

Sportfishing Knowledgeable anglers head for Zihuatanejo from December through March, when marlin, dorado, sailfish, and other big game fish come within a few miles of shore. According to the experts, the San Andreas Fault cuts deep canyons not far from the shoreline, creating ideal conditions for large fish that demand plenty of space. The **Ixtapa/Zihuatanejo Billfish Classic** tournament held in January and the May **International Sailfish Tournament** both attract serious sportfishers and produce record-breaking catches—recently an angler landed a thousand-pound marlin after battling for several long hours. Sportfishing boats, from *pangas* (small skiffs) to cabin cruisers, are available for charter at the fishing cooperative in Zihuatanejo (Paseo del Pescador, 42056), and **Servicios Turísticos Acuáticos,** which has no office. For information, call 44162; representatives roam the marinas and check in for messages. Boats and captains can be reserved in advance through **Ixtapa Sportfishing Charters** (717/424.8323; fax 717/424.1016), and **Aeromexico Vacations** offers fishing packages (800/245.8585).

Time Zone Ixta/Zihua is on Mountain Time, one hour ahead of California and two hours behind New York.

Restaurants/Clubs: Red   Hotels: Blue

Shops/ Outdoors: Green   **Sights/Culture: Black**

Tours Local travel agencies offer tours of the two towns as well as excursions to **Isla Ixtapa** and more remote beach towns. One of the nicest tours is to **Troncones,** a coastal village 10 kilometers (six miles) north of Ixtapa. The beaches on this part of the coast are perfect for solitary strolls, and the water is usually calm enough for swimming. There is one small hotel here, **La Casa de la Tortuga** (70732; fax 43296) with a good restaurant, **El Burro Borracho** ($; 70732). Countryside tours go to tropical fruit plantations and lagoons, where bird watching is excellent in the early morning and evening. Most hotels have tour desks, or check with **American Express** (Krystal Ixtapa, Paseo Ixtapa, just west of Paseo de las Garzas, 30853) or **F4 Tours** (Los Patios Shopping Center, Paseo del Palmar and Paseo Ixtapa, Ixtapa, 31442).

Visitors' Information Center The **Oficina de Turismo** (Tourism Office) is in Ixtapa at **Plaza Ixpamar** (Paseo Ixtapa, between Paseos del Palmar and de las Garzas), Suite 18. It is open Monday through Friday. For information, call 31270, fax 30819.

Phone Book

Fire 47551

Hospital General de Zona 8 Av Morelos
    (just southwest of Hwy 200), Zihuatanejo....42285

Police..47551, 47171

Red Cross 42009

Ixtapa

Designed with tourism in mind, Ixtapa consists of a hotel zone along a gorgeous beach, plus two golf courses, a marina, and several small shopping plazas. The town has no center, and gives little sense of being in traditional Mexico, but it's the perfect place to kick back and relax without worrying about missing out on anything.

1 Playa Linda Total escape is possible at this relatively undeveloped beach, which is backed by groves of coconut palms, glistening sand, and the jungle. Horses are available to rent by the hour or the day, and a few *palapas* (palm-roofed stands) on the beach serve drinks and snacks and sell handicrafts. Boats depart from here for Isla Ixtapa from dawn to dusk. ◆ Carretera a Playa Linda (west of Paseo de las Garzas)

2 Isla Ixtapa Known as "Isla Grande," this jungle island just off the coast is a wildlife preserve of sorts, though only the gulls and pelicans can withstand the steady stream of sun worshipers, skin divers, and bird watchers who come here from Playa Linda. Day-trippers have three beaches to choose from: Cuachalalate, the main beach with *palapa* restaurants (try the fish at **Paraiso**) and a dive shop; Varadero, where you can rent snorkels and masks and dine at other restaurants (try **El Marlin**); and Playa Coral, a haven where fish and turtles congregate in the clear waters. It's a 10-minute boat ride to the island from Playa Linda (buy a round-trip ticket and don't miss the last boat back, which leaves before dusk).

3 Playa Quieta The boats for Isla Ixtapa, which used to leave from here, now depart from Playa Linda. The beach is open to the public, but most of the facilities are run by **Club Med Ixtapa.** ♦ Carretera a Playa Linda (west of Paseo de las Garzas)

4 Club Med Ixtapa $$$$ Although the beach may be quiet, its famous all-inclusive resort is not. A 20-minute drive from Ixtapa's hotel zone, this club is one of the "family villages" for nearly every age, from 10 months to 11 years. Children and adults both get into the **Circus Workshop,** where they learn to fly on a high trapeze, and at the end of a week, guests and talented GO's (the staff) put on a great show, complete with makeup, funky wigs, and costumes. The days are packed with snorkeling, tennis, volleyball, archery, and other activities. Meals are served buffet style, and while not every dish is a gourmet delight, many are well above average, with outstanding breads and pastries baked fresh daily. ♦ Carretera a Playa Linda (west of Paseo de las Garzas). 43340, 43380, 800/258.2633

5 Punta Ixtapa Bulldozers and the sound of hammers have chased away the iguanas and armadillos on this natural point at the western end of Bahía del Palmar, which is well on the way to becoming a luxurious residential development, with lots costing up to $1 million and houses expected to go for $1.5 million. The construction will take to the end of the decade to complete. The complex includes the beaches Don Rodrigo and Cuata, where rocks jut from the sea just offshore, and abuts Playa Linda, just two kilometers (one mile) away. ♦ South of Carretera a Playa Linda

6 Marina Ixtapa A channel at the end of Playa del Palmar leads yachts into this gorgeous marina complex. Condominiums with Mediterranean and hacienda-style architecture edge the 622 yacht slips, which accommodate vessels of up to one hundred feet long. Restaurants and shops are clustered around a handsome terra-cotta–colored lighthouse, and its 18-hole golf course provides a scenic landscape. ♦ Paseo Ixtapa (west of Paseo de las Garzas)

Within Marina Ixtapa:

Club de Golf Marina Ixtapa (Marina Ixtapa Golf Course) Ixtapa's second 18-hole course was designed by Texan Robert von Hagge. The championship-caliber par-72 course, said to be the most challenging in Mexico because of its topography of sand dunes and undulating greens, measures approximately 6,900 yards from the back tees. The greens are designed to incorporate a

variety of pin areas that can be used to determine the difficulty of the course; walking the course is not allowed here, but there are 125 carts to help you navigate the layouts. Those interested in other sports or activities may use the clubhouse, tennis courts, swimming pool, gym, spa, and restaurant. More than a mile of canals run through the course, allowing condo owners to take water taxis to the greens. ♦ Daily. 31410; fax 30825

Beccofino ★★★★$$$ The name in Italian means fine beak, or, colloquially, the ability to discern good taste. Indeed, owner Angelo Rolly Pavia has used excellent taste in this restaurant reminiscent of the Italian Riviera. The view of handsome yachts in the marina evokes a mood of extravagance, and this is definitely the place to go all out. The menu, in Italian and Spanish, is an adventure for those unfamiliar with the cuisine, but even the uninitiated can appreciate swordfish ravioli or shrimp in pink pepper sauce. Meatless meals include a sublime cannelloni with spinach and cheese and pasta Beccofino with pesto and peas. There's a daily special for every course, and a tempting array of desserts, including tropical fruit tarts. Imported wines include the popular Batasiolo Pinot Grigio, Chiantis, and Champagnes, and a bracing grappa that is sure to clear your head (for the moment, that is). ♦ Italian ♦ Daily breakfast, lunch, and dinner. Reservations recommended. 31770

Bucanero's ★★★$$$ It's a toss-up as to which marina restaurant is best. At this one, the dining room sits a few steps above the outdoor terrace and has wide windows looking out to the marina. It's more pleasant to sit outside, however, if you can tolerate the envious looks of those waiting in line for a table. The seafood is masterfully prepared—be sure to have the squid if it's on the menu, or any of the pastas. This is the best marina restaurant for breakfast, and enjoying a plate of sliced papaya and pineapple or a full repast of salmon and eggs here is a great way to start the day. ♦ Seafood/International ♦ Daily breakfast, lunch, and dinner. Reservations recommended. 30916

7 Playa del Palmar The center of Ixtapa's tourism zone, this two-milelong stretch of sand is backed by more than 10 luxury hotels. In pretourist times there was only wild grass growing to the edge of the sand; thick groves of coconut palms now provide a junglelike setting. Several *morros* (rocky islands) lie offshore, creating exquisite silhouettes against the sunset. The surf here can get rough, so swimmers should take note of the daily conditions announced by the flags: red, dangerous; yellow, use caution; green, go ahead and swim. ♦ Paseo Ixtapa (between Paseo de la Roca and Marina Ixtapa)

8 Carlos 'n' Charlie's ★$$ Dancing beneath the stars goes on throughout the night in this branch of Carlos Andersen's chain of zany cafes where fun is king. The Mexican decor offers a few surrealistic touches, and the fare is the usual ribs, seafood, and regional dishes. ♦ Mexican ♦ Daily lunch and dinner. Paseo Ixtapa (west of Paseo de las Garzas). 30085

8 Best Western Posada Real $$ A simple, chain-style lodging with 110 small, nondescript rooms, this most affordably priced Ixtapa hotel sits on the same beach as the upscale giants. Two large pools, beach *palapas*, and grassy gardens provide ample relaxation areas, while the two adjacent restaurants are among the rowdiest around (choose your room accordingly). The hotel's housekeeping is not as good as it should be; check your room carefully before settling in. Note that it's the farthest hotel from Ixtapa's shopping centers, so unless you're an energetic walker—or not a shopper—you may spend as much on taxis as you save on your room. ♦ Paseo Ixtapa (west of Paseo de las Garzas). 31685, 31745, 800/528.1234; fax 31805

8 Euforia Disco The action at this all-night disco doesn't even get started until nearly midnight. A high-tech laser display and sound system plus floor fog make this a popular hangout for the young crowd. ♦ Cover. Daily in August and at Christmas and Easter; out-of-season hours vary. Paseo Ixtapa (west of Paseo de las Garzas). 31190

9 JJ's Lobster & Shrimp ★★★$ A great spot for people watching, this small, funky restaurant isn't fancy, but it serves good food at reasonable prices. The lobster bisque is excellent, as is the fresh fish with spinach and mushrooms. **JJ's Junk Food Joint,** right next to the lobster house and under the same ownership, is a good spot for pizza, burgers, and spaghetti. ♦ Seafood/International ♦ Daily

breakfast, lunch, and dinner. Paseo Ixtapa (west of Paseo de las Garzas). 32494

10 DoubleTree Hotel $$$ You can't miss this hotel, one of the monoliths on the beach. It features a giant pool with a swim-up bar and 281 large, comfortable rooms that have bougainvillea streaming from the balconies. Bright flowers are painted above every arch, while wood carvings and floral arrangements add touches of elegance. The lobby bar is a relaxing place for a cocktail before dinner, and the umbrella-topped tables are perfect for sitting under the massive skylights. ♦ Paseo Ixtapa (west of Paseo de las Garzas). 30003, 800/222.TREE; fax 31555

11 Krystal Ixtapa $$$$ The beachfront hotel has transformed vacationing into a fine art form. One of three highly respected properties designed and operated by Mexico City's de la Parra family, this well-maintained hotel has 254 comfortable rooms and suites with exceptional views of the ocean and beach. The oversized lobby has classic and modern Mexican touches, striking wall hangings, and embroidered cushions, while sitting areas are bathed in sunshine from the broad skylights. Clusters of trees and flowers fill the rambling grounds, and a huge pool meanders around a grand sundeck. With a variety of daytime activities available, along with several intimate bars and cafes, there's always something to keep you busy. A meal plan is available. ♦ Paseo Ixtapa (just west of Paseo de las Garzas). 30333, 800/231.9860; fax 30216

Within the Krystal Ixtapa:

Bogart's ★★$$$$ This expensive, elaborate restaurant is a shrine to the late Humphrey Bogart and his much-loved movie *Casablanca*. Life-size posters of Bogey, romantic piano music, subdued lighting, ceiling fans, and white-on-white Moroccan-style architecture help set the scene. The somewhat pretentious decor and attitude are carried through in the elaborate menu, which includes a vast array of flambéed entrées and desserts. Highlights include the Casablanca Supreme (chicken breast stuffed with lobster), and a combination salad with bacon, nuts, lettuce, and tomatoes in a warm vinaigrette dressing. ◆ International ◆ Daily dinner. Reservations recommended. 30333

Christine An elegant yet fun disco is housed in a lovely building. The round dance floor is surrounded by ficus trees, and tiny flashing lights crisscross the floor. During the floor show, waiters dance along with the most flamboyant laser light show around. Stars shine through the glass-domed ceiling, while US stars perform on-screen in the most current video clips. ◆ Cover. Daily. 30333

11 Hotel Dorado Pacífico $$$ A soaring 15-story atrium lobby with glass elevators and splashing fountains leads to a long swimming pool with a swim-up bar. The 285 rooms and suites all face the ocean side and have sliding glass doors that lead to small balconies. The suites have mini-bars, spacious sitting areas, and fold-out couches, and all rooms have blond wood furnishings and tile floors. Rooms with two beds are a rarity here; most have one double or a double bed and a fold-out couch (those are billed as triple rooms). Families are welcome, and there's a separate wading pool and two water slides for kids. The cafeteria offers large buffets, and it's a great spot for a late-night snack of french fries and gazpacho before heading to the discos. ◆ Paseos Ixtapa and de las Garzas. 32025, 800/448.8355; fax 30126

Within the Hotel Dorado Pacífico:

La Cebolla Roja ★★$$ Grilled meats and fish are the specialty at this alfresco dining area right on the sand. Candles flicker in hurricane lamps, and the crashing waves provide the music. Try the mixed grill, with a sampling of Mexican-style meats. ◆ Mexican/Seafood ◆ Daily dinner. 32025

11 Raffaello ★★★$$$ A pale pink Mediterranean terrace surrounded by twinkling lights creates the perfect setting for dinner. Italian specialties include beef *piccata*, baked octopus, and the delicious pasta Raffaello (a blend of pasta, bacon, and ham in a green chili sauce). ◆ Italian ◆ Daily lunch and dinner. Paseo Ixtapa 6 (at Paseo de las Garzas). 32386

12 La Puerta Mall At one time this property was part of a large hacienda surrounded by thousands of coconut palms. The hacienda has been replaced by some fine shops and restaurants in a series of Spanish-style one-story stucco buildings arranged around a courtyard (none of Ixtapa's shopping malls is of the glitzy glass-and-chrome variety so popular in Cancún). As the first mall on the strip, it is now battling competition from at

least three other plazas. ◆ Daily. Paseo Ixtapa (between Paseos del Palmar and de las Garzas)

Within La Puerta Mall:

Mamma Norma Pizzeria ★★$$ This tiny cafe is consistently recommended as the best pizza place in Ixtapa (and they deliver!). The Mexican pizza is topped with beans and chorizo (sausage), the marinara comes with tuna, sardines, and chopped egg. There's also a great choice of salads (all with vegetables cleaned with purified water). Photos of Italy line the walls, and meals are accompanied by recorded Italian tunes. ◆ Italian ◆ Daily lunch and dinner. 30274

Naturalísimo 99% Natural ★$ Drink your juice the healthy, natural way, or have the bartender add a jigger of rum. Billed as a natural foods restaurant, this cheery cafe also serves beef, chicken, and pork, as well as great cheese-and-avocado sandwiches on homemade wheat bread. There is a full bar, and the bakery offers take-out breads and sweet rolls. ◆ Sandwiches/Bakery ◆ Daily breakfast, lunch, and dinner. No credit cards accepted. No phone

Mic-Mac A vast array of embroidered T-shirts and dresses (including a fine selection of Maria de Guadalajara cotton gauze designs), Guatemalan belts, and gorgeous postcards fill this small shop, owned by the same people who have the larger La Fuente in Los Patios. ◆ Daily; closed at midday. 31733

El Infierno y La Gloria ★★★$$ Despite its name, which means means "hell and glory," this restaurant/cantina puts all the emphasis on the latter. The dining rooms are filled with statues, paper flowers, and cutesy folk art, and the walls are covered with murals

depicting scenes from a Mexican pueblo, including portraits of amorous couples on balconies as well as a wall-size Moses. The menu runs the Mexican gamut from enchiladas to chicken in mole sauce, with generous portions served by waiters who are friendly without being overbearing. ♦ Mexican ♦ Daily breakfast, lunch, and dinner. 30272

12 Los Patios In the row of shopping centers across from the hotels, this one stands out for its excellent folk art shops and galleries. The building is a two-story, U-shaped, rust-colored affair. ♦ Daily. Paseo Ixtapa (between Paseos del Palmar and de las Garzas)

Within Los Patios:

Golden Cookie Shop ★★★$ At breakfast time in high season you're almost destined to stand in line for a seat at this German bakery and cafe, but it's worth the wait. Owners Esther (from Singapore) and Helmut (from Germany) Walters serve great breakfasts of eggs, hash browns, and melt-in-your-mouth sweet rolls. But chef Helmut really shines with his bratwurst, knockwurst, chicken curry, *nasi goreng* (an Indonesian rice dish with vegetables), and fried bananas. The pastries, strudel, and cookies are beyond compare, and you're not likely to find homemade rye bread and thick deli sandwiches anywhere else in town. ♦ International/Bakery ♦ M-Sa breakfast, lunch, and dinner; closed 3-6PM. Second floor. 30310

La Fuente This is surely the only place you'll find lacquered wicker desks and tables sporting smiling wicker jaguar faces, or three-foot-high blown glass vases. Hand-painted plates rest upon distressed antique buffets and dining tables; mirrors with embossed tin frames hang on the wall. The shop carries only the best Mexican folk art and furnishings, most of which you may long to ship home. ♦ Daily; closed at midday. First floor. 30812

Galería San Angel Owner Rosa Elena Quesnel de Vitard has filled her small gallery with a sampling of some of Mexico's finest artists, including religious paintings by Jorge Ritter, designer of the Mexican pavilion murals at the 1964 New York World's Fair. Hand-tooled crosses made of silver and cedar designed by Brother Gabriel Chávez de la Mora of Cuernavaca, surrealistic brass boxes and mirrors by Enrique Zavala, and filigreed replicas of the gold jewelry found at the Zapotec temples at Monte Albán in Oaxaca are also available here. ♦ Daily; closed at midday. First floor. 43611

Santa Prisca If silver is your passion, don't miss this gallery and shop. The jewelry, hand-crafted in the silver-mining town of Taxco, is elegant and unusual, and the display of Aztec masks will make you a collector. ♦ Daily; closed at midday. First floor. 43857. Also at: Mercado de Artesanía Turístico, 5 de Mayo (between Juan Alvarez and Catalina González), Zihuatanejo. 30709

12 Plaza Ixpamar Yet another small shopping center, this one is distinguished by the black iron gate and archway at its entrance, behind Los Patios. Many of the spaces here have yet to be rented out, but it's a cool, shady place to wander through the existing shops. The tourism office is located here. ♦ Daily. Paseo Ixtapa (between Paseos del Palmar and de las Garzas)

Within Plaza Ixpamar:

El Amanecer This two-story shop is chockablock with reasonably priced folk art and crafts from all over Mexico. An extensive collection of expressive terra-cotta angels from Metepec covers one wall; rustic clay candelabra have a woodlike shine, the result of a technique developed by Don Heron Martinez of Puebla. Rows of embroidered dresses hang by the windows, and tables are covered with wood and clay skeletons, magic powders, and *milagros* (religious charms). ♦ Daily; closed at midday. 31902

13 Presidente Inter-Continental Ixtapa $$$$ An upscale all-inclusive hotel, this was one of the first hostelries built in Ixtapa, and it wears its age well. From the street all you see is the newer high-rise, dubbed "the computer card" by some because of its tiny square windows. But once past the tower you have a view of the true hotel, with a front plaza and iron gazebo, carved stone entryways, and colonial-style fountains. There are a total of 420 rooms, most with tile floors, marble countertops, rattan furniture, large balconies, and king-size beds on request. The newer building has a glass elevator and great views of the sea. The food is above par for an all-inclusive accommodation. It's popular with Mexican families. ♦ Paseo Ixtapa (between Paseos del Palmar and de las Garzas). 30018, 800/327.0200; fax 32312

14 Mercado Turisticos Ixtapa The vendors who once plied their wares on the sidewalks and beaches now congregate in this rather dark and gloomy tile-roofed artisans' market across from the **Sheraton Ixtapa Resort.** It's well worth a visit here for the requisite T-shirts and souvenirs and the sampling of folk art from Guerrero artisans. Bargaining is expected. ♦ Daily. Paseos Ixtapa and del Palmar. No phone

15 Sheraton Ixtapa Resort $$$ The sound of water splashing in fountains in the open-air atrium lobby immediately calms stressed-out visitors. A tropical landscape of pools, beaches, and gardens provides plenty of room for privacy, though you may prefer to relax on your balcony and survey the scene from above. The entire 331-room hotel was designed for pleasure and relaxation, with spacious rooms in cool, soothing colors. The pool is the best in the hotel zone, with plenty of shallow water for kids and a huge swim-up bar where you can feast on shrimp or spiced coconut meat. There are four restaurants to choose from, plus 24-hour room service; a traditional (expensive) Mexican fiesta with buffet dinner is presented every Wednesday. ♦ Paseo Ixtapa (just south of Paseo del Palmar). 31858, 800/325.3535; fax 32438

Within the Sheraton Ixtapa Resort:

La Fonda ★★★$$ If you came to Mexico for the food, then this is the place for you. Here it's called gourmet Mexican, with such specialties as ceviche, *chicharrón de queso* (grilled cheese rinds), quesadillas, *huitlacoche* (a mushroomlike fungus cultivated in corn husks), and squash blossoms. The dining room is reminiscent of a colonial plaza, with walls washed in soft blue, yellow, and pink, huge star-shaped piñatas hanging from the ceiling, and a fountain at the entryway. The strains of Mexican ballads, sung and strummed by a guitarist in the adjacent lobby bar, complete the dining experience. ♦ Mexican ♦ Daily dinner. 31858

Veranda ★★$ Dining in the open atrium lobby under bright white suspended tents has a cool, cosmopolitan feeling. The Mexican breakfast buffet is set up for early birds, who choose from fruit, fresh juices, pastries, and cereals before digging into such Mexican specialties as *chilaquiles* (corn tortillas in sauce), quesadillas, *huevos rancheros,* and much more. Those who don't want that much spice in their life may opt for pancakes, eggs and bacon, or club sandwiches with fresh-roasted turkey. This is the perfect place to escape the mid-day sun. ♦ Mexican/International ♦ Daily breakfast, lunch, and dinner. 31858

16 Campo de Golf Ixtapa (Ixtapa Golf Club) Designed by Robert Trent Jones Jr., this green oasis with palm trees scattered alongside cool reflecting lakes and ponds makes for an exciting game of golf. (It's a natural refuge for flamingos, cranes, parrots, iguanas, and the occasional crocodile, too.) The 18-hole course is 6,898 yards, par 72, with a capacity for 250 players. Clubhouse facilities include showers and lockers, a pro shop run by golf pro Eladio Esquivel, a boutique, and a restaurant-bar. Adjacent to the clubhouse are five lighted, professional-size tennis courts and a large swimming pool with a bar and lounge area. Other amenities include caddies, electric carts, and a roving bar cart to quench your thirst on the course. Golf tournaments are held here in November and June. ♦ Daily. Paseos Ixtapa and de las Golondrinas. 31062

17 Villa del Lago $$$ It's a golfer's dream to stay in this elegant six-suite bed-and-breakfast right next to the sixth tee; there's also a small pool overlooking the rolling greens and the lake. The villa was once the home of local architect **Raul Esponda,** which he designed to reflect the best in traditional Mexican style. Heavy, carved wooden doors open into the main house's dining room, library, and lounge; French doors lead to the gardens and suites. Although all of the accommodations are first-rate, our favorite is a two-story affair with a private patio looking out to the course. You can enjoy breakfast on a patio, poolside, or on the second-story dining-room terrace, the best place for spotting birds in the treetops or the crocodiles that live in the lake. Dinner is available upon request. Rates are by the night or week, and golf packages are available. Families take over the entire compound at times; reserve early for the best rooms. Nightlife consists of stargazing from the terrace while sipping a drink, but taxis will whisk you off to restaurants, bars, and discos just five minutes away on Playa del Palmar. ♦ Reservations recommended. Retorno de las Alondras 244 (off Paseo de las Golondrinas). 31482; fax 31422, 619/575.1766 in the US

Crocodiles submerged in ponds at Ixtapa Golf Club are measured each year by zoologists; the big ones (over 4 meters/13 feet) get new accommodations at the Mexico City Zoo.

Local lore has it that Zihuatanejo received its name from one of Spanish conqueror Hernán Cortés's captains. When the captain reached Bahía de Zihuatanejo, his guide told him the area was called Cihuatlán in the Nahuatl language, meaning "the place of women." The captain added the Castilian suffix *nejo,* meaning small and insignificant, to the name—which may be why the conquerors left the area alone.

18 Westin Brisas Resort Ixtapa $$$ Sitting on its own little bay on Playa Hermosa, this 428-room pyramid-shaped hotel provides the ultimate in privacy. The air is filled with the sounds of exotic birds who live in the nearby jungle; pleasant walkways meander past swimming pools with waterfalls. Guests in the lanai rooms have ocean views from their hammocks; those in the **Royal Beach Club** have use of a private lounge where complimentary continental breakfast and afternoon cocktails with hors d'oeuvres are served. Not to be overlooked are the standard rooms, which are still luxurious compared to other hotels. Nonsmoking rooms are available. Fresh flowers and fruit are brought in daily, and a shady beach *palapa* is reserved at your request. Every restaurant in the complex is excellent, and shoppers get their fix at high-end galleries and boutiques. Some guests never leave the grounds; this hotel is a destination in itself. ♦ Off Paseo Ixtapa (just west of Paseo de la Roca). 32121, 800/228.3000; fax 30751

Within the Westin Brisas Resort Ixtapa:

El Mexicano ★★$$ Gourmet Mexican food tastes even better on a tree-lined patio decorated in bold colors. Jumbo prawns in tamarind sauce are outstanding, and the baby abalone in chili chipotle sauce is a memorable appetizer. For a different approach to fish, try the cream of coriander seafood dishes. ♦ Mexican ♦ Daily dinner. Reservations recommended. 32121

Portofino Restaurant ★★★$$$ When you're in the mood to splurge on a special evening, this restaurant offers intimate dining with crystal, candlelight, and the best Italian food in town. Offerings include scrumptious beef scallopini and the biggest and freshest shrimp you've ever eaten. The antipasto buffet not only looks good, but it has all the familiar tastes of your favorite trattoria in Rome. Save room for dessert—the choices seem endless, but try the sabayon dressed with fresh strawberries. ♦ Italian ♦ Daily dinner. Reservations recommended. 32121

19 Villa de la Selva ★★★$$$ Take all the time you wish and linger over a Spanish coffee or a glass of Cognac high on the southern hills

overlooking Playa Hermosa and the impressive **Westin Resort.** Once the lovely home of an ex-president, this elegant hacienda has been converted into a series of dining rooms, each with open terraces and views of the sea. Classic Mexican dishes and outstanding steaks are on the menu, along with a great wine list. ♦ Mexican/International ♦ Daily dinner. Reservations recommended. Paseo de la Roca (south of Paseo Ixtapa). 30362

Zihuatanejo

Though Zihuatanejo can no longer be called a fishing village, it's still one of the most traditional towns on Mexico's Pacific Coast. Fishermen beach their skiffs on the sand after bringing in the day's catch, and families gather along the waterfront *malecón* for evening strolls. The town has a good public market, great Mexican and seafood restaurants, and a wonderfully relaxed ambience. Inexpensive and moderately priced hotels (along with three luxurious small inns) line the hills facing **Zihuatanejo Bay,** above long, clean beaches and calm water. Visitors tend to get hooked on Zihua and return year after year to their favorite rooms and restaurants.

20 Puerto Mío $$$ Few hotels can claim their own cove and marina; this one has all that and more. Hacienda-style buildings in pale pastel colors perch on the side of a steep bluff that appears to be climbing into the sky. All 31 rooms and suites have unparalleled views of Bahía de Zihuatanejo and are gorgeously furnished with folk art; some have private hot tubs. The rooms in the mansion atop the property's highest hill are enormous, with gauze canopies draping over the beds, shells embedded in the bathroom walls, and vibrant handwoven cotton fabrics contrasting with white stucco walls. Swimming pools seem to flow over the edge of the cliff; barrel cacti tower beside fuchsia bougainvillea, giving the property a surrealistic effect that combines desert with jungle. Note, however, that it's a long hike uphill to some of the rooms; transport, by open-air jitney, is available but unreliable. A plus: The **Zihuatanejo Scuba Center** has its main shop here with five boats departing from the center's private pier. ♦ Andador Contramar (south of Noria). 42748, 888/389.2645; fax 42048, 43624

Within Puerto Mío:

Restaurant Puerto Mío ★★★$$$ The terrace and formal dining rooms overlooking the small cove help make this a special place at sunset; as night falls, torches are lit along the cliff tops over the sea. Begin your meal with a salad of sliced tomatoes and full-bodied Oaxacan cheese, or delicate shrimp crepes. Move on to fresh tuna with pepper sauce, or snapper with peanut sauce, or whatever fresh fish the chef has prepared. ♦ Nouvelle Mexican/Seafood ♦ Daily breakfast, lunch, and dinner. 42748

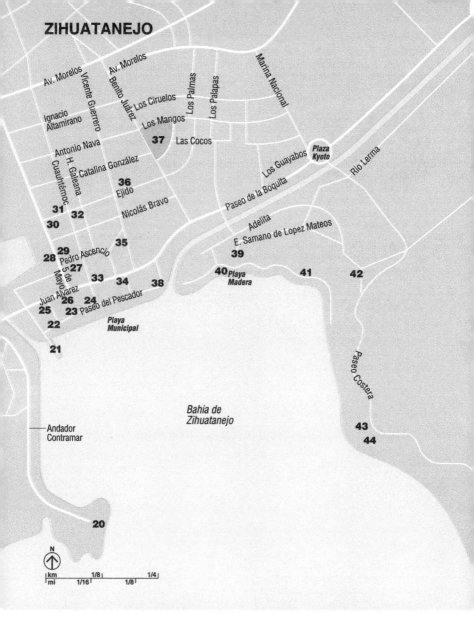

ZIHUATANEJO

21 Muelle Municipal (Municipal Pier)
Cruise ships, fishing boats, and yachts all
anchor off this short wooden pier, which
also is a favorite spot for evening strolls.
There is a white obelisk monument marking
the beginning of Paseo del Pescador is just to
the right of the pier; the navy is headquartered
to the left, next to the fishing cooperative.
Fisherfolk beach their *pangas* along this
stretch of sand and stash their gear in blue
wooden lockers. They pull out before dawn
and return before noon with their catch.
If fresh fish isn't what you had in mind for
a souvenir, check out the adjacent display
of coral and shells at the open-air **Mercado
Conchas Marina** (Seashell Market). ♦ Paseo
del Pescador

22 Paseo del Pescador A decorative brick
promenade runs from the municipal pier
the length of downtown Zihua and the Playa
Municipal (or Playa Principal), where locals
sun on the sand and play in the waves. Open-
air seafood restaurants line the walkway from
the pier to the basketball court at the foot
of Cuauhtémoc, where there always seems
to be a game under way. A small stage at the
water side of the court is used for musical
performances on Sunday evenings, and the
wide brick plaza on the street side of the court
serves as a gathering spot. More cafes appear
as the road leads eastward to the **Museo
Arqueológico de la Costa Grande.** The
walkway extends along the cliffs to Playa
Madera; there are benches for those who wish

to simply gaze out to sea. Be careful, because the waves can come crashing in during high tide. ♦ Between Playa Madera and Muelle Municipal

22 La Sirena Gorda ★★★$$ Owner Luis Muñoz knows his way around a fish, especially when it's wrapped in a fresh corn tortilla. Fish tacos are his specialty and shouldn't be missed. Fillings include smoked sailfish, shrimp topped with crumbled bacon and onion strips, conch with nopales cactus, and *pescado al pastor* (fish roasted on a spit and served with fresh cilantro). Chances are you'll keep coming back until you've sampled them all; there also are hefty burgers and fish dinners. The restaurant's name means "fat mermaid"; the lovely sea creature is depicted in paintings and drawings done by creative customers. Early risers can watch the anglers head out to sea while lingering over a breakfast of eggs or fish tacos. ♦ Seafood ♦ M, Tu, Th-Su breakfast, lunch, and dinner. Paseo del Pescador (just east of Muelle Municipal). 42687

23 Casa Elvira ★$$ Locals and travelers fill the outdoor tables here on weekend afternoons and feast on large seafood platters of red snapper, lobster, shrimp, and octopus. The parade of people on the *paseo* is visible from most tables, as is a saltwater aquarium mimicking the local underwater scenery. If you're tired of fish, there's also good spaghetti, a grilled meat platter, and cheese-filled *chiles rellenos*. The quality of the food is unpredictable; stick with the less expensive items on the menu. ♦ Seafood/Mexican ♦ Daily lunch and dinner. Paseo del Pescador (between Cuauhtémoc and Muelle Municipal). 42061

24 Casa Marina Several of Zihua's nicest shops are clustered in this one building. **La Zapoteca** is filled with handwoven wool rugs in ancient Zapotec designs and a good selection of Oaxacan folk art. The walls at **El Jumil** are covered with antique and modern masks, while pottery, baskets, and weavings are displayed at **Manos**. Bookworms will want to browse through the used books at **Cafe La Marina**, a small pizza place. ♦ Daily. Paseo del Pescador 6 (at Cuauhtémoc). 42373

25 Garrobos ★★$ Though not on the waterfront, this informal cafe is one of Zihua's better seafood eateries. You can count on fresh dorado, tuna, snapper, or whatever's in season, served with white rice, a small salad, and fresh bread. The basic Mexican dishes such as enchiladas and tacos are also good. ♦ Mexican ♦ Daily. Juan Alvarez (between Cuauhtémoc and the lagoon bridge). 46706

26 Mamacita's ★★$ Desperate readers in search of something to read can't resist stopping by this small cafe several times during their visits. The shelves of used paperbacks are impressive, the food (sandwiches, snacks, beer) less so, but the characters hanging about are always interesting. ♦ American ♦ Daily noon-8PM. Juan Alvarez (between Cuauhtémoc and the lagoon bridge). No phone

27 El Patio ★★★$$$ Candles shimmer in an intimate garden dining area perfect for quiet conversations. The street side of the restaurant serves as a bar in high season and a dining room at other times. Precious hand-painted Talavera vases and plates are displayed in antique china cabinets, and blue-and-white tiles from Oaxaca line the counters of the open kitchen. Dinners begin with complimentary *gorditas* (appetizer-size corn patties with chopped lettuce, meats, onions, and cheese). Mexican specialties include a *nopalito* (cactus) salad and shrimp-filled *chiles rellenos;* seafood shines in the tuna brochette. There's live music in the high season, including Andean flutes or Spanish flamenco. ♦ Mexican/Seafood ♦ Daily breakfast, lunch, dinner. 5 de Mayo 3 (at Pedro Ascencio). 43019

28 Mercado de Artesanía Turístico Vendors who used to ply their wares on the beach have set up shop in this four-blocklong market with 255 permanent stands. Clean, shaded, and filled with fascinating goods, the market is a great place to learn about local folk art. Artists paint colorful scenes of village life on bowls and plates, or glue tiny seashells into statuettes. T-shirts abound, and though they may seem light and flimsy, they're perfect for this humid climate and dry quickly. A careful shopper will find items from most of Mexico's craft centers (including a wide variety of silver jewelry designs), and some skillful bargaining could yield some worthy treasures. ♦ Daily. 5 de Mayo (between Juan Alvarez and Catalina González). No phone

29 Iglesia de la Virgen de Guadalupe (Church of the Virgin of Guadalupe) Zihua's main church is a simple one, with a metal roof and ceiling fans. A box is set by the front door with a sign in English requesting donations for the church's ongoing refurbishing. ♦ 5 de Mayo (between Pedro Ascencio and Nicolás Bravo)

30 Paul's ★★★$$ Paul Karrer, the Swiss chef/owner of this pretty bistro, has developed a loyal following for his unusual menu. Few other places around serve escargot, sashimi, duck breast, and fresh quail, and though shrimp is common, his version, with a light dill sauce, is superb. A relocation of the restaurant was under consideration at press time, so check to make sure the address is still correct. ◆ International ◆ Daily dinner. 5 de Mayo (between Nicolás Bravo and Ejido). 42188

31 Boutique D'Xochitl Known for her elaborate style of dress, Xochitl was an Aztec queen in the time of Cuauhtémoc. Modern women can dress equally extravagantly in flowing gauze skirts by Maria de Guadalajara and appliquéd jackets by Girasol, two of Mexico's top designers of resortwear. This boutique carries both lines, plus glamorous hats and accessories to complete the look. ◆ Daily. Cuauhtémoc and Ejido. 42131

32 Nueva Zelanda ★★★$ First-rate breakfasts plus great sandwiches, *tortas,* and enchiladas keep the seats full throughout the day. Diners check their choices on a printed menu/order form, and waiters deliver the orders quickly. Sit at the counter and watch the waiters put papaya and water or milk in the blender for thick *licuados* (fruit drinks). ◆ Mexican/American ◆ Daily breakfast and lunch. Cuauhtémoc (between Nicolás Bravo and Ejido). 42340. Also at: Los Patios, Paseo Ixtapa (between Paseos del Palmar and de las Garzas), Ixtapa. 30838

33 Ruby's Joyería y Galería Jewelry and accessories in silver, gold, and precious gems are displayed, with prices ranging from downright cheap to thousands of dollars. Lots of jewelry shops line this pedestrians-only stretch, but this store has the highest-quality pieces, many signed by the artist. ◆ Daily; closed at midday. Cuauhtémoc 7 (between Juan Alvarez and Pedro Ascencio). 43990

33 Zihuatanejo Scuba Center Zihua has earned a cult following for its outstanding diving. Manta rays, eagle rays, and the occasional shark or humpback whale provide that extra jolt of excitement divers crave, and with at least 28 dive sites to choose from, deep-sea devotees find enough variety to satisfy them. This place is run by Ed Clarke, an ex-San Francisco business executive, and Juan Barnard Avila, a marine biologist. Both are experienced certified divers and run a first-class, safe operation. Divers must have a certification card and are taken in small groups to sites that include coral gardens and underwater caves. Certification courses are available. The center's main operation is at Puerto Mio, but divers can stop by this conveniently located branch to view underwater videos, schedule their dive trips, and rent and purchase equipment. ◆ M-Sa. Cuauhtémoc 3 (between Juan Alvarez and Pedro Ascencio). 42147; fax 44468. Also at: Puerto Mío, Andador Contramar (south of Noria). 42748

34 Hotel Avila $ The rooms on the beach side of this immaculately kept budget hotel have the best seats in town for viewing the scene along the Paseo del Pescador. Two large terraces with upholstered couches, tables, and chairs face the sea; from this lofty perch you have a panoramic view of Bahía de Zihuatanejo. Each of the 27 large, white rooms has two double beds, giant showers, ceiling fans, and powerful air-conditioners (which you need only in the height of summer). Sliding glass doors open onto balconies and patios, providing a nice sea breeze. Rooms on the street side aren't nearly as nice, since you lose the breeze and gain traffic noise. The restaurant downstairs is a good spot for a quick bite or cool drink. Since this is the only downtown hotel right at the beach, it fills up quickly in the winter months. ◆ Juan Alvarez 8 (between Vicente Guerrero and Cuauhtémoc). 42010; fax 43299

The bark of the *cuachalalate* tree, which grows wild in the jungle, has long been used to treat kidney ailments.

Every day around 7PM in Zihuatanejo, hundreds of swallows circle the town and land on the telephone wires near the movie theater. They chatter and twitter together for about 45 minutes, then fly away to their nighttime habitat. No one knows why they come to this particular spot, but for as many years as anyone can remember this has been an evening ritual. Strangers learn the hard way not to park their cars under the telephone wires.

Restaurants/Clubs: Red Hotels: Blue

Shops/🌳 Outdoors: Green Sights/Culture: Black

35 El Buen Gusto A steady stream of people enter this bright pink house to peruse shelves filled with delicious *bolillos* (crusty rolls), dense sugar cookies, and flaky pastries. Resist temptation and buy only what you can eat within the day, then return tomorrow to see what new treats are fresh from the oven. ♦ Daily. Vicente Guerrero 8 (between Juan Alvarez and Augustín Ramírez). 43231

35 Coco Cabaña It's fun to browse through this boutique's large selection of Mexican folk art, complete with whimsical animals from Oaxaca, unique Guerrero masks, and handwoven cloth from Chiapas. Prices are a bit higher than in the bigger cities, but the quality and variety are excellent. ♦ Daily. Vicente Guerrero and Augustín Ramírez. 42518

35 Coconuts ★★★$$ The trees at this elegant outdoor restaurant sparkle with tiny white lights. The building surrounding the courtyard is a remodeled 1865 hacienda, its stucco walls, arches, and niches providing a pretty background. The establishment's good (and well-deserved) reputation for its international menu and friendly bar has made it a favorite among visitors and locals. The chef uses what's fresh from market and sea, creating great seafood dishes with herb sauces. Try the legendary bananas flambé. The restaurant is closed during the rainy season, so call ahead. ♦ International ♦ Daily dinner; closed August through November. Reservations recommended from December through April. Augustín Ramírez 1 (between Pedro Ascencio and Vicente Guerrero). 42518

Lights, Camera, Action

Mexico has always entranced both national and international filmmakers, providing the backdrop for Westerns, adventures, and plenty of romance films. The following are some of the films that have been shot in Mexico or that tell a story about Mexicans.

Bring Me the Head of Alfredo Garcia (1974) Director Sam Peckinpah is at his most bizarre in this film of a drunken dropout's odyssey through Mexico.

El Mariachi (1993) With a minuscule budget, independent filmmaker Richard Rodriguez used unknown actors to produce this well-received movie about a young man's attempts to become a mariachi.

El Norte (1983) A Guatemalan brother and sister make their way through hostile territory in Mexico and the US in this touching and enlightening tale of illegal immigration that stars Jack Nicholson.

Juarez (1939) Paul Muni stars as the Mexican liberator President Benito Juárez, who fought to free Mexico from European rule under Austrian archduke Maximilian and his wife Carlota (Bette Davis).

Like Water for Chocolate (1992) Author Laura Esquivel's novel of magical love, sensuality, and cooking comes to the screen under the direction of Alfonso Aral.

Medicine Man (1992) Sean Connery and Lorraine Bracco search for a cancer cure and attempt to save the Amazon's rain forest, though they're actually in the jungles of southern **Veracruz.**

Night of the Iguana (1964) **Puerto Vallarta** was never the same after Richard Burton and Elizabeth Taylor carried on their off-screen affair during the filming of this sultry Tennessee Williams play.

The Old Gringo (1989) The era of Pancho Villa is gorgeously depicted in this film version of Carlos Fuentes's novel, starring Jane Fonda, Gregory Peck, and Jimmy Smits.

Predator (1987) Arnold Schwarzenegger muscles his way through the steamy jungles outside Puerto Vallarta to conquer a gross alien from outer space.

Revenge (1989) Kevin Costner loses out to Anthony Quinn in a fatal love triangle set outside Puerto Vallarta.

Romancing the Stone (1984) The jungles and colonial towns of Veracruz fill in for Colombia, where Kathleen Turner, Michael Douglas, and Danny DeVito battle each other and standard movie *banditos* while searching for a mysterious green jewel.

10 (1979) Dudley Moore pursues Bo Derek through the fantasy world setting of **Las Hadas** in **Manzanillo.**

Treasure of the Sierra Madre (1948) John Huston directed his son Walter, along with Humphrey Bogart and Tim Holt, in the film version of B. Traven's tale of an ill-fated search for gold.

Under the Volcano (1984) Albert Finney masterfully depicts the drunken British ex-consular agent from author Malcolm Lowry's classic novel about an alcoholic expatriate in Mexico.

36 Tamales y Atoles Any ★★★$
Traditional Mexican cooking doesn't
get any better than this. On Thursday
and Saturday the restaurant presents the
pozolero, a feast featuring *pozole* (a stew
of hominy and chicken or pork), homemade
tamales, *chiles rellenos,* and a variety of
side dishes. The daily menu features several
kinds of tamales—cornmeal wrapped around
beef, chicken, pork, or fruit and steamed
in corn husks. Also worth sampling are the
quesadillas, corn tortillas folded around a
variety of fillings—*flor de calabaza* (squash
flowers) with cheese, grilled chilies with
cheese, chorizo (sausage), or mushrooms.
Die-hard fans stop by frequently to check
out the daily specials. The large room is
rustic, decorated with large clay pots and
vases and murals depicting scenes from
a small-town general store. ◆ Mexican
◆ Daily breakfast, lunch, and dinner.
Ejido and Vicente Guerrero. 47373,
47303

37 Mercado Central Here housewives fill
their shopping bags with seasonal vegetables,
fresh meat, poultry, seafood, and medicinal
herbs. There's also a wide variety of tropical
fruits, including papaya, coconut, bananas,
and tamarind. The candy made with tamarind
can be sugary sweet; for something really
different, try the candy dusted with powdered
dried chilies. The streets around the market
are filled with artisans' shops and stands.
This is a good place to look for huaraches
and leather sandals. ◆ Daily. Benito Juárez
and Antonio Nava. No phone

38 Villamar ★★★$ Better known by
locals as "Joaquin's place," after owner/
chef Joaquin Vasquez, this beachside
restaurant is the best spot to dig your
toes in the sand while eating or sipping
a cappuccino. Formerly the chef at **Casa
Elvira** (see page 82), Joaquin brought
his talents to his own place, where well-
prepared local seafood stars on the menu,
along with steaks, fajitas, and barbecued
ribs. Diners can choose to eat inside the
dining room or at sidewalk tables, but
on the beach the flickering firelight of
flambéed shrimp seems particularly
romantic. ◆ Seafood ◆ Daily lunch and
dinner. Paseo del Pescador 2 (east of
Vicente Guerrero). 44719

**38 Museo Arqueológico de la Costa
Grande (Archaeology Museum)**
Inaugurated in 1992, this small museum is
located in a handsome river-rock building
at the end of Paseo del Pescador, practically
on the sand. Displays include paintings of
the pre-Columbian Cuitlateca peoples and
a collection of artifacts from archaeological
sites in the state of Guerrero. ◆ Admission.
Tu-Su. Paseo del Pescador (east of Vicente
Guerrero). 32552

39 Bungalows Pacíficos $ High on a hill
overlooking the bay, this small hotel offers
large patios where guests can sit among the
wild indigenous plants and catch the breezes
and vistas of Zihuatanejo. The six apartmentlike
rooms are simple, with twin beds and kitchens.
Owner Anita Hahner Chimalpopoca is friendly
and full of useful information and suggestions,
and the best part of staying here is getting to
know her (made easier because she speaks
English, Spanish, and German). She is vitally
interested in the archaeology of the area and
has been collecting artifacts for more than 20
years. Playa Madera is at the base of a long,
downhill climb, and you can reach town along
the cliffside path from here. ◆ Eva Samano de
Lopez Mateos (south of Adelita). 42112; fax
42110

40 Playa Madera This sunbathing spot,
 the smallest beach along the bay, is named
for its early days as a loading point for logs
(*madera* means timber) that were cut from
the surrounding jungle and exported. A
number of small inexpensive hotels and
cottages dot the shore and the bluff above.
Unless the tide is extraordinarily high you
can walk from downtown to this beach
along a man-made path. ◆ East of Paseo
del Pescador

41 Kau-Kan ★★★★$$$ This establishment
is owned by Ricardo Rodríguez, one of
Zihua's best-known chefs (formerly at **La
Casa Que Canta** in Zihuatanejo and **Champs-
Elysées** in Mexico City) and set on a slight hill
overlooking the beach. Rodríguez's venture
boasts an outdoor terrace with handsome
carved wooden railings, indoor dining rooms
with arched doorways, and a rooftop terrace.
Though the restaurant is easier to find in
daylight, it takes on a special glow at night,
when twinkling white lights and candles lend
an unmistakable air of romance. The service
is professional and efficient, and the menu
features seafood with unusual touches, such
as robalo (a white fish) with *guajillo* chili

strips and *mantarraya* (manta ray) with black butter. The wine list includes some imports, and the exotic fruit sorbets make a perfect ending to a superb meal. ♦ Seafood ♦ Daily lunch and dinner. Playa Madera. 48446

42 Villas Miramar $$ Popular with snowbirds on long-term stays, this 17-room hotel has one building overlooking Playa Madera and another set amid gardens across a small street. The rooms are a good value, with simple decor, air-conditioning, phones, and televisions. The shaded pool is a popular gathering spot for afternoon cocktails. The coffee shop–style restaurant is open for all three meals. ♦ Adelita (north of Paseo Costera). 42106; fax 42149

42 Hotel Irma $ A true taste of Mexico set on a cliff above Playa Madera, this casual hotel has pink granite walls, red-tile floors, brick archways, and 72 simple rooms, some of which have been remodeled with light wooden furnishings and freshly painted walls. Try for one on the top two floors; they have breezy terraces and views of the sea. Not all rooms are air-conditioned, but all have fans and TVs (local stations only). The least expensive rooms face the gardens or have windows that look out on the inside corridors. Guests can use the beach facilities at the **Fiesta Mexicana** hotel on Playa la Ropa, or descend a long stairway to the beach below the **Irma**. Excellent Mexican food is served at **El Zorito's**, but the coffee shop is just average. ♦ Adelita (just north of Paseo Costera). 42025; fax 43738

43 La Casa Que Canta $$$$ Considered one of the most beautiful hotels in Mexico, and a member of the Small Luxury Hotels of the World, this place lives up to its name—the house of song. Each of the 24 suites (7 with private pools) is named after a popular Mexican ballad, and each has a mood of its own. The cool white-on-white decor is accented with gorgeous furnishings from Michoacán, engraved and painted by hand into fanciful scenes. The arms of a couch are carved into bright red-and-yellow parrots; soft blue monkeys swing on a nightstand. Several rooms have wooden desk chairs decorated with reproductions of Frida Kahlo paintings; all have telephones, but TV sets are nonexistent. Children under the age of 16 are not allowed. The walls surrounding the property are made of rough adobe and give off

a pleasant faint, earthy aroma of straw and clay. In addition to the beach, there are fresh- and saltwater swimming pools. Breakfast and lunch are intimate affairs, served on the private balconies or at the guests-only *palapa* cafe; dinner is served with advance reservations. ♦ Paseo Costera (south of Adelita). 42722, 42878, 800/525.4800; fax 42006, 47040

44 Villa de la Roca $$$ Yet another one-of-a-kind inn, this bed-and-breakfast offers five delightful suites with king-size beds, sitting rooms with cushy couches, and private terraces with views of the ocean and of the pool, which cascades from its location in front of the large, open-air living room to the terrace below. A full American breakfast is served in the dining room, which affords guests the same panoramic view. ♦ Paseo Costera (south of Adelita). 44793

45 Playa la Ropa (Beach of Clothes) Centuries ago one of the trading ships from the Orient floundered and sank in Bahía de Zihuatanejo, and for days afterward fine silks and rich clothing washed ashore—hence the name. Many say this is the best swimming beach in town, and it's usually filled with locals and guests from adjacent hotels. Several hotels and cafes are located right on the sand, and a few more are nestled in the hillside overlooking the road above the beach. ♦ West of Paseo Costera

On Playa la Ropa:

Villa del Sol $$$$ Take all the ingredients of a great Mexican hotel—comfortable beds, tropical ambience, luxurious amenities, complimentary coffee and croissants with your wake-up call, and purified water—and add a friendly staff and 45 spacious rooms and suites with delicate transparent white gauze draperies around the beds, a sitting area, and a terrace with hammocks. Put it all on the most beautiful beach in Zihuatanejo, and the result is this hotel, a member of the Small Luxury Hotels of the World and Relais & Châteaux. The property sits in the middle of Playa la Ropa, and nine of the newest suites have private plunge pools overlooking the beach. Hand-painted tiles, fountains, and Mexican art decorate the rooms and public spaces, with winding, shady paths leading to the three pools, two tennis courts, and the **Villa del Sol Restaurant,** where the meals will make a substantial dent in your wallet. Outsiders are welcome to use the hotel's private beach area and lounge chairs for a fee; the restaurant is open to the public. Proper attire is required—no bathing suits in the restaurant, no shorts after 6PM. A MAP plan (rates include breakfast and dinner) is enforced in high season (15 November through 30 April) and optional in the summer. Children over 14 are welcome during winter, and younger children are accepted during the summer season. ♦ 42239, 800/223.6510, 888/389.2645; fax 42758

Hotel Paraiso Real $$ Located on Playa la Ropa next to a mangrove forest where crocodiles, squirrels, birds, and turtles add to the jungle ambience, this small hotel is perfect for escapists with an interest in ecology and nature. Six rooms face the beach, while the other fourteen are surrounded by gardens. Unnatural distractions are kept to a minimum; rooms have no phones or TVs. Due to the proximity of the wild crocs, children under 12 are not admitted. The hotel has a small restaurant and bar, and water sports centers on the beach rent kayaks and catamarans. The owners also operate the **Zihuatanejo Scuba Center**, so dive trips are easily arranged. ♦ Mailing address: Zihuatanejo Scuba Center, Calle Cuauhtémoc 3, Zihuatanejo 40880, Guerrero, Mexico. 42147; fax 42147

Rossy ★★$ The two floors of lawn chairs, tables, and inviting hammocks are all open to the cool ocean breezes at this eatery at the far end of Playa la Ropa. Feeling adventurous? Try limpets (a mollusk that lives on the rocks) in a soup or cocktail. The cold beer and excellent coffee are amazingly low in price. ♦ Mexican/Seafood ♦ Breakfast, lunch, and dinner. 44004

46 Playa Las Gatas (Nurse Shark Beach) At the southern end of Playa la Ropa is a peninsula; on its seaward side is the **Faro de Potosí** (Potosí Lighthouse); on the bay side is a beach that locals consider the most beautiful in the entire bay. Local tradition has it that a Tarascan king built the breakwater of rocks that protects the lush palm-lined beach to create a private beach for his daughter. Unless you're a mountain goat, you must get here by boat (catch one from the downtown pier). There are several *palapa* restaurants here specializing in lobster, charcoal-broiled red snapper, clams, and oysters; the best is **Chez Arnoldo.** Scuba, snorkeling, and other water sports equipment is available for rent.

Bests

Julia Ortiz Bautista
Owner-Manager, Job Representaciones, a Centralized Reservations Office for Hotels, Villas, Bungalows, and Furnished Apartments

Bucanero's restaurant—Located at **Marina Ixtapa,** a favorite place for breakfast, lunch, or dinner, with the best international food.

Stay at **Villa del Lago** bed-and-breakfast—Elegant six-bedroom residence right on the **Campo de Golf** with golf or tennis packages available; separate rooms or the whole house can be rented.

Beccofino restaurant—Owned/managed by Raly, an Italian who will prepare real Italian food for you.

La Sirena Gorda—The best place for seafood tacos in a friendly ambience.

To celebrate your wedding anniversary in the most intimate and romantic place, go to **Puerto Mío** or **La Casa Que Canta** for a tropical drink and admire the sunset and the **Zihuatanejo Bay;** then go to the prestigious **Villa del Sol** restaurant for dinner and ask for the suggestions of the chef for a variety of international and Mexican delicacies, accompanied by soft music and the rhythmic sounds of the gentle surf.

Kau-Kan restaurant—Breakfast, lunch, or dinner in an open-air *palapa* right on **Playa Madera**— exquisite food. The catch of the day is the major feature of the varied menu.

Take a day and venture to **Playa Linda** for horseback riding close to nature.

Enjoy real Mexican *atole* (a warm drink made with ground rice or corn) and tamales at **Tamales y Atoles Any** in the heart of **Zihuatanejo;** also, if you're looking for a casual but elegant Mexican restaurant, go to **El Patio** beside the cathedral.

Buy a beautiful Mexican dress or a jacket at **Boutique D'Xochitl** in downtown Zihuatanejo.

For cappuccino, go to **Nueva Zelanda** in Zihuatanejo.

Ask for the best Mexican fiesta in the **Sheraton** hotel.

Take your children and organize a mini-golf tournament at the mini-golf club in **Ixtapa** (behind the shopping arcade).

Enjoy a beautiful sunset in the most sophisticated place overlooking the ocean at the **Villa de la Selva** restaurant in Ixtapa.

For silver or souvenirs go to **Arely's,** located in **Los Patios** shopping arcade.

If you are looking for handicrafts, try the flea market in Ixtapa or Zihuatanejo.

Visit **Marina Ixtapa** and watch the variety of boats in their own dock. Elegant restaurants, boutiques, and bars are also available.

For teenagers, there's a nice open-air ambience at **Carlos 'n' Charlie's.**

Acapulco

Acapulco has been synonymous with glamour, wealth, and fame since the 1950s, when Rita Hayworth, Eddie Fisher, Errol Flynn, Cary Grant, and their friends made it a Hollywood hideaway. Even today it is de rigueur for celebrities to stop here at least once during their careers, adding their names to the roster recited by taxi drivers and tour guides. Given the number of private enclaves and guarded retreats, few travelers actually see Acapulco's famous guests, but somehow their presence keeps the city's legendary glamour alive.

The real Acapulco is a city with nearly a million residents sprawling inland from from a gorgeous curved bay, which the Spaniards discovered in 1521. By 1616 they had constructed **Fuerte de San Diego** (Fort San Diego) to guard their galleons bearing treasures from China and the Philippines en route to Europe. Acapulco remained a major Spanish port until the War of Independence (1810-21); once the Spaniards were banished it dwindled to obscurity. A paved road from Mexico City to Acapulco was opened in 1922, but it wasn't until the 1950s that the region again garnered worldwide fame. Tourism has since become the main industry, and the bay is now lined with enough hotel rooms for all comers, including average tourists with unremarkable names.

Sometimes, however, progress has its price: Acapulco's tourism boom in the 1960s and 1970s left scars on its scenery; the local government has spent much of the 1990s cleaning up the city's streets, neighborhoods, hotel zones,

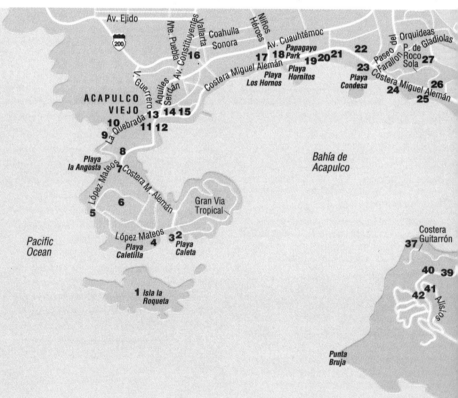

and bay. New sewage lines have been installed, and clean-up patrols keep the beaches and bay free of trash. Still, if you wander a few streets inland from the bay, you find some of the worst living conditions in urban Mexico. Hurricane Pauline brought worldwide attention to the plight of the city's working class in 1997, when hundreds were left homeless after floods and mudslides. The tourist zone recovered almost immediately, but months passed before residents had running water, electricity, and roofs over their heads. Much remains to be done here before all of the city's residents have reasonable living conditions—it's a part of Acapulco that few tourists see.

Touristic Acapulco is divided into several districts, each with its own distinct character. On the west side of the bay, **Acapulco Viejo** (Old Acapulco) and the **Playa Caleta** (Caleta Beach) area were once the center of glamour, but have settled into a comfortable obscurity, attracting laid back and nostalgic visitors. **Costera Miguel Alemán**, lined with high-rise hotels, shopping malls, restaurants, discos, and beach bars, runs parallel to the bay's shoreline, with a golf course, **Centro Acapulco** (Convention Center), and lavish hillside houses on the east end. Tourists seeking the familiar will be comfortable here amid such brand-name eateries as the **Hard Rock Cafe**, **Planet Hollywood**, and **McDonald's**. The hills along **Carretera Escénica**, from the Costera southeast to the airport, are dotted with spectacular homes and resorts, most hidden from sight. Gourmet restaurants and exclusive discos command stunning views. The beach side of this scenic road is the site of a mega-development in progress called **Acapulco Diamante**, which will stretch for miles. When finished (after the turn of the century), the area will include deluxe resort hotels and multimillion-dollar homes.

An aura of monied narcissism seems to pervade the sultry sea air, and influences the local ambience. *Acapulqueños* and their guests follow a schedule far different from what fast-paced US residents are accustomed to. Early morning doesn't exist, except for the working class. Breakfast is a late-morning affair, after 10AM or so. Lunch doesn't start until three, and it seems gauche to dine before nine. The night really begins at midnight, when revelers of all ages gather at discos and clubs. Sleep is an afterthought, and siestas are imperative if you plan to keep up with the pace. And there are other ways to spend your time and money. The shopping, for everything from sandals to sculptures, is excellent. Sunbathing is the daytime activity of choice. Dining can be as adventurous as you wish, be it fish tacos, or flaming filet mignon. Acapulco is home, at least part time, to many who have seen and done it all. Still, they keep returning for more.

La Pedrera

32   Parque Nacional del Veladero

Niños Héroes de Veracruz

28
31
29
30   Cristobál Colón
33   Cap. J.
34 Sebastián
laya acos
35
Ortíz Monasterio
36

200

Carretera
38 Escénica

Costera arina Vieia
Calita
43

Playa Pichlingue

Blvd. Puerto Marqués

200

Bahía de Puerto Marqués

Playa Marqués

PUERTO MARQUES   to airport

44

45 →

code 74 unless otherwise noted.

...etting to Acapulco

...irport

Aeropuerto Internacional Juan N. Alvarez (Juan N. Alvarez International Airport) is 22 kilometers (14 miles) southeast of downtown Acapulco. The airport handles both national and international flights, but airport services such as car rentals and shops are open only when flights are arriving and departing.

Airport Services
Airport Information 669476

Airlines
Aeroméxico	851705, 851600, 800/237.6639
Alaska Air	800/426.0333
America West	800/235.9292
American	669248, 810161, 800/443.7300
Continental	609063, 669034, 800/525.0280
Delta	841428, 669032, 800/221.1212
Mexicana	845083, 841215, 800/531.7921

Getting to and from Aeropuerto Internacional Juan N. Alvarez

By Bus Transportation is provided from the airport by *colectivo* (van) direct to your hotel; rates are set by the zone and range from $5 to $12. No public buses run to the airport.

By Car The drive to downtown Acapulco from the airport takes about 25 minutes. **Carretera Escénica** runs along the hills east of the bay past Acapulco Diamante and the **Las Brisas Hills** area. The road name changes to **Costera Miguel Alemán** north of the Las Brisas Hills, and continues to run along the center of the bay, called the **"Costera,"** to **Acapulco Viejo** and **Playa Caleta.**

The following car-rental agencies have counters at the airport; they are open only when flights are arriving and departing.

Avis	841633, 842581, 800/331.1212
Budget....................................	810596, 800/527.0700
Dollar......................	843066, 843769, 800/800.4000
Hertz	858947, 856889, 800/654.3131

Rental cars are also available at most hotels in Acapulco.

By Taxi Taxis await passengers in front of the airport. The fare to downtown Acapulco is about $12.

Getting Around Acapulco

Buses Buses are inexpensive and convenient to most tourist destinations. Look for the yellow stands and blue *parada* (bus stop) signs—some even include a pay phone and mailbox and have color-coded maps of the bus routes mounted on the wall. Buses marked *Base-Costera-Zócalo-Hornos* run along the length of the main tourist zone to the

zócalo in Acapulco Viejo and the beach below the cliffs of **La Quebrada.** (Avoid those labeled *Cine Rio* unless you want to take the congested trip through downtown Acapulco.) Those marked *Base-Caleta* run to Playa Caleta at the southwest tip of the bay.

Driving Traffic can be terribly congested in Acapulco, especially along the Costera and downtown. Parking is limited on the Costera; the best option is at the hotels and shopping centers. Unless you plan to explore the beaches outside town or are staying in Acapulco Diamante, you don't need a car; taxis and buses are easy to use and inexpensive.

The car-rental agencies at **Aeropuerto Internacional Juan N. Alvarez** (listed above) also have offices in hotels.

Taxis Taxis are the easiest and cheapest means of travel around Acapulco. You can usually flag down a cab on the main boulevard any time of day or night. Taxis parked in front of hotels (by the sign marked *sitio*) can cost more than the ones cruising the streets, especially during the slow seasons. You can run up quite a tab traveling to the hotels and restaurants in the area around the **Westin Las Brisas Hotel** and Acapulco Diamante, so always establish the price with the driver before climbing in.

FYI

Accommodations Room rates in Acapulco run the gamut from very inexpensive small inns in Acapulco Viejo and Playa Caleta to very expensive places (starting at $200 a night) at the Westin Las Brisas Hotel and Acapulco Diamante. Reservations are essential during Christmas, Easter Week, and Mexican national holidays.

Consulates
US Consular Agent Continental Plaza, Costera Miguel Alemán (between Paseo del Farallon and Hernando Cortés) 840700

Publications There are few English-language tourist publications available. Hotels and travel agencies should have a copy of *Acapulco Magic*, a magazine published in English and Spanish.

Shopping Artisans' markets and shopping malls line the Costera, selling everything from serapes to fine art. Best buys include resortwear, casual clothing, silver jewelry, and sandals.

Street Plan The city is divided into the old and new sections, connected by the Costera Miguel Alemán, a broad waterfront boulevard that winds around the bay from east to west.

Time Zone Acapulco is on Mountain Time, one hour ahead of California and two hours behind New York.

Tours Most hotels have their own travel agents. Many others are available throughout Acapulco, including:

American Express	845555, 841520
Turismo Caleta	846570
Viajes Dorado Pacífico	863280

Scuba diving trips are available through **Nautilus Dive Shop** (Costera Miguel Alemán 450, between Av la Aguada and Camino la Pínzona, 831108).

Visitors' Information Center The **Oficina de Turismo** (Tourism Office) is open daily. It's located on Costera Miguel Alemán (Centro Acapulco, Costera Miguel Alemán and Victoria, 847050, 844973). The **Acapulco Convention and Visitors' Bureau** is open Monday through Friday and is located in the Oceanic 2000 building at 3111 Costera Miguel Alemán (at Yucatán) 848554; fax 848134.

Phone Book

Fire...841111

Hospital General Av Adolfo Ruiz Cortinez
  (west of Hwy 95) 851730

Locatel (24-hour hotline for legal and medical
  emergencies, and other information) 811100

Police...850650

Red Cross..814101

1 Isla la Roqueta Ten minutes by skiff from Playa Caleta is this long, forested island with a hilltop lighthouse (a 20-minute climb) from which there's an incomparable panoramic view of Acapulco Bay. The island is a great place for hiking (if the weather's not too warm), and the beach is popular for sunbathing, swimming, and snorkeling. Boats for the island depart all day both from Playa Caleta and a small dock beside the **Mágico Mundo** aquarium. There's also a 45-minute glass-bottom boat cruise that includes a peek at the underwater *Virgen de Guadalupe* statue.

On Isla la Roqueta:

Palao's Restaurant ★$ A giant peaked *palapa* (palm-roofed hut) covers this Polynesian-style restaurant on the shore. You can eat indoors or out to the sounds of salsa or mariachi music, and although the Mexican and seafood dishes are predictable, the setting is lovely, especially in the early evening. For boat information, check with your hotel's tour desk or with the young boys on Playa Caleta who hawk trips to the restaurant. ◆ Mexican/Seafood ◆ Daily lunch and dinner. No phone

2 Playa Caleta Once the hangout for the glamour set, this park and the surrounding residential and shopping neighborhoods are typically overlooked by tourists. But the area has much to offer for those seeking a sampling of traditional Mexico. The beach here is immensely popular with locals, who seem to cover every grain of sand on weekends. City buses travel regularly between the Costera, the main plaza, and Playa Caleta. ◆ Gran Via Tropical and Costera Miguel Alemán

3 Mágico Mundo Marino A combination amusement park, aquarium, and beach club, this place is packed with families on the weekends. The indoor and outdoor exhibits include displays of tropical fish, turtles, alligators, and seals frolicking and splashing. Windows let you see both above and below the waterline. Other diversions include a water slide, swimming pool, sheltered saltwater cove, jet skis, Windsurfers, a scuba school, and a lookout tower with a telescope that lets you survey Isla la Roqueta (US quarters are accepted for the telescope). ◆ Admission. M, W-Su. Av Adolfo López Mateos (just west of Costera Miguel Alemán). 831215, 831193

4 Boca Chica Hotel $$$ European and US travelers seeking charm and tranquillity instead of glitz keep rediscovering this small pink-and-white inn, built into the hillside over a small bay next to Playa Caleta. Once a favorite of the Hollywood crowd, the hotel lost much of its following in the 1970s and 1980s as fancier spots opened on the Costera and the east bay. But Miguel Angel Muñoz, son of the original owner, is intent on keeping the hotel as inviting as ever. The 45 rooms are simply furnished and air-conditioned, though guests may prefer to keep their doors open to the sea breezes. Satellite TV is gradually appearing in the rooms, but most guests prefer to spend their time at the secluded beach, where the water is crystal clear, and snorkelers collect shells along a rocky point (nonguests can spend the day here for a small fee, which is credited toward the purchase of refreshments at the restaurant). If that's not enough, Playa Caleta is within easy walking distance, and the rest of Acapulco is readily accessible by public bus. Rates in the high season include breakfast and a choice of lunch or dinner. ◆ Playa Caletilla 7 (south of Av Adolfo López Mateos). 836601, 836741, 800/346.3942; fax 839513

Within the Boca Chica Hotel:

Marina Club ★★$$ Those in the know make the trip regularly to this seaside restaurant to enjoy the unlikely marriage of two cuisines. The Mexican chef spent several years in Japan, and the sushi and sashimi are prepared to order from the freshest fish. For a north-of-the-border variation, try the

Philadelphia rolls with salmon, cream cheese, and cucumber. The wasabi, seaweed, and even the rice are all imported (Mexican rice doesn't stick together as well as Japanese). The Mexican food is just as good, judging by the number of locals here, and the mango mousse shouldn't be missed. ◆ Mexican/Japanese ◆ Daily breakfast, lunch, and dinner. 836601, 836741

5 Hotel Los Flamingos $$ This hotel was built in the 1930s, when most of Acapulco's visitors were very rich and sailed in by yacht. It wasn't until the 1950s that it became a Shangri-la for the "Hollywood Gang." The select group, including Cary Grant, John Wayne, Johnny Weismuller, Roy Rogers, Errol Flynn, Red Skelton, and Richard Widmark, loved it so much they bought it for a short time (fond memories are kept alive in the photo gallery in the hotel lobby). It's still a charmer, with one of Acapulco's most beautiful gardens and pool areas. The food is good, the 46 rooms are clean, and the atmosphere is tranquil. Though no longer the luxury hotel it once was, it's perfect if you want peace, a view of the sea, and a five-minute drive to downtown. ◆ Avs Adolfo López Mateos and Costa Grande. 820690; fax 839806

6 Coyuca 22 ★★★$$$$ This converted villa offers elegant dining in four open terraces that look down the side of the mountain at the lights of Acapulco. Eating in the beautifully lighted garden is like visiting a good friend who just happens to prepare divine lobster and steaks. Two fixed-price dinners are offered each evening along with à la carte menu items; seafood preparations are your best choice. ◆ Seafood/Steak ◆ Daily dinner; closed May through October. Reservations required. Av Coyuca 22 (between Avs de la Suiza and Alto Monte). 835030, 823468

7 Holiday Inn Hotel and Suites $$ Holiday Inn renovated the **Villas La Marina** property in 1996, creating a charming small inn with only 90 rooms and suites. Rock-and-brick stairways lead under bougainvillea-draped archways to single-story white buildings interspersed with gardens and a small heated pool. An elevated walkway leads over the road to the waterfront; shuttle service is available to the hotel's beach club. Facilities include a restaurant, gift shop, and tour desk. ◆ Costera Miguel Alemán 222 (between Av la Aguada and Camino la Pínzona). 823620, 800/465.4329; fax 828480

8 Mariscos Mi Barquito ★★$$ The climb up several flights of stairs to the top of this house on a hill is rewarded with a cool breeze, spectacular view, and wonderful food. At this true Mexican seafood cafe meals include ceviche the consistency of soup (order fish ceviche with shrimp floating on top), plus a hot seafood soup worthy of high praise. Snapper, octopus, shrimp, shark, and the daily catch are prepared a variety of ways. Lunch for hours as *acapulqueños* do, giving yourself time to sample several dishes. The restaurant's white facade and blue lettering make it easy to spot near the foot of the street to La Quebrada. ◆ Seafood ◆ Daily lunch. Av Adolfo López Mateos 30 (between Av de las Playas and La Quebrada). 823595

9 La Quebrada Cliff divers plunge from this 130-foot cliff night and day carrying flaming torches into a small pocket of the rushing sea. (See "Perilous Plunges," page 93.) ◆ Daily. La Quebrada (between Av Adolfo López Mateos and Vicente Guerrero)

10 El Mirador Plaza Las Glorias $$ When this place was first built by Teddy Stauffer, he invited his Hollywood cronies to come discover Acapulco—making the hotel *the* hangout for the stars. Over the years its luster faded, and the only real attraction was a glamorous history and a great location overlooking the rocks and cliffs of La Quebrada. Today the 81 renovated rooms, many with kitchenettes and balconies, attract those who appreciate the view and the reasonable prices and don't mind the absence of a beach. There are three pools, one of them by the sea. Although the room rates are inexpensive by Acapulco standards, you can run up a hefty taxi tab from here visiting the beaches and restaurants on the Costera. ◆ La Quebrada 74 (between Av Adolfo López Mateos and Vicente Guerrero). 831155, 831221, 800/342.2644; fax 824564

Within the El Mirador Plaza Las Glorias:

La Perla $$ Although this restaurant/ nightclub is a popular spot for a drink, it's known for one show only—La Quebrada's cliff divers (see "La Quebrada" above). The menu features lackluster versions of basic Mexican dishes, so come for the show and dine elsewhere. Call ahead for current information on show times and try to arrive 15 minutes early for a good seat. ◆ Mexican ◆ Admission. Daily. 831221

Restaurants/Clubs: Red   **Hotels:** Blue

Shops/ ♟ Outdoors: Green   **Sights/Culture:** Black

11 Hotel Misión $ With only 27 rooms and a courtyard that's always in bloom, this charming 19th-century hacienda-turned-hotel is one of the nicest places to stay in Acapulco Viejo. The biggest drawback is the lack of air-conditioning or a pool; pluses include the traditional Mexican character of the place, with its hand-painted tiles and wrought-iron banisters, and plenty of fans to stir the breeze. The courtyard restaurant serves breakfast for hotel guests only; even if you don't stay here stop by for lunch on Thursday, when everyone is welcome to partake of the traditional *pozole* feast, featuring stew made from hominy and chicken or pork, along with trays of *botanes* (appetizers). ♦ Felipe Valle 12 (between Bretór Juárez and La Quebrada). 823643; fax 822076

12 Pesca Deportiva (Commercial Boat Docks) Fishing enthusiasts come here to watch the big commercial boats unload their catch. This is also a docking point for tour boats and a favorite promenade for Mexican families who enjoy tourist watching as much as tourists enjoy observing them. For a day of deep-sea fishing, visit the Sociedad Cooperativa Turisticas office across from the *zócalo* (central plaza). First-timers might feel more comfortable making arrangements through their hotel. ♦ Costera Miguel Alemán and Plaza Alvarez. 821099

13 Plaza Alvarez Also called the *"zócalo,"* Acapulco Viejo's central plaza is opposite the city's fishing harbor and is filled with aged trees providing shade and thick, low branches for young climbers. Shoeshiners do a thriving business in the cool shadows, local women trade gossip while children play nearby, and men meet at outdoor cafes and discuss life

over a game of dominoes and cups of coffee. The atmosphere is relaxed and a world apart from the luxury hotels in "new" Acapulco. The **Catedral Nuestra Señora de la Soledad**, constructed in 1930, faces the plaza. ♦ Costera Miguel Alemán (between I. de la Llave and Iglesias)

14 Sanborn's ★★$$ This full-service boutique/restaurant/bookstore is *the* best choice for homesick US travelers. The familiar glass cases offer everything from books and magazines to jewelry and trinkets. For a great breakfast, order hotcakes and coffee at the lunch counter, or drop in for a lunch of enchiladas or quesadillas. A more modern branch is at Playa Condesa. ♦ American/Mexican ♦ Daily breakfast, lunch, and dinner. Escudero (between Costera Miguel Alemán and José María Morelos). 26167. Also at: Costera Miguel Alemán 1226 (between del Prado and Picúda). 844465

15 Fuerte de San Diego (Fort San Diego) The only bit of history intact from Acapulco's beginnings is this star-shaped fort. Strategically placed on a hill next to the army barracks in 1616, its vantage point enabled soldiers to spot a distant pirate ship and fire mounted cannons before the marauders got too close. The original fort was destroyed in the 1776 earthquake, then rebuilt before 1800. Mexican troops drove out the Spanish and took over the fort in 1818. Today the fort's moat separates it from houses, shops, and cafes. Under the direction of Mexico City's **Museo de Antropología** (Museum of Anthropology), the fort has been restored and houses the **Museo Histórico de Acapulco** (Acapulco Historical Museum). Exhibits include displays on the arrival of the *conquistadores* and Acapulco's history as a port for galleons bearing imports from the Far East. Note the model of the *Galeón de Manila,* an 18th-century sailing ship that harbored in the port between trips to China. ♦ Admission. Tu-Su. Costera Miguel Alemán (east of Escudero). 823828

Perilous Plunges

One of **Acapulco's** most popular year-round attractions is the high divers at the cliffs of **La Quebrada.** Hundreds of tourists watch the young, muscular divers from terraced viewing platforms. This daring feat is even more spectacular at sunset, when the divers, often in pairs, carry flaming torches as they plunge 130 feet into the sea.

After kneeling and praying at a small shrine, each diver in turn stands poised on the cliff's edge, arms pointing down, muscles tense with concentration as he studies the timing and rush of the crashing surf. At the right moment he leaps forward and hurtles down in a graceful swan dive, slipping into the water

as it rushes into a small cove. One wrong move could be fatal.

This dangerous spectacle, performed by a select fraternity of trained men, dates back to 1934. But who's to say when it all began? Maybe pre-Columbian Indians tested their strength against the powerful sea in the same way.

To witness this memorable sight, you can climb up to the observation point, where you will be charged a small fee. Or you can enjoy one of the best vantage points for the show on the terrace of the adjacent **La Perla** at the **Plaza Las Glorias** hotel, which overlooks the cliffs. For more information, call 831155, 831221.

16 Mercado Municipal For a look at the life of *acapulqueños*, take an hour or two to wander through the public market where locals shop for necessities. There's no touristy glitz, just everyday goods displayed in a labyrinth of stalls where meats and vegetables, leather goods, hand-carved wooden items, baskets, and baubles are sold. A huge flower market has blossoms, roots, herbs, and potions for any purpose. Pottery and leather sandals are real bargains, but you're better off going to a reputable uptown jewelry store for silver. Come early in the morning, since many vendors call it a day by 1PM. ◆ Daily. Avs Constituyentes and Hurtado de Mendoza

17 Chiles' Verdes ★★$$ At first glance, this dining spot has the appearance of a trendy **Carlos 'n' Charlie's** restaurant. But once you settle in for lunch (which doesn't really get going until 3:30PM), you discover a true Mexican hangout. Businesspeople huddle at tables under ceiling fans, devouring hefty portions of such Mexican dishes as *molcajete* (marinated strips of meat served with melted cheese) and enchiladas. The restaurant sits at the edge of the auto-repair district, not a scenic or picturesque neighborhood, although those who wander the back streets will get a much more authentic picture of Acapulco than they'll ever see on the Costera. ◆ Mexican ◆ Daily lunch and dinner. Malaespina 20 (between Costera Miguel Alemán and Av Cuauhtémoc). 855276

18 Papagayo Park A natural treasure ignored by most tourists, this park is named for a hotel that once was a waterfront resort. The main attraction here is a children's amusement park, with bumper boats and life-size reproductions of the space shuttle *Columbia* and a Spanish galleon. The playgrounds, peaceful pathways, and the aviary, where tropical birds perch for photos along winding paths, make the 52-acre park worth a stop. ◆ Costera Miguel Alemán (between Magallanes and Aviles)

19 Plaza las Glorias Paraíso $$$ Within walking distance of Acapulco Viejo but still on the main hotel strip, this place is immensely popular with families and tour groups. The Plaza las Glorias chain took over this older Radisson hotel a while back and completely remodeled the 422 rooms, now decorated with pastel fabrics and light wood furnishings. Even the grandest suites are moderately priced compared to those at nearby hotels, and special packages make this one of the best bargains in town. The large restaurant serves a good breakfast buffet, though other meals are average. Two drawbacks: The elevators are noisy and the pool is small. One plus: The largest of Acapulco's artisans' markets is next door. ◆ Costera Miguel Alemán 163 (west of Esclavo). 855596, 800/342.2644; fax 855543

20 Howard Johnson Maralisa Hotel and Beach Club $$ Once a beach club for a luxurious hotel, this place is now a member of the famous US chain. Much of the hotel's grandeur has faded—the tile work and stone lion fountains look worn and neglected, and the guest rooms have an outdated decor, with furnishings of dark wood and garish green bathrooms. But the rates are remarkably low for this area, and with only 90 rooms and balconies overlooking the two small pools, the setting is a pleasant reprieve from its massive neighbors. The small restaurant with views of the sea serves all three meals. ◆ Alemania and Costera Miguel Alemán. 856677, 800/446.4656; fax 859228

21 Plaza Bahía Shopping Center Take a break from the heat in this air-conditioned mall, with three floors of shops and cafes. Clothing stores include familiar names such as **Benetton, Esprit,** and **Dockers,** and the movie theater usually shows first-run US hits with Spanish subtitles. If you need a pharmacy, eyeglasses, money changer, photo shop, travel agent, or souvenirs, take a look. ◆ Daily. Costera Miguel Alemán 123 (just east of Hernando Cortés)

ACAPULCO PLAZA
Beach Resort & Plaza Suites

21 Acapulco Plaza Hotel $$$ If you're looking for a hotel that has something going on all the time, check out this beachside high-rise complex. There's a wonderful tropical atmosphere, from the parrots and macaws screeching by a waterfall in the lobby to the splashing fountains next to the pools. The two towers beside the hotel house time-share units, while the main pyramid-shaped building is operated by the Fiesta Americana chain and has 506 rooms and suites. All the usual amenities are offered, including a bilingual staff and two large pools. The health club has exercise equipment, saunas, steam baths, Jacuzzis, and massage. Tennis buffs can play into the evening on the hotel's four outdoor, lighted courts. Four good restaurants and an assortment of bars make dining and drinking a special event. ◆ Costera Miguel Alemán 123 (just east of Hernando Cortés). 859050, 800/343.7821; fax 855285

Rudic art Gallery

22 Galería Rudic Owner Myrtille Rudic de Rullán displays a fine collection of Mexican artwork in her attractive gallery. Sculptor Armando Amaya's, expressive women pose at the gallery's entrance; if it hasn't sold yet, you must see the lithe bronze man riding a soaring manta ray, by Gustavo Salmones. Painter Alejandro Camarena captures Mexico in scenes from plazas, and rotating exhibits provide a glimpse of the country's exciting art scene. ◆ M-Sa; closed at midday. Pinzón 9 (north of Costera Miguel Alemán). 844844

23 Continental Plaza $$$ Though this hotel received a much-needed face-lift a while back, its 390 rooms will never be elegant. The grounds, however, are spectacular, with landscaping grown thick and junglelike over the years, and pools that wind under bridges and along rock paths in a seaside maze. The hotel is also used as a time-share property. ◆ Costera Miguel Alemán (between Paseo del Farallon and Hernando Cortés). 840909, 800/882.6684; fax 842081, 842120

Within the Continental Plaza Hotel:

Tony Roma's ★★★$$ The proliferation of US chain restaurants in Mexican resorts can be overwhelming; surely you didn't travel to Acapulco for a Big Mac. But sometimes the longing for home-style cooking does overtake even the most stalwart adventurer. When that happens, head here. The meats are imported, so you can get ribs, steaks, and burgers just like those back home, and you can be sure the bountiful salads are prepared with purified water. With a subdued, spacious sense of relaxed dining, this is a refuge for homesick travelers who've grown tired of raucous bars. ◆ American ◆ Daily lunch and dinner. 843348

24 Fiesta Americana Condesa $$$ One of the old standbys along the Costera, this high-rise hotel with 500 rooms and suites underwent a much-needed renovation a few years ago. Though it can't compare with the glitzier, newer hotels in Diamante, it is still the queen of the Costera, beloved for its giant *palapas*, cordial service, and good meals in the restaurants. The beach is one of the most active along the bay, offering every imaginable water sport. ◆ Costera Miguel Alemán 1220 (between del Prado and Paseo del Farallon). 842828, 800/343.7821; fax 841828

25 Paraíso/Paradise ★★$$ Another wild place for vacationers who have left restraint at home, especially if they're under 30. If you don't know how to dance, you'll do it anyway, and if it's your birthday, who knows what will happen? Seafood is the specialty, and portions are large. The music is loud, the waiters are crazy, and the salsa is hot.

◆ Seafood ◆ Daily lunch and dinner. Costera Miguel Alemán and del Prado. 845988

26 Cafe Pacífico ★★★$$$ Pianist Ricardo Arcos is the main attraction at this small restaurant and lounge, which starts filling up with his fans after midnight. Before then, this is the perfect setting for romantic dining, with flames leaping from chafing dishes as solicitous waiters flambé shrimp with Pernod or Cognac, or sauté fresh spinach with bacon. With fewer than 10 tables, the dining room fills up quickly after 9PM, though you won't mind waiting while Ricardo's playing. ◆ Continental ◆ Daily dinner. Costera Miguel Alemán and del Prado. 842538 ext 241

27 Villa Vera Hotel and Raquet Club $$$$ One of the first to entertain Hollywood's "in" crowd, this hotel was built in the 1950s by Carl Renstrom, a wealthy Nebraska inventor and businessman, as a villa for his family. He later added five smaller villas for business associates, and the hotel soon became a tropical hideaway for the celebrities of the day. In more recent years it has suffered through several changes in ownership, and housekeeping and maintenance have grown lax. Still, some loyal guests wouldn't stay anywhere else. Set on a quiet hillside away from the bustle of downtown, the hotel has 80 rooms (many with small private pools), a restaurant, three red-clay tennis courts, and a fitness center. Thick trees and lavish gardens around the property provide privacy and a sense of seclusion. ◆ Lomas del Mar 35 (north of del Prado). 840333; fax 847479

28 Club de Golf Acapulco This public nine-hole course is the scene of tournaments throughout the year. Located next to the **Centro Acapulco,** it's not as aesthetically pleasing as the course at the **Acapulco Princess** (see page 99). No carts are allowed. ◆ Daily. Costera Miguel Alemán (east of del Prado). 840781

29 Elcano $$$ The most exciting hotel on the strip is actually one of the oldest, thoroughly remodeled under the direction of architects **Carlos Villela** and **Ramiro Alatorre.** The glamour of the 1950s is re-created with a unique design and style—a nautical blue-on-white scheme that echoes the sky and sea. The 340 rooms are filled with creature comforts—sloping navy blue–tiled back-rests for the firm double and king-size beds, slatted wood lounge chairs on the balconies, high-backed white wicker chairs at the marble-topped dining tables, and both air-conditioning and fans. Blue-and-white patterns in the tile floors carry the nautical theme throughout the hotel and are even used around the pool. The health club has the latest in fitness machines, and the beauty salon is always crowded. The hotel has an ideal location, set back against the bay a few blocks from the **Centro Acapulco,** blessedly removed from the frenetic noise of the Costera.

Most enchanting of all is the hotel's artwork. Artist Cristina Rubalcava, a Mexican expatriate living in Paris, created a series of paintings evoking the myths and memories of Acapulco. She painted the cliff divers of **La Quebrada** hurtling toward mermaids in the sea, and Rita Hayworth dancing on the beach, encircled by a boa trailing the words of a favorite song, "La Boa." The paintings hang in the guest rooms and are printed as complimentary postcards for guests. If you're not staying here, you can still see some of Rubalcava's work in **La Victoria** restaurant (on the premises) and on the wall facing the elevators at pool level. ✦ Costera Miguel Alemán 75 (east of del Prado). 841950; fax 842230

Within the Elcano:

La Victoria ★★★★$$ A romantic, tranquil gourmet restaurant that rivals any in the city. Arrive before 10PM and you'll be serenaded by the soulful guitarist performing in the cocktail lounge; after that a spirited trio entertains diners. Seafood stars on the menu, from the piquant ceviche to shrimp in Champagne sauce, crab cakes, and grilled salmon. The desserts are incomparable; stop in for a *café español* and a sweet treat with some friends so you can try them all. ✦ Seafood/International ✦ Daily dinner. Reservations recommended. 841950

Bambuco ★★★★$$ A classy seaside cafe with impeccable service, this restaurant draws a local following for power breakfasts of *huevos rancheros* and mushroom omelettes. The mix of vacationers and power brokers gives the cafe a cosmopolitan feel, relaxed yet buzzing with seemingly important conversations. The lunch and dinner menu includes some of the selections from **La Victoria** (including the desserts), plus salads and sandwiches. ✦ Mexican/International ✦ Daily breakfast, lunch, and dinner. 841950, 842230

29 Copacabaña Hotel $$$ This 1950s-style hotel is one of the hottest spots on the beach, and it's close to the action downtown, too. Everything here is done on a grand scale: The huge bar has a large dance floor where guests can dance to a live band on the beach under the stars; and the slightly worn 480 rooms have bizarre yellow, green, and orange color schemes and large terraces with great views.

Many families from Mexico City return yearly. There's a restaurant that serves adequate Mexican meals. ✦ Luis Maya 11 (south of Costera Miguel Alemán). 847730, 42155, 800/221.6509; fax 846268

30 Mariscos Pipo ★★$$ Locals consistently cite this casual cafe as one of the best spots for moderately priced fresh seafood, as well as for lunch near the **Centro Acapulco.** Fishing nets, shells, and other nautical implements decorate the dining room, where regulars feast on huge seafood cocktails and fried or grilled fish fillets. ✦ Seafood ✦ Daily lunch and dinner. No credit cards accepted. Costera Miguel Alemán and Victoria. 840165. Also at: Almirante Breton 3 (between Costera Miguel Alemán and Bretór Juárez). 838801, 823237

30 Super Super For your not-so-basic shopping spree, this enormous supermarket has just about everything you might be craving—and some you probably never dreamed of. The fruit counter provides an introduction to the more bizarre tropical fruits, including the gorgeous hot-pink *pitajaya* and papayas as big as watermelons. The deli counter offers take-out chicken with mole, as well as flan, various salsas and salads, and a selection of imported goods that is truly astounding. ✦ Daily, 24 hours. Costera Miguel Alemán and Victoria. No phone

31 Centro Acapulco (Convention Center) One of the largest convention centers in Mexico, it hosts business meetings, concerts, and cultural events throughout the year. The famous acrobatic **Papantla Flyers** have become a fixture on stage here, thrilling audiences as they leap from a tall pole and fly in ever-enlarging circles attached to a rope. Just as the upside-down flyer gets perilously close to the ground, the rope is totally unfurled, and he lands gracefully on his feet. **Ballet Folklórico** is presented Tuesday and Sunday nights during the winter season. For the lively crowd, the center's **Disco Laser** offers what its name suggests: flashing lights, live and taped music, and a lot of fun; things get rolling about 11PM. There are several crafts and gift shops on the beautifully landscaped grounds with artwork from around the country. ✦ Costera Miguel Alemán and Victoria. 847050; fax 846252

32 Su Casa ★★★$$ You'll feel right at home at this aptly named terrace restaurant, one of the prettiest spots for dining with a view of the bay. It's in the home of owners Shelly and Angel Herrera, who greet even first-time guests as good friends. The Herreras play with their menu constantly, depending on what's freshest at the markets, adding such dishes as shrimp grilled with bananas and pineapple or chicken marinated in a blend of juices. Standard selections include a good porterhouse steak, enchiladas with tomatillo sauce, and shrimp sautéed with garlic. Come in time for a sunset margarita. ♦ Seafood/Mexican ♦ Daily dinner. Av Anahuác 110 (north of Monterrey). 844350

33 CICI Parque Acuatico (CICI Water Park) Families settle in for the day at this amusement park where water is the greatest attraction. Children (and a few adults) scream as they speed down water slides, watch trained seals and dolphins cavort, and play in a swimming pool with built-in wave action. Toddler-size attractions include small slides, gentle waterfalls and fountains, and a relaxing river ride. Adults can set up housekeeping in cool, shaded areas, and for refreshments the park's many snack bars rise to the occasion. ♦ Admission. Daily. Costera Miguel Alemán and Cristóbal Colón. 848033, 848210

34 Restaurant Suntory Acapulco ★★$$$ This low-key restaurant specializes in *shabu-shabu* (beef and vegetables dipped in steaming broth), *teppanyaki* (meat, seafood, and vegetables cooked at the table on a sizzling hot plate), and sukiyaki (meat, bean curd, and vegetables). If you want to try something really fresh, catch your own crayfish from the tank and have it prepared for you at tableside. The restaurant is part of a worldwide, high-quality chain that originated in Mexico City in 1970. ♦ Japanese ♦ Daily lunch and dinner. Reservations required. Costera Miguel Alemán 36 (between Yucatán and Santa Maria). 848088, 848766

35 Jai Alai Frontón The latest nighttime entertainment in a city that thrives on nightlife is at this massive, jai alai stadium. The building also holds an off-track betting establishment where gamblers can place their wagers on horse races and other sporting events, broadcast via satellite TV. ♦ Admission. Jai alai games held Th-Su at 9PM from December through August. Costera Miguel Alemán and Ortíz Monasterio. 811650, 811654

36 Hyatt Regency Acapulco $$$$ Set at a quiet stretch of beach on the east side of Bahía de Acapulco (Acapulco Bay), this older property was completely renovated in 1996. The 690 rooms, all with great views of the sea, have floral furnishings and small writing tables; those on the two **Regency Club** floors have access to a private lounge where complimentary continental breakfast and afternoon wine and cheese are served daily. The verdant grounds are thick with palms and dotted with pools, above-average cafes, and bars. One restaurant, **El Isleño**, serves authentic kosher cuisine, and there is a synagogue on the grounds. ♦ Costera Miguel Alemán 1 (just south of Ortíz Monasterio). 691234, 800/233.1234; fax 843087

37 Acapulco Sheraton Hotel $$$ The dramatic lobby, with floor-to-ceiling windows along the entire ocean side, provides views that won't quit. Furniture and carpets are rich in teal, burgundy, and purple. Even the lobby bar piano is painted a shiny rich burgundy. Striking sculptures are scattered about; note the *Neptune* in the lobby and another in the **Bahía Restaurant.** The 197 rooms and 15 suites are very comfortable, with soothing colors, tile floors, luxurious bathrooms, and air-conditioning. The least expensive rooms face the gardens; rooms with water views are in the expensive range. One peculiarity is the manner in which you must get to your room: If you're staying in one of the 13 villas, you must take as many as three elevators and crossover walkways to get there. A funicular brings guests from the lower sections of the property to the upper levels. One swimming pool is set in a garden, and a second is near the beach. The hotel is built on the side of the hill overlooking Playa Secreto (where a former Mexican president is said to have brought his mistress for romantic interludes). ♦ Costera Guitarrón 110 (west of Carretera Escénica). 812222, 800/325.3535; fax 843760

38 Extravaganzza Acapulco's discos are legendary for their lavish decor, stylish clientele, and psychedelic special effects. This place lives up to its name, with an unbelievable dose of nonstop music, flashing lights, floor fog, and fireworks. Smile nicely at the doorman; on busy nights he decides who gets in and who doesn't. Don't come here dressed in shorts, T-shirts, or sandals. ♦ Cover. Daily. Carretera Escénica (southwest of Costera Guitarrón). 847154, 847164

39 Señor Frog's ★★★$$ Set atop a cliff facing Bahía de Acapulco, this place is as popular with local VIPs as it is with partying tourists. The food is bountiful and delicious, with an emphasis on barbecued ribs and chicken, Mexican platters, and seafood. On Thursday afternoons, *pozole,* a hominy stew, is the requisite meal, and lunches last until sunset. Several tables are permanently reserved for prominent local dignitaries, who gather religiously for this elaborate meal. It traditionally begins with a plate of *botanes* (appetizers), including tamales, *taquitos,* and hunks of Oaxacan cheese, then continues with the main course of *pozole.* Finish with dessert and you'll be full until the next day. The place really kicks into action at night, when the music is raucous, the crowd rowdy, and the tequila flowing abundantly. ♦ International/Mexican ♦ Daily lunch and dinner. La Vista Shopping Center, Carretera Escénica and Almejas. 848020, 848027. Also at: Costera Miguel Alemán 999 (at del Prado). 841285

40 Madeiras ★★★★$$$$ Within walking distance of the **Westin Las Brisas Hotel,** this open pavilion built of rich hardwoods offers you one of the most sumptuous meals in the city. Thanks to the large, open windows, cooling breezes and sparkling views of the Acapulco shoreline complement an elegant setting, and the food is out of this world. The four-course prix-fixe menu has a gourmet listing that runs from a starter of Thai pasta to terrific cold soups to main dishes that include veal tips in white wine—all topped off with a superb selection of desserts and coffee. Reservations can be difficult to get, so many people make them months in advance—yes, it's that good. ♦ International ♦ M-Sa dinner. Reservations required. Carretera Escénica (south of Almejas). 844378

40 Miramar ★★★$$$$ A bit less swank than the neighboring **Madeiras,** this classy restaurant is still one of Acapulco's more elegant dining spots. Tables with flickering candles are set on a series of terraces facing the bay. Courtly waiters in black suits (despite the lack of air-conditioning) uncork imported wines and help diners choose among the pâtés and seafood cocktails and the duck, salmon, and beef specialties. Ask for a table at the edge of the terraces, away from those set for large (and often noisy) groups. ♦ International ♦ Daily dinner. Reservations required. Carretera Escénica (south of Almejas). 847874

40 Ristorante Casa Nova ★★★$$$$ From the moment you step into the grand entrance with its immense flower arrangement, you know you are in for an elegant dining experience. Steps lead you down the mountainside to the restaurant where you can dine in indoor air-conditioned comfort or on an outdoor terrace; both have spectacular views of the bay. The extensive menu presents perfectly prepared pastas, plus such international delicacies as fresh Norwegian salmon and thick New Zealand

lamb chops. ♦ Italian/Continental ♦ T-Su dinner. Reservations required during winter. Carretera Escénica 5256 (between the airport and Westin Las Brisas). 846815/16

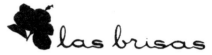

41 Westin Las Brisas Hotel $$$$ This elegant 267-room grande dame is more than 30 years old, but still holds her reputation as the loveliest hotel in Acapulco. With grounds of 110 acres, the property is built into the contours of a mountain ensconced in fuchsia blossoms, pink hibiscus, feathery vines, and tall trees. The small casitas (villas) continue to lure honeymooners and others with romance on the mind. There are private pools at 253 of the bungalows. The resort is sparkling white, dashed with its hallmark pink color scheme, pink-and-white four-wheel-drive vehicles, and fresh pink flowers floating in pools. The **Royal Beach Club** casitas are the most recently renovated accommodations.

The hotel pampers its guests, and many come back year after year. On the fifth visit, you receive a discreet, hand-painted sign, notifying all who pass by that your casita has been named in your honor (at least for the duration of your stay). A breakfast of fresh fruit, sweet rolls, and hot coffee is deposited daily in the "magic box" (in a wall with a double opening) to greet you each morning.

The streets of this small village are steep, and hardy guests can get good cardiovascular exercise just walking to the lobby; or you can pick up the phone and dial for a four-wheel-drive vehicle, which arrives at your bungalow within minutes and take you anywhere on the grounds. The 1996 renovation incorporated wheelchair ramps and rooms accessible to those with disabilities. The grounds include **La Concha,** a private seaside beach club, a spa and health club, an art gallery, a variety of boutiques, a deli, and tennis courts. At the very top, the **Capilla de Paz** (Chapel of Peace) sits 1,300 feet above sea level. The three restaurants are closed to nonguests except for special events. A service charge covering all tips (for waiters, porters, etc.) for your stay is included in the bill. The four-wheel-drive vehicles are available for rent from the hotel. ♦ Carretera Escénica 5255 (at Alisios). 841580, 800/228.3000; fax 842269

42 Spicey ★★★$$$$ You're sure to find something you've never tasted before on the menu at this trendy spot. The chef mixes Thai, Chinese, Mexican, and European ingredients to create unusual combos such as *chiles rellenos* with mango sauce, smoked salmon spring rolls, and chateaubriand with a sauce of sake and sun-dried tomatoes. You can have a plain grilled steak or fish fillet if you

like, though you'd be missing out on the fun. Go with a group and sample several entrées. The air-conditioned dining room is a blessing when it's hot, though many diners prefer the outdoor terrace with its stunning bay view.
♦ Pacific Rim ♦ M-F lunch and dinner; Sa-Su dinner. Carretera Escénica (south of Almejas). 811380

43 Acapulco Diamante A massive resort development that stretches along the coastline from the **Westin Las Brisas Hotel** all the way to the **Acapulco Princess Hotel** near the airport, this is like a second, self-contained city within the city limits of Acapulco. By early in the next century, the area will include luxury private home developments and condo complexes, two marinas, three 18-hole golf courses, and several hotels, including a small, exclusive **Quinta Real** scheduled to open as we went to press. The bright orange sculpture at the entrance to **Diamante** near the airport is called *Pueblo del Sol* and was created by sculptor Pal Kepenyes. (To view Kepenyes's work, especially his jewelry, check with local galleries or call his studio at 843738.)
♦ South of Carretera Escénica

43 Camino Real Diamante $$$$ A winding, rocky road twists past palatial private homes toward a jewel-toned bay. Green-tile roofs and creamy stucco walls echo the colors of the surrounding terrain; natural rock platforms and lounging areas perch above the sea. The buildings afford water views from the 156 superdeluxe rooms, each decorated in moss green, beige, aqua, and lavender. Amenities include sandalwood-scented toiletries, deep bathtubs, hair dryers, shaving mirrors, and satellite TV. Elevators transport guests to the pools, two restaurants, fitness center, and tennis court; fitness buffs may prefer to get their exercise climbing the steps from the beach to the lobby and rooms.
♦ Catita and Costero Marina Vieia. 661010, 800/722.6466; fax 661111

44 Acapulco Princess Hotel $$$$ Over the years this pyramidal palace has become an Acapulco landmark. Its three high-rise white towers are visible from the main road and loom over the sands of Playa Revolcadero. Despite its intimidating overall size, which includes 1,019 rooms and suites, the hotel has consistently garnered a glowing, well-deserved reputation for luxury and excellent service. Rooms vary in size and amenities, but all have floor-to-ceiling sliding glass doors leading to private terraces, dressing areas with sinks and vanities separate from the bathrooms, and cane furnishings upholstered in tropical prints. Guests tend to stake out their favorite spots around the 480-acre grounds and five meandering pools; they also claim their favorites among the seven restaurants (some open only in high season)

and multiple lounges and bars. For those who want long, quiet walks on the beach, the hotel offers white sand dotted with tall trees; the surf can be rough, however, and swimming is discouraged. Golfers have a choice of two courses—a 6,400-yard course designed by Ted Robinson, and an 18-hole, par-72 course designed by Robert Trent Jones Jr. Tennis tournaments, games, and lessons are held at the nine outdoor and two indoor tennis courts. The shopping arcade includes fine jewelry, folk art, and clothing boutiques. Note that the hotel is a long way from the Costera, and the Dine Around Plan (with credits at the hotel's restaurants) is mandatory during the high season. ♦ South of Carretera Escénica. 691000, 800/223.1818; fax 691016

44 Pierre Marqués Hotel $$$$ Built in 1957 as J. Paul Getty's hideaway, this is now a luxurious hotel within the **Acapulco Princess** compound and open only during high season from November through February. In decor, the 344 rooms, suites, villas, and bungalows, all with balconies or patios, resemble those at the **Princess**, though this hotel has a much more private and peaceful atmosphere. There are three pools and two restaurants, and a complimentary shuttle travels between the two hotels; all of the facilities are available to guests at either hotel. ♦ South of Carretera Escénica. 691000, 800/223.1818; fax 691016

45 Vidafel Mayan Palace $$$ Another grand-scale project that will eventually have more than a thousand rooms, a water park, monorail, and other attractions, this time-share resort and hotel is located on the spectacular Playa Revolcadero. You get a sense of the scope of the project from the magnificent entryway, where gigantic replicas of Maya carvings set in green marble niches, a long reflecting pool, and polished black-and-white marble floors give the hotel a museumlike appearance. The huge swimming pool extends past waterfalls and boulders to the beach, where it parallels the sand. Many of the 380 rooms have kitchens or kitchenettes, dining areas, and sofa beds. Facilities completed thus far include an 18-hole golf course, 12 tennis courts, and three restaurants. ♦ South of Carretera Escénica. 690102, 800/843.2335; fax 620008

Oaxacan Coast

Oaxaca is one of Mexico's most fascinating states. With its wealth of local cultural traditions, the area is more reminiscent of Guatemala than Mexico City. The **Sierra Madre del Sur** mountains ripple through the state, dividing the coast from the eponymous capital city. The mountains are dotted with wood fires from tiny, traditional villages, while the coast is covered with a smattering of city lights and the dust created by bulldozers at several growing resort developments.

Oaxaca is one of Mexico's poorest states, and *oaxaqueño* immigrants are the backbone of the agricultural labor force in both California and Mexico. Nevertheless, while economically poor, Oaxaca is rich in natural resources and cultural treasures. Mexico aficionados know and love the city and state for its food, folk art, archaeology, and indigenous character.

Oaxaca has been on the explorers' maps since the *conquistadores* arrived in the 1570s and found thriving Zapotec and Mixtec cities atop the mountains. In the valley below, the Spaniards and their descendants, along with their Indian laborers, built some of Mexico's finest colonial churches and palaces. Today, the ruins of **Monte Albán** and **Mitla** and the colonial city of **Oaxaca** are must-sees on most travelers' lists.

Developers left Oaxaca alone until 1974, when **FONATUR**, the national agency for tourism development, put the **Bahías de Huatulco** on their short list of future resorts. **Puerto Escondido**, 65 miles northwest up the Oaxacan coast, was already established as a laid-back hideaway for die-hard surfers and explorers. Two decades later, Huatulco is on the coastal resort map, though it

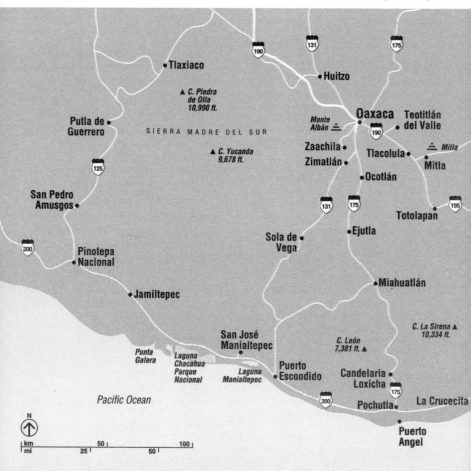

hardly rivals the other **FONATUR** resorts of Cancún and Los Cabos. The resort area encompasses 52,000 acres, 40,000 of which are supposed to be set aside as nature preserves, if developers can be held in check. Puerto Escondido has grown more slowly, without the infrastructure of a planned resort. Both are attracting more and more travelers, though they're not yet swamped with charter flight hordes. Get here soon.

Puerto Escondido

Succulent seafood, awesome waves, uncrowded beaches, and an all-pervasive mañana attitude—these, in a nutshell, are what Puerto Escondido has to offer. There are no glitzy hotels, brand-name restaurants, or cruise ships here, just one-of-a-kind hostelries tucked along small bays and up steep residential streets facing the sea, a lineup of palm-roofed cafes on the sand cupping **Bahía Principal**, and a fleet of white, yellow, and green skiffs poised at the edge of the blue bay, their sterns pointed toward forested coves.

Like Huatulco, Puerto Escondido hardly seems as though it's in the state of Oaxaca at all. Unlike other towns in the region, it contains no significant archaeological sites and has no folk art villages nearby; instead, the foothills of the **Sierra Madre del Sur** hide rivers, hot springs, waterfalls, coffee plantations, and Zapotec and Mixtec villages. Established as a port in 1928, Puerto Escondido, which means "hidden port," did not even have a paved road connecting it to Oaxaca City until the 1960s; tourist development, including an airport, took root in the 1980s, but, even so, Puerto Escondido remains a small town. There are probably fewer than 10,000 permanent residents (the official census figure of 16,000 includes surrounding towns), and the population is at its height in winter, when snowbirds flock to inexpensive second homes and hotels. Others who return annually include young blond Californians and Australians, middle-aged ex-hippies, and 50-something retirees. Mexican nationals and Europeans work on their tans here in July and August, giving the town a nice international feeling. Surfers are here year-round, and assemble en masse for the surfing tournament held every November. With its laid-back attitude and weather as sunny as its disposition, Puerto Escondido suits both regular visitors and locals just fine.

Palomares

Matías Romero

Lachivixa

▲ C. Piedra Larga
9,350 ft.

Ixtepec

Juchitánde
Zaragoza

Magdalena
Tequisistlán   Tehuantepec

Salina
Cruz

Punta
Chivo

Golfo de
Tehuantepec

When Fidel Castro came to power in Cuba in 1959, Mexican president López Mateos voted against Cuba's expulsion from the OAS (Organization of American States) and retained diplomatic relations with the new government.

Area code 958 unless otherwise noted.

Getting to Puerto Escondido

Airport

Aeropuerto de Puerto Escondido (Puerto Escondido Airport) is located two miles west of Puerto Escondido's tourism zone. There are daily flights to Puerto Escondido from Oaxaca City; these flights are occasionally canceled, however, if not enough seats are sold. You must go to the airport to make any changes to your ticket; call ahead to make sure the airline counters are open, since most airport businesses are open only when flights are arriving or departing.

Airlines

Aeromorelos 20653

Mexicana......................20098, 20414, 800/531.7921

Getting to and from Aeropuerto de Puerto Escondido

By Bus Transportation from the airport to hotels is provided by *colectivos* (vans); fares run from $2 to $4. *Colectivos* and taxis are available only around flight arrival and departure times. No public buses run between the airport and town.

By Car The drive between the airport and Puerto Escondido on **Carretera Costera (Highway 200)** takes about 10 minutes.

There is only one car-rental agency with a counter at the airport; it's open only when flights are arriving and departing.

Budget 20312, 800/527.0700

By Taxi Taxis await passengers in front of the airport. The fare to town is about $5.

Bus Station (Long Distance)

Puerto Escondido's **Estrella Blanca** bus station (20427) is on **Avenida Oaxaca** one block north of the Carretera Costera. First-class buses travel between here and Mexico City, Pochutla, Acapulco, Oaxaca, and Huatulco. Smaller second-class bus lines have terminals on **Avenida Hidalgo.**

Getting Around Puerto Escondido

Puerto Escondido's hotels and businesses are located in several areas. West of town near the airport is **Playa Bacocho,** a beach area with a few higher-end hotels just off the Carretera Costera. About one mile east of Playa Bacocho, **Avenida Alfonso Peréz Gasga,** called **Avenida Gasga,** intersects the Carretera and runs south to the paved *adoquinado,* the **Pedestrian Zone** (aka the **PZ**) just off **Playa Principal,** the town's main beach. The hill that leads to the PZ is lined with moderate and budget hotels, while the PZ itself is home to shops and restaurants. North of the Carretera, Avenida Gasga is called **Avenida Oaxaca,** the main road

running into the city, where the market, post office, and bus stations are located. Southeast of the PZ is **Playa Marinero,** another beach and the site of more hotels and restaurants, and farther south yet is **Playa Zicatela,** the most famous beach in Puerto Escondido. It's possible to walk along the sand from Playa Zicatela to Playa Principal, though it's a hot half-hour stroll. The easier way of getting around is to hike up to the Carretera Costera and take the buses marked *Mercado,* which stop at the Gasga intersection.

Specific street addresses are rare in Puerto Escondido; many places list their address as the name of the street s/n (*sin numero,* or without number). Street signs are nearly nonexistent, and there are no maps with street names. Most addresses include the area.

Buses Local buses and co-op taxis charge about 20¢ and run along Carretera Costera, the highway separating the PZ and downtown.

Driving Rental cars are available at hotels, but are not necessary unless you want to drive to deserted beaches outside of town.

Taxis Plenty of cabs are available and are usually parked in front of the hotels and beaches and at both ends of the PZ; settle on a fare before getting in.

FYI

Accommodations Lodging places in Puerto Escondido are small and inexpensive for the most part. Hotels are clustered above Playa Bacocho, on the hills above the PZ, and along Playa Marinero and Playa Zicatela.

Publications There are few English-language tourist publications available. The information stand in the PZ (see "Visitors' Information Center," below) distributes a small map of the area and some leaflets for hotels and restaurants.

Shopping Small artisans' markets and shops line the PZ, offering jewelry, sportswear, hammocks, and Guatemalan textiles. Several shops carry folk art from Oaxaca, but the selection is limited.

Time Zone Puerto Escondido is on Central Time, two hours ahead of California and one hour behind New York.

Tours The following travel agencies offer moderately priced tours of the surrounding area, including bird watching trips to area lagoons; day excursions to the **Atotonilco** hot springs, the fishing town of **Puerto Angel,** the **Centro Mexicano de la Tortuga** (National Mexican Turtle Center) in **Mazunte,** and Huatulco; and overnight trips to Oaxaca City.

Agencia de Viajes Bahia Escondida
Posada Real, Av Benito Juárez 1, Playa Bacocho
....20095

Erickson Travel Agency
Av Gasga ....20126, 20389; fax 20126

Turismo Rodimar
Av Gasga 905-B ....20737; fax 20737

Visitors' Information Center The **Oficina de Turismo** (Tourism Office) is conveniently located on **Avenida Benito Juárez** at the Carretera Costera near Playa Bacocho (20175). The office is open Monday through Friday from 9AM to 3PM and 6 to 8PM and Saturday from 10AM to 1PM. Only scanty assistance is provided, however. There is also an information kiosk (no phone) at the foot of Avenida Gasga at the PZ; the kiosk's hours are erratic, but it is scheduled to be opened Monday through Friday from 10AM to 2PM and 4 to 7PM.

Local travel agencies (see "Tours," above) are the best source of tourist information.

Phone Book

Hospital Centro de Salud, Av Gasga 20549
Police 20721, 20498

1 **Posada Real** $$ If the owners paid as much attention to the rooms as they do to the grounds, this resort-style property would be the best place in town. A 100-room hotel and long swimming pool sit at the edge of a broad cliff top lawn overlooking the beach, and there isn't a finer place around for watching the sunset. White lounge chairs are set invitingly under palms inhabited by flocks of chirping birds, and in high season a trio plays romantic ballads in the background as the sun melts into the sea. Equally enchanting is the hotel's

Cocos Club, a swimming pool, restaurant, and bar complex at the foot of the cliffs by the beach. Unfortunately, the tiny rooms—with no balconies, dull green decor, and an erratic hot water supply—are less enticing. Still, regulars addicted to their chosen seats on the lawn wouldn't stay anywhere else. ◆ Av Benito Juárez (south of Hwy 200). 20133, 20237, 800/528.1234; fax 20192

Within the Posada Real:

Cocos Club Both hotel guests and outsiders are welcome to use the facilities here, although outsiders are required to purchase a meal or drinks at the restaurant. The club is worth visiting at least once for its clean, raked beach and landscaped, lagoonlike pool area. Lunch is served by the pool and in the *palapa* (palm-roofed) restaurant; the best seats in the house are the faux leopard skin–covered swings at the bar. The food is unremarkable—stick with the sandwiches—but the piña coladas and margaritas are exceptional. The club is at the bottom of a steep hill by the hotel; taxis sometimes wait by the restaurant for passengers. ◆ 20133, 20237

1 **Hotel Aldea del Bazar** $$ White mosque-style domes and minarets set the tone at this unusual hotel and spa. Like its sister property in Puebla, this place has a Middle Eastern/New Age ambience and attitude. The 47 white rooms are sparsely decorated, with orange

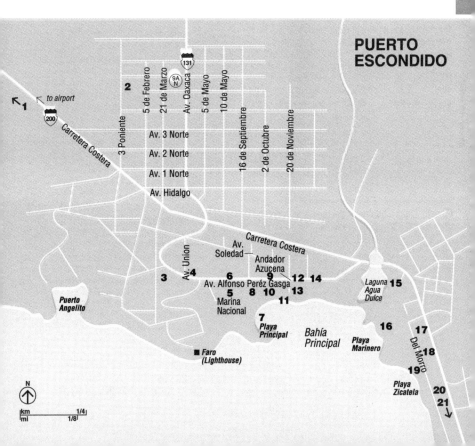

PUERTO ESCONDIDO

to airport

Carretera Costera

2

5 de Febrero
21 de Marzo
Av. Oaxaca
5 de Mayo
10 de Mayo
16 de Septiembre
2 de Octubre
20 de Noviembre

3 Poniente

Av. 3 Norte

Av. 2 Norte

Av. 1 Norte

Av. Hidalgo

Carretera Costera

Av. Union

Av. Soledad

Andador Azucena

3   4
         6   9   12   14
Av. Alfonso Peréz Gasga
      5   8   10   13
Marina   11
Nacional

Puerto Angelito

7
Playa Principal

Faro (Lighthouse)

Bahía Principal

Playa Marinero

Laguna Agua Dulce   15

16   17
                 18
            19

Playa Zicatela   20
                  21

N

km   1/4
mi   1/8

bedspreads offering a spark of color. The beds have slanting cement backrests that, when padded with pillows, are comfortable for reading or watching television. The best rooms face the long swimming pool and wide lawns, which have white, tentlike awnings for shade. At one end of the pool is the restaurant; service and food quality are spotty, but it's a nice place to relax over a cup of herbal tea and a plate of sliced papaya. ♦ Av Benito Juárez and Hwy 200. 20508

Within the Hotel Aldea del Bazar:

Centro Temazcalteci Spa Prehispánico

Set in a separate white building to the side of the hotel, the spa is centered around an Aztec-style *temazcal* sweat lodge, an oval-shaped structure with rather uncomfortable cement benches. Once the guests, sans clothing, are seated inside, a white-robed attendant hands in a bucket of steeping herbs and a ladle. Guests splash the water on a bed of hot rocks, while tapes of drumming and chanting provide otherworldly background music as the guests gradually melt down. Follow the sweat with a cold shower and massage or mud mask. You'll either feel renewed or ready for a nap. ♦ Daily by appointment. 20508

The Wild Side

The coastline north of Puerto Escondido is dotted with lagoons that delight bird watchers. **Laguna Manialtepec** is a favored destination for boat tours in the early morning and evening, when egrets, ibis, pelicans, and herons come to feed along the mangroves. Daylong tours go up the coast to **Laguna Chacahua Parque Nacional,** where roseate spoonbills, ibis, and wood storks are protected in a natural preserve.

The tour inland to the **Atotonilco** hot springs is another popular excursion. After a drive to the village of **San José Manialtepec,** participants travel by horseback through a river valley, crossing the river several times to reach the natural hot springs. The dusty, hot adventurers have time to soak in the springs and splash in the river before returning by horseback to San José and by van to Puerto Escondido.

All travel agencies in the area offer the same basic tours, though serious bird watchers should ask to join a group guided by Michael Malone, an experienced ornithologist, or another qualified guide.

L.L.B.

2 El Mercado The market, which has both open-air and enclosed sections and sprawls over several blocks, is the heart of the traditional downtown area. One section is devoted to artisans' stands, another to vegetable stalls, another to counters displaying fresh chickens and slabs of beef, and yet another to several luncheonettes. It's a long walk from the beach; take one of the buses marked *Mercado* that run along the Carretera Costera. ♦ Daily. 3 Poniente and Av 6 Norte. No phone

Hotel Castillo de Reyes

3 Castillo de Reyes $ With only 26 rooms, this hotel feels like a private home. Don Fernando, the manager, holds court at the outdoor table near the lobby and treats his guests as friends. The small rooms, shaded by palms and cooled with ceiling fans, are decorated with animal skins, garish masks, and coconut shells. There's no pool or restaurant. ♦ No credit cards accepted. Av Gasga (west of Av Union). 20442

4 Paraiso Escondido $ A veritable folk art museum, this hotel zigzags up a hillside in a series of rock-walled buildings above the PZ. Each of the 20 rooms, all with air-conditioning, is distinctively decorated with built-in desks, small balconies with French doors, wrought-iron key holders by the doors, and a variety of adornments, including copper plates and tiled murals on the walls. On one level there's an altar to St. Francis, complete with candles and religious statues; on another a suspended wooden bridge leads to a *mirador* (lookout point). A wading pool for kids sits beside the main pool, and the restaurant, which is the only disappointment, is open for all meals. ♦ No credit cards accepted. Avs Gasga and Union. 20444

4 Hotel Nayar $ A monument to the bland architecture of the 1970s, this property consists of a golden-yellow building with 41 similarly colored rooms. Only 15 of the units have air-conditioning; all have wood-louvered windows with no screens, tiny TV sets with local reception, two soft beds, and yellow-tiled bathrooms separated from the bedrooms by plastic shower doors. The pool is a bit of a walk from the rooms, and the restaurant fare is below average. Still, the rates are extremely low, the facilities are clean, and the PZ is a short walk away. ♦ Only Mexican bank credit cards accepted. Av Gasga 407 (just east of Av Union). 20113, 20319; fax 20319

5 Oro de Monte Albán Gorgeous replicas of the gold jewelry found in the tombs at Oaxaca's **Monte Albán** ruins are displayed in glass cases in this tiny, air-conditioned branch of a Oaxaca City–based chain of shops. ◆ Daily. Av Gasga (east of Marina Nacional). 20530

5 Tienda Omar Friendly fisherman Don Chuy will sell you postcards and stamps and even post your mail. This is a true variety store, with bathing suits, playing cards, sunglasses, day packs, and some nice Talavera ceramics. ◆ Av Gasga 502 (between Av Soledad and Marina Nacional). 20286

Within Tienda Omar:

Pesca Deportiva If you're interested in angling for marlin, dorado, or sailfish, Don Chuy will arrange for a local fisherman to take you out in a small launch (get one with a *sombra,* or shade) and will provide all the necessary fishing gear. Sailfish are most abundant from November (when the annual fishing tournament is held) until May. ◆ 20286

5 Wipe Out Bar Want a little Bob Marley with your sunset? Check out this second-story bar (enter through the gift shop below) overlooking the Playa Principal. A surfers' hangout with a raffish air, the bar hosts reggae and rock 'n' roll bands every night. ◆ No cover charge. Daily 7PM-1AM; music from 9:30PM to 1AM. Av Gasga (between Av Soledad and Marina Nacional). No phone

6 Artesanía The quality of the folk art in this small shop is better than at most others; the prices are higher as well. Great finds include shoes of leather and Guatemalan cloth, Guatemalan bags and shirts, and one-of-a-kind silver jewelry. ◆ Daily. Av Gasga 707 (between Av Soledad and Marina Nacional). No phone

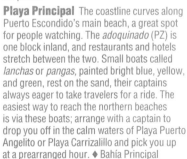

7 Playa Principal The coastline curves along Puerto Escondido's main beach, a great spot for people watching. The *adoquinado* (PZ) is one block inland, and restaurants and hotels stretch between the two. Small boats called *lanchas* or *pangas,* painted bright blue, yellow, and green, rest on the sand, their captains always eager to take travelers for a ride. The easiest way to reach the northern beaches is via these boats; arrange with a captain to drop you off in the calm waters of Playa Puerto Angelito or Playa Carrizalillo and pick you up at a prearranged hour. ◆ Bahía Principal

On Playa Principal:

La Posada del Tiburon ★★★$ This lovely place has an excellent location right on the sand, as well as cheerful waiters and superb food. The delicious and unique specialties include fillet of fish in a creamy lemon sauce and *filete relleno*—the catch of the day filled with octopus, shrimp, and conch. Meat and chicken dishes come with baked potato, steamed veggies, and rice. Special touches, including predinner tostadas with a spicy garlic sauce and homemade

garlic bread, will more than satisfy. This restaurant is a great find. ◆ Mexican/Seafood ◆ Daily breakfast, lunch, and dinner. 20789

8 La Luna A bit of Bali on the Mexican coast, this shop is filled with Balinese and Indian sundresses and shirts and gorgeous paintings of Indonesian country scenes. The clothing is well made and perfect for Puerto Escondido's tropical climate. ◆ Daily. Av Gasga (between Andador Azucena and Av Soledad). 20929

8 Bamboleo Like its neighbor, this shop has tons of tasteful Balinese and Indian clothing, including a good selection of sarongs. ◆ Daily. Av Gasga (between Andador Azucena and Av Soledad). 20993

9 La Galería ★★★$ A bit more refined than the beachside restaurants, this eatery sits above the sidewalk under a tile A-frame roof. Heavy wood tables are arranged on a clean brick floor, and outstanding—albeit expensive—paintings by the owner cover the walls. Dense whole-wheat bread and herbed butter begin the meal, followed by excellent salads (including one with hunks of apple and sharp cheese on a bed of lettuce). Among the pasta offerings are an unusual blend of fettuccine, roquefort cheese, and spinach, and a great fettuccine with shrimp. Soft jazz plays in the background, contributing to a dining ambience that is more tranquil than you'll find elsewhere in the PZ. ◆ Italian ◆ Daily dinner. No credit cards accepted. Av Gasga (between Andador Azucena and Av Soledad). No phone

10 Cafe Cappuccino ★$ The evening news on TV brings crowds into this simple cafe, where the sweets are the best items on the menu. The *Tres Marias* sundae—three flavors of ice cream covered with chocolate sauce and nuts—is sure to beat the heat, and the apple, pineapple, and cheese pies are all homemade. Among the most popular meals are the seafood platters and burgers, plus milk shakes. ◆ Mexican/American/Desserts ◆ Daily breakfast, lunch, and dinner. No credit cards accepted. Av Gasga (between Andador Azucena and Av Soledad). 20334

10 Zicatela Some of the area's best souvenir T-shirt designs can be found at this air-conditioned shop. Shorts, sunglasses, bathing suits, and some beach paraphernalia are also on the shelves. ◆ Daily. Av Gasga (between Andador Azucena and Av Soledad). No phone

---

Restaurants/Clubs: Red   **Hotels:** Blue
Shops/ Outdoors: Green   **Sights/Culture:** Black

LOS CROTOS

10 Los Crotos ★★$ Locals say the seafood and Oaxacan dishes are better here than anywhere else in the PZ, although both quality and reputation have slipped recently. The dining room is located a few steps down from the sidewalk; tables covered in orange cloths are clustered under ceiling fans. Outside, the tables are under *palapas* just above the beach; unfortunately, the smell of brackish water sometimes wafts up from the nearby lagoon. Begin your meal with a *jarra de agua papaya* (a big pitcher of papaya juice with purified water and ice) and a cocktail glass stuffed with fresh shrimp. Entrées worth trying include tamales *oaxaqueños* (cornmeal stuffed with meat and spices then wrapped in corn husks), chicken in a red mole sauce, *lengua de ternera* (marinated calf tongue), and shrimp with a garlic-and-chili sauce. ♦ Mexican/Seafood ♦ Daily breakfast, lunch, and dinner. Av Gasga (between Andador Azucena and Av Soledad). 20025

11 Restaurant Bar & Pizza da Claudio ★$ Thanks to the many Italian expatriates who have settled here, Puerto Escondido has an amazing number of Italian restaurants. This place, also called **"The Spaghetti House,"** sits right by the Playa Principal and serves a wide array of pastas and pizzas. The best deal is the nightly pizza or pasta dinner special, which includes salad, dessert, and coffee. For a different twist on the local fish dishes try the *maccheroni al sugo di pesce,* a fish fillet with capers, tomatoes, and pasta. Two-for-one mixed drinks are offered in the early evening. ♦ Italian ♦ Daily lunch and dinner. Andador Azucena (south of Av Gasga). 20005

12 Mario's Pizzaland ★★$ Enjoy a simple but satisfying meal at this casual Italian eatery with green walls, green-and-white checkered tablecloths, and ceiling fans. The nightly dinner special, which includes salad, pasta, and beverage, is the best deal around, considering the high quality of the food. The *spaghetti alla Maria* (with olive oil, garlic, and dried red peppers) is a pleasant change from Mexican food, while the *spaghetti alla Mario* (with mushrooms, bacon, and cream) is sure to sate the most voracious appetite. There also are five vegetarian pizza selections, and both meat and vegetable lasagna are served nightly. ♦ Italian ♦ Daily lunch and dinner. Av Gasga and Andador Azucena. 20570

13 Mercado de Artesanías A row of artisans' stands lines the street to the beach, offering an opportunity for shoppers to bargain. The selection is pretty much the same at all the stalls—woven purses, leather belts, pottery, hammocks, and carved wooden figurines—but quality varies, so inspect prospective purchases carefully. ♦ Daily. Andador Azucena (south of Av Gasga). No phone

14 Hotel Casa Blanca $ If you don't mind street noise and simple accommodations, this small hotel smack in the middle of the PZ is the perfect place to stay. The white building with cobalt-blue trim houses several businesses on the street level, with most of the 21 guest rooms located upstairs. The best rooms have balconies above the PZ, offering a front row view of passersby, but light sleepers might prefer those at the back of the house. Only some rooms have air-conditioning; all have two or three beds, open closets, small dressers, TVs, lightweight curtains that don't block the sun, and large bathrooms with no shower curtains. Lounge chairs are set around the small pool, and there's a jug of purified water in the hallway for all to use. The latest innovation is room service; the poolside restaurant is open daily except at the lunch hour. ♦ Av Gasga 905 (east of Andador Azucena). 20168

CASA BLANCA

15 Carmen's Patisserie ★★★$ It's impossible to resist the aroma of baking bread the first time you pass by this place, and once you've sampled Carmen's pastries, you're hooked. The dining room is as simple as can be—a cement floor, a few rickety wooden tables and chairs, and a wall lined with books and months-old newspapers. The menu is equally simple—a giant bowl of fruit smothered with yogurt and granola, massive cheese-and-avocado sandwiches on whole-wheat rolls, and pastries filled with ham and cheese. Patrons make their choices, then settle in over fresh-brewed coffee or fresh orange juice and read or chat. Customers wander through all day for mango or cinnamon pastries, spinach rolls, and those feather-light, whole-wheat buns. ♦ Bakery/Cafe ♦ M-Sa breakfast and lunch; Su breakfast. No credit cards accepted. Entrada Playa Marinero (south of Hwy 200). No phone

16 Playa Marinero As Puerto Escondido's main bay curves east, the name of the beach along its edge changes from Playa Principal to Playa Marinero. This is the best of Puerto Escondido's swimming beaches; the waves that crash on Playa Zicatela to the southeast are broken by a rocky point at the edge of the bay, and though it's important to watch the surf and undertow, the water is usually calm enough for bodysurfers and cautious swimmers. Vendors rent sun umbrellas and chairs along the sand, and roving salesman stop by with their jewelry and straw hats. ♦ Bahía Principal

17 Hotel Santa Fe $$ This place used to be the best hotel in town, known both for its lovely architecture and its amiable service. But the maintenance has slipped, the 51 rooms and eight bungalows tend to be dusty and musty, and some of the staff are downright discourteous. The property consists of several colonial-style buildings with tiled stairways and bougainvillea-draped arches clustered around a small pool that could use a good cleaning. The rooms are still attractively decorated, with handwoven multicolored spreads and drapes, pretty tiles on the baseboards and in the bath, carved wood furnishings, and both air conditioners and fans. Each of the bungalows has a living room, kitchen, and bedroom. The gift shop is excellent, and the restaurant an enduring favorite. ♦ Del Morro (west of Hwy 200). 20170, 20266, 800/849.6153; fax 20260

Within the Hotel Santa Fe:

Restaurant Santa Fe ★★★$ Even nonguests enjoy a meal or two at this pleasurable restaurant, especially in the morning and at sunset. The dining room overlooks the north end of Zicatela beach, and it's a joy to linger over fragrant coffee and homemade whole-wheat toast as the beach comes to life. Boys on horseback seek customers for early morning rides, children climb the rocky point at the edge of the beach to watch the fishing boats come in, and a cool sea breeze flutters the palms. Try the *chilaquiles* (tortillas fried with eggs and chicken) or *huevos rancheros* (fried eggs served over a corn tortilla with spicy tomato sauce) at breakfast, and the seafood cocktails at dinner. The service is friendly and efficient. ♦ Mexican/American ♦ Daily breakfast, lunch, and dinner. 20170, 20266

17 Hotel Estudios Tabachín del Puerto $$ Six apartments surround the patio, shaded by the tree that lends this place both its name and its charm—*tabachín* is the local word for the flamboyant tree. You'll feel at home in an apartment filled with shelves of paperback books and artwork and clocks on the walls. In second- and third-floor units, the ocean is visible above the roof of the **Hotel Santa Fe.** The largest apartment—with two bedrooms, living room, and kitchen—contains king, queen, and single beds. Owner Paul Cleaver (or don Pablo as he's known in Puerto) is a knowledgeable and affable host. He also owns a small posada about 90 minutes north of Puerto Escondido in the pueblo of Nopala. Guests here can arrange day trips or overnight stays. ♦ Del Morro (west of Hwy 200). 21179; fax 21179

18 Hotel Flor de Maria $ Of all the budget hotels in town, this is by far the best. The credit goes to Maria and Lino Francato, Italians who met in Canada and moved to Puerto Escondido to open their idea of the perfect hostelry. Attuned to foreign tastes, the Francatos know how to please their clientele, making sure the 24 immaculately clean rooms have screens on the windows, plenty of hot water, a sufficient number of electric outlets and lights, and comfortable mattresses. There are large jugs of purified water on every floor for all to use. Lino applies his artistic talents in decorating the lovely rooms, painting pictures of parrots and pink or blue faux headboards right on the walls. Guests gravitate day and night to the rooftop terrace, which has a small swimming pool, plenty of tables and chairs, and hammocks hanging under a *palapa*. There are no TVs in the rooms, but there is one in the rooftop bar, open in the high season; guests congregate there to watch sporting events and movies. The beach is a few steps down a sandy road, and the best bakery in town is just across the street. ♦ Del Morro (west of Hwy 200). 20536; fax 20536

Within Hotel Flor de Maria:

Restaurant Flor de Maria ★★★★$ Only a true Italian chef could make manicotti like Maria's, with fresh spinach and ricotta cheese stuffed in pasta shells as light as crepes. Transplanted gringos take note of the specials posted on a board outside the restaurant door, and word quickly spreads when Maria is making pork roast with mashed potatoes, liver and onions, cabbage rolls, or gnocchi—not to mention cheesecake with strawberries, flaky lemon pie, or chocolate tiramisù. Candlelight flickers on linen-covered tables, Pavarotti croons in the background, and conversation flows easily between strangers. You must have at least one dinner here. ♦ Italian/American ♦ Daily breakfast, lunch, and dinner. 20536

19 Playa Zicatela Zicatela is a mecca for surfers from around the world, who must ride the Mexican Pipeline, as this stretch of beach is called, at least once in their lives. The Pipeline's waves form perfect rushing water tunnels; photos of surfers completely encircled by 10-foot waves hang in Zicatela's campgrounds and cafes. A surfer statue sits beside a walkway that runs the length of the beach, and when the waves are up scores of surfers grab their boards and run barefoot from their rooms to the sea. Strolling this beach is a joy during the day but it's not safe to walk alone. Avoid the beach at night, as muggings and robberies are not unheard of. The sea is also very dangerous and best left to pros; a story always seems to be circulating about the surf's latest victim. ♦ Del Morro

20 Hotel Arcoiris $ An old favorite on Playa Zicatela, this sprawling three-story inn has 26 rooms, each with two double beds, ceiling fans (no air-conditioning), and a balcony equipped with a hammock hook—but, alas, no hammock. A jungle of trees, flowers, and vines flourishes around the swimming pool and the stairways to the rooms. **La Galera** restaurant on the third floor faces Zicatela's famed sunsets. Stop by for the early evening Happy Hour; perhaps a fisherman will share his catch, prepared by the chef. This is a convivial place, filled with surfers year round and Canadian and American snowbirds from December to May. ♦ Del Morro (west of Hwy 200). 20432; fax 20432

20 La Gota de Vida ★★★$ Right across from the beach is this small cafe with a lunch counter and tables overlooking the surf. A vegetarian's delight, the menu features vegetable tamales, soy burgers, hummus, big salads, steamed broccoli and cauliflower, wheat-germ bread, and inexpensive daily specials. There's a wide selection of juices and *licuados* made with yogurt. ♦ Vegetarian ♦ Daily breakfast, lunch, and dinner. Del Morro (west of Hwy 200). No phone

21 El Cafecito ★★$ This branch of **Carmen's Patisserie** (see page 106) is the most popular restaurant on Zicatela. Patrons fill the few indoor and sidewalk tables from early morning until sunset, dining on bowls of fresh fruit with granola and yogurt, huge cheese-and-avocado sandwiches, and irresistible sweet rolls and cookies. ♦ Bakery/Cafe ♦ Daily breakfast, lunch, and early dinner. Del Morro (west of Hwy 200). No phone

A Capital Excursion

It's almost impossible to resist a side trip from the coastal cities of **Huatulco** or **Puerto Escondido** to **Oaxaca,** the capital city of the Mexican state of the same name. Nearly everyone—from food lovers and folk art collectors to archaeology and history buffs—will find attractions and activities of interest here.

If you have a full week for your vacation, consider starting and ending it at the coast and spending the middle two or three days in the city. Small planes fly daily between Oaxaca and Puerto Escondido or Huatulco; the moderately priced trip takes about 20 minutes from either city and is far more comfortable than the dizzying drive up the mountains—a 272-kilometer (169-mile) full-day trip by car or bus on winding mountain roads from Huatulco to Oaxaca (don't make this dangerous ride at night).

Foodies hooked on Oaxacan tamales, cheese, and the region's seven varieties of mole—from the rich black mole of chocolate, chili, and spices to yellow mole of *pipian* seeds—are in their glory in the capital city. Firewater fans will want to savor Oaxaca's famous mezcal, distilled from the local maguey cactus, whose flavors run the gamut from cremes of nut, coffee, peach, and the woody-flavored seven herbs *(siete hierbas)* to those with the maguey cactus worm marinating in the bottom of the bottle. Those who eat the worm are said to become drunk, although this may be because they've upended the entire bottle to get at the worm. You can sip the sauce in most establishments, but some like to drink with the locals in saloons such as the **Casa de Mezcal,** south of the main square (Flores Magon 209, no phone), with its swinging doors and masculine clientele. Visitors from other parts of Mexico spend much of their time wandering the streets in this area, where tiny shops around the **Mercado Benito Juárez** specialize in the state's best food, drink, and handicrafts. Oaxaca, along with

Michoacan and **Jalisco,** has one of the country's best selections of handicrafts: Here you'll find hammocks, embroidered items from each of Oaxaca's seven regions, and a fabulous selection of earthenware and glazed pottery.

Cafes around the classically picturesque *zócalo,* or main square, serve frothy Oaxacan chocolate, plates of *chapulines* (grasshoppers fried with chili, salt, and herbs) with cold Negra Modelo beer, and wonderful tortilla soup topped with soft, white Oaxacan cheese.

Breakfast is best at the sidewalk tables at the **Marqués del Valle** hotel's restaurant (north side of the square, 951/44803), where you can sip your *cafe de olla* (coffee made in a clay crock with cinnamon and brown sugar) or *cafe con leche* (coffee with hot milk) while watching the plaza come to life. For a mid-afternoon lunch, take a table on the second-story balcony at **El Asador Vasco** (west side of the square, 951/44755) or stop in at **La Casa de la Abuela** (Av Hidalgo 616, 951/63544). Many visitors take advantage of the panoramic view from the bar of the **Hotel Victoria,** located just northwest of the city center (Cerro del Fortin 1, 951/52812) to enjoy the sunset over an evening cocktail.

Visiting shoppers are kept busy with the city's excellent variety of stores, including **Artesanías Chimalli** (García Vigil 513, north of the main square, 951/42101), **Victor's** (Porfirio Díaz 111, north of Av Independencia, 951/61174), **Corazón del Pueblo** (Macedonio Alcalá 307, between Mariano Matamoros and Nicolas Bravo, 951/30547), **Aripo** (García Vigil 809, north of the main square, 951/33030), and **La Mano Magico** (Macedonio Alcalá 203, between Av Morelos and Mariano Matamoros, 951/64275). The selection is great and prices are low at the women's cooperative **Mujeres Artesanas de las Regiones de Oaxaca,** or **Maro** (5 de Mayo 204, between Av Morelos and

Murguía, 951/60670), and proceeds go directly to the artisans.

Those who have extra time can make excursions to the many folk art villages surrounding Oaxaca city. Among the most popular are **Arrazola** (Hwy 145, west of the Zaachila road) and **San Martín Tilcajete** (off Hwy 175, 21 km/13 miles south of Oaxaca), both specializing in the painted copal-wood animals rendered in wild shapes and colors. **San Bartolo Coyotepec** (Hwy 175, 23 km/14 miles south of Oaxaca) is famous for its burnished black pottery; **Teotitlán del Valle** (north of Hwy 190, east of Oaxaca) has been producing handwoven wool rugs and serapes of exceptional quality for generations.

A trip to one of the weekly market towns surrounding Oaxaca will prove that time, indeed, stands still in some places: People still barter for sheep, goats, and squealing piglets, while the main market bursts with timeless utilitarian objects, from the plastic to the sublime. If in Oaxaca on a Thursday, don't miss **Zaachila's** fabulous market, 18 kilometers (11 miles) south of Oaxaca. Here horse and cart are still among the principal means of transportation, and townspeople breakfast, gossip, and sell with verve and dignity within the grand marketplace. Another excellent market is that of **Tlacolula**, held on Sunday, when the streets of Oaxaca are quiet—sometimes downright deserted. In striking contrast, Tlacolula's bustling market draws buyers and sellers from the surrounding towns. You can combine your Sunday market stop with a visit to the ruins of Mitla (see below) and an obligatory ogling at the famous Tule tree, which is thought to be at least 2,000 years old. This giant cypress, called *ahuehuete* by the locals, is over 40 meters in girth. Local schoolkids with offical-looking badges will point out dozens of figures formed by the tree's twisted trunk.

All first timers to the area must visit **Monte Albán,** the city and ceremonial site first constructed by the Zapotec around 600 BC and later refined by the Mixtec; the site, about 8 kilometers (5 miles) southwest of Oaxaca, is open daily and admission is free on Sunday. The bookstore/giftshop there is excellent, and the restaurant overlooking the valley of Oaxaca has decent fare and attentive waiters. The archaeological site of **Mitla,** with its Art Deco–like geometric designs, is also a must-see; it's located 40 kilometers (25 miles) southeast of Oaxaca and is open daily. Admission is free on Sunday.

The city itself offers plenty to see.

Culture lovers will want to take in the **Regional Museum of Oaxaca** (Macedonio Alcalá and Gurrión, 951/62991; closed Monday; free on Sunday), famous for its collection of priceless jewels discovered in **Monte Albán's Tomb 7.** This museum is found within the six-block complex of the church and convent of **Santo Domingo,** currently undergoing a million-peso face-lift that may outdo its original splendor. The completed complex also will contain exhibition space, botanical gardens, offices, and a cafe. Other lovely museums are the **Rufino Tamayo Museum of Pre-Hispanic Art** (Morelos 503, between Porfirio Díaz and Tinoco y Palacios, 951/64750; admission; open M, W-Su). Both are housed in former colonial residences. The Baroque facade of the **Catedral de Oaxaca** (Plaza de Armas and Av Independencia), built in 1535, remains intact.

You'll want to stay at least one night in Oaxaca, if only to experience one of its wonderful small hotels. The **Camino Real Oaxaca** ($$$$; 5 de Mayo 300, at Murguía, 951/60611; reservations 800/722.6466; fax 951/60732) sets the standard for colonial-style inns. The 91 rooms are housed in a 16th-century convent that's a national monument; its gardens, patios, and restaurant are works of art. The hotel presents an excellent folkloric dance show and buffet dinner every Friday night.

El Hostel de la Noria ($$; Av Hidalgo 918, 951/47844; fax 951/63992) is a newer offering near the plaza, with 43 rooms in a colonial-style building. Also recommended are the **Principal** ($; 5 de Mayo 208, between Av Morelos and Murguía, 951/62535), a colonial house with 16 comfortable rooms and lots of character, and **Las Golondrinas** ($; Tinoco y Palacios 411, between Nicolas Bravo and Ignacio Allende, 951/68726), a sprawling 24-room inn whose many, multicolored patios are bursting with potted plants. Most hotels in the city fit in the budget or moderate categories; you can lodge in comfort and subdued style and still save money on a room.

If you're in the state of Oaxaca, don't miss a trip to the capital city. Even those who have been back dozens of times find new pleasures here.

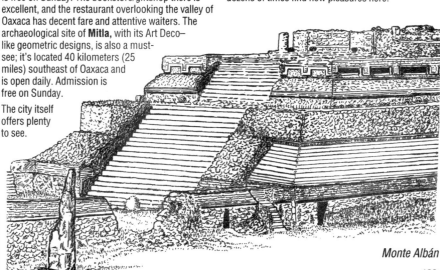

Monte Albán

L.L. BRENGELMAN

109

Huatulco

It's easy to understand why tourism developers cast their eyes upon Huatulco. They must have been riveted by the sight of nine stunning, pristine bays at the wooded base of the **Sierra Madre del Sur** mountains. Surprisingly, this section of the **Oaxacan Coast** was virtually untouched until 1974, when the Mexican government chose the **Bahías de Huatulco** for development. The major hotels are clustered around **Bahía Tangolunda**; less expensive hotels are located near **Bahía Chahué** and **Bahía Santa Cruz**, which also has a marina. The highway-side town of **La Crucecita** is designed to look like a traditional Mexican pueblo and has interesting street life and a few inexpensive hotels.

Actually, the resort area of Huatulco is as low-key as you can get and still have first-class accommodations. Dining out and shopping have yet to take hold, and with most of the big hotels—such as **Club Med**, the **Sheraton**, and the **Royal Maeva**—having adopted all-inclusive plans to some extent, guests can stay put and simply relax if they wish. The scenery is utterly gorgeous, so it's easy to slide into a trance while gazing at the mountains and sea. If you're feeling livelier, Huatulco is the perfect base for nature lovers to explore the mountains and bays along the 18-mile coastline (see "Boating to the Bays," page 114). Do you fancy snorkeling or scuba diving amid the tropical fish? Want to expend some energy jet skiing, windsurfing, or parasailing? Prefer to loll in a hammock under the palms? Or are you in the mood to enjoy the wildlife in a nature preserve, or admire the great spectacle of a natural blowhole? It can all be found among the bays—for now, at least. Although development has slowed in Tangolunda, Santa Cruz, and La Crucecita since the first building spurt, plans continue to emerge for the six undeveloped bays.

At the top of the mountains, the city of **Oaxaca** beckons with its traditional temptations—the food and the fiestas, the archaeology and the folk art (see "A Capital Excursion," page 108). Don't resist. Riding in a small plane (or a slow bus) to the city, 1,550 meters (5,085 feet) above sea level, is an experience not to be missed. And the rewards, once you reach the top, are unmatched.

Area code 958 unless otherwise noted.

Getting to Huatulco

Airport

Aeropuerto Bahías de Huatulco (Bahías de Huatulco Airport) is located about 16 kilometers (10 miles) west of Huatulco's hotels and towns. The airport handles both national and international flights, though on many days only one or two flights are scheduled. Most international flights involve a connection in Mexico City. Airport services such as car rentals and shops are open only when flights are arriving and departing.

Airlines

Aeromorelos 10336

Mexicana 10208, 70251, 800/531.7921

Getting to and from Aeropuerto Bahías de Huatulco

By Bus Transportation is provided from the airport by *colectivo* (van) direct to your hotel; rates are set by the zone and range from $6 to $10. No public buses run to the airport.

By Car The drive from the airport to Huatulco's three main areas takes about 30 minutes. **Highway 200** runs east from the airport and has clearly marked exits for **Santa Cruz, La Crucecita,** and **Tangolunda.**

The following car-rental companies have counters at the airport and are open only when flights are arriving and departing.

Budget 10036, 70034, 800/527.0700

Dollar 10055, 800/800.4000

National......................10293, 10051, 800/328.4567

By Taxi Taxis await passengers in front of the airport. The fare to Tangolunda is about $15, to La Crucecita about $10, to Santa Cruz about $12.

Getting Around Huatulco

Walking between Tangolunda, Santa Cruz, and La Crucecita is not possible; you must drive, or take a cab, bus, or boat. Highway 200 connects all three areas and is clearly marked with turn-offs to each area. The best, and least expensive, way to get around is by public bus.

Buses Huatulco's main bus station is in La Crucecita (Av Gardenia 1201, at Calle Ocotillo, 70261). There is first-class bus service to Oaxaca (seven hours) and Puerto Escondido (three hours). The public bus from Tangolunda Bay to Santa Cruz and La Crucecita runs frequently between 6AM and 7PM.

Driving Traffic is minimal in Huatulco and driving is easy, once you understand the layout of the three areas. Most hotels have car-rental desks, and street parking is readily available.

Taxis Cabs are plentiful and are usually parked in front of larger hotels, as well as around the plazas in Santa Cruz and La Crucecita. Fares are regulated and are listed in hotel lobbies and at some taxi stands.

FYI

Accommodations Although the hotels in Tangolunda are generally expensive, most offer an all-inclusive rate or a meal plan. This option is worth thinking about because none are within walking distance of other restaurants. Hotels in Santa Cruz are more moderately priced and within easy walking distance of the marina. La Crucecita's hotels are the least expensive and are fairly close to Chahué Bay.

Cruises and Water Sports The bays are Huatulco's main attraction, and several companies offer boat cruises and rent water sports equipment.

Tequila Catamaran (Blvd Chahué, La Crucecita, 70580, 70728) offers catamaran cruises of varying lengths of time, including a full-day tour with stops for snorkeling and sunbathing.

Triton Dive Center (Marina Santa Cruz, 70844) has scuba and snorkeling trips available.

Publications Few English-language tourist publications are available, but hotels and travel agencies may have a copy of *Huatulco,* a brochure published in English and Spanish.

Shopping Huatulco's shops are beginning to take advantage of the wealth of folk art produced in the state of Oaxaca. The items they do carry are greatly overpriced, though some are of exceptional quality. The best folk art, jewelry, and sportswear can be found in small La Crucecita shops.

Time Zone Huatulco is on Central Time, two hours ahead of California and one hour behind New York.

Tours Most hotels have their own travel agents who can book boat and nature tours. (See "Boating to the Bays," page 114). Among the companies offering tours of the region, including trips to Puerto Escondido and Oaxaca city, are:

Bahías Plus Carrizal and Guanacaztle, La Crucecita
....70216, 70932

Cantera Tours Hotel Sheraton, Blvd Benito Juárez 227
....10055

Visitors' Information Center The **Oficina de Turismo** (Tourism Office) is operated by SEDETUR, the Oaxaca State Tourism Department. It's located in the **Plaza San Miguel** on **Boulevard Benito Juarez** (east of Blvd Tangolunda) in Tangolunda Bay. The office is open weekdays from 9AM to 5PM (71542; fax 71541).

Phone Book

Hospital Centro Medica Flamboyan and Carrizal, La Crucecita 70687, 70104
Police 70009
Red Cross 71188

Tangolunda

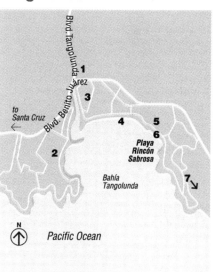

Pacific Ocean

The centerpiece of Huatulco tourist development, **Bahía Tangolunda** (Tangolunda Bay), is home to all the major hotels and the 18-hole golf course. The action is totally within the hotels; the commercial center at the entrance to the area is virtually vacant. Most hotels offer all-inclusive plans—really the most practical option because there are few restaurants in the area. Taxi drivers abound, eager to take you to **Santa Cruz** and **La Crucecita.** If you're watching your pesos, use the public bus; it runs frequently during daylight hours and passes right by the hotel entrances. The **Sheraton** and **Quinta Real** are the most friendly to visiting nonguests; the others are either all-inclusive or so exclusive that nonguests are not allowed to wander about.

1 Campo de Golf Tangolunda This 18-hole, par-72, championship golf course sprawls through a valley surrounded by forested foothills. Golfers must angle their balls around trees and over difficult water obstacles; the 13th hole is on an elevated green overlooking the **Sheraton's** beach. After the ordeal, you may welcome the good, if expensive, lunch served by the clubhouse. ♦ Daily. Blvds Benito Juárez and Tangolunda. 10037

2 Club Med Huatulco $$$$ Extending over a 50-acre spread at the edge of Bahía Tangolunda, the resort clusters its 500 rooms in four small villages, each marked with a bright purple, blue, pink, or yellow tower. The water sports facilities—kayaks, Windsurfers, snorkeling gear, and a large pool—are the best in the area. So are the meals—lavish spreads of such gourmet delights as pâté, salmon, homemade breads, roast beef, and trays of fresh vegetables and fruit. There's a **Teen Club** with activities geared to two age groups (12-14 and 15-17), along with **Circus Workshops** and seasonal specialty weeks. ♦ Advance booking required Blvd Benito Juárez (west of Blvd Tangolunda). 10033, 10101, 800/258.2633

3 Quinta Real $$$$ Designed by **Ricardo** and **Roberto Elias** this architectural stunner rises on a hill above Tangolunda Bay. The white domed buildings, with only 27 suites, are designed for those who want the ultimate in seclusion. Some suites have private swimming pools that are cleverly hidden from view; those without a pool have whirlpools and terraces with fabulous ocean views. The rooms have wood-beam ceilings, framed Guatemalan and Oaxacan textiles, and hand-crafted armoires hiding televisions. The hotel has a large swimming pool and beach club, and an excellent restaurant. ♦ Blvd Benito Juárez (just east of Blvd Tangolunda). 10428, 800/445.4565; fax 10429

Within the Quinta Real:

Restaurante Las Cupulas ★★★★$$$ Be sure to savor at least one meal in this elegant dining room with its ornate chandeliers, hand-crafted dishes, and innovative menu. For an all-out feast start with sea bass tartare or puff pastry stuffed with cream cheese and nopal cactus, move on to the mixed green salad topped with fried brie or the coriander bouillabaisse, and then experience true Oaxacan black mole covering a braised chicken filled with almonds, raisins, and peaches. You won't find such dishes (or such professional service) anywhere else in Huatulco. ♦ Mexican/International ♦ Daily breakfast, lunch, and dinner. 10428

4 Sheraton Huatulco $$ This most full-scale of Tangolunda's hotels has five-story buildings terraced around the pool and gardens. Pleasantly decorated in a pink-and-rose color scheme, the 348 rooms have black Oaxacan pottery, mini-bars, satellite TV, and tubs as well as showers. If you opt for the all-inclusive plan (nightly room rates are also offered), you'll have a choice of menu items from the two restaurants or the theme buffets (such as Italian or Mexican) offered at dinner. Amenities include four tennis courts, a children's nursery free to the under eights), a playground, two expensive restaurants, and the best silver shop in Tangolunda. ♦ Blvd Benito Juárez (east of Blvd Tangolunda). 10055, 800/325.3535; fax 10113

The Napoleonic Law—guilty until proven innocent—still rules in Mexico.

5 Don Porfirio ★★$$ The best restaurant outside of the hotels in Tangolunda is this steak and lobster house. True, the ambience isn't elegant; the tables are set at the edge of an open kitchen and along the sidewalk facing the street, and there is no air-conditioning. The prices for grilled lobster are higher than at the restaurants in La Crucecita and Santa Cruz. But for a reasonable price, you can dine on the Oaxacan sampler plate of cheese, tamales, guacamole, pork, and beef. This is your best dining option if you want to stay in the hotel zone, and many diners get a charge out of the house specialty, lobster flambéed with mescal. ♦ Seafood ♦ Daily lunch and dinner. Blvd Benito Juárez (east of Blvd Tangolunda). 10001

Within Don Porfirio:

Noches Oaxaqueñas ★★★$$ The owners of **Don Porfirio** give visitors an opportunity to sample Oaxacan culture at this dinner theater–type showplace that they've opened as a kind of annex to the restaurant. Guests pay an admission fee to see the show and can order drinks, *botanes* (appetizers), and full meals from **Don Porfirio**'s menu. A Guelaguetza show featuring folkloric dances from throughout Oaxaca state is presented on weekend nights, with young dancers doing breathtaking routines in traditional costumes. Decorated like a hacienda, the showroom has both a main dining room and a balcony and is blessedly air-conditioned. Those who haven't seen similar shows in Oaxaca city or are new to the state's culture will better appreciate their surroundings after spending an evening here. ♦ Oaxacan ♦ F-Su nights. 10001

6 Royal Maeva $$$ With volleyball nets and water aerobics classes in the pool and theme nights featuring raucous music and games, this all-inclusive resort is the liveliest hotel in Tangolunda. (Beware of accommodations close to the pool—the noise can be quite irritating.) The 300 surprisingly spacious and comfortable rooms have heavy cotton drapes and spreads in soft pastels. Meals are served buffet style or at the sit-down-and-be-served Italian restaurant, where the pastas are homemade. Room service is also available. ♦ Blvd Benito Juárez 227 (east of Blvd Tangolunda). 10000, 800/466.2382; fax 10220

7 Zaashila $$$$ Formerly operated by the Omni chain, this exclusive hotel sits on a hilltop overlooking the bay. The several terra-cotta–and-white buildings with bright cobalt-blue walls are terraced down a hillside, creating an architecturally stunning effect (though a fresh coat of paint and better maintenance would make the place even more delightful). Private pools sit outside the 32 luxury suites, and these, as well as the 98 rooms, are all sumptuously decorated with comfortable upholstered wicker chairs with ottomans, green wrought-iron tables, and double sinks and tubs. Guests enjoy the dome-shaped, *palapa* (thatched-palm)–shaded outdoor restaurants and bars beside the two swimming pools and one tennis court, but it's a bit of a hike down the hill to the beach. The dinner restaurant, **Chez Binni**, serves good continental cuisine in an open-air setting. ♦ South of Blvd Benito Juárez. 10460, 888/727.4452; fax 10461

La Crucecita

Situated inland from **Santa Cruz** and **Chahué Bays**, La Crucecita is the commercial center of Huatulco and the best place in the area for shopping, dining, and local color. The large (by small-town standards) central plaza has pathways edged in blooming shrubs that lead to the *kiosko* (gazebo). Bordering the plaza are streets lined with shops and sidewalk cafes, while the side streets house the bus station, long-distance phone office, self-service laundries, and small markets. If you're staying in **Tangolunda** or **Santa Cruz**, you'll want to come here at least once to sample the restaurants and observe small-town Mexican life.

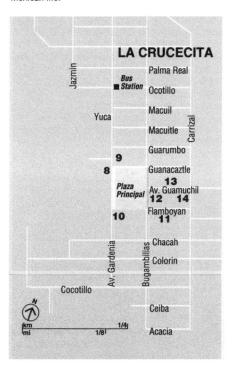

8 Hotel Posada Flamboyant $ At almost twice the price of any hotel by the plaza, this place with 67 rooms and 4 suites with kitchenettes still falls in the inexpensive category. The interior is painted in soft shades of blue and yellow; the rooms have tile floors, walls inset with painted tiles, and two firm twin beds, air-conditioning (which can be appallingly noisy), and satellite TV. The swimming pool is in a garden off the second floor, and there is a guarded parking lot, a travel agency, and a small coffee shop. ♦ Av Gardenia (between Chacah and Ocotillo). 70113, 70105; fax 70121

9 Paradise This collection of side-by-side shops includes a clothing boutique with sundresses and shorts from India and a folk art gallery. The pottery, masks, and wood carvings here are of a higher quality than those in the artisans' markets. ♦ Daily. Av Gardenia and Guarumbo. 70648

10 Restaurante Maria Sabina ★★$ It's hard to resist the aroma of sizzling shrimp wafting from the outdoor grill at this sidewalk cafe. Here is the place to try regional dishes such as Oaxacan mole, and a cup of frothy hot chocolate. ♦ Mexican ♦ Daily lunch and dinner. Flamboyan and Av Gardenia. 71039

11 Museo de Cultura Oaxaqueña More a shop than a museum, this space has become a working artists' haven and the best place in the area for visitors to watch the weavers, carvers, and potters from Oaxaca's highlands. The shop displays a delightful array of tin mirrors and frames, woolen rugs and tapestries, gleaming black pottery, and cleverly painted wooden figures. ♦ Daily. Flamboyan 216 (between Carrizal and Bugambilias). 71403

12 Plateria Maitl Patient browsing will yield some good finds and unusual designs amid the rows of silver earrings and necklaces filling the glass cabinets in this small shop. Make sure your purchase is stamped "925"—it means you're buying real silver and not an alloy of nickel and tin called "alpaca." ♦ Daily. Bugambilias (between Flamboyan and Guamuchil). 71223

13 Mercado 3 de Mayo Like the artisans' stands in Santa Cruz, this market area is filled with the same tired T-shirts, rugs, and pottery figurines. But the selection is a bit larger here, and you can bargain for good prices on carved animals from Oaxaca. ♦ Daily. No credit cards accepted. Av Guamuchil (between Carrizal and Bugambilias). No phone

14 Hotel Las Palmas $ Budget travelers are pleased to discover this inexpensive small hotel a half-block from the plaza. All 10 rooms have air-conditioning and fans, private bathrooms with showers, two firm single beds, and small TVs. A 15-room addition was scheduled for completion as we went to press. **El Sabor de Oaxaca,** the adjacent restaurant, is excellent; it's under the same ownership but has its own entrance. ♦ Av Guamuchil 206 (between Carrizal and Bugambilias). 70060; fax 70057

14 El Sabor de Oaxaca ★★★★$ The best place in town to sample Oaxacan cuisine is at this pretty, rainbow-hued restaurant, where hand-sculpted vases are perched in bright yellow niches in the blue walls, and the tables are covered with yellow, orange, and green cloths. The *plato oaxaqueño especial* for two persons covers the highlights of the menu, with good-sized portions of Oaxacan cheese,

chorizo, tamales, seasoned pork and beef, and guacamole. Other choices are the green, yellow, and black mole (the color is determined by the spices used in the sauce) and *chapulines,* Oaxaca's legendary fried grasshoppers. Soft jazz adds to the ambience. A patio extension to the restaurant was in the planning stages at press time. ♦ Mexican ♦ Daily breakfast, lunch, and dinner. Av Guamuchil 106 (between Carrizal and Bugambilias). 70060

Santa Cruz

Santa Cruz was established as the waterside tourism center for the area, but it still looks like a town that's never taken hold. The marina is filled with *pangas* (small skiffs) and yachts whose captains are eager to take tourists on bay cruises for lower prices than those offered by the travel agencies. The town consists of a dreary artisans' market beside a central plaza, several commercial buildings that house offices and the area's three banks, and a few small hotels and restaurants.

Boating to the Bays

Nature is **Huatulco**'s biggest attraction, and much of it has been left alone thus far. The most difficult decision you'll make during your stay here is picking your favorite among the nine bays and 36 beaches along the 18-mile coastline. Boats to most of the bays depart from some of the hotels, as well as from the marina at **Bahía Santa Cruz.** Several bays offer tourists casual restaurants and water toy rentals, while others are almost completely deserted. Starting from the east, the first bay is **Bahía Conejos,** named for the rabbits that once lived here undisturbed. Conejos is likely the next bay slated for development, but for now it's a pleasant escape near the hotel zone, with a few *palapa* (palm-roofed) restaurants on the beach and decent snorkeling. Next comes **Bahía Tangolunda** and its shoreline of lavish hotels. Visitors interested in jet skiing, diving, parasailing, and other water activities will find the most services here. **Bahía Chahué** is the next in line; some call it the

"people's beach." Until recently, hammocks hung from palms beside simple campgrounds where budget travelers set up housekeeping. But Chahué is now being developed. A road leads from **Crucecita** to the beach, where a large parking lot has been constructed. Several small hotels have risen on the few paved streets by the bay; the modest 19-room **Posada Chahué** (70945; fax 71240) is still a favorite with budget travelers. **Santa Cruz** is the site of the marina and of **Playa la Entrega,** a pretty beach just a few minutes' boat ride from the town of Santa Cruz. Entrega is one of the best areas for snorkeling and scuba diving since a coral reef lies just offshore. The beach is fairly peaceful, with a few *palapa*-shaded restaurants, some ragged snorkeling gear for rent, and plenty of tropical fish around the bay's rocky points. A natural blowhole called **La Bufadora** puts on a great show between Playa la Entrega and **Bahía Organo,** named for the organ cacti that rise on the hills over the water. At the tourist-oriented **Bahía Maguey,** vendors rent snorkeling gear and kayaks to the dozens of people climbing out of tour boats. Several simple restaurants serve great seafood cocktails and grilled fish. **Bahías de Cacaluta, India,** and **Chachacual** are remote and peaceful; Chachacual has been set aside as a nature preserve. The last in the lineup, **Bahía San Agustín,** is a favorite of scuba divers, who find turtles and large pelagic fish in the rocks around **Isla San Agustín** in the bay.

If you're planning a long tour of the bays, be sure your boat has a *sombra,* or shade cover. Life jackets are required on all tour boats, and passengers must keep them on at least until the boat passes the port captain's office at the edge of Bahía Santa Cruz.

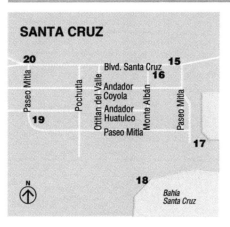

SANTA CRUZ

15 Hotel Castillo Huatulco $ The 121 rooms and suites in this resort-style hotel, across the street from the marina, are somewhat dark and uninviting, with cream-colored walls, brown floors, and dark blue drapes and bedspreads. But the grounds are nice, with a long pool framed by several buildings. The restaurant is open for all meals, and drinks and *botanes* (snacks) are served in the lobby bar. Beside the hotel is a commercial space with airline offices, travel agencies, and shops. Shuttles to the beach are available, and the public bus stops across the street. ◆ Blvd Santa Cruz and Paseo Mitla. 70051, 70251; fax 70131

16 Artisans' Market If you want to shop for souvenirs in Santa Cruz, this small outdoor market facing the plaza is the only place. The vendors are particularly nice and usually eager for sales, but their selection is predictable—hammocks, T-shirts, glass and wood statues of fish, and a few Guatemalan textiles. ◆ Daily. No credit cards accepted. Blvd Santa Cruz (between Paseo Mitla and Monte Albán). No phone

17 Sociedad Cooperativa Turística (Tourism Cooperative) Boat captains do their best to entice tourists who are wandering around the waterfront to take a ride along the bays. Some have fairly flashy presentations—snapshot albums filled with candid photos of travelers snorkeling, sunbathing, and swimming. Though some people say you can bargain here, the captains maintain that the cooperative has set firm prices for the tours. The cheapest way to see the bays is to ask for transport to and from a particular bay that has a good beach and cafes. Longer tours—a half-hour, an hour, or more—cruise along the coast and make stops for snorkeling and lunch, if the passengers wish. The captains do not take credit cards or traveler's checks, but if you arrange your trip through a travel agency (usually more expensive) you can pay in whatever form you prefer. ◆ Daily. Paseo Mitla (south of Blvd Santa Cruz). 70081

17 Tipsy's Food, drink, water sports, and boat cruises are available at this full-service beach club on the shores of Santa Cruz Bay. Activities include waterskiing rentals and classes, bay tours, snorkeling, fishing, kayak rentals, and beach volleyball. Or guests can just hang out on the beach in lounge chairs under umbrellas; towels and a freshwater shower are available. The indoor and outdoor restaurant offers *botanes* and appetizer platters, along with with seafood salads, grilled onions, fajitas, and guacamole, plus full steak and seafood dinners. ◆ Daily. Paseo Mitla (south of Blvd Santa Cruz). 70127

18 Restaurant Avalos Doña Celia ★★★$ Superb seafood is served at this waterfront cafe, the last in a series of similar restaurants at the edge of the bay. Look for the one with blue awnings and blue-and-white checkered tablecloths and settle in for a fine meal. Good choices are the spicy *sopa mariscos* (seafood soup) and the *plato huatulqueño*, a plate of shrimp and octopus sautéed with chilies and onions. Fish and seafood are prepared several ways—grilled with garlic and oil, sautéed with almonds, or deep-fried. It's worth leaving the hotel zone to linger over a meal here. ◆ Seafood ◆ Daily breakfast, lunch, and dinner. Playa Santa Cruz (south of Paseo Mitla). 70128

19 Hotel Marlin $ The rates are low and the ambience mellow at this 29-room bright pink inn, where you can choose between inexpensive rooms with fans or slightly more expensive ones with air-conditioning. There's a big pool right by the hotel restaurant and the **Magic Circus** disco next door. ◆ Paseo Mitla and Andador Huatulco. 70055; fax 70546

20 Meigas Binniguenda $ A favorite among those seeking privacy, low room rates, and soothing surroundings, this was one of the first hotels in the area and originally housed the investors, architects, and engineers who developed Huatulco. The 74 rooms have ample closet, dresser, and shelf space, large tables and heavy wooden chairs next to French doors that open to tiny balconies, and huge showers. Waterfalls cascade into the pool day and night, and groves of bamboo and palms shade the gardens. The restaurant, open for all meals, is very good, especially for breakfasts of *huevos oaxaqueños* (fried eggs on tortillas, covered with melted Oaxacan cheese); an all-inclusive meal plan is available. Construction has begun on 100 additional rooms, and the hotel operates a beach club on Santa Cruz Bay. It's a five-minute walk to restaurants and services in Santa Cruz. ◆ Blvd Santa Cruz and Paseo Mitla. 70777; fax 70284

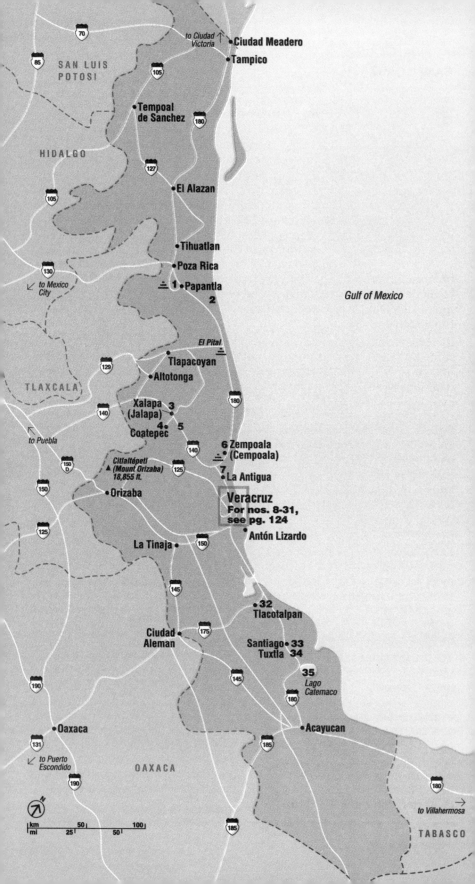

San Luis Potosi

70

85

Hidalgo

105

127

130
↙ to Mexico
City

105

Tempoal de Sanchez

180

El Alazan

Tihuatlan

Poza Rica

⚎ 1 **Papantla**
2

to Ciudad
Victoria ↑ • **Ciudad Meadero**

• **Tampico**

105

Gulf of Mexico

El Pital

Tlapacoyan

• **Altotonga**

129

Tlaxcala

140

Xalapa 3
(Jalapa) •
4 •
Coatepec 5

150 D

150

Citlaltépetl
▲ **(Mount Orizaba)**
18,855 ft.

125

• **Orizaba**

to Puebla

180

6 **Zempoala**
⚎ • **(Cempoala)**
7
• **La Antigua**

Veracruz
For nos. 8-31,
see pg. 124

140

125

La Tinaja •

150

• **Antón Lizardo**

145

• 32
Tlacotalpan

Ciudad
Aleman

175

Santiago • 33
Tuxtla 34

35
Lago
Catemaco

145

180

190

• **Oaxaca**

131

↙ to Puerto
Escondido

190

Oaxaca

• **Acayucan**

185

180

→ to Villahermosa

⊕
N

km
50   100
25   50
mi

185

Tabasco

Veracruz

The Mexican state of Veracruz is blessed with an abundance of natural gifts. Mexico's highest peak, **Cilaltépetl** (also called **Mount Orizaba**), poses between sky and land, high above rivers, rain forests, and coffee plantations. **Lago Catemaco** at the south is Mexico's third-largest lake. The port city of Veracruz is one of the most profitable in the nation, and oil pumps boom on the southern coast.

The 430-milelong state of Veracruz ripples along the **Gulf of Mexico** coast, somewhat isolated and definitely independent in character. The Olmec, Mexico's oldest known culture, scattered several multiton carved rock heads in Veracruz back around 1200 BC. Later, the Huastec, Otomí, Maya, and Totonac civilizations left their marks on the region. Then Hernán Cortés and his galleons sailed into Veracruz port in 1519. Cortés bestowed the name of Vera Cruz (True Cross) upon the fertile territory, where his ships could be hidden in deep rivers, and his men could be well fed. Not long after, he found La Malinche, the woman who led Cortés's army through her country to Spanish victory.

In 1683, attacks by the pirate Lorenzcillo led the Spaniards to construct a stone wall and seven *baluartes* (bastions) around the port and growing city. Invaders have pressed against her shores ever since: Veracruz has been the backdrop for three foreign invasions (one French, two from the United States) and is the birthplace of the Mexican Constitution. Two controversial and flamboyant Mexican presidents—Venustiano Carranza and Antonio López de Santa Anna—were born here, as was composer Augustín Lara. In character and style the state and its eponymous port city are a world unto themselves, overlaid with foreign influences. The Olmec heads have distinct negroid features, which implies possible contact with Africa, and African slaves are known to have arrived with Cortés. Also, visiting *Cubaños* say they feel as if they're in Havana when they walk down the *malecón* in **Veracruz City**; maybe that's because decades ago, Pearson & Company, an American engineering firm, designed the waterfronts in both those cities.

In character, the *veracruzaños* are lively, sentimental, and ribald. Veracruz gave the world the traditional song *La Bamba,* later made famous in the US by Richie Valens. City dwellers are called *jarochos,* supposedly after a small town where the residents speak in a distinctively rude style. *Jarocho* music is among Mexico's finest, but it's not the only music played in Veracruz. There's nothing better than wandering through the city's **Plaza de Armas** while marimbas, mariachis, *jarocho* groups, and military bands play simultaneously.

Tourists from the US and Canada have yet to catch on to Veracruz, but plenty of visitors from within Mexico favor it as a destination. In addition, sailors from all over the world arrive at the port, and the region is a favorite among European and Australian backpackers. Adventure travelers can't resist climbing **Mount Orizaba** or rafting Veracruz's nine mighty rivers, and archaeology buffs are drawn by the pyramids at **El Tajín** and the scores of smaller sites. But sun worshipers be forewarned: Despite its 430-milelong coastline, the state isn't a beach resort. The shore here is reminiscent of that of south Texas, packed with brown sand so hard it can withstand the weight of VW Beetles and pick-up trucks. But if you appreciate nature, culture, and character, don't miss Veracruz.

Area code is 29 unless otherwise indicated.

Getting to Veracruz

Airport

The small (one terminal) **Aeropuerto Internacional Heriberto Jara** (Heriberto Jara International Airport) handles national and international flights, though international passengers currently clear customs and change planes in Mexico City. Airport businesses such as car-rental agencies and shops are typically open only around the times planes depart and arrive.

Airport Services

Information 349008

Airlines

Aeroméxico 350833, 350142, 800/237.6639

AeroLitoral 350701

Mexicana................................322242, 800/531.7921

Getting to and from Aeropuerto Internacional Heriberto Jara

By Bus Transportation from the airport direct to hotels in Veracruz City is provided by *combi* (van); rates are set by zone and range from $6 to $8. No public buses run to the airport.

By Car The drive to downtown Veracruz from the airport takes about 15 minutes; take **Avenida Miguel Alemán** north from the airport exit. To reach the beach hotels south of town take **Avenida Ejercito Mexicano (Carretera Boticaria-Mocambo)**.

The following car-rental agencies have counters at the airport; they are open only when flights are arriving and departing.

Avis..311580, 800/331.1212

Dollar 355231, 800/800.4000

By Taxi Taxis await passengers in front of the airport. The fare to downtown Veracruz is about $10.

Train Station

The Veracruz train station—**Estación de Ferrocarriles Nacionales de Mexico** (Montesinos and Av de la República, 323338)—was one of the first in the country, and the trains that run here seem as old as the station. The cars are typically dirty and uncomfortable, and the service is laboriously slow; the trip to Mexico City takes about 12 hours (as opposed to 6 hours by car or bus).

Getting Around Veracruz

Most of the important sights in downtown Veracruz are easily covered on foot. The best way to get around the state and the city is to hire a tour guide and driver, or rent a car and carry good road maps.

Buses Within the city, public buses run regularly along **Boulevard Manuel Avila Camacho,** the main waterfront thoroughfare from downtown to the outlying hotels. Open-sided wooden trolleys, replicas

of mule-driven vehicles used in the city in the 1800s, also run along the waterfront. The drivers sometimes comment on the sights, but do not offer formal tours. Reaching the outlying attractions in the state is more complicated, since bus service consists mainly of second-class buses that stop frequently en route. The **Terminal de Autobuses** (main bus terminal; 376790) in Veracruz City is at Avenida Díaz Mirón 1698 (between Av Aragon and Tuero Molina). The main bus lines covering the state are **ADO** (375522) and **UNO** (350783).

Driving Driving is fairly simple in both the city and the state of Veracruz, though the city streets do get congested on weekdays.

The car-rental agencies at **Aeropuerto Internacional Heriberto Jara** (see above) also have offices in city hotels.

Taxis Plenty of cabs are available; they usually park in front of the hotels, plazas, and beaches.

FYI

Accommodations Room rates in Veracruz are among the lowest in the country, especially at the downtown hotels. Rates are typically a bit higher at the hotels on the better beaches east of downtown. Reservations are essential during Carnival, Easter Week, and Mexican national holidays.

Climate Veracruz summers are hot and humid, while spring and fall are milder. High, wild winds called *nortes* blow from November through March, making the air feel cool even though the temperatures are high. Hurricane season usually occurs in September and October.

Publications Few English-language tourist publications are available. The tourism office (see "Visitors' Information Center," below) sometimes has copies of *Turisteando,* a small pamphlet with hotel and restaurant listings. Since the majority of tourists here are Mexican nationals, much of the existing visitors' information is written in Spanish.

Shopping Shops carrying high-quality folk art appear to be nonexistent in Veracruz City, where seashell knickknacks abound in the ticky-tacky artisans' market on the *malecón.* Vendors in the plaza sell pretty straw fans and figurines woven from vanilla beans. Locally grown coffee beans make another good gift.

Street Plan **Paseo del Malecón** (also named **Insurgentes**) runs along the downtown waterfront, becoming Boulevard Manuel Avila Camacho as it jogs at right angles at **Muro de Pescadores** (Fishers' Wall). The boulevard runs south of town past beaches and residential areas to the hotels at **Playa Mocambo** and on to the town of **Boca del Río.**

Time Zone Veracruz is on Central Time, two hours ahead of California and one hour behind New York.

Tours Visitors to Veracruz can choose from a wealth of fascinating excursions offered by an abundance of travel agencies ready to transport travelers in air-conditioned comfort. Finding an English-speaking guide can be a challenge, however. Most tours are quite reasonably priced, and more of a bargain if you can find others to share the cost. Among the most popular day-trip destinations are the village of **La Antigua**; the Totonac ruins of **Zempoala**; **Xalapa**, Veracruz's capital city; the picturesque town of **Tlacotalpan**; the **Los Tuxtlas** region; and **Lago Catemaco**. **El Tajín**, the archaeological site, can also be toured in a a day from Veracruz, but it's an exhausting journey of about five hours each way, and visitors are better off making an overnight excursion. Agencies also offer river rafting, sportfishing, mountain climbing, diving excursions, and a variety of city tours. For information contact the following:

Centro Reservaciones de Veracruz ....
.................................356422; 351607; fax 356423

Martín Sandoval Tours 353915

Veraventuras ....28/189579; fax 28/189680 in Xalapa

VIP Tours......................219975, 223315; fax 223315

Visitors' Information Center Veracruz City's **Oficina de Turismo** (Tourism Office) is located in the **Palacio Municipal** (City Hall; Plaza de Armas, 321999) and is open daily. The **Direccion General de Turismo del Estado de Veracruz** (State Tourism Office) is in Xalapa (Blvd Cristobal Colón 5, 28/128500 ext 130; fax 28/125936) and is open Monday through Friday.

Water Sports Though the water in the Gulf of Mexico isn't nearly as clear and inviting as that of the nearby **Caribbean**, it does attract serious divers. A series of reefs runs south along the shore from the port area to Boca del Río; another sits offshore from the town of Antón Lizardo, 20 kilometers (12 miles) southeast of Veracruz City. Shipwrecks in both areas are added attractions. There are a few dive shops in the city; for information contact **Dorado Divers** (Blvd Manuel Avila Camacho 865, 314305; fax 314305) or one of the agencies listed under "Tours" above.

Sportfishing enthusiasts are also drawn to the gulf's fertile waters, where they find an abundance of snapper. To arrange an excursion, contact the **Club de Yates** (Yacht Club; Blvd Manuel Avila Camacho and Paseo del Malecon, 320917).

Phone Book

Hospital IMSS Av Cuauhtémoc and Cervantes y Padilla, Veracruz City 349697, 322833, 380664

Red Cross...375500

Visitors' Information 321999

Central Veracruz State

Citlaltépetl (Mount Orizaba), a challenge irresistible to many mountain climbers, rises above central Veracruz State in a rich agricultural area where coffee, mango, and banana plantations dot the countryside and rivers rush through valleys to the sea. The ruins of **El Tajín** are this region's biggest attraction, drawing archaeology buffs from all over

the world. **Papantla,** the town nearest the ruins, is known for its *voladores* (flying dancers), who perform at fiestas and cultural centers throughout Mexico. **Xalapa,** the capital of the state of Veracruz, draws travelers to its excellent anthropology museum. While organized tours are available from Veracruz City to the ruins and cities of the center, most explorers will want more time than tours allow to discover the area's hidden waterfalls and traditional villages.

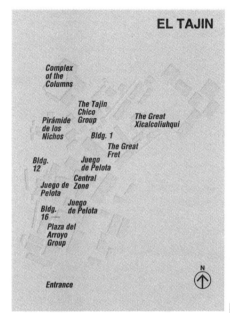

EL TAJIN

Complex of the Columns

The Tajin Chico
Pirámide Group   The Great
de los   Xicalcoliuhqui
Nichos   Bldg. 1
            The Great
            Fret
Bldg.   Juego
12   de Pelota
        Central
Juego de Zone
Pelota
        Juego
Bldg.   de Pelota
16 —
Plaza del
Arroyo
Group

N

Entrance

1 El Tajín Set amid a forest of banana and mango trees in a tropical valley, this is the most important archaeological site in Veracruz. Archaeologists are reluctant to say which group actually constructed the buildings scattered over some 16 square miles here, since those excavated thus far show influences of the Olmec, Huastec, Otomí, Maya, and Totonac civilizations. **El Tajín** was at its height in the Classic Period (AD 300 to 900), and the Totonac inhabited the site when the Spanish arrived there in 1785. Since excavations began in 1934, archaeologists have identified more than 200 buildings and numerous ball courts, although only about 20 structures have been excavated, and most of them have not yet been fully restored. **El Tajín** is not easily reached. It lies some 225 kilometers (140 miles) northwest of the city of Veracruz, and there are few tourist services in the area. Visitors either spend the night in the town of Papantla, 12 kilometers (seven miles) east of **El Tajín** (buses run from Papantla to the ruins) or make the arduous 10-hour round trip from Veracruz. Crowds are virtually nonexistent at the site, so visitors may roam about and photograph the buildings in relative solitude. The small visitors' center at the entrance has a restaurant, gift shop, rest rooms, and three-dimensional models that give visitors some idea of the enormous size of the site. Guides, some of whom speak English, are available here as well; it's worth the additional fee to have one escort you, since the few explanatory signs are printed in Spanish, and many of the edifices look like nothing more than green mounds with bits of columns and steps poking through the overgrowth. Be sure to bring water, snacks, bug repellent, and a hat. ♦ Admission; free on Sunday and holidays. Daily. Hwy 130 (12 km/7 miles west of Papantla). No phone

Within El Tajín:

Pirámide de los Nichos (Pyramid of the Niches) The most famous building at **El Tajín** is this exotic stone-and-adobe structure. The edifice is composed of six levels stacked in a pyramidal triangle. Each level contains rows of recessed niches; there are 365 niches in all, representing the number of days in the year. The residents of **El Tajín** are believed to have burned fires in all the niches—the flames flickering against the crimson and blue paint that once covered the building must have been awe-inspiring. A stairway that visitors are no longer allowed to climb leads to the top of the pyramid.

Juego de Pelota (Ball Court) There are at least 9 ball courts in **El Tajín** (some guides place the figure at nearly 20), reflecting the Olmec influence. Some archaeologists say this may have been a center for the game, in which two teams competed in a sport much like today's soccer—except that this game typically culminated in human sacrifice. Bas-relief panels on the walls around the court depict warriors following the rituals of the game.

Edificio de las Columnas (Building of the Columns) Visitors are allowed to climb the stairway to the top of this pyramid, where you can get a sense of **El Tajín** as an actual city. From the vantage point at the top, it's evident that the buildings—now under great mounds of earth covered with grass and trees—are laid out with a certain symmetry. This particular structure is believed to have been one of the last pyramids built at the site.

Los Voladores (Flying Pole Dancers) Though the *voladores* come from Papantla, the best place to see them perform is at the ruins. Their pole, 30 meters high, sits in front of the visitors' center near the entrance; if you hear the sound of flutes, head in that direction. The dancers are Totonac Indians, dressed in red, blue, and white vests and pants and wearing conical hats decorated with ribbons and tiny mirrors. Five dancers climb to the top of the pole, where one stays on a platform at the top, playing a flute and dancing. The other dancers, with ropes tied around their waists, drop backward from the top of the pole and spiral down, spinning around and around as they gradually unwind their ropes. ♦ Donation. No set schedule, but the dancers typically perform daily at midday

2 **Papantla** The nearest town to **El Tajín**, Papantla is best known for its *voladores* (flying pole dancers) and its fields of *vanilla planifolia,* the vanilla plant. A large concrete vanilla bean marks the entrance to the city, where the souvenir of choice is a flower or figurine made from intertwined vanilla beans. Few outsiders would visit this town of some 160,000 residents were it not for its proximity to the ruins; services are minimal, and the hotels less than inviting. Still, staying here beats trying to drive from Veracruz and back in one day. ♦ Hwys 130 and 180 (235 km/147 miles north of Veracruz City)

Pirámide de los Nichos, El Tajín

L.L. BRENGELMAN

Within Papantla:

Hotel Premier $ The best choice among the town's few hotels is this modern 20-room inn, built in 1990. The rooms have air-conditioning, telephones, and TVs; some have balconies that look out over the main plaza. There's no restaurant, but there are a few small cafes nearby. ♦ No credit cards accepted. Enrique 103 (at the main plaza). 784/21645, 20080; fax 784/21062

3 Xalapa (Jalapa) Capital of the state of Veracruz, Xalapa is called the "City of Flowers" and the "Athens of Mexico." Set in the hills northwest of Veracruz City, the city is home to one of Mexico's finest museums (**Museo de Antropología de Jalapa,** see below), the state government offices, and the **University of Veracruz.** Narrow old streets wind up and down the city's hills, making driving here unpleasant, especially on weekdays. But it's worth spending a night or two anyway—you can easily devote half a day to the museum and another half to other sights in the area. The heart of the city is the pretty **Parque Júarez,** which has lovely rose and gardenia gardens. On a clear day you'll see **Citlaltépetl** (Mount Orizaba) on the horizon. Wander the streets and alleyways, and stop for coffee at one of the cafes along Callejón del Diamante, a narrow pedestrian alley where the college students congregate. ♦ Hwy 140 (104 km/64 miles northwest of Veracruz City)

Within Xalapa:

Museo de Antropología de Jalapa (Jalapa Museum of Anthropology)
Architect **Edward Durrell Stone,** who also designed the Kennedy Center in Washington, DC, created this magnificent home for artifacts found at the many archaeological sites in Veracruz. The first piece you see upon entering the low-lying gray stone building is a gigantic Olmec head, one of seven in the museum's collection. Each of these heads, which weigh up to 27 tons, represents the face of a warrior with negroid features; all have different expressions.

The museum is laid out in several descending levels, each with a courtyard garden filled with bamboo, ferns, and large sculptures. Each level is devoted to artifacts from a particular culture—either Olmec, Huastec, or Totonac—and the pieces displayed are among the finest you'll see anywhere. There's a small book-shop near the entrance, and a cafe on the second floor. ♦ Admission. Tu-Su. Av Jalapa and 1 de Mayo. 28/150920

Hotel María Victoria $ A favorite of tour groups, this hotel has 96 rooms and 18 suites in an unattractive white-and-pink high-rise building just one block from the plaza. The rooms are large, clean, and serviceable; many have good views of the plaza and city streets. The pool is a major plus on muggy days, and

the restaurant serves adequate meals. ♦ Av Zaragoza 6 (between Allende and Sebastián Camacho). 28/186011; fax 28/180501

La Casona del Beaterio ★★$ Close to the plaza and decorated with old photos of Xalapa, this casual eatery is the best place in the neighborhood for hearty meals of chicken or beef served with beans, rice, and fried plantains. Be sure to sample the *picaditas* (small rounds of fried cornmeal filled with beans). ♦ Mexican ♦ Daily breakfast, lunch, and dinner. Av Zaragoza 20 (between Carrillo Puerto and Revolución). 28/182119

La Casa de Mama ★★$ A few blocks from the plaza, this attractive blue-and-white restaurant sits on a busy thoroughfare (take advantage of the valet parking if you're driving). Regulars swear the *queso fundido* (melted cheese served with tortillas) is the best in the state, and the seafood and meat dishes are served in generous portions. ♦ Mexican ♦ M, Su lunch; Tu-Sa lunch and dinner. Blvd Manuel Avila Camacho 113 (between Avs Adolfo Ruíz Cortines and Jalapa). 28/173144

Fiesta Inn $$ This 120-room chain hotel is a good base for those with cars who want easy access in and out of town. It's on the highway at the southeast entrance to the city. The modern buildings, with faux colonial-hacienda facades, have thoroughly up-to-date interiors, with powerful air-conditioning, English-speaking clerks, and large rooms with satellite TV, phones, bathtubs, and showers. The pool is tucked away in a nice garden, and the restaurant is better than you'd expect at a chain hotel. Another advantage is the US phone number for reservations, a rarity in these parts. ♦ Hwy 140 and Blvd Cristóbal Colón. 28/127920, 800/343.7821; fax 28/127946

4 Coatepec Villages and towns that depend upon coffee production dot the landscape of northern Veracruz. This is one of the most pleasing, with cobblestone streets, restored colonial mansions, and the aroma of roasted coffee. Gardenias bloom in outdoor gardens, orchids thrive in greenhouses, and mangos, sugarcane, and coffee grow in abundance. If you have time to visit only one of the coffee towns, choose this one. ♦ 15 km/9 miles southeast of Xalapa

Within Coatepec:

Posada Coatepec $$$ One of the most charming small inns in Mexico, the posada makes for a luxurious base camp from which to explore the region. Formerly a private home, it now offers 24 guest rooms and a free-standing villa. Each room is individually decorated with folk art, hand-

HOTEL

POSADA
COATEPEC

painted tiles, wood-beamed ceilings, and furnishings and rugs crafted in the area; all have air-conditioning and satellite TV. The villa is a complete two-story house with a big front lawn, two bedrooms, dining and living rooms, and a full kitchen in a separate building. The restaurant **María Enriqueta** is open for all meals and offers both regional and international cuisine. The grounds and pool are beautiful. ◆ Hidalgo 9 (at Aldama). 28/160544; fax 28/160040

Within Posada Coatepec:

Veraventuras One of the best adventure-tour agencies in the region has an office at the posada and another in Xalapa. Guides offer river-rafting, bird watching, and ecotourism trips to the rivers, waterfalls, colonial cities, and haciendas in the state of Veracruz. ◆ 28/160544; fax 28/160040. Also at: Santos Degollado 8, Int. 8, Xalapa, Veracruz 91000. 28/189579, 28/189779; fax 28/189680

5 Hacienda El Lencero A gorgeous restored country estate just southeast of Xalapa, the hacienda is well worth a leisurely visit if only to enjoy its atmosphere of genteel country living. The estate is named after a Spanish soldier who owned the property in the mid-1500s, when it encompassed some 4,000 acres of ranch land. Its more famous resident was Antonio López de Santa Anna, who served as the president of Mexico 11 times and purchased this country refuge in 1842. In 1981, the state acquired the hacienda and 16 acres of land around it and gradually began restoring the buildings and their furnishings. Today the whole complex of main house, chapel, stables, and outbuildings, is a museum and one of the finest restored haciendas in the country. Mexican, European, and Asian antiques fill the rooms, causing some to call it the "Museum of Furniture." The chapel, main house, and servants' quarters are surrounded by ancient oaks, their branches covered with epiphytic plants. It's easy to spend two hours here, especially if you engage the (free) services of one of the excellent guides (who speak only Spanish). ◆ Admission. Tu-Su. Hwy 140 (14 km/9 miles southeast of Xalapa). No phone

---

The average Mexican consumes more than half a kilo (about one pound) of tortillas per day.

Restaurants/Clubs: Red **Hotels:** Blue
Shops/ Outdoors: Green **Sights/Culture:** Black

6 Zempoala (Cempoala) Much more accessible than **El Tajín,** the Totonac ruins of **Zempoala** date primarily from the Classic Period (AD 300-900), though some were built in the 14th and 15th centuries. The site is unimpressive when compared with **El Tajín,** however, and while a half-dozen buildings have been restored there are no signs identifying or describing them. The site is thought to have been a ceremonial and astronomical center for the Totonac, who still inhabited the buildings when the Spaniards appeared in 1519. Cortés is said to have set up temporary headquarters in the **Templo Mayor** (Main Temple), a modest pyramid facing the entryway. The **Templo de las Caritas** (Temple of Little Faces) was once decorated with clay skulls and faces. For many, the most significant structure is the **Circle of the Equinox,** believed to be a center of cosmic energy. The waist-high ring of pillars seems unremarkable, but believers visit it by the hundreds on the winter solstice (21 December), when they say they sense the presence of an otherworldly power.

The ruins sit in the small village of the same name; in fact, many of the humble houses along the dirt streets stand beside overgrown mounds that could cover pre-Columbian buildings. Visitors pay their fee at a small shack at the entrance to the ruins, where guides are sometimes available. There are rest rooms by the entrance, but no food concessions; bring your own water, snacks, and toilet paper. ◆ Admission; free Sunday and holidays. Daily. Hwy 180 (40 km/25 miles north of Veracruz City). No phone

7 La Antigua An enormous ceiba tree at the entrance to this town bears the sign "La Ceiba de la Noche Feliz" (The Ceiba of the Happy Night). Legend has it that when Hernán Cortés first arrived in the state of Veracruz he found refuge here in a protected part of Río Huitzalpan and tied his ships up to this tree. Over the centuries the river has meandered away from this spot and is now closer to the center of the small present-day village. Among the noteworthy sights in La Antigua are the modest white-and-blue church at the entrance to the village—said to have been the first Catholic church in the Americas—and the ruins of the **Casa de Cortés** (House of Cortés) in the center of the village, which is not what its name implies. While some say Cortés lived in the house when he first arrived in the Americas, more knowledgeable guides describe it as an administrative headquarters and storage place for goods being shipped back to Spain. A long suspension bridge hangs over the river; at the base of the bridge vendors sell fresh mangos carved into flowers and trinkets made from the wood of coffee trees. ◆ Hwy 180 (28 km/17 miles north of Veracruz City)

Veracruz City

8 Castillo de San Juan de Ulúa (Castle of San Juan de Ulúa) As fascinating as it is gray and foreboding, this fortress has served as a dock, fort, prison, and presidential home since it was built by the Spaniards in the late 1600s. Isolete de San Juan de Ulúa, the islet on which the castle stands, was named by explorer Juan de Grijalva, who discovered it on the feast day of St. John the Baptist (24 June) in 1518. German engineer J. Frank is credited with having designed the enclosed fortress, which was completed in 1692; for much of the next two centuries its cannons repelled invasions by pirates and the French and American navies. In the late 1800s the fortress was a horrid, deadly prison; the small bridge that led to the *castillo* was dubbed **El Puento de los Suspiros** (Bridge of Sighs) because those who crossed it knew they would never escape the disease, famine, and flooding for which the prison was infamous. In 1915 Mexican President Venustiano Carranza claimed **San Juan de Ulúa** as a presidential residence, and it now serves as a museum.

The drive to the fort is interesting as well, taking you through the port area and huge lots filled with trucks and storage tanks for wheat, aluminum, sugar, and molasses, which leaves a lingering scent in the air. ♦ Admission. Daily. Av San Juan de Ulúa (northeast of Av Miguel A. de Quevedo). 385151

9 Edificios de Correos y Telégrafos (Telegraph and Post Office Buildings) Neo-Classical in style, these adjoining buildings were designed by **Salvador Echegaray** in the 1920s, as was the solemn gray **Aduana Maritima** (Maritime Customs House) next door. These impressive buildings, along with the tiled train station, all face the Plaza de la República and the Plaza de la Concordia, both of which have fountains and benches and are perfect for a break from touring. ♦ Av de la República (just southeast of Montesinos). No phone

10 Plaza de Armas Visitors quickly become addicted to Veracruz's main plaza (also referred to as the *zócalo*), one of the liveliest in a country filled with great parks. The plaza teems with people, music, and vendors throughout the day, but it truly comes to life after the military band lowers the flag to the Mexican national anthem at twilight. From then until near dawn the action gets more and more intense, as mariachis, marimba players, and regional groups play side by side at outdoor cafes. There's always something happening here. Students from local dance schools perform the local *danzón* on Tuesday, Thursday, and Saturday nights, swaying in a style that's similar to Cuban ballroom dancing. And you never know what sort of band might take hold of the center stage, which replaces the kiosk common in most Mexican plazas. Birds roosting in the palm and laurel trees add their chirping to the clamor, while church bells chime seemingly whenever they please. The plaza is framed by the **Palacio Municipal** (Municipal Palace; home of the tourist information office), the **Catedral Veracruz** (Veracruz Cathedral), and a variety of hotels and restaurants. ♦ Av Independencia (between Zamora and Av M. Lerdo)

11 Hotel Colonial $ Popular with tour groups who want to be close to the plaza, this property has 208 rooms and suites in various stages of repair. Guests face a tough decision here—those who desire a room overlooking the plaza must take into consideration the accompanying noise, which lasts well into the wee hours of the morning. Rooms at the back of the hotel look out onto walls or the enclosed parking lot, or have no windows at all and seem stuffy even with air-conditioning. The swimming pool is indoors, on the second floor in a dreary room, but the restaurant is cool and colorful and has some tables outside by the plaza. ♦ Av M. Lerdo 117 (between Avs Zaragoza and Independencia). 320193, 324313; fax 322465

11 Hotel Imperial $$ The grande dame of the plaza's hotels (built in 1794) is remarkable for its stained-glass elevator and skylight and its Old World ambience. Some of the 421 rooms and suites have been remodeled, and the best units are the bilevel suites at the front of the hotel, which feature iron balconies and claw-foot tubs; all rooms have telephones and satellite TV. While the small indoor pool doesn't encourage lounging, it's a good size for swimming laps. The hotel's sidewalk cafe is one of the busiest spots on the plaza in the evenings. ♦ Av M. Lerdo 153 (between Avs Zaragoza and Independencia). 311741, 311866

12 Quality Inn Calinda Veracruz $$ Managed by the Calinda chain, this establishment is the nicest hotel right at the plaza. The colonial-style exterior has a pleasing peach-and-cream color scheme, and the 166 rooms and suites have immaculate white walls and mint-green furnishings. The pool is tiny, but the second-story terrace restaurant is the ideal spot for watching the goings on in the plaza below. ♦ Avs Independencia and M. Lerdo. 312233, 311124, 800/228.5151; fax 315134

VERACRUZ CITY

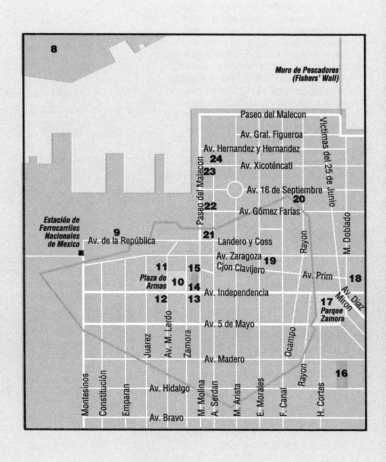

8

Muro de Pescadores
(Fishers' Wall)

Paseo del Malecon

Av. Gral. Figueroa

Av. Hernandez y Hernandez

24 Av. Xicoténcatl

23

Av. 16 de Septiembre

22 20 Av. Gómez Farías

Estación de
Ferrocarriles
Nacionales
de Mexico

9 Av. de la República

21 Landero y Coss

Av. Zaragoza 19

11 15 Cjon Clavijero

Plaza de
Armas 10 14 Av. Prim 18

12 13 Av. Independencia 17
Parque
Zamora

Av. 5 de Mayo

Av. Madero 16

Av. Hidalgo

Av. Bravo

Paseo del Malecon

Victimas del 25 de Junio

M. Doblado

Rayon

Av. Diaz Miron

Juarez
Av. M. Lerdo
Zamora
Ocampo
Rayon

Montesinos
Constitución
Emparan
M. Molina
A. Serdan
M. Arista
E. Morales
F. Canal
H. Cortes

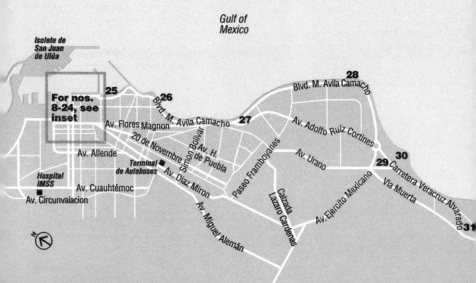

Gulf of
Mexico

Isolete de
San Juan
de Ulúa

25

28

Blvd. M. Avila Camacho

26

For nos.
8-24, see
inset

Av. Flores Magnon

27

Av. Adolfo Ruíz Cortines

30

29

Carretera Veracruz Alvarado

Av. Allende

20 de Novembre

Simon Bolivar

Av. H.
de Puebla

Paseo Framboyanes

Av. Urano

Via Muerta

31

Terminal
de Autobuses

Av. Diaz Miron

Hospital
IMSS

Av. Cuauhtémoc

Av. Circunvalacion

Calzada
Lazaro Cardenas

Av. Ejercito Mexicano

Av. Miguel Alemán

N

13 Cafe del Portal ★★★$ Though not directly facing the plaza, the sidewalk tables at this landmark cafe are the most popular seats in the neighborhood. Gentlemen in sport shirts or guayaberas take the same seats at the same time each day to indulge in coffee and gossip, while weary office workers ritualistically stop in for a cup of caffeine and a piece of *budín* (bread pudding with raisins and cinnamon topped with chocolate sauce). The cavernous inside dining room grows cacophonous at lunchtime, when the *comida corrida* (a low-cost full meal) draws crowds. Don't miss the sepia photos of earlier times on the walls. This popular cafe was previously affiliated with **Gran Cafe de la Parroquia** (see page 126), and infrequent visitors still get the two confused. Both are worth visiting. ♦ Mexican ♦ Daily breakfast, lunch, and dinner. No credit cards accepted. Av Independencia and Zamora. 312759

14 Catedral de Nuestra Señora de la Asunción (Cathedral of Our Lady of the Assumption) This moderately elaborate parish church was designated a cathedral in 1963, although it lacks the two towers typical of buildings with such standing. The original stone structure was completed in 1731, but additions and improvements, including a dome covered with Pueblan tiles and five naves, weren't finished until 1809. ♦ M. Molina and Av Independencia. 324829

15 La Paella ★★$ One of the least expensive restaurants on the plaza, this narrow cafe decorated with bullfighting posters and photos of Spain serves great paella (of course), along with good regional cuisine. Try to snag one of the few tables by the front windows overlooking the street. ♦ Spanish ♦ Daily breakfast, lunch, and dinner. Zamora 138 (between Avs Zaragoza and Independencia). 320322

16 Mercado Hidalgo One of the best Mexican markets, this block-deep, indoor and outdoor emporium is filled with fascinating objects and scenes. The artfully arrayed produce stands contain the region's best offerings— giant mangos, tiny bananas, fragrant papayas, and pineapples. Parrots and canaries are displayed in bamboo cages; iguanas tethered with leather leashes await their demise in a cauldron of boiling water (locals love tender iguana meat). Stands outside the market feature roasted coffee beans from the various coffee plantations in the north; purchase a few different kinds for a sampling. ♦ Daily. Soto (between Avs Madero and Hidalgo). No phone

17 Parque Zamora This small urban park consists mostly of pretty tree-lined paths lined with benches. Dances are held here on Sunday evenings, though you might spot a few couples swaying to the marimba beat of an unscheduled musical performance nearly any time of the week. ♦ Avs Diaz Miron and Independencia

18 Capilla del Santo Cristo del Buen Viaje (Chapel of Christ of the Good Voyage) Since the time of the Spaniards, sailors have been stopping by this small white chapel before setting off to sea. The building, which looks much like a Spanish mission church, once stood outside the city walls. The walls have since fallen, and the city has grown around the chapel, which now serves as a neighborhood church. ♦ M. Doblado (between Avs Prim and 20 de Noviembre). No phone

19 Museo de la Ciudad (City Museum) A typical 19th-century Veracruz mansion has been turned into a good museum devoted to the history and people of the city. Of particular interest are the exhibits on Carnival and other regional customs and the African room dedicated to the slaves brought to Veracruz by the Spaniards in the 16th century. ♦ Admission. Tu-Sun 9AM-3PM. Av Zaragoza 397 (between F. Canal and E. Morales). 318410

20 Bastión de San Diego (Bastion of St. James) This 17th-century bastion—one of the few remnants of the system of forts and stone walls that the Spaniards erected around the city—now houses a small museum. The stars of the collection are 64 pre-Columbian and colonial-era artifacts known as "the jewels of the fishermen." Though various legends surround the discovery of this cache of figurines and jewelry, all versions of the story claim that a fisherman found them in a sunken ship. The government confiscated the pieces from him in 1976 and put them on display here. ♦ Admission. Tu-Su. Bounded by Avs 16 de Septiembre and Gómez Farías, and Rayón and F. Canal

RESTAURANTES PARDIÑOS

21 Pardiños ★★★★$$ A pink colonial-era building with white awnings houses this fine seafood restaurant, which many say is the best in the city. Bright cobalt-blue paint frames the streetside windows in the white dining room, where ceiling fans manage to stir the air enough for comfort. The waiters kindly explain the menu, which is packed with such regional dishes as *salpicon de jaiba* (a blend of shredded crab, cilantro, and onion) and the traditional *huachinango veracruzano* (red snapper baked with a sauce of chilies, tomatoes, and capers). The seafood-stuffed coconut is packed with octopus, crab, and white cheese, and the lobster comes with the meat already cut up and restuffed in the shell.

The original **Pardiños** restaurant, near the beach in Boca del Río, opened in 1950 and is also a delightful place to eat. ♦ Seafood ♦ Daily lunch and dinner. Landero y Coss 146 (at Paseo del Malecón). 317571, 314881. Also at: Zamora 40, Boca del Río. 860135

22 Gran Cafe de la Parroquia ★★★$
You just can't say you've done Veracruz until you've indulged in the coffee ritual at this venerable cafe. The coffee starts out in elegant chrome-and-brass urns from Turin, Italy, and then is poured into large aluminum kettles. Waiters roam the vast dining hall with their pots, filling tall glasses with an inch or two of the potent brew. The customer then raps the glass with a spoon, the signal for another waiter with a kettle of steaming hot milk to arrive. The customer signals how much milk he or she wants to make the perfect *cafe lechero*, and the ritual is complete. Toasted *bambas* (sweet rolls dusted with sugar) are the ideal coffee accompaniment, though there are plenty of sandwiches and regional entrées on the menu as well. ♦ Regional ♦ Daily breakfast, lunch, and dinner. No credit cards accepted. Av Gómez Farías 34 (at Paseo del Malecón). 322584. Also at: Paseo de Malecón 340 (at Av 16 de Septiembre). 321855

23 Paseo del Malecón One of the most interesting and picturesque places to stroll in downtown Veracruz is along the port's waterfront. Navy ships, fishing boats, tour boats, and skiffs all rock side by side, and if you're here at the right time you might see fishermen unloading tons of fresh shrimp. A massive monument to the fishing industry sits in a small park opposite the waterfront, and vendors hawk *volobanes* (delicious puff pastries filled with ham, cheese, fish, or pineapple) from wheeled carts. ♦ Between Muro de Pescadores and Landero y Coss

23 Hotel Emporio $$ A spectacular view of the port and lavish decor featuring crystal chandeliers and gorgeous murals covering the walls make this the most appealing hotel downtown. The **Presidential Suite,** at the top of the 202-room high-rise, comes complete with a bright red hot tub and staggering views and costs less than a deluxe room in the newer hotels outside town. The standard rooms are also great bargains. Other perks on the premises: three swimming pools, a full gym with sauna, a business center, and a good restaurant. ♦ Paseo del Malecón 210 (at Av Xicoténcatl). 320022; fax 312261

24 Faro Venustiano Carranza (Venustiano Carranza Lighthouse) The second lighthouse in Veracruz has been transformed into a museum dedicated to native son Venustiano Carranza, who served as president of Mexico from 1917 to 1920 and was one of the authors of Mexico's Constitution. The museum includes rooms furnished as his office and bedroom, using furniture from his home, and other memorabilia, including a diagram of his bullet-ridden body (he was assassinated in 1920). ♦ Free. Tu-Su. Paseo del Malecón (between Avs Hernández y Hernández and Xicoténcatl). No phone

25 La Bamba ★★$$ Of the many seafood restaurants along the waterfront, this place stands out for its food and ambience. The building sits on stilts above the water right by the most popular beach in town, and music either blares over the loudspeakers or is provided by musicians seeking tips. The fish- and shellfish-based menu features lobster, shrimp with garlic, and several preparations of the ubiquitous pompano and red snapper. Stop by for a weekend lunch, and you'll find yourself dining amidst local families. ♦ Seafood ♦ Tu-Su lunch and dinner. Blvd Manuel Avila Camacho and Zapata. 325355

26 Acuario Veracruz (Veracruz Aquarium) Designed by **Hiroshi Kamio** and opened in 1992, this aquarium, set within a waterfront shopping mall, is the finest in Mexico. Visitors enter through a small tropical forest complete with waterfalls, ferns, and resident toucans, then pass by ponds filled with turtles. It's easy to become mesmerized by the many tanks of fresh- and saltwater fish—don't miss the dainty seahorses, exotic lionfish, and prehistoric-looking piranhas. Kids enjoy the enormous pilot whale skeleton and the tables of shells, skulls, and bones they can touch and examine. ♦ Admission. Daily. Blvd Manuel Avila Camacho and Av Xicoténcatl. 327984

Within the Acuario Veracruz:
VIPS ★$ A cool, comfortable spot for everything from ice cream to steaks, this coffee shop–style restaurant is part of a national chain. The sandwiches, soups, and enchiladas are remarkably good, though the dining room is rather sterile. The restaurant's shopping area stocks all the basics, from aspirin to batteries to snacks. ♦ Mexican/American ♦ Daily breakfast, lunch, and dinner; F-Sa open 24 hours. 328011

27 La Casita Blanca/Museo Augustín Lara

This was the home of Veracruz native Augustín Lara, one of the most venerated composers in Mexico. At the core of Mexican popular culture in the 1930s and 1940s, Lara's music expressed the soulful, sensual rhythm of his city. He is best known for his song *Veracruz,* written in 1936, which has become the unofficial anthem of the city and state and moves sentimental souls to tears. In 1992 Veracruz honored its native son by turning the musician's modest white house into a museum. Among the items on display are a copy of his trademark white piano, along with photos and mementos of his career. ◆ Admission. Tu-Su. Av Adolfo Ruíz Cortines and Blvd Manuel Avila Camacho. No phone

27 La Mansion ★★★$$

More elegant than most local restaurants, this steak house adjoins and shares the same address as the home of composer Augustín Lara. The ambience here is refined, yet comfortable, and the steaks are the best in town. The seafood also is well prepared, especially the tender grilled lobster. This is a good spot for a special night out; gentlemen will feel more comfortable in a jacket and tie, though they are not required. ◆ Steak house/Seafood ◆ Daily dinner. Av Adolfo Ruíz Cortines and Blvd Manuel Avila Camacho. 311338

28 Fiesta Americana Veracruz $$

Of all the Veracruz hotels built to accommodate business travelers in recent years, this one stands out as a great place to vacation as well as conduct meetings. The massive terra-cotta structure looks somewhat intimidating from the street, since it sits on a long stretch of undeveloped beach (other hotels are expected to sprout up here eventually). Inside, though, it's an oasis of comfort and serenity, with vast marble halls and 233 rooms and suites, most with balconies and ocean views. The rooms are the most modern in town, with voice mail and direct-dial phones, satellite TV, bathtubs and showers, in-room safes, and a sensor that turns off the lights and the air-conditioning when you leave the room. The **Café La Fiesta** beside the indoor/outdoor swimming pool hosts a bodacious buffet breakfast every morning, and serves wonderful green salads (hard to find in these parts), decent hamburgers, and a great *pescado relleno* (fresh fish wrapped around crab and shrimp and topped with melted cheese) at lunch and dinner. The more formal **El Delfín** restaurant is the place for thick steaks, lobster, and tempting pastries. ◆ Blvd Manuel Avila Camacho and Bacalao. 898989, 800/343.7821; fax 898904

29 World Trade Center Expover

Nearly everyone uses the English name of this modern convention center, which forms the hub of a hotel and shopping center complex. Along with meeting rooms and halls, the center has a cafe and travel agency. The enclosed, air-conditioned **Las Americas** shopping center next door is a great place to escape the midday heat. ◆ Av Adolfo Ruíz Cortines 3497 (at Hwy 180). 214186, 377107; fax: 214186, 377107

29 Continental Plaza $$

As at most of Veracruz's new hotels, business travelers are the main clientele here. However, tourists and vacationers may find they can take advantage of reasonably priced package deals and end up with a luxurious room for less than they expected. The 235 rooms and suites are decorated in pale pastels, and the lavish pool area makes up for the lack of a beach. Pluses include easy access to the highways and airport, an on-site restaurant, and plenty of shopping opportunities at the plaza next door. ◆ Av Adolfo Ruíz Cortines 3497 (at Hwy 180). 890505, 800/342.2644; fax 890501

30 Mocambo $$

Once the most lavish resort in the area, this property has been overshadowed by its newer neighbors. The 123 rooms and suites are comfortable, if unimaginatively decorated, but the grounds are still wonderful, with a jungle of trees and flowers surrounding the pool. The restaurant, **La Fragata**, is worth finding for its courteous service and proximity to the gardens, which are terraced down a hillside to the city's best beach. ◆ Blvd Adolfo Ruíz Cortines 4000 (at Hwy 180). 220333, 220205; fax 220212

31 Boca del Río

Not long ago this small fishing village on the mouth of the Río Jamapa was considered a distant outpost, a day trip for city dwellers. Now Veracruz has spread right to the edge of Boca del Río. The town is best known for its seafood cafes, packed along narrow streets by the waterfront. Stop by the original **Pardiños** (see page 125) for a sampling of the local cuisine. ◆ Hwy 180 (south of Veracruz)

Although the site may not be open for tourism until early in the next century, in 1994 a major discovery was made of a "lost" pre-Columbian city on the gulf coast northwest of Veracruz. Named El Pital, after the nearest village, the ancient city sprawls over 40 square miles and originally had more than a hundred structures—including some pyramids over 130 feet high—that had been completely hidden by dense jungle vegetation. It will take archaeologists many years to completely uncover the city.

Southern Veracruz State

Tropical forests, lakes, lagoons, and river valleys make southern Veracruz a naturalist's paradise. Volcanoes and mountains rise above the countryside, where small rural roads travel from sea level to an altitude of 5,000 feet. Traditional little villages sit beside wide, wild rivers lined with tropical plants; botanists say there are at least 3,000 different species in the region. Travelers typically head south from **Veracruz City** to **Lago Catemaco,** Mexico's third-largest lake. A stop at the town of **Tlacotalpan** is imperative for its gorgeous, well-preserved, colonial-era buildings and the traditional lifestyle of its inhabitants. **Santiago Tuxtla** and **San Andres Tuxtla** are typical southern towns surrounded by tobacco plantations. The big attraction here, though, is Lago Catemaco, ringed by small villages and hideaway hotels. City dwellers regularly escape the coastal heat for Catemaco's fresh mountain air, soothing, verdant scenery, and excellent cuisine based on the fish from the lake and nearby rivers.

32 Tlacotalpan So picturesque and culturally unique is this small town that it should be protected as a historic landmark. Located at the edge of the Río Papaloapan (Papaloapan River), Tlacotalpan was a thriving river port after the Spaniards arrived in the 16th century, when vessels from Cuba, Cartagena, and Europe brought furnishings, musical instruments, and other luxury items into Mexico. The town's prosperity dwindled in the 19th century, when the railroad replaced the river as the country's main means of transporting goods. But Tlacotalpan's residents never lost pride in their town, and to this day they continue to follow age-old customs and traditions. Thus, the milkman still delivers his milk from the back of a burro, and plant vendors drag wagons loaded with blooming roses down cobblestone streets. Most of the buildings in town are well preserved and painted in the traditional manner: in vivid blues, yellows, pinks, and greens. Residents are proud to show visitors their homes, which are usually filled with European-style paintings and wood and wicker furnishings hand-crafted locally. The town is particularly captivating in early February during the **Fiestas de la Candelaría** celebrations. Photographers beware: You'll have a hard time dragging yourself away. ◆ Hwy 175 (south of Hwy 180)

33 Santiago Tuxtla Founded in 1525, this small town filled with white stucco mansions was once the regional capital of southern Veracruz. A huge Olmec head weighing some 40 tons was found here; perhaps its weight has kept it from being moved to a major museum, as it sits right in town, a reminder of the region's

cultural roots. Movie fans may recognize the pretty main plaza, featured in the film *Romancing the Stone.* The market, located right across the street from the plaza, is filled with regional produce including thumb-size bananas and large juicy mangos. ◆ Hwy 180 (southeast of Hwy 175)

Within Santiago Tuxtla:

Museo Regional Tuxteco (Regional Museum of the Tuxtlas) Facing the main plaza and housed in a colonial mansion, this small museum holds a modest display of Olmec artifacts. ◆ Admission; free Sunday. Daily. Circuito Angel Carbajal and Parque Juárez. 294/70196

Hotel Castellanos $ Travelers longing to spend a night or two in small-town bliss will be delighted with this one-of-a-kind hotel, where the characters played by Kathleen Turner and Michael Douglas hid out in the film *Romancing the Stone.* The white building with its circular brick tower faces the main plaza; inside, a domed ceiling covers the spiral stairway leading to the 53 simple rooms, some with balconies facing the plaza. The hotel has a small cafe, and there are several other modest eateries in the neighborhood. ◆ No credit cards accepted. Comonfort and Av 5 de Mayo. 294/70200, 294/70300, 294/70400

34 San Andres Tuxtla The neighboring town to Santiago Tuxtla has a similar style of architecture, and is known among cigar aficionados for its *puros* (handmade cigars). The most famous factory is **Tabacos San Andres** (Blvd 5 de Febrero 10, 294/21200; fax 294/21628), which offers free tours Monday through Saturday. The locally grown tobacco is said to produce some of the finest cigars in the world, and the San Andres label is respected internationally. The best of the cigars are quite expensive; for a more modest souvenir pick up a box of the vanilla-scented cigarillos. ◆ Hwy 180 (east of Santiago Tuxtla)

35 Catemaco The combination of gorgeous mountain scenery and Mexico's third-largest lake makes this a popular vacation destination for city dwellers and folks from all over Mexico. The region is known for its tranquillity, nature preserves, and *brujos* (witches), whose customs are said to date back to pre-Columbian times. Locals are unwilling to impart much information on the witches themselves, but don't hesitate to capitalize on the phenomena in naming their businesses. The town is also known for its celebration of the Feast of St. Carmen on 16 July, when pilgrims arrive by the thousands. You can't visit Catemaco without taking a boat tour of Lago Catemaco; check with the **Cooperativa de Lanchas** (Boat Cooperative; Blvd de Malecón, 294/30662, 294/30081). Tours of an hour or more take you to several islands in the lake, including Monkey Island, where a colony of macaques has lived since they were brought here from Thailand in 1979. Though it's easy to visit Catemaco on a day trip from Veracruz, you might want to spend a night or two at one of the fine inns on the lake. ♦ Lago Catemaco

Within Catemaco:

Restaurante 7 Brujas ★★★$ The best seats in town are in the second-floor, open-air dining room of this seafood restaurant located across the street from the lake. One of the specialties is *carne de chango,* which translates directly as monkey meat but is actually smoked pork. Most diners stick with the seafood—*mojarra en chili y limón* (white fish with chilies and lime), *jaibas rellenas* (stuffed crabs), or *langostinos* (lake crayfish). As the menu says: *¡Todo esta Riquisimo!* (Everything is delicious!). Musicians play typical *jarocho* tunes on guitars and harps, and diners don't restrain themselves from jumping up to dance. ♦ Seafood ♦ Daily lunch and dinner. Blvd de Malecón. 30157

Casa Hotel Playa Azul $ Excellent bird watching is an added attraction for early risers at this jungle-shrouded hotel. Serious bird-watchers settle in for days during the winter months, when up to 80 species can be spotted. The hotel's 80 rooms are comfortably furnished with blue walls, two double beds, floor-to-ceiling windows, and heavy drapes.

Amenities include a pool, restaurant, bicycle rental, and ecological tours (for an added fee). ♦ Carretera a Sontecompan (east of Hwy 180). 294/30001; fax 294/30042

Hotel La Finca $ One of the prettiest hotels on the lake, this property has 20 rooms in air-conditioned cabanas by the shore. The restaurant is popular with tour groups during the day, but in the evening the buses leave, the birds come out, and you feel as if you're surrounded by nature. ♦ Hwy 180. 294/30322; fax 294/30430

 Nanciyaga Officially known as the **Proyecto Ecologico Educacional Nanciyaga** (Ecological and Educational Project Nanciyaga), this tropical rain forest reserve is privately owned and has been gently developed as a sort of New Age retreat. Dirt pathways lead through the forest to a circle of simple shacks on stilts, where visitors may camp overnight for a fee. Near the huts is a replica of a *temazcal* sweat lodge; farther down the path is a large natural pool of crystal-clear spring water. Visitors can sign up for mineral baths, mineralized mud facials, massage, drum classes, chiropractic sessions, and even spiritual cleansing sessions with a shaman, or walk the rain forest trails as long as they wish. Nanciyaga was the setting for Sean Connery's film *Medicine Man;* at the entrance to the forest are two fiberglass trees courtesy of Hollywood. There is a small vegetarian cafe and a stand selling herbal potions and charms. You can reach the park on a boat tour from Catemaco or from the road. ♦ Admission. Daily. Carretera Catemaco Coyame (east of Hwy 180). 294/30199, 294/30666

Made in the Shade

The ubiquitous *palapa* (a large palm-frond hut) found along Mexico's coasts has existed since the days of ancient cultures. Maya drawings and carvings from the first century show *palapas* shading kings and peasants alike, both on land and in dugout canoes. Two thousand years later, the *palapa* is an integral architectural feature of the most glamorous hotels in **Puerto Vallarta** and **Cancún** and is the requisite beach shelter along the **Pacific,** the **Caribbean,** and the **Mar de Cortés.**

A basic, traditional *palapa* is made from a tree trunk and topped with a roof of palm fronds, which are nailed or tied on an umbrella-shaped framework of poles. (Large *palapas* also have upright supports for the circumference of the roof, which are ideal for hanging hammocks.) Resort and restaurant designers have taken the *palapa* to new heights with soaring 30-foot-tall palm-frond roofs shaped like pyramids, A-frames, and arches. It can take months to cover these elaborate wood-beam frames with

palm fronds. Many modern *palapa* artists shun palms in favor of zacate, a thin, long grass from the state of **Campeche** that's sewn into strips that wrap easily around the most intricate designs. When constructed properly, a well-made *palapa* can last 20 years or more, and many can even withstand tropical storms.

Yucatán Peninsula

The 43,000-square-mile Yucatán Peninsula sits like an independent nation bordered by the **Gulf of Mexico**, the **Caribbean Sea**, and the wilderness of Guatemala and Belize. The peninsula bears the slashes of *sacbes* (ancient limestone roads) connecting the ruins of the Maya ceremonial centers of **Chichén Itzá**, **Uxmal**, and **Cobá**. Today asphalt highways link the peninsula's three states—**Campeche, Yucatán,** and **Quintana Roo**—with Mexico City and the national government. The connection seems almost superficial, however. In character, cuisine, and geography, the Yucatán Peninsula is more Caribbean, European, and Maya than Mexican.

Campeche, on the Gulf of Mexico, is the peninsula's unknown territory, a stretch of impenetrable jungle covered with Maya ruins and bordered by a coastline known more for its ports than its beaches. Hurricane Roxanne dealt Campeche a cruel blow in 1995, hitting the region not once but twice in its path through the gulf. The state was devastated, with all major roads flooded for days. Most roads are back to normal now, but the state's oil and agricultural industries will take longer to recover.

Yucatán state is wedged between Campeche and Quintana Roo, in the center of the northern coast where the Gulf of Mexico meets the Caribbean. Spanish *conquistadores* built **Mérida**, the capital of Yucatán, atop the ancient Maya city **T'Ho**. Of all Mexican cities, it best reveals the similarities and differences between the ancient Maya and their Spanish, French, and Mexican conquerors. The largest city on the Yucatán Peninsula, it is a

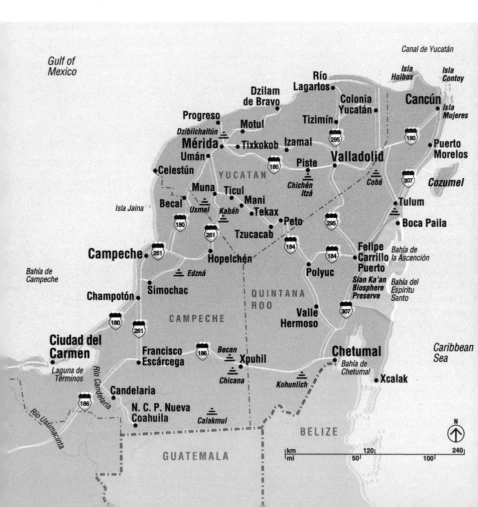

great launching point for a Yucatán adventure, with monuments, markets, and museums serving as an introduction to the peninsula's history and mystique.

The state of Quintana Roo is largely composed of a limestone shelf covered with scrubby jungle and white sand beaches that line a chain of coral reefs in the Caribbean. This region was the province of pirates, smugglers, and Maya villagers until developers set their sights on **Cancún** in the early 1970s. Within two decades, Cancún has become the nation's number one tourist destination, with the nearby island resorts of **Cozumel** and **Isla Mujeres** getting their share of attention as well. Travelers in search of a secluded and much less tourist-oriented retreat head for the sparsely populated beaches and Maya outposts along Quintana Roo's mainland coast, which stretches south of Cancún to the capital city of **Chetumal** and the border of Belize.

Mérida

Beyond the distinction of probably being the safest and most European capital city in Mexico (and possibly Central America, too), Mérida encompasses all that is fascinating about the **Yucatán Peninsula.** Gracious and ebullient, *meridanos* (as the 700,000 or so inhabitants of the city are called) embrace both neighbors and strangers with genuine goodwill. Narrow brick streets shaded by laurel trees pass by Moorish palaces and archways dating back to the time of the Spanish *conquistadores*, who built their 16th-century capital from the rubble and ruins of the ancient Maya capital, **T'Ho.** Bits of limestone blocks from temples destroyed in 1542 can still be detected in the walls of 16th-century Franciscan churches where the Maya of today follow the Catholic rituals their ancestors resisted 400 years ago. Approximately 500,000 Maya were killed by the Spanish, led by Francisco Montejo, in a 15-year battle for control of Mérida's land, commerce, and soul. But the Maya spirit is resilient, and their descendants retain a distinct Indian appearance and an ancient language that is still spoken in traditional villages and along the city streets.

The history of this area is alive and very much a part of the culture, architecture, and social life of Yucatán's capital city. Nowhere is this more evident than in the central plaza, which has remained Mérida's heart from the time of **T'Ho,** through the conquest, and into today. Maya men from tiny villages outside the city drape colorful hammocks on their shoulders and entreat tourists to buy their wares. Businessmen with distinctly European appearances read Spanish newspapers while having their shoes shined by Maya boys. Young girls in miniskirts and high heels stroll past Maya women who are wearing lavishly embroidered shifts and selling woven bracelets and shawls.

A mural depicting the violent and vivid blending of the Maya and Spanish peoples into the Mexican race is painted on a wall of **Palacio Municipal** (City Hall); portraits of the tormentors and benefactors who controlled Yucatán's political and religious evolution hang in the **Palacio Gobierno** (Government Palace). *Meridanos* of all ethnic ancestry gather by the plaza to watch folk dancers perform a wedding dance or to listen to festive marimbas and military bands.

The city's European heritage and proximity to the Caribbean give it a flavor and look of its own. Mérida's cuisine is a mix of Yucatecan, continental, and Middle Eastern fare, the third due to the large number of immigrants from that part of the world. Residents dress for the tropics, the men in short-sleeved guayabera shirts that hang loose outside their trousers. Everyone, including politicians and bankers, forgoes suits and ties and wears guayaberas to civic events. The lightweight, intricately woven Yucatecan hammock is preferred over the bed by many residents, and even the most elegant homes have hammock hooks in the walls.

Europe's impact on Mérida is most evident along **Paseo de Montejo,** a boulevard lined with laurel, tamarind, and various flamboyant trees, and a procession of palatial mansions. The city was a center of wealth and power during the late 1800s. *Hacendados* (hacienda owners) controlled vast parcels of land, running corn and cattle plantations with the labor of indentured Indians. Henequen, a strong fiber from the agave plant that is used for making rope, became a valuable export in the 1900s; agave fields flourished in the peninsula's heat, and vast fortunes grew from its cultivation. The *hacendados* created city neighborhoods fashioned after the Champs-Elysées, commissioning French and Italian engineers and architects to design pompous, ornate homes, which they filled with imported marble, crystal, and antiques. Many of these mansions still stand along the Paseo de Montejo and surrounding streets, though some have fallen into unfortunate disrepair. The frothy cream-and-white **Palacio Cantón** is one of the best preserved of these homes and now serves as the **Museo Regional de Antropología** (Regional Anthropology Museum).

Perhaps the best way to fully appreciate Mérida's charms is to hire a *calesa* (horse-drawn carriage) for a Sunday afternoon ride, when traffic is lightest. Start at the main plaza and head north on **Calle 60** past the parks to Paseo de Montejo and its side streets, then southwest to the **Parque Centenario.** Keep your camera handy, for Mérida is filled with picturesque places.

Area code is 99 unless otherwise indicated.

Getting to Mérida

Airport

Aeropuerto International de Mérida (Mérida International Airport) is 6 kilometers (4 miles) southwest of the city, and the single terminal handles both national and international flights. Airport services such as car rentals are available only when flights are arriving or departing.

Airport Services
Information 461372

Airlines
AeroCaribe	461678, 286790
Aeroméxico	279455, 461400, 800/237.6639
Aviacsa	461378, 269087, 800/284.2622
Aviateca	461296, 258059, 800/327.9832
Bonanza	460564, 260609
Mexicana	461332, 277421, 800/531.7921
Taesa	461826, 202077, 800/328.2372

Getting to and from Aeropuerto Internacional de Mérida

By Bus *Colectivos* (vans) run from the airport to downtown and to major hotels. Fares range from $2 to $5, depending on the location of your hotel.

By Car The airport is a 15-minute drive from the hotel district. **Avenida Itzaes** runs north from the airport to town and intersects the numbered streets (calles), which is where most of the hotels are located.

The following car-rental companies have counters at **Aeropuerto Internacional de Mérida** but are open only when flights are arriving and departing.

Avis	252525, 800/331.1212
Hertz	840020, 800/654.3131
National	461394, 800/328.4567

By Taxi Taxis wait in front of the airport; the fare to the hotels ranges from $4 to $10.

Getting Around Mérida

Most of Mérida's hotels, museums, plazas, and other attractions are within walking distance of each other. If you need transportation, your best bet is to use the public buses, which run frequently through downtown.

Buses The **Terminal de Autobús** (main bus station; Calle 70, No. 5555, at Calle 71) has daily first-class bus departures for **Chichén Itzá, Uxmal,** the coast, Campeche, Villahermosa, Palenque, and Mexico City. Call 232287 for information. Second-class buses depart from the terminal at **Calle 69** (between Calles 68 and 70). Buses to **Izamal** and **Progreso** depart from the terminal at **Calle 62** (between **Calles 67** and 65).

Driving A car is unnecessary in the city, but does come in handy if you plan to tour the ruins and towns in the countryside. Many tourists rent a car just for one or two days and park at their hotels (which have free parking lots) while in the city. Downtown traffic is often very congested weekdays, and the pattern of one-way streets can be confusing. If you do drive, try to avoid the area around the market, where trucks, buses, and cars converge in an intimidating mass. Most hotels can arrange car rentals.

The following car-rental agencies have offices in Mérida and at the airport:

Avis 282828
Executive 233732
National 232493

Taxis Cabs are available at hotels but do not circulate around Mérida looking for fares. Instead, they congregate at taxi stands *(sitios)* at most of the city's parks and major churches and by **La Catedral.** To request a cab, call 285322 or 231221.

FYI

Accommodations Mérida is filled with wonderful inexpensive to moderately priced, family-operated hotels, many located in colonial-style buildings with flower-filled courtyards. Some of the budget properties lack air-conditioning, televisions, and swimming pools. More modern, chain hotels have opened near the Paseo de Montejo and offer all the luxuries high-end travelers expect at very reasonable rates. Reservations are essential around Christmas, Easter, and during Mexican holiday weekends.

Consulates
US Consulate Paseo de Montejo and Av Colón..........
....255011

Publications *Yucatán Today* is an English-language monthly magazine filled with tourist tips. It's available at hotels, shops, and the tourist information office.

Shopping A great shopping city, Mérida has one of the best public markets in Mexico. Tourist-oriented shops line Calle 60 and are scattered on the side streets around the plaza and public market. Some shops close at midday, and many of the small ones are closed Sundays (see "Favorite Folk Art Finds in Mérida," page 138).

Street Plan Mérida's streets were originally laid out in a grid (small side streets added over the years have altered the layout somewhat), with even-numbered streets running north-south and odd-numbered streets running east-west. Calle 60 is the main street. Street addresses are difficult to find, since the numbers do not follow a logical order. Always ask for landmarks and cross streets when requesting directions.

Time Zone Mérida is on Central Time, two hours ahead of California and one hour behind New York.

Tours Most hotel desks and tour companies can arrange trips to the ruins of **Uxmal** and **Chichén Itzá** and sightseeing tours of Mérida.

Discover Mérida is a tourist bus with two-hour sightseeing tours of the city; it departs daily from **Parque Santa Lucía.** For information and tickets, contact your hotel's front desk or call 272476, 276119.

Ecoturismo Yucatán runs group and customized cultural, adventure, and bird watching tours on the Yucatán Peninsula and in southern Mexico, Belize, and Guatemala. It is located at Calle 3, No. 235 (between Calles 32-A and 34). 252187; fax 259047.

Mayaland Tours operates hotels at **Uxmal** and **Chichén Itzá** and offers bus tours with overnight stays at the ruins, as well as other package tours that include reduced rental-car rates. Their day tours in Mérida include a fascinating circuit of colonial neighborhoods and churches by horsedrawn carriage; an early-morning walking tour; and a bus tour to colonial-era convents in the countryside. For information, contact them at the **Plaza Americana** (Fiesta Americana Mérida, Av Colón, Suite 1A, 250621, 250622, 800/235.4079; fax 250087.

Yucatán Trails has English-speaking travel agents to assist with local tours and information and reservations for destinations throughout Mexico, as well as reservations to get you home. Their office is at Calle 62, No. 482 (between Calles 59 and 57). 282582, 285913; fax 244919.

Visitors' Information Center The **Oficina de Turismo** (Tourism Office) is in the **Teatro José Peón Contreras**. Open daily, it is located at Calle 60 (between Calles 59 and 57). 248386, 286547.

Phone Book

Fire...249242
Hospital O'Horan 238711
Police...252555
Red Cross...249813

1 Plaza Mayor Mérida's main plaza, surrounded by monuments to commerce and Christianity, is at its best on Sunday, when the surrounding streets are closed to vehicular traffic, and *meridanos* dressed in their best gather to spend most of the day in a whirl of music, color, and festivity. Vendors selling plastic Donald Ducks, embroidered baby clothes, and peace symbols on leather neckbands set up stands along the plaza's periphery. Carts sit at every corner, offering tamales, homemade potato chips, corn on the cob, and sweet meringues. Teenagers ogle their friends from balconies in the **Palacio Gobierno,** while toddlers race about with joyful abandon under the adoring gazes of adults. The plaza is less enchanting on other days, when traffic noise on the narrow streets remains a constant distraction. But it's always a pretty place to relax, study your map, and get a shoeshine. ♦ Bounded by Calles 60 and 62, and Calles 63 and 61

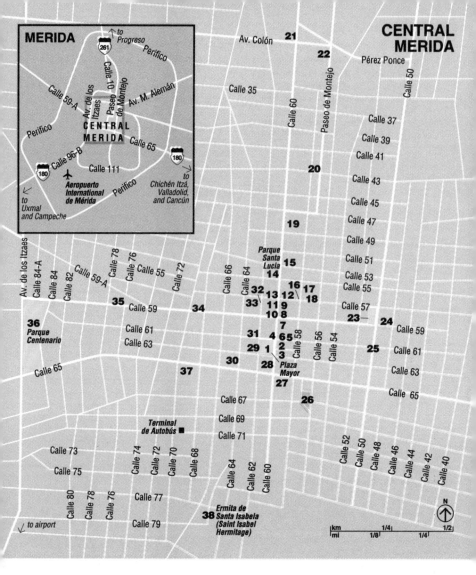

2 La Catedral

Looking more like a prison than a church, this cathedral is said to be the oldest in North America. It was built by Maya laborers over a 36-year period in the late 1500s out of stones and rubble from the ancient Maya city **T'Ho.** Much of the present floor is made of marble tombstones from the 1800s. Narrow gunnery slats shed the only natural light inside this Gothic monolith lined with altars to the Virgin and saints. Statues of benefactors, noted doctors, and priests stand near the entrance, along with supplicants sitting on the floor, begging for coins.

The cathedral lacks the ornate glitter and gold normally seen in Mexican churches, supposedly because it was looted during the revolution. Religious pictures, rosary beads, and *milagros* (tiny silver, gold, or tin replicas of human body parts to pin on a statue of the saint who helped heal your wounds) are sold at two small stands by the front doors. ♦ Calle 60 (between Calles 63 and 61). No phone

3 Museo de Arte Contemporáneo Ateneo de Yucatán (MACAY)

This former colonial-era seminary has been remodeled into a stunning contemporary art museum with a courtyard sculpture garden and several exhibition areas. The political paintings of Fernando Castro Pacheco and modernistic abstract paintings of Fernando Garcia Ponce are on permanent display. Temporary exhibits include photography, ceramics, and graphic arts. Both the reconstructed building and the exhibits are well worth seeing. ♦ Admission, free Sunday. M, W-Su. Pasaje de la Revolución (between Calles 58 and 60). 283258, 283236; fax 283204

4 Palacio Gobierno

Designed by engineer David Casares, this 100-year-old palace houses state offices. The inner courtyard is filled with perfect palms and ferns in tall terracotta vases that line the gray tile floor; netting over the courtyard keeps the pigeons out. Be sure to note the mysterious gray, red, and yellow mural, *Evolución Social de Hombre de Yucatán* (The Social Evolution of Man in Yucatán), painted by Yucatecan artist Fernando Castro Pacheco in 1972. A regal ballroom upstairs, graced by crystal chandeliers and a grand piano, serves as a gallery for Pacheco's moving and startling portraits of Yucatán's historical personages and social themes. Several wrought-iron balconies face the plaza from off the ballroom and are a nice spot for a breather.

The mood here is formal and sedate. Visitors are expected to act with decorum, except on Sunday, when the liveliness of the plaza prevails. Small newsstands and cafes line the covered arcade along the front of the palace, where you can pick up a copy of *The News* (a Mexico City–based, English-language paper) and a cup of *tamarindo* sorbet. ◆ Daily. Calles 61 and 60. No phone

5 Pan Montejo There are several branches of this bakery around the city, but this is the best of those near the plaza, with shelves of cookies, breakfast pastries, and breads, and a select display of special treats at the counter. Don't miss the nut tarts. ◆ Daily. No credit cards accepted. Calle 61 (between Calles 58 and 60). 231174

5 Museo de la Ciudad de Mérida (City Museum) Housed in a former convent and hospital, this museum holds the prints, drawings, photos, and models of early Mérida. The building was one of the first structures built after the Spanish conquest. ◆ Admission. Tu-Sa; closed at midday. Calles 61 and 58. 262258

6 Gran Hotel $ Built in 1901, Mérida's first hotel is grand indeed, with Greek pillars, tile floors, wrought-iron banisters along curving stairways, and two levels of balconies looking down on the central courtyard. The hallways are filled with gorgeous antiques and china cabinets displaying porcelain brought to Mérida by European immigrants in the early 1900s. The noise coming from nearby **Parque Hidalgo** has been diminished by heavy sliding glass doors on the rooms facing the park, and

air-conditioning has been added to some of the 33 rooms. Enormous carved wooden beams frame the windows in the high-ceilinged rooms, which have one or two double beds, modern tile showers, small closets, tiny televisions, and standard furnishings (the good antiques are in the public spaces). Purified water is available in large dispensers on each floor. This is a great place to absorb the atmosphere of old and new Mérida both, surrounded by history inside the hotel and the jumble of traffic and parks outdoors. ◆ Calle 60, No. 496 (between Calles 61 and 59). 247730; fax 247622

Within the Gran Hotel:

El Patio Español ★★$ Tables are set beside the courtyard and in small dining rooms inside the hotel, giving a pleasant respite from the sun. The food is surprisingly good for a hotel cafe; try the excellent *sopa de lima* (a large bowl of savory broth with shredded chicken, strips of fried tortillas, and slices of lime), served with warm *bolillos* (rolls). The paella and Yucatecan dishes are also very good. ◆ Yucatecan/International ◆ Daily. 247730

7 Parque Hidalgo Calle 60 north of the plaza is lined with hotels, restaurants, and parks, none more popular than this courtyard (sometimes called **Parque Cepeda Peraza**) with benches and a small gazebo. Sidewalk cafes and aged hotels frame the walkways, and marimbas play throughout the day. On Saturday and Sunday night young people wait up to an hour in long lines wrapping around the plaza to get into the most popular movie theater in town, where first-run Spanish-language films are screened. The park is a great spot to linger over a coffee or beer, write postcards, and watch the scenery. Artisans sometimes set up tables here, and hammock sellers are always present. ◆ Calles 60 and 59

On Parque Hidalgo:

Giorgio ★$ Part of the attraction of this popular, though simple, cafe are its reasonably priced pizzas and pastas. Another lure is the ongoing parade of vendors, travelers, and locals through the park. ◆ Italian ◆ Daily lunch and dinner. No phone

Hotel Caribe $ A longtime favorite on **Parque Hidalgo**, this converted three-story colonial home has a fantastic central courtyard. The 56 rooms, decorated in soft pastels and floral prints, have telephones and air-conditioning. Most are set back around the courtyard and don't have a view of the plaza, but they're quieter than those facing the street. The rooftop pool area gives a nice view of downtown. The outdoor cafe is the least expensive place to eat at the park, but the service is excruciatingly slow. ◆ Calle 59, No. 500. 249022, 800/555.8842; fax 248733

8 Iglesia de la Tercera Orden (Church of the Third Order) The Jesuits set up a miniature dynasty here in 1618, building a Baroque, carved-stone church, a boys' school, a theater, and the **Parque de la Maternidad** (Mother's Park). A close look at the church's outer walls facing Calle 59 reveals Maya latticework designs in the stones, which were taken from the rubble of the ancient Maya capital, **T'Ho.** ♦ Calle 59 (between Calles 58 and 60)

8 Parque de la Maternidad (Mother's Park) This small, quiet park has a graceful, white statue of the Madonna and Child surrounded by S-shaped benches known as *confidenciales*. It's one of the prettiest places to escape from the activity on the street. ♦ Calles 60 and 59

9 Teatro José Peón Contreras Designed by engineer Enrique Deserti in 1908, when *meridanos* were thoroughly enamored with European design, this ornate Italianate theater has a sweeping Carrara marble staircase and frescoed dome. (Deserti also created the **Palacio Cantón,** home of the **Museo Regional de Antropología,** see page 139.) Art shows are sometimes held in the lobby, and the **Ballet Folklórico** (Folkloric Ballet) of the **Universidad Autónomo de Yucatán** (University of Yucatán) puts on a weekly show using music and dance to depict the history of the state. ♦ Admission for show. Shows: Tu. Calle 60 and Callejon Congresso. 243954

Within the Teatro José Peón Contreras:

Oficina de Turismo (Tourism Office) English- and Spanish-speaking clerks armed with an immense knowledge of their city staff this excellent tourism office. Brochures and pamphlets are kept behind the desk, so you must ask for what you need and sign the guest book. ♦ Daily. 248925

Cafe José Peón ★$ This pretty indoor/outdoor cafe would be ideal if the food were better; stick with the coffee, espresso, cappuccino, and desserts, especially the carrot cake. Still, it's a peaceful place to sit—the street it fronts is closed to traffic. ♦ Cafe ♦ Daily breakfast, lunch, and dinner. No phone

---

Restaurants/Clubs: Red   Hotels: Blue

Shops/♆ Outdoors: Green   **Sights/Culture:** Black

10 Amaro ★★$ Vegetarian and Yucatecan dishes are served under shade trees at this small eatery, one of the few places where you can find steamed veggies and brown rice. ♦ Vegetarian/Yucatecan ♦ Daily lunch and dinner. No credit cards accepted. Calle 59 (between Calles 60 and 62). 282451

La Bella Epoca

11 La Bella Epoca ★★$$ Mérida's best tables for a leisurely, sumptuous dinner are set on the small second-story balconies of this elegant yet casual restaurant. While the menu is perhaps a bit too ambitious, offering Mexican, Yucatecan, Middle Eastern, and vegetarian fare, the chef manages to prepare most dishes fairly well. His roster of regional Mexican specialties is particularly impressive—for a savory tour of the country's cuisine, start with *sikil-pak* (a dip of pumpkin seeds and grilled tomatoes and onions), followed by *pollo pipian* (chicken with a sauce of ground pumpkin seeds), and finish with the *crepas cajetas* (crepes with caramel sauce) for dessert. The ambience is less enchanting if you can't get a balcony table. ♦ Continental/Mexican/Yucatecan ♦ Daily lunch and dinner. Calle 60 (between Calles 59 and 57). 281429

11 Universidad Autónomo de Yucatán (University of Yucatán) A Moorish archway straddles a street corner where students congregate before class. Beyond it sits a bare patio that's center stage for the university's musical concerts on Friday nights. This university was established in 1831 on the site of Mérida's first university, built by the Jesuits in 1618. In and around the library are portraits of the school's founders and patrons (such as Andres Quintana Roo and Cepeda Peraza, both highly revered generals) and a mural telling the story of the reconstruction and reopening of the university by Governor Felipe Carillo Puerto in 1941. The school has a fine intensive Spanish program and a Maya studies course for foreigners. ♦ Calles 60 and 57. 283329

12 Casa del Balam $$ You don't realize the charm that lies within this seven-story, 54-room hotel until you walk past the drab facade and up a red-tile path to the entrance and courtyard filled with ferns, bougainvillea, and palms. "House of the Tiger" would be by far the best hotel in downtown, were it not for the traffic noise at this corner. To cut down on the din, all rooms have double-paned windows and air-conditioning, which definitely help. All rooms also have satellite TV, small refrigerators, wrought-iron headboards, red-and-white tile floors, woven blue spreads, and touches of Old Mexico. You'll be charmed by the cane-backed rocking chairs in the rooms and courtyard, and the inner balconies where you can almost forget the city outside. Guests have free use of the 18-hole golf course and tennis courts at the country club **La Ceiba**, about 20 minutes from the hotel. **Buganvilias** is a simple dining room where the waiters appear to have lived their entire lives, bearing trays of typical hotel fare. If you're not staying here, stop in for a cool drink in the courtyard and soak in the atmosphere of Old Mérida. ◆ Calle 60, No. 488 (at Calle 57). 228844, 800/624.8451, 800/555.8842; fax 245011

Within Casa del Balam:

Kiuik Curios This tiny shop carries an above-average selection of embroidered dresses, painted wooden animals, and reproductions of antiquities. ◆ Daily. 248844

13 El Pórtico del Peregrino ★★★★$$ Romance and tranquillity are guaranteed at this small restaurant, which doesn't look like much from the street. Once you walk down a narrow passageway, though, you're in a tropical garden where vines wrap around tree trunks and candlelight casts a peaceful glow. Just off the garden is an air-conditioned dining room furnished with antiques; another cool room by the street provides a nice spot for lunch. *Berenjenas al horno* (baked eggplant layered with tender chicken, melted cheese, and a savory tomato sauce) is the best dish in the house. The chicken-liver shish kebab also has a loyal following. There is a mainstream selection of grilled chicken and fish dinners. ◆ Middle Eastern ◆ Daily lunch

and dinner. Calle 57, No. 501 (between Calles 60 and 62). 286163

13 Cafetería Pop ★$ Plain, simple, and unadorned, this is tops in Mérida for fresh-brewed coffee and breakfast served all day long. Students and professors from the nearby university congregate at its 12 tables; however, the proprietors discourage loitering during the busiest hours of the morning and do not sell beer or wine unless it's ordered with a meal. Hamburgers here are better than most in town, and the restaurant makes a good pit stop for a cup of coffee and a slice of cake or pie when your energy flags. ◆ American/Mexican ◆ Daily breakfast, lunch, and dinner. Calle 57, No. 501 (between Calles 60 and 62). 286163

14 Parque Santa Lucia One of the prettiest of Mérida's many parks, this small spot across from the **Iglesia de Santa Lucia** fills with locals and guests for the Thursday night concerts and the Sunday flea market and book sale. ◆ Calles 60 and 55

15 Hotel Trinidad Galería $ Those drawn to the bizarre and unusual will enjoy this eccentric hotel, owned by Manolo Rivero, an avid collector of antiques and modern art. The lobby is filled with potted palms (one sporting a stuffed monkey), and 17th-century statues are scattered along the rambling hacienda's stairways and corridors. Eclecticism reigns in the 30 rooms, with a jumble of mismatched antique chests and beds. Some rooms are huge, with king-size beds and windows overlooking the courtyards, while others are as small and simple as a monk's cell. Under a century-old tree there's a long lap pool. Rivero has a second 62-room hotel of the same name a block away, designed in an equally unconventional style, and guests there have use of this hotel's swimming pool. Beverages and snacks are available at the small cafe. ◆ Calle 60 (between Calles 53 and 51). 232463; fax 242319

16 Posada Toledo $ Europeans and budget travelers are justifiably enamored of this hotel in a converted colonial mansion. The 23 rooms have high wood-beamed ceilings, antique furnishings, hardwood floors, and tiled baths. All rooms have air-conditioning, but only a few have windows to the street; it's common for guests seeking fresh air to keep their doors open to the central courtyard. Two rooms at the front of the hotel have been converted into a master suite with pale blue walls, ornate woodwork along ceilings and doors, a crystal chandelier, air-conditioning, and a separate living room. The rate for this palatial suite is far less than for a typical double room in a more modern hotel; it could be the perfect honeymoon suite for the right couple. There is no restaurant. ◆ No credit cards accepted. Calles 58 and 57. 231690; fax 232256

Favorite Folk Art Finds in Mérida

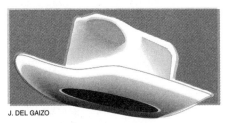

J. DEL GAIZO

The **Yucatán Peninsula** is well known for its distinctive regional folk art—particularly its hammocks and clothing (designed to alleviate the discomfort of the tropical heat) and the woven blankets and hand-crafted pottery incorporating Maya symbols and portraits of gods. Savvy visitors begin their journeys through the peninsula with a trip to the local market to buy a hammock for beach siestas, and a *jipi* (straw hat) to shade their brows while climbing the ruins. The market and surrounding shops in Mérida are the best sources for regional crafts, but good buys can also be found in **Cancún, Cozumel,** and in most town squares, where vendors from the area display their wares, including the following three favorite Yucatecan creations.

Hammocks

Woven of flimsy, multicolored strings in a loose yet supple hanging cradle, the Yucatecan hammock is coveted the world over for its comfort, durability, and beauty. Silk hammocks are works of art and cost a fortune. Nylon hammocks are tough yet silky, and they don't fade or shred in the sun. Cotton is the most common and least expensive material used. (Henequen and other scratchy fibers are unacceptable for a hammock, unless you have ascetic tendencies.) Yucatecan hammocks come in three sizes: *sencillo* (designed for one person, but often not large enough for the average gringo's body), *doble* (to hold two people snugly or one comfortably), and *matrimonial* (big enough for two adults and a child).

If you have the time and transportation, consider visiting a hammock weavers' town, such as **Tixkokob,** east of Mérida. Hammock looms sit on nearly every front porch, and families are delighted to show you their techniques and wares. Often the man of the family is in the city, wandering through the plaza with his pile of homemade hammocks, but the women and children genuinely enjoy visitors and will most likely invite you into their homes to practice swinging in their family hammocks strung across the living space. If you can't get away from Mérida but still want to shop knowledgeably, visit **El Aguacate** (Calle 58, No. 604, 286429) near the market district or **La Poblana** (Calle 65, No. 492, 216503)—both shops will take the time to show you how their hammocks are made and discuss the qualities of each variety.

Jipis

These popular hats (commonly called Panama hats by tourists) are made from the fibers of the jipijapa plant, grown in **Campeche.** They are crushable, bendable, wonderfully wearable lightweight straw hats that are perfect for the Yucatán climate; a well-made *jipi* will hold up for years. Judge its quality by the coarseness of the fiber and the tightness of the weave. Soft, tightly woven hats of the highest caliber are surprisingly expensive and not really necessary for casual use. Try the middle grade and stay away from cheap, loosely constructed hats, unless you plan to dispose of it after your trip. *Jipis* are woven in dark, damp caves in the small towns within the state, Campeche, including **Becal,** on **Highway 180** between Mérida and the city of Campeche. In Mérida, you'll find good examples of the various *jipis* at **La Casa de los Jipis** (Calle 56, No. 526, no phone).

Guayaberas

Foreign men who spend a lot of time in the Yucatán almost always end up adopting the guayabera look, which makes great sense given the heat. Guayaberas are shirts that button up the front to an open neck and collar, have short sleeves, and hang outside the trousers. They typically are made of lightweight cotton, but also come in polyester (which destroys their breathing ability). The shirt fronts are usually embroidered in the same color thread as the shirt (white is the most traditional color, but blue is very popular as well) or pleated with tiny tucks. Custom-tailored and off-the-rack guayaberas are available in Mérida at **Camisería Canul** (Calle 59, No. 496, 230158), **Guayaberas Jack** (Calle 59, No. 505, 286002), and other shops in the same neighborhood.

17 Cafe Alameda ★$ Join the local businessmen in their guayaberas at this small cafe where the breakfast of choice is beef shish kebab with pita bread. The menu also includes a wide range of Middle Eastern dishes such as hummus, tabbouleh, and stuffed grape leaves, as well as plenty of other selections for vegetarians. Locals typically linger over their copies of the daily paper at the front tables while tourists from nearby budget hotels gather in the back patio.
♦ Middle Eastern/Yucatecan ♦ Daily breakfast

and lunch. No credit cards accepted. Calle 58, No. 474 (between Calles 57 and 55). 283635

18 Hotel Mucuy $ Mérida has an outstanding selection of budget hotels, and this one is right up there both for its low price and its ambience. Much of its charm is due to the hospitable hosts, Alfredo and Ofelia Comín. The building's architecture isn't as remarkable as that of the colonial-style hotels, but the 24 rooms are comfortable and immaculate; all have ceiling fans and face a charming garden. There's a communal refrigerator, bookshelf, and clothesline, and tables and chairs are grouped by the garden. The hotel arranges some of the most economical trips to the ruins available in town; tours are available for hotel guests only. Advance reservations with a deposit are a good idea around holidays and in August, when European travelers converge here. There is no restaurant. ♦ No credit cards accepted. Calle 57, No. 481 (between Calles 56 and 58). 285193, 237801; fax 237801

19 La Casona ★★★$$ A peaceful courtyard filled with trees and vines is the setting for this fine Italian restaurant. Though Yucatecan and Mexican dishes are available, you're best off sticking with the wide selection of pastas—ravioli stuffed with spinach, five kinds of lasagna (including vegetarian and mushroom), canneloni, and manicotti. The wine list includes several Chiantis, and espresso and cappuccino are good finales. Dining in courtyard restaurants does have its drawbacks; apply bug repellent beforehand. ♦ Italian ♦ Daily lunch and dinner. Calle 60, No. 434 (between Calles 49 and 47). 238348

20 Paseo de Montejo The Champs-Elysées of Mérida, this boulevard has a landscaped central divide and wide, shaded sidewalks perfect for a leisurely stroll. Though not as elegant and picturesque as it was in its prime, it's still a prestigious address. Some families whose ancestors built the palatial mansions along the Paseo have been unable to maintain them and have let several fall into disrepair. But others have been restored as corporate headquarters, and the Paseo is coming back to life. Most significant to the renaissance is the opening of two elegant hotels, the **Hyatt Regency Mérida** and the **Fiesta Americana Mérida** (see below). ♦ Between Calle 47 and Av 31

20 Museo Regional de Antropología (Regional Anthropology Museum) The museum is located inside the frothy cream-and-brown **Palacio Cantón,** a grand and suitable home for the state's impressive collection of Maya art and artifacts. The palace was built in 1911 for Governor General Francisco Cantón Rosado (who enjoyed it for only six years before dying in 1917) and was used as a school of fine arts in the 1930s. In

1948 it became the official residence of the Governor of Yucatán and in 1977 was transformed into the museum. Allow plenty of time to examine the building, with its Doric and Ionic columns, sweeping white marble staircases, crystal chandeliers, and Beaux Arts ornamentation, as well as the displays themselves.

The histories of the Maya and Yucatán are covered extensively. Of special interest are the exhibit of the wooden boards used to press Maya children's foreheads into a sloping shape to make them beautiful and the models of significant structures at **Chichén Itzá** and **Uxmal.** The second floor is devoted to temporary exhibits; past shows have included artifacts from the **Templo Mayor** site in Mexico City. The museum has an excellent bookstore, though much of the literature is in Spanish. ♦ Admission; free Sunday. Tu-Su. Calle 43 (between Paseo de Montejo and Calle 58). 230557

21 Hyatt Regency Mérida $$ The tallest hotel in town at 17 stories, this elegant, mirrored tower has 300 luxurious rooms with in-room movie channels on satellite TV, in-room safes, 24-hour room service, and handsome European-style furnishings. Though the rooms are quite grand, the windows do not open, and some may find them claustrophobic. Amenities include a fitness center and pool and a full-scale business center. The **Peregrina Bistro** offers good buffets and international meals, and there's an in-house *pastelería* (pastry shop). Drinks and tea are served in the lobby's several seating areas, a serene spot for reading and visiting with friends. ♦ Calle 60, No. 344 (at Av Colón). 420202, 421234, 800/233.1234; fax 257002

22 Fiesta Americana Mérida $$ Built in the style of Mérida's Neo-Classical mansions, this handsome five-story, pale peach hotel blends beautifully with the Paseo's architecture and attitude. Each of the 350 rooms has a tiny iron-railed balcony facing the city or the pool and tennis court in the courtyard. Decorated in green, mauve, and blue and with gorgeous paintings of nearby ruins, the rooms have safes, mini-bars, satellite TV, and, to accommodate business travelers, three phones with fax ports. There are also several meeting rooms and a business center. The lobby is set above street level and is accessible from the Avenida Colón entrance to **Plaza Americana;** escalators whisk guests up toward the hotel's dome-shaped, stained-glass ceiling and marble fountains. The service throughout the hotel is outstanding. Live piano music accompanies the lavish breakfast buffets and afternoon tea at **Cafe Montejo,** the hotel's restaurant. ♦ Paseo de Montejo 451 (at Av Colón). 421111, 800/343.7821; fax 421112

Within the Fiesta Americana Mérida:

El Mural ★★★★$$$ The first thing you notice upon entering this elegant restaurant is the whimsical mural covering one long wall. Study the scene of Mérida street life closely, and you'll see Jacques Cousteau holding a turtle-shaped balloon, Mexican singer Maria Felix standing with Albert Einstein, and local comic Cholo linking arms with Mikhail Gorbachev. A trio of musicians serenades diners; culinary offerings include appetizers of Yucatecan *queso relleno* (cheese stuffed with raisins and ground beef) or lobster *pozole* (hominy stew), and such entrées as Mexican or imported steaks, fish fillets wrapped around *chaya* (similar to spinach), or ravioli spiced with chipotle. The excellent fare and top-notch service make this restaurant well worth visiting. ♦ Nouvelle Mexican ♦ M-Sa lunch and dinner. 421111

Plaza Americana Travelers staying in the neighborhood's luxury hotels find all the services they need here. Clothing and jewelry boutiques, souvenir shops, travel agencies, and money-exchange stands fill this street-level commercial center beneath the **Fiesta Americana**. The center has become an important part of tourism development at the north end of the city. Two bus lines with express service to Cancún pick up passengers here; for schedules contact **Nuevos Horizontes** (234443) or **Super Expresso** (250910).

Within the Plaza Americana:

Sanborn's ★★$ This branch of the Mexico City landmark looks like every other in the country, with a great bakery and candy counter, an excellent selection of newspapers and magazines, a pharmacy, a lavish array of jewelry and gifts, and a dependable restaurant. One level above the shop, the restaurant has a separate nonsmoking section (still a rarity in Mexico). The menu offers a sprinkling of dishes from throughout the country—mole from Puebla and *pozole* from Jalisco—and a good choice of sandwiches, salads, and soups. Deafening music impedes conversation. ♦ Mexican ♦ Daily breakfast, lunch, and dinner; open until 1AM. 252522, 256835

There are more than a thousand known Maya archaeological sites in the state of Yucatán.

Though conquered and subjugated by the Spaniards and their mestizo descendants, the Maya of Yucatán gathered in 1847 to begin waging a bloody guerrilla war against their oppressors. More than half the Maya population of the peninsula died in the War of the Castes, which lasted until 1901.

23 Los Almendros ★$ Locals and travelers pack this eatery at lunchtime for traditional Yucatecan and Maya meals that last for hours. Along with its branches in Ticul and Cancún, the restaurant has been serving the same basic menu for nearly three decades—*pok-chuc* (pork chop grilled with spices), *cochinita* or *pollo pibil* (pork or chicken baked in banana leaves), *pavo de relleno* (turkey stuffed with olives, capers, raisins, and cheese), and other regional fare. The cavernous dining room echoes with spirited conversations, and the menu is printed with photos and English descriptions for neophytes. Though the quality of the food is not what it once was, you may want to start your culinary education here because of the modest prices, then move on to some of the smaller Yucatecan restaurants in the city. ♦ Yucatecan ♦ Daily breakfast, lunch, and dinner. Calle 50-A, No. 493 (between Calles 59 and 57). 285459

24 Iglesia Mejorada (Church of Improvement) Modeled after a Spanish church of the same name, this massive, intimidating structure was built in 1640 by the Franciscans and used as a hospital in the mid-1800s. Though rarely open, it is interesting from the outside, looming over the pretty plaza and brick streets of the church's namesake neighborhood. The side streets are filled with lovely mansions from the turn of the century; most are run-down and some are abandoned, but it's not difficult to imagine how grand it all must have been. ♦ Calles 50 and 59

24 Museo de Artes Populares (Museum of Popular Arts) An impressive collection of folk art fills the rooms of this transformed colonial hacienda. Of particular interest are the conch-shell carvings, hammock looms, and pottery reproductions of Maya huts. The upstairs galleries display a large collection of costumes and masks from Chiapas, Oaxaca, and Michoacán. ♦ Free. Tu-Su. Calle 59 (between Calles 48 and 50). No phone

25 El Arco de los Dragones In the 17th century the Spanish fortified the city by building a massive stone wall around it with 13 arched gates. One of the few remaining arches looms over Calle 61 by the overgrown wall and grounds of a deserted Spanish military base. Moorish in design, the arch has three spires on top and gated guard stations at each side (*dragones* means guard in Spanish). ◆ Calles 61 and 50

26 Mercado Municipal You haven't really been to a Mexican municipal market until you've tried to absorb this overwhelming labyrinth of commerce. (Do *not* bring your car into this area.) The enclosed market, a block square, itself is fairly predictable, with the lower floor occupied by Maya women and children hawking trinkets and other items, while the men sell dead chickens and pigs. However, the second floor houses an artisans' market filled with treasures, most of which can also be found in the rows of tiny shops lining the surrounding streets. The second floor is where you're bound to get lost at least once, trying to find the section devoted to hammocks, *jipis* (straw hats), regional clothing, and woven bags.

The main mail and telegraph offices are located in two dark and forbidding 19th-century stone buildings in the middle of a traffic island at the north side of the market, further complicating the nightmarish maze for drivers. ◆ Daily. Calle 56 (between Calles 69 and 65)

27 Mercado de Artesanías García Rejón (Artisans' Market) Embroidered dresses and *huipiles* (blouses), brightly striped woven belts, henequen hammocks and bags, and pottery decorated with Maya designs fill this arts-and-crafts market. Many of the products are machine-made and flimsy, but you can find one-of-a-kind treasures if you're patient and persistent. ◆ Daily. Calles 65 and 60

28 Casa de Montejo (House of Montejo) Francisco Montejo Jr., the son of Mérida's conqueror, began building the family palace in 1549, using Maya laborers and artisans and rubble from **T'Ho**. An appalling reminder of this heritage can be seen at the entrance of the building in the stonework portraits of Spanish soldiers in full imperial regalia standing on Maya heads. Successive generations of Montejos occupied the house until the 1970s, when the Mexican bank **Banamex** had it remodeled by the renowned architect **Augustín Legoretta** and turned it into its Mérida headquarters. Little remains of the inner house, which had been refurbished during the late 19th century in the ornate French style of the day. Visitors can stroll the inner gardens and cash traveler's checks during banking hours. ◆ M-F. Calle 63 (between Calles 60 and 62)

Awesome Izamal

When Pope John Paul II visited Mexico in August 1993, he held a momentous audience with the indigenous peoples of Mexico and Central America in this town 72 kilometers (45 miles) east of Mérida. Wearing their traditional dress, Maya and mestizo groups from all over the region met in the main plaza in a gathering of at least 3,000 (the official estimate, considered low by observers). One of the oldest cities in Mexico, Izamal holds particular importance both to the Maya and to those of the Catholic faith because of its Maya temples and impressive convent and monastery.

Izamal was once ruled by the ruthless Bishop Diego de Landa, a Franciscan zealot responsible for nearly obliterating the Maya in the 1700s. Along with torturing and killing thousands of Maya, Diego de Landa burned their sacred codices, the written history of Maya culture. The monastery at Izamal was built from the rubble of a Maya temple and *cenote* (natural well) wall that were dismantled by Maya slaves under the direction of Fray Juan de Mérida, a Franciscan monk who also supervised the construction of several churches. Northeast of the plaza, the ruins of the Maya temple **Kinich Kakmó** rise atop a hillside with an astounding view of the flat countryside. On a clear day, you can see **Chichén Itzá.**

Known as the "Ciudad Amarillo," for the unrelenting yellow color scheme of its buildings, Izamal got a fresh coat of paint and other improvements for the pope's visit. The town is becoming a stop on organized tours of the area, and a **Parador Turistica** (Tourism Center) near the entrance road to town includes a museum, restaurant, artisans' shops, and other attractions. The restaurant **Kinich Kakmó** (Calle 27, No. 299, between Calles 28 and 30, 995/40153) is the perfect spot to sample Yucatecan cuisine. Owner Miriam Azcorra has created a charming courtyard setting for her restaurant, which stands practically in the shadow of the ruins. Stop for lunch on the way to **Chichén Itzá.**

Tours to Izamal are available in Mérida through **Mayaland Tours** (Plaza Americana, Fiesta Americana Mérida, Paseo de Montejo 451, at Av Colón, Suite 1A, 250621, 250087, 800/235.4079). On Sunday, a train tour to Izamal departs from the Mérida railroad station and includes a bus tour of the town and lunch at the Parador Turistico; for information, call 249495, 249677, or inquire at your hotel's tour desk. The town of Izamal is well worth visiting—it combines much of Yucatán's history in a picturesque colonial setting. Make sure you have plenty of film!

29 Palacio Municipal (City Hall) A true city hall, always bustling with activity, this building was constructed in 1542 as the town's headquarters and jail. Throughout the next four centuries, the original wooden building was rebuilt and replaced several times by other structures. The current pretty yellow palace with its ribbonlike white trim was finally completed in 1928, with finishing touches such as an ornate archway from a nearby Dominican convent and a clock tower that chimes on the quarter hour. On Sunday and several evenings during the week, the street is roped off and a wooden stage is erected for performances of a traditional wedding dance or concerts by a local band. ♦ Daily. Calle 62 (between Calles 63 and 61). No phone

30 Casa de las Artesanías The selection at the folk art shop in this restored monastery is enough to satisfy even the most die-hard shoppers. Baskets, weavings, pottery, glassware, embroidery, wood carvings, furniture painted with whimsical designs—it's all here, at reasonable, set prices. The quality of the goods is better than much of what you find at the market, though most items here are manufactured. Be sure to check out the building itself and the courtyard in the back, where art exhibits are often held. The monastery is also used for art and Maya-language classes and houses a small display of musical instruments. ♦ Daily. Calle 63, No. 513 (between Calles 64 and 66). 235392, 286676

31 Cafe Louvre ★$ More interesting for its ambience than its food, this cafe has two small doors on the street leading into an outer coffee shop buzzing with conversation. At first glance, the back room looks like a beige dungeon filled with men reading newspapers and families in a feeding frenzy. Once your eyes adjust to the dim light and your ears adjust to the cacophony, it seems more like a train terminal where you can sit and drink coffee for hours watching the working class at rest. On Calle 62 north of the cafe are some marvelous Art Deco buildings, including a deserted theater made of glass bricks. ♦ Mexican ♦ Daily breakfast, lunch, and dinner. No credit cards accepted. Calle 62, No. 499-D (between Calles 61 and 59). 245073

32 Hotel Colón $ If you're going to enjoy your stay here, you have to overlook the ravages of time and appreciate the architectural novelties incorporated in the 1920s design of one of Mérida's first hotels. Whether you're a guest or a visitor, be sure to check out the tiled *baños de vapor* (steam baths). Separate areas for women and men have elaborate hand-painted tile showers and narrow rooms with shallow pools surrounded by benches, where bathers soak in the steam. (Baths are open to nonguests for a fee and are rumored to be popular for secret liaisons.) The swimming pool in a back garden is one of the nicest in town. The rest of the 63-room hotel is eclectic, starting with the huge painted plaster dogs guarding the front desk. Rooms have tattered red-and-gold brocade bedspreads and drapes, and the yellow-and-blue tile stairways and arches are faded and chipped. Still, a stay here is an experience you'll never forget. A coffee shop provides light meals and snacks. ♦ Calle 62, No. 483 (between Calles 59 and 57). 234355, 234508; fax 244919

33 Alberto's Continental Patio ★★★★$$ For more than 30 years Alberto, Nery, and Pepe Salum have served exquisite Lebanese meals in a carefully restored home built in 1727. Giant rubber trees shade a central patio, yet allow diners to see the  stars at night. Two inner dining rooms are decorated with antique religious statues and paintings, gilded mirrors, copper pots, and candles sparkling in hurricane lamps on the heavy wooden tables.

The menu runs the full range of fish, beef, and fowl, with a good selection of Maya specialties. For a Yucatecan feast order the complete dinner of ceviche, *sopa de lima* (lime soup), broiled snapper with achiote sauce, fried bananas, and coconut pie. But the chef's true love is Lebanese fare; try a subtly spicy hummus or tabbouleh followed by cabbage rolls stuffed with ground beef. Finish with a cup or two of their thick dark Turkish coffee, and you'll be sure to stay up all night. ♦ Lebanese/Mexican ♦ Daily lunch and dinner. Calle 64, No. 482 (between Calles 59 and 57). 285367

34 Casa Mexilio $ This turn-of-the-century stone-and-stucco structure has been transformed into a distinctive guest house with eight rooms, each with a character of its own. All have some combination of white walls, canopy beds, hand-painted porcelain

---

Restaurants/Clubs: Red
Shops/♥ Outdoors: Green

Hotels: Blue
Sights/Culture: Black

sinks, antique wardrobes, black and terra-cotta pots dangling from ropes, and Mexican and Guatemalan textiles and rugs. Rooftop gardens provide wonderful overviews of the city and environs, from the cathedral's spires to the outlying jungle. Breakfast (included in the room rate) is served in a second-story dining room filled with antiques; future plans include the addition of an innovative dinner menu. The resident cats lounge beside a small pool in the shaded courtyard. The neighborhood is quiet, and it's usually easy to find parking on the street. At press time the owners were remodeling a building across the street into **Estudio,** a combination art gallery, artists' studio space, and three-room guest house. ♦ Calle 68, No. 495 (between Calles 59 and 57). 282505, 800/538.6802; fax 282505

South of the Border Books

Here's a list of good reads that will give you some insight into the people and culture of Mexico.

Art & Architecture

Art and Time in Mexico: From the Conquest to the Revolution, by Elizabeth Wilder Weismann (Harper & Row, 1985)

Casa Mexicana, by Tim Street-Porter (Tabori & Chang, 1986)

Folk Treasures of Mexico, by Marion Oettinger (Harry N. Abrams, 1990)

Gardens of Mexico, by Antonio Haas (Rizzoli, 1993)

Mexico: Splendors of Thirty Centuries (Metropolitan Museum of Art, 1990)

A Treasury of Mexican Folkways, by Frances Toor (Crown, 1967)

Biography

Passionate Pilgrim, by Antoinette May (Paragon House, 1993)

Cookbooks

The Art of Mexican Cooking, by Diana Kennedy (Bantam, 1989)

Mexican Regional Cooking, by Diana Kennedy (HarperCollins, 1990)

Mexico's Feasts of Life, by Patricia Quintana (Country Oak Books, 1989)

Tastes of Mexico, by Patricia Quintana (Tabori & Chang, 1986)

Cultural Commentary

Children of Sanchez, by Oscar Lewis (Random House, 1979)

Conversations With Moctezuma, by Dick J. Reavis (Quill, 1990)

Distant Neighbors: A Portrait of the Mexicans, by Alan Riding (Random House, 1984)

Five Families, by Oscar Lewis (Basic Books, 1979)

God and Mr. Gomez, by Jack Smith (Watts, Franklin, 1982)

Into a Desert Place, by Graham Macintosh (Graham Macintosh, 1988)

A Labyrinth of Solitude, by Octavio Paz (Grove Press, 1985)

Living Maya, by Walter F. Morris (Harry N. Abrams, 1987)

The Maya, by Michael Coe (Thames and Hudson, 1987)

The Mexicans: A Personal Portrait of the Mexican People, by Patrick Oster (Harper & Row, 1989)

Mexico, Places and Pleasures, by Kate Simon (HarperCollins, 1988)

Mexico: Some Travels and Some Travelers There, by Alice Adams (Prentice Hall, 1990)

Mornings in Mexico, by D.H. Lawrence (Penguin Books, 1960)

The Reader's Companion to Mexico, edited by Alan Ryan (Harcourt Brace & Co., 1995)

So Far From God, by Patrick Marnham (Viking, 1985)

Time Among the Maya, by Ronald Wright (Grove/Atlantic Monthly Press, 1989)

Travelers' Tales Mexico, edited by James O'Reilly and Larry Habegger (Traveler's Tales, 1994)

Viva Mexico: A Traveller's Account of Life in Mexico, by Charles Flandrau (Eland Books, 1985)

Fiction

Aztec, by Gary Jennings (Avon, 1981)

Like Water for Chocolate, by Laura Esquivel (Doubleday, 1994)

Mexico, by James A. Michener (Random House, 1992)

The Old Gringo, by Carlos Fuentes (HarperCollins, 1986)

Under the Volcano, by Malcolm Lowry (NAL-Dutton, 1984)

History

The Conquest of New Spain, by Bernal Díaz (Shoe String, 1988)

A Forest of Kings, by Linda Schele and David Freidel (Willam Morrow, 1990)

Incidents of Travel in Yucatán, by John Lloyd Stephens (Dover, 1843)

A Short History of Mexico, by J. Patrick McHenry (Doubleday, 1962)

Sons of the Shaking Earth, by Eric Wolf (University of Chicago Press, 1962)

Science

Log from the Sea of Cortez, by John Steinbeck and E.F. Ricketts (Penguin, 1977)

Reef Fishes of the Sea of Cortez, by Alex Kerstich (Sea Challengers, 1989)

Day Trip Discoveries

The countryside surrounding Mérida is filled with fascinating diversions—Maya ruins, secluded gulf coast beaches, historic haciendas, and enchanting small towns. All are easily reached in day trips from the city. About 34 kilometers (21 miles) north of Mérida lies the port city of **Progreso,** where the coast is lined with small hotels and the summer homes of well-to-do *meridanos.* En route to Progreso are the ruins of **Dzibilchaltún,** a small archaeological site within a nature preserve that includes a *cenote* (a natural well) where you can take a refreshing swim.

Another pleasant coastal destination is **Celestún,** a tiny fishing village 91 kilometers (56 miles) west of the city. The rivers and lagoons around Celestún are a nature preserve for the thousands of pink flamingos that nest here, while areas of the beach are protected for sea turtles, which return every summer to lay their eggs. Bird-watchers can hire boat captains to take them through the lagoons—the sight of flocks of flamingos in flight is truly breathtaking. Restaurants along the beach specialize in the freshest seafood imaginable; don't miss the ceviche, crab claws, and shrimp. There are a few small budget hotels in town; check at the tourist office in Mérida for room availability.

For the most part, Yucatán's henequen haciendas lie crumbling in the countryside, but a few have been restored and are open for tours. The most established one is **Hacienda Yaxcopoil** (Hwy 261, 32 km/20 miles south of Mérida, no phone). The hacienda was built in the mid-1800s, first as a cattle ranch and then as a plantation for henequen, which was grown to make rope. The original house and outbuildings have been restored and are open to the public daily; there's an admission fee. **Hacienda Kancabchen** (24 km/15 miles northeast of Mérida, 840193, 840174 in Mérida) is open for tour groups only and features a restored 1903 home, chapel, and gardens. The organized tours include a traditional Yucatecan dinner and rodeo show along with a tour of the grounds. The main attraction at the restored main house at **Hacienda Teya** (Hwy 180, 13 km/8 miles east of Mérida, 281885, 281889) is its restaurant, open daily for lunch. **Hacienda Temozón** (19 km/12 miles south of Mérida on the road to Uxmal, 443637; fax 448484) has been restored and has a restaurant that serves regional cuisine.

Hacienda Katanchel (Hwy 180, 26 km/16 miles east of Mérida, 234020, 800/223.6510; fax 234000) is a restored 17th-century hacienda that has become the most exclusive, and expensive, hostelry in the region, with 30 luxurious suites, a swimming pool, and a gourmet restaurant set amid 650 forested acres. Other haciendas are being similarly restored, and the area will soon offer travelers a circuit of small country inns.

35 Hotel Residencial $ A logical and comfortable stopping place for those traveling by car is this Pepto-Bismol pink, French Colonial–style hotel. The formal entrance leads into a courtyard with a small kidney-shaped swimming pool, though the noise and traffic of arriving and departing guests impede poolside relaxation. White pillars and wrought-iron railings support the balconies on the four floors above. The decor within the 66 guest rooms is far less opulent than the exterior, but the air-conditioning and showers are powerful, and the mirrored closet is big enough to store a year's supply of clothes. There is also a restaurant, and nearby are a gated parking lot and a pretty little neighborhood park. ♦ Calle 59, No. 589 (between Calles 59-A and 78). 244844, 243099; fax 240266

36 Parque Centenario A fantastic display of youthful merriment and family togetherness takes place every Sunday at this botanical-zoological amusement park, which was inaugurated in 1910 at the western edge of Mérida. Rides in the amusement area are designed for children and Maya adults (many of whom tend to stand little more than four feet tall). There's a sky ride that dangles 10 feet above a shallow lake. Shaded brick pathways wander past the zoo's interesting collection of indigenous monkeys, lizards, and snakes. The park sits at a corner where traffic from the airport and points east veers into downtown. Behind it is an interesting cemetery and residential area. ♦ Free. Daily. Av de los Itzaes (between Calles 65 and 59). 285815

32000[""]

32000[""]

37 Hotel D'Champs $ This thoroughly modern hotel (by far the nicest within walking distance of the bus station) pays tribute to Mérida's French period with its architectural details mimicking the ornamentation of the mansions of Paseo de Montejo. A pale gray–and-peach color scheme carries throughout the lobby and into the 90 rooms decorated in floral pastels. The dining room and bar sit off a garden at the end of a long swimming pool. White wrought-iron tables under shade trees provide a good spot for enjoying a cool drink before returning to your room for a quiet siesta. Large groups are often booked here. ♦ Calle 70, No. 543 (between Calles 67 and 65). 248655, 248829; fax 236024

38 Ermita de Santa Isabela (Saint Isabel Hermitage) The botanical gardens alongside this Jesuit hermitage, built in the mid-1700s, are filled with Maya figurines, stone fountains, wishing wells, and indigenous flowers and trees, many labeled with their Spanish names. Located in a quiet neighborhood with brick roads, the hermitage was a popular resting spot for travelers en route to Campeche in the 1800s and was restored in 1966. ♦ Calle 65 Diagonal (between Calles 79 and 77)

Bests

Roberta Graham de Escobedo
Cofounder/Manager, Ecoturismo Yucatán

Enjoy the small-town, family-oriented atmosphere of "Mérida en Domingo" (Sunday in Mérida), when the downtown streets are closed off to traffic and free entertainment is found in many parks, along with stands selling colorfully embroidered Maya dresses.

You haven't had a real Yucatecan meal until you've tried the fiery *habañero* chili pepper—the hottest chili in the world.

A boat ride up the estuary to observe the pink flamingo colony in the sleepy fishing town of **Celestún** is a must for bird-watchers and nature lovers.

A refreshing dip in the small *cenote* (natural well) **Xlacah** at the ruins of **Dzibilchaltún,** only 30 minutes north of **Mérida,** is a great way to end your visit to the site. Many local Maya enjoy this cooling spot with their families.

Don't miss visiting the **MACAY,** Yucatán's **Museum of Contemporary Art,** to see what's happening in the creative arts here. Both local and national artists are featured in its ever-changing exhibits.

Take time to drive slowly through some of Mérida's older residential neighborhoods to admire the spectacular turn-of-the-century architecture that abounds. A trip back in time.

Every Thursday evening at 9PM at the **Parque Santa Lucia,** both locals and tourists gather for the weekly *serenata* of Yucatecan dancing, music, and poetry. Don't miss it!

Alfonso Escobedo
Founder/Director, Ecoturismo Yucatán

Alberto's Continental Patio in **Mérida** makes the best Lebanese food, their tahini being a delight to enjoy with some crunchy *kak* sesame bread. A chat with Don Alberto is almost as good as the food he serves.

A walk on Mérida's elegant **Paseo de Montejo**—a trip back in time to the turn of the century, with its elegant mansions and lovely old trees.

No visit to Mérida is complete without a ride in a *calesa,* horse-drawn carriages dating back to the French influence on Yucatán's culture.

What more fascinating way to pass an evening than to watch people in the **Plaza Grande,** old men having their shoes shined, children dashing around the flower gardens, young lovers sharing a common bench, even a "bag lady" or two.

One of the reasons Mérida is considered a romantic town is the regular Thursday evening concert, or *serenata,* held at the **Santa Lucia** park, offering Yucatecan dancing, poetry, and guitar trios in a colonial setting under the laurel trees.

Stopping outside one of the many colonial churches on a Saturday night will most often yield a peek into a wedding in process.

"Mérida en Domingo," when the downtown square and nearby streets are closed off to vehicles, offers a wonderful opportunity for visitors and local families alike to stroll and enjoy the free public concerts and stands of local food and crafts that are there for the browsing every Sunday of the year.

Don't forget your snorkel equipment if you stay at beautiful **Akumal Beach** south of **Cancún.**

Can you imagine sitting on a park bench but not being able to put your arms around your lover? The *confidenciales* (benches) of Mérida are designed in an "S" shape so you end up looking into the eyes of your bench partner instead of sitting side by side. Quite an innovation.

Los Almendros restaurant in Mérida is the best place in town to savor the world-famous Yucatecan cuisine—especially yummy is the stuffed cheese and the turkey oriental style.

Uxmal

Hidden in the rolling green hills of the **Puuc** territory (*puuc* is Maya for hill), Uxmal is **Yucatán**'s most architecturally beautiful Maya site. Its pyramids and palaces are decorated with incredibly ornate and intricate latticework friezes that from afar look like delicate lace held up against the azure sky. The elliptical and enchanting **Pyramid of the Magician** echoes the form of the surrounding terrain, looming above the angular planes and geometric designs of the **Quadrangle of the Nuns**.

Tour guides will tell you that Uxmal means "thrice built"; archaeologists, however, have found that it was occupied and rebuilt at least five times.

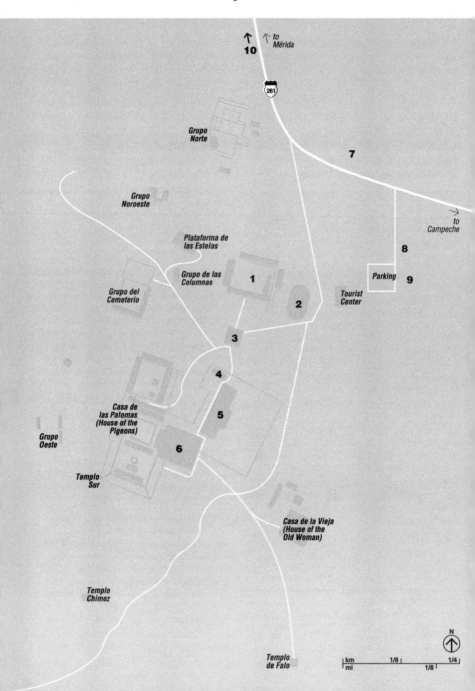

The area first flourished in the seventh century and was abandoned and reoccupied sporadically through the ninth century. A tribe known as the Tutul Xiú invaded Uxmal in the early 10th century and held on for about 400 years, a period of war and strife between the Yucatán's Maya tribes. When the Spaniards arrived in the mid-15th century, Uxmal was essentially deserted.

Archaeologists have yet to completely understand why Uxmal was inhabited and deserted so many times. One clue can be found in the abundance of masks and sculptures of the snout-nosed rain god, Chac. The people had good reason to fear and revere Chac, for water is scarce here. There are no *cenotes* (natural wells in the limestone terrain), which soak up rainwater. And though the Maya dug *chultunes* (cisterns) for collecting water during the infrequent storms, drought may well have driven them away.

Most travelers visit Uxmal for just a few hours on day trips from Mérida, 50 miles north, and also stop at other major sites in the Puuc region. For a far more rewarding visit, spend the night near the ruins; you'll be able to explore them early in the morning and evening, when the tour groups are gone, and you can return at night for the sound-and-light show, the best of its kind in Mexico. The colorful display brings out architectural details easily missed in daylight, and the site takes on an eerie sense of mystery, especially in the glow of the moon. Uxmal is open daily; there is an admission fee (free on Sunday) and an extra charge for using a video camera. The sound-and-light show is presented twice nightly—once in Spanish and again in English.

Area code 99 unless otherwise noted.

1 Cuadrángulo de las Monjas (Quadrangle of the Nuns) The Spaniards named this group of four buildings surrounding a central plaza. Archaeologists suspect the Maya used it as a school for the military or royalty, housing the students in some 70 small rooms. A fine example of a corbeled arch marks the main entrance at the south side. The facades are strikingly ornate, with stone latticework friezes at the top of each building, interspersed with masonry masks, snakes, and miniature representations of the *na* (a classic Maya hut), still seen in villages throughout the Yucatán Peninsula.

2 Pirámide del Adivinador (Pyramid of the Magician) Said to be the only Maya structure built in an ellipse, this graceful, beautiful pyramid faces west toward the setting sun and stands 92 feet high. Its western stairway slopes at a 60° angle; the eastern stairway is even steeper, but the view is worth the climb. A doorway shaped like the grotesque face of Chac leads into the small temple at the top (you pass through his mouth). Several legends purport to explain the origin of the pyramid—some say it was built in one night by a magical dwarf, others that it housed a magician dwarf king who overthrew an evil leader with cunning, trickery, and the help of a giant bat speaking for the gods. The original pyramid was rebuilt five times, each new version covering the last and maintaining the basic oval form. The best times to take photos are at sunrise and sunset, when the limestone walls take on a golden glow. At night, in the full moonlight, the pyramid has an ethereal beauty that could never be captured on film.

3 Juego de Pelota (Ball Court) Set within viewing distance from **Uxmal**'s major buildings, this was the site of ritualistic games involving human sacrifice. This court is far smaller than the one at **Chichén Itzá** and has not been restored.

4 Casa de las Tortugas (House of the Turtles) The upper cornices of this small, simple temple are embedded with a turtle motif. Some of the seven tiny rooms inside have platforms about 16 inches high. Archaeologists have yet to figure out the purpose of these platforms.

The most economical meal in Mexico is the *comida corrida*, a fixed-price meal that includes soup, salad, entrée, rice, dessert, and a drink. The lunch is usually available throughout the afternoon at small cafes and restaurants favored by locals.

Restaurants/Clubs: Red **Hotels:** Blue

Shops/ Outdoors: Green **Sights/Culture:** Black

On the Road to Ruins

Several small and fascinating Maya sites are scattered along the highways south of **Mérida** and around **Uxmal.** You can cover most of them on a day trip from Mérida or spend the night at **Uxmal** for more time to explore. The most popular route is a circular drive beginning south of **Uxmal** on **Highway 261.** Some sites are undergoing excavation; some structures may be roped off. A small admission fee is charged at all the sites, except on Sunday, when admission is free.

Once connected to **Uxmal** 22 kilometers (14 miles) northwest by a now overgrown limestone road called a *sacbe,* **Kabah** is fascinating for its **Palacio de los Mascarones** (Palace of the Masks) and **Codz-Pop** temple, both covered with hundreds of hook-nosed images of the rain god Chac. An unnamed road marked with signs for the ruins turns east off Highway 261 south of Kabah. **Sayil,** five kilometers (three miles) southeast, contains a restored three-story palace. Reliefs of Chac adorn the second level of the palace, along with a replica of the Descending God, who is normally associated with **Tulum. Xcapak,** two kilometers (one mile) southeast, is a small site with three barely rebuilt structures. **Labná,** another six kilometers (four miles) south, is marked by a large ceremonial arch with two reproductions of the classic *na* (Maya hut) and the ubiquitous Chac. All sites are open daily and charge small admission fees except on Sunday.

About 29 kilometers (18 miles) northeast of **Labná** are the **Caves of Loltún,** an underground system of enormous caverns and passageways with Maya sculptures interspersed with surrealistically shaped stalactites. The name Loltún means "flower of the rock," possibly referring to the petal-shaped rooms off one corridor. Visitors must take part in a guided tour of the caves and are not allowed to wander about alone. Tours are offered daily (check at the information desk at **Uxmal** for tour hours), and there is an admission fee.

Mani is a contemporary Maya town at the northeast point of the Maya route loop and is infamous as the site where Fray Diego de Landa, a Spanish Franciscan zealot, burned nearly all the Maya books and documents. The huge 16th-century church and monastery in the center of town was built in an amazingly short seven-month period with the labor of the Maya, who were beaten for honoring their gods. Mani also has the *cenote* where the wicked mother of the magical dwarf who (maybe) built the **Uxmal** pyramid is said to live. Legend has it that she would make the well run dry and demand that babies be tossed in as a sacrifice in return for water.

Ticul, a Maya town near the intersection of Highway 261 and **Highway 184,** is a good place to stop for lunch, though the traffic is horrendous. Its main restaurant, **Los Almendros** (★★$; Calle 23, No. 207, 997/20021), has a reputation for serving the best Yucatecan cuisine around, and the prices are moderate. The outdoor patio is pleasant when there's a breeze. **Arte Maya,** at the west side of town on **Calle 23,** is a must-see gallery of Maya sculptures, created by a cooperative of artists who trained with the late master of Maya carving, Wilbert Gonzalez.

---

5 Palacio Gobierno (Palace of the Governor) Considered by some to be the finest example of pre-Hispanic art in Mesoamerica, the 320-footlong palace is separated by three corbeled arches, creating narrow passageways or sanctuaries. The intricate friezes along the uppermost section of the palace are made up of geometric carvings overlaid with plumed serpents and Chac masks. What looks like a carved chain at the top cornice is actually a representation of undulating serpents, whose heads once protruded from the corners, but now are gone. The limestone mosaics decorating the building are said to have required more than 20,000 individually cut stones set into a rubble core. The Spaniards gave the palace its current name, but it is believed the Maya used it as a center for astronomy. The building faces east, toward Venus, and every eight years the planet rises on the horizon to a point that is aligned with the palace's main door.

6 Pirámide Grande (Great Pyramid) Also called the **"Pyramid of the Macaws"** for the carvings of birds in flight that decorate its walls, this pyramid rises 65 steps in 9 levels above the **Palacio Gobierno.** Though the view from the **Pirámide del Adivinador** is said to be the finest at **Uxmal,** photographers should climb up here for panoramic shots of the city's buildings set against the impenetrable jungle. From here you can see rounded mounds overgrown with grass and trees, probably covering even more buildings waiting to be excavated.

7 Hotel Hacienda Uxmal $$$ This was the first hotel at **Uxmal,** and it feels like a private hacienda where the Maya housekeepers, porters, and waiters are considered part of the family. The 80 rooms are furnished with wood-and-wicker rocking chairs, dressers, and headboards. Air-conditioning and cable TV with movie channels have been added to most of the rooms; hot water is usually abundant. Tropical flowers and trees shade the swimming pool. The restaurant has improved considerably since it opened and offers breakfast, lunch, and a three-course dinner. Snacks are served at the poolside bar in high season. ♦ Hwy 261. 280840; fax 234744. For reservations: Plaza Americana (Fiesta Americana Mérida, Paseo de Montejo 451, at Av Colón), Suite 1A, Mérida. 250621, 250622, 800/235.4079; fax 250087

8 The Lodge at Uxmal $$ The most comfortable, beautiful rooms by the ruins were completed in 1997 at this lodge that stands directly across from their entrance. Hardwood doors carved with Maya designs open into spacious quarters with stained-glass windows, red-tile floors, ceiling fans, air-conditioning, televisions, small refrigerators, and hand-crafted wooden furnishings. Rooms at the ends of each building have curved windows facing the lawns and a pool that flows around a grassy island graced with mature trees. Meals are served under a large *palapa* beside a second pool. Nonguests who lunch at the restaurant are allowed to use the pool for free—a blessing after climbing pyramids. ♦ South of Hwy 261. 280840; fax 234744.

For reservations: Plaza Americana Local (on Av Colón), Suite 1A. 250621, 250622, 800/235.4079; fax 250087

9 Villa Arqueológica $$ Club Med manages a hotel by the ruins, a very popular choice with European travelers and tour groups. A two-story white stucco building framing the swimming pool houses 44 small, air-conditioned guest rooms. The dining room serves the best food at the site. ♦ South of Hwy 261. 247503, 800/555.8842

10 Rancho Uxmal $ Your only option for inexpensive rooms near the ruins is this simple 20-room inn with a very good restaurant and a swimming pool (filled only during high season). The rooms have soft mattresses, fans, and private bathrooms with hot showers. Four rooms have air-conditioning and cost a bit more. It's a 45-minute walk to the ruins, but you may be able to catch a ride or flag down a bus; buses traveling to Mérida from the ruins will drop you off at the hotel. ♦ No credit cards accepted. Hwy 261 (about 3 km/2 miles north of Uxmal). For reservations: Rancho Uxmal, Calle 26, No. 156, Ticul, Yucatán 97860, Mexico. 997/20277

Campeche

Nestled between the **Gulf of Mexico** and the jungles of **Quintana Roo,** Campeche is the most overlooked of the three states on the **Yucatán Peninsula.** The capital city, also called Campeche, is the most frequently visited part of the state, although only about 50,000 tourists make it here each year. In the early 1500s, the capital was an entry point to the peninsula for the Spanish, who fortified it against pirates in the 1600s with *baluartes* (massive stone walls and gates) that still surround the city.

Much of this state is wild and sparsely inhabited, with a population of only about 700,000. Few roads run to the south and east, where many of the animals that have disappeared from the peninsula—jaguars, ocelots, and deer—roam undisturbed in natural preserves. Maya sites, many of which have barely been explored, are hidden in the rainy jungles to the south and the dry plains to the north.

The largest Maya burial ground on the peninsula is on **Isla Jaina** off Campeche's northwest coast, which is closed to tourists. Some of the most beautiful statues, carvings, and jewelry from the Maya world have been found in burial jars on the banks of Jaina's rivers; most of those treasures are now in museums and collections around the world. **Edzná** is the most frequently visited Maya site in the state and sits south of the highway between Campeche and **Uxmal.** Built and inhabited between 300 BC and AD 900, **Edzná** is best known for its **Temple of Five Stories,** a stepped pyramid with intricate details. Nearby, the site of **Xtampak** is undergoing sporadic excavation, as are **Becan, Chicana, Xpuhil,** and **Calakmul** in the southern part of the state. Tourism services are scarce in this area, though the sites can be reached on a long day trip from either the capital city or **Chetumal,** on the Quintana Roo coast.

Most of the capital's urban attractions can be seen in a day and are concentrated along the waterfront and the main plaza (bounded by Calles 55 and 57, and 10 and 5). The **Baluarte de San Carlos** (Av 16 de Septiembre and Calle 67, no phone) has a small museum of the city's history. It is open Tuesday through Sunday and charges an admission fee. **Baluarte de Santiago** (Av 16 de Septiembre and Calle 51) surrounds a lush botanical garden, while **Baluarte de la Soledad** (Calles 8 and 57, no phone) offers a sweeping view of the town and waterfront from its gun towers, and an enclosed collection of stelae from the state's many Maya archaeological sites. It is open Tuesday through Sunday. Campeche's **Catedral** (Calles 55 and 10) was constructed from 1650 to 1850 and is far more ornate and Gothic than the one in Mérida. The **Museo Regional de Campeche** (Calle 59 (between Calles 16 and 14, 981/69111) was originally built for the royal governor in 1804 and houses a respectable collection of artifacts from Maya ruins. The museum is open Tuesday through Sunday, and there is an admission fee.

The best hotel in the city is the waterfront **Ramada Inn Campeche** ($$; Av Ruíz Cortinez 151, at Calle 59, 981/62233, 800/272.6234), the least expensive hotel in the Ramada chain. Fishing is one of Campeche's leading industries, which means seafood stars on local menus.

Chichén Itzá

The most famous of the Maya sites, **Chichén Itzá** covers about four square miles of jungle, and the area surrounding the ruins has been cleared and planted with green lawns. Hordes of tourists arrive by the busload from Mérida and Cancún, swarming over the sacred buildings. Tour bus engines drone incessantly as their drivers wait in air-conditioned comfort. But there is a way to appreciate **Chichén Itzá**'s grandeur with some sense of isolation— just be at the gates the minute they open (8AM). Shutterbugs who wish to

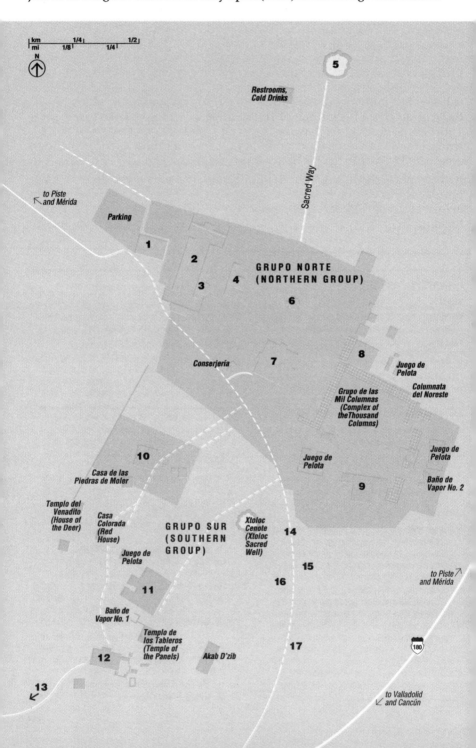

photograph the ruins sans humans should definitely arrive early. Then take a break at midday, when the crowds are at their peak, and return in the mid-afternoon, about the time the out-of-towners are loading up for their journey back to the cities. Naturally, this schedule works best if you spend the night at one of the captivating hotels nearby.

Giving yourself a couple of days to fully explore **Chichén Itzá** allows you to follow its development chronologically and architecturally. The ceremonial center of **Chichén Itzá** went through several incarnations. At the far southern edge of the site are the oldest buildings, believed to have been constructed around AD 400–600, during the Maya Classical Period. In AD 900, the site was invaded by the Itzá, a Maya tribe from the south associated with the Aztec. The Itzá were then joined by the Toltec from around Mexico City in the latter part of the 10th century; the combined groups altered existing buildings and constructed others in a style blending elements from both cultures. The buildings in the **Grupo Sur** (Southern Group), including **El Caracol**, show the beginnings of Toltec influence, with pure Maya elements. Those in the north group have distinct Toltec designs, emphasizing war, struggle, and sacrifice in the carvings. **Chichén Itzá's** most famous buildings, especially **El Castillo** temple, were completed in this era.

A dirt road divides the north and south groups; if you have the time, spend one day at each. If you have only a day to see **Chichén Itzá**, plan on spending at least four hours at the site and more if you wish to climb the several steep buildings and survey the scenery. Guides are available at the entrance and will entertain you with a mix of fact, folklore, and fantasy for a reasonable sum. Wear comfortable shoes and sunscreen, and carry a bottle of water.

The evening sound-and-light show has been completely revamped, with improved technical systems and a more factual text. The show is worth seeing, plus it gets you into the ruins at night (though you are not allowed to wander about). Wear insect repellent and carry a flashlight. There are two entrances—one from the main parking lot, the other from the south road leading to the hotels. **Chichén Itzá** is located on **Highway 180** between Mérida and Cancún, and is open daily. There is an admission fee, except on Sunday. The nightly sound-and-light show is presented twice each evening, once in Spanish and once in English.

Area code 985 unless otherwise noted.

1 Main Entrance The Mexican government has prettied up the entryways to many major archaeological sites, putting in parking lots (with parking fees), restricting vendors to permanent stalls, and creating a central gathering place for groups. At **Chichén Itzá**, you enter through a cement corbeled arch to a central shopping and dining area with rest room facilities adequate for busloads of tourists. Backpackers can check their gear at the ticket counter. A large model of the site gives you a good overview of what you will see. Facilities include an excellent bookstore, an ice-cream parlor, a jewelry store, a decent restaurant, and a small museum where several carvings from the buildings are protected from the elements.

Within the Main Entrance:

Cultur Servicios (Shopping Center) This large store is divided into several small shops. There are two excellent sections selling books on the Maya and Mexico, a camera and film department, and a money-exchange counter (however, it offers a dreadful exchange rate for US dollars). You must purchase each item at its corresponding counter. ◆ Daily. No phone

Restaurante Ruinas de Chichén Itzá ★★$ Better than would be expected, this cafeteria-style restaurant serves breakfast all day (including a refreshing fruit plate), plus tourist-oriented treats such as fried chicken, spaghetti, and tuna sandwiches. Some tables are scattered away from the rest under big trees, a perfect spot for writing postcards. ◆ Cafeteria ◆ Daily. No phone

2 Juego de Pelota (Ball Court) This ball court may be the largest in the Maya world, at 272 feet long and 99 feet wide. Sheer cut stone walls run the length of the court on each side, and stone rings protrude near the top of the walls. The game played in this court is believed to have resembled soccer.

Players used their heads, shoulders, and feet (but not their hands) to pass a small rubber ball through the rings. It seems the games ended in ritual sacrifice, though it still is not clear whether the winners or losers lost their heads. Sacrifice to the gods was, after all, considered to be an honor, though it may be hard to imagine people playing their hearts out to make such an offering. The acoustics of the court are excellent; a person can hear whispering or clapping at the other end of the court, though the chatter and yelling from your fellow visitors may frustrate your attempts to replicate this experiment.

J. DEL GAIZO

3 Templo del Jaguar (Temple of the Jaguar) A chamber at the base of this temple is decorated with frescoes of warriors in elaborate regalia, with some of the original green and red paint intact. Beehives hang from the ceiling, perhaps allowed to remain in the hope that they will discourage visitors from loitering in the chamber and leaning on the walls, thus rubbing off the paintings. A jaguar sculpture in the middle of the chamber, the last such intact carving at **Chichén,** has oversized claws and a leering grin much like that of the Cheshire cat. The standing jaguar's back is flat, making a tempting perch for souvenir photos. Consider the cumulative damage of thousands of tourists straddling this ancient cat and refrain from adding to the destruction.

4 Tzompantli Four walls carved with hundreds of skulls surround a platform four feet high littered with more freestanding skulls, some with red paint present. This is probably where the heads of enemies and ball players (see above) were displayed, impaled on stakes. Carvings of warriors and serpents can be seen on the wall facing the **Templo de los Guerreros** (Temple of the Warriors).

El Castillo

5 Cenote (Sacred Well) A wide dirt road, once paved with limestone, leads north from the main cluster of ruins to this oval-shaped sinkhole measuring 198 feet long, 194 feet wide, and 69 feet deep from ground level to the water's surface; the water is at least 90 feet deep. The upper sides of the *cenote* are clogged with tree roots and vines, but the limestone walls become slick and slippery closer to the water.

It was first believed that young female virgins were hurled into these waters to appease the rain gods, but diving archaeologists have since discovered skeletons belonging to individuals of all ages and both sexes. Some believe that the society's castoffs (the sick, old, or degenerate) were sacrificed here to the rain god. Another story is that men, women, and children were all thrown into the well to satisfy the gods in the early morning. The slippery walls were impossible to climb, and most could not swim well enough to survive until noon. Those who remained on the surface were lifted from the water to relate the stories of what they had learned from the spirits in the water. Thousands of artifacts of gold and jade, items highly precious to the Maya, have also been found in the murky depths, which undoubtedly hold more treasures. Several underwater archaeological digs have taken place here, including one headed by Jacques Cousteau. A refreshment stand and rest rooms are located by the *cenote*.

6 El Adoratorio de Venus (The Temple of Venus) Serpent monsters with human heads coming out of their mouths are carved along the stairways. It is believed these carvings represented the planet Venus. The temple is also known as the "Temple of Chac Mool," for a statue of this figure that was buried inside (now displayed at the **Museo de Antropología** in Mexico City). A large Chac Mool (a stone carving), patched with cement, stands beside the temple.

7 El Castillo (The Castle) Also known as the "Temple of Kukulcán," the grandest of Chichén Itzá's ceremonial buildings (loosely called pyramids) looms 98 feet above ground in a regal mass of gray limestone befitting its name. It dominates the site in stark symmetry and tells us much about the Maya concept of time. Four stairways facing the cardinal directions have 91 steps each. Visitors can climb the west stairway, a steep and somewhat frightening ascent and an even more terrifying descent; you can hold on to the rusted chain running down the center. The steps in the four stairways, combined with the

J. DEL GAIZO

single step up to the temple at the top, total 365. Fifty-two panels on the sides represent the years of the Maya calendar, while the 18 terraces each represent a month of the religious year (each month consisting of 20 days, plus a 5-day month, equaling 365).

The building is topped by a temple to Kukulcán (known as "Quetzalcoatl" in other parts of Mexico), the deity that led the Toltec on their migration to Yucatán, and who is represented by a feathered snake. Archaeologists have discovered a more ancient temple inside the pyramid. A slippery, damp stairway leads from a small doorway under the north steps up to an altar holding two statues. One is a Chac Mool, a stone carving of a reclining figure with a dish on his chest—where the hearts of sacrificed victims were placed in offerings to the gods; the other is a bejeweled red tiger that originally wore a mosaic disc of jade and turquoise, now in the **Museo de Antropología** in Mexico City. The inner temple is open to the public only a few hours in the morning and again for a few hours in the afternoon. Those prone to claustrophobia should take heed: The stairs are narrow, dark, and winding, and most days there is a line of tourists going both ways, making the trip somewhat frightening.

A great stone serpent head protrudes from the base of the stairway. At the spring and fall equinox (21 March and 21 September), the afternoon light and shadows strike the stairway and form a picture of Kukulcán undulating out of his temple and wriggling down the pyramid to bless the fertile earth. The engineering skill that went into this amazing project boggles the mind. Thousands of people travel to **Chichén Itzá** to witness the sight, particularly in the spring, since there is always the chance that the fall rains will spoil

the spectacle. It's wise to make hotel reservations well in advance—a year ahead is not unreasonable.

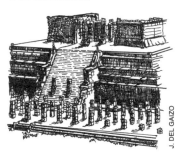

J. DEL GAIZO

8 Templo de los Guerreros (Temple of the Warriors) Also known as the "**Temple of a Thousand Columns,**" this sits east of **El Castillo.** Stand near the open-mouthed serpent's head at the northwest corner of **El Castillo** for a great photo of the ornate serpent and the towering pyramid juxtaposed against a lineup of white limestone pillars. The temple is much like the **Temple of Venus** in the Toltec center of **Tula** north of Mexico City. Archaeologists speculate the Toltec carried plans for the building from their homeland to **Chichén Itzá** when they traveled to Yucatán and overtook the Maya in AD 900. The columns, running in straight rows in front of the temple and along its southern side, are carved with reliefs of warriors on all four squared-off facades. Rising above the columns, the temple has several distinctive characteristics. The side of the front stairway is shaped in a corbeled arch, and masks of the rain god, Chac, protrude from the sides of the stairway. A reclining Chac Mool sits near the top of the steps, and carvings of serpents, jaguars, and warriors are still visible on the walls.

Piste

The archaeological site of **Chichén Itzá** sits at the edge of Piste, a small village where more and more tourist shops and visitors' services are opening each year. Acting as the service center for the ruins, Piste already has a gas station, a bank (where it may be difficult to change large traveler's checks—bring along the cash you will need), and several restaurants and hotels.

For the most part the restaurants are geared toward the tour bus trade and are alternately packed full or totally empty. **Pueblo Maya** (★; 985/62777), a tourist attraction on the main road through town, is the best choice for a reasonably priced buffet lunch served in a mock Maya village with artificial streams and artisans' workshops. Less touristy (though it does cater to bus groups) is **Hacienda Xaybe'h** (★★; 985/10039), with a large dining room serving

buffet meals, an outdoor pool available to those who dine in the restaurant, and a good gift shop.

Piste's hotels have lower rates than those right at the ruins, and most are within easy walking distance of the site. The **Pirámide Inn** (Carretera Mérida-Valladolid, 985/62462) has 44 motel-like rooms, a large pool and courtyard, a good restaurant, and information on tours to other Maya sites. The best budget hotel in the area is the **Hotel Dolores Alba** (99/285650; fax 99/283163 in Mérida), on the highway south of the ruins toward **Valladolid.** The basic rooms, some with air-conditioning, are more than adequate, and hammocks hang beside the small pool. Breakfast and dinner are served in the lobby restaurant. The owners are extremely accommodating—they'll drive you to the ruins in the morning and flag down buses en route to Valladolid or **Mérida** for you to continue on your travels.

9 El Mercado South from the **Templo de los Guerreros,** a narrow pathway leads to this little-visited cluster of ruins. A large, columned portico extends to the north side forming two parallel galleries. In one of these is an altar with bas-reliefs. In the rear is a courtyard surrounded by columns, which some suspect may have been covered with palm thatch and used as a market area.

10 Grupo Sur The old road from Mérida used to cut right through **Chichén Itzá,** dividing the ruins in the north from those in the south. A pathway now leads from the remains of this road to the **Southern Group** (also called the "Central Group"). There is a refreshment stand at the beginning of this trail, with tables and chairs shaded by a *palapa* (thatched-palm hut).

10 El Osario (The Tomb of the Great Priest) Working when funding is available, archaeologists have unearthed from a mound of rubble at this site at least seven skeletons with artifacts that would have been buried with high priests. After removing the artifacts and bones, they have begun reconstructing the main edifice covering the tombs. Though the reconstruction has been going on for over two years, the building is still roped off, and visitors are not allowed to climb the steps to the top. Other structures in the area are being excavated and may also be roped off.

J. DEL GAIZO

11 El Caracol (The Observatory) To some, this is the most beautiful building in the Maya world. A circular tower sits atop two tiered platforms, with small windows facing the four cardinal points. A spiral staircase inside the platforms winds to the top, but it is not open to the public. The name means "the snail" and supposedly refers to this staircase. The building is believed to have been used by astronomers. It is particularly beautiful late in the day, when its tower glows gold in the light of the setting sun.

La Malinche was the Indian mistress, adviser, and interpreter who aided Hernán Cortés in his conquest of Mexico. Today, the pejorative term *malinchismo* refers to a person's preference for all things foreign.

12 Casa de las Monjas (House of the Nuns) The Spaniards believed virgins who were destined to be sacrificed lived in this building, and thus they gave it this monastic name. Climbing the pyramid gets more difficult every year, as the limestone steps continue crumbling, but the view is well worth the fright. Crouch behind the small door at the top for a spectacular photo of **El Caracol** and **El Castillo.** There are several small chambers at the base of the building in back. Guides say the pyramid will soon be roped off and climbing prohibited.

13 Chichén Viejo A pathway just west of the **Casa de las Monjas** leads to the oldest ruins of **Chichén Itzá,** which are only partially excavated. The farther you wander on this isolated jungle path, the more you begin to understand what it must have been like when early explorers first stumbled upon the ruins. Overgrown mounds on both sides of the path are labeled with rickety signs that point out the **Temple of the Phallus** and the **Temple of the Lintels.** The carvings on these buildings are similar to those found in the Puuc region of **Uxmal,** with lacy latticework and distinctive Chac masks. Maya guides are usually waiting at the beginning of the path, and can lead you deep into the jungle, away from the tourist-oriented parts of **Chichén Itzá** into a world that seems untouched by modern influences.

14 Southern Entrance The old road that once carried traffic through **Chichén Itzá** leads to a rear entrance of the ruins and past a few hotels to join the main road again. Area Maya residents still use the road as a shortcut, riding their bikes over dirt ridges and ruts past a steady stream of tourists. In the high season Maya women hang clotheslines by the tour buses and sell T-shirts, blankets, and shawls. Several tour companies park their buses just outside the back gate, where you can pay the entrance fee and come and go from the ruins to the hotels. Guests at the three hotels along this road have easy access to the ruins and can take a break at midday to swim, eat, and sleep.

HOTEL
MAYALAND

15 Hotel Mayaland $$$ Enchanting and unrelentingly romantic, this hotel sits in a hundred-acre jungle of red ginger blossoms, fuchsia bougainvillea, and towering trees. Inside the 95 rooms, located in a three-story main building and in traditional Maya *nas* (huts) scattered about the grounds, mosquito nets hang over beds that have Maya designs carved in their mahogany frames. Wooden shutters cover screened windows, ceiling fans lazily stir the tropical air, and low-slung cane and mahogany chairs sit on front porches. All rooms have air-conditioning and TVs; some at the front of the main building enjoy a breathtaking view of **El Caracol.** A separate section of 24 Maya villas is reserved for groups and has its own pool and driveway from the main highway; another 100 rooms are planned here.

The main pool is the perfect escape from the midday heat, and basic meals are available at the three restaurants, but they get a bit crowded with day-trippers. After the tour buses pull away, however, and the sun sets behind the ruins poking through the jungle, there isn't a more romantic place to stay. ◆ West of Hwy 180. 985/10077; fax 985/10129. For reservations in Mérida: Mayaland Tours, Plaza Americana, Suite 18A , Mérida, Yucatán 97000, Mexico. 250621, 250622, 800/235.4079; fax 250087

16 Hotel Hacienda Chichén $$ So mysterious they seem almost haunted, the 20 air-conditioned rooms here are located in small cottages scattered about the grounds, many with secret paths leading from their porches into the jungle to **Chichén Viejo.** The rooms were built for the archaeologists originally excavating the ruins in the early 1900s, and when you open the wood shutters to the sounds of the jungle at night you feel as though you've journeyed back to another era. Three suites have been added in cottages resembling the older buildings. The main building and stone archway in front of it are the remains of a 17th-century hacienda, complete with a small Catholic church said to be the oldest on the peninsula. The pool is much newer, though it's surrounded by rock walls and trees that seem to have been there forever.

The hotel is open all year, and advance reservations are strongly advised. Meals are served in the central dining room and on the main building's porch looking over the grounds. An old railroad track runs by the church into the jungle, serving as a path to the ruins. Another trail runs to **El Caracol** from behind the cottages. The Maya workers at the hotel can guide you along these walks during their off-hours (for a tip). ◆ West of Hwy 180. 10045. For reservations in Mérida: Calle 60, No. 488, Mérida, Yucatán 97000, Mexico. 99/248844, 800/624.8451; fax 99/245011

17 Villa Archeológica $$$ One of several hotels built by the government near archaeological sites and managed by Club Med, this place is typically filled with tour groups from the **Club Med** in Cancún, though individual guests are welcome. The 32 small, air-conditioned rooms are decorated with local folk art, and there's a good library on the Maya. The pool is a cool, shaded spot perfect for relaxing after climbing the ruins. There's also a good French restaurant—the most expensive dining spot around. ◆ West of Hwy 180. 800/555.8842

Bests

Alicia del Villar de Blanco
Entrepreneur

Mérida This city of bleached-white roofs and sparkling clean streets has a charm that's hard to describe. It's one of the safest places in Mexico, probably because there is no drug problem among the young; the family structure is very solid, and adolescents feel wanted and cared for here. Mérida has impressive historical sites: the ornate **Cathedral;** the **Palacio Gobierno,** a beautiful 17th-century building housing city offices; the **Teatro José Peón Contreras,** an architectural jewel; the **Universidad Autónomo de Yucatán;** and **Paseo de Montejo,** which is filled with elaborate mansions and happy inhabitants.

Chichén Itzá Along with **Palenque** and **Tikal,** this is one of the most extensive Maya archaeological sites. Grandiose temples, pyramids, a ball court, and other structures speak highly of a most amazing and ancient civilization. Among many achievements, the Maya invented the concept of "zero," an exercise in abstract thought that the Europeans started using in the early Middle Ages, when the Maya were already in decline. The **Temple of Kukulcán,** also known as **"El Castillo,"** is magnificent and is the focus of a biannual equinox in March and September, when the play of light from the setting sun suggests a serpent undulating down the principal staircase. You'll also see ancient steam baths, a ceremonial ball court with amazing acoustics, temples to Venus and the Jaguar, and much more.

Uxmal All the majesty and grandiosity of **Chichén Itzá** cannot compare with the rare beauty of **Uxmal,** where the creators outdid each other in their artisanship. Delicate structures are graced with a stone filigree not seen anywhere else in the world. Among the many buildings worth touring are the **Pyramid of the Magician;** the **Quadrangle of the Nuns,** with rooms resembling Spanish cloisters; and the **Governor's Palace,** one of the most stunning pre-Columbian structures. Every night there is a spectacular hourlong light-and-sound show, in Spanish at 7PM and in English at 9PM.

Izamal This harmoniously built colonial city 72 kilometers (45 miles) east of Mérida is famous for its immense **Convent,** built by **Diego de Landa** in the 16th century atop an ancient Maya pyramid. You reach it by climbing the pyramid's original steps. Three platforms make the complex asymmetric, and it's surrounded by many arches.

Cancún

Cancún is designed to dazzle and mesmerize, to fill visitors' days with sun, sea, and shopping, and their nights with a whirl of music, dining, dancing, and gazing at star-filled skies. Reality is held at bay by an onslaught of sensations. Palms wave lazily beside shimmering pools; parasailers float high above the shore; neon-bright windsurfers skim the surface of the sea like graceful birds. Swimmers and snorkelers move leisurely from their towels to the water and back, skin glistening with oil and sweat.

Standing on the beach you'd hardly know you were in Mexico, save for the occasional drift of Spanish. Margaritas and guacamole are popular snacks by the pool, but it's not as though you have to adapt to another culture. In fact, Cancún has a culture all its own, a hybrid of modern Mexican and American trappings with little indigenous influence. Thirty years ago, the 13-milelong island was an undeveloped strip of white, talcum-fine sand. But thanks to its natural attributes—beautiful beaches, reefs for snorkeling and scuba diving, proximity to the Maya ruins, and adequate space and facilities—it was selected by FONATUR, the government agency charged with improving Mexico's tourist facilities, as the country's first multimillion-dollar experiment in resort development. Ground was broken for the first hotel in 1970, and the area has been booming ever since. Today there are some 120 hotels, with more than 22,000 rooms.

Cancún was created to lure and captivate vacationers, and it does just that. Many visitors set up housekeeping in vacation-ownership properties; some bask in sublime luxury at the area's glitziest hotels. The wise ones take advantage of the abundance of package deals and charter flights that make Cancún accessible to middle-income tourists. The only ones left out of the picture are budget travelers; as a rule, the lack of interest is mutual.

Cancún aims to soothe its guests without straining their sensibilities. Tourists congregate on the island, a stretch of white sand shaped like the number "7" and framed by the **Caribbean Sea** and a series of lagoons. US franchises crowd **Paseo Kukulcán**, the single road running the length of the tourist zone. Multiple shopping plazas offer name brands recognized all over the world. Cancún aims to please everyone, albeit in a homogenized, white-bread way.

Most of Cancún's nearly 350,000 residents live beyond the island hotel zone in a mainland city that was, like the resort, also nonexistent 30 years ago. The city and hotel zone are connected by Paseo Kukulcán and a man-made strip of land. Most visitors venture into downtown Cancún at least once, strolling through the tourist-oriented shops and restaurants on **Avenidas Tulum** and **Yaxchilán.** But the downtown area is almost completely overshadowed by the hotel zone; in the past few years, several wonderful restaurants have either closed or moved closer to the hotels. Others survive, thanks to their great reputations. The city is certainly worth exploring and has actually become more interesting in recent years as the province of budget travelers and locals.

One of Cancún's greatest advantages is its position as a convenient, accessible gateway to the Mexican **Caribbean** and the **Yucatán Peninsula.** Those who travel the region frequently jet in and out of Cancún, using the resort area as a launching pad for further exploration and spending a night or two in comfort at both ends of their journeys. There are as many ways to get out of Cancún as there are to get in. Ferries and tours frequently head east across the Caribbean to **Isla Mujeres**, a traditional favorite of the getaway traveler. Public and tour buses ply the roads from Cancún to the Maya ruins of **Chichén Itzá, Cobá,** and **Tulum,** all within a day's trip. Rental cars whiz along the 80-milelong **Cancún-Tulum Corridor (Highway 307),** headed to more secluded

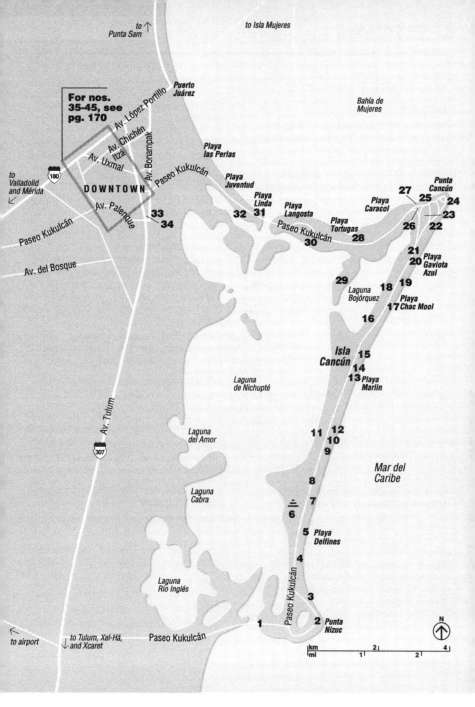

For nos. 35-45, see pg. 170

paradises. If you have at least a week's vacation, rent a car for a day or two and explore. Once you are about 10 miles out of town, surrounded by scrubby jungle interspersed with thatch-roofed Maya huts, you will come to see Cancún as the aberration that it is. But you'll also understand why the handful of bankers and politicians who flew over the eastern wilderness of the Yucatán Peninsula in the late 1960s settled on this area as the perfect place to create a tropical paradise.

Area code 98 unless otherwise noted.

Getting to Cancún

Airport

Aeropuerto Internacional de Cancún (Cancún International Airport) is 10 kilometers (six miles) west of **Punta Nizuc,** the southern end of the hotel zone, and 14 kilometers (nine miles) south of Cancún. The airport has one terminal that handles both domestic and international flights.

Airport Services

Information...845839

Airlines

AeroCancún 850225, 860228

AeroCozumel and AeroCaribe 842020, 860162

Aeroméxico 843571, 860018,
....800/273.6639 in the US

American 860055, 841907,
....800/433.7300 in the US

Aviacsa 860093,874214

Aviateca.................843938, 800/327.9832 in the US

Continental ....860006, 800/525.0280 in the US

Lacsa ....873101, 875101, 800/225.2272 in the US

Mexicana 874444, 860068,
....800/531.7921 in the US

Northwest ....860046, 800/225.2525 in the US

Taesa ....860208, 860206, 800/328.2372 in the US

United ....8601025, 800/241.6522 in the US

Getting to and from Aeropuerto Internacional de Cancún

By Bus Minibuses run from the airport into the downtown area and to the hotel zone and cost far less than individual taxis.

By Car The airport is about a 15-minute drive from the hotel district (depending on the location of the hotel). The exit road from the airport runs into Paseo Kukulcán and the hotel zone.

The following car-rental agencies have counters at **Aeropuerto Internacional de Cancún.**

Avis ....830803, 860222, 800/331.1212 in the US

Budget ......840204, 860026, 800/527.0700 in the US

Econo-Rent.....................................876487, 860171

Dollar........860153, 860179, 800/800.4000 in the US

By Taxi Taxis are available directly outside the baggage claim area. The fare to the hotel zone is about $5 to $10.

When Hurricane Roxanne blew through the Mexican Caribbean in 1995, Cancún was spared any serious damage, but the coast from Puerto Morelos to the border with Belize was hit hard.

Getting Around Cancún

Sidewalks and a bicycle path run along the short arm of the hotel zone's "7" shape, but for the most part Paseo Kukulcán is friendlier to cars than to pedestrians. The longer north-south leg of the "7" has some scenic stretches on the lagoon side of the road; the hotel side is filled with ramps and driveways and is not a safe place to stroll absent-mindedly. Except when traveling short distances, you're best off taking a cab or bus.

Buses *Ruta 1* and *Ruta 2* city buses go to the beaches along Paseo Kukulcán and to Punta Nizuc in the hotel zone. *Ruta 8* goes to **Puerto Juárez** and the ferry to Isla Mujeres. The fare is less than 50¢ for both. Catch the bus on Avenida Tulum, or at stops along Paseo Kukulcán. **Autocar Cancún** and **Turicun** buses travel the length of the hotel zone into downtown until midnight and are the least expensive way to get around. Bus stops are marked, though these buses will stop nearly anywhere you flag them down.

The bus station is located in downtown Cancún near the intersection of Avenidas Tulum and **Uxmal.** Call 845542 or 843948 for schedule information.

Driving Driving is easy in the hotel zone, since there is only one road along the hotel strip. Stick with posted speed limits, as traffic police are abundant. However, driving in the downtown area can be confusing if you wander the side streets. It's best to park on Avenida Tulum or Avenida Yaxchilán.

The car-rental agencies at **Aeropuerto Internacional de Cancún** (listed above) also have offices in hotels.

Taxis Cabs wait at most hotels and can be easily flagged on the street.

FYI

Accommodations Cancún's hotels are among the most expensive in the country, with rates beginning at $250 or more per night for many of the properties. Several hotels offer packages for honeymooners, golfers, and families; some have packages that include airfare. Always ask about these and any special promotional rates when booking a room. All-inclusive properties are becoming very popular, though guests tend to miss out on trying local restaurants by eating all meals in the hotel. The least expensive hotels are located in downtown Cancún.

Consulates

Canadian Consulate Plaza Caracol and Paseo
Kukulcán ....83360; fax 833232

US Consulate Plaza Caracol and Paseo Kukulcán
....820272

Cruises and Water Sports There are more than a dozen boat tour and water activity operators in the hotel zone, and countless opinions about the quality and price of their services. Talk with as many people as possible before you choose a company; much depends on the crew aboard a particular ship. Among the more popular boat trips are day tours to Isla Mujeres with snorkeling, lunch, and shopping, or evening tours with dinner and a show; submarine excursions at the reefs; snorkeling trips; and sunset cruises. Scuba diving trips are common, but dedicated divers will be disappointed; the nearby reefs have been loved to death. If you're serious about diving, go to **Cozumel** or one of the dive resorts south of Cancún.

Most marina operations rent wave runners, kayaks, Windsurfers, and other water toys. The following companies have proven track records:

Aqua Tours Paseo Kukulcán (Km 6.5)............830400

Aqua World Paseo Kukulcán (Km 15.2) 852288

Marina Aqua Ray Paseo Kukulcán (Km 10.5)
....831763

Publications *Cancun Tips* publishes both a large magazine and a smaller coupon book seasonally. Both have good maps and information on restaurants and activities; both can be found at the airport, hotels, and tour agencies.

Dining Cancún is an expensive place to dine, and the options aren't as fantastic as you might expect. Most locals rattle off the same half-dozen restaurant names when asked what's best; many are located in the finer hotels. Chain take-out joints abound, as do fun-oriented chain restaurants, including the **Hard Rock Cafe, Planet Hollywood, Outback Steakhouse, Tony Roma's**, and on and on, eliciting the occasional feeling that you can't escape the US. The more traditional Mexican restaurants are scattered through the hotel zone and downtown. Those that serve lunch may not open until 1 or 2 PM.

Shopping Cancún has numerous shopping malls and plazas, most offering the same selection of sports- and resortwear, sporting goods, and jewelry. Brand names including **Benetton, Ralph Lauren, Dockers,** and **Guess?** are common, and the prices aren't significantly lower than in the US. Artisans' markets are located in both the hotel zone and downtown and display rather generic T-shirts, sombreros, and serapes. Fine Mexican folk art is hard to find here; small shops with carved masks, hand-painted pottery, and glassware are typically located in the back corridors of the malls.

Street Plan Paseo Kukulcán runs the length of the hotel zone from **Club Med** to the outskirts of downtown, where it merges with **Avenida Cobá.** Most shops and restaurants listed in the downtown section of this chapter are on Avenidas Tulum and Yaxchilún or on the cross streets between them. Some of these cross streets, most one block long, share the same name; for example, there are two named **Crisantemos** and two named **Claveles.**

Time Zone Cancún is on Central Time, one hour behind New York and two hours ahead of California.

Tours Archaeological travel agencies and tour companies are plentiful in Cancún. Most offer the same basic trips with assorted themes and amenities. Probably the single most popular

excursion is a trip down the mainland coast to the Maya ruins of **Tulum,** with a stop at **Xel-Há,** an underwater preserve. The **Chichén Itzá** trip is popular and enjoyable, although the drive can be somewhat grueling, since it takes about three hours each way if the tour bus travels the old road. This is cut to two hours if the bus uses the toll road. If you're an archaeology buff, consider spending a night near the ruins rather than trying to see everything in one day. **Xcaret** has become a top destination for day-trippers from Cancún; if you splurge on the pricey admission, you may as well spend the whole day.

Check your hotel's tour desk for an overview of your options, and ask fellow travelers about their experiences with the different companies.

Mayaland Tours (Party Center, Paseo Kukulcán, Km 9, 830679, 830691; fax 830708) operates hotels in **Chichén Itzá** and **Uxmal** and has several options for short and extended explorations, including a car-rental package combined with stays at the company's hotels. Their **Chichén Itzá** tour includes meals at the **Mayaland Hotel** and transportation in comfortable, double-decker buses.

Maritur (Av Nader 42-5 or the Meliá Cancún Hotel, Paseo Kukulcán, Km 16, 873839; fax 871713) offers tours to all attractions in the region with excellent guides.

Visitors' Information Center The **Oficina de Turismo** (Tourism Office) (Av Tulum 26, between Avs Cobá and Uxmal, 848073; fax 840437) is open daily from 9AM to 9PM. The **Cancun Tourism un Conveations Bureau** has an office at Avenidas Cobá and Nader, 846531. Brochures are available by calling toll free 800/CANCUN8.

Phone Book

Fire...841202

Hospital Americano Viento 15 (off Av Tulum)
....846133, 846430

Police..841913

Red Cross..841616

Total Assist (24-hour assistance) Claveles 5 (west of Av Tulum) 841092, 848116

1 Restaurant Río Nizuc ★★$ A small fishing cooperative provides the catch of the day at this rustic restaurant beyond the hotel zone. The anglers have built a wooden walkway to this eatery along the mangrove-lined shore. Order the whole fish (you can choose from snapper, grouper, or dorado—whatever's in season) either grilled, fried, or *tikin-xic* (Maya style, baked in banana leaves). The meals and drinks (including the popular Cuba Libres made of rum, Coca-Cola, and lime) are inexpensive, and the experience more authentically Mexican than most in Cancún. ♦ Seafood ♦ Daily lunch. Paseo Kukulcán (east of Hwy 307). No phone

2 Club Med $$$$ This 300-room resort claims one of the most spectacular and isolated fingers of land at the far southern end of the hotel zone, jutting between Laguna de Nichupté and the Caribbean on Punta Nizuc. It's close to the airport and the highway to **Tulum,** yet far enough from downtown Cancún to make visiting there a special excursion. The all-inclusive system here is one of the best values around, since restaurant tabs and hotel rates in Cancún are high by Mexican standards. Scuba divers and water sports enthusiasts get their money's worth and can easily spend a week exploring the sea from the compound without getting bored. The rooms (which are actually downright spartan) and facilities aren't as nice as at some of the newer Club Meds. Side trips to **Chichén Itzá** and Cobá with meals and overnight stays at the excellent Club Med–run **Villas Arqueológicas** are well worth the extra charge. Unfortunately, the complex has no facilities for children under 12. ♦ Paseo Kukulcán (east of Hwy 307). 852409, 800/CLUB.MED; fax 852290

3 Westin Regina $$$$ This hotel gets major points for its attention to detail. From the outside, the soaring structure seems almost forbidding, but inside, the 385 guest rooms are delightfully comfortable and luxurious, with windows that open and allow you to be lulled to sleep by the cool breezes and the sounds of the surf. The mini-bar in each room has a sink, and ice machines are located on every floor. The shower is in a separate stall from the bathtub, and toiletries include laundry soap. Though far from most of the restaurants and shops in the hotel zone, this property is close to the airport and Highway 307 and has two restaurants and three bars. It sits between the sea and the lagoon, with deep blue swimming pools on both sides (the property has five pools and four hot tubs). The surf gets rough here, and though the rocky point looks like a perfect snorkeling spot, it isn't; the waves make it difficult to keep your snorkel clear of water. The hotel's lagoon-side pool is a calmer spot for reading and relaxing in the sun, and is the best spot for viewing the sunset. ♦ Paseo Kukulcán (east of Hwy 307). 850086, 800/228.3000; fax 850296

For the Birds

Several spots near Cancún keep bird lovers reaching for their binoculars.

Isla Contoy, 30 kilometers (19 miles) north of **Isla Mujeres,** is a nearly four-milelong national wildlife preserve where more than 70 species of birds inhabit swamps and lagoons undisturbed. Pink flamingos migrate to the island in April, and sea turtles lay their eggs on the beaches from June through August. In the past, Isla Contoy was a popular day trip and overnight camping destination, but government officials declared it off-limits to tourists in 1993 in order to protect its flora and fauna. After a few months boat tours were again permitted, but people are no longer allowed to step onto the island itself and must be content to cruise along its edges. Boat excursions to Isla Contoy from Isla Mujeres or Cancún generally include a bird-watching cruise along the island's edge and a stop for snorkeling and swimming. The trip is at least 1.5 hours from Isla Mujeres, and 3 hours from Cancún. For comfort, choose a boat with a bathroom, sun covering, life jackets, and cold drinks. The ride can be rough if the winds are up. Check at the **Fishermen's Cooperative** (Cooperativa de Pescadores) office (Av Gustavo Rueda Medina, 987/70274) on Isla Mujeres or **Asterix Isla Contoy Tour** in Cancún (864847; fax 864755) for information. Be forewarned: The ban on tours to the island could be reinstated at any time.

Thousands of flamingos visit **Río Lagartos** (Alligator River), actually an estuary, every spring and summer during mating season. The national park, 259 kilometers (161 miles) northwest of Cancún, is also home to egrets, herons, cormorants, and an occasional falcon or hawk, attracting birders and naturalists year-round. The flamingos are the big draw, however, filling the sky with a rush of pink feathers in flight. The alligators (for which the area was named) were hunted into near-extinction and are now protected. Check with travel agents in Cancún for trips to Lagartos. If you want to go on your own, you'll need to rent a car. The trip takes about four hours each way, through the towns of **Valladolid** and **Tizimín.** The park has few facilities.

The **Sian Ka'an Biosphere Reserve** on the **Boca Paila Peninsula** south of Cancún is another prime bird-watching spot. Day trips to the preserve can be arranged through **Amigos de Sian Ka'an** (Apdo 770, Cancún, Quintana Roo 77500, Mexico, 98/849583; fax 98/873080). It's not a good idea to visit the reserve on your own, as there are no boats for hire to explore the lagoons, which are the highlight of the trip. The day tours begin at the **Cabañas de Ana y José,** (south of the ruins on the Boca Paila Rd) in **Tulum.** Participants travel by van to Boca Paila, then board small boats and cruise through the channels and lagoons past Maya ruins and waterways. The tours take about 3.5 hours.

SUN ✿ PALACE

4 Sun Palace $$$$ Taking the wallet-free theme to new heights of luxury, this all-inclusive hotel offers amenities more typical of the glitzy pay-as-you-go hotels, including in-room whirlpool tubs, ocean views from all the rooms, and a variety of suites and combinations of interconnected rooms to accommodate families and friends. As in most all-inclusive resorts, the emphasis here is on food, drink, and fun, with a choice of restaurants and bars, and scheduled activities such as aerobics and volleyball. The hotel's health club is a major plus, with its state-of-he-art exercise equipment and indoor lap pool. The room rates, which include meals, are lower than those at many neighboring hotels, and package deals including airfare are sometimes available. Tours to surrounding ruins are free with certain packages or can be arranged for an additional fee. The company operates two other all-inclusive properties in the area—**Beach Palace,** also in the hotel zone, and **Moon Palace,** on the coastal highway near Puerto Morelos. ◆ Paseo Kukulcán (Km 20). 851555, 800/346.8225; fax 852040

5 Royal Solaris Caribe $$$ Formerly an intimate hideaway, this property has expanded into two towers, with a total of 500 rooms. Curved walls and arches frame and separate alcoves in the public areas and rooms, giving a sense of privacy and space. A Mediterranean theme prevails in the architecture and decor—the stark white walls against the blue sea and sky call to mind hillside villas on the Greek isles. The property now includes time-share units and villas and has become quite popular with families. There are seven restaurants, and a spacious lounge with lockers for guests whose planes are departing after check-out time. There is also a health club and the largest pool on Cancún. ◆ Paseo Kukulcán (Km 20.5). 850100, 800/368.9779; fax 850354

 5 Playa Delfines The road widens near this wildly gorgeous stretch of beach, allowing drivers to pull to the shoulder and park. There's always a gathering here at sunset, when the waves crash against the sand, giving those strolling along the beach a sense of the sea's awesome power. Swimming is not recommended unless the water is calm. ◆ Paseo Kukulcán

6 Ruinas del Rey Though the ruins came first, their location next to the **Caesar Park Cancún** golf course makes them look like an afterthought. The small temples and burial site (built between AD 1200 and 1500) were first excavated in 1954 and restored in 1975. They're not that impressive if you've been to the larger Maya sites. ◆ Daily. Paseo Kukulcán (Km 17)

7 El Pueblito $$ Dwarfed by the competition in size and style, this is the least expensive hotel on this stretch of beach, yet it is also more attractive than you might expect. Colonial-style buildings in white stucco with bubble gum–pink trim are staggered down a hillside beside five swimming pools with the requisite volleyball net and swim-up bar. On the south side of the complex a water slide flows from the top of the hill to the bottom. The 239 rooms are far from luxurious, but most have balconies facing the pools or the sea, and all have cable TV and phones. A good choice for those on a budget who care more about being near a fabulous beach than staying in a fancy room. The rate includes meals and taxes, yet still beats most room rates in Cancún. ◆ Paseo Kukulcán (Km 17.5). 850797; fax 850731

CÆSAR PARK

8 Caesar Park Cancún Beach & Golf Resort $$$$ This pyramid-shaped structure looms from atop a slight rise above a 700-yardlong beach, and everything about the place exudes luxury. The 530 rooms and suites have in-room safes, voice mail, mini-bars, private ocean-view terraces, and a sleek, pastel decor. **Royal Beach Club** rooms and suites have ceiling fans along with air-conditioning, coffee makers, and marble bathrooms; other suites are equipped with Jacuzzis. A series of seven swimming pools cascades toward the beach. Other perks include two tennis courts, a well-equipped fitness center, a **Kids' Club,** two hot tubs, and a water sports center. The five restaurants offer a choice of Mexican, Japanese, Italian, and American fare. ◆ Paseo Kukulcán (Km 17). 818000, 800/228.3000; fax 818080

Within the Caesar Park Cancún Beach & Golf Resort:

Caesar Park Cancún Golf Club This 18-hole, par-72 course was designed by the Aoki corporation. The manicured greens run along the shores of Laguna de Nichupté (the 72 sand traps certainly fit in with the natural landscape!). Guests of the hotel can take advantage of golf packages or reduced green fees; the course is open to nonguests as well. ◆ Daily. 818000

Restaurants/Clubs: Red   **Hotels:** Blue
Shops/ 🍃 Outdoors: Green   **Sights/Culture:** Black

9 Fiesta Americana Condesa $$$$
Offering spectacular sea views from every vantage point, the terra-cotta buildings at this 502-room property are surrounded by gardens, streams, waterfalls, and swimming pools. Cool marble floors, pale wood furnishings, and plant-filled balconies make the rooms comfortable havens. The dramatic sky-high *palapa* (thatch-roofed hut) covering the escalators and lobby gives the place a truly Mexican feel. The cafe and the French and Italian restaurants are far better than you'd expect in a hotel, and you can work off the calories on the three tennis courts or in the health club. The long, uncrowded, white sand beach is perfect for solitary walks. Spring for an oceanfront room with a hot tub on the terrace—you're worth it. ♦ Paseo Kukulcán (Km 16.5). 851000, 800/343.7821; fax 81800

10 Meliá Cancún $$$$ A waterfall glistens against the slick black triangular entrance to this sophisticated hotel, and a jungle of vines trails eight stories down a glass pyramid atrium to dense gardens and splashing fountains. Those craving pampering are soothed in the full-scale spa, one of the few in Cancún to offer a wide array of body treatments, including massages in outdoor cabanas under the stars. The amply air-conditioned fitness center is equally impressive, with state-of-the art equipment. The wide beach is perfect for long walks. The 492 rooms, renovated in 1997, have marble floors, wonderful slanted upholstered headboards (great for reading) and private terraces or balconies with sea or lagoon views. The 220-yard, 18-hole golf course adds a pleasant swath of green to this section of the hotel zone, which is becoming terribly jumbled and crowded. There are three restaurants, one of which serves a bountiful breakfast. The hotel is popular with European travelers. This chain also operates the less opulent **Meliá Turquesa** ($$$$; Paseo Kukulcán, Km 12, 832544; fax 851029). ♦ Paseo Kukulcán (Km 16). 851160, 800/336.3542; fax 851263

11 la dolce vita ★★★★$$$$ Locals and Cancún regulars have long included this restaurant on their short lists of best places to dine. Many of the touches that worked downtown have been recreated here; the dining room is both pretty and sophisticated, with candles flickering in hurricane lamps, soft jazz playing in the background, and waiters gliding by unobtrusively in white uniforms with pink vests and bow ties. Plants are scattered about, and an outdoor terrace faces the lagoon. Among the appealing appetizers on the northern Italian menu are a smooth cream of lobster soup, carpaccio, and escargots with artichokes. Veal ravioli, red snapper in puff pastry, and pasta with lobster medaillons and shrimp are just a few of the pasta temptations. Gourmet pizzas baked in a wood-burning oven have been added to the menu in response to tourists' desire for more casual fare. ♦ Northern Italian ♦ Daily lunch and dinner. Reservations required in high season. Paseo Kukulcán (Km 14.6). 80161

12 Marriott Casa Magna $$$$ Often cited as the most lavish property in Cancún, this white palace of a hotel manages to be both opulent and comfortable. The 450 rooms and 38 suites (some nonsmoking) are fully equipped with all amenities, including irons and ironing boards and direct-dial long-distance phone service. In the lobby, padded bar stools face a high, arched window with sea views; the rooms soothe the eyes with pastel carpets and comforters, and plenty of lounge chairs await guests by the apparently endless pool. The **Club Amigos** children's center offers bilingual TV programming as well as books and games.

Of the six restaurants and bars within the hotel, **Mikado** stands out for its innovative Thai cuisine, including chicken satay and pad thai, along with some Japanese dishes such as sushi and *teppanyaki*. ♦ Paseo Kukulcán and Retorno Chac. 852000, 800/223.6388; fax 851731

12 Golfito en la Pirámide Man-made family diversions are rather scarce in Cancún, so this large miniature-golf park is a welcome addition, especially when you're looking for something to do with the kids after dark. A white pyramid marks the entrance, and there are 36 holes in two separate courses, with plenty of water traps to challenge the grown-ups. ♦ Admission. Daily. Paseo Kukulcán (Km 14). 831230

13 Ritz Carlton $$$$ Decidedly European in decor and service, this pale pink hotel looks understated from the road, but the beveled glass doors opening into the lobby dispel such perceptions. Glistening crystal chandeliers, gleaming marble floors, and French Provincial furnishings project an opulent style that is reflected throughout the property. All 369 rooms and suites have televisions and mini-bars hidden inside elegant armoires; glassed-in showers separate from the bathtubs; and balconies looking out on the pool, beach, and formal landscaped gardens. Within the building, the hallways leading to the guest rooms face an eight-story central atrium with a stained-glass dome ceiling. The service throughout the hotel is excellent; it's better still in the private **Club Lounge,** where gourmet treats are offered throughout the day, and secluded seating areas overlook the atrium. Use of the health club, steam rooms, and saunas are all included in the room rate; massage is extra. Locals have discovered the **Club Grill** restaurant, beloved for its extraordinary desserts and romantic dance music in the lounge. If you are accustomed to impeccable service and European style, this is the place for you. ◆ Retorno del Rey 36 (at Paseo Kukulcán). 850808, 800/241.3333; fax 851015

14 Casa Turquesa $$$$ More like a private villa than a hotel, this hostelry has 31 elegantly furnished suites set behind a guarded gate. Oceanfront balconies with private hot tubs, in-room CD players and VCRs, huge dressing rooms, and an abundance of Caswell-Massey toiletries raise the level of comfort. Striped blue-and-white awnings shade guests by the swimming pool and on the pristine white beach, and there's a charming restaurant for those who want to extend the tranquil mood to mealtimes. A member of the Small Luxury Hotels of the World, this establishment is less fussy than the **Ritz Carlton,** but still exudes an air of grand luxury. ◆ Paseo Kukulcán (Km 13.5). 852924, 800/525.4800; fax 852922

15 Plaza Kukulcán This enclosed, air-conditioned plaza has the usual sprawl of sportswear, jewelry, and folk art shops and trendy bars and restaurants, as well as two movie theaters and Cancún's only bowling alley. ◆ Daily. Paseo Kukulcán (Km 13). 852200, 852304

Within Plaza Kukulcán:

Cenacolo ★★$$ The name, loosely translated, means a gathering of artists, poets, and writers, though at this restaurant it's hard to discern the artistic leanings of the patrons, all of whom are wolfing down plates of pasta. Locals seem willing to venture into the hotel zone for fried calamari with aioli, *pasta puttanesca* (with an anchovy, tomato, and olive sauce), and seafood fettuccine. Outdoor tables overlook the traffic and lagoon; indoors is more clublike, with regular patrons mingling at the bar. ◆ Italian ◆ Daily lunch and dinner. 872888, 853603

Ruth's Chris Steak House ★★★$$$$ The prices seem astonishingly high for a simple steak dinner at this esteemed eatery, but these are no simple steaks. Thick as a Dickens novel, they're imported from the US, custom aged, cut by hand, and cooked in butter (should you need a bit more fat). Side dishes cost extra, and the martinis and manhattans are made with imported liquor, which comes dear in Mexico. Still, the restaurant (part of a chain that originated in New Orleans) is extremely popular, especially with Americans who enjoy the outdoor terrace. ◆ Steak house ◆ Daily lunch and dinner. Reservations recommended in high season. 852702, 853301

16 Flamingo Plaza If you're feeling the least bit homesick for US-style shopping, you'll be comforted by the layout and content of this modernistic, Maya-themed mall. Many of the shops are name-brand outlets (**Gucci, Disney**), with a few bargains amid the high-priced trendy togs. A food court contains a dazzling (or appalling) array of familiar chain pizza, sandwich, and burger stands. ◆ Daily. Paseo Kukulcán (Km 11.5). 832855, 832945

Within Flamingo Plaza:

Artland You'll get an abbreviated education in Maya culture just by studying the works of art on display at this gallery, which specializes in batik items and rubbings of Maya carvings. There are also paintings of the ruins, many with printed explanations of the Maya deities. ◆ M-Sa. 832855, 832945

Gold's Gym Yes, this is a branch of the bodybuilding emporium that turns out muscled, bronzed gods in LA. There's even a display of its workout wear, in case you want hip souvenirs. Daily and weekly rates are available for tourists. ◆ M-F until 10PM; Sa-Su until 9PM. 832933

The city of Cancún is designed along a pattern called "the broken plate." Urban areas are arranged in independent sections, each with its own schools, shopping centers, services, and parks. These self-contained neighborhoods are called *supermanzanas* (super city blocks). Some addresses include a designation such as SM 28, which tends only to confuse the casual tourist. Try to stick to main avenues and their cross streets when getting addresses.

Xcaret It's a maze of Mexican curios, from tacky coconut-shell gorillas bearing tequila bottles to *muñecas* (painted pottery dolls) by Oaxacan artist Josefina Aguilar. Check out the rain sticks—three-foot-high bamboo poles strung on the inside with beads that sound like falling rain when the poles are inverted. ♦ Daily until 10PM. 832855

Los Castillo The Castillos are known throughout Mexico for the superb silver jewelry crafted at the family workshop in Taxco. Once you've seen their work, you'll be able to judge the quality, or lack thereof, of the silver items displayed in numbing abundance all over town. ♦ Daily. 850882

17 Continental Villas Plaza $$$$ You can't miss this lineup of 26 pink villas and a 635-room hotel curving along the boulevard across from the businesses on Laguna Bojórquez. The location is ideal, at the beginning of the hotel zone's busiest stretch of hotels, restaurants, and shops; there are water sports facilities on both the Caribbean and the lagoon, as well as a pool. Looking like a strawberry whipped-cream confection on a thin strip of land between the road and the beach, the resort has seven restaurants and bars, including **Le Buffet,** which serves nightly all-you-can-eat spreads. The pastel color scheme carries through into the light and airy rooms and suites. The hotel presents one of the better *Ballet Folklórico* shows nightly. ♦ Paseo Kukulcán (Km 11). 831022, 800/882.6684; fax 851403

18 Gypsy's ★★★$$$$ Dinner shows are inevitable in a place like Cancún, where nearly anything goes in the drive to outshine the competition. This place showcases outstanding flamenco dancers at the dinner hour, who dazzle diners with their stomps and swirls in a handsome *palapa* above Laguna de Bojórquez. Red-and-yellow tablecloths and matador capes swinging from the ceiling are meant to evoke visions of Old Spain. But the show is more important than the cuisine, which seems geared to satisfying a full house. A decent paella and Spanish chorizo (sausage) fulfill the menu's obligations to the motherland. There's also a daily breakfast buffet, but be forewarned: Like many bargain breakfasts offered around town, this one is staffed by personable time-share salespeople. ♦ Spanish/Seafood ♦ Cover. Daily breakfast, lunch, and dinner. Paseo Kukulcán (Km 10.5). 832120, 832018

Cancún accounts for 19 percent of Mexico's total tourism income.

19 Hyatt Cancún Caribe $$$$ Elegant, sophisticated, and quieter than most Cancún hotels, this is one of the few in the tourist zone to have earned Mexico's Gran Turismo rating, which means that it exceeds the standards for five-star hotels. The classiest of the 198 rooms are in the villas, with private pools, Jacuzzis, and lounges, and gorgeous settings atop a limestone bluff overlooking the sea. The decor is an opulent blend of golden marble pillars and floors, black wrought-iron banisters, and dark, carved wooden hutches and étagères. Resident peacocks spend much of their time outside lying by the glass doors. The beach is narrower than most, but is also more dramatic, thanks to the limestone boulders jutting out of the sea. ♦ Paseo Kukulcán (Km 9.5). 830044, 800/233.1234; fax 831514

Within the Hyatt Cancún Caribe:

Blue Bayou ★★★$$$$ The sounds of a flowing waterfall mingle with soft jazz and murmured conversations in this elegant restaurant filled with tropical plants. Spicy creole and Cajun dishes are the specialties, and the menu also offers plenty of Mexican and grilled fish dishes that are a little easier on the palate. The blackened steaks are thick, tender, and delicious. Be sure to save room for the sublime pecan pie. Stop by the adjacent cocktail lounge for an after-dinner drink and some live jazz. ♦ Creole/Cajun ♦ Daily dinner. Reservations recommended. 830044

20 Misión Miramar Park Inn $$$ Overshadowed by its fancier neighbors, this 189-room inn is popular with Mexican and American families. Kids become bilingual in the long swimming pool that flows from the beach to the narrow passage between the buildings. The rooms are serviceable and more typical of Mexican hotels than most in Cancún; they have red-tile floors, rattan furnishings, and mini-bars. Couples of all ages enjoy dancing at the casual **Batachá** nightclub in front of the hotel, and two restaurants serve reasonably priced tacos, enchiladas, and burgers. ♦ Paseo Kukulcán (Km 9). 831755, 800/555.8842; fax 831136

21 Coral Negro Mercado de Artesanías (Black Coral Artisans' Market) This outdoor handicrafts market has stand after stand selling similar cotton blankets, T-shirts, gauze dresses, and souvenirs, with a few special finds buried among the knickknacks. The taco and *torta* stands where the market's vendors eat have the cheapest food in the zone. ♦ Daily. Paseo Kukulcán (Km 9). 830758

22 Forum by the Sea Yet another shopping mall—though this one is more lavish than the rest—has been squeezed into the neighborhood. The building is circular in design, with a glass elevator rising from the sidewalk entrance to the third-level shops. You will find many of the same brand-name clothing vendors as at the other malls; there's also a soaring two-story **Hard Rock Cafe** (818120). ◆ Daily. Paseo Kukulcán (Km 9). 832486

Within Forum by the Sea:

Rainforest Cafe ★★★$$$ Yes, it's part of another US chain, but at least the theme is nature rather than rock 'n' roll. With a Disney-style jungle theme, the restaurant features life-size robotic elephants and gorillas, floor-to-ceiling saltwater aquariums, waterfalls, an overabundance of vines, the sounds of thunder and rainfall, and a delightful cooling mist spraying from various flower beds. The overall ambience makes for a refreshing break from the bright, hot sun; linger over a smoothie or "designer juice" at the bar when the heat gets you down. The food is good and abundant, but appallingly pricey; you'll pay dearly for a salmon fillet with soy and mustard vinaigrette over fettuccine, Cajun chicken, banana cheesecake, or even a simple burger. There is a children's menu and plenty of distractions to keep the young ones happy. ◆ American ◆ Daily lunch and dinner. 818130

23 Centro de Convenciones (Convention Center) Cancún couldn't have made it as a world-class destination without a central convention center and facilities for major international events. The center, which opened in 1994, is in the middle of Punta Cancún, the widest piece of land between the sea and the lagoons, anchoring the intersecting lines of the hotel zone. Still to come is the 50-story **Cancún Tower** (pictured at right), designed by the Mexican architectural firm **Arqcan**. Construction of the tower began in 1993 and was halted soon after; there's no sign that it will ever be completed. ◆ Paseo Kukulcán

Within the Centro de Convenciones:

Centro Cultural del Instituto Nacional de Antropología y Historia (Cultural Center of the National Institute of History and Anthropology) This small museum contains stone carvings, pottery, and other artifacts from the region's archaeological sites. ◆ Admission. Tu-Su. No phone

Cancún After Dark

Cancún is a late-night town, where the clubs and discos hit their stride around midnight. The dress codes at discos include no shorts or sandals, and the more elegant your clothing, the easier your admittance. Cover charges can run more than $12 per person, and drinks are extraordinarily expensive. High-tech light and laser shows, fog machines, and fireworks are typical special effects, with each disco striving to outdo the other.

The more casual and less expensive spots normally have a US slant, specializing in rock 'n' roll and burgers and beer. Here's a rundown on the current hot spots (all are open daily and have a cover charge unless otherwise noted):

Azúcar A tropical decor, upscale clientele, and live bands make this a popular club for devotees of the salsa, rumba, and lambada. The dancers are as much fun to watch as the band. ◆ Paseo Kukulcán (east of Playa Linda). 830441

Batachá This small local club offers Cuban and Caribbean bands under a *palapa* (thatched-roof hut). ◆ Misión Miramar Park Inn, Paseo Kukulcán (Km 9). 831755

La Boom The light shows and special effects are updated frequently, making this one of the trendiest and most crowded nightspots. Another plus is an all-you-can-drink special. ◆ Paseo Kukulcán (east of Av Bonampak). 831152

Christine's High on elegance, this is an enduring favorite of the well-dressed, glamorous disco set. ◆ Krystal Hotel, Paseo Kukulcán. 831793

Dady'O The cavelike club with high-tech lasers and lights bouncing off the ceilings and walls keeps the young crowd overstimulated. ◆ Paseo Kukulcán (Km 9.5). 833134

Planet Hollywood Arnold Schwarzenegger is one of the owners of this club, part of the international chain. It's got all the standard features—a restaurant, movie memorabilia (including the motorcycle from *The Terminator*), music videos, and dancing to one of Cancúns best DJs. ◆ Flamingo Plaza, Paseo Kukulcán (Km 11.5). 850723

Up & Down It's a gourmet restaurant, romantic nightclub, and state-of-the-art disco all in one. Wear your glitziest outfit here—no shorts or sandals are allowed. ◆ Paseo Kukulcán (Km 16.5). 852910

24 Camino Real $$$$ When it first opened, this was the most elegant of the Cancún hostelries, and more than two decades later it is still in a class of its own. Located on the tip of Punta Cancún, the hotel is striking, with bold unadorned white walls angled against walls of magenta, cobalt blue, and purple. To get to their rooms, guests must be willing to cover significant territory on foot en route from the lobby, four restaurants, pool, and beach. Accommodations are either in the original 296-room building, which features staggered terraces facing the sea, or the 17-story, 85-room **Royal Beach Club**, where original folk art adorns the walls and corner suites have hot tubs. All the rooms have marble floors, tropical furnishings, and great toiletries; some have hammocks hanging on the terraces. A saltwater lagoon on the grounds enhances the tropical mood and gives snorkelers a chance to swim with colorful fish. Windsurfing is exceptionally good off the hotel's beach. ♦ Paseo Kukulcán. 830100, 800/722.6466; fax 831730

Within the Camino Real:

Maria Bonita ★★★$$$ Ask anyone who lives in Cancún for the best restaurant in the hotel zone, and this classy Mexican spot is always at the top of their lists. Designed like a rambling hacienda with several rooms painted blue, pink, and yellow, the restaurant has plenty of space to accommodate both large parties and intimate dinners beside gardens and arches. The menu is packed with irresistible samplings of gourmet regional Mexican cuisine that will lure you back again. Don't miss the wild mushroom and shrimp casserole, cactus flower salad, chicken with almond mole, or poblano chilies stuffed with lobster and *huitlacoche* (a mushroomlike fungus grown on corn). ♦ Mexican/International ♦ Daily dinner. Reservations recommended. 830100 ext 8060

25 Fiesta Americana Coral Beach $$$$ The 11-story, salmon-colored hotel is a palatial 602-suite affair that dominates the clutter on Punta Cancún. In the atrium lobby, potted palms and a stained-glass dome soar above sitting areas, and the energy level is reminiscent of Grand Central Terminal at rush hour. Still, when a string quartet plays during Happy Hour at the lobby bar, all seems tranquil and sedate.

Designed to accommodate large meetings, small conventions, and the overflow from the main convention center, the property features a 660-footlong swimming pool, a fully equipped health club and spa, a water sports marina, and an outdoor glass elevator that swoops up from the beach to the 11th-floor penthouse suites. The standard suites have a spacious bedroom a few steps above a small seating area leading to a private balcony; master suites have private hot tubs in

the bathrooms and an abundance of marble. The decor is subdued Mediterranean/Art Deco with arches and pillars; 13 lounges and bars are scattered throughout the many levels that break up the building's vastness. Despite its size, the hotel excels in service, maintenance, and charm. ♦ Paseo Kukulcán (Km 9). 832900, 800/343.7821; fax 833076

Within the Fiesta Americana Coral Beach:

Coral Reef ★★★$$$$ A sumptuous feast at this romantic restaurant begins with smoked salmon with kiwi-and-peach sauce or lobster bisque. Move on to a main course of fresh yellowtail Grenoblese (sautéed with limes and white wine and topped with capers), and end with the incredible caramelized apples on puff pastry topped with vanilla ice cream. Enjoy your meal against a background of classical music, candlelight, well-dressed waiters, and plush decor. ♦ Seafood/Continental ♦ Daily dinner. Reservations recommended. 832900

La Joya ★★★$$$$ A modest stairway leads from the hotel lobby into this restaurant; the more dramatic entry is from the street, where curved stained-glass windows glow brightly. The multitiered dining room bustles with activity and conversation; musicians stroll from table to table playing Mexican favorites as waiters stride by bearing trays loaded with regional Mexican cuisine such as lobster *pozole* (a hominy stew normally made with chicken or pork) or one of the other dishes that tweak traditional recipes with unusual ingredients. Seafood, meat, and pasta share equal billing on the menu, but none of the preparations is boring: The cioppino sports artichoke bottoms, the chicken appears in oyster sauce, and the pepper steak boasts green peppercorns from Madagascar. Somehow, it all works. ♦ Mexican/International ♦ Daily dinner. Reservations recommended. 832900 ext 4200

26 Plaza Caracol Several shopping centers blend into each other in the crowded commercial zone on Paseo Kukulcán near the convention center. Glass walls and twinkling lights make this one stand out. It's also the only mall in this collection to be entirely enclosed and air-conditioned. Nearly 300 shops and restaurants create a confusing jumble of eating and buying options in the plaza's two sections, Caracol I and Caracol II. Famous names such as **Gucci, Ralph Lauren,**

Guess, and even **McDonalds** are represented, among the jewelry, T-shirt, and handicrafts shops. It pays to tour the entire place once before buying anything (assuming you can find your way back to your first choice). The shops selling Mexican folk art and souvenirs are located along an isolated hallway on the second floor of Caracol I. ♦ Daily. Paseo Kukulcán. 831038, 832450

Within Plaza Caracol:

Casa Rolandi ★★★$$$ The classiest of the plaza's restaurants has several dining rooms with vines hanging from copper pots, Spanish guitar music playing in the background, and a mesmerizing saltwater aquarium with a spectacular selection of fish. The Italian-Swiss owner has several restaurants in the Mexican Caribbean resorts, most specializing in pizza. Here, the wood-burning ovens are used to roast chicken, duck, and fresh fish, giving them a unique moistness and flavor. Appetizers include a melt-in-your-mouth salmon carpaccio and mussels in white wine. Pasta comes stuffed with shrimp, smothered in cream, and tossed with a decent pesto. The salad/antipasto bar provides a meal in itself. Try the mango mousse for dessert. ♦ Swiss/Italian ♦ Daily lunch and dinner. 831817

Amigo's Cuban cigars are the specialty at this tiny tobacco shop, and you can tell by the quantity being carted off by your fellow shoppers that they intend to bring some of Havana's best back home. Take heed, however: Cuban cigars are not allowed through US Customs. ♦ Daily. 832805

Iguana Wana ★★$$ If you're determined to bypass all the US franchise restaurants and still have an inexpensive, quick meal, this may be your best bet. The menu selections should satisfy just about everyone in your group, with choices from Caesar salad to spicy shrimp to vegetarian dishes to *carnitas enchiladas*. There are also decent pastries, frozen yogurt, and strong espresso; the only drawback is the noise level, which can be deafening in the often crowded white-and-green dining room. ♦ International ♦ Daily breakfast, lunch, and dinner. 830829

Artesano Stuck away from the crowds on the plaza's second floor, this small shop has one of the best collections of Mexican folk art in Cancún (which suffers from a strange lack of high-quality folk art stores). You'll find hand-painted vases and bowls, tin mirrors and frames, and an ever-changing array of souvenirs. ♦ Daily. 833471

Galería Sergio Bustamante You've seen copies of the master's works in every handicrafts shop on the island; now view the originals in this gallery. Bustamante first gained attention with his life-size papier-mâché, copper, and brass sculptures of flamingos, lions, and giraffes. This gallery goes beyond these images, displaying the artist's newer paintings and sculptures, many involving sea life. Bustamante also has expanded his collection by designing jewelry; his enameled gold and silver pieces are as pricey as his art objects. ♦ M-Sa. 834353

26 **100% Natural** ★★$$ What a find. This is absolutely the best place to go when you've had your fill of heavy meals and alcohol and crave vitamins. *Licuados* (blended fruit drinks) are made with yogurt, milk, or orange juice in cleverly named combos such as "El Vampiro" (made of beet, celery, and carrot juices). Purists are delighted with the steamed vegetables over brown rice. And those desiring a heavy dose of protein and fat can go for the hamburger topped with a fried egg. Ravenous after a night of dancing and bar hopping? Stop in at 3AM for scrambled eggs with spinach and cheese or a broccoli omelette before crashing until noon. The waiters are consistently cheerful regardless of the time of day, and the clientele seems genuinely happy to be feasting on fresh, simple, satisfying meals. ♦ American/Mexican/Health food ♦ Daily breakfast, lunch, and dinner. Plaza Terramar, Paseo Kukulcán. 831180. Also at: Av Sunyaxchén 62-64 (between Av Yaxchilán and Saramullo). 843617; Plaza Kukulcán, Paseo Kukulcán (Km 13). 852904

Chilies are the most popular seasoning in the world—and Mexicans make great use of the chili in their native dishes. Some chilies pack a surprisingly powerful punch, however, and if you happen to eat one that ignites your tastebuds, the best antidote is not to guzzle down that ice-cold *cerveza*, but to eat dairy products, such as milk, yogurt, and ice cream, or starchy foods like tortillas, bread, and rice.

26 La Mansión Costa Blanca This serene, classy shopping center is painted a garish pink, which detracts from its Moorish arches and domes. The center is on the lagoon side of the maze of malls at Punta Cancún, however, and the shaded stairways and walkways are a peaceful escape from the neighboring noisy bars and restaurants. There are mostly galleries and exclusive folk art shops here; unfortunately, they tend to change ownership and names frequently. ◆ Daily. Paseo Kukulcán. 841272

Within La Mansión Costa Blanca:

El Mexicano ★★★$$$ If you want a first-class floor show with dinner, a night here is a must. Mariachi, folkloric dancing, and tropical Caribbean shows are interspersed with excellent dance music. This well-established restaurant moved from the plaza's second floor to the first and expanded to seat 300. The large dining room, whose decor is reminiscent of a hacienda, does a big business in groups, but singles and couples needn't feel out of place. Appetizers, entrées, and desserts cover the spectrum of Mexico's cuisine, and if you feel your food isn't spicy enough, you can always spoon on the green salsa made from the fiery *habañero* chili, onion, and lime. Save room for the *crepas cajeta* (thin crepes filled with caramel sauce, topped with chopped nuts, and flambéed with liqueurs) prepared tableside. The lunch buffet is reasonably priced, but the place is more charming at dinnertime and is better saved for a romantic night of dining and dancing. ◆ Mexican ◆ Daily lunch and dinner. 832220

Celica Hand-painted pottery and ceramic vases, plates, and jars are artfully arranged in this small gallery. ◆ Daily. 820120

27 Xcaret Terminal You can't miss the wildly painted buses parked here, waiting to board passengers bound for **Xcaret**. The ecological amusement park, located 69 kilometers (43 miles) to the south, is heavily promoted throughout the area, with billboards and advertisements all over the place. You can get information and buy your tickets here. ◆ Daily. Paseo Kukulcán. 833143; fax 833324

27 Fiesta Americana $$$$ Though smaller and older (and less expensive) than the chain's other hotel zone properties, this 281-room hotel is a charmer. Buildings of terra-cotta, gold, and rose frame the free-form pool, which is surrounded by thick bushes and trees. The rooms face the sea or lagoon and have carpeting, small balconies, and a rather dark decorating scheme that is slated for refurbishing. There are two restaurants, and the hotel is right across the street from Plaza Caracol. ◆ Paseo Kukulcán. 31400, 800/343.7821; fax 32502

PRESIDENTE
INTER·CONTINENTAL®
HOTELS AND RESORTS

28 Presidente Inter-Continental $$$$ Some Cancún regulars return here year after year for the friendly, accommodating attitude that has been this establishment's hallmark since it opened. The rectilinear hotel remains an architectural delight despite the addition of a 10-story tower, overlooking the original building's pyramidal roof, inset with rectangles painted a vivid pink. All of the 298 rooms are renovated on a regular basis; if possible, splurge on one on the **Club** floors, where complimentary continental breakfast, afternoon hors d'oeuvres, and after-dinner pastries and coffees are served in private lounges.

The grounds and beach are wonderfully secluded, since the property's neighbors are private residences rather than other large hotels. The pool is one of Cancún's best, with a waterfall cascading by the swim-up bar (stand under the waterfall for a great shoulder massage). The two restaurants are consistently good, especially for breakfast, which is served in **El Caribeño** by the pool. If you get to the beach early enough, claim one of the *palapas* with plastic lounge chairs for the right amount of sun and shade. The smaller swimming pool set near the tennis court is a good place to sunbathe in relative solitude. ◆ Paseo Kukulcán (Km 7.5). 830200, 800/327.0200; fax 832602

29 Club de Golf Cancún One of the few golf courses in the world with a Maya shrine, this layout was designed by Robert Trent Jones Jr. when Cancún was just beginning to emerge as a tourist mecca. Now, more than two decades later, the 18-hole course (par 72) has some competition, but it remains a beautiful greenbelt surrounded by private homes on an island in Laguna Bojórquez, connected to the hotel zone by a bridge. The club, formerly called **Pok-Ta-Pok**, has two tennis courts, a restaurant, and a bar. Temporary memberships are available and can be arranged through most hotels. ◆ Daily (last tee-off at 4PM). South of Paseo Kukulcán. 830871; fax 833358

"Solitude—the feeling and knowledge that one is alone, alienated from the world and oneself—is not an exclusively Mexican characteristic. All men, at some moment in their lives, feel themselves to be alone. And they are. . . . Solitude is the profoundest fact of the human condition."

Octavio Paz, *The Labyrinth of Solitude*

30 Carlos 'n' Charlie's ★★★$$ This is the original of the several Grupo Andersen restaurants in Cancún. (It is located right next to one of the newest ones, **El Shrimp Bucket**, 832710). Between the two, loyal clients get their fill of bountiful shrimp, chicken, and barbecued rib meals, ice buckets stuffed with bottles of cold beer, and music loud enough to drown out both thought and conversation. This formula is immensely popular with both locals and tourists, and lines form outside all the restaurants on Saturday nights. If you're more interested in the food than the social scene, stop in for lunch with a view of the lagoon. The nighttime cover charge is waived if you dine here before dancing on the crowded floor. Other restaurants in the chain include **Señor Frog's** (Paseo Kukulcán, Km 9.5, 831092), **Guadalajara Grill** (Paseo Kukulcán, Km 4.5, 832931), and **Carlos O'Brian's** (Av Tulum 107, 841659). ♦ Mexican/American ♦ Daily lunch and dinner. Paseo Kukulcán (Km 5.5). 830846

31 Playa Linda Many of the sightseeing boats, specialty cruises, fishing boats, and ferries to Isla Mujeres depart from this dock. The complex includes a taco stand, a long-distance telephone and fax office, and representatives of most of the cruise companies. ♦ Paseo Kukulcán (Km 4.5)

At Playa Linda:

Isla Mujeres Shuttle Travelers used to have to go to Puerto Juárez, northeast of Cancún, to catch the ferry to Isla Mujeres. Now they can take this shuttle, which costs a bit more than the ferry but is far more convenient. The boat departs here, then stops at Playa Tortugas (also in the hotel zone) before heading to the island. The trip takes about 20 minutes from Playa Tortugas to Isla Mujeres; the schedule changes frequently, but the boat generally leaves about five times daily between 8AM and 6PM. The company also advertises a shuttle to Cozumel, which actually entails a 45-minute bus ride from Playa Linda to Playa del Carmen and a 30-minute ferry ride across to Cozumel. Experienced travelers can make the trip for less money using public transportation; first-timers might appreciate the guidance. ♦ Daily. 831963, 833583

Atlantis Submarine Landlubbers get a peek at Cancún's underwater delights on tours aboard this submarine. Just in case the sea life demurs, divers accompany the sub and swim outside the portholes, scattering food to attract the fish. The company has claimed a section of coastline and sea at Isla Mujeres for its **Destination Atlantis** park, complete with artificial and natural reefs underwater and a restaurant and bar on land. ♦ Daily. 833021

32 Plaza Nautilus A few gems lurk in this easily overlooked roadside mall. Parking is a bit of a hassle, and many of the storefronts are empty. But it is convenient for those staying in this area, and does have the standard selection of souvenir shops. ♦ Daily. Paseo Kukulcán (Km 3.5). 831903

Within Plaza Nautilus:

Trattoria da Arturo ★★★$$$ More locals than tourists fill the dozen or so tables in this intimate eatery. The antipasto cart—with its impressive array of marinated seafood and vegetables—is reason enough to dine here. Though it's difficult to restrain yourself, save room for the red snapper en papillote, the grilled portobello mushrooms, or pasta with salmon. The service, cuisine, ambience, and soft blue-and-white decor make this the perfect spot for your romantic, last-night-of-vacation dinner. ♦ Italian ♦ Daily lunch and dinner. Reservations recommended. 832063, 832382

33 Los Almendros ★★$$ Sister to eateries of the same name in Mérida and Ticul, this restaurant draws the crowds at lunch, when locals settle in for lengthy meals of *pollo pibil* (chicken baked in banana leaves), *poc-chuc* (charcoal-broiled pork), and *pavo escabeche* (turkey with garlic and cinnamon). For the full effect, order the *combinado Yucateco*, which has these dishes plus *longaniza* (sausage). All meals are served with spicy marinated red onions, a bowl of black beans, warm tortillas, and salsa. Portions are small, so order liberally, and accompany your meal with a bottle of León Negro or Negro Modelo beer. ♦ Yucatecan ♦ Daily lunch and dinner. Avs Bonampak and Sayil. 871332

34 Plaza de Toros (Cancún Bullring) Professional bullfights are held here every Wednesday afternoon during the high season. Tickets are available at most hotels. ♦ Avs Bonampak and Sayil. 848372

During the war against Spain, the Virgin of Guadalupe was awarded the rank of general.

When requesting a song by a guitarist who wanders from cafe to cafe, expect to pay about $3 per tune, or $5 for two songs. Some musicians will also perform on an hourly basis.

Restaurants/Clubs: Red   **Hotels:** Blue
Shops/ ♥ Outdoors: Green   **Sights/Culture:** Black

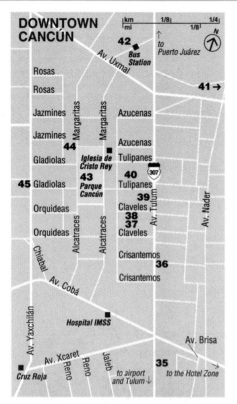

DOWNTOWN CANCÚN

35 Hotel Calinda America $$ Well located at the edge of downtown near the hotel zone, this bland 177-room property has some advantages over other downtown choices. The rooms, though nondescript, are spacious, clean, and quiet; the pool is large and set in a garden away from traffic noise; and there's complimentary shuttle service to the beach. The restaurant serves decent Mexican and American meals, and other downtown eateries are within walking distance—though you must cross some busy intersections with confusing traffic patterns. **Mayaland Tours,** which offers rental-car packages and bus trips to the ruins, has an office here. ♦ Av Tulum (between Avs Sayil and Cobá). 847500, 800/555.8842; fax 841953

36 Ki Huic The main market for handicrafts spreads behind Avenida Tulum in a maze of stalls that can leave shoppers bewildered and overwhelmed. If you're serious about searching for treasures and bargaining over prices, allow yourself at least two hours to make your way past hundreds of cotton blankets, polyester dresses, gaudy T-shirts, and bizarre displays of jeweled bugs. Examine your selections carefully; much of the junk sold here will fall apart the first time it's washed, worn, or used.

Don't start bartering until you're really sure you want that priceless pottery Chac Mool,

then jump in with polite determination. Many vendors will try to make you name your price first, but you're better off getting an amount from them, then cutting it in half. It helps to walk away if you're getting nowhere, and never pay more than 70 percent of the quoted price. It also helps if you gang up with other shoppers and purchase several items from the same seller, requesting a discount for your mass purchase. ♦ Daily. Av Tulum (between Avs Cobá and Uxmal). 843347

37 Rosa Mexicana ★★$$ Instead of serving nachos as appetizers, this classic Mexican restaurant offers *nopalitos,* the traditional salad made from the small buds of the nopal cactus combined with onion, pepper, cilantro, vinaigrette, and crumbled white cheese. Another salad has chunks of jicama and orange slices sprinkled with lime juice, salt, and ground chilies. The red snapper is smothered in cilantro, while the chicken is served in a ground-almond sauce or covered with a mole *poblano* with an incomparable taste. Desserts include papayas baked with honey and cheese, and a nut cake drenched with rum. If you're beginning to wonder if Cancún really is in Mexico, come here for a gratifying immersion in the country's flavors and smells. ♦ Mexican ♦ Daily dinner. Reservations required for patio seating. Claveles 4 (west of Av Tulum). 846313

38 Hotel Antillano $ Tucked on a side street just off Avenida Tulum, this 48-room inn is quieter than others in the neighborhood. The rooms have white walls, red-tile floors, sinks outside the bathrooms, and TVs with only local reception. There's a small pool in an interior courtyard, and plenty of restaurants in the neighborhood (though none on the premises). ♦ Claveles 1 (west of Av Tulum). 841532; fax 841878

39 Fama A general department store with a bit of everything, this place has racks and racks of magazines and paperbacks in English and Spanish, including a good selection of books and guides on the Yucatán Peninsula. Postcards, film, and sundries cost less here than in the hotels, and there's a good exchange rate for those cashing US traveler's checks or dollars. ♦ Daily. Av Tulum 105 (between Claveles and Tulipanes). 841839

40 El Pescador ★★★$$ For more than a decade, this restaurant has proven that you don't need fancy gimmicks and frenetic activity to be a success in a highly competitive market. Good food, well prepared and reasonably priced, is what keeps customers coming back. Though the tables are placed as close as can be in the two dining rooms and on the sidewalk patio, there still isn't nearly enough seating for all the locals and visitors willing to wait indefinitely for what many consider the best fish dinners in town. The decor is simple: Wooden tables are placed close together and paper streamers add a colorful touch. For a treat, have the lobster ceviche appetizer (which costs about the same as an entrée). The menu and prices are the same for lunch and dinner, but you'll have a better chance of beating the crowd if you show up around noon. The owners have a second restaurant at Plaza Kukulcán, which follows the same successful formula. ♦ Seafood ♦ Daily lunch and dinner. Tulipanes 28 (between Av Tulum and Alcatraces). 841227. Also at: Plaza Kukulcán, Paseo Kukulcán (Km 13). 852200

41 Yamamoto ★★★$$ This Japanese eatery has been a favorite of both locals and tourists for years, and with good reason. The chefs take full advantage of the abundance of fresh fish from the region, preparing artful platters of sushi and sashimi. The cooked dishes are equally satisfying, and the dining room a serene escape. ♦ Japanese ♦ Daily lunch and dinner. Av Uxmal 31 (between Avs Bonampak and Nader). 873366, 847828

41 Locanda Paolo ★★$$ The gregarious, gracious owner, comfortable setting, and great pastas make this restaurant a favorite with locals. ♦ Italian ♦ Daily lunch and dinner. Av Uxmal 35 (between Avs Bonampak and Nader). 872627

42 Plaza Caribe $ Savvy bus travelers (the bus station is right across the street) take advantage of the air-conditioned coffee shop in this 140-room Best Western–managed hotel when their plans go awry. Others who need to stay close to the bus station can enjoy the nice swimming pool and the friendly clientele. Be sure to ask for a room in the back, away from street noise. ♦ Av Tulum 36 (at Av Uxmal). 841377, 800/555.8842; fax 846352

43 Parque Cancún Since Cancún is a new city that lacks both history and social traditions, its main plaza likewise lacks soul—it feels like an afterthought on the part of city planners. Consisting of blocklong concrete slabs and a statue of Francisco Madero, the first publicly elected president of Mexico, the plaza is at its best on Friday and Saturday nights, when free concerts are presented and local families turn out to socialize. ♦ Margaritas and Alcatraces

44 La Habichuela ★★★$$$ Peacock-style, white wrought-iron chairs and spacious tables are set in a romantic, tranquil garden that's watched over by a statue of Pacal, the Maya ruler of Palenque. The tables are covered with white-and-pink linen, tiny white lights sparkle in the trees, and soft, contemporary jazz plays almost imperceptibly in the background. Lobster, prepared nearly any way you can imagine, comes in three sizes—regular, jumbo, and monstrous—but the dish that made this restaurant famous is the *cocobichuela* (lobster and shrimp in a light curry sauce served in a coconut shell). The waiters call it *el plato de los reyes Mayas* (the dish of the Maya kings). For complete decadence, end your meal with *crepas Brazil* (a combo of featherlight crepes, Cognac, nuts, butter, and caramelized sugar), flambéed tableside, of course. The pseudo-Maya theme is continued with symbolic bas-reliefs and excellent reproductions of Maya personages in small arched niches in the walls. The service is impeccable, the food sublime, and the location—just two blocks off the dreaded, noisy Avenida Tulum—both convenient and peaceful. If you're going to go all out for a special night, do it here. ♦ Seafood/Nouvelle Mexican ♦ Daily lunch and dinner. Reservations required in high season. Margaritas 25 (between Gladiolas and Av Uxmal). 843158

45 Pericos ★★★$$$ Wacky, weird, and wild, this is the ultimate let-loose-and-play saloon/restaurant. Dressed-up skeletons dangle from ceilings and walls, patrons perch on leather saddles at the bar, waiters hurry about with trays of drinks and gun belts slung across their chests à la Pancho Villa, and marimbas reverberate with a joyful sound. Unlike many such spots, this place carries off the gaiety in quite a genuine and entertaining way, amusing a wide cross section of Cancún tourists and residents. From the front, the building is covered with palm fronds, making it look run-down, while inside it looks like a hacienda, with a fountain, a formal staircase, and a balcony from which to view the bizarre goings-on below. Flaming entrées such as shish kebabs and coffee drinks loaded with liqueurs are served by waiters in firefighters' uniforms for some added drama. ♦ Mexican/American ♦ Daily lunch and dinner. Av Yaxchilán 71 (between Chiabal and Marañon). 843152

Mexican writer Octavio Paz (1914-1998) won the Nobel Prize for literature in 1991.

Isla Mujeres

Just eight miles northeast of Cancún, Isla Mujeres is the perfect destination for those seeking peaceful surroundings, moderate prices, and the atmosphere of a small Mexican town. Unlike Cancún, the island has no high-rise hotels, discos, or shopping malls, and few distractions from its main attraction: the beach. Visitors quickly settle into a languid routine, alternating between the sand and sidewalk cafes. Some who initially plan to spend a night or two end up extending their stays, convinced they've discovered the ideal tropical hideaway on "Isla," as the island is called by both locals and travelers.

The name of this small spot of land in the Caribbean means "Island of Women." There are several versions of how the island got its name. Some say it was because of the island's preponderance of Maya statues of women and shrines to Ixchel, the goddess of fertility. Others says the pirates left their wives and girlfriends here before the men went off to loot ships in the Caribbean. The island was more popular with pirates than with the *conquistadores*, and was a hideaway for pirate ships in the early 19th century. Tourists began arriving in the 1970s as Cancún was being developed, and continue to find it one of the least expensive Caribbean destinations in Mexico.

The five-milelong, two-and-a-half-mile-wide island can be explored easily on a rented moped or by taxi in four hours or less, leaving plenty of time for relaxation. Ferries from Cancún and **Puerto Juárez** deposit their passengers at the waterfront area of the island's downtown; nearly all attractions are within walking distance. North of the pier is **Playa Norte** (North Beach), also called **"Playa Cocoteros"** or **"Playa Cocos,"** the most popular beach on the island. Several *palapa* (palm-roofed) restaurants on the beach serve fresh fish, cold

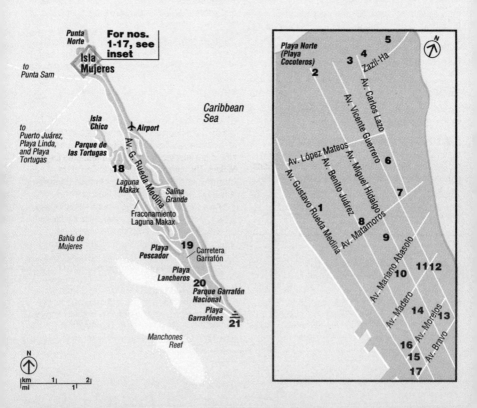

drinks, and snacks. At the far north end of Playa Norte, a small bridge leads to the remains of a crumbling hotel. Once the keystone resort for the island, the hotel suffered serious damage from Hurricane Gilbert in 1988; since then various projects have been considered for the property, but none has succeeded. South of Playa Norte, back by the ferry pier, is the island's downtown, a jumble of unnamed streets with homes, restaurants, and shops in various states of repair. You can spend an hour or two wandering, watching a basketball game in the plaza, and browsing the shops for souvenirs, which tend to be less expensive here than in Cancún.

The most popular Isla Mujeres day trip is to **Parque Garrafón Nacional** (Garrafón National Park), more commonly called **El Garrafón.** Located near the island's southern tip, this underwater preserve is teeming with tropical fish. Nearby are the ruins of the **Hacienda Mundaca,** an early–19th-century fortress. At the far southern tip of the island is **El Faro** (The Lighthouse) and a small cluster of Maya ruins. Once you've seen these few attractions, there's nothing more to do than sun on the beach, swim in the sea, or wander the streets in town.

Area code 987 unless otherwise noted.

Getting to Isla Mujeres

Ferry

All travelers to Isla Mujeres must arrive by ferry from the Cancún area, since the island has no airport. **Isla Mujeres Ferry Pier,** located at the southeastern edge of the town of Isla Mujeres, is the entryway to the island. A passenger ferry (70618) runs from Puerto Juárez to Isla Mujeres every hour on the half hour from 6:30AM to 8PM daily. The least expensive ferry takes about 40 minutes each way; the fare is about $2; a one-way trip on the express ferry takes 15 minutes. The fare is about $3. The more expensive **Shuttle Isla Mujeres** (833448, 833583 in Cancún) departs from the **Playa Linda** and **Playa Tortugas** docks in Cancún's hotel zone. There also is a car ferry that leaves from nearby **Punta Sam** (north of Cancún) five times a day.

Getting Around Isla Mujeres

Most of the island's hotels and tourist services are within easy walking distance of the ferry pier.

Bicycles and Mopeds With few rental cars available on the island, travelers instead rent mopeds, bicycles, and golf carts to reach attractions outside town. Rentals are available at most hotels.

Taxis Taxis line up at the pier to transport those with too much luggage to haul through the heat. The fare to hotels is less than 50¢.

FYI

Accommodations There are no chain hotels on Isla Mujeres, only small, casual inns with low rates and few frills. The island remains one of the least expensive Mexican coastal destinations, which makes it a popular getaway. Reservations are essential from November through Easter Week and during August, when European travelers fill the hotels. The hotel association on the island is represented by **Four Seasons Travel** in the US. They can book rooms far more efficiently than the average traveler and are a great source of information. Call 800/552.4550.

Cruises and Water Sports Activities on Isla are limited to snorkeling, swimming, and scuba diving. Vendors on Playa Norte rent snorkeling gear and beach umbrellas; thus far, water toys such as Jet Skis and Para-Sails have not marred the island's peaceful ambience. Scuba diving operators have dive shops and equipment rentals in town; see listings below.

Publications The *Islander* provides goods map and information on restaurants and activities and is available at hotels.

Shopping Small souvenir shops, boutiques, and artisans' stands line Avenida Miguel Hidalgo. Best buys include T-shirts and wall hangings batiked with Maya designs, purses and belts from Guatemala, and carved masks and wooden animals from Oaxaca.

Street Plan One main road runs the length of the island. It's called **Avenida Gustavo Rueda Medina** at the north end, from Playa Norte past the ferry pier to the intersection with **Fraconamiento Laguna Makax.** The name then changes to **Carretera Garrafón,** and the road runs past **Parque Garrafón Nacional** to the southern tip of the island. In town, **Avenida Miguel Hidalgo** is the main shopping and dining street; it runs east to west and is intersected by several small streets running south to north.

Time Zone Isla Mujeres is on Central Time, two hours ahead of California and one hour behind New York.

Visitors' Information Center The **Oficina de Turismo** (Tourism Office) is located on the second floor of the **Plaza Isla Mujeres** (Av Miguel Hidalgo, between Avs Matamoros and López Mateos, 70316). It's open Monday through Friday from 8AM to 5PM.

Phone Book

Medical Service 70477
Police 70082
Red Cross 70280

1 Posada del Mar $ With the greatest expanse of lawns and the best swimming pool on the island, this hostelry is a long-time favorite of Isla regulars. The 40 well-maintained rooms are simple but comfortable; they have plenty of closet space and tables and chairs, and are repainted frequently. The louvered windows let in the sea breeze, so you almost never need to use the air-conditioning. A *palapa* bar by the pool has swinging seats, hammocks, and comfy tables and chairs; customers are well cared for by the bartender Miguel. ♦ Av Gustavo Rueda Medina 15A (between Avs Matamoros and López Mateos). 70444, 70120; fax 70266

Within the Posada del Mar:

Pinguino ★★$$ The tables set on a balcony above the sidewalk at this popular eatery are good spots for people watching; those set under the trees are pleasantly private. Breakfast includes great homemade whole wheat bread and granola with fruit and yogurt. At dinner, the lobster tail is superb. Live bands play here on weekend nights in the high season. ♦ Mexican ♦ Daily breakfast, lunch, and dinner. 70444

2 Chimbo's ★★$ Islanders sit in hammocks, the swinging seats at this restaurant and bar on the beach, where sunset is celebrated with piña coladas and general merriment. Fried fish, ceviche, and salsa and chips keep sunbathers and swimmers fueled—needless to say, the dress code is minimal. Music booms from loudspeakers at night, when travelers kick off their sandals and rock on the sand. ♦ Mexican/Seafood ♦ Daily lunch and dinner. Av Miguel Hidalgo (west of Av López Mateos). No phone

The Cora Indians from the state of Nayarit have their own version of the origin of the revered Mexican chilies. Legend has it that a man named Narama was attending a banquet when he suddenly jumped on the table. His testes turned into chilies, and he sprinkled the spicy seeds onto the food. The guests had their first taste of the spice of life, and it has been an important part of the culture ever since.

Restaurants/Clubs: Red   **Hotels:** Blue
Shops/ Outdoors: Green   **Sights/Culture:** Black

3 Hotel Cabañas María del Mar $$ The accommodations options are extensive at this sprawling complex on Playa Norte. All the rooms have fans and air-conditioning, refrigerators, hammock hooks (bring your own hammock), and a combination of double and single beds. The Cabañas section has 15 rooms (2 per building) with *palapas* and large front porches in a garden area. The 24 Tower rooms face the beach and feature private terraces. Nicest of all are the 18 Castle rooms, with blue-and-white–tile floors and carved wooden furnishings. The hotel draws many return guests, thanks to its casual, friendly ambience, good location, and variety of facilities and extras, including a pool, a restaurant, tours, moped rental, and complimentary continental breakfast. ♦ Av Carlos Lazo 1 (west of Av López Mateos). 70179, 70211; fax 70273, 70156

4 Buho's ★★$ A favorite hangout for locals and tourists, this casual restaurant has tables on the sand as well as in an alcove dining room, and a big *palapa*-covered bar that's one of the top nightspots on the island. Breakfast features *huevos motuleños* (eggs served on a corn tortilla) and platters of fresh papaya, pineapple, and watermelon. At lunch and dinner the catch of the day is grilled at an outdoor kitchen by the tables. This is a good place to linger over a cool drink any time of day. (Eavesdroppers are rewarded with local gossip.) ♦ Mexican/Seafood ♦ Daily breakfast, lunch, and dinner. Av Carlos Lazo (west of Zazil-Ha). 70301

5 Na Balam $$$ From the beach, all that can be seen of this small inn are glimpses of cream stucco buildings peeking through a profusion of palms. The 31 pretty air-conditioned rooms are decorated with folk art from Chiapas and have green tile floors, white walls, and patios or balconies. The newest section sits across the road from the beach around an oval pool. ♦ Reservations required, especially for August and holidays. Zazil-Ha 118 (north of Av Carlos Lazo). 70279, 800/223.6510; fax 70446

Within Na Balam:

Zazil-Ha ★★$ The French toast and coffee are reason enough to stop here for breakfast; choose a table under the palms or in the cool dining room. Chef Armando bakes wonderful whole-grain breads daily, and uses fresh herbs, fruits, and spices in his catch-of-the-day creations. Try the fresh fish with *chaya* (a spinach-like green) or the shrimp with mangoes. There are always a few great vegetarian entrées and several salads on the menu. ♦ Mexican/Health food ♦ Daily breakfast, lunch, and dinner. 70279

6 El Mercado Isla's small public market is a good place to pick up fresh papayas, mangoes, coconuts, and pineapple for a do-it-yourself fruit plate. Get here early for the best selection. ◆ Daily. Av Carlos Lazo (between Avs Matamoros and López Mateos). No phone

7 Artesanías El Nopal Gorgeous embroidered *huipiles* (loose-fitting blouses) from Oaxaca and Guatemala hang from the ceiling at the island's most colorful shop. The wooden shelves are packed with white-on-white embroidered blouses, black pottery, and lacquered boxes. The wooden tables and chairs in **El Nopalito,** the shop's cafe, are covered with paintings of flowers and birds. Breakfasts include fresh papaya and bananas with yogurt, scrambled eggs with tomatoes, and freshly baked breads. ◆ Shop: M-Sa. Cafe: Daily breakfast. Avs Vicente Guerrero and Matamoros. 70555

8 Cafecito ★★$ The pretty aquamarine-and-white building stands out in this neighborhood; inside, you'll find the best coffee on the island. Breakfast offerings include fresh fruit crepes and a variety of egg dishes served with flaky croissants. The dinner menu features fish prepared several different ways. Stop by after dinner for coffee, crepes with vanilla ice cream and chocolate sauce, and conversation with the locals who hang out here. ◆ Cafe ◆ M-W, F-Sa breakfast and dinner; Su breakfast. No credit cards

accepted. Avs Benito Juárez and Matamoros. No phone

9 Arriba ★★$ Vegetarians and others who prefer healthful, low-fat meals enjoy the cuisine at this second-story spot. The salads have a wider array of fresh veggies than you usually find in Mexico; vegetables also are stir-fried and served in tempura platters. The Caribbean rice with ginger, vegetables, and egg is a cheap, filling meal that can also be ordered as a side dish with poultry or fish. ◆ Health food ◆ Daily dinner. No credit cards accepted. Av Miguel Hidalgo (between Avs Mariano Abasolo and Matamoros). 70458

Hotel Belmar

10 Hotel Belmar $ The 12 rooms in this small hotel are among the nicest in town, with large tiled bathrooms, satellite TV, and in-room phones. The one suite has a hot tub and full kitchen. Two drawbacks: The noise from the restaurant (see below) can be a bit disruptive, and the aromas keep you in a permanent state of hunger. ◆ Av Miguel Hidalgo 110 (between Avs Madero and Mariano Abasolo). 70430; fax 70429

Sleeping Beauties

Las Cuevas de los Tiburones Dormidos (The Caves of the Sleeping Sharks) are Isla Mujeres's most famous underwater attraction. The caves, about five kilometers (three miles) northeast of the island in the open sea, were first discovered by Carlos García Castilla, a local fisherman who came upon them while diving for lobster. He noticed that the sharks in the area seemed unusually lethargic and found some within the caves actually sleeping with their eyes open (since sharks have no gills, normally they must be constantly

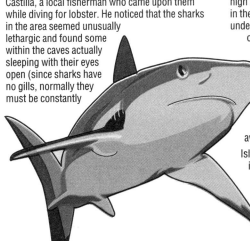

on the move to oxygenate their bloodstream). Jacques Cousteau, Ramon Bravo, Mexico's leading shark expert, and a diving expedition from *National Geographic* magazine all studied the phenomenon and attributed the sharks' somnolent state to the high salinity of the water and lack of carbon dioxide in the caves. The steady currents through the undersea warrens supply the animals with the oxygen they need.

The sleeping sharks are a big attraction for scuba divers, but only the most experienced should attempt the dive. You must descend at least 80 feet under water to see the sharks (which may or may not be there when you are), and there's also the possibility of encountering wide-awake, hungry sharks as well as sleepy ones.

Isla Mujeres has several other good dive sites, including the coral reefs at **Los Manchones** at the southern end of the island. Local dive shops conduct tours to The Caves of the Sleeping Sharks and other locations. They are **Bahía Dive Shop** (Av Gustavo Rueda Medina 166, at Av Morelos, 70340), **Buzos de Mexico** (Avs Gustavo Rueda Medina and Madero, 70131), and **Coral Scuba Center** (Av Matamoros 13-A, at Av Gustavo Rueda Medina, 70763; fax 70371).

Within Hotel Belmar:

Rolandi's ★★★
The convivial courtyard here is a great place to stop for thin-crust pizza, garlic bread, and cold beer. Or order a full meal—we recommend the fish carpaccio

RESTAURANT-BAR-PIZZERIA

appetizer, followed by calzone stuffed with lobster or pasta with squid, and coconut ice cream with Kahlua or lemon ice with fresh melon for dessert. ♦ Italian ♦ Daily lunch and dinner. 70430

11 Hotel Francis Arlene $ The Magaña family keeps a close eye on this homey small hotel, one of the friendliest places to stay on the island. The 18 rooms have tiled floors, ruffled bedspreads, small refrigerators, and either ceiling fans or air-conditioning; some have kitchenettes. Guests help themselves to coffee and fresh fruit in the morning, and find the resident manager's family friendly and resourceful. A 12-room addition was scheduled to be completed at press time. There's no restaurant on the premises, but several are within walking distance. The windward beach is one block away. ♦ No credit cards accepted. Av Vicente Guerrero 7 (between Avs Madero and Mariano Abasolo). 70310, 98/843302 in Cancún; fax 70310, 98/843302 in Cancún

12 Hotel Perla del Caribe $$ You can't get much closer to the sea than the balconies of this modest 90-room hotel on the island's windward side. The three-story building borders a small pool and sandy lounging areas set back from a seaside sidewalk. The simple rooms have dark wood furnishings, orange drapes, telephones, and radios, but no TVs. The bathrooms have a musty smell, the product of years of damp sea air, but the views and sound of the surf can't be beat. An in-house restaurant serves basic meals throughout the day. ♦ Avs Madero and Vicente Guerrero. 70306, 70507, 800/258.6454; fax 70011

13 La Loma The reliable standby for quality folk art, this shop is packed with hand-carved masks, jewelry from Chiapas, painted animals

from Oaxaca, and *huipiles* (blouses) and fabrics from Guatemala. ♦ Daily. Av Vicente Guerrero 6 (at Av Bravo). 70223

14 Casa del Arte Mexica Walk through the corbeled arch entryway into this gallery and peruse the exceptional selection of limestone carvings and rubbings of Maya designs. There's also an array of batik T-shirts and sarongs. ♦ Daily. Av Miguel Hidalgo 6 (between Avs Morelos and Madero). 70459

15 Van Cleef & Arpels The name might be familiar, especially to those accustomed to cruise ship ports, but the jewels displayed in this shop are not ones you would find in more cosmopolitan areas. The shop is licensed to the name only; the gold baubles are designed independently. The emeralds, rubies, and diamonds are certainly dazzling, however, and the prices quite reasonable. ♦ M-Sa. Avs Morelos and Benito Juárez. 70299

15 Goodies This ice-cream parlor, ideally located just up the street from the pier, lures quite a few hot and thirsty day-trippers with its cheery mint-green decor and soda fountain counter. Ice-cold Gatorade, tropical fruit *paletas* (ice pops), and ice-cream cones and sundaes keep customers cool. ♦ Daily. Av Morelos (between Avs Gustavo Rueda Medina and Benito Juárez). No phone

16 Panadería La Reina The aromas from this bakery are enough to stimulate the most finicky of appetites. Stop by first thing in the morning or at 5PM—the times when the freshest items are set out—and stock up on goodies for your room. ♦ No credit cards accepted. M-Sa. Avs Morelos and Benito Juárez. 70419

17 Mirtita's ★$ Ceiling fans whir in this Formica-filled coffee shop where fishermen, shopkeepers, and travelers sit in orange plastic chairs and read newspapers while they eat. The food is basic, filling, and cheap; try *huevos mexicanos* (eggs scrambled with onions, tomatoes, and peppers) or the chicken sandwich. ♦ Coffee shop ♦ Daily breakfast and lunch. No credit cards accepted. Av Gustavo Rueda Medina (between Avs Bravo and Morelos). 70232

17 Hotel Gomar $ A great choice, especially if you're hauling luggage from the pier, is this four-story hotel right across from the waterfront. The 16 rooms are painted a rather vivid pink, and have pink drapes, two double beds, and clean bathrooms. TVs are available for an extra charge. The rooftop terrace has a wonderful view of the town and sea. Only four of the rooms face the sea, however; try to reserve one in advance. The hotel lacks a restaurant, but there are several on the same block. ♦ No credit cards accepted. Av Gustavo Rueda Medina 150 (between Avs Bravo and Morelos). 70541

18 Puerto Isla Mujeres
$$$ Gorgeous and secluded, this upscale resort opened in 1995 to rave reviews from visitors and locals alike. The complex, beautifully designed by architect **Enrique Díaz Marta,** is centered around a marina and yacht club

and aims to meet the needs of those traveling by boat as well as by land. The 26 rooms are scattered throughout several cream-colored buildings with terra-cotta roofs set around a swimming pool and lawn. Meticulous attention to detail makes them among the nicest accommodations in the region. The two-story villas have private terraces; whirlpool tubs in the upstairs bathroom; entertainment centers with cable TV, VCRs, and CD players; mini-bars upstairs and down; ceiling fans; air-conditioning; and hand-crafted wood furnishings with cushions covered in bright, hand-loomed fabrics. Coffee and croissants are slipped through a service door every morning. The resort has a beach club accessible by land or sea with three pools, a water sports center, and a restaurant. There's also a restaurant on the main property. ♦ Fraconamiento Laguna Makax (west of Av Gustavo Rueda Medina). 70485; fax 70093

19 Hacienda Mundaca Isla Mujeres was a favorite hideaway for Fermin Mundaca de Marechaja, a Spanish pirate who made a fortune transporting slaves from Africa to Cuba in the early 19th century. It's said that Mundaca fell in love with a local girl, and when he lost interest in piracy and slave transport, he decided to retire here and woo her. Mundaca built the young woman a beautiful hacienda with tropical gardens and rock archways, but still failed to win her affection; she married an islander. The ruins of Mundaca's hacienda are open to the public, who can wander through the rock arch and among broken walls overgrown with vines and shrubs. ♦ No charge. Daily. Carretera Garrafón and Fraconamiento Laguna Makax. No phone

20 Dolphin Discovery Just north of Garrafón, dolphins frolic in the water at **Pirate's Village,** an educational center and restaurant. Advance reservations must be made to swim with the dolphins, who are well cared for by marine biologists. Visitors needn't get in the water, however, but can pet and learn about the gentle mammals without getting wet. A **Dolphin Express** adventure cruise departs from Cancún daily and includes continental breakfast, lunch, shopping, and snorkeling. If you're already on Isla, call ahead for hours and reservations. ♦ Daily. Carretera Garrafón

(south of Fraconamiento Laguna Makax). 98/831448 in Cancún, 70596 on Isla Mujeres

20 Parque Garrafón Nacional (Garrafón National Park) The snorkeling at this underwater preserve near Isla Mujeres's southern tip is far better than what you'll experience off the beaches of Cancún. It's a little more difficult, however, because you enter the water by climbing over limestone rocks rather than strolling in from the sand. The water gets crowded, especially after tour boats from Cancún discharge passengers around noon each day. Nonetheless, this is the best place on the island to stop for a swim. The park has dressing rooms, showers, food and souvenir concessions, and equipment rentals. The owners of **Xcaret** water park south of Cancún have taken over management of **Garrafón** and will surely spruce the place up and add new attractions. ♦ Admission. Daily. Carretera Garrafón (south of Fraconamiento Laguna Makax). No phone

21 El Faro y Las Ruinas (Lighthouse and Maya Temple) At the south end of the island, a lighthouse stands on a rocky promontory. From here, a path leads to a small Maya ruin, which is thought to have been built as an observatory honoring the moon goddess Ixchel. The lighthouse keeper sells cold drinks and handwoven hammocks to explorers who venture down the dirt road to his home (the road is navigable by moped if you take it slowly). There's a parking lot before you reach the lighthouse. ♦ Daily. Carretera Garrafón (south of Fraconamiento Laguna Makax). No phone

Cozumel

It takes barely 30 minutes to fly from Cancún over the multicolored, mesmerizing **Caribbean Sea** to Cozumel. Behind you, hotel towers glisten in the light of the sun. Ahead, waters wash over shimmering white sands, and slender palms reach toward the cloudless blue sky. Millions of exotic fluorescent fish float gracefully with the currents near jagged, milky-white reefs through fertile feeding grounds.

Nature is Cozumel's calling card, and she presents it unpretentiously. No flash, no glitter, no glitz. No race to see how many hotel rooms can fit on a parcel of land. No need to embrace fast-food emporiums; some that have tried have failed, though the **Hard Rock Cafe** and **Planet Hollywood** do a good business with the cruise-ship crowds. Cozumel's protectors have set a limit of 7,000 hotel rooms for the island, only half of which have been constructed thus far. Most of the businesses and some 55,000 inhabitants are concentrated in the town of **San Miguel** on the west side of the island; resorts and private villas line the soft white sand beaches to the north and south. A chain of coral reefs runs 13 miles along the southwestern shore, creating a windbreak that allows the Caribbean to flow peacefully in glittering turquoise bays.

At 24 miles long and 9 miles wide, Cozumel is Mexico's largest island. Only three percent of the island is developed; the rest is wild jungle (covering a base of gray limestone) populated by iguanas, foxes, deer, and other animals. The windward side is pounded by the open sea foaming above rocky cliffs. To the north, marshes, swamps, and lagoons shelter snow-white herons and

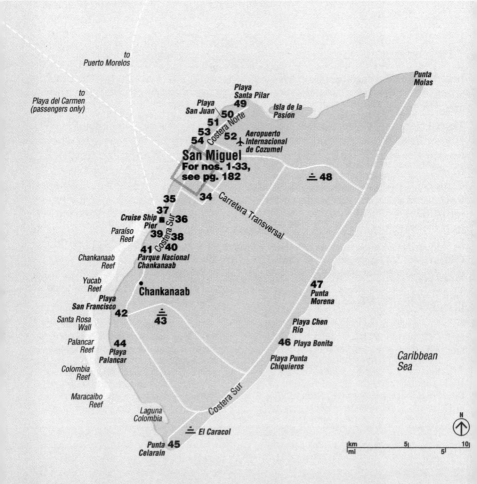

terns. An unknown number of Maya temples lie crumbling imperceptibly under a veil of ancient vines.

You can't halt progress completely, however, even in Cozumel. Many locals were horrified when construction began on a new cruise ship pier at **Paraíso Reef** in 1995, despite warnings about harm to the reef. The pier is due to be completed in 1999, and another pier is said to be on the way. With at least 650 cruise ships sailing to the island annually, the existing facilities are considered inadequate. *Cozumeleños* received another shock when seven traffic lights were installed on the island in 1997, but are delighted that they now have two gas stations and three large supermarkets. A new underwater park is planned for **Colombia Lagoon** at the south end of the island. But thus far, no plans are in the works for new, large hotels or other structures that would intrude on the island's peace.

More than 100,000 visitors fly into Cozumel's airport each year, many bearing scuba gear. Since the early 1960s, after Jacques Cousteau called it a diving mecca when filming the nearby **Palancar Reef**, divers have swarmed here, making the island one of the top five scuba destinations in the world. The additional 400,000 tourists that arrive on cruise ships fill San Miguel's restaurants and shops with a crush of eager spenders. Hotels are booked far in advance for Thanksgiving, Christmas, and Easter, when the temperature averages a comfortable 82 degrees, and the sun is almost guaranteed to shine daily.

The crowds are far smaller in the summer, when the rain, humidity, and mosquitoes hit their peak. However, visitors willing to withstand these minor incoveniences are treated to reduced hotel rates, uncrowded beaches, water temperatures over 80 degrees, and the unforgettable sight of mother sea turtles lumbering to shore to lay their eggs. Hurricanes are a concern in September and October; Hurricane Gilbert hit the island with a vengeance in 1988, and Hurricane Roxanne rattled the islanders in 1995, though you'd hardly believe the tales of destruction now. Cozumel recovered with amazing speed, and even the fragile coral reefs that suffered the wrath of high winds are growing back.

The island is laid out logically, and it's difficult to get lost or confused. Hotels along the northwest shore are favored by families and recluses who want to relax in the sun on uncrowded beaches and are willing to travel to town for bar hopping, shopping, and people watching. The majority of Cozumel's most popular restaurants and shops line San Miguel's **Avenida Rafael Melgar**, also known as the *malecón*. Dedicated shoppers will likely return several times to browse and buy; those looking for rowdy watering holes will find them here. Culture seekers should visit the excellent **Museo de la Isla de Cozumel** and spend time in the **Plaza Juárez**, where local families congregate to visit and watch their children play.

South of town are resorts that cater to divers who want to be close to the reefs. The snorkeling is better here than off the north shore, and the main road is lined with restaurants, hotels, and bars. The action is lively, youthful, and somewhat frenetic, except at the **Presidente Inter-Continental** and other self-contained retreats, where peaceful pampering is the norm. Drives along the windward side of the island are the most popular day trips. Many visitors soon weary of looking for excitement and stimulation, however, and settle into the island lifestyle, taking advantage of Cozumel's simple, relaxed, laid-back attitude, as the sun, sea, and tropical heat work their magic ever so subtly.

Area code 987 unless otherwise noted.

Getting to Cozumel

Airport

Aeropuerto Internacional de Cozumel (Cozumel International Airport) is on the north edge of San Miguel. The airport handles both national and international flights at one terminal.

Airlines

AeroCozumel and AeroCaribe 23456

Continental 20847, 800/525.0280

Mexicana 22945, 800/531.7921

Getting to and from Aeropuerto Internacional de Cozumel

By Bus Aero Transportes minibuses run from the airport into town and to the hotels for a low fare. Taxis cost a bit more but are a good choice if you are in a hurry or don't want to stop several times before reaching your destination.

By Car Cozumel's airport is a five-minute drive from downtown. The airport road goes west to Avenida Rafael Melgar; turn right or left, depending on where your hotel is located.

Volkswagen Beetles are common rental cars, but air-conditioned sedans are not readily available. If you want air-conditioning, it's best to reserve a car in advance. The following car-rental agencies have counters at **Aeropuerto Internacional de Cozumel** but are open only when flights arrive and depart.

Avis.............................20099, 800/331.1212

Budget 20903, 800/527.0700

National 23263, 800/328.4567

Pay Less 24744

Rentadora Cozumel...21120

By Taxi Taxis await travelers at the airport. The fare to downtown is $2 to $5.

Getting Around Cozumel

It's not necessary to have a car for your whole stay in Cozumel, since taxis are abundant and inexpensive.

Bicycles and Mopeds Mopeds are a common mode of transportation for both locals and visitors, and it seems as if there is a moped rental booth on every street corner. However, many of these small bikes are in dreadful, unsafe condition, and they usually break down at the most inopportune times. Check the vehicle carefully before you take off and make sure the tires have sufficient air and tread. Always wear a helmet (it's illegal to drive without one) and obey the traffic laws and right-of-way rules as if you were driving a car.

Buses There is no public bus service in Cozumel.

Driving With so few roads, driving is easy here. However, traffic gets congested on Avenida Rafael Melgar, especially when cruise ships disgorge hundreds of passengers in town. Finding a parking place can be difficult; there is a pay lot near the church on **10 Avenida Sur** (between 1 Sur and Av Benito Juárez).

The car-rental agencies at **Aeropuerto Internacional de Cozumel** (listed above) also have offices in hotels and in town.

Taxis Taxis are available at the hotels and can also be flagged on the street. Cab fares are regulated and are surprisingly inexpensive. Meters are not used, however, so agree on the fare with the driver before the taxi starts moving.

FYI

Accommodations Most of Cozumel's hotels are reasonably priced, and there is a good selection of budget properties. Hotels on the south, leeward side of the island are closer to the reefs and therefore more diving-oriented than those at the north end. Many of the hotels offer dive and honeymoon packages (some including airfare). Always ask about these and any special promotional rates when booking a room. The least expensive hotels are located in San Miguel.

Consulates American Consultation (13 Sur and 15 Av Sur, 20654) provides a liaison with the consulates in Mérida and Mexico City and can assist travelers with legal problems and translations.

Ferries The passenger ferry to **Playa del Carmen,** on the mainland, departs daily from the ferry pier (Avs Rafael Melgar and Benito Juárez, 21588). The schedule changes frequently and is posted at the pier. Trips last 30 to 45 minutes, depending on the boat. Independent boat operators also offer trips from Cozumel to the mainland departing from the pier. Look at the boat before you pay; the seas can be rough, and a journey in a small boat will likely leave you and your luggage drenched.

The car ferry leaves from the cruise ship pier (Costera Sur, south of 21 Sur) to **Puerto Morelos** on the mainland several times during the week. The trip takes three to four hours. For information, call 20950.

Publications The *Blue Guide to Cozumel,* published seasonally in English, is filled with helpful tips; it's available at the airport, hotels, and tour agencies.

Shopping Cozumel has some excellent folk art shops and an abundance of curio and import shops catering to cruise-ship passengers and stocked with sportswear, beach toys, and diving gear.

Sportfishing The sportfishing off Cozumel is spectacular, with tuna, dorado, wahoo, marlin, and sailfish in plentiful numbers from March through July, and record catches of billfish peaking in April and May. Fishing is not allowed inside the reefs along the western shores, but there is a channel between the reef and Playa del Carmen where sailfish abound. Cozumel hosts a **Billfish Release Tournament** and a

Marlin Tournament in May, attracting top names in sportfishing circles. Light-tackle fishing for tarpon and bonefish in the flats at the north end of the island is also popular. Boats can be chartered at **Club Náutico de Cozumel** marina and the **La Caleta** marina behind the **Presidente Inter-Continental Cozumel** hotel. To choose a sportfishing charter, wander through the marinas as the boats come in and ask other customers whether they enjoyed their outings. Check the fishing gear provided, and keep in mind that a bathroom and a shaded area make the trip far more comfortable. Tour agencies and hotel desks can arrange sportfishing charters, or contact the following companies and captains:

Capt. Felipe Quinones 21817

Capt. Nacho Euan ....20545; fax 20445

Cozumel Angler's Fleet ....20113; fax 21135

The Sharp Hook.............................24349; fax 23282

Time Zone Cozumel is on Central Time, two hours ahead of California and one hour behind New York.

Tours Most hotels have tour desks offering trips to **Tulum** and **Chichén Itzá** on the mainland, either in small chartered planes or via ferry and bus. The plane trips are a much better option in terms of time and scenic value—few sights are as spectacular as the gray limestone temples of **Tulum** rising above the aquamarine sea. Tours to the ecological park **Xcaret**, including transportation and admission, are very popular. Tours on Cozumel include journeys to the windward side of the island and party boats that cruise the coast with a stop at **Parque Nacional Chankanaab** (Chankanaab National Park) for swimming and snorkeling. **Barbachano Tours** represents more than 30 hotel, condo, and villa properties and frequently offers packages including airfare, accommodations, and scuba diving. For more information, call 800/327.2254.

The following companies also offer tours:

American Express Av Coldwell 385 (at 11 Sur) 20725

Aviomar 6 Norte (between 15 Av Norte and 10 Av Norte) 20477, 20588

Fiesta Cozumel 11 Sur and 30 Av Sur 20433, 21044

Visitors' Information Center There is a tourist information booth at the ferry pier (Avs Rafael Melgar and Benito Juárez, no phone), which is open daily. The tourist information office is on the second floor of the **Plaza del Sol** facing the main square (20972).

Phone Book

Ambulance 20639

Clinica Cozumel
(24-hour, English-speaking medical care),
15 Av Norte 320..........................23545; fax 42222

Hospital
11 Sur (between 20 Av Sur and 15 Av Sur) 20140

Police ....00 (for critical emergencies), ...20092, 20409

Red Cross..21058

Scuba Emergencies 5 Sur, No. 21B (at 5 Av Sur) 22387

1 Ferry Pier Tourists and workers arrive from the mainland at a long concrete pier that intersects Avenida Rafael Melgar. The ferry for Playa del Carmen departs daily from 4AM-8PM.
♦ Avs Rafael Melgar and Benito Juárez. 21588

2 Avenida Rafael Melgar Better known as the *malecón*, this waterfront walkway is Cozumel's busiest street. Mopeds, VW Beetles, and Jeeps angle into every available parking space and cruise the avenue in a slow procession. Police officers halt the parade as pedestrians stream across the four-lane street, often oblivious to the traffic. This is Cozumel's version of downtown, where everyone ends up sooner or later to eat, shop, and eye their fellow revelers. It is the main paved road around the island, but is called Rafael Melgar only in the town of San Miguel. Outside of town it becomes Costera Sur or Carretera a Chankanaab to the south, and Costera Norte to the north. Even with the name changes, you can't get too confused since it is the only road parallel to the waterfront.

2 Las Palmeras ★$ The best seats on the waterfront are at this bustling open-air cafe looking across to the ferry pier. Bottles of Tehuacan mineral water sit on each table, but be aware that you'll be charged for the whole bottle if you open it. The view is better than the food, so stick to simple, inexpensive fare—scrambled eggs and white toast at breakfast, sandwiches and soups at lunch and dinner. Better yet, eat your main meal elsewhere and just come here for coffee and ice cream. ♦ Mexican/American ♦ Daily breakfast, lunch, and dinner. Av Rafael Melgar (between 1 Sur and Av Benito Juárez). 20532

Presidential elections in Mexico are held every six years in July, and the victor takes office in December. The last six months of the outgoing leader's term is called *El Año de Hidalgo* (the year of the nobleman). It is a time of extreme uncertainty, when the president typically pushes through unpopular programs and paybacks with little regard for how they will affect the country. For example, during this period in 1982, then-president López Portillo nationalized the banks, creating economic panic.

Restaurants/Clubs: Red   **Hotels:** Blue
Shops/♥ Outdoors: Green   **Sights/Culture:** Black

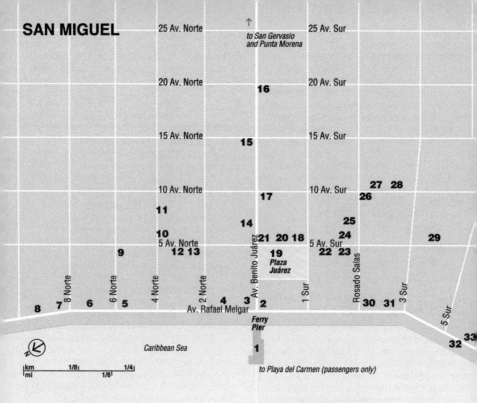

SAN MIGUEL

25 Av. Norte • to San Gervasio and Punta Morena • 25 Av. Sur

20 Av. Norte • **16** • 20 Av. Sur

15 Av. Norte • **15** • 15 Av. Sur

10 Av. Norte • **17** • 10 Av. Sur • **27 28**

11 • **26**

14 • **25**

10 • **21 20 18** • **24** • **29**

5 Av. Norte • **22 23**

9 • **12 13** • 5 Av. Sur

19
Plaza Juárez

8 Norte • 6 Norte • 4 Norte • 2 Norte • Av. Benito Juárez • 1 Sur • Rosado Salas • 3 Sur • 5 Sur

8 • **7** • **6** • **5** • **4** • **3** • **2** • **30 31** • **32** • **33**

Av. Rafael Melgar

Ferry Pier

Caribbean Sea • **1**

km / mi • 1/8 • 1/4 • 1/8

to Playa del Carmen (passengers only)

3 Explora Sportswear with a safari theme fills this small store, which gets impossibly crowded when more than 10 customers squeeze in. The T-shirt designs are strikingly different, with gorgeous silkscreen paintings of lobsters, angelfish, and crabs under the store's slogan: "Nature at its best." The shop also has practical, sturdy hiking shorts and pants. ♦ Daily. Av Rafael Melgar (between Av Benito Juárez and 2 Norte). 20316

4 Casablanca Jewelry shops abound on Cozumel, and this place is one of the most impressive, with a staggering array of emeralds, diamonds, and sapphires in the raw or set in gold. The jewelry is arranged elegantly by type of gemstone in freestanding and wall-mounted display cases. The salespeople are knowledgeable about gems and extremely courteous. ♦ Daily; closed at midday. Av Rafael Melgar (between Av Benito Juárez and 2 Norte). 20982

Cozumel's nonnumbered streets, Rafael Melgar and Rosado Salas, are named after doctors.

The striking brown-and-white–striped Splendid Toadfish, which exists only in the reefs off Cozumel, can suck down another fish in six milliseconds, making it one of the fastest eaters in the world.

5 Museo de la Isla de Cozumel (Cozumel Museum) The former **La Playa** hotel, which housed guests in relative luxury at the turn of the century, now is home to an excellent museum worth visiting for an hour or two. The first floor has sea and reef exhibits (including wonderful specimens of coral), and an island ecology display. A large map highlights the areas reserved as parklands. One of the most fascinating exhibits is on the second floor, where photographs, dioramas, and old newspaper clippings show Cozumel's history. In the courtyard, an exhibit on the Maya includes a typical Maya house, called a *na,* with rounded walls, thatch roof, and hammocks as the main furnishings. The museum has a breezy cafe for breakfast and lunch on the second-floor roof overlooking the *malecón,* and a small gift shop. ♦ Admission. Daily. Av Rafael Melgar (between 4 Norte and 6 Norte). 21434

6 Pizza Rolandi ★★★$$ The courtyard of this Swiss-Italian pizzeria is the most enjoyable spot in town for a leisurely lunch or dinner. Locals and visitors alike congregate here day after day, unable to get enough of the distinctive cuisine. These pizzas are highly unusual, made on a crust that resembles light and airy pita bread. Toppings are as typical as olive oil, tomatoes, basil, and cheese, or as outlandish as a combo of mushrooms, asparagus, and ham. The homemade coconut ice cream topped with amaretto or cassis is the perfect sweet treat any time of day or night. For a total blowout, have the banana supreme, a full-scale banana split flamed with Cointreau. ♦ Swiss/Italian ♦ M-Sa lunch and dinner. Av Rafael Melgar 23 (between 6 Norte and 8 Norte). 20946

7 Los Cinco Soles Allow yourself plenty of time to browse through the many rooms in this folk art shop with an excellent selection of crafts from all over Mexico. One room is filled with resortwear, including a large selection of gauze dresses, blouses, and skirts made by Maria of Guadalajara. Fanciful *nacimientos* (nativity sets) and pottery figurines are sold at prices far lower than in Cancún. ♦ Daily; closed at midday. Av Rafael Melgar 27 (between 8 Norte and 10 Norte). 22040

7 Pancho's Backyard ★★★★$$
Owner Pancho Morelos has created a tranquil courtyard restaurant behind his shop, **Los Cinco Soles,** with water burbling in stone fountains, and flowering vines wrapping around white archways and pillars. Enhancing the traditional Mexican setting are *equipale* tables and chairs, made of leather surfaces in bases of woven slats. The hand-painted pottery dishes and blown-glass goblets are samples of the wares sold in the store, as are the candleholders and statues. His health-conscious menu emphasizes Mexican dishes prepared with a minimum of oil and a deft sprinkling of spices. Mexican wines from the **Calafia** and **Santo Tomás** wineries in Baja are featured and accompany the fragrant *chiles rellenos* wonderfully. ♦ Mexican ♦ Daily lunch and dinner. Av Rafael Melgar (between 8 Norte and 10 Norte). 22141

8 Galería Del Sol Watercolors, oil paintings, and sculptures depicting island themes are artfully arranged in this serene gallery. Featured are local artists, including Gordon Gilchrist, whose etchings of Maya temples and pyramids are coveted by collectors. ♦ M-Sa; closed at midday. Av Rafael Melgar (between 8 Norte and 10 Norte). 20170

9 Manuel's Hammocks During the day, you can usually find retired police officer Manuel Azueta on the front porch of his bright blue house, weaving thin strands of cotton and nylon into hammocks. They may cost more than those found at the flea market, but the quality is well worth the price, and you're likely to get a lesson in weaving, along with some memorable snapshots. ♦ Most mornings and late afternoons. 5 Av Norte (between 4 Norte and 6 Norte). No phone

10 Bakery Zermatt Fresh crusty *bolillos* (rolls), cheese danish, chocolate croissants, thick pizza by the slice, and two walls of shelves filled with other sweet selections make it tempting to visit this aromatic place at least once a day. No preservatives are used, so buy only what you can eat immediately, then come back for more. ♦ Daily. 4 Norte and 5 Av Norte. 21384

11 La Veranda
★★$
Ownership has changed at this classic Caribbean-style wooden cottage, unusual for Cozumel, which sits behind a  landscaped garden on a quiet side street. The comfortable indoor dining room has a large bar and pleasant dining area, where fish fillet in mango sauce, jerked chicken, and stir-fried veggies are served graciously. ♦ Seafood ♦ Daily dinner. 4 Norte (between 10 Av Norte and 5 Av Norte). 24132

12 Batik Factory One section of this shop displays batik T-shirts and wall hangings with underwater coral and fish scenes and depictions of Maya deities. Another room features hand-carved masks and other folk art. ♦ Daily; closed at midday. 5 Av Norte (between 2 Norte and 4 Norte). 21960

13 Artesanías El Ocelote Among the small shops that fill Cozumel's main streets and sell the same manufactured handicrafts, this one has a better-than-average selection. Offerings include purses and belts from Guatemala, Yucatecan hammocks, silver jewelry, and clay figurines. ♦ Daily. 5 Av Norte (between 2 Norte and 4 Norte). No phone

14 Morgan's ★★★$$ Locals and tourists alike consistently return here for a special night out. This former customs house has been paneled on the outside with lacquered mahogany planks; inside, a nautical theme prevails with a glow of candlelight and brass. White linens, crystal, and silver cover the tables, and the wine list is better than most on the island. The menu leans toward continental specialties—coq au vin, chateaubriand, crepes suzette—and top-quality steaks. Try the avocado, melon, and shrimp salad for an appetizer, followed by a wonderful Caesar salad and fresh fish or lobster, and finish with one of the flaming desserts. Guitarists play romantic ballads during dinner. ♦ Continental ♦ Daily lunch and dinner. Av Benito Juárez (between 10 Av Norte and 5 Av Norte). 20584

15 Sonora Grill ★★$$ If your fishing yields a catch, bring your prize here for a dinner you won't forget. The chef in the open kitchen can turn your offering into a veritable fish feast—a heaping platter of grilled and fried fillets, along with bread, tortillas, rice, salad, baked potatoes, and vegetables. Of course, you don't have to provide the main course, and you don't even have to eat fish. They also serve a hefty dish of fajitas, carne *asada* (marinated and grilled meat), and grilled lobster. The second-story restaurant gets a nice breeze through the windows and is quieter and more relaxing than those along the sidewalk below. ♦ Seafood/Mexican ♦ Daily breakfast, lunch, and dinner. Av Benito Juárez and 15 Av Norte. 23620

16 La Mission ★★$$ This place has developed a faithful following among the scuba set, who know they'll be fed generously for a reasonable price. Watch the cooks at the open grill to get an idea of the sizable portions and decide which tempting entrée will best satisfy your appetite. Lobster is a popular choice, along with Mexican combination plates heaped with tacos, enchiladas, refried beans, and rice. The dining room is open to the street and is festively decorated with stained-glass lamps, red-and-white checkered tablecloths, and Mexican pottery. You won't leave here hungry. The owners have opened a second restaurant, **La Langosta Loca** (Rosado Salas, between 10 Av Sur and 5 Av Sur, 23518), which seems equally popular. ♦ Mexican/Seafood ♦ Daily dinner. Av Benito Juárez 23 (between 20 Av Sur and 15 Av Sur). 21641

17 Iglesia Inmaculada Concepción (Immaculate Conception Church) Cozumel's main Catholic church is just a block off Plaza Juárez. Religious processions and concerts by the church choir are held in the pedestrian walkway on Benito Juárez. The church has a spectacular stained-glass mural of the Archangel Michael standing on a devil engulfed in flames. ♦ Av Benito Juárez (between 10 Av Sur and 5 Av Sur)

18 Flea Market To find the best array of tawdry souvenirs, browse this collection of stalls near the plaza—you can easily find it from the sound of blaring disco music and the large "Handicrafts" signs. Amid the trinkets are old Spanish coins, Cuban cigars, bizarre stone reproductions of Maya carvings, and amber jewelry imbedded with fossils. ♦ M-Sa; some stands closed at midday. 5 Av Sur (between 1 Sur and Av Benito Juárez). No phone

19 Plaza Juárez Graceful flamboyant trees frame the central plaza with feathery leaves and brilliant orange blossoms. Children race up and down the stairs of the white wrought-iron gazebo, where local bands perform on Sunday. It seems the whole town turns out for these weekly concerts, which sometimes include impromptu dances. Hot dogs, french fries, and sodas are sold from stands around the edge of the concrete plaza, while balloon and cotton candy vendors entice children. Don't miss this display of small-town life, a reminder that although Cozumel seems to be filled with foreigners, it is classically Mexican at heart. ♦ 5 Av Sur (between 1 Sur and Av Benito Juárez)

20 Agencia de Publicaciones Gracia English-language magazines, newspapers, and books are available at this small shop on the plaza. There's a good selection of books on Mexico and the Maya as well. ♦ Daily. 5 Av Sur (between 1 Sur and Av Benito Juárez). 20031

21 Estilo Caribeño You'll be tempted to fill your carry-on bags with pink, purple, and green wine goblets, hand-painted plates and bowls, and other treasures from this gem of a shop. The prices are a bit high, but so is the quality. ♦ Daily. 5 Av Sur (between 1 Sur and Av Benito Juárez). 20935

22 Gallito Sol ★★★$$ Unusually stylish by Cozumel standards, this nicely designed restaurant lends a welcome elegance to the dining scene. The *palapa* roof is made with

slender strands of zacate grass, and the linen-covered dining tables surround an indoor garden. The chef prepares regional Mexican dishes with a twist: octopus *escabeche* (made with a marinade similar to that of ceviche and containing octopus instead of turkey), chicken with *flor de calabaza* (squash blossoms), and tequila ice cream. There's a bar (generously stocked with imported liquors) decked out with chrome-and-wicker chairs and glass-topped tables, and a few outside tables at the edge of the pedestrian walkway are shaded by white umbrellas. ◆ Nouvelle Mexican ◆ Daily dinner; late-night bar. 5 Av Sur 148 (between Rosado Salas and 1 Sur). 25238

23 Cocos Cozumel ★★★$ You may well end up having breakfast here nearly every morning—owners Daniel and Terri Ocejo's coffee alone is worth a visit. Some may opt for typical US breakfasts of eggs and hash browns, but you shouldn't miss their eggs scrambled with chilies and served with cheese sauce atop a fried tortilla, the enormous cream-cheese muffins, and the egg tacos. Another plus: The Ocejos run a library of sorts, with shelves stacked high with used paperbacks that they sell for a few pesos. ◆ Mexican/American ◆ Daily breakfast from 6AM; closed from mid-September through mid-October. 5 Av Sur 180 (at Rosado Salas). 20241

24 Roberto's Of the many black-coral shops on Cozumel, this one stands out for its gorgeous carvings of hammerhead sharks, angelfish, and marlin by artist Roberto Franco. Branches of the fragile and precious coral—which look like dead brown ferns—hang in the back workshop. There is some dispute over the sale of this endangered species; expert divers say the supply from local reefs has all but disappeared, and those searching for it must go down 300 feet or more to find it, risking their lives in the process. Still, the demand is high, Cozumel's divers and jewelers make a handsome living dealing in black coral, and their work is impressive. Be aware, however, that you may have some problems bringing a purchase back into the US. ◆ M-Sa; Su evenings. 5 Av Sur (between Rosado Salas and 1 Sur). No phone

25 Prima Trattoria ★★★$$ Albert and Ceci Domínguez started their business with a pizza parlor that has evolved into a wonderful trattoria with a rooftop garden. The owners grow their own salad ingredients and bake the pizzas and garlic bread in a wood-burning brick oven; try the Chicago-style pizza. Among the pastas is a sublime lobster fettuccine. You'll find that the submarine sandwiches, liberally sprinkled with a garlicky oil dressing, are big enough to serve two small eaters. Takeout and hotel delivery are available; also, the **Prima** deli next door sells imported cheeses and meats, sandwiches, and

homemade breads. ◆ Northern Italian ◆ Daily 3-11PM. Rosado Salas 109 (between 10 Av Sur and 5 Av Sur). 24242

26 La Chozá ★★★$ Often cited by locals as the best Mexican restaurant in town, it offers *chiles rellenos* with shrimp filling; Veracruz-style jumbo shrimp (sautéed with tomatoes, onions, and peppers); chicken covered with mole sauce; and *puerco entomado con rajas* (pork chunks with grilled peppers). The menu changes daily; specials include *cochinita pibil* (a savory Yucatecan dish of pork chunks marinated with sour orange juice and slowly baked in banana leaves). Finish your meal with a fragrant cup of *cafe de olla* (rich Mexican coffee simmered with cinnamon and sugar). The *palapa* restaurant is casual yet stylish—meals are served on pretty blue-and-white pottery, and giant tasty margaritas come in hand-blown glasses that are edged in sapphire blue. ◆ Mexican/Yucatecan/Seafood ◆ Daily breakfast, lunch, and dinner. Rosado Salas 198 (at 10 Av Sur). 20958

27 Cafe Caribe ★★$ Coffee beans roasted under this label appear in restaurants around town (and on market shelves to take home as souvenirs). Sip an espresso or a cappuccino, or select from among nearly a dozen specialty drinks while indulging in a dense chocolate cake, flaky pecan pie, or whatever other desserts the baker comes up with each day. This small cafe is a good place to swap stories with fellow travelers while waiting for the sugar and caffeine to kick in. ◆ Coffeehouse ◆ Daily 7AM-1PM and 4-10PM. No credit cards accepted. 10 Av Sur (between 3 Sur and Rosado Salas). 23621

28 Joe's ★★$$ Billed as a lobster pub, this is better known for the salsa, jazz, and reggae bands that play here late nearly every night. Dining tables are set in a back patio, while the small stage and dance floor are inside by the bar, where it gets incredibly hot once the dancing starts. ◆ Seafood ◆ Daily dinner. 10 Av Sur 229 (between 3 Sur and Rosado Salas). 23275

In the early 1900s a group of workers on Cozumel found an ivory statue of the Archangel Michael wearing a crown of gold. The discovery was made on 26 September, the day of the Feast of Saint Michael. In honor of this fortuitous coincidence, the island's main settlement was named San Miguel.

29 Villa Las Anclas $$ This is an excellent option for those wishing to set up house while on vacation. Seven apartments—each complete with a kitchen, living room, and two bedrooms (up a spiral staircase) with writing desks and bookshelves, and plenty of room to spread out—are offered at this small inn. Though not near the water and lacking a pool, it is cooled by lots of shade trees and has a pretty garden. There are several nice, small restaurants in the neighborhood, which is close to the *malecón*, yet quiet. ♦ 5 Av Sur 325 (between 5 Sur and 3 Sur). 21403; fax 21955

30 Pepe's Grill ★★★$$$ The best tables in the house are in the upstairs dining room looking out onto the *malecón*, where you can feast on shrimp, steaks, and pasta in a romantic, nautical setting. The shrimp brochette has nine large shrimp grilled with chunks of green pepper, tomatoes, and onion, and is served with a baked potato and vegetables. *Spaghetti portofino* is prepared tableside in a copper chafing dish with bacon, white wine, and shrimp. There's also a decent salad bar. This restaurant is said to have the best prime rib on Cozumel, but be prepared to pay dearly. Save room for the tangy lime pie, one of the best versions of this ubiquitous island dessert. ♦ Seafood/Steak ♦ Daily dinner. Reservations recommended. Av Rafael Melgar (between 3 Sur and Rosado Salas). 20213

The Undersea World of Cozumel

Cozumel's greatest attractions lie underwater along the southwest side of the island, where a 13-milelong series of coral reefs harbors more than 230 species of tropical fish. Yellow, purple, orange, and white sponges and corals grow in fantastic formations, creating canyons, mountains, and plateaus, a striking backdrop for electric-blue queen angelfish, violet-and-jade–striped parrot fish, and thousands of neon-pink and yellow wrasses.

Scuba divers drift effortlessly with the current in the 70 to 80 degree water past brain-shaped coral the size of small buildings. Visibility is usually good to about a hundred feet and can reach twice that in some areas.

Brown-and-white–spotted moray eels slither in the reefs, while silvery barracuda glide by just out of reach. And the schools of divers in their fluorescent gear, bubbles streaming above them in the sky-blue water, are often joined by giant bronze Nassau groupers.

More than 30 dive shops on Cozumel offer trips to about 40 dive sites with a range in depth that should please both seasoned divers and neophytes. Many of the shops have joined together to form the **Cozumel Association of Dive Operators (CADO),** a much-needed organization that strives to improve safety conditions for divers and to protect marine ecology. Divers are instructed to stay off the fragile coral, which is easily destroyed when struck by a diver's fins or stroked by a careless admirer. (It's illegal to remove anything from the reefs, which are a national underwater preserve; thus, watchful divers can find incredibly large lobsters and crabs scuttling about, and even a loggerhead turtle or two.)

CADO offers classes for divemasters on emergency procedures and supports the island's emergency clinic and recompression chamber by contributing $1 from every diver's fee. The clinic is open 24 hours daily (5 Sur 21B, between 5 Av Sur and Rafael Melgar, 22387, 21430; fax 21848). Two other recompression chambers have also opened.

With so many dive shops competing for clients here, you can afford the luxury of comparison shopping. Herding a dozen or more divers over reefs crowded with other groups is quite common during the peak seasons. Find out how many people go out on the shop's boats, and whether you have a choice of dive sites. Several shops offer six-pack boats, carrying a half-dozen divers to the sites of their choice; individual trips are also available. Certification courses are offered, or you can take a resort course, a shorter lesson that includes a shallow dive. The following operators are respected members of **CADO:**

Aqua Safari ♦ Av Rafael Melgar (between 7 Sur and 5 Sur). 20101; fax 20661

Blue Bubble Divers ♦ 5 Av Sur and 3 Sur. 21865

Caribbean Divers ♦ Av Rafael Melgar and 5 Sur. 21080; fax 21426

Del Mar Aquatics ♦ La Ceiba, Costera Sur (south of 21 Sur). 21833

Dive House ♦ Fiesta Americana The Reef, Costera Sur (south of 21 Sur). 21953

Dive Paradise ♦ Av Rafael Melgar 601 (between 11 Sur and 7 Sur). 21007; fax 21061

Pro Dive ♦ 5 Av Sur and Rosado Salas. 20221

31 Mi Casa This gallery of Mexican house-wares has a select collection of hand-painted pottery, tableware, and vases, pewter and silver frames, brass hurricane lamps, and bas-relief plaques of Pacal, an ancient Maya ruler. It also has an excellent selection of books on the Maya and their culture, many in English. ◆ Daily. Av Rafael Melgar 271 (between 3 Sur and Rosado Salas). 21472

Plaza Las Glorias

32 Plaza Las Glorias $$$$ This has the best location of any hotel on the island, since it's right on the beach but also within easy walking distance to downtown. It's also a location favored by hurricanes and high winds. The pool sits right above the water and two small beaches. The 160 rooms—all with satellite TV and mini-bars—include 148 junior suites with separate sleeping and living areas, a queen-size foldout couch, bathtubs, hair dryers, and terraces with ocean views. A dozen deluxe suites feature hot tubs on the terrace. There's a lavish brunch with made-to-order omelettes served daily in the poolside *palapa* restaurant. Guests, who tend to be young, athletic, and feisty, compete with the youthful, energetic staff members at beach and pool volleyball, limbo contests, and other fun-filled activities. The dive shop is a branch of **Aqua Safari.** ◆ Av Rafael Melgar (between 7 Sur and 5 Sur). 22400, 26446, 800/342.AMIGO; fax 21937

33 Aqua Safari This excellent dive shop celebrated its 30th anniversary in 1996, certainly a record for a Cozumel business. Owner Bill Horn is known for running a safe shop, and his divemasters make a point of lecturing on safety and ways to protect the sea's fragile environment. The shop offers a full range of services to divers, from equipment sales and rentals to customized dive trips. Afternoon dives are discounted for those who want even more after a two-tank morning dive. ◆ Daily. Av Rafael Melgar 40 (between 7 Sur and 5 Sur). 20101; fax 20661. Also at: Plaza Las Glorias, Av Rafael Melgar (between 7 Sur and 5 Sur). 23362

Within Aqua Safari:

Safari Inn $$ Divers looking for basic, no-frills accommodations at below-budget prices will find a friend in owner Bill Horn, who also owns the dive shop downstairs. The 12-room, three-story hotel has comfortable mattresses, big showers with plenty of hot water, high-powered air-conditioning, and good screens on the windows. One of the rooms has bunk beds and enough room for five close friends.

Overall, this is a good choice for those who prefer to spend their money on dive trips rather than hotel amenities. There is no restaurant. ◆ 23101, 20101; fax 20661

33 Jeanie's Waffle House ★★★$ Jeanie and Raul DeLille have carved a nice niche in the local restaurant scene with their water-front cafe. The small dining room faces the water, and the few tables ouside are pleasant when there's not too much foot traffic on the sidewalks. Jeanie bakes wonderful desserts, and they've added pastas, sandwiches, tamales, and fish to the menu. But the main attraction is the fresh-baked waffles, topped with nuts, strawberries, chocolate syrup, or served with egg breakfasts all day long. ◆ Waffles/International ◆ Daily breakfast, lunch, and dinner. Av Rafael Melgar 40 (between 7 Sur and 5 Sur). 20545

34 Parque Arqueológico de Cozumel (Cozumel Archaeological Park) An attraction far from downtown and the beaches, this park seems to have been built as a diversion for cruise-ship passengers who arrive here by the busload. Lushly landscaped, it has replicas of 65 of Mexico's most famous archaeological finds, including the five-foot-high stone head attributed to the Olmec civilization and replicas of Maya relics. If you haven't visited archaeological sites on the mainland, you may find the park interesting. Wear bug repellent if you visit in the rainy season (June through September). ◆ Admission. Daily. Bounded by 50 Av Sur and 40 Av Sur, and 5 Sur and 3 Sur. No phone

35 Hotel Barracuda $$ One of the least expensive hotels near the reefs, this pink 50-room property sits on a ledge above the sea. The no-frills rooms have small refrigerators, televisions, and seafront balconies; dive boats pick up clients at the hotel's small cement dock. There's nothing fancy about the place, but it's within walking distance of town, has good snorkeling just offshore, and is frequented by friendly dive groups. ◆ Av Rafael Melgar 628 (at 11 Sur). 20002; fax 20884

36 La CoCay ★★★$$$ Hidden in a residential area away from the tourist zone, this small restaurant draws rave reviews from locals. In an open kitchen where he can view his regulars sampling new creations, the French chef prepares stylish renditions of escargots and veal. The fudge torte with ice cream and berry sauce is not to be missed. ◆ Mediterranean ◆ Daily dinner; closed from mid-September through mid-October. 17 Sur and 20 Av Sur. 25533

36 Fiesta Inn Cozumel $$ Proximity to the water and town, plus reasonable room rates, make this small hotel on the inland side of the coastal road an excellent choice. Several understated two-story buildings frame plush green lawns and a huge swimming pool (guests walk through a tunnel under the road to reach the beach). Most of the 180 rooms face the pool (35 face the sea), and the dark decor is quaint—brown paisley bedspreads, blue drapes, blue-and-brown–tile floors, and large showers and tubs. There's a dive shop, a good restaurant, and a bar featuring karaoke. You'll find soda and ice machines in the hallways, and you can order **Pizza Hut** pizzas and other fare through room service. ♦ Costera Sur (just south of 21 Sur). 22811, 22900, 800/343.7821; fax 22154

37 Scuba Club Dive Resort $$$ This dedicated divers' hotel, formerly known as the **Galápago Inn,** has several packages that include room, meals, and diving at reasonable rates, and is often filled with groups from US dive shops. The small, white-stucco inn has 60 rooms facing the inner courtyard and others in a two-story building looking out to sea. Rooms 36 through 41 have particularly nice views. One wonderful feature is the beachfront *palapa* with 12 hammocks hanging underneath—a perfect spot for relaxing and fantasizing about the creatures you've seen on your dives. There's a small pool above the beach. The dive shop, run by **Del Mar Divers,** is well equipped for shuttling boatloads of divers back and forth to the reefs. ♦ Costera Sur (between 21 Sur and 19 Sur). 20663, 800/847.5708

Within the Scuba Club Dive Resort:

Scuba Club Restaurant ★★$$ A casual yet good second-story eatery overlooking the beach, it offers huge sandwiches and burgers, great french fries, and bountiful Mexican specialties. ♦ Mexican/American ♦ Daily lunch and dinner. 20663

38 La Ceiba $$$ Most guests choose this hotel for the sunken airplane located a hundred yards offshore, which serves as an artificial reef and attracts swarms of tropical fish. The hotel is named after the *ceiba* tree (there's an old one growing by the pool), which was sacred to the Maya. The majority of the 115 rooms are in an 11-story tower; many need refurbishing. The rooms in an adjacent two-story section are in better shape, and have tile baths, bizarre orange, yellow, and brown wall hangings, and king-size beds. The dive shop rents tanks for shore

dives and also offers boat trips. The restaurant faces the water and serves decent Mexican cuisine. ♦ Costera Sur (south of 21 Sur). 20812, 20379, 800/437.9609; fax 21833

39 Presidente Inter-Continental Cozumel $$$$ Of all the hotels on the island, this one does the best job of seducing guests into never leaving the grounds. Set beside the jungle on a gorgeous sheltered cove, the hotel offers several levels of accommodations: modern rooms in a high-rise tower; moderately priced rooms buried in gardens by the marina and a lagoon; and the best in the house, with private terraces hidden behind palms just steps from the sand. Go all the way, if you can, and reserve one of these spacious rooms with sleek, light cedar furnishings, bright purple, pink, and blue touches in the decor, a dining table by the window overlooking the sea, a large terrace with lounge chairs, and private pathways leading to the beach.

The snorkeling is excellent along this stretch of rocky shore, especially at the southern end, where stone stairways lead down into the water filled with sergeant majors and angelfish, and at another rocky ledge by the *palapa* restaurant. A dive shop on the premises runs trips to nearby reefs. Though the hotel has 253 rooms and suites and is often full, you never feel crowded, since there is a long beach north of the central swimming pool and cove, and private sunbathing areas are set apart under small *palapas*. The hotel has always excelled at personalized, gracious service, and returnees are greeted like old friends by staff, many of whom have been around for years. ♦ Costera Sur 3 (south of the cruise ship pier). 20322, 800/327.0200; fax 21360

Within the Presidente Inter-Continental Cozumel:

El Caribeño ★★★$$ A fabulous breakfast buffet is served under an enormous *palapa* by the beach. The cheese danish and croissants are addictive, the array of tropical fruits beautiful and delicious, and the made-to-order waffles so crisp and light you'll be tempted to return for more. The lunch menu has a healthy, exotic flare, and includes a fragrant lemon-pepper pasta salad topped with grilled prawns, a grilled chicken breast with chili mayonnaise, and green *chiles rellenos* with shrimp filling. It's hard to resist the fresh onion-filled popovers served at lunch (if you smile sweetly, your waiter will bring more). Even if you're not staying at the hotel, consider stopping here for a leisurely breakfast or lunch, followed by a nap on the beach. ♦ Mexican/American ♦ Daily breakfast, lunch, and dinner. 20322

Beyond Your Basic Bean Burrito

The cuisine of Mexico is far more varied than most travelers realize—it has been influenced by the ancient Aztec and Maya, the Spanish *conquistadores*, the French occupation, and the modern-day invasion of expatriates and travelers from the United States, Europe, and the Far East. The Indians provided corn and beans, the basics from which all Mexican cuisine emerges. Beef and cheese came from the Spanish; spices and coffee arrived on trading ships from Africa and the Far East. To get the real flavor of Mexico, bypass such internationally generic fare as hamburgers and pizza and seek out the authentic regional food, which varies throughout the land.

Beans, rice, corn, tortillas, and chilies (some mildly spiced, some fiery hot) are eaten throughout Mexico, but even these staples vary in preparation and flavor. In some areas, cooked pinto beans are mashed and fried; in others they are served as a runny soup. Other differences come from products indigenous to the area. **Sonora,** for example, is the source of prime beef raised on the state's wide-ranging cattle ranches. Coastal areas are known for seafood cocktails (such as ceviche) and fish preparations, which again vary according to the types of local chilies and vegetables. **Yucatán** cooks season meats and fish with sour orange juice, wrap them in banana leaves, and bake them; in **Veracruz** red snapper is smothered with a zesty sauce of onions, tomatoes, capers, and green peppers.

Most major cities and resorts have one or two restaurants specializing in the regional cuisines of Mexico, where travelers can sample *pozole* (hominy stew) from **Jalisco,** mole from **Puebla,** and delicate cheeses from **Oaxaca.** For the least-expensive representation of local dishes, try the *comida corrida* (the set menu). These multicourse midday feasts typically include soup, beans, rice, and an entrée of fish, poultry, or meat, as well as coffee and dessert. Lunch is the main meal of the day, usually consumed at one or two in the afternoon, followed by a siesta; dinner is a light meal served after 8PM.

For those who are not interested in trying the unknown, here's a glossary of common Mexican foods:

Achiote Annatto seeds or oil; used for flavor and color.

Antojitos Appetizers; also called *botanes*.

Carne Asada *Carne* (meat) usually refers to beef. *Carne asada* is a grilled and marinated strip of beef served with beans, rice, tortillas, and guacamole.

Cerveza There are many popular brands of *cerveza* (beer) in Mexico, including Tecate, Dos Equis, Corona, Carta Blanca, and Superior. Always try the regional beers, such as Montejo in Yucatán and Pacifica in **Mazatlán.**

Ceviche A seafood cocktail of raw fish, lobster, conch, or shrimp pickled in lime juice with chopped onions, tomato, and cilantro. (As a rule, raw fish is not the safest food to eat unless you know it is fresh and was caught in unpolluted waters).

Chayote A member of the squash family and one of the most common vegetables in Mexico, usually served steamed or boiled with carrots.

Chilaquiles Pieces of corn tortillas cooked in a savory broth; sometimes served with eggs and cheese.

Chile Relleno A green chili (of the Anaheim variety) stuffed with cheese and/or meat, and covered with a corn batter and baked or fried.

Cilantro The leaves of the coriander plant (also known as Chinese or Mexican parsley). This herb is commonly used in salsas and guacamole.

Flan Caramel or fruit-flavored custard.

Guacamole Mashed avocado with cilantro and lemon juice; some varieties include onion, garlic, tomato, and/or sour cream.

Huachinango a la Veracruzano Traditionally made with red snapper in a sauce of tomatoes, green peppers, capers, and onion.

Huevos Mexicana Eggs scrambled with diced onion, green pepper, and tomato.

Huevos Rancheros Fried eggs on steamed corn tortillas covered with a tomato-based sauce.

Huevos Revueltos Scrambled eggs.

Jugos Juices made right on the spot at juice stands. Try papaya, mango, and orange.

Licuados Drinks made from water, ice, and pureed fruits; usually the cup is dipped directly into the mixture, which is stored in large glass bottles. The flavors are determined by the region and may include watermelon, papaya, strawberry, or pineapple. *Licuados* are wonderfully refreshing, but it's hard to tell if they are made from purified water unless you're in a tourist-oriented restaurant.

Limonada Lemonade made with fresh lemon juice, sugar, and water; purified water is used at most restaurants and bars.

Mole A sauce used on meats and vegetables, it originated in Puebla and Oaxaca and is made from a blend of spices and, usually, bitter chocolate.

Pozole A hearty stew made from pork or chicken and hominy.

Salsa A blend of tomatoes, onions, hot peppers (most often jalapeños, though the type may vary with the region), lemon or lime juice, and seasonings. Salsas come in a range of flavors and degrees of spiciness; taste a drop before adding it to your food.

Sopa de Tortilla Seasoned chicken-broth–based soup with thin strips of deep-fried corn tortillas, chunks of cheese, avocado, and sprigs of cilantro.

Tamales Cornmeal paste formed around a filling of seasoned meat, chicken, vegetables, or fruit, then wrapped in corn husks and steamed.

40 Fiesta Americana The Reef $$$ Ideal for those who want seclusion, this hotel is located at the edge of the jungle across from a pristine white beach. All 172 rooms and suites in the main building look toward the sea, though only those on the upper floors have ocean views. The scenery at the rear of the hotel is spectacular as well, especially in the morning, when birds flock to the mangrove trees. The modern rooms pamper guests with firm, king-size mattresses, satellite TVs, big bathtubs, mini-bars, in-room safes, and a calming pink-and-green color scheme. Those opting for one of the four parlor suites also enjoy dining areas and kitchenettes. Tropical casita suites are set behind the hotel amidst jungle growth and are designed to blend with the landscape while providing great accommodations for divers. The entrance to each casita has sinks and lockers for dive equipment, and with four bedrooms in each unit, divers or families can share the cost. The **Reef Beach Club** is an elaborate affair, with mini-*palapas* lined up along the sand, a shaded restaurant and bar, and Windsurfer and jet-ski rentals. There's a metal bridge over the road, so guests needn't dodge the traffic. Packages including meals, diving, and tours are available, and advance reservations are strongly advised. ◆ Costera Sur (south of 21 Sur). 22622, 800/343.7821; fax 22666

Within the Fiesta Americana The Reef:

Dive House Scuba divers, take note—this hotel is about as close as you can get to Cozumel's legendary reefs, some of which are just a few minutes away by boat. The dive operation here is excellent and offers **PADI** certification, resort courses, and all the dive services you need. ◆ Daily. 22622

41 Parque Nacional Chankanaab (Chankanaab National Park) Snorkelers, swimmers, and landlubbers can take part in the reef action without strapping on scuba gear. The Mexican government has created a wildlife sanctuary at this saltwater lagoon, where green-and-blue parrot fish, neon-orange starfish, and fragile pastel-pink anemones are visible from paths around the water. The bay is also full of colorful critters, who swim right up to shore. The cove is an ideal spot for snorkeling; the fish have been protected for so long here that they don't fear humans. Rusted cannons, anchors, and statues of Christ and the Virgin Mary encrusted with coral are scattered upon the white sand floor.

The park is also a botanical garden, with more than 350 species of flowers, vines, and trees from 22 countries (along with 417 species of plant life found on Cozumel) lining the pathways. There is a small museum with relics from shipwrecks, and a mock Maya village with replicas of Maya carvings painted in bright yellows and blues, as they might have been originally. Facilities include four dive shops with snorkeling, scuba, and camera equipment rentals, the **La Laguna** restaurant (serving great ceviche, seafood cocktails, and fish fajitas), several gift shops, lockers, restrooms, and showers. Try to avoid going to the park when the cruise ships are in port, as the place fills up. ◆ Admission. Daily. Costera Sur (south of the cruise ship pier). No phone

42 Diamond Resort $$$$ About as elaborate as an all-inclusive can be, this self-contained resort sits on its own at Playa San Francisco. In a village setting of two-story, *palapa*-roofed buildings, the 300 rooms are large and comfortable, with TVs, balconies or terraces, and large bathrooms, but very few have water views. Amenities include several pools, tennis courts, water sports, aerobics classes, and nighttime entertainment. Divers are particularly happy here because many of the best reefs are close to the property. Meals are served buffet style, and there are plenty of uninspired selections. If you want complete escape, this may be your place. But if you're interested in more sophisticated dining, as well as shopping and exploring, you'll have to rent a car or spend lavishly for cabs. ◆ Costera Sur (Km 16.5). 23443, 800/858.2258; fax 24508

43 El Cedral This temple was the first Maya ruin sighted by Spanish explorers on Cozumel in 1518, and is supposedly where the island's first Catholic Mass was held. Apparently the Spaniards destroyed most of the site, and it is believed that the US Army Corps of Engineers finished the damage during WWII while building the island's airstrip. All that remains is a crumbling, gray limestone building with a stubborn tree growing in its center. The temple is the island's agricultural center, and hosts an annual fiesta on 1-3 May. ◆ 3 km/2 miles east of Costera Sur

Mecca of the Maternal Maya

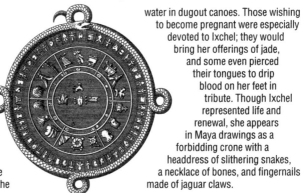

Ixchel, the Maya goddess of fertility, childbirth, medicine, and the moon, was believed to have resided on Cozumel, which the Maya called *Ah-Cuzamil-Peten* (Island of the Swallows). Women from throughout Maya lands were expected to make the pilgrimage to the island at least once in their lives, an arduous and sometimes dangerous trip that took them from their homes to the mainland coast, and then across the water in dugout canoes. Those wishing to become pregnant were especially devoted to Ixchel; they would bring her offerings of jade, and some even pierced their tongues to drip blood on her feet in tribute. Though Ixchel represented life and renewal, she appears in Maya drawings as a forbidding crone with a headdress of slithering snakes, a necklace of bones, and fingernails made of jaguar claws.

44 Playa Palancar This pretty white sand beach is a perfect hideaway. The Palancar Reef, a dramatic coral formation and one of the most popular diving spots off Cozumel, begins offshore from here, too far away to reach by swimming, however. Still, the snorkeling is terrific, and the setting is idyllic, especially if you're lucky enough to have the beach to yourself. ♦ West of Costera Sur

45 Punta Celarain The five-kilometer (three-mile) drive down the rutted dirt road to this solitary lighthouse can be a rough and deserted one, and should not be attempted during the rainy season. On the way you'll pass a tiny Maya ruin, so small it appears to have been built to house the *aluxes* (tiny Maya fairies). It's believed that the ruin's shell-shaped design, with holes at the top, served to warn of imminent storms, as the high winds passing through the holes would emit a sound resembling a foghorn. You will also drive by a forested lagoon; if you see a break in the foliage, hike through to the water for a glimpse of graceful white herons and terns gliding by peacefully.

At the end of a rocky point you'll find the lighthouse, which Primo and Maria Garcia have been tending for more than three decades. They sell simple lunches of fresh ceviche and fried fish on the patio outside their home. Offer Primo a tip and he'll allow you to climb the winding staircase to the top of the lighthouse, where the 360° view of scruffy green jungle, languid ocher lagoons, and endless cerulean sea will take your breath away. The lagoons and beaches here are being restored as an ecological park with trails and more access roads. ♦ South of Costera Sur

46 Playa Bonita The windward side of the island has several spectacular beaches, but at most of them the sea is too rough for swimming. The water is fairly calm at this spot, though, and you'll also find a restaurant and water sports rentals. ♦ Costera Sur (Km 37)

47 Punta Morena A deserted building on an isolated beach called Chen Rio serves as the base camp for a group of biologists striving to protect the endangered sea turtles that visit Cozumel every summer to lay their eggs. The Mexican government has placed the turtles under its protection and enacted a heavy fine for the capture or sale of the creature or its eggs. Still, turtle meat is considered both a delicacy and a staple of the islanders' diets, and the eggs are valued for their alleged aphrodisiacal properties. The biologists and the **Museo de la Isla de Cozumel** (see 182) have run educational programs to enlighten the locals about the turtles' plight and enlisted them in guarding the eggs against poachers. Several years ago, tourists were able to watch the mother turtles laying their eggs at night, and were even allowed to bring the unhatched eggs to a hatchery, where baby turtles were released into the sea 60 days later. The tours have been curtailed; check at the museum for information, and you may be given a permit to visit the area when the turtles are there. If you're on the windward side in the summer, stop at the building and ask to see the baby turtles; tips in support of the program are much appreciated. ♦ Costera Sur (south of Carretera Transversal)

48 San Gervasio This collection of small temples and columns, believed to have been the ceremonial center of Maya life on Cozumel from AD 300 to 1500, was excavated in 1986 and has undergone considerable restoration to become a fascinating, if somewhat limited, introduction to the Maya world. Try to visit the site just as it opens or closes, when the birds and iguanas are active. A *palapa* roof covers the entryway, where there are artisans' stands, rest rooms, snack shops, and guides for hire. Archaeologists reconstructing the ruins believe there are some 380 buildings here, though only about a dozen are visible, some with their original paint. One building is called "Las Manitas" for the small red handprints marking the walls. Nine small structures standing in a cluster include a temple, palace, and ossuary, where human remains were found. The building labeled *Estructura Los Nichos* (Building of the Niches) may have been a temple to the goddess Ixchel. There is still much to be learned about this site and other ruins around the island; archaeologists think more than 2,000 Maya homes and temples may lie beneath the jungle growth. ♦ Admission, free Sunday. Daily. 10 km/6 miles northeast of Carretera Transversal

49 Paradisus $$$$ The spacious, cool lobby filled with plants and ceiling-to-floor windows facing a swimming pool and the sea is a good introduction to the all-inclusive hotel's amenities. A pyramid-shaped *palapa* shades the main pool's swim-up bar, and *palapa* beach umbrellas line a private stretch of sand that runs north into wild jungle. A second pool set back from the sea is a quieter spot for swimming laps and lounging. The hotel is the northernmost property on Cozumel, removed from traffic and peripheral noise. The sense of privacy and seclusion here pleases visiting dignitaries as well as vacationers. The room rate includes meals, activities, and tips, and two children under the age of 12 can stay in the room at no extra charge. Meals are served buffet style, though guests can opt to have dinner in the more formal **Cafe Paraíso,** which offers menu service.

The 149 rooms have tan marble floors, blond cane furnishings, floral pastel linens, mini-bars, and vanities with sinks separate from the bathrooms. Deluxe rooms have large balconies with tables and chairs. Spring for a room overlooking the ocean; those facing inland have a rather drab view of the road and jungle. Activities include horseback riding, nightly shows put on by the hotel's staff, water sports, a fitness center, and children's programs. ♦ Costera Norte (Km 5.8). 20411, 800/336.3542; fax 21599

50 Sol Cabañas del Caribe $$$ Nine tiny cottages line a small cove shaded by palms and hibiscus. Named after flowers, the stucco cabanas were among Cozumel's original

lodgings, built in the 1960s to serve the few lucky trailblazers who had the wherewithal to make it to the island before it was discovered by the outside world. Remodeled in 1997, the cabanas have tiled baths, two double beds and a foldout couch, kitchenettes, and front porches where parents can relax while watching the kids on the beach. A small wading pool is a safe spot where the little ones can play, and the water in the cove is shallow and calm. A pair of tan-and-white, two-story buildings house 48 modern rooms with a brown-and-tan color scheme. The resort is well hidden from the road and lacks both TV and telephones—a plus for those seeking a true escape. ♦ Costera Norte (north of Blvd Aeropuerto). 20017, 20161, 800/336.3542; fax 21599

Within Sol Cabañas del Caribe:

Windsurfing School Windsurfing champion Raul De Lille represented Mexico in the 1991 Pan-American Games in Cuba. When not practicing with the pros, he teaches windsurfing in the calm waters off **Sol Cabañas**'s beach. He thinks that Cozumel is ideal for beginners, who spend more time prone in the warm water than upright on their boards. The rates for instruction are very reasonable and the equipment top-notch. Kayaks and other water sports gear are available for rent. ♦ Daily. 20017; fax 21942

Restaurante Gaviotas ★★★$$ Artificial lights illuminate a natural saltwater pool under the restaurant's deck, where sleek silvery fish (with the ungainly name of Bermuda grunts) swim. It is one of the prettiest restaurant settings on the island, and the nightly specials are a good choice—particularly the *sopa maya* (black bean soup) and the *pollo pibil* (chicken baked in banana leaves). This place has a mountain-lodge feel, and locals tend to congregate at the bar, which is far more peaceful than most of those in town. ♦ Mexican ♦ Daily breakfast, lunch, and dinner. 20161

51 Playa Azul Hotel $$$ A complete remodeling has transformed this small place—one of the oldest hotels on the island—into a charming hostelry popular with European and Mexican families. The 31 rooms in two- and three-story white stucco buildings have brown-tile floors, floral blue linens, balconies, air-conditioning, and telephones, but no TVs. The hotel also lacks a swimming pool, though it does face a nice beach and calm sea with good snorkeling. The large restaurant is open for all meals, and tours, diving, and sportfishing can be arranged. ♦ Costera Norte (Km 4). 20199, 20043; fax 20110

51 Club Cozumel Caribe $$$$ This somewhat run-down all-inclusive resort compound has 260 rooms, a long beach, two swimming pools, a disco, and group activities scheduled throughout the day and night. Rooms in the nine-floor tower section have seen better days, but have balconies looking out to the water or the jungle. Those in a newer two-story section have tile baths, double beds, and terraces. Lockers are provided at the dive shop for your scuba gear so you don't have to lug it around. Meals are served in an open-air dining room or around the pool, and consist of generous, if somewhat boring, buffets. Nightly entertainment includes tropical dance shows, while your days can be filled with aerobics, volleyball, Spanish lessons, and windsurfing classes (for an extra charge, the club provides a day-care center so that parents can participate in these activities). Excursions to ruins on the mainland cost extra. Also, diving is not included in the rate, but the cost for a two-tank dive here is somewhat less than what the dive shops in town charge. Although the hotel often has special package rates that include reduced airfare, divers should note that it's a long boat ride to reach the reefs. ♦ Costera Norte (north of Blvd Aeropuerto). 20100, 20055, 800/327.2254

52 La Cabaña del Pescador ★★$$$$
The chefs at this place wisely apply their talents to one simple and sumptuous meal—steamed lobster served with melted butter, rice, vegetables, and bread. The restaurant is set back from the road in a tropical garden where geese and ducks wander by a small stream. The simple dining room is made from lacquered poles topped with a *palapa*. Dim light radiates from lightbulbs inside baskets hanging from the ceiling and oil lamps on the tables, while ceiling fans stir the tropical air. Guests choose their lobster from a tray on the front counter, and the price is determined by the lobster's weight. The same owners have another restaurant, **El Guacamayo,** next door, serving salads, crab, conch fritters, and grilled fish at dinner nightly. ♦ Lobster ♦ Daily dinner. Costera Norte (north of Blvd Aeropuerto). No phone

53 Condumel $$ Built of local limestone embedded with seashell fossils, this 10-unit condo complex has reproductions of the Maya gods Ixchel and Chac on the walls and a mock corbeled arch at the entrance. Hammocks are provided for sleeping, or you can use the firm king-size mattresses. The kitchens are decorated with tiles hand-painted with flowers and vegetables and have refrigerators stocked with the basics, plus stoves, toaster ovens, microwaves, and coffeemakers.

Air-conditioning is available, but the combination of ceiling fans and sea breezes is normally enough to keep you cool. Outside, tables and chairs perch on rocky points, and a

ladder hangs from the limestone shelf above the sand into the water. This is a good deal for a group or family: The rates for the condos, some of which can sleep up to five people, are about the same as for one double room at the beachfront hotels. Maid service is available, and you can also have a cook prepare your meals. ♦ Costera Norte (north of Blvd Aeropuerto). 20892; fax 20661. For reservations: Box 142, Cozumel, Quintana Roo 77600, Mexico

54 Club Náutico de Cozumel Grandiose yachts sporting satellite dishes dwarf dive and tour boats berthed for the night in the island's largest marina. Take a walk along the docks, particularly in the late afternoon, when the boats are all coming in for the night. ♦ Puerto de Abrigo, Costera Norte and Blvd Aeropuerto. 21024

Bests

Sharon Morales
Owner, Los Cinco Soles

The drive around the windward side of the island stopping at the southern lighthouse, **Punta Celarain,** where the lightkeeper's wife makes the best fresh conch ceviche. Afterward, climbing to the top of the lighthouse—fantastic view.

Listening to the shrieks of the parrot flocks in the early morning as they circle before flying to the mainland to feed for the day.

Savoring the *sopa de frijol* (black bean soup) at the very romantic **Pancho's Backyard** restaurant.

The fresh smell of soap on the Maya people as they head to the market in the morning.

Snorkeling at **Yucab Reef,** one of a chain of reefs on the leeward (west) coast—an incredible variety of tropical fish.

March 21, watching the children's Spring Parade.

The Sunday night fiesta in the plaza or main square.

Elizabeth Wenger
President, Four Seasons Travel

Cobá—Taking an early morning stroll along **Lake Cobá,** watching the local shop owners feed the "Nictaha" crocodiles who inhabit the area, and bird watching along the paths of the ruins.

Tulum Corridor—Turning down every road that leads to the coast off the main highway to Tulum, finding uninhabited beaches and reefs and going snorkeling.

Chichén Itzá—Take the two-day journey! It is well worth it. Go early in the morning and beat the bus tours. You have to climb **El Castillo,** inside and out.

Cozumel—Eating *tampiqueños* on the square at **Las Palmeras** restaurant. This is thin slices of beef steak, with peppers and onions, uniquely Mexican spiced.

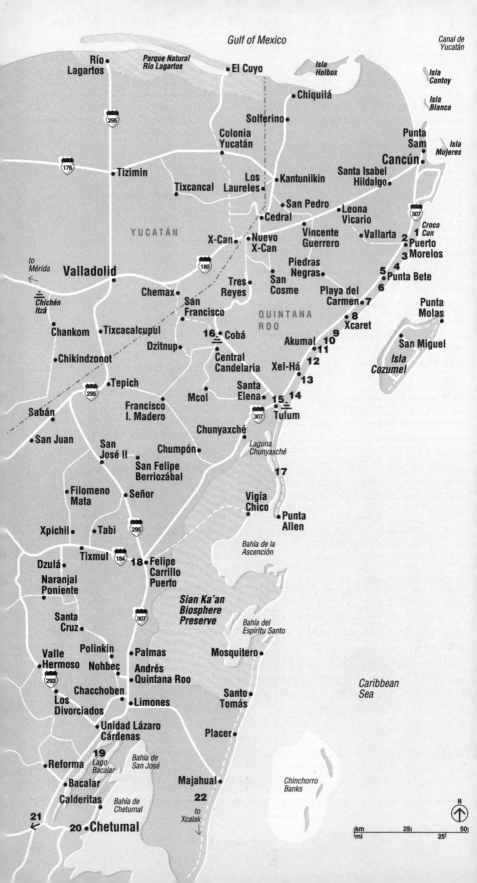

The Quintana Roo Coast

The **Caribbean** coast of Quintana Roo was once a secret Eden, cherished by a fanatical cult of adventurers eager to explore the 451 kilometers (280 miles) of virgin beaches and coral reefs stretching from Cancún to **Chetumal** at the Belize border. But Cancún's success has filtered south, and the white, sandy beaches lined with swaying palms have been discovered by developers, travel agents, and tour guides. **Highway 307**, once a two-lane ribbon of asphalt rippling through a jungle that harbors parrots, monkeys, and crumbling Maya ruins just yards from the sea, has become a four-lane (in parts) thoroughfare for taxis, trucks, and Jeeps—a freeway to paradise.

The first hundred miles south of Cancún has been dubbed the **Cancún-Tulum Corridor.** It was an area targeted by the government and investors as the logical extension of Cancún, and it's now sprinkled with marinas, golf courses, condo villages, and one-of-a-kind resorts. Sections of the coast were hit hard by the rains and winds of Hurricanes Opal and Roxanne in 1995, but reconstruction began immediately after the rains ended. Within weeks shattered windows and collapsed *palapas* (palm-roofed huts) were replaced, and the trees that had been stripped by salty winds sprouted new leaves.

The corridor's attributes have long been familiar to Cancún regulars and travelers wandering off the beaten path. Archaeology buffs flock to the Maya ruins of **Cobá** and **Tulum;** divers and snorkelers treasure the hidden coves at **Akumal;** and explorers delight in the series of unmarked dirt roads leading from the highway to secluded hotels. Now mainstream tourists ply the corridor as well, buying time-shares in state-of-the-art vacation communities such as **Puerto Aventuras**, a 900-acre development with a marina, golf course, and condos galore. The town of **Playa del Carmen** has become a destination unto itself, with ferries to Cozumel, dozens of budget hostelries, and **Playacar**, another full-scale resort development. In addition, tour buses stream down from Cancún to **Xcaret**, an underwater archaeological park with plenty of attractions for day-trippers. In 1998, the Cancún-Tulum Corridor was renamed **Riviera Maya**. Over the next few years, a concerted tourism development effort is expected to add 10,000 new hotel rooms in this area.

Realizing that development posed a potential threat to the **Yucatán Peninsula**'s wildlife and ecology, the Mexican government teamed up with the **United Nations Educational, Scientific, and Cultural Organization (UNESCO)** in 1987 to create the **Sian Ka'an Biosphere Preserve**, which protects 10 percent of Quintana Roo's jungle and coastline. Starting just south of the Cancún-Tulum Corridor, **Sian Ka'an** incorporates the 35-kilometer (22-mile) **Boca Paila Peninsula**, a magnet for explorers who crave the isolation of undeveloped Quintana Roo. Several small resorts and fishing camps are in the preserve, attracting nature lovers and escapists willing to drive down long, bumpy dirt roads to reach their idea of heaven.

The southern half of Mexico's Caribbean coast is beginning to feel the overflow from the north, as the pioneers who created resort hideaways near Cancún 20 years ago flee to less crowded shores. The **Xcalak** (pronounced *Eesh*-ca-lak) **Peninsula**, at the far southern tip of the state, has caught the attention of those seeking endless swaths of sand, plots of reasonably priced land, and the chance to create or re-create a tropical retreat. At press time, state government was putting in a paved road down the peninsula, and plans for major hotel developments were in the works. If you're interested in seeing what the Quintana Roo coastline looked like pre-Cancún, visit Xcalak—soon.

Area code 987 unless otherwise noted.

Getting to the Quintana Roo Coast

Airport

The nearest international airport to the Quintana Roo coast is in Cancún; see page 158 for information.

Ferry

A passenger ferry from Cozumel arrives at the pier in Playa del Carmen about a dozen times a day. The trip takes 30 to 45 minutes, depending on the boat and weather conditions, and the fare is about $2.50.

A car ferry from Cozumel comes to **Puerto Morelos** about six times a week; the cost is approximately $15 each way. For the latest schedule, call 20827.

Getting Around the Quintana Roo Coast

Airlines There are a few small airstrips on the coast; the largest is in Playa del Carmen. Private planes and small airlines fly from here to Cozumel, Isla Mujeres, Uxmal, Xcalak, and remote areas. For information, call **Aero SAAB**, 30804; fax 30501.

Buses It's easy to travel by bus down the coast of Cancún to Chetumal. The drawback comes when you reach your bus stop, as many of the coastal attractions are a mile or more off the highway, a difficult walk if you're lugging heavy bags. Enterprising taxi drivers cruise the bus stops along Highway 307 and can take you to your ultimate destination. (Be sure to settle on the fare before you hop in.)

Playa Express buses run frequently to Playa del Carmen and **Tulum** from Cancún's downtown bus terminal (Avs Tulum and Uxmal, 841984). From Playa del Carmen's bus station (Avs Benito Juárez and 5), connections can be made to **Felipe Carrillo Puerto, Lago Bacalar,** and Chetumal to the south, and Valladolid, Piste, and Mérida to the west. Bus travel along the coast is inexpensive, and you can reach most places for under $10.

Driving The best way to tour Mexico's Caribbean coast is by auto. Most rental cars in the area are four-wheel-drive vehicles or VW Beetles. Four-wheel drive is not necessary except during the rainy season, but comes in handy if you want to drive off the beaten track. You can sometimes get better rates if you make arrangements in advance. If you want air-conditioning or a four-door sedan, reserve well ahead of your arrival. The following agencies have desks at the Cancún airport:

Avis ....830004, 860222, 800/331.1212 in the US

Budget ......840204, 860026, 800/527.0700 in the US

Econo-Rent....................................876487, 860171

National ....860152, 851000, 800/328.4567 in the US

Rental cars are also available at some coastal hotels and in Playa del Carmen.

FYI

Accommodations The Quintana Roo coast is dotted with rustic campgrounds, small, inexpensive hotels, and even lavish resorts, and room rates are far lower than those in Cancún. Electricity and hot water (a rarity in these parts just five years ago) are standard at all but the most out-of-the-way places. In remote hotels, electricity may be available only a few hours a day, and power outages are common, so bring along a flashlight and drinking water.

Reservations are necessary from November through April and again in August. If making reservations by mail, write at least two months in advance. Many of the hotels along the coast are represented by two US agencies that can book rooms through toll-free reservations numbers. For information, contact **Turquoise Reef Resorts** (800/538.6802) or the **Playa del Carmen Hotel Association** (800/GOPLAYA).

Shopping Artisans' markets dot the roadside on Highway 307, offering the same selection of cotton blankets and T-shirts with Maya designs. The best folk art shops are in Playa del Carmen.

Telephone From Cancún to Puerto Morelos the area code is 98; from south of Puerto Morelos to Tulum, 987; from **Tulum** to Chetumal, 983. But telephone service is still a novelty along the coast, and service is erratic and unreliable—phone numbers change frequently, and winds, rain, and sea air play havoc with lines, so numbers are often out of service. Some remote hotels do not have phones; some use numbers in Cancún for reservations.

Time Zone The Quintana Roo coast is on Central Time, two hours ahead of California and one hour behind New York.

Tours Most outfits offering archaeological tours are based in Cancún. Most offer the same basic trips with assorted themes and amenities. Probably the single most popular excursion is a trip down the mainland coast to the Maya ruins of **Tulum,** with a stop at **Xel-Há,** an underwater preserve.

Visitors' Information Center There is a visitors' information booth in Playa del Carmen (Plaza Principal, 20856). The hours are erratic.

Phone Book

Centro de Salud (Health Center) Av Benito Juárez and Calle 15, Playa del Carmen 21230

Hospital General Av Andres, Chetumal 983/21932

Police Chetumal 983/62329

Police Playa del Carmen 20205

1 Croco Cun Don't let the hokey name fool you. This is actually a zoological park that specializes in breeding morolette crocodiles and releasing them in areas where they have become almost extinct. Guides are eager to give you an in-depth lesson on the reptile's lifestyle and habitats and will let you hold a baby croc if you so desire. Interspersed among the crocodile ponds are exhibits of nearly all the species of animals that once inhabited the peninsula—spider monkeys, badgers, deer, wild pigs, pheasants, and peccaries, plus a scarlet macaw from Chiapas.

The snake exhibit is enough to keep you out of the jungle forever, and the indigenous tarantulas are appallingly large. The zoo also has a family of hairless dogs called *xoloscuintli,* descendants of those that lived with the ancient Aztecs. Allow a couple of hours for your tour and wear plenty of insect repellent. There is a small restaurant serving meals and snacks, and a gift shop. ◆ Admission. Daily. Hwy 307 (Km 33). 98/844782

2 Puerto Morelos The car ferry to Cozumel leaves from this small village of 3,000 residents (5,000 if you count part-timers with vacation homes and condos). When the ferry arrives and departs, the town's sandy streets are filled with cars and trucks waiting in line. Once they're gone, it returns to its natural somnolent state. Neighbors gather at the concrete main plaza to gossip and watch their children play while fishermen beach their boats on the sand nearby.

The town has remained remarkably unscathed by the rampant development taking place around it. However, if you walk down the streets to the north and south of the town, you'll see neighborhoods of new homes and condos. There are precious few hotels and restaurants, and no tourist attractions, except for a spectacular coral reef just 500 yards offshore. It's beloved by fisherfolk and renowned for its abundance of shipwrecks, making it a big lure for divers. ◆ Hwy 307 (Km 36)

In Puerto Morelos:

Posada Amor $ Just one block from the beach, this blue, white, and pink two-story building houses the oldest hotel and restaurant in Puerto Morelos. The 19 rooms have simple cement-slab beds covered with thin mattresses, dark drapes to keep sunlight away from late sleepers, and ceiling fans. Half the rooms have private baths, but only six have hot water. ◆ Javier Rojo Gómez (southeast of Hwy 307). 10033; fax 10178

Within Posada Amor:

Posada Amor Restaurant ★★$ The two dining rooms of this simple restaurant make up the town's main gathering spot. Stick to the Mexican meals such as *huevos rancheros* (fried eggs served over a corn tortilla with spicy tomato sauce) and *carne asada* (grilled marinated beef) if you want to sample their best offerings. The Sunday buffet is a big hit with travelers and locals and a great place to meet people. ◆ Mexican ◆ Daily breakfast, lunch, and dinner. 10033

Caribbean Reef Club $$ Talk about hideaways. There's nothing in sight but long stretches of empty beach and the endless sea. The Mediterranean-style villa has 21 rooms and suites, all facing a deep blue swimming pool and the beach. The rooms have marble floors, satellite TV, air-conditioning, ceiling fans, cane-backed chairs, glass-topped tables, and kitchens with microwave ovens; some suites have fireplaces. A boat is available for snorkeling and fishing trips, but you may just want to wander on the long secluded beaches, take an occasional dip in the pool, or while the hours away swinging in a hammock on your terrace. ◆ South of the ferry pier. 10191; fax 10190. For reservations: Apdo 1526, Cancún, Quintana Roo 77500, Mexico. 800/322.6286 in the US; fax in Cancún 98/832244

Within the Caribbean Reef Club:

Caribbean Reef Club Restaurant ★★★★$$ Set away from the villa on a pathway bordered with red hibiscus and fuchsia bougainvillea, this white, open-air restaurant has a wooden patio overlooking the beach and an indoor dining room with arched windows and seating nooks facing the sea. Chef Ray Whittingham, who honed his craft in Jamaica, England, and France, is particularly proud of his Caribbean dishes—coconut shrimp, blackened fish with a spicy shrimp or lobster sauce, and a superb lime pie. Travelers with less adventuresome taste buds are happy with burgers and steaks imported from the US, served with fresh vegetables cooked al dente. The air-conditioned dining room fills with transplanted Americans on weekend evenings; the tables on the outside deck have great views of the sunset. Both visitors and locals congregate in the restaurant's bar. ◆ Caribbean/Mexican ◆ Daily lunch and dinner May-Dec; daily breakfast, lunch, and dinner Jan-Apr. 98/832636

Rancho Libertad $$ The cabana-by-the-beach concept reaches new heights with these two-story *palapa*-covered buildings set right on the sand. This adults-only hotel has 13 rooms with hanging beds (like hammocks with mattresses), big bathrooms with five-gallon jugs of purified water, green cement floors, ceiling fans, and electric bug repellent dispensers that have little odor. Breakfast (included in the rate) is served in the communal dining room and lounge area; guests are welcome to use the kitchen facilities and refrigerator for other meals. Diving and snorkeling tours are available, as is massage. Yoga and body work groups sometimes book the whole place for workshops, taking advantage of the large sand-floored meeting area under the main *palapa*. ♦ No credit cards accepted. South of the ferry pier. 987/10181, reservations in the US 719/685.1254, 888/305.5225

Wet Set The most established dive operation in town offers scuba and snorkeling trips to the reefs with certified dive masters. Kayaking and fishing trips are also available. ♦ Daily (hours are erratic). The main plaza. 987/10198, 987/10191

3 Jardín Botánico Dr. Alfredo Barrera Marin (Dr. Alfredo Barrera Marin Botanical Garden) Bug repellent is a must for a tour through this well-tended jungle composed of many of the peninsula's indigenous trees, most labeled in Spanish. Try to visit early in the day, when the birds are chipper and the humidity is low. ♦ Admission. M-Sa. Hwy 307 (Km 38). No phone

3 Rancho Loma Bonita This small ranch, out of sight from the road, offers horseback riding on wonderful trails through the jungle and along the coastline. The horses are in good condition, and it's a joy to ride along the edge of the sea with no other human in sight. ♦ Daily. Call in advance for reservations to ensure that horses are available for all the members of your party. Most Cancún hotels and tour companies can arrange your equestrian excursion as well. Hwy 307 (Km 42). 98/875423, 98/875465 in Cancún

4 Maroma $$$$ So exclusive you won't be let past the gate without advance reservations, this 36-room inn has garnered rave reviews for its seclusion, architecture, and restaurant. The white buildings are sculpted with arches and domes, and all the rooms face the ocean. Blue lounge chairs sit on the white sand like isolated statues. The region's best chefs praise the restaurant here for its innovative preparations of fresh fish and an impressive wine list. ♦ Hwy 307 (24 km/15 miles south of Puerto Morelos). 987/44729; fax 98/842115 in Cancún

5 Punta Bete One of the prettiest stretches of beach in this area is home to one of the most beloved hideaways on the coast, plus a couple of small campgrounds. A large concrete archway on the east side of the highway marks the entrance to **La Posada del Capitán Lafitte**, the beach's only hotel (see below), which sits by the sea about two kilometers (one mile) east at the end of a dirt road. Another resort, **Kailuum**, formerly located here, was shut down by Hurricane Roxanne in 1995. ♦ Hwy 307 (Km 52)

At Punta Bete:

La Posada del Capitán Lafitte $$ Stucco bungalows with window fans and oceanfront porches line a wild beach where ocean breezes preclude any need for air-conditioning. No wonder guests return annually for their dose of tranquillity. One of the first resorts along this coast, it remains one of the area's best. Offering the complete antithesis to Cancún's glitz, the resort is laid-back and unpretentious. The 43 rooms are simple (electricity and hot running water are the only amenities); the gameroom has satellite TV. The full-service dive shop runs trips to nearby reefs. Breakfast and dinner are included in the rate. ♦ Closed September and October. East of Hwy 307. No phone. For reservations: Turquoise Reef Resorts, Box 2664, Evergreen, CO 80439. 303/674.9615, 800/538.6802; fax 303/674.8735

Within La Posada del Capitán Lafitte:

Capitán Lafitte Restaurant ★★$ A true variety of fare is the hallmark of this spot— including chilled soups, curried chicken, and a weekly lobster night. Meals are served under a *palapa* overlooking the water by waiters who instantly learn your name and memorize your preferences. ♦ Mexican ♦ Daily breakfast, lunch, and dinner; closed September through October. No phone

6 Shangri-La Caribe $$$ European groups seem particularly fond of this 70-unit beachside property. The accommodations are located in one- and two-story cabanas that resemble Maya huts, with whitewashed stucco walls, shaggy *palapas,* and hammocks hanging on the front porches. The dive shop is well equipped, and diving here, though not as spectacular as off Cozumel, can be addictive. The pool is a good spot to gather and revive, and the restaurant serves excellent hamburgers and seafood. ♦ Hwy 307 (Km 56). No phone. For reservations: Turquoise Reef Resorts, Box 2664, Evergreen, CO 80439. 303/674.9615, 800/538.6802; fax 303/674.8735

6 Las Palapas $$$ Similar to the **Shangri-La Caribe** (above) in architectural style, this hostelry has 55 spacious bungalows, each with a thatch roof, two double beds, a desk by the window, and two hammocks on the front porch. The property is a self-contained paradise, with two restaurants (breakfast and dinner are included in the rates), an absolutely gorgeous beach, a pool, a gameroom, and a dive shop. You can walk along the beach to Playa del Carmen, about 20 minutes south, or hire a cab or rent a car for trips to the ruins. Many European guests just stay put for days on end, which isn't a bad idea. ♦ Hwy 307 (Km 58). 30584, 800/467.5292; fax 30458

7 Playa del Carmen The largest community between Cancún and Chetumal (with about 40,000 inhabitants), this beach town has evolved from a backpacker's hangout to a full-scale resort destination. Development was inevitable here, given the location: Cancún is less than an hour's drive north; Cozumel is 30 minutes east via the ferry; and the ruins of **Tulum** and **Cobá** are less than an hour's drive south. "Playa" (as the place is known locally) has the longest stretch of uninterrupted beach along the corridor; it also has the most tourist services, including banks, bus stations, a small airstrip, markets, pharmacies, and auto parts stores. Avenida Benito Juárez is the main street leading from the highway to the ferry pier. South of the pier is the massive Playacar development.

The town's center is the waterfront plaza at the ferry dock, complete with a church, kiosk, playground, and sidewalk cafes. North of the plaza is Avenida 5, the first street parallel to the beach and a pedestrian walkway closed to vehicular traffic. New restaurants and shops open and close at an astounding rate along this stretch, yet the sound of hammers is constant, since it seems as if everyone who comes to town decides to open some sort of business. Playa's hallmark inexpensive bungalow hotels have given way to more refined establishments. At the same time, unbridled construction has created a hodgepodge of architectural styles, from simple thatch-roofed cabanas to three-story cement hulks. Fancy Italian restaurants, boutiques selling Balinese batiks, coffeehouses, Cuban cigar shops, liquor stores featuring dozens of brands of tequila, and every trendy commercial enterprise imaginable can be found in storefronts painted in vivid oranges, pinks, and blues.

Budget travelers can still find inexpensive rooms with hammocks hanging over the sand. These accomodations (as well as budget restaurants) are still good deals relative to the rest of the area, but they're scarcer and cost more than they once did. In spite of the development, however, the town's laid-back character endures—many shops are open only in the morning and evening. If you're looking for gorgeous beaches, moderate prices, convenient bus service, and a youthful see-and-be-seen crowd, this is your best choice on the coast. ♦ Hwy 307 (Km 68)

In Playa del Carmen (businesses are listed north to south):

Chichan Baal Kah $$ This gorgeous seven-unit apartment complex opened in late 1995 and became an instant hit. The adults-only property (children under 16 are not allowed) features fully furnished units with large master bedrooms,

living/ dining rooms, kitchenettes, and patios. The pool is set amid ferns and palms, and daily maid service is available. A restaurant is under construction beside the inn; others are within easy walking distance. The complex is just one of many Turquoise Reef Resorts' properties in the area; apartment-style units are also available in the group's nearby **Quinta Mija** and **Casa Jacques** complexes. ♦ Calle 16 and 5 Av Norte. 31252; fax 30050. For reservations: Turquoise Reef Resorts, Box 2664, Evergreen, CO 80439. 303/674.9615, 800/538.6802; fax 303/674.8735

Condotel El Tucan $ Though not on the beach, this handsome hotel is one of the nicest in town, with four-story, sand-colored buildings surrounding a junglelike garden and pool area. The 67 units are individually decorated; all have tiled kitchens with mini-refrigerators and electric stove burners, as well as large balconies with hammocks and lounge chairs. The least expensive rooms are studios with one double bed; the largest suites sleep 8 to 10 people in three bedrooms and a living room with a futon couch. Breakfast at the comfortable *palapa*-roofed restaurant is included in the room rate; lunch and dinner (not included) are also served. ♦ 5 Av Norte (between Calles 14 and 16). 30417, 800/467.5292; fax 30668

Hotel Mosquito Blue $$$ Pretty and peaceful, this small Mediterranean-style inn is a welcome addition to Playa's hotel scene. The subdued blue-and-white color scheme is

H O T E L

accented by deep green lawns against the pool, lacquered mahogany French doors and furnishings, and soft gray and green tiles. Eight standard rooms, eight luxury rooms with balconies, and eight junior suites all face the courtyard and pool; they have air-conditioning, satellite TV, in-room safes, and four-poster king-size beds. A lounge area on the second floor is equipped with a large movie screen with Dolby sound, where Italian films are shown; the lounge also boasts a stylishly designed library area that's a cool, comfortable spot to read and relax. The restaurant, **Tiramisù,** offers a tranquil setting for all three meals. ♦ 5 Av Norte (between Calles 12 and 14). 31245, 31335; fax 31337

Hotel Baal Nah Kah $$ Once a charming home, this three-story palapa-roofed structure has become Playa's first bed-and-breakfast. Guests in the five rooms may use the large living room, complete with aviary, a full kitchen, and balconies strung with hammocks. The rooms vary in size and amenities; some have air-conditioning, and one has a kitchenette. A small restaurant next door serves breakfast (included in the room rate). ♦ Calle 12 (between 1 Av Norte and 5 Av Norte). 30110; fax 30050

Da Gabi ★★★★$$ A blessed oasis of calm off the crowded Avenida 5, this Italian restaurant is the best of the new crop of gourmet eateries. Two palapas cover several levels of tables draped with deep red cloths. Soft jazz plays in the background, and candles flicker under soft light from conch-shell lamps. Pizzas (try the Napoletana with anchovies, mozzarella, and fresh tomatoes) are served hot from a brick oven that turns out a steady stream of take-out and delivery orders. The menu features a refreshing spinch salad, fettuccine with mussels and shrimp, chicken breast with mushrooms, several steaks, and a good tiramisù. ♦ Italian ♦ Daily dinner. Calle 12 (between 1 Av Norte and 5 Av Norte). 30048

Blue Parrot Inn $$ An old-timer by Playa standards, this hotel has 45 rooms housed in small cabanas and thatch-roofed stucco buildings right on the sand. The older rooms have been remodeled and have fans and air-conditioning. Those in two newer buildings have air-conditioning, but no TV or telephones. The beachfront restaurant is an enduring favorite of local expats, especially during Happy Hour. Later in the evening, movies and music videos are shown in a second-story bar with a sand floor and beanbag chairs. The mood throughout is low-key, friendly, and comfortable. Reservations must be made through the US office, though if you're in the area, call the hotel or drop in to see if a room is available. ♦ Calle 12 and 5 Av Norte. 30083; fax 30049. For reservations: 635 W Wisconsin Ave, Orange City, FL 32763. 904/775.6660, 800/634.3547; fax 904/775.1869

Tank-Ha Dive Center Scuba diving operations have opened all over town, but this one has been around for years, offering certified divemasters, quality rental gear and boats, and exciting open water and *cenote* (sinkhole) dives. They may charge a bit more than other shops, but the first-rate service—from divemasters to rentals—are worth the extra bucks. ♦ Daily. 5 Av Norte (between Calles 8 and 10). 30302; fax 31355

Plaza Rincón del Sol This bright-pink shopping center is a delight, with Colonial arches, landscaped terraces, and a few lovely shops. ♦ Daily. 5 Av Norte and Calle 8. 30110

Within Plaza Rincón del Sol:

Xop Every item in this gallery is made by a truly talented Mexican artist. It's worth a stop here just for the hand-crafted jewelry: The gorgeous amber found locally is set in earrings with porcupine quills, wild boar tusks, and boa constrictor ribs; amber pendants embedded with fossilized insects hang from intricate silver necklaces; Maya gods with opal eyes are cast in silver pins. There is also an outstanding selection of masks from Guerrero and carved wooden *santos* (saints). All items can be packed for shipping. ♦ M-Sa. 30110

El Vuelo de los Niños Pajaros An unusual array of hand-crafted notepaper and cards, wood sculptures, masks, embroidered vests, and blouses is artfully displayed in this small shop. Check out the selection of Latin music, too. ♦ Daily. No credit cards accepted. 30445

La Parrilla ★★$$ Sizzling platters of beef, chicken, and vegetable fajitas keep locals and travelers coming back to this open-air cafe set beside the sidewalk at the edge of the plaza. Pasta creations are prepared tableside while cooks assemble tacos, brochettes, and sandwiches in the open kitchen. The cafe has become wildly popular and lines form outside for dinner in high season. ♦ Mexican ♦ Daily breakfast, lunch, and dinner. 30687

Albatros Royale $ This is one of the prettiest hotels along the beach, with 31 basic—yet comfortable—rooms in two-story buildings. Each has a king-size bed or two doubles, a large bathroom, a cool tile floor, simple (pine and plastic) furniture, a thatch roof, and a balcony complete with an orange-and-yellow hammock. Sea breezes and ceiling fans provide all the cooling you need. The beach is at the edge of the property, and breakfast at the nearby **Pelicano Inn** (see page 201) is included in the room rate (which may increase during holiday periods). There are also plenty of other restaurants and shops within a few blocks. ♦ Calle 8 (east of 5 Av Norte). 30001, 800/538.6802; fax 30002

La Calaca The quality of the items packed into this shop is not as high as at some other places, but there are some treasures amidst the masks, lacquered boxes, and jewelry from throughout Mexico. ♦ Daily; closed at midday. 5 Av Norte (between Calles 6 and 8). 30177. Also at: 5 Av Norte and Calle 4. 30177

Temptations Balinese skirts, trousers, and dresses are all the rage in Playa these days, and this shop, one of the first to carry them, may have the best selection. ♦ Daily. 5 Av Norte (between Calles 6 and 8). 30385

Pelicano Inn $ The old beloved but run-down **Cabañas Albatros** have been replaced by this wonderful inn located right on the sand. The 23 rooms are housed in two-story stucco buildings with *palapa* roofs and balconies. All have a white-on-white color scheme with built-in desks and shelves, ceiling fans, safes, and large showers. The restaurant serves breakfast (included in the room rate), lunch, and the best coffee, espresso, and cappuccino in town. Thus far, the rates have remained quite low given the facilities, but they could rise, especially during holiday periods. ♦ Reservations recommended (the rooms fill up quickly). Calle 6 (east of 5 Av Norte). 30001, 800/538.6802; fax 30002

Within the Pelicano Inn

Ronny's ★★★$$ Americans craving thick steaks and juicy burgers are delighted to find this beachfront restaurant where imported beef highlights the menu. Fish and chicken are also available. Finish with one of the outstanding ice-cream creations. ♦ American/Steak house ♦ Daily lunch and dinner. 62471, 30996

Hotel Alejari $ The lush landscaping adds an isolated, junglelike air to this 29-room, two-story inn. Some rooms have air-conditioning and kitchenettes and cost a bit more; less expensive ones are cooled with ceiling fans. A few family-size duplex units have bedrooms upstairs and down, and some rooms face the sea. A restaurant is on the property; several others are within easy walking distance. There's no pool, but you're only half a block from the beach. ♦ Calle 6 (east of 5 Av Norte). 30374; fax 30005

Sabor ★★$ Melinda Burns, pastry chef extraordinaire, spoils her fans with an irresistible array of desserts. The few small tables in her tiny cafe are almost always filled with loyal patrons sampling dense chocolate cake, flaky pecan pie, creamy cheesecake, coconut flan, or whatever other treat appears on the shelves that day. A full breakfast menu, fruit salads, and sandwiches are also available. ♦ American/Desserts ♦ Daily breakfast, lunch, and dinner. No credit cards accepted. 5 Av Norte (between Calles 2 and 4). No phone

El Chino ★★$ When you've grown weary of the tourist scene, head away from the beach to the locals' part of town and this traditional eatery. Tables covered in white-and-orange cloths overlaid with clear plastic line the long *palapa* dining room, where the TV on the bar airs soccer matches and national news. Children run about as if the place was a playground, while several generations of their families gather over huge shrimp cocktails, platters of fresh ceviche, and grilled shrimp. Standard home-style Mexican cooking is the draw—try the enchiladas *suizas,* burritos, tacos, or fajitas. Most meals cost less than an appetizer would at fancier establishments. Order the flambéed crepes for dessert if only to watch the eyes of the children as the lights are turned out and the room illuminated with blue fire dripping into the skillet from a curving orange peel. ♦ Mexican ♦ Daily lunch and dinner. Calle 4 (between 10 Av Norte and 15 Av Norte). No phone

Mom's $ With rates that are among the lowest in town, this hotel has become an informal information center and gathering spot as well as a place to stay. The 20 simple rooms have brown-tile floors, built-in desks, and huge showers. Two rooms have air-conditioning; the others have fans. The small pool is a welcome amenity, since it's a 10-minute walk to the beach. The upstairs bar has a pool table and a bulletin board for messages; the downstairs restaurant serves down-home US-style breakfast and dinner, including meat loaf with mashed potatoes and country-fried steak with gravy. ♦ No credit cards accepted. 30 Av Norte and Calle 4. 30315; fax 30315

La Chozá ★★★$$ This branch of the venerable Cozumel restaurant is one of the best places in town for traditional Mexican and Yucatecan meals. Stenciled decorations and folk art fill the walls in the pleasant dining room; it's also nice to sit at one of the sidewalk tables and watch the world go by. Try the *chiles rellenos* with seafood filling, the chicken in mole sauce, or any of the daily specials. ♦ Mexican ♦ Daily lunch and dinner. No credit cards accepted. 5 Av Norte (between Av Benito Juárez and Calle 2). 30327

Máscaras ★★$$ Overshadowed by the many new Italian restaurants in Playa, this small cafe is still favored by sentimental locals and travelers who miss the old Playa. It's a delight to sit at the outside tables on weekend nights, when the townspeople gather in the plaza just across the street. Try the marinated calamari, gourmet pizzas made in wood-burning ovens, or seafood brochette. ♦ Italian ♦ Daily lunch and dinner. Av Benito Juárez and the main plaza. 62624

Muelle de Cruceros (Ferry Pier) Two ferry companies operate boats to Cozumel from Playa del Carmen. **Cruceros Maritimos del Caribe** (21942) runs the *Mexico* and *Mexico III,* both fast, air-conditioned boats that make the 30-minute trip 10 times daily. **Naviera Turistica** (21824, 21913) pilots the traditional *Cozumeleño* ferry, which departs eight times a day. The ferry boat has open-air decks and is less expensive, but the trip takes 15 minutes longer. Several stands by the pier sell tickets. The street to the ferry is closed to traffic; there's a parking lot at Avenida Benito Juárez and Avenida 10 that is open daily 24 hours. ♦ 5 Av Sur (south of Av Benito Juárez)

At Muelle de Cruceros:

Señor Frog's ★$ Part of Carlos Andersen's chain of popular eateries, this restaurant sits on one of the most valuable pieces of real estate in town, right at the foot of the ferry pier. The decor is cluttered with posters and piñatas, and the food pleases unadventuresome eaters seeking large portions of barbecued ribs and chicken or big, messy burgers. The Mexican dishes are only lightly spiced. ♦ Mexican/American ♦ Daily lunch and dinner. No phone

Playacar Playa del Carmen's peaceful isolation ended when construction began on this 880-acre upscale resort community in the early 1990s. The property sprawls along the coastline south of the ferry pier and includes several large, all-inclusive hotels catering to European package-tour groups, an 18-hole golf course, private villas and condos, and an air-conditioned shopping mall. Construction continues on more hotels and homes along the golf course and the beach, where bits of Maya ruins are protected by jungle growth. ♦ Hwy 307 (south of Av Benito Juárez)

Within Playacar:

Plaza Antigua New on the scene in 1997, this shopping mall is designed to look like a many-colored hacienda. The enclosed multilevel building is blessed with powerful air-conditioning—shop here during the midday heat, when you can sit beside splashing fountains and feel as if you've been transported to cooler climes. The plaza was still being finished at press time, and phones were not yet installed. When completed, it will include several folk art and souvenir stores, clothing boutiques, jewelry shops, and a food court. ♦ Daily 9AM-9PM. 10 Av Sur

Within Plaza Antigua:

Toscani ★★★$$
One of precious few air-conditioned restaurants in the area, this refined dining room is  located on the second level of the plaza. Heavy linens, delicate crystal, and candlelight

enhance the feeling of elegance, and everyone dresses in their very best to dine here. Carpaccio of salmon, fish, or beef starts the meal, followed by homemade pastas, baked fish in saffron sauce, several cuts of imported beef, or chicken in a pastry crust. Though newly opened at press time, this restaurant is sure to be the best choice for a special night out. ♦ Italian ♦ Daily dinner. 31526

Continental Plaza Playacar $$$ Built on the scale and in the style of a Cancún hostelry, this was the massive Playacar development's first hotel, and it's usually filled with travelers on package deals and group tours. The 188 large rooms (including 62 suites with kitchenettes) have woven cotton spreads on the king-size and double beds, and pastel-colored, tropical-flower prints on the couches and chairs, as well as air-conditioning, satellite TV, telephones, and mini-bars. There are two good restaurants, noteworthy for their breakfast and dinner buffets. The pool flows around islands connected by bridges, and the beach stretches uninterrupted for miles to the south. There's a water sports center on the beach, travel agency, gift shop, tennis court, and room service. ♦ Reservations required. 30100, 800/882.6684; fax 30105

Diamond Resort $$$$ With attractive, two-story *palapas* that spread down a slight hill toward the beach, this all-inclusive resort is far nicer than most. The 300 rooms have air-conditioning and ceiling fans, TVs and phones, big bathtubs and showers, and small balconies. The dining room is on the second story of an enormous thatch-roofed building where all meals are bountiful buffets; hot dogs and hamburgers are served in a smaller snack shop by the beach. Recreational pastimes include all water sports, tennis, volleyball, bicycling, and basketball. There's also a schedule of other activities—such as aerobics and stretch classes—throughout the day. Tours to the ruins are available at an additional cost. The main drawback is the location, at least a 15-minute walk from downtown Playa. ♦ 30339, 800/642.1600; fax 30348, 800/858.2258

Caribbean Village $$$$ Run by the same company as the **Diamond Resort** (see above), this all-inclusive facility is set in the midst of Playacar's 18-hole golf course, about a 10-minute walk from the beach. The 300 rooms have air-conditioning and ceiling fans, TVs and phones, big bathtubs, and showers. The fully supervised kids' program frees parents to make use of the links, the full-service beach club and scuba operation, and three bars. All meals, which are served buffet-style in the club's restaurant, and many activities are included in the rate; ask about golf packages. ♦ 30434, 800/858.2258; fax 30437

XCARET

Wild Breeding Aviary

Caballerizas Horse Stables

Spanish Chapel

La Cocina

Botanical Garden

Xcaret Museum

Underground River

Underground Rivers Entrance

Parking

Theater

Archaeological Zone

Tropical Aquarium

Maya Village

Underground River

Underground River

Archaeological Zone

Jaguar Islands

Archaeological Zone

Inlet

Caribbean Sea

La Laguna Restaurant

Blue Lagoon

Beach

Boat Dock

Beach

Bay

La Peninsula Restaurant

Rivers Exit

Changing Rooms

Dolphins

Natural Pools

N

Playacar Golf Course Designed by Robert Von Hagge, this 18-hole, 7,200-yard layout was carved out of the middle of the jungle. Facilities include a putting green, driving range, pro shop, and clubhouse. The course is open to the public. ♦ 30624, 800/642.1600

8 Xcaret Nature underwent a drastic transformation during the creation of this park, which bills itself as "nature's sacred paradise." The once-secret inlet (the name, pronounced *Eesh*-ca-ret, means "little cove" in Maya) with temples, underground caves, and secluded snorkeling spots, has been transformed into an "eco-archaeological park." Artificial beaches and lagoons are etched into the limestone, lush tropical flowers and trees grow along landscaped paths, and *palapas* shade restaurants overlooking the Caribbean. Even those who initially resented the bulldozing and blasting that created this "natural" setting are beginning to come around. Fact is, the place is absolutely gorgeous and nearly mesmerizing when uncrowded. And the owners appear to respect nature, now that it matches their dreams: Tropical and regional birds are sheltered from humans in a lush aviary; Caribbean corals and fish grow in aquariums; and cocoons turn to butterflies in a net-covered garden amid waterfalls and fountains.

On average, the park gets more than 1,000 visitors daily. The most controversial attraction is the "dive with dolphins" program, which is limited to 30 individuals a day on a first-come, first-served basis. Dolphin devotees line up long before opening time in the hopes of being among the chosen few. The underground river trip—in which participants float through caves—is another big hit. Also on the grounds are white-sand beaches along sheltered lagoons, a collection of restored and natural Maya ruins, and a

203

hacienda-style horse stable where you can arrange rides along the beach or watch horses perform. The park is open Thursday nights for *Xcaret Night*, featuring a walk along candlelit paths to a Maya village display, a high-quality dinner buffet, and a spectacular music and folkloric dance performance.

Lockers, showers, and rest rooms are in the main building, which also houses a museum and an excellent gift shop. The four restaurants are all good, though somewhat expensive; the best is the Mexican-style **La Cocina** near the horse stable. Tours and transportation to **Xcaret** are readily available in Cancún, Playa del Carmen, and Cozumel. ♦ Admission; additional fee for dolphin dive, snorkel and mask rental, and horseback riding. Daily; Th dinner shows. Hwy 307 (Km 72). 98/830654; fax 98/833709

9 Cabañas Pamul $ One of the traditional hideaways along the coast, this complex has grown steadily without disturbing its loyal guests. The heart of the complex is the seven-bungalow hotel, a cluster of peach-and-white buildings on the sand. The rooms have tile floors, ceiling fans, two double beds, and 24-hour hot water and electricity. Meals are served under a large *palapa;* as might be expected the menu features fresh fish and tropical fruit, though some say this place also has the best burgers on the coast. A full-service dive center has equipment for shore and boat dives. The adjacent trailer park is one of precious few in the area; tent camping is also allowed. There's a small market at the entrance to the complex, so those seeking to stay put need never leave the grounds. ♦ Hwy 307 (Km 85). 62691; fax 43240. For reservations: Apdo 83, Playa del Carmen, Quintana Roo 77710, Mexico

10 Puerto Aventuras One of the first master-planned megaresorts on the coast, this 900-acre development is a peaceful escape, especially for yacht travelers. Gone are the aggressive time-share salespersons who used to practically attack anyone who entered the grounds. Now the three hotels in the development are all undergoing ownership changes and renovations, and the only real estate sales involve full-ownership condos and villas. The most important feature of this project is a 250-slip marina, a needed addition to these shores. Another attraction is a golf course, where 9 of a proposed 18 holes are ready for play. The resort has a tranquil feeling, and the renovated hotels should provide plenty of space for those who want to get away from it all. ♦ Hwy 307 (Km 98). 35110, 35180; fax 35182

In Puerto Aventuras:

Papaya Republic ★★★★$$ Hector and Malena Mestre have created a jungle paradise at the edge of the Aventuras development, and it's well worth searching out. Their restaurant sits beside the sea, with a giant *palapa* covering the main dining room and tables scattered about outside just above the sand. The ambitious menu includes superb fresh ceviche, fish fillet with mustard sauce, tender calamari stuffed with caviar and crab, Thai soup, and whatever new recipes Hector invents. The jungle theme is carried out with jaguar-print tablecloths, wooden masks on the walls, and a live menagerie of monkeys, deer, and birds who've gravitated to the property. Count on lingering over a long lunch or becoming entranced by jungle sounds during dinner. Call ahead if you're planning a group celebration or if you want a special menu. ♦ Mexican/Continental ♦ Daily lunch and dinner. 35170, 35191

Museo Pablo Bush Romero (Pablo Bush Romero Museum) Centro Educacional de Deporte Acuatico y Maritimo (CEDAM; the Mexican Underwater Explorers' Club), was founded in 1958 largely through the efforts of Pablo Bush Romero, an explorer, adventurer, and diver with a strong love for his country's Caribbean coast. He played a major role in the funding and creation of this scuba museum, which was inaugurated in 1988; his likeness stands near the entrance. Divers will be fascinated by the early copper hyperbolic chamber with leather seals where divers underwent recompression. The museum's displays also include artifacts found at the wreck of the *Mantanceros,* a Spanish merchant ship that sank off this coast in 1741 (no one knows for sure why the craft went down). The collection of glass beads, gold coins, rusted cannons, poker chips and dominoes, and religious statues from this and other shipwrecks (including the *Nicolosa,* which sank in 1527 and was discovered off Punta Cancún in 1959) gives an eerie sense of what life at sea must have been like in the past, when pirates and rival nations waged war against each other with cannonballs. This is must-see for divers and history buffs. ♦ Admission. Daily; closed at midday. No phone

Mike Madden's CEDAM Dive Center This is one of the best areas in the world for cave and *cenote* (underground well) diving and the site of expert Mike Madden's **Professional Association of Dive Instructors (PADI)**–approved facility, which offers equipment rentals and sales. An abundance of spectacular dive sites are within a 10-minute boat ride. Those who've spent considerable time under water here say you can dive twice a day for a week and always find something new. The fish are large and abundant, and divers typically see giant rays and sea turtles, including the legendary turtle said to be as big as a Volkswagen Beetle. ◆ Daily. Casa del Mar

11 **Akumal** Mediterranean villas, basic bungalows, and modern hotels line the shores of this natural bay, once the nesting ground for thousands of sea turtles (the name is Maya for "land of the turtles"). The sea turtles still return to the coast for their annual migration but have moved to more isolated spots north and south of the Akumal hotels, away from humanity.

This was a Maya community and a coconut plantation long before tourism hit these shores, but all that remains of the original village is a settlement of Maya workers at the entrance to the area's first resort. Explorers discovered the wreck of the *Mantanceros* offshore in 1926, and it was here that Pablo Bush Romero headquartered **CEDAM** in the 1950s. Several side roads lead from the highway to the resorts, which have an assortment of complicated names. ◆ Hwy 307 (Km 105)

At Akumal (resorts are listed north to south):

Akumal Cancun Resort & Beach Hotel $$ Part laid-back, part comfortably modern, this small resort attracts a loyal repeat clientele. Many of the staff members have been around for years, and the place has an agreeable, friendly feeling. The 91 rooms were renovated after Hurricane Roxanne; none has a TV set or telephone, but many have balconies opening out onto views of the garden or the sea. The pool is small, but the beach is a broad crescent against the calm Caribbean. Both all-inclusive and nightly rates are available. If you don't have a car, the all-inclusive rate, which includes transport to and from **Cancún International Airport** and three meals daily, is a good deal. ◆ 30841; fax 30842

Hotel Club Akumal Caribe & Villas Flamingo $$ A two-story villa sits at the tip of a rocky point, marking the northern boundary of this sprawling resort complex that includes four villas, three condominiums, 40 bungalows, and a small hotel with 21 rooms. **Cannon House,** the main villa, is the most luxurious of the accommodations, followed by a line of suites set back from the beach behind lush landscaping. The bungalows, some of which housed the divers

who explored shipwrecks for **CEDAM** back in the 1950s, are set right on the sand, their thatch roofs replaced by red tile. The hotel is at the south end of Playa Akumal and has a private pool. Two full-service dive shops, three restaurants, an ice-cream stand, gift shops, and a small market are also part of the complex. ◆ 59012; fax 59019. For reservations: Akutrame, Box 13326, El Paso, TX 79913. 915/584.3552, 800/351.1622; fax 915/581.6709

Within Hotel Club Akumal Caribe & Villas Flamingo:

Lol-Ha ★★$ The best of the three restaurants here, this is a large, open-air, thatch-roofed dining room set above the sand on stilts. Breakfast is a feast that can easily hold you until dinner, especially if you consume all the sweet rolls and cookies in the basket set on each table along with your omelette or *huevos Mexicanos* (eggs scrambled with tomatoes, onion, and green peppers). Dinners include thick charcoal-grilled steaks, lobster, and seafood, all served in generous portions with vegetables, rice or potatoes, and bread. Flaming desserts are a specialty. ◆ Seafood/Mexican ◆ Daily breakfast and dinner. No phone

12 **Chemuyil** Local families gather on the beach along this gorgeous cove on weekend afternoons for hours of frolicking and feasting on the simple meals prepared at the beach's *palapa* bar and restaurant. The bay used to be a wonderful snorkeling spot but has become a bit murky. The south end of the beach is a campground where travelers can pitch tents, hang their hammocks, or camp out of their vehicles for weeks on end. Circular *palapas* at the center of the beach are available for rent so you can hang your hammock in the shade for the day or overnight—but there are no locks. Facilities include indoor showers and rest rooms, which apparently explains the admission fee. ◆ Admission. Hwy 307 (Km 109). No phone

MARAVILLA NATURAL
XEL·HA
CANCUN

13 **Xel-Há** An underwater preserve famous for its excellent snorkeling, the park is located in a natural *caleta* (cove), where limestone rocks and ridges submerged in the sea provide an ideal gathering spot for giant parrot fish and schools of other tropical fish that breed here. Nonsnorkelers can spot turtles and tropical fish even as they stroll down the landscaped paths around the lagoons. A small museum has some relics from ships wrecked offshore. Several restaurants scattered about the park serve decent sandwiches and fish dinners,

and there are hammocks hanging under palms, showers, changing rooms, and lockers. Snorkeling equipment and underwater cameras are available for rent, and there is a large gift shop. Usually part of tours from Cancún to **Tulum,** the site gets ridiculously crowded from noon until 3PM. ◆ Admission. Daily. Hwy 307 (Km 122). 98/849422 in Cancún

14 Casa Cenote ★★$ Worth searching for, this restaurant is perched beside Tancah, one of the largest *cenotes* on the Yucatán Peninsula. Lark and Gary Phillips's eatery is the most popular along the coast among Americans with homes in the area. The Phillips prepare excellent casual fare—great chicken fajitas, nachos topped with chicken or pork, and juicy hamburgers. All the beef, chicken, and cheese is imported from the US. On Sunday, there's a multicourse barbecue feast that lasts through the afternoon.

After (or better yet, before) a meal, take a dip in the *cenote*. It begins in a lagoon and runs out to sea, creating a fish trap of sorts just offshore, where the snorkeling is superb. Three manatees are said to live in the sinkhole, but they are extremely shy and tend to stay out of sight when humans are around. ◆ American/Mexican ◆ Daily lunch and dinner until sunset. Hwy 307 (Km 127). No phone

TULUM

↑ Bldgs. 57-59

Wall
Watchtower
House of the Cenote
Altars
Great Platform
Temple of the Wind
Wall
Great Palace
Tickets
House of the Columns
Temple of the Descending God
Parking/ Entrance
Ceremonial Platform
Stela 2
El Castillo (The Castle)
Bldg. 20
to Hwy. 307 ←
Temple of the Initial Series
Temple of the Frescoes
Bldg. 13
Bldg. 54
Watchtower
Wall
Wall
Map not to scale

15 Tulum The setting is absolutely gorgeous. Crumbling alabaster limestone temples rise from a grass-covered cliff above the Caribbean. Fuchsia bougainvillea and purple Wandering Jews twist around cracks and

along stone stairs. Huge, fluffy clouds the color of new-fallen snow float in the dark blue sky, which is frequently crossed by rainbows.

The city is the only Maya site built right by the sea. Though lacking the pomposity and grandeur of **Chichén Itzá** or **Uxmal,** it is the prettiest archaeological setting you're likely to see. The cluster of some 60 small structures is surrounded by a 3,000-footlong wall more than 20 feet thick in parts (*tulum* means "wall" in Maya) that dates from the Maya Post-Classic Period (circa 900 to 1500). Explorer Juan Grijalva and his crew were the first Spaniards to sight it as they sailed down the Caribbean coast in 1518, and Spaniard Gonzalo Guerrero lived here and married a Maya princess. Their children were the first mestizos in the Yucatán. Bishop Diego de Landa, who singlehandedly destroyed most of the recorded Maya history during the Spanish conquest, wrote that **Tulum** had 600 inhabitants in the mid-1500s; by the end of the century, it was completely deserted. The architecture shows the influence of the Toltec, a tribe from central Mexico that dominated the Maya during the Post-Classic Period. Few of the buildings spread over the 16-acre grassy plateau have significant carvings or architectural aspects, and the most distinctive buildings have been roped off as the stairs and carvings have deteriorated.

In the past, tour buses parked right beside the ruins, discharging fumes and noise. The entrance and parking lots now have been moved closer to the highway, and the area around the ruins is gradually returning to its original jungle state. The new entrance is a formal affair, with a fee charged for parking. Visitors enter the park through an enormous building filled with shops, restaurants, bars, and artisans' stands. The ruins are a 10-minute walk along pathways bordered by jungle undergrowth; a shuttle bus plies the route as well, for an additional fee. You can easily tour the site in an hour; however, those interested in studying the buildings closely and soaking up the scenery should plan on staying at least two hours and should try to get here by 9AM, before the tour groups arrive. Guides with varying degrees of expertise are stationed at a booth behind the entrance building. ◆ Admission and an additional fee for the use of video cameras; free Sunday and holidays. Daily. Hwy 307 (Km 131). 988/31505

At Tulum:

El Castillo (The Castle) Rising three stories above a steep cliff overlooking the sea, this structure must have been an incredible sight in its prime, when it was painted in vivid blues, reds, and whites. The Maya frescoes that once covered the building are long gone, but the crumbling edifice is still astounding. The stairs to the top are roped off, which is unfortunate since the view inland over the city is spectacular. Two windows on the seaward side of the third story reportedly housed beacons that guided mariners safely through the reef to shore. An experiment by Mexico's **Instituto Nacional de Antropología y Historia** (**INAH;** National Institute of Anthropology and History) in 1985 proved that lights shining from the two windows create a beam that points straight to a natural opening in the reef. Two serpent columns run up the stairway to the top of the building, where there are carvings of the Descending God.

Templo del Dios Descendente (Temple of the Descending God) Most of the images of the Descending God have been found at **Tulum.** This distinctive deity is depicted upside down, with his head pointed to the ground. His wings suggest that he may represent the Bee God (an important deity in this honey-producing region). Those who believe the Maya either came from another planet or had contact with extraterrestrial beings say the Descending God is proof that some creatures visited earth from space. One of the best carvings of the god is over the doorway of this temple, just north of **El Castillo.** Walk farther north to the edge of the cliff on a small point for a good overview of the site. A natural bay sits at the bottom of this cliff and is accessible from a pathway at the bay's west end. This is a nice spot for a cooling swim, though there are no showers or rest rooms.

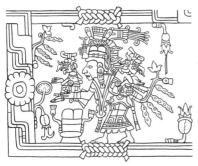

Templo de los Frescos (Temple of the Frescoes) Palm-thatch awnings shade a series of faded paintings on the inner and outer walls of this structure. Depicting the major Maya gods of rain and the moon, the frescoes are difficult to make out, but the flecks of red paint give you an idea of how the buildings looked when the city was in its prime.

16 Cobá This was possibly the largest city-state on the Yucatán Peninsula during the Maya Post-Classic Period. At its peak, from 400 to 1100, the community covered 81 square miles, encompassed five lakes (its name means "rippling waters" in Maya), and was the home of some 50,000 people.

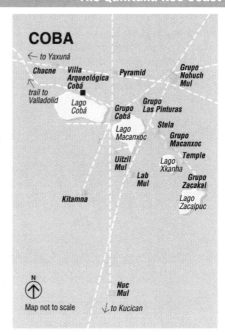

COBA

← to Yaxuná

Chacne Villa Arqueológica Cobá Pyramid Grupo Nohuch Mul

trail to Valladolid Lago Cobá Grupo Cobá Grupo Las Pinturas

Lago Macanxoc Stela

Uitzil Mul Lago Xkanha Grupo Macanxoc Temple

Lab Mul Grupo Zacakal

Kitamna Lago Zacalpuc

N

Map not to scale

Nuc Mul

↓ to Kucican

Archaeologists estimate that 6,000 structures are spread throughout the site, which today is literally buried in the jungle. Less than five percent of the buildings have been excavated, and the sites worth visiting are spread along unmarked trails that seem to disappear into the vegetation.

The maps available at the entrance station are very difficult to follow. To ensure a safe tour, it is well worth hiring a guide. Bring water and bug repellent, wear sturdy shoes, and try to avoid exploring during midday, when the sun's heat turns the jungle into a steam bath.

All those precautions aside, this place is worth more than a quick run-through. It's one of the few spots where you can wander relatively safely through the jungle and possibly run across a spider monkey or peccary. Once you're away from the entrance, the sounds of buzzing bugs and chortling birds seem almost deafening, then a ghostly silence falls. The sun filters through enormous ferns and palms, and the earth has a pungent, almost primeval aroma. The view from atop any of the pyramids is breathtaking, and from the highest, **Nohuch Mul,** you can begin to grasp the immensity of the ancient city. Though it's hard to detect, the site once had a network of *sacbes* (white limestone roads) connecting it with **Tulum** and other Maya cities in the region. There is a small refreshment stand at the entrance to the ruins, but if you're planning to spend considerable time walking around, you might want to carry some snacks.
♦ Admission; free Sunday. Daily. 42 km/26 miles northwest of Hwy 307

At Cobá:

Grupo Cobá The first set of ruins inside the entrance includes the 79-foothigh **Iglesia** (Church), so named by the Spanish because the Maya placed offerings at the top and lit candles to their gods. Archaeologists have yet to discover what the Maya called this shrine. The group includes several smaller buildings around a patio.

Grupo Nohuch Mul No matter what else you see at **Cobá**, you must make it to the tallest pyramid discovered on the Yucatán Peninsula, rising 12 stories above the jungle floor. It takes a hardy climber to make it up the pyramid's 120 narrow limestone steps to the temple on top, and whatever breath you have left after the climb will be taken away by the panorama before you. From the top of the pyramid, also called "El Castillo" (The Castle), you can see other ruins poking through the dense vegetation, as well as the lakes that gave the city its name.

This pyramid is often compared to one in Tikal in Guatemala, which is similar in height and shape, but more ornate in decoration. The temple at the top of **Nohuch Mul** has a carving of the Descending God (the trademark of **Tulum**). The longest *sacbe* in the known Maya world begins at the pyramid's base and runs southwest for 99 kilometers (62 miles) to Yaxuná, near **Chichén Itzá.** Archaeologists and anthropologists are unsure whether these *sacbes* were used as commerce routes or ceremonial pathways. It is believed that the Maya did not use the wheel, yet these roads would seem ideal for transporting the heavy limestone blocks used in construction, as well as items for trade.

Grupo Las Pinturas Polychromatic murals from the Maya Post-Classic Period are still visible on the walls of the largest pyramid in this group of ruins. There is also a large stela—a tall limestone pillar carved with important dates and local events. Stelae are found at nearly all Maya sites, and many are scattered along the pathways here; most, like this one, depict a Maya warrior standing atop his captives.

16 El Bocadito ★$ If you're trying to keep expenses down, your best dining option near **Cobá** is this small indoor/outdoor restaurant. Home-style Mexican and Yucatecan cooking are the specialties here; the portions are generous and the prices astonishingly low. The buses going inland and to the coast stop here, so it's a good place to rest while you wait for your ride. There are also eight basic rooms for rent, with double beds, ceiling fans, and cold showers (which provide some relief from the oppressive heat). The hotel fills up quickly and has no phone, so check about a room before you head for the ruins. ♦ Mexican/Yucatecan ♦ Daily breakfast,

lunch, and dinner. The road to the ruins. For reservations: Apdo 56, Valladolid, Yucatán 97780, Mexico. No phone

16 Villa Arqueológica Cobá $$ There are many good reasons for spending the night at Cobá, one being the opportunity to partake of the gracious hospitality at this small inn nearly buried in vegetation on the shores of Lago Cobá. This is one of a chain of hotels built by the Mexican government and operated by Club Med at major archaeological sites. Forty small, air-conditioned rooms are arranged in a two-story white stucco building framing a pool and courtyard where bougainvillea and ferns seem to grow wild. Authentic Maya carvings and Mexican folk art make the hotel's corridors and dining room resemble a museum. The excellent library contains most of the classic texts on the Maya; some are in English. ♦ Reservations are recommended, as the hotel often fills up with tour groups from Cancún. No phone. For reservations: 5/2033086 in Mexico City, 800/CLUB.MED in the US

Within Villa Arqueológica Cobá:

Restaurant Villa Arqueológica Cobá ★★$$ This is by far the best place to eat at the ruins, with a menu that supplements the usual fresh seafood and Yucatecan specialties with pâtés and quiche. The tables by the pool are a pleasant spot for breakfast. ♦ Mexican/French ♦ Daily breakfast, lunch, and dinner. No phone

17 Boca Paila Peninsula The paved road south of the parking lot on this peninsula runs past small sandy paths leading to campgrounds, fishing cooperatives, and a few private homes. After four kilometers (two miles), a narrow spit of land splits from the mainland, and a dirt road leads to the small settlement of Punta Allen at the southern tip of the 22-milelong peninsula. In 1987, **UNESCO** and the Mexican government designated the peninsula a World Heritage Site, part of the International Man and the Biosphere program. The entire peninsula and 10 percent of Quintana Roo's wildlands have been incorporated into the 1.3-million-acre **Sian Ka'an Biosphere Preserve.** The fishing camps and existing resorts along the peninsula are included in the preserve, and their ecological impact is closely monitored.

An assortment of small campgrounds and hotels lines the first 16 kilometers (10 miles) south of **Tulum.** As with the rest of the coast, this stretch of road has seen considerable development in the past few years as new cabana complexes rise along the sand. Even with the additional rooms, you can't count on finding a lodging place here on the spur of the moment, especially during high season; try to reserve in advance or secure lodging early in the day.

Past this collection of small properties, the road becomes rutted, bumpy, and eerily remote; don't venture on unless you've brought water, a jack, a good spare tire, and plenty of patience. And don't even think about trying to traverse this road when it's raining. It takes about three hours to travel the length of the peninsula, longer if you stop to appreciate the innumerable idyllic beaches. A wooden bridge crosses a channel between the sea and the lagoons on the mainland side of the peninsula. This is a good place to stop for a rest and look for some of the hundred-odd species of birds that inhabit this area. Your last stop on the peninsula is Punta Allen, a fishing village with a few unnamed restaurants and exclusive fishing resorts, where guests are often flown in by private plane from Cancún or Cozumel. ◆ South of Hwy 307

On the road to the Boca Paila Peninsula:

CABAÑAS AT THE BEACH

Zamas $ One of many properties to open along this road in the late 1990s, this small collection of cabanas stands out for its design and its innovative restaurant. The 12 rooms are housed in *palapa*-roofed buildings with enormous showers tiled in bold orange and blue and double beds draped in mosquito nets. The restaurant, ¡**Que Fresco!**, is a colorful collage of tiles and brightly painted tables and chairs facing the sea; it is open for all three meals. The menu includes crepes, banana pancakes, tostadas with melted cheese and black beans, and a different mole each day. The beach here is lovely, with small hills covered with sea grasses. ◆ No credit cards accepted. 5 km/3 miles south of Tulum ruins. For reservations: Apdo 49, Tulum, Mexico 77780; reservations in the US 303/674.9615, 800/538.6802; fax 303/674.8735

Cabañas Ana y José $$ This family-owned hotel is a longtime favorite of **Tulum** devotees. Several two-story buildings house the 16 rooms. All the rooms in the front building by the beach are great; the downstairs rooms in the remaining buildings lack cross-ventilation. All units have ceiling fans, private bathrooms, and hot water. The facilities, including the best restaurant in the neighborhood, are immaculately clean and

well maintained, but not luxurious. The one suite is the exception: The perfect semirustic honeymoon hideaway, it has an enormous balcony overlooking the sea, a huge bathroom with a big bathtub, a CD player and stereo, a king-size bed, and a couch and comfy chairs. There is a dive shop on the premises, and bike rentals are available. The owners have built 2 more hotels in the area: **El Meson** ($) with 8 air-conditioned rooms on Highway 307 at the crossroad to Cobá; and **La Rañanitas** ($$), with 16 air-conditioned rooms and a swimming pool on the Boca Paila Road, 9 kilometers (6 miles) south of the ruins. All share the same phone and fax numbers. ◆ No credit cards accepted. 7 km/4 miles south of Tulum ruins. 12004, 98/806022 in Cancún; fax 12004, 98/806021 in Cancún

On the Boca Paila Peninsula:

 Sian Ka'an Biosphere Preserve It's hard to experience the real magnitude of the preserve, as little of it is accessible by road. In Maya, the name means "where the sky is born."
The preserve encompasses 62 miles of beach, two large Caribbean bays, freshwater and saltwater lagoons, mangrove swamps, unexplored jungle, and a system of canals built by the Maya less than a century after the birth of Christ. At least 20 Maya temples have been discovered, and about a thousand residents, primarily Maya, live here. The biosphere project aims to keep the people on the land, supporting themselves by fishing, farming, and working at the low-environmental-impact tourist centers along the peninsula. Travelers are expected to stay on the road and not wander indiscriminately into the jungle.
Amigos de Sian Ka'an, a volunteer organization based in Cancún, offers tours of the preserve. Some hotels in the area also offer tours; ask about boat excursions, which offer the best views of birds and Maya ruins. ◆ For information and tours, write: Amigos de Sian Ka'an, Apdo 770, Cancún, Quintana Roo 77500, Mexico. 98/849583; fax 98/873080

Boca Paila Fishing Lodge $$$$ The big attraction here is the superb fishing in the lagoons, flats, and open water for bonefish, tarpon, snook, and snapper. The resort has eight white stucco cabanas on the beach, which accommodate up to 18 guests and have rattan furnishings, hot water, and 24-hour electricity; some units have screened porches. Weekly rates include fishing and all meals; rates are lower for nonanglers sharing a room with someone who's fishing. Naturalists are content to walk the long beach and boat through the lagoons searching for some of the 330 species of birds that have been spotted along this part of the peninsula.

♦ Reservations required, especially from November through mid-June. 27 km/17 miles south of Tulum. No phone. For reservations in the US: Frontiers International Travel, PO Box 859, Wexford, PA 15090-0959. 800/245.1950; fax 412/935.5388

Cuzan Guest House $ Travelers who make it to the end of the road will discover this delightful little hostelry. The best of the 12 rooms here are in two Maya-style huts with private baths; six other rooms are in tepee-shaped buildings with concrete floors and shared baths. The restaurant is the best in Punta Allen, and fly-fishing and boat tours are available. ♦ No credit cards accepted. 57 km/35 miles south of Tulum. No phone. For reservations: Apdo Postal 24, Felipe Carrillo Puerto, Quintana Roo 77200, Mexico. 983/40358; fax 983/40383

18 Felipe Carrillo Puerto Located at the intersection of highways going northeast to Cancún and northwest to Mérida, this is a town of about 40,000 residents, with a large public market, a gas station, stores, and a fascinating history. Known as Chan Santa Cruz during the War of the Castes (1847-1901), the town was the central meeting place for Maya rebels and refugees fleeing oppression by the hacienda owners around Mérida who treated the Indians like slaves. The Maya revolted against the governments of Mexico and Yucatán, using guerrilla tactics that nearly won them the war, though half the Indian population of the peninsula died in the struggle. Chan Santa Cruz was the site of the *Talking Cross,* which had been carved into a mahogany tree and appeared to speak prophecies. Actually, the Indian priest Manuel Nahuat provided the voice from behind a curtain and was believed to be translating messages from the gods. Mexican soldiers destroyed the cross, but the Maya carved other crosses and hid them in their villages, continuing to hold that the gods spoke through these symbols. The town's name was changed to honor the socialist governor of Yucatán who instituted social reforms in land distribution, Indian rights, and education in the 1920s, and was assassinated by a rival political party. ♦ Hwy 307 (Km 226)

19 Lago Bacalar The second-largest lake in Mexico (after Lago de Chapala near Guadalajara), this 35-milelong body of water is often called the "Lake of Seven Colors." Fresh and salt waters mix here, creating varying shades of turquoise and blue that contrast vividly with the deep-green jungle along the shores. The lake is popular with Mexicans, but hasn't caught on with foreign travelers. If you're exploring the southern part of the peninsula, however, this is the perfect base camp. The setting and accommodations are far more attractive than those in Chetumal, and you can tour the Xcalak Peninsula or the ruins of **Kohunlich** from here in a day trip. ♦ Hwy 307 (between Hwys 186 and 293)

At Lago Bacalar:

Rancho Encantado $$$ Lush tropical gardens and lawns bordering the shores of Lago Bacalar frame this luxurious retreat. Each of the 12 palm-roofed casitas (scattered far enough apart for privacy) has its own bath, sitting area, and tiled wet bar with refrigerator and coffeemaker. There are no TV sets, but the front porches with their requisite hammocks are perfect for watching the area's abundance of birds. The casitas and the main dining room are decorated with wool rugs from Oaxaca, carved hardwood furnishings, and excellent reproductions of Maya sculptures. The bill of fare emphasizes fresh vegetables and fruits grown on the grounds, homemade breads, and fresh fish; breakfast and dinner are included in the room rate. Guests enjoy swimming and snorkeling in the lagoon and exploring the surrounding region. The management is the best source of information on the many unrestored Maya archaeological sites scattered throughout the area. Special tours can be arranged in advance through their US office. ♦ Km 340. 983/80427; fax: 983/80427. For reservations in the US: PO Box 1256, Taos, New Mexico 87571. 505/776.5878, 800/505.6292; fax 505/776.2102

20 Chetumal There's little reason to come here unless you're traveling on to Belize and Central America. It seems strange that the capital of Quintana Roo is at the southern end of the state, 380 kilometers (236 miles) from Cancún, but the city was a seat of power nearly a century ago and was by far the most populated part of the eastern peninsula until Cancún came along. Today the population stands at about 50,000, whereas Cancún's is approximately 400,000.

On the border between Mexico and Belize, near the Bahía de Chetumal and the mouth of the Río Hondo, Chetumal has a run-down Caribbean flavor, with a hint of mystery and an underlying suggestion of danger (a holdover from its smuggler days, when guns and ammunition frequently passed back and forth across the border). Businesspeople who must journey here to visit government offices do so reluctantly, since the accommodations and ambience are less than ideal.

If you do visit Chetumal, spend some time along Boulevard Bahía, which runs along the bay and features pleasant restaurants and bars and a pretty waterfront park. The downtown area looks dilapidated and unsavory, even though it was rebuilt after Hurricane Janet nearly destroyed it in 1955. Salsa, reggae, and marimba music blares from boom boxes in shops and restaurants, and the crowds on the street are a mix of Mexicans, Caribbean islanders, Middle Easterners, and Belizeans. Take some precautions when roaming the streets and don't bumble around like a tourist waiting to be taken for a ride. ♦ Hwy 186 (east of Hwy 307)

In Chetumal:

Los Cocos $ An old, reliable standard, this bland hotel has 60 slightly musty but serviceable rooms with noisy air-conditioning, along with two restaurants and a large pool set in a lush garden. The in-house travel agency is helpful. ♦ Av Héroes 138 (at Héroes de Chapultepec). 983/20544; fax 983/20920

Hotel Continental Caribe $$ Newer than the **Los Cocos,** this place has an atrium lobby with a fountain, a courtyard swimming pool, a serviceable restaurant, and 64 modern rooms with good air-conditioning. ♦ Av Héroes 171 (between Héroes de Chapultepec and Mahatma Gandhi). 983/21100

Sergio's ★$ For those who live along the coast and have little access to "exotic fare" such as pizza and thick grilled steaks, this is a necessary stop. It's also the place to come for catching up on local gossip. ♦ American ♦ M-Sa lunch and dinner. Alvaro Obregón 182 (at Av 5 de Mayo). 983/22355

Emiliano's ★★$ The best seafood in town is served at this large restaurant that's immensely popular with locals at lunchtime. Try the seafood pâté, the ceviche, or the seafood cocktail to start; the gigantic seafood platter is a favorite entrée. ♦ Seafood ♦ Daily lunch and dinner. Av San Salvador 557 (at Calle 9). 983/70267

21 Kohunlich Some 67 kilometers (42 miles) west of Chetumal, this isolated Maya site is particularly interesting for its portrayals of the Sun God on the **Pirámide de los Máscarones** (Pyramid of the Masks). The largest of these stucco bas-reliefs is 10 feet tall, with bulging round eyes, a prominent flared nose, and an extended tongue. The 10-square-mile site is the focus of sporadic excavations; it is estimated that there are some 200 buildings in the area, though only 5 have been uncovered. Usually deserted except for the watchman, the site is overgrown with foliage. Bring water and bug repellent, and don't wander far from the entrance. ♦ Admission; free Sunday and holidays. Daily. South of Hwy 186. No phone

22 Xcalak Other than the **Sian Ka'an Biosphere Preserve** (see above), the last remaining undeveloped portion of the Quintana Roo coastline is this thin, 40-milelong peninsula that ends at the border of Belize. The peninsula's main community is at the south end of a 30-milelong rutted dirt road (rumors say it may someday be paved), with a few private homes, campgrounds, and fishing co-ops scattered along the way.

The Chinchorro Banks, 29 kilometers (18 miles) east of the peninsula, is exciting territory for scuba divers. There are some three dozen shipwrecks along the 24-mile reef. Divers are prohibited from taking anything from the wrecks, and the government sometimes closes the area if looting is suspected. Fishermen in the towns of Majahual and Xcalak take divers to the reef in their boats, and local dive resorts also offer transportation. The weather and rough seas often force the cancellation of Chinchorro excursions, but the diving is superb closer to shore as well.

When visiting the peninsula, start out early, bring water and a good spare tire, and plan on stopping often to take in the scenery. Make reservations in advance if you plan on spending the night, since Xcalak's popularity is growing. If you don't have reservations, give yourself time to return to Bacalar, Chetumal, or Felipe Carrillo Puerto before dark if the coastal resorts are full. A major "eco-tourism" development on the peninsula is in the planning stages. ♦ Southeast of Hwy 307

On the Xcalak Peninsula:

Costa de Cocos $$ Literally at the end of the road, this small resort provides one of the last true hideaways on the Quintana Roo coast. Owners María and Dave Randall worked four years to build a clean, comfortable haven near the fishing co-op, in a region where running water, flush toilets, and electric lights are still rarities. The 12 palm-roofed cabanas have all those modern niceties as well as tile bathrooms, comfortable mattresses, screened doors and windows, bookshelves stocked with an eclectic assortment of paperbacks and magazines, and hammocks hanging both indoors and out.

There is a restaurant on the grounds, and breakfast and dinner are included in the room rate. The resident divemaster takes divers and snorkelers to dozens of spectacular sites along the reef, which is just a 10-minute ride from shore; tanks, air, weights, and some dive gear are available for rent at the resort. A 25-foot boat is used to take divers to Chinchorro upon request. Local skiff captains offer longer trips to the village of San Pedro on Belize's Ambergris Cay. ♦ Xcalak. For reservations: Turquoise Reef Group, Box 2664, Evergreen, CO 80439. 303/674.9615, 800/538.6802; fax 303/674.8735

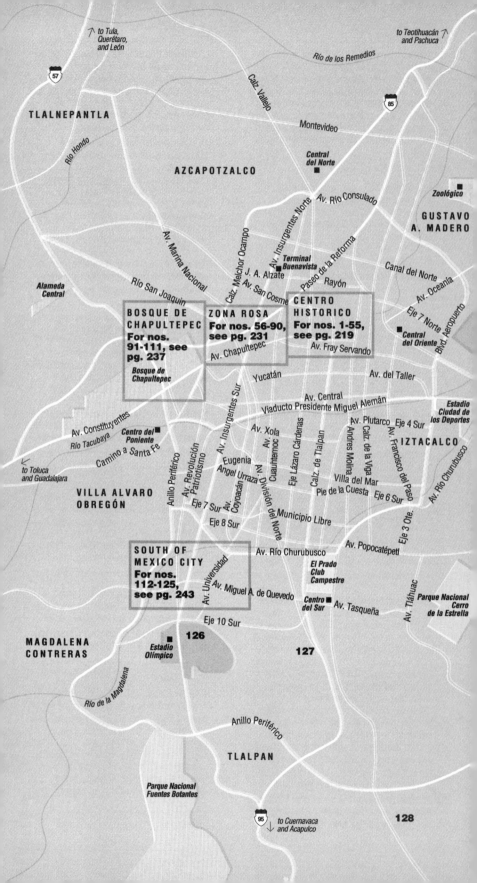

↑ to Tula,
Querétaro,
and León

to Teotihuacán ↑
and Pachuca

57

85

Río de los Remedios

Calz. Vallejo

Montevideo

TLALNEPANTLA

Río Hondo

AZCAPOTZALCO

*Central
del Norte*

Av. Río Consulado

Zoológico

**GUSTAVO
A. MADERO**

Av. Marina Nacional

Av. Insurgentes Norte

Calz. Melchor Ocampo

Canal del Norte

Av. Oceanía

*Alameda
Central*

Río San Joaquín

*Terminal
Buenavista*

J. A. Alzate

Av. San Cosme

Paseo de la Reforma

Rayón

Eje 7 Norte

Blvd. Aeropuerto

*Central
del Oriente*

**BOSQUE DE
CHAPULTEPEC
For nos.
91-111, see
pg. 237**

**ZONA ROSA
For nos. 56-90,
see pg. 231**

**CENTRO
HISTORICO
For nos. 1-55,
see pg. 219**

*Bosque de
Chapultepec*

Av. Chapultepec

Av. Fray Servando

Av. del Taller

Yucatán

Av. Constituyentes

Río Tacubaya

Av. Central

Viaducto Presidente Miguel Alemán

*Estadio
Ciudad de
los Deportes*

Av. Xola

Av. Plutarco

Eje 4 Sur

Andrés Molina

Calz. de la Viga

Av. Francisco del Paso

IZTACALCO

*Centro del
Poniente*

Camino a Santa Fe

Av. Insurgentes Sur

Av. Cuauhtémoc

Eje Lázaro Cárdenas

Calz. de Tlalpan

Villa del Mar

Eje 6 Sur

← to Toluca
and Guadalajara

Anillo Periférico

Av. Revolución
Patriotismo

Eugenia

Ángel Urraza

Av. Coyoacán

Av. División del Norte

Pie de la Cuesta

Eje 3 Ote.

Av. Río Churubusco

**VILLA ALVARO
OBREGÓN**

Eje 7 Sur

Municipio Libre

Av. Popocatépetl

Eje 8 Sur

**SOUTH OF
MEXICO CITY
For nos.
112-125,
see pg. 243**

Av. Universidad

Av. Río Churubusco

*El Prado
Club
Campestre*

Av. Miguel A. de Quevedo

Av. Tláhuac

*Parque Nacional
Cerro
de la Estrella*

*Centro
del Sur*

Av. Tasqueña

Av. Tláhuac

Eje 10 Sur

126

127

**MAGDALENA
CONTRERAS**

*Estadio
Olímpico*

Río de la Magdalena

Anillo Periférico

TLALPAN

*Parque Nacional
Fuentes Botantes*

95

↓ to Cuernavaca
and Acapulco

128

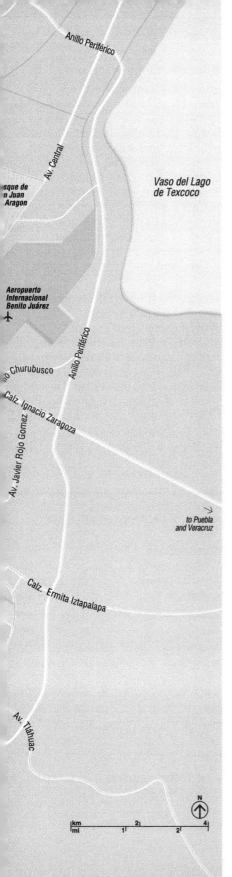

Anillo Periférico

Av. Central

Vaso del Lago
de Texcoco

sque de
n Juan
Aragon

Aeropuerto
Internacional
Benito Juárez

o Churubusco

Anillo Periférico

Calz. Ignacio Zaragoza

Av. Javier Rojo Gomez

to Puebla
and Veracruz

Calz. Ermita Iztapalapa

Av. Tláhuac

N

km   2   4
mi   1   2

Mexico City

The nearly 700-year-old capital of Mexico is one of the world's great cities. Never mind the newspaper headlines that declare it a contaminated, corrupt, overcrowded, mad, bad, and dangerous place. Mexico City is all of these things to some degree, just like any big city, but it's also one of the most intriguing, vibrant, and stimulating metropolises in the world.

This metropolitan area of 23 million people (one-fourth of Mexico's entire population) grew from the ruins of **Tenochtitlán**, the religious, political, and economic center of the Aztec civilization, founded in 1325. According to legend, the Aztecs, who were in search of a home base, were told by their gods to look for an eagle eating a snake atop a nopal cactus; they found what they were seeking on a snake-infested island in the middle of **Lake Texcoco** and named the area "the place of the cactus fruit" (the eagle eating the snake later became the emblem for the country). Within two centuries the Aztec Empire had grown so powerful its influence stretched across much of what is today Mexico and Central America.

Word of the Aztec city's wealth spread to Hernán Cortés, and in 1519 the Spanish conquistador arrived, troops in tow, to find 300,000 inhabitants and magnificent temples, avenues, and marketplaces—a city so splendid it conjured up images of Venice for Bernal Díaz del Castillo, whose journals are a record of the conquest. Emperor Montezuma and his people welcomed the Spanish with gifts of gold, but Cortés wanted much more. Within two years he was destroying palaces and massacring the indigenous people, wiping out much of the city; over a longer period of time, diseases brought by the Europeans eliminated even more of the population. Mexico City was constructed from the rubble of Tenochtitlán—its churches and municipal buildings are made with stones from the Aztec's sacred temples, and many traces of the ancient peoples can still be found in the area.

The foundation of present-day Mexico City was laid during the three centuries of Spanish rule; sanitation reforms were instituted, and a spectacular European-style city arose, including a very Parisian main boulevard, the **Paseo de la Reforma**. This blending of Spanish and Indian styles has resulted in an architectural collage: Bold, avant-garde structures rub shoulders with Moorish and Baroque colonial buildings, and both stand atop remnants of Tenochtitlán that are occasionally unearthed. Such contrasts are the nature of Mexico City, where children beg for pesos in the same streets on which wheelers and dealers meet to shape the country's future, and where fascinating murals and green plazas are often lost in a haze of pollution, noise, and traffic snarls. This chaotic and discordant mélange has been a lure for numerous artists and writers: John Dos Passos, Evelyn Waugh, Ernest Hemingway, D.H. Lawrence, Langston Hughes, and Jack Kerouac all spent time here, finding plenty of grist for their musings.

To discover the soul of the city, you have to browse through the markets that spill onto the streets, offering a rich cornucopia of sights, sounds, and smells. These *mercados* are the bustling social hub of life here, and the people who congregate daily are as colorful as the fresh fruits, vegetables, and flowers they come to buy. You must also sample the bars and cantinas of **Plaza Garibaldi**, where mariachi music and shots of tequila are the order of the day. And no matter how little time you have to explore Mexico City, don't miss the world-class **Museo Nacional de Antropología** (National Museum of Anthropology); the **Zócalo**, downtown's vast main square; or the **Palacio Nacional**, home of Diego Rivera's dramatic and poignant murals. To get to know Mexico City requires patience, determination, and a bit of inquisitiveness. One must sift through the chaff of crime and grime to find its essence—a city with a history as rich as that of any Maya ruin.

Area code 5 unless otherwise noted.

Getting to Mexico City

Airport

The **Aeropuerto Internacional Benito Juárez** (Benito Juárez International Airport) is located in the northeast section of the city, about a 30- to 60-minute drive (depending on traffic) from the **Centro Histórico** and the **Zona Rosa**. Like a small city unto itself, the airport has separate terminals for national and international flights. It takes at least 15 minutes to walk from one end of the airport to the other (a trek many travelers must undertake to catch connecting flights). The terminals are connected indoors, and the cavernous airline ticket counter area is filled with gift shops, pharmacies, bookstores, liquor stores, currency exchange offices, banks, and nearly every service a traveler could desire. A bridge connects the airport with the **Marriott Aeropuerto**; the hotel's restaurant is a good place to linger if you have a long layover.

Porters are available at the baggage carousels, as are free luggage carts. However, you cannot take the carts into the main area of the airport or to the airport's multilevel indoor parking lot. The luggage storage room is in the national terminal next to Gate A.

Airport information kiosks are located in both terminals, as are branches of the Mexico City tourism office.

Airport Services

General Information	762.4011
Tourist Information	762.6773
Security	571.3600

Airlines

Aeroméxico	228.9910, 800/237.6639
American	209.1400, 800/443.7300
America West	95/800/235.9292 in Mexico, 800/235.9292
Continental	280.3434, 800/525.0280
Delta	202.1608, 800/221.1212
Mexicana	325.0990, 800/531.7921
Taesa	227.0700, 800/328.2372
United	627.0222, 800/241.6522

Airport Accommodations It can be difficult to get same-day flight connections at the Mexico City airport, and travelers often have to spend a night in the city between flights. If your layover is short, consider staying close to the airport rather than riding for 30 minutes or more each way to a downtown hotel. Hotels near the airport include:

Marriott Aeropuerto ($$$) ....230.0505, ...800/228.9290; fax 230.0134

Hotel Aeropuerto ($)...............785.6928, 785.5318; ....fax 784.1329

Hotel Rizaor ($)..................726.9998; fax 654.3840

Holiday Inn Plaza Dali Hotel ($$)............768.2020, ...800/465.4329; fax 552.0895

Getting to and from Aeropuerto Internacional Benito Juárez

By Car All major car-rental companies have desks at the airport, but driving from the airport into the city is definitely not advised. The traffic is horrid, and you won't need or want a car while staying in the city. The following car-rental companies have counters at **Aeropuerto Internacional Benito Juárez** and are open 24 hours daily.

Avis 588.8888, 762.1166, 800/331.1212

Budget 566.6800, 800/527.0700

Dollar 207.3838, 800/800.4000

By Metro There is a metro (subway) station at the airport, about a 10-minute walk past the national terminal. The station is on *Metro Lines 5, 1,* and *9;* if you speak Spanish, clerks at information booths in the metro station will tell you what lines to take to reach your destination; if you don't, the clear and plainly posted metro maps should get you where you're going.

By Taxi **Transporte Terreste,** a well-organized taxi service, offers set rates for trips into Mexico City. Buy a prepaid ticket from one of their booths, located at both the national and international luggage areas and near the airport exits. The fare to most inner-city hotels is about $8 per cab (not per person). Pay no more than the price on the ticket, which is good for up to four passengers going to the same destination with luggage weighing no more than 25 kilos (55 pounds) each. Count your change, as there have been reports of cashiers short-changing arrivals. Do not take rides from the unlicensed, unauthorized taxi drivers who boldly solicit passengers in the airport. To get to the airport from the city, hail a taxi at your hotel; make sure the meter is working, get an estimate of the fare anyway, and ask for the *aeropuerto.*

Bus Stations (Long-Distance)

There are four major bus stations: **Central del Oriente** (East Terminal; Calzada Ignacio Zaragoza and Av Ingeniero Eduardo Molina, 767.5877); **Central del Norte** (North Terminal; Eje Central, between Avs Instituto Politecnico and Fortuna, 587.5973); **Central del Sur** (South Terminal; Calzada Taxqueña 1320, at Canal de Miramontes, 689.9795); and **Central del Poniente** (West Terminal; Avs Sur 122 and Río Tacubaya, 271.4519).

Buses depart for and arrive from all parts of the country at these terminals, though the direction the bus is headed doesn't necessarily correspond with the terminal's location. All the bus stations are cavernous, with restaurants, bus and city information offices, and taxi stands. The **Oficina del Turismo** (Tourism Office) in the Zona Rosa (see "Visitors' Information Center," page 217) has bus maps.

Train Station

The **Terminal de Ferrocarriles Nacionales de México** train station (commonly called the **Terminal Buenavista**) is located on **Avenida Insurgentes Norte** (at Mosqueta, 547.1084). Trains depart daily for many of Mexico's major tourist destinations. Many are badly in need of refurbishing, though some are in good condition. Don't even think about taking anything but a first-class train, however—the rest are murderously slow, unclean, and sometimes dangerous.

Getting Around Mexico City

This is not a city to drive in, but taxis and the public transit system are efficient and relatively inexpensive alternatives.

Buses Buses run throughout Mexico City and are a great way to get around cheaply during non–rush hours. The **Oficina del Turismo** (Tourism Office) in the Zona Rosa (see "Visitors' Information Center," page 217) has bus maps. Maps are also posted at stops, which are marked with a green-and-white sign with a picture of a bus and the route number. The most useful route for tourists runs along the Paseo de la Reforma from the Zócalo to **Bosque de Chapultepec;** these buses are labeled *Zócalo, Reforma,* or *Lomas.*

Driving Driving within Mexico City is a horror best left to bus and cab drivers. There's absolutely no need to rent a car if you're staying in the city and visiting attractions in the metropolitan area. If you plan on touring farther afield, ask the car-rental company for the office closest to the highway leading to your destination and depart from there, or else have the car delivered to your hotel and get on the road before 6AM.

Rental cars are included in the smog-reduction program that prohibits vehicles from being used one day per week (as designated by license plate numbers). Be sure to ask the rental company which day your automobile will be barred from city streets.

The car-rental agencies at **Aeropuerto Internacional Benito Juárez** (listed above) also have offices in Mexico City.

Metro Mexico City's subway system is cheap, quick, clean, and efficient, though intimidating at first and often crowded even in off hours. Despite the apparent chaos, the metro system is easy to use. Buy a ticket (or a book of 10 if you plan to use the system extensively) and pop it into the slot to open the barrier. The metro runs the length and breadth of the city; to change lines, follow the signs that read *correspondencia.* Trains run from early morning until after midnight, and tickets, maps, and information are available at all stations. See the inside back cover of this book for the metro map.

To cut down on crimes against women, the metro now has cars reserved for female travelers during weekday rush hours, 6-10AM and 5-8PM.

Taxis Cabs come in different shapes and sizes: the cheap street taxis (usually VW Beetles or sedans that are being painted a bright, ecological green as they switch to unleaded gas) and the large, black sedans that wait outside the tourist hotels. In general, the hotel sedan taxis charge by the distance and have drivers who speak English, know the city well, and have room for four or five passengers, making them expensive. Street taxis charge by a usually reliable meter *(taximetro)*, but can only hold a maximum of three passengers. If the meter is broken—and probably even if it isn't—confirm the fare before taking off. Not all taxi drivers know the city well; if the address you want is off the beaten track, try to find out what some of the major landmarks are near your destination. The safest option is to use hotel taxis or buses. There was a rash of robberies in street taxis in 1997; passengers were driven at gunpoint to banks to withdraw cash with their ATM or credit cards, or robbed of all their possessions and left at some remote location.

FYI

Accommodations Mexico City has hotels for every budget and taste. The Centro Histórico offers the best selection of economical lodgings, while the Zona Rosa and Bosque de Chapultepec neighborhoods are filled with moderate and expensive places. Room rates at some expensive hotels start at $200 a night. Business travelers fill the larger hotels during the week, so reservations are strongly advised.

Climate Mexico City's infamous smog is its most important climatic factor. Combined with the city's altitude (7,240 feet), the pollution can make breathing difficult. The smog is at its worst in the winter months, from mid-November through January, when smog alerts are common. In general the city's climate is mild, with temperate days and cool evenings. You'll need a sweater or jacket in winter. Rain is common between May and October and seems to be the worst in August and September, when streets often flood after a downpour. The rain has its benefits, however, since it clears the air so well a bit of blue sky will actually peek through the yellow smog.

Embassies

The following English-speaking countries maintain embassies in Mexico City:

Australia 5/531.5225

Canada 5/724.7900

New Zealand 281.5486

UK 207.2449

US 211.0042

Publications Mexico City has two daily English-language newspapers, *The News* and the *Mexico City Times*. The *Daily Bulletin,* an English-language tourist information paper, is available at tourist information offices and some hotels.

Shopping Shoppers have no trouble unloading their pesos at the city's markets, boutiques, and galleries. The best overall shopping district is the Zona Rosa, where upscale shops and an excellent artisans' market can easily occupy browsers for several days. The government-operated **FONART** stores scattered around the city are excellent sources of high-quality folk art from across the country.

Street Plan Though Mexico City is indeed enormous, it's actually not difficult to figure out where you're going. Most of the major attractions are located in the Centro Histórico, the Zona Rosa, and Bosque de Chapultepec, all connected by the Paseo de la Reforma. It's a good idea to use public buses or to take a bus tour of the city when you first arrive to get a grasp of the layout. Though the metro is by far the city's easiest mode of transportation, it is a little disorienting since its path is mostly underground.

Telephone You'll quickly notice how many people use cellular phones in Mexico City. That's because the city's phone system is notoriously dreadful. Telephone numbers frequently change or become inoperable—it's not unusual to talk with someone on the phone one day and not be able to reach them at the same number the next.

Businesses are frequently listed under the name of a corporation rather than the business name, so calling information (dial 04) is often an exercise in futility. Hotel operators and concierges are your best sources of assistance with telephone numbers, since they usually keep an updated list of numbers for restaurants and tourist attractions.

Time Zone Mexico City is on Central Time, two hours ahead of California and one hour behind New York.

Tours Most large hotels have their own travel agents who can provide up-to-date information on tours of the area, including visits to the ruins at **Teotihuacán** and the floating gardens of **Xochimilco**. **Tren Turistico** (512.1012) offers 30-minute narrated tours of the Centro Histórico aboard replicas of 1920s-style, open-air wooden trolleys. The tours in English are at 11AM. Tickets are sold and tours begin in front of the **Museo de la Ciudad de México** (Mexico City Museum; Pino Suárez 30, at República de El Salvador). The trolleys depart every half-hour from 10AM to 6PM Tuesday through Sunday, and a one-day ticket allows you to get off and reboard as often as you wish.

Gray Line Tours offers excursions both within and beyond Mexico City. This reliable company has years of experience, offers multilingual commentary, and will pick up and drop off clients at their hotels. The office (Londres 166, at Florencia) is open daily. Call 208.1163, 208.1304, or 533.1666 for an English-speaking agent.

Visitors' Information Center The **Departamento de Turismo del Distrito Federal** (Mexico City Tourism Office), located in the Zona Rosa (Amberes 54, at Londres, 525.9380, 525.9384; fax 525.9387), is open daily. Many members of the helpful staff speak English and can provide information on hotels, restaurants, and events.

LOCATEL (658.1111) is City Hall's 24-hour information line. In addition to emergency assistance, it provides information on lost people, possessions, or vehicles, as well as the addresses and phone numbers of city museums.

Phone Book

Fire 08

American British Cowdray (ABC) Hospital
Av Observatorio (between 132 Sur and 136 Sur) 230.8000

Hospital Angeles de Pedregal Camino a Santa Teresa 1055 (at Ruta de la Amistad) 652.1188

Police 08

Tourist Help emergency assistance provided by the Mexico Ministry of Tourism..................250.0123

Tourist Help—Procuraduria General de Justicia del Distrito Federal (24-hour, English-speaking legal assistance) 625.8761, 625.7020

Centro Histórico (Historic Center)

There is no better way to plunge into the heart of Mexico City than by heading to the **Zócalo,** the vast main square in the center of downtown that has been the hub of city life since the Aztec founded their capital here in 1325. When the Spanish conquerors, led by Hernán Cortés and his native-born mistress, La Malinche, arrived in 1519, they smashed the Aztec temples and palaces and built the public square and beautiful colonial palaces you see today. Aztec ruins are still being discovered here. When the subway system was being built in the 1970s, construction had to be constantly halted because of the hundreds of archaeological artifacts unearthed daily. The **Museo y Ruinas Templo Mayor** (Great Temple Museum and Ruins), on the northeastern edge of the Zócalo, houses the most important of these artifacts.

Although this part of the city is called the Centro Histórico, it isn't just about history and museums; it's the liveliest and most colorful part of Mexico City. The city has begun refurbishing the neighborhood, and several buildings are undergoing restorations. Huge wall murals painted after the 1910 revolution, popular bohemian theaters, and restaurants offering everything from tacos and enchiladas to grasshoppers and iguana steaks are found throughout the area. There are also palaces, museums, churches, and shops, not to mention the largest pawnshop in the Americas.

This is no longer much of a residential district—earthquakes, subsidence (the city was built on a lake bed and is slowly sinking), and congestion have caused many people to move away. But that hasn't reduced the neighborhood's bustling street life: Stalls offer everything from mariachi tapes to skimpy underwear; organ-grinders play for the crowds; lottery vendors all claim to have the winning tickets for sale; and vats of corn on the cob smothered with mayonnaise, chili powder, lime juice, and salt are peddled on street corners. The city is making an effort to move these street vendors into organized markets, but they are not going willingly, and the character of the neighborhood would be changed dramatically if they did: It's the mixture of the distant past and contemporary life that makes this area so special.

1 Zócalo With each side measuring 792 feet, this is the largest square in the Americas and the second-largest in the world (Moscow's Red Square is the largest). Formerly planted with gardens and trees, the plaza was the meeting place of viceroys and presidents; today the trees are gone and the square is an enormous gray cement slab with few seats and a rather inhospitable aura. Government ministries are now scattered throughout the city, but the president still has his official headquarters here in the **Palacio Nacional.** The section of the plaza facing the palace sometimes becomes a temporary home to protestors of various persuasions who set up tent cities and congregate for rallies. In the middle of the square, the Mexican flag is raised every morning and lowered every evening accompanied by a full military salute and horns and drums. For the ultimate taste of Zócalo life, visit on the weekend or during the Independence Day festivities on 15 and 16 September, when thousands of people pour into the square and make merry. ♦ At Francisco I. Madero and 20 de Noviembre

At the Zócalo:

Metro Zócalo The best subway station for visiting the Centro Histórico is in the middle of the plaza and offers a mole's-eye view of Mexican life. Its walls are lined with architectural drawings of the capital, and kiosks are staffed by potbellied men selling tickets and grudgingly handing out free maps. In recent years, vendors have been moved from the corridors to a market at the entrance in an attempt to reduce congestion. This is one place in the city where you should keep a tight hold on your wallet, not to mention your wits.

2 Palacio Nacional (National Palace) The palace was built in 1521 by the *conquistador* Hernán Cortés on the ruins of Emperor Montezuma's palace and aviaries. Although it has been chopped and changed many times and was seriously damaged in 1692 by an enraged mob that wanted the Spanish to leave Mexico, it still dominates the whole east face of the Zócalo. The building has always been at the forefront of revolutions and coups. In fact, the very bell that started the War of Independence against the Spanish in 1810 is hanging above the central doorway; it is rung in commemoration of that struggle every 15 September by the president. ♦ Zócalo (between Pino Suárez and Moneda)

Within the Palacio Nacional:

Diego Rivera Murals The 1910 revolution against the dictatorship of Porfirio Díaz ushered in a new era of Mexican art. Public buildings became easels for young painters, many inspired by the Russian revolutionary and poet Mayakovsky. Diego Rivera painted 550 square yards of murals in the **Palacio Nacional** between 1929 and 1951. He covered the first-floor corridor with enormous, instructive panels illustrating the lives of each of the country's indigenous peoples before the Spanish conquest. The murals depict the great Aztec market in nearby Tlatelolco, Tarascan fishermen with their voluminous butterfly nets

on Lake Patzcuaro, the preparation of cocoa and tequila, and more. In the last of the corridor panels, Rivera delighted in shocking his public by portraying Hernán Cortés as a syphilitic hunchback suppressing the natives and getting rich off the pickings of the New World.

Palacio Nacional

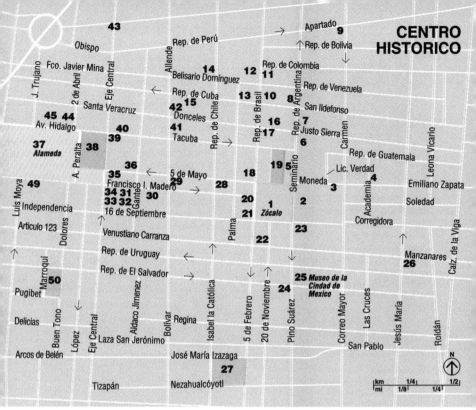

The three walls of the palace's main staircase are a Mexican history lesson covering the last 500 years; scenes range from the conquerors brutally subjugating the glorified Aztec to life in Mexico in the 1950s. There are myriad details, and it takes a true history buff or a knowledgeable guide to pick out all the characters. For example, the *Struggle of the Classes* on the south wall includes portraits of such diverse subjects as Rivera's wife, the painter Frida Kahlo; her sister Cristina; and Karl Marx, who is shown pointing the way to a glowing future. Rivera was a card-carrying Communist for many years, although he was often thrown out of the party for being too disruptive. ♦ Free. Daily

3 Museo Nacional de las Culturas (National Museum of Cultures) The first mint in the Americas is now a museum with exhibits from around the world, and a 1938 mural in the entrance hall painted by Rufino Tamayo (1899-1991) to celebrate the 1910 revolution. The building is located on one of the oldest streets in the city, Moneda, which was also home to the Americas' first printing press and first university. ♦ Free. M-Sa. Moneda 13 (between Correo Mayor and Seminario). 512.7452

4 Museo José Luis Cuevas Works by this avant-garde multimedia artist, considered one of Mexico's best contemporary artists, are displayed here. In addition, the **Sala Picasso** contains several drawings and paintings by the Spanish master, while other exhibit halls

feature temporary shows of modern art. ♦ Admission. Tu-Su. Academia 13 (between Emiliano Zapata and República de Guatemala). 542.8959

5 Fuente Modelo de la Ciudad de Mexico (Fountain Model of Ancient Mexico City) This impressive outdoor model depicts Mexico City (then called Tenochtitlán) as it was before the Spanish arrived in 1519. The model, with its miniature temples, canals, lakes, and palaces, stands directly in front of the real ruins of the **Templo Mayor** (Great Temple), creating an awe-inspiring snapshot of the Aztec civilization at its most glorious. It is hard to imagine the city could ever have been so small and even harder to imagine that it was constructed in the middle of a lake, linked to the mainland by a series of causeways. ♦ Seminario (between Zócalo and Tacuba)

Mexico City's dining habits are reflected in restaurant hours, which may seem strange to travelers from the US. Some places don't open for breakfast until 9 or 10AM, while some business executives have a late breakfast. Lunchtime starts at 1PM and lasts until 4 or 5PM, though some places stay open as late as 8PM to accommodate early diners. Many of the more exclusive restaurants don't even open for dinner until 8PM, and are busiest around 10PM.

6 Museo y Ruinas Templo Mayor (Great Temple Museum and Ruins) The

Spaniards built their New World capital on top of razed Aztec temples, and over the centuries Aztec artifacts appeared whenever anyone stuck a spade into the ground. However, it wasn't until 1978 that the site of the most important twin temples to the Aztec gods of rain (Tlaloc) and war (Huitzilopochtli) was properly excavated. The museum is the only one in the world dedicated solely to the Aztec. Designed by **Pedro Ramírez Vázquez** (who was also responsible for the **Museo Nacional de Antropología** and the modernistic **Basilica de Guadalupe**), it is an eight-room treasure trove of more than 3,000 Aztec splendors, ranging from the monolithic sculpted stone of the moon goddess Coyolxauhqui (on the second floor) to the *tzompantli* (skull rack), where warriors displayed the heads of their decapitated prisoners. The museum collection includes the obsidian knives used to cut out the hearts of sacrificial victims, and the tributes, such as shells, chocolate, and cochineal dye, that the Aztec demanded from subjugated vassals. Unfortunately, the exhibits are labeled in Spanish only. ♦ Admission; free Sunday. Tu-Su. Seminario 8 (between Moneda and Justo Sierra). 542.4784

Within the Museo y Ruinas Templo Mayor:

Bookshop Although small, this store has a very wide range of reference books on Mexico and its pre-Hispanic civilizations and art; many are in English. The stock also features posters, tapes, postcards, magazines, and gifts. ♦ Tu-Su. 542.4784

7 Ex-Colegio de San Ildefonso (Former College of St. Ildefonso) Founded in 1588

as a school for Jesuit novitiates, this college is famous for the murals painted around its patio. In the late 1920s, Mexico's enlightened minister of education, José Vasconcelos, commissioned young painters to cover the walls of public buildings with their own interpretations of Mexico and its revolution.

The results of this program surprised the painters as much as they did the government. Wealthy students who were vehemently opposed to the left-wing politics of the muralists did everything they could to sabotage their art, including defacing the works in progress at night. (Murals differ from frescoes, which have been around since the Renaissance, in that they are painted on dry walls rather than wet plaster.) Nor did the new revolutionary government get what it expected; José Clemente Orozco (1883-1949) was always skeptical about the success of the revolution, and his murals here—*Justice and the Law* (1923) and *The Church and Reaction* (1924)— imply that the golden age was still a long way off. The building has been renovated and turned into one of the most outstanding museums in the city, inaugurating such exhibits as the internationally acclaimed *Splendors of Thirty Centuries,* a stunning collection of pre-Hispanic artifacts. Check with the tourist office or museum for information on the current exhibit. ♦ Admission. Tu-Su. Justo Sierra 16 (at República de Argentina). 702.2834

Within the Ex-Colegio de San Ildefonso:

Anfiteatro Bolívar (Bolívar Amphitheater) Diego Rivera painted his first mural, *The Creation,* here in 1922. He managed to protect himself from the students' jeering by locking himself and his assistants inside the building. In what was originally a church cupola and organ loft and is now a stage backdrop, he painted a mural that is far from his best. It is important, however, because it marks the beginning of his career as a muralist. In the lobby, a 1933 work by Fernando Leal (1896-1964), an often-overlooked 20th-century muralist, depicts Simón Bolívar as an exemplary revolutionary astride his white horse. The entrance fee for the main museum covers this place, too; just ask permission from the guard at the door. ♦ Justo Sierra 14

8 Secretaría de Educación Pública (SEP; Ministry of Education) The painting of

murals on public buildings reached its greatest glory with Diego Rivera's massive work in the education minister's headquarters. Although lesser-known artists such as Jean Charlot and Amado de la Cueva had a hand in the work, most of the 250 panels, which cover 18,000 square feet, are the result of Rivera's gargantuan effort. All three floors, the staircases, and the elevators are painted with murals that cover the spectrum of Mexican culture. The first floor is the site of the largest and best-known mural, which presents visions of daily country and industrial life; the second floor concentrates on the Mexican states; and the third represents Mexico's heroes, arts, and trade. ♦ Free. M-F all floors; Sa-Su first floor only. República de Argentina 28 (at González Obregón). 657.3801

9 El Taquito ★★$$ This traditional
restaurant, once the domain of famous bullfighters, has seen many other luminaries—including Pope Paul VI and Marilyn Monroe (on separate occasions)—

pass through its doors. Beef, tequila, and bonhomie are the main ingredients of a meal here. Come with a healthy appetite and try the *botanes* (appetizers) such as *tostaditas con guacamole* (chips with guacamole) and *chicharrónes* (fried pork skins) before moving on to the huge beef dish, *carne a la tampiqueña*, which comes with beans, rice, avocado, and enchiladas. Live music is played from 2 to 10PM. ♦ Mexican ♦ M-Sa breakfast, lunch, and dinner; Su lunch and dinner. Carmen 69 (between República de Bolivia and Apartado). 526.7699, 526.7885

10 **Casa de Aduana (Customs House)** Stop by the former Customs House (now part of the Education Ministry) on the southeast corner of the attractive Plaza de Santo Domingo to see David Alfaro Siqueiros's mural *Patricians and Patricides*. Although he painted it on the walls of the Baroque staircase between 1945 and 1971, long after the revolutionary government had softened its political stance, the mural still reflects the artist's arch-Stalinist views. Siqueiros was the last of the hard-line revolutionary muralists; his loyalty to the tradition is seen in this work's uncompromisingly dynamic colors and postures. ♦ M-F. República de Brasil (between González Obregón and República de Venezuela). No phone

11 **Palacio de la Inquisición (Inquisition Palace)** The much-feared Inquisition court—set up by the Catholic Church to keep dissenting citizens in line with the Spanish crown—operated in Mexico between 1571 and 1820. What you see today is a beautiful building, rebuilt in the early 18th century, which looks like an Italianate palace; it was turned over to the **Universidad de Mexico**'s medical school in 1854. Today it houses the nine-room **Museo de Medicina** (Medicine Museum), with displays of everything from pre-Hispanic herbal cures to current anticholera vaccines. There's also a reconstruction of a 19th-century apothecary's shop. ♦ Free. Daily. República de Brasil 33 (at República de Venezuela). 529.6416

12 **Plaza y Iglesia de Santo Domingo (Santo Domingo Plaza and Church)** This charming rectangular square and its church evoke the essence of Mexico City's Centro Histórico, with its mixture of traditional and modern life. In 1520 the powerful Dominican religious order chose this land as the site of its first great convent and church. The present church, finished in 1736, is a beautiful Baroque replacement of the original, which deteriorated from the unrelenting water seepage. The structure is all that remains of a large group of monastic buildings that were pulled down in the anti-Catholic purges of the mid-19th century. ♦ República de Brasil (between González Obregón and República de Perú)

Frida Fervor

J. DEL GAIZO

Frida Kahlo (1907-54) has become the best-selling Latin American painter of all time, outstripping even her husband, muralist Diego Rivera. Well known by artists, intellectuals, and collectors in her day, her work achieved public notoriety only in the 1980s. *Newsweek* dubbed her "a highbrow version of the Elvis phenomenon," and she has also been the subject of a Broadway musical. Her powerful, painful self-portraits are favorites with collectors, and one of her paintings (*Self Portrait with Loose Hair,* 1947) sold for more than $1 million, breaking the auction record for Latin American art.

Part of the fascination with Kahlo's art lies in her persona—one of independence, outspokenness, honesty, strength, and anguish—and her passionate and fascinating life in postrevolutionary Mexico. She was the friend of many major artistic and political figures, including Tina Modotti, Edward Weston, André Breton, Leon Trotsky, José Clemente Orozco, David Alfaro Siqueiros, and, of course, Rivera. Her paintings, however, are what have inspired her cultlike following. Her ability to reveal her soul on canvas has turned her into a modern feminist icon.

Born in **Coyoacán** to a German-born photographer father and Mexican mother, Kahlo began painting in her teens, already vowing to marry Rivera, 20 years her senior. After surviving polio as a child, she later saw her dreams slip away when, at the age of 19, her backbone, pelvis, and leg were shattered in a bus crash. She slowly recovered, but was never able to have children (although she never stopped trying), and she spent many years bedridden. To strengthen her spine, she wore binding corsets, and the continual pain she suffered from her injuries is one of the subjects of her paintings, which feature such harrowing images as her own face studded with nails, circlets of thorns around her neck, and her spine depicted as a crumbling Greek column.

Although surprisingly few of Kahlo's works are on view in **Mexico City,** her enchanting house in Coyoacán is open to the public (Londres 247, at Allende, 554.5999). Other places to see her work are in the studio she shared with Rivera, **Museo Estudio Diego Rivera** (Diego Rivera and Av Altavista, San Angel, 616.0996) and the **Museo de Arte Moderno** (Paseo de la Reforma and Calzada Mahatma Gandhi, Bosque de Chapultepec, 211.8045). All three are open Tuesday through Sunday and charge admission. Kahlo's likeness also appears in many of Rivera's murals, most prominently in those in the **Palacio Nacional.** To learn more about her life, read *Frida,* by Hayden Herrera, or Marta Zamora's *Frida Kahlo: The Brush of Anguish.*

13 Portal de los Evangelistas (Portal of the Evangelists) Along the west side of the Plaza Santo Domingo runs an arcade of makeshift stalls where modern-day public scribes carry on the ancient tradition of assisting illiterates who want help writing their love letters and legal documents. ♦ Plaza de Santo Domingo (between González Obregón and Belisario Domínguez)

Hostería de Santo Domingo

14 Hostería de Santo Domingo ★★★$$
This very traditional lunchtime restaurant has been open for more than a century and is busiest on weekends, when extended families come to eat and listen to strolling musicians. The speciality here is *chile en nogada* (*poblano* chili peppers stuffed with dried fruits, nuts, and meat, and covered with a rich cream sauce and pomegranate seeds). Traditionally eaten from August through September, the dish is available here year-round. ♦ Mexican ♦ Daily breakfast, lunch, and dinner. Belisario Domínguez 72 (at República de Chile). 510.1434

15 Cicero Centenario ★★★★$$$$
Downtown's hippest restaurant is located in a restored 17th-century mansion. Victorian and colonial-era antiques decorate the many dining rooms and the streetside cantina, a popular after-work watering hole. The menu features some of the best regional Mexican cuisine in the city, from such ordinary (yet delicious) offerings as guacamole and *chicharrón* (fried pork skins) to *pollo en pipián verde* (chicken in pumpkin seed sauce) and dishes featuring different versions of mole sauce. ♦ Mexican ♦ M-Sa lunch and dinner. Reservations recommended. República de Cuba 79 (between República de Chile and Allende). 521.7866. Also at: Londres 195 (between Génova and Amberes), Zona Rosa. 533.3800

16 Hotel Catedral $ A real find for those who want to stay close to the Zócalo, this six-story inn has 116 surprisingly quiet rooms with one or two double beds and TVs with local channels. Rooms on the top floor have a good view of the **Catedral Metropolitana** (at right), and some have tubs as well as showers. The restaurant is popular with local businesspeople, and there's a guarded parking lot next door, handy for guests traveling by car. ♦ Donceles 95 (between República de Argentina and República de Brasil). 521.6183, 521.8581; fax 512.4344

17 Bar León Fans of Latin music will find few better places in the city to go dancing. From the nondescript entrance, head into the dance hall to sweat, drink, and dance the night away. ♦ Cover. M-Sa until 3AM. República de Brasil and Donceles. 510.3093

18 Monte de Piedad (National Pawnshop) This four-story pawnshop was founded in 1775 as a charitable institution by Romero de Torres, one of the country's richest silver-mine owners. The site, once home to Aztec palaces, is now invaded by browsers and brokers looking through room after room of family junk and treasures. Since the economic crisis in Mexico, the shop has seen a sharp increase in business, as people of all financial backgrounds seek to raise some extra cash. ♦ M-Sa. Monte de Piedad 7 (at 5 de Mayo). 518.2006

19 Catedral Metropolitana (Metropolitan Cathedral) Mexico City's main cathedral (pictured on page 270) took 250 years to complete—and it shows. It is the largest cathedral in Mexico, although certainly not its most beautiful, displaying a hodgepodge of styles imposed by the many architects involved in the design. It was begun in 1573 as a Baroque copy of Salamanca's 16th-century cathedral. In the late 18th century, the Spanish architect **Manuel Tolsá** adorned the central doorway with a clock and sculptures representing faith, hope, and charity. There are three grand doorways leading into the dimly lit interior. The 390-footlong vaultlike space has 16 small chapels, including one dedicated to St. Isidro Labrador (the Black Christ) and one to the miraculous Virgin. The most marvelous of them all is the Baroque **Chapel of the Kings** at the end of the nave; this gilt altarpiece was completed in 1737 after seven years of work by Sevillian craft worker Jeronimo de Balbas, who was known throughout Spanish dominions as the master of his day. The choir is set in the middle of the nave and houses two 3,000-pipe organs constructed with metalwork from the city of Macao. Underneath it is a crypt that holds more than 3,000 bodies, including most of Mexico's archbishops. ♦ Zócalo (between Seminario and Monte de Piedad)

Within the Catedral Metropolitana:

El Sagrario (Sacristy) This later addition to the eastern side of the cathedral shows the Andalusian influences of its architect, **Lorenzo Rodríguez,** who labored from 1749 to 1760 on the intricate Baroque facade. Both the cathedral and the sacristy were built on the marshy ground of former lake beds, and each has tilted as it sinks deeper and deeper into the bog; reinforcement efforts are under way continually.

20 Majestic $$ Overlooking the square, this building that looks like a former Spanish palace, but dates from the early 20th century, is one of the most charming and well-placed hotels in the city, with a stone fountain in the lobby, a glass roof over the central courtyard, and heavy carved wooden doors and decorative tiles throughout. The 85 guest rooms, however, are modern in style. Some face the Zócalo and offer an interesting vantage point on the activity below (except during holidays, when the view is obscured by lighted decorations that are hung over the windows). ♦ Francisco I. Madero 73 (at Zócalo). 521.8600, 800/528.1234; fax 512.6262

Within the Majestic:

Majestic Restaurant ★★★$$ Even if you're not a guest at the hotel, don't miss the top-floor terrace restaurant, which has both a superb view of the Zócalo and the best Sunday brunch in Mexico. Eggs can be prepared in front of you, tortillas are hand-patted to order, and the jugs of fresh fruit juices are constantly refilled. Delicious *chilaquiles* (tortillas fried with eggs and chicken in sauce) and *machaca* (dried beef) are kept warm on hot plates. The terrace fills quickly on weekend mornings, and the inside dining room isn't nearly as interesting as the view from outside, so try to arrive early. ♦ Mexican ♦ Daily breakfast, lunch, and dinner. Seventh floor. 521.8600

GRAN HOTEL

21 Gran Hotel de Cuidad de Mexico $$$ One of only two hotels right on the Zócalo, this 125-room hostelry is a fun place to stay if you want to be in the center of the action. The elegant Art Nouveau building, complete with a stained-glass dome by Jacques Gruber, was originally built as a department store at the turn of the century; the wrought-iron elevators, sweeping terraced floors, and bird cages all seem more appropriate for a Parisian hotel. The rooms are gradually being refurbished and vary considerably in style and view. Some face the walls of other buildings; some face the Zócalo. The fourth-floor rooftop restaurant looks out over the square, while the first-floor **Del Centro** restaurant, run by the steak house chain Delmonico's, is a favorite lunch spot for professionals and politicians. ♦ 16 de Septiembre 82 (at Zócalo). 510.4040; fax 512.6772

22 Palacio de Hierro (Iron Palace) One of Mexico City's two oldest department stores, it has been competing with its rival **Liverpool** on the same intersection for more than a century. Both were established by Frenchmen and are still partially owned by their founding families, although their style is now more north-of-the-border than European. This store was constructed of iron (hence its name), and the central gallery has a stained-glass roof and a wrought-iron balcony, all the rage in the 1870s. Selling a good range of US and Mexican brand names, it is considered expensive by local standards. There are other branches around town, all of which are bigger, but not such architectural jewels. ♦ Daily. 20 de Noviembre 3 (at Venustiano Carranza). 747.3108

23 Corte Suprema de Justicia (Supreme Court of Justice) President Lázaro Cárdenas commissioned this structure as the court building in 1935, although it looks more like a colonial palace. Cárdenas offered the job of painting the murals to José Clemente Orozco, one of the three great postrevolutionary muralists. Orozco's highly ironic portrait, *Injustice of Justice* (1941), at the top of the stairs, proved too much even for Cárdenas's liberal government, and the rest of the commission was handed over to US artist George Biddle, who painted *War* (1945) at the library's entrance. ♦ Free. M-F. Pino Suárez (between Venustiano Carranza and Moneda). No phone

24 Iglesia y Hospital de Jésus (Church and Hospital of Jesus) A hospital and church mark the site where Montezuma, the Aztec emperor, and Hernán Cortés, the Spanish conqueror, are said to have met for the first time. To commemorate the occasion, Cortés ordered that the first Mexican hospital be built here in 1524 and that his remains be interred in one of the church walls (to the left of the chancel). The choir loft was painted from 1942 to 1944, not with the usual religious allegory, but with José Clemente Orozco's *Apocalypse,* a bold artistic commentary on World War II. ♦ República de El Salvador and Pino Suárez

25 Museo de la Ciudad de Mexico (Mexico City Museum) The Counts of Calimaya, former owners of this elegant colonial palace, borrowed from Aztec sculpture and incorporated a serpent's head into the building's cornerstone. Today this beautiful structure is a stuffy, historical museum of the city, an important project executed without much imagination. One of the few highlights is the top-floor studio of landscape painter Joaquin Clausell (1886-1935). Here he cleaned his brushes on the walls, creating from the strokes a variation on his watercolors, which show the halcyon, smog-free days of Mexico City in all its glory. ♦ Free. Tu-Su. Pino Suárez 30 (at República de El Salvador). 542.0487

Restaurants/Clubs: Red   **Hotels:** Blue
Shops/♥ Outdoors: Green   **Sights/Culture:** Black

¿Habla Español?

Relax. Mexicans don't assume that gringos speak Spanish, and most will be pleased of you try. Here are some basics to get you started.

Hello, Good-Bye, and Other Basics

Good morning	*Buenos días*
Good afternoon	*Buenas tardes*
Good evening	*Buenas noches*
How are you?	*¿Cómo está usted?*
Good-bye	*Adiós*
Yes	*Sí*
No	*No*
Please	*Por favor*
Thank you	*Gracias*
You're welcome	*De nada*
I beg your pardon/	*¿Perdón?/*
Excuse me	*Con permiso*
I'm sorry	*Lo siento*
I don't speak Spanish.	*No hablo español.*
Do you speak English?	*¿Habla usted inglés?*
I don't understand.	*No comprendo/* *No entiendo.*
Do you understand?	*¿Comprende?/¿Entiende?*
More slowly, please.	*Más lento, por favor.*
I don't know.	*No sé.*
My name is . . .	*Me llamo . . .*
What is your name?	*¿Cómo se llama?*
miss	*señorita*
madame, ma'am	*señora*
mister	*señor*
good	*bueno/a*
bad	*malo/a*
open	*abierto/a*
closed	*cerrado/a*
entrance	*la entrada*
exit	*la salida*
push	*empujar*
pull	*jalar*
What time does it open/close	*¿A qué hora se abre/cierra?*
today	*hoy*
tomorrow	*mañana*
yesterday	*ayer*
week	*la semana*
month	*el mes*
year	*el año*

Hotel Talk

I have a reservation.	*Tengo una reservación.*
I would like	*Quisiera*
a double room	*una habitación doble*
a quiet room	*una habitación tranquila*
with (private) bath	*con baño (privado)*
with air-conditioning	*con aire acondicionado*

Does that price include breakfast? taxes?	*¿Está incluído en el precio el desayuno? los impuestos?*
Do you accept traveler's checks?	*¿Acepta usted cheques de viajero?*
Do you accept credit cards?	*¿Acepta tarjetas de crédito?*

Restaurant Repartee

Waiter!	*¡Mesero!/¡Camarero!*
I would like	*Quisiera*
a menu	*una carta*
a glass of	*un vaso de*
a bottle of	*una botella de*
The check, please.	*La cuenta, por favor.*
Is a service charge included?	*¿Está incluído el servicio?*
I think there is a mistake in the bill.	*Creo que hay un error en la cuenta.*
lunch	*la comida*
dinner	*la cena*
tip	*la propina*
bread	*el pan*
butter	*la mantequilla*
pepper	*la pimienta*
salt	*el sal*
sugar	*el azúcar*
soup	*la sopa*
salad	*la ensalada*
vegetables	*las verduras/vegetales*
cheese	*el queso*
beans	*los frijoles*
meat	*la carne*
chicken	*el pollo*
veal	*la ternera*
fish	*el pescado*
seafood, shellfish	*los mariscos*
pork	*la carne de cerdo/ de puerco*
ham	*el jamón*
dessert	*el postre*

As You Like It

cold	*frío/a*
hot	*caliente*
sweet	*dulce*
dry	*seco/a*
broiled, roasted	*asado/a*
baked	*horneado/a*
boiled	*hervido/a*
fried	*frito/a*
raw	*crudo/a*
rare	*jugoso/a*
medium	*medio/a*
well done	*bien cocido/a*
spicy	*picante*

Thirsty No More

black coffee	un café negro
"American-style" coffee	un café americano
coffee with hot milk	un café con leche
milk	la leche
tea	un té
fruit juice	un jugo de fruta
water	el agua
purified water	la agua purificada
mineral water	una agua mineral
ice	el hielo
without ice	sin hielo
beer	una cerveza
red wine	un vino tinto
white wine	un vino blanco

Sizing It Up

How much does this cost?	¿Cuánto cuesta esto?
inexpensive	barato/a
expensive	caro/a
large	grande
small	pequeño/a
long	largo/a
short	corto/a
old	viejo/a
new	nuevo/a
used	usado/a
this one	esto
a little	un poquito
a lot	mucho

On the Move

north	norte
south	sur
east	este
west	oeste
right	derecho/a
left	izquierdo/a
highway	la carretera/autopista
gas station	la gasolinera
Go straight ahead.	Siga todo derecho.
here	aquí
there	allí
bus stop	la parada de autobuses
bus station	el estación de autobuses
train station	el estación de ferrocarril
subway station	el estación de metro
airport	el aeropuerto
tourist information	información turística
map	una mapa
one-way ticket	un boleto de ida
round-trip ticket	un boleto de ida y vuelta
first class	primera clase
second class	segunda clase
smoking	fumar
no smoking	no fumar
Does this train go to. . . ?	¿Va este tren a. . . ?
Does this bus go to. . . ?	¿Va este autobús a. . . ?
Where is/are. . . ?	¿Dónde está/estan. . . ?
How far is it here to. . . ?	¿Qué distancia hay from desde aquí hasta. . . ?

The Bare Necessities

aspirin	la aspirina
Band-Aids	unas curitas
barbershop	la peluquería
beauty shop	la salón de belleza
condom	un condón
dry cleaner	la tintorería
laundromat, laundry	la lavandería
post office	el correo
postage stamps	unas estampillas, timbres
postcard	una tarjeta postal
letter	una carta
sanitary napkins	unas toallas femininas
shampoo	el champú
shaving cream	la espuma/ crema de afeitar
soap	el jabón
tampons	unos tampones
tissues	un pañuelo de papel/Kleenex
toilet paper	el papel higiénico
toothpaste	la pasta de dientes
Where is the bathroom?	¿Dónde está el baño?
Where are the toilets?	¿Dónde están los sanitarios?
Men's Room	Caballeros/Señores
Women's Room	Damas/Señoras

Days of the Week (usually lowercased in Spanish)

Monday	Lunes
Tuesday	Martes
Wednesday	Miércoles
Thursday	Jueves
Friday	Viernes
Saturday	Sábado
Sunday	Domingo

Numbers

zero	cero
one	uno
two	dos
three	tres
four	cuatro
five	cinco
six	seis
seven	siete
eight	ocho
nine	nueve
ten	diez

26 Mercado La Merced This vast produce center covers several streets east of the Zócalo and is Mexico City's biggest market. If you don't see what you want here, most likely it can't be found anywhere. To get there, take the metro (Line 1) and hop off at the **Merced** station. Sunday is the busiest day. Keep a close watch on your wallet and purse here. ♦ Daily. Bounded by Roldán and Jesús María, and República de Uruguay and Manzanares

27 Museo Charrería The most Mexican of sports, *charrería* (much like a rodeo, but with more pomp and circumstance) is honored here in the former **Montserrat Church,** a Baroque 18th-century construction. Spurs, saddles, spangled bolero jackets, and tight trousers embroidered with gold and silver, as well as historical documents, pistols, and wide-brimmed sombreros are all on display. ♦ Free. M-F. Isabel la Católica 108 (between Nezahualcóyotl and José María Izazaga). 709.4838

28 Hotel Gillow $ The location of this budget travelers' hangout, midway between the Zócalo and the **Alameda** (see page 227), couldn't be better, and the price can't be beat. The 110 rooms are large and comfy, and many have new tile and marble bathrooms and new carpets and drapes. Most windows face walls or an air shaft, but that does cut down on the street noise. The interior courtyard and fountain are covered with a glass skylight, and tables and chairs are scattered about for lounging. There is a coffee shop on the first floor. ♦ Isabel la Católica 17 (between Francisco I. Madero and 5 de Mayo). 518.1440; fax 512.2078

29 Ritz $ Although in the heart of the city, this attractive Art Deco hotel with 125 rooms is quiet and peaceful, offering a pleasant restaurant and a family atmosphere. The hotel uses the reservation facilities of the Best Western chain and is popular with those traveling on business. ♦ Francisco I. Madero 30 (between Isabel la Católica and Bolívar). 518.1340, 800/528.1234; fax 518.3466

30 Palacio de Iturbide The first palace built on this spot belonged to one of the original Spanish conquerors. Then in 1779 the Mexican architect **Francisco Guerrero y Torres** (1727-92) was commissioned to build the most sumptuous palace in Mexico City to remind the owner, Don Pedro de Moncada, of his family home in Palermo, Italy. A masterpiece of civil Baroque architecture, the facade is constructed of *tezontle* (a reddish volcanic stone) interspersed with the local gray stone; the two materials complement each other and provide a surface for the elaborate sculptured adornments. In 1821 the owner offered the palace to the short-lived and flamboyant hero of the Independence movement, Agustín Iturbide, who accepted the office of emperor from the palace's

balcony. It now belongs to the Banamex banking corporation, which uses the fine interior patio to exhibit its superb art collection; the gallery is open to the public. There is also a small shop to the right of the main doorway selling art books (some are in English) and posters. ♦ Free. M-F; also Sa-Su when there's a special exhibit in the gallery. Francisco I. Madero 17 (between Bolívar and Gante). 518.2187

31 Iglesia de San Francisco Construction of this important Franciscan church was begun in 1524, shortly after the conquest. Its monastery was demolished according to the anticlerical laws of the 19th century, and the addition of two wide streets cut swaths through the property, easing access to the congested downtown. Still, it is a good example of the exuberant Churrigueresque architectural style, its facade studded with reliefs and sculptures. Set off the street in a courtyard, this is also one of the most peaceful places to escape from the street bustle. ♦ Francisco I. Madero (between Gante and Eje Central)

32 Pastelería Ideal This immensely popular pastry shop takes up several floors and is an institution with a long history. In addition to the mind-boggling array of mouthwatering concoctions, there are fabulous cakes for *quinceañeras* (elaborate 15th-birthday celebrations), street parties, first communions, and weddings. On the second floor you can see these towering creations with 12 or more tiers, a display of Mexican kitsch in its purest form. ♦ Daily. 16 de Septiembre 18 (between Gante and Eje Central). 510.0052

There is one car for every 5 residents in Mexico City, one car for every 2.5 inhabitants in Madrid, and one car for every 0.8 persons in Los Angeles.

33 Prendes ★★$$ Typical of the best of the Centro Histórico, this restaurant relies on nostalgia and a tradition that dates back to 1892, rather than the menu, to lure the crowds. The walls are lined with murals (by the important revolutionary painter Dr. Atl, and by Julio Castellanos, who is known for his metaphysical drawings) of celebrities and former patrons such as Pancho Villa and Walt Disney. The politicians and political watchers have all since moved on to other pastures, but the restaurant is still packed at lunchtime and on Sunday, when the house special, *paella valenciana*, is served. ◆ Mexican ◆ Daily lunch and dinner. 16 de Septiembre 10 (between Gante and Eje Central). 512.7517

34 La Torre Latinoamericana (Latin American Tower) A famous landmark since 1956, this glass-needle tower—47 floors and 532 feet high—was the first Mexican structure to be built on an earthquake-resistant foundation and has survived the subsequent tremors unscathed. There is a top-floor lookout and a restaurant, **Muralto,** which serves lunch and dinner. Unfortunately seldom is the air clear enough to see the city without its cap of smog; the view is often more dazzling at night. ◆ Admission. Daily. Eje Central and Francisco I. Madero. 510.2545

35 Sanborn's Casa de los Azulejos ★★$$ Legend has it that this structure was built after a father bet his wild son that he would never earn enough money to build a house of tiles. How the son proved him wrong! The Pueblan tile-covered building, constructed in the 1730s, was once the home of the Counts of the Valley of Orizaba and has been a drugstore with a restaurant and soda fountain since 1903. The dining room is a great place to consume hefty servings of Mexican staples, including the wonderful *chilaquiles* (tortillas fried with eggs and chicken in sauce). In the restaurant's stairwell is a fine example of artist José Clemente Orozco's early work, the mural *Omniscience* (1925). **Sanborn's** is also a department store of sorts, with a pharmacy, an excellent newsstand, and a fine bakery and candy counter. ◆ Mexican ◆ Daily breakfast, lunch, and dinner. Francisco I. Madero 4 (at Condesa Marconi). 512.2300. Also at: Niza and Hamburgo, Zona Rosa. 525.3741

36 Bar L'Opera ★★★$$ For a taste of Belle Epoque Mexico, spend an evening at this wonderful after-theater restaurant, where you can enjoy drinks at the splendid bar or have a full meal. The food isn't great (except for the *huachinangoà la veracruzana*, with tomatoes and onions), but the atmosphere is, with street musicians and organ-grinders serenading diners in the midst of magnificent turn-of-the-century decor. Service is formal, and the old-fashioned waiters would never dream of giving the bill to a woman. Indeed, until 1975, women weren't admitted at all. ◆ Mexican/French ◆ Daily lunch and dinner. 5 de Mayo 10 (at Filomeno Mata). 512.8959

37 Alameda Named after the *alamos* (poplars) that once grew here, this place was built on drained marshes in the 16th century as an elegant park for Spanish nobles. Later it became the site of Inquisition burnings. Again a park, it's now one of the most popular spots in the city on Sunday, when it fills with families, young lovers who meet here to woo without parental supervision, popcorn vendors, cotton candy peddlers, and men who sell caged birds, carrying long poles that can hold up to 30 cages at a time. ◆ Bounded by Angela Peralta and Dr. Mora, and Avs Juárez and Hidalgo

38 Palacio Nacional de Bellas Artes (National Palace of Fine Arts) Known by locals simply as "Bellas Artes," this huge theater complex took 30 years to build and combines Art Nouveau design on the outside and Art Deco inside, both liberally punctuated by pre-Hispanic motifs. **Adam Boari,** the Italian architect, began work on the Carrara marble exterior at the turn of the century, but his plans fell victim to the 1910 revolution.

Palacio Nacional de Bellas Artes

Federico Mariscal completed the interior in 1932. Many of Mexico's foremost muralists were invited to paint the walls of the upper floors: Rufino Tamayo worked on the second floor between 1952 and 1953 after the three giants—Diego Rivera, David Alfaro Siqueiros, and José Clemente Orozco—had completed their third-floor murals. Rivera was originally commissioned to paint *Man at the Crossroads* for New York City's Rockefeller Center; horrified at the mural's socialist undercurrents, the sponsors destroyed it. Rivera, undaunted, made this copy from his drawings.

The Tiffany crystal stage curtain shows the local volcanoes Ixtaccíhuatl and Popocatépetl and is normally displayed before appearances by the renowned **Ballet Folklórico.** The gardens in front of the building, destroyed in 1994 during the installation of an underground parking facility, have been replanted now that the lot is complete. ♦ Free; admission for shows. Murals: Tu-Su. Shows: W night, Su morning and night. Tickets to the shows are sold 48 hours in advance at the palace or at most hotels and travel agencies. Av Juárez (between Eje Central and Angela Peralta). 521.9225, 521.3633

Within the Palacio Nacional de Bellas Artes:

Bookshop This extensive bookshop sells boxed sets of Frida Kahlo and Diego Rivera memorabilia, as well as the excellent Education Ministry publications (available in Spanish only, although some are worth buying for the pictures alone) at very low prices. With posters, piles of books, diaries, and a variety of gifts, it is a great place to find a memento of Mexico's rich artistic past. ♦ Daily. 521.9760

Café del Palacio ★★$$ Take a moment to sit here quietly after viewing the palace's overwhelming murals. This small cafe by the entrance to the bookstore is the perfect spot to sip a cappuccino, enjoy a small salad or a sweet, or write postcards (you can mail them right across the street). ♦ Cafe ♦ Tu-Su lunch and dinner. 521.0807

39 Dirección General de Correos (Post Office) Built in 1902 by Italian-born architect **Adam Boari,** this Florentine-style structure is still the city's chief post office. There is a small **Museo Postal y Biblioteca** (Postal Museum

and Library) on the second floor. ♦ Free. M-F. Eje Central and Tacuba. 510.2999

40 Museo Nacional de Arte (National Museum of Art) Italian architectural tastes influenced much of the construction in turn-of-the-century Mexico City, and it was the Italian architect **Silvio Contri** who designed this building as the **Palace of Communications and Public Works** between 1904 and 1911. A statue of King Carlos IV of Spain astride a horse, sculpted by Manuel Tolsá, sits in front of the structure; locals call it *El Caballito* (The Little Horse).

Today the building houses Mexico's greatest 19th- and 20th-century works of art. The 20th-century collection is outstanding, chronicling the period when Mexicans began creating for themselves and not for European patrons. Pieces range from the acidic political critiques of Julio Ruelas and José Guadalupe Posada to the drawings and paintings of the muralists, the anguished self-portraits of Frida Kahlo, and works of young contemporary artists. ♦ Admission. Tu-Su. Plaza Tolsá and Tacuba. 512.7320

40 Los Girasoles ★★★$$$ Take a seat at one of the sidewalk tables at this trendy eatery before the traditional lunch hour (2PM) and settle back to enjoy a fabulous show. The restaurant's owners include several local media celebrities who rarely show up now that the place has gained a name for itself. The menu features traditional Mexican dishes, including *cochinita pibil* (pork baked in banana leaves), *chapulines* (fried grasshoppers), chicken with mole, and red snapper with a tomato-based sauce. Choose a beer from the same region as your main course, a shot of smooth tequila, or a nonalcoholic *limonada* (lemonade). If the sidewalk terrace is busy you may be banished to one of the dining rooms inside the restored colonial house. ♦ Mexican ♦ Daily lunch and dinner. Reservations recommended for lunch. Plaza Tolsá 8 (at Tacuba). 510.0630

41 Café de Tacuba ★★★$$ Housed in an old convent, this long-standing cafe and restaurant was established in 1912 and has kept its original, attractive tiled walls. A favorite after-theater spot, it offers Mexican favorites such as tamales, *chilaquiles* (tortillas fried with eggs and chicken in sauce), and enchiladas, plus coffee and cakes, which are great for capping off a busy day. The long dining room becomes noisy during lunchtime, when businesspeople wait in line for a seat and everyone seems to be table hopping. It's best to arrive unfashionably early (before 2PM) for lunch. ♦ Mexican ♦ Daily breakfast, lunch, and dinner. Tacuba 28 (at Allende). 518.4950

42 Teatro de la Ciudad (City Theater) Founded in 1912, this popular theater presents everything from revue shows to international opera companies. The resident folk dance company, the **Ballet Folklórico Nacional de México,** rivals the troupe that performs at the **Bellas Artes;** both performances are worth seeing. For performance listings see *The News,* the English-language daily paper. At press time the theater was closed until further notice, but the troupe will perform at other venues in the city. ♦ Tickets available at the box office M-F, and at hotel tour desks. For information on performance locations: 294.4928. Donceles 36 (between República de Chile and Allende). 510.2197

43 Plaza Garibaldi This square is surrounded by several great bars and clubs, but the big attraction takes place every evening from 7PM to 2AM and all day Sunday, when mariachi bands congregate to play their wailing songs of love and treachery for anyone willing to pay. Often hired to serenade girlfriends or celebrate marriages and birthdays, mariachis are professionals and don't come cheap; they are an indispensable part of macho Mexican culture, in which the man is the victim of a faithless woman. The groups consist of violin, trumpet, and guitar players and a heart-wrenching vocalist. Any lover worth his salt should know the songs so well that he will sing along (foreigners will be forgiven for their ignorance). The plaza is most fun late at night, but although the safety situation has been somewhat improved by gas lamp–style street lights around the plaza, this neighborhood is still not a place to wander around at night. Take a cab back to your hotel, preferably with a group. Several blocks south of the plaza, on busy Eje Central, young mariachis seek business from passing motorists by jumping into traffic in their tight, black bolero jackets and trousers to convince the drivers of their prowess. ♦ Eje Central (between República de Perú and República de Honduras)

44 Museo Nacional de la Estampa (National Museum of Printmaking) The art of printmaking, particularly lithography and etching, reached its peak in Mexico during the last century with the advent of newspaper cartoons, caricatures, and spoofs. Such works quickly became the nation's most accurate and acerbic forms of political commentary, as can be seen in the work of José Guadalupe Posada on the second floor of this museum. Also displayed here are silkscreen prints and engravings. There's hardly room to do the art form justice, since the building is small and dedicates half of its space to temporary exhibits of works by young printmakers and retrospectives on the masters, but it does provide a thought-provoking introduction. Set in a courtyard between two churches that sink visibly deeper into the subsoil every year, the museum has managed to stand its ground. ♦ Admission. Tu-Su. Pl de la Santa Veracruz (between Av Hidalgo and Santa Veracruz). 510.4905

45 Museo Franz Mayer Formerly the **Hospital of San Juan de Dios** and later an orphanage, this elegant 16th-century mansion has been converted into one of the city's finest museums, housing the private collection bequeathed to Mexico by German art enthusiast Franz Mayer upon his death in 1975. Although cited as a collection of "applied art," in which all the pieces were practical and meant for everyday use, the exhibits are far from mundane. You'll get a glimpse into the lifestyle of the ruling classes of the colonial era who had the means to gather the best products of the known world, including Talavera ceramics, silks and screens from China, solid silver altarpieces, Philippine marquetry, and English mahogany furniture. There's also a collection of fine arts. ♦ Admission; free Sunday. Tu-Su. Pl de la Santa Veracruz (between Av Hidalgo and Santa Veracruz). 518.2267

Within the Museo Franz Mayer:

Bookshop The museum boasts a small but well-supplied bookstore with a broad selection of art magazines, architectural tomes, elegant coffee-table books, postcards, and guides, some in English. ♦ Tu-Su. 518.2267

El Patio ★★$ This lovely cafe sits on a beautiful and breezy colonial courtyard. It's a calm place to recover from museum fatigue while sipping a cappuccino, indulging in a sweet, or lunching on a salad and rolls, all to the strains of classical music. ♦ Cafe ♦ Tu-Su lunch. 518.2267

46 Best Western Hotel de Cortés $$ This pleasant hotel has 29 rooms and suites set around a charming colonial-style patio. One of the nicest lodging places in the **Alameda** area, it has been modernized in ways that make it more comfortable without sacrificing the original ambience. The windows facing the busy street, for example, are double-glazed to seal out much of the noise, and the large bathrooms have marble sinks and powerful showers. The Baroque stone structure was originally built in the 18th century as the **Hospice de San Nicolás de Tolentino,** a guest house for Augustinian monks; atop the front gateway is a stone figure of San Tomás de Villanueva, patron saint of the needy. The government confiscated the building from the Catholic Church after the 1910 revolution, and it became a private hotel in 1943. The courtyard restaurant is a pleasant spot for a break from the city streets. This hostelry is considered a real find by many culture-oriented travelers, and it fills up quickly. ♦ Av Hidalgo 85 (at Paseo de la Reforma). 518.2121, 800/528.1234; fax 512.1863

47 Pinacoteca Virreinal de San Diego (Viceregal Art Gallery of San Diego) The former **Convent of San Diego** houses an impressive museum of 16th- and 17th-century ecclesiastical art. The collection of works by colonial masters includes pieces by Oaxacan-born artist Miguel Cabrera, who, between 1740 and 1765, painted some of Mexico's greatest religious art. ♦ Admission; free Sunday. Tu-Su. Dr. Mora 7 (between Colón and Av Hidalgo). 510.2793

48 Museo Mural Diego Rivera (Diego Rivera Mural Museum) This museum was built specifically for Rivera's huge mural *A Sunday Afternoon in the Alameda,* formerly housed in the **Hotel Prado,** which was destroyed after the 1985 earthquake. Fortunately, the mural remained undamaged and was carefully moved across Avenida Juárez to a new home overlooking its subject—the **Alameda.** Among the many people depicted enjoying the park are the young artist himself, whose portrait is between the figures of his wife, artist Frida Kahlo, and a skeletal nobleman. Behind and around the central figures are characters from Mexico's glorious and not-so-glorious past, including former presidents, emperors, enemies, and heroes. ♦ Admission; free Sunday. Tu-Su. Balderas and Colón. 510.2329

49 Museo Nacional de Artes e Industrias Populares (National Museum of Popular Arts) More a shop than a museum, this vast warehouse displays arts and crafts from all over the country. Everything is on sale at reasonable prices, and there's a far greater selection of unusual artwork than in the tourist shops of the Zona Rosa. Much to the disappointment of folk art collectors, who can't resist a visit here each time they're in the city, the building was closed indefinitely for extensive remodeling at press time. ♦ Av Juárez 44 (between Dolores and Luis Moya). 521.6679; fax 510.3404

50 Mercado San Juan This market hawks not only unusual cure-alls, but the best and freshest produce around. In fact, chefs from Mexico's top restaurants invariably come here to buy their ingredients, choosing from a selection that ranges from wild mushrooms and suckling pigs to exotic tropical fruits (such as the pink-fleshed *pithaya*) and *chihuahua* cheese made by Mennonites. There's also a mind-boggling array of chilies, herbs, and spices. ♦ Daily. Ayuntamiento (between Buen Tono and Marroquí)

51 Montserrat ★★$ Located just across Balderas from the **Mercado La Ciudadela,** this inexpensive, casual restaurant is a great place to stop after shopping. Different *comidas corridas* (inexpensive full meals) are offered daily, and Mexican specialties such as *pollo a la Mexicana* (chicken with a tomato, onion, and green pepper sauce) and *carne asada a la tampiqueña* (marinated beef) can be ordered off the menu. Soups, enchiladas, seafood dishes, and fresh fruit drinks are all available. ♦ Mexican ♦ Daily breakfast, lunch, and dinner. Balderas 96 (between Ernesto Pugibet and Ayuntamiento). 521.5128

52 Mercado La Ciudadela (Citadel Market) A citadel that was built by the Spanish in 1807 to hold their enemies during the War of Independence now houses a library and has lent its name to this arts-and-crafts market. With more than 300 stalls selling ceramics, glassware, masks, and a hundred other items, the market is a good choice when shopping for gifts. Overshadowed by the Zona Rosa's more accessible **Mercado Artesanía,** it tends to get overlooked, but those in the know swear the prices here are lower. Among the specialties available are huge wooden masks from the state of Guerrero depicting sirens, mermaids, animals, dragons, devils, and skeletons. A few workshops have been set up in and around the open-air market so you can see the crafts being made. ♦ Daily. Balderas and Ayuntamiento

53 Paseo de la Reforma The elegant, broad avenue commonly referred to as "Reforma" was designed in the 1860s by Carlota, wife of the short-lived Austrian emperor of Mexico, Maximilian. To the north and south there are many wonderful museums, shops, and markets that are often overlooked by tourists. ♦ Between Av Constituyentes and Canal del Norte

53 Fiesta Americana Reforma $$$ Known for its amenable service and dependable rooms, the location of this chain hotel is ideal for those who enjoy walking, since you're about midway between the Zona Rosa and the Centro Histórico on the pleasant Paseo de la Reforma. The 610-room hotel has a fully equipped health club and sauna (but no swimming pool) and four restaurants. ♦ Paseo de la Reforma 80 (at Ramírez). 705.1515, 800/343.7821; fax 705.1313

54 Monumento a la Revolución (Monument to the Revolution) At the turn of the century, an ambitious plan to build a new legislative palace was set in motion by the dictator/president Porfirio Díaz, but his project was interrupted by the 1910 revolution, which toppled him the following year. Work on the structure ceased until 1930, when its design was altered by the architect **Carlos Obregon;** later it became a monument to the revolution. Today the building houses a museum with a permanent exhibition on the history of the monument and the revolution itself. ♦ Free. Tu-F. Plaza de la República and Av Juárez. 566.1902

55 Museo de San Carlos The Neo-Classical **Buenavista Palace** was designed as a private home at the beginning of the 19th century by architect **Manuel Tolsá.** Emperor Maximilian handed it over to General Bazaine and his French troops in 1865. In 1968 the beautiful palace became a museum housing a large and impressive collection of European masters from the 14th to the 19th centuries, including works by Berruguete, Botticelli, Cranach the Elder, Rubens, Goya, and Reynolds. ♦ Admission; free Sunday. M, W-Su. Puente de Alvarado 50 (at Ramos Arizpe). 566.8522

Zona Rosa

The Zona Rosa (Pink Zone) was once the city's ritziest district, with elegant town houses, smart shops, and exclusive restaurants. In the 1970s and 1980s it degenerated into a shadow of its former self, but today it is undergoing a renaissance—some streets have been closed to traffic and filled with modern sculptures and trendy cafes, and trees have been planted everywhere. Only a few streets wide and a few deep, this tiny area boasts boutiques, antiques shops, and shopping malls linking one street to another. It's just a short journey along the **Paseo de la Reforma** to all the main sights, and the restaurants have more international offerings than in the rest of Mexico City. The area is at its best after 8PM, when the city's best-dressed denizens stroll the sidewalks and claim the best tables at world-class restaurants.

56 Ballet Teatro del Espacio (Ballet Theater of the Space) Zona Rosa's dance theater is the home of one of the best companies in Mexico, under the direction of Gladiola Orozco and Michel Descombey. Performances and contemporary dance classes are offered. ♦ Admission. Performances: Th-Sa. Hamburgo 218 (between Varsovia and Praga). 207.3729

57 Westin Galería Plaza $$$ This deluxe, refined hotel with 450 rooms and suites provides comfort, quiet, and top-notch service within a block of Reforma and the landmark **El Angel** monument. The rooms are among the

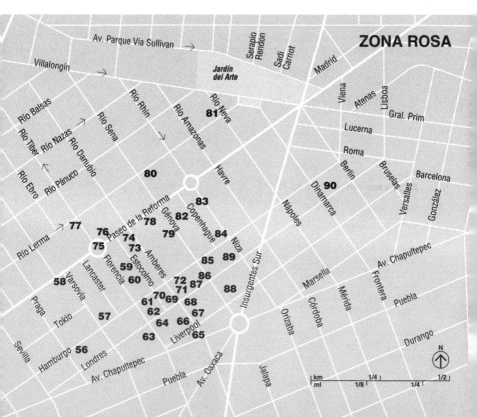

ZONA ROSA

nicest in the city, decorated in pastels with light wood furnishings, and have hair dryers, lighted makeup mirrors, in-room safes, and remote-controlled TVs. One floor is reserved for nonsmokers. Other pluses include an executive section with fax machines in the rooms, three international restaurants, a rooftop pool, and a breezy lobby. ♦ Hamburgo 195 (between Lancaster and Varsovia). 211.0014, 800/228.3000; fax 207.5867

58 Yug ★★★$ Don't let the name deter you from stopping in for granola and homemade yogurt with mango and papaya juices, or the creamed spinach soup, which soothes the shakiest stomach. The enormous menu includes inexpensive whole-wheat sandwiches and superhealthful salads of alfalfa, carrots, watercress, and button mushrooms. Vegans be forewarned: Mayonnaise and creamy salad dressings accompany everything. ♦ Vegetarian ♦ M-Sa breakfast, lunch, and dinner; Su lunch and dinner. Varsovia 3 (at Paseo de la Reforma). 533.3296

59 Tourist Help–Procuraduria General de Justicia del Distrito Federal The narrow house built by **Rafael Quintanilla** in 1930 is the beleaguered tourist's refuge. Open 24 hours a day year-round, the office's English-speaking public prosecutors can help you report crimes, such as theft, and fill out forms you will need to make claims with insurance companies. ♦ Daily 24 hours. Florencia 20 (between Hamburgo and Paseo de la Reforma). 625.7020. Also at: República de Argentina 14 (at San Ildefonso), Centro Histórico. 625.8761

60 Coloniart This is the best of a cluster of antiques stores on pretty and quiet Estocolmo. Although the charming shop has set hours, it opens at the whim of the owners; serious collectors should call ahead to browse through the fascinating collection of crosses, crucifixes, altarpieces, Pueblan vases, and heavy Spanish furniture. ♦ M-Sa. Estocolmo 37 (between Hamburgo and Paseo de la Reforma). 514.4799, 525.8928

61 Duca d'Este ★★★$ Situated at the intersection of two busy streets, this is an elegant perch for people watching any time of day through the floor-to-ceiling windows while sipping a cup of Earl Grey and nibbling a slice of flaky apple strudel or strawberry cake. Pick up some rich butter cookies, berry tarts, or syrupy flan for an in-room treat. ♦ Cafe

♦ Daily breakfast, lunch, and dinner. Hamburgo 164B (at Florencia). 525.6374

62 Da Raffaello ★★$$ A loyal clientele packs this small Italian restaurant at lunchtime. Many come for the simple yet perfectly cooked linguine with clams. For a fine dinner, try the saltimbocca (veal medaillons with ham, mozzarella, and red wine), followed by a dessert of zabaglione Marsala. It's wise to make reservations; ask for one of the highly coveted window tables. ♦ Italian ♦ Daily lunch and dinner. Reservations recommended. Londres 165 (at Florencia). 207.7016

63 Casa de Prensa Yearning for the *Wall Street Journal* or the latest *GQ*? Peruse the excellent selection of international newspapers and magazines here, and pick up a few attractive Mexican postcards as well. ♦ Daily. Florencia 57 (between Liverpool and Londres). 525.7865

64 Mercado de Artesanías (Artisans' Market) This cornucopia of Mexican arts and crafts sells everything, including silver, serapes, pewter, ceramics, fabrics, and clothes. Spangled sombreros fight for space with hammocks. Locksmiths, butchers, grocers, and cobblers also have stalls, but the market is geared toward international tourism, and the prices and stock reflect this. A convenient place to begin and end a trip to Mexico, it gives an overview of the country's crafts, but is more expensive and less fun than buying direct from the artisans. Definitely haggle over prices here. ♦ Daily. Londres 154 (between Amberes and Florencia). No phone

65 Fonda El Refugio ★★★★$$ One of the best-recognized Mexican restaurants in the city, this place specializes in regional cuisine from throughout the country. English-speaking guests are presented a menu describing the dishes and their origins, which helps when you're faced with such offerings as *manchamanteles* (which loosely translates as "tablecloth spotters"). This dish, prepared only on Tuesday, originated in Puebla and consists of fried chicken mixed with apples, sweet potatoes, bananas, pineapples, and a red pepper sauce. To counteract the spices, order a *jarra* (pitcher) of *agua fresca* (a drink made from purified water and flowers or fruit). Coffee is prepared in the traditional *cafe de olla* style—ground beans from Chiapas are simmered in a clay pot with brown sugar, cinnamon, and cloves. The restaurant is a delight from the moment you enter the pretty cornflower-blue building; be sure to tour the premises and take note of the intricate hand-painted tiles, hand-embroidered tablecloths, and traditional pottery and glassware. ♦ Mexican ♦ Daily lunch and dinner. Reservations recommended. Liverpool 166 (at Amberes). 525.8128

66 Krystal Zona Rosa $$$$ A tall, modern, 330-room hotel with an ideal location and attentive staff, this is a great choice for both business and pleasure travelers. **Krystal Club** guests are treated to complimentary breakfasts, newspapers, and evening hors d'oeuvres, but even those in the regular rooms feel pampered by the powerful showers, firm mattresses, and evening turndown service. The outdoor pool isn't very conducive to lounging, but does come in handy for workouts. The hotel has become overwhelmingly popular with business travelers, who find the suites with fax machines and large desks perfect for setting up their temporary offices. ♦ Liverpool 155 (at Amberes). 228.9928, 800/231.9860; fax 211.3490

Within the Krystal Zona Rosa:

Kamakura ★★★$$$ A small stream runs past the front door into this Japanese garden restaurant and sushi bar filled with bamboo, polished pebbles, and brooding Buddhas. For the full experience, take a seat at one of the *teppanyaki* tables—where Spanish-speaking Japanese chefs display refined artistry in slicing and grilling vegetables, meats, and seafood on the tabletop grill—or at the long bar where sushi is prepared. Show restraint when ordering, as the portions are quite large. For the total experience, visit with a group of friends and plan to spend several hours savoring your meal, from the *cassis* and Champagne aperitif to the warm sake finish. ♦ Japanese ♦ Daily lunch and dinner. 228.9928

67 Tané Probably the best silver shop in the country, it has a well-deserved reputation for carefully crafted and beautifully designed jewelry and silver sculptures. With an exclusive storefront backed up by metal doors and a gun-toting guard at the gate, the store exudes opulence. ♦ M-Sa. Amberes 70 (between Liverpool and Londres). 511.1422

68 Quality Inn Calinda Geneve $$ Opened in 1907, this hotel is filled with character and antiques, from the manual Underwood typewriters and oil paintings on display in the lobby to the heavy wooden furnishings in the rooms. Depending on your point of view, the 320 rooms are charmingly old-fashioned or

simply out of date. Street noise can be a problem; ask to see a few rooms before you choose. **El Jardin,** the hotel's original restaurant, has been restored so stop by for a look; the iron-and-glass ceiling, brick floors, and stained-glass windows are classic remnants of the Zona Rosa's era of grandeur. ♦ Londres 130 (between Génova and Amberes). 211.0071, 800/221.2222; fax 208.7422

69 Los Castillo The Castillo brothers, famous silversmiths of Taxco, have a shop in the heart of the Zona Rosa. Although they have no workshop on site, there is a fine display of the family's work, ranging from full chess sets to moderately priced earrings and necklaces. Many of their pieces, such as silver and turquoise earrings modeled after Aztec headdresses, employ pre-Hispanic designs and semiprecious stones. ♦ M-Sa. Amberes 41 (between Londres and Hamburgo). 511.8396

70 Plaza del Angel Stone archways frame the entrance to this hacienda-style plaza linking Londres to Hamburgo (a favorite shortcut in the rainy season). Antiques shops are the main attraction, along with a few small cafes. ♦ Daily. Between Londres and Hamburgo

Within Plaza del Angel:

Mercado de Antiguedades (Antiques Market) On weekends the interior plaza becomes an open-air antiques market where vendors from outside the city come and set up their stalls. Almost everything is sold on Saturday, from Persian rugs and Pueblan ceramics to children's books featuring the cartoon character Tintin and tin trays from the 1950s. On Sunday the focus turns to antiquarian books, maps, and documents. The many antiques shops surrounding the plaza and on nearby streets are open during the week, so you can shop around and compare prices before visiting the market on the weekend. ♦ Sa-Su. No phone

Miniaturas Originally housed in a closet-size space that could barely hold three customers, the shop has moved to slightly roomier quarters. Miniature nativity scenes, *calaveras* (skeletons), and whole armies of soldiers fill glass cabinets and shelves; buyers make their selections by number and order at the counter. The miniature tableaux of everything from barroom scenes to weddings are addictive; many customers return to see what's new every time they're in the city. ♦ M-Sa. Hamburgo 150. 514.1405

All of Mexico City's public museums have free admission on Sunday, when they are packed with local families. Go early if you wish to study the exhibits in peace. Many of the museums are closed on Monday.

Maximilian and Carlota: Mexico's Martyred Monarchs

Two of the most ill-fated characters in Mexico's history are the 19th-century Austrian archduke Maximilian and his Belgian wife, Charlotte, who changed her name to the Spanish equivalent, Carlota. His life ended at the age of 35 in front of a firing squad, while she went mad in the Vatican pleading for his release, and lived the rest of her life locked up in a Belgian castle (she lived to be 87).

The young couple came to Mexico in 1863 at the bidding of both conservative Mexicans, who wanted to see a European-style monarchy replace the disorganized politicians who had run the country since 1820, and Napoléon III, who was trying to extend his empire overseas. Although Maximilian asked for a plebiscite to make sure the people wanted him for their emperor, it soon became obvious that the results had been rigged, and the Mexicans were not a bit interested in having a European ruler. No one met them upon their arrival, and Maximilian's liberal ideas (including restoring communal property to Indians and toughening child-labor laws) and his insistence on courtly manners and rigorous protocol were greeted with a surprised irritation.

Within a year, Napoléon had grown embarrassed by his puppet rulers, and, under international pressure, withdrew the French troops that were supporting them. In response, Maximilian retreated for longer and longer periods to **Cuernavaca,** where he

fathered his only child by a gardener's wife, while Carlota sought solace with the remaining imperial guard officers. Oblivious to public opinion and against common sense, they decided to stay in Mexico; Carlota returned to Europe only to beg for support. Arriving in Rome, she burst into the Vatican on the verge of madness and refused to leave (making her the only woman to spend a night there). Meanwhile, Maximilian had retreated to the city of **Queretaro,** where he hoped to find loyalists, but instead was besieged, captured, and tried.

Since Maximilian had shown no leniency to the Mexicans who had fought against his rule, they in turn showed none toward him. He was court-martialed as a traitor to Mexico and was handed the death sentence by Benito Juárez, the president-in-exile of Mexico who had been deposed by the French troops. Maximilian was killed on 19 June 1867. Carlota lived for another 60 years, insane and still claiming to be empress of Mexico.

Today, little trace of the doomed couple is visible in Mexico, except for the **Paseo de la Reforma** in **Mexico City;** Carlota had ordered this broad boulevard built to remind her homesick husband of Europe. In a grand sweep, the road leads from **Bosque de Chapultepec** to the **Alameda,** and during their brief and unhappy reign it allowed Carlota to watch her husband's carriage come and go.

71 Oficina de Turismo del Districto Federal (Federal District Tourism Office) Well positioned in the heart of the Zona Rosa, the tourist office, which has many English-speaking staffers, is ready to help with all queries. They distribute the free English-language newspaper the *Daily Bulletin,* as well as up-to-date information on hotels, restaurants, and events. ♦ Daily. Amberes 54 (at Londres). 525.9380, 525.9384; fax 525.9387

72 VIPS ★$ Forgive the ugly decor of this bookshop/cafe and enjoy being cossetted by the maternal waitresses. The menu offers hearty breakfasts, steak sandwiches, enchiladas, and *chilaquiles* (tortillas fried with eggs and chicken in sauce), plus hamburgers and salads. ♦ Mexican ♦ Daily breakfast, lunch, and dinner. Hamburgo 126 (between Génova and Amberes). 207.7094

72 Plaza Rosa A shopping mall with the latest designer clothing, sporting goods, and gift shops, as well as a couple of restaurants, this is a good place to see what's in vogue in one of the most style-conscious cities in the world. ♦ M-Sa. Hamburgo (between Génova and Amberes)

73 Galería Sergio Bustamante This bright, open gallery is the perfect setting for Bustamante's fanciful ceramic sculptures. His original idea—the ceramic eggs from which emerge fully plumed birds and beasts—has so often been pirated and cheaply imitated that he now concentrates instead on larger pieces, including full-length mirrors out of which surreal animals poke their heads. Bustamante has added hand-crafted jewelry to his collection, incorporating surrealistic themes in bold earrings, necklaces, and pins. ♦ M-Sa. Amberes 13 (between Hamburgo and Paseo de la Reforma). 525.9059

74 Champs-Elysées ★★★★$$$$ This French restaurant knows what it is doing and does it consummately well. Reserve a table with a window seat at lunchtime, order the *filet de boeuf avec béarnaise* (beef fillet with a shallot, butter, and wine sauce) or the fresh salmon with flageolet beans, and then move on to a dessert of guava sorbet for a long afternoon of great dining. Mexico's politicians and movers and shakers eat here regularly, largely because of the superb menu, but also to see and be seen. ♦ French ♦ M-Sa lunch and dinner. Reservations recommended; jacket and tie required. Paseo de la Reforma 316 (at Amberes). 525.7259

74 Champs-Elysées Boutique This is a gourmet take-out delicatessen selling the sybaritic pleasures of its sister restaurant. Among the delights available are extra-virgin, first-pressing olive oil; miniature quiches; and baguettes filled with foie gras, bacon and avocado, Parma ham, or duck with chutney. It's all wildly expensive. ♦ M-Sa. Paseo de la Reforma 316 (at Amberes). 525.7259

75 "El Angel"/El Monumento a la Independencia ("The Angel"/Monument to Independence) This 118-foot-tall monument to Mexico's independence from Spain is a glorious golden-winged angel. Representing victory, it has been the unofficial symbol of the city since its completion by the architect **Rivas Mercado** in 1910. ♦ Paseo de la Reforma and Florencia

76 María Isabel Sheraton $$$$ This deluxe hotel has the best possible view of **El Angel.** Situated on the north side of Reforma next to the **US Embassy,** it is perfect for those who want to be near, but not quite in, the Zona Rosa. There are 752 rooms and suites (including enormous penthouse suites with spectacular views of the city), and three restaurants—two formal, the third more casual. Other amenities include a pool and fitness center, special floors for business travelers, and state-of-the-art business services. ♦ Paseo de la Reforma 325 (between Río Danubio and Río Tiber). 207.3933, 800/325.3535; fax 207.0684

77 Las Delicias ★★$$ A favorite among foreign tourists for its folk art–inspired decor as well as its food, this eatery serves classic Mexican dishes with flair. One of the popular specialities is shrimp *a la tequila,* sautéed tableside in white wine, lemon juice, and onions, and then doused with a shot of tequila before serving. The *mole poblano,* made with chocolate, almonds, and peanuts, is excellent. Mariachi groups play every afternoon and evening. ♦ Mexican ♦ Daily lunch and dinner. Río Tiber and Río Lerma. No phone

78 Cine Latino Movie theaters in Mexico are cheap and popular, and this is a local favorite, showing North American, European, and Mexican art-house films. The selections are a step above the usual mainstream Hollywood flicks and range from the latest Mexican hit to Kurosawa. English-language films are screened in English with Spanish subtitles. ♦ Daily; showtimes vary. Paseo de la Reforma 296 (between Génova and Amberes). 525.8757

79 La Gondola ★★$$ From its dark interior, this restaurant spills out into a sidewalk cafe along a pedestrians-only street. The tables are set up under a canvas roof, and classical music (sometimes live) plays in the background. The pleasant atmosphere is reminiscent of a busy Italian trattoria, right down to the white-aproned waiters. The specialty is spaghetti Vivaldi, made with fresh vegetables. ♦ Italian ♦ Daily lunch and dinner. Reservations recommended. Génova 21 (between Hamburgo and Paseo de la Reforma). 514.0743

Les Moustaches

80 Les Moustaches ★★$$$$ Across Reforma between the **British** and **US Embassies** sits a smart restaurant that lives up to its name—every single waiter, and even the owner himself, sports a mustache. While over the top in both expense and ostentation, this dining spot does, nevertheless, serve excellent abalone and wonderful desserts. Formal in style and service, the restaurant is particularly popular with Cognac-sipping businessmen bearing cellular phones; the waiters and clientele have little tolerance for casually dressed tourists. ♦ International ♦ M-Sa lunch and dinner. Jacket and tie required (except at Saturday lunch). Río Sena 88 (at Río Lerma). 533.3390

Mexico City and Tokyo are the world's largest cities. The population of Mexico City is greater than the combined populations of Denmark, Finland, and Norway.

81 María Cristina $ On the north side of Reforma, a 10-minute walk from the Zona Rosa, you'll find the most attractive medium-range hotel in the city, where loyal guests return time and again. The 156 rooms and suites are comfortable and come equipped with telephones, TVs, in-room safes, and mini-bars. Master suites have in-room hot tubs. It's definitely a place for holiday-makers and families rather than expense-account business travelers—the pace is gentle, and the price is reasonable. The garden provides a relaxing spot to sit after a hard day of shopping and sight-seeing, and nearby **Jardín del Arte** hosts art shows on weekend afternoons and is a pretty place to stroll amid locals and few tourists. The hotel's only drawback is its inferior restaurant. ♦ Río Lerma 31 (at Río Neva). 566.9688, 703.1787; fax 566.9194

82 Copenhague This tiny, narrow street in the Zona Rosa has nothing but restaurants. In one block (open to pedestrian traffic only) there are about a dozen, each with a distinct style and menu and nearly all with sidewalk patios. It is quite possible to move from one to the other enjoying a drink here, lunch there, and coffee somewhere else. ♦ Between Hamburgo and Paseo de la Reforma

82 Piccadilly Pub ★★$$$ Hardly a replica of a typical British pub, it belies its name by serving only Mexican beers. At least the menu is genuine—with the nearby **British Embassy** providing a lot of business, the fare has to remain authentic. Choose among Welsh rarebit, shepherd's pie, porterhouse steak, trifle, and strawberries and cream. The owner, Jane Pearson, is a British expatriate. ♦ British ♦ M-Sa lunch and dinner; Su lunch. Copenhague 23 (between Hamburgo and Paseo de la Reforma). 514.3740

83 El Mesón del Perro Andaluz ★★$$$ Directly opposite the **Piccadilly Pub** is a similarly nostalgic restaurant, but this one caters to the Spanish community. As popular for a drink or light lunch as it is for a full-blown feast, the place takes pride in its seafood and light, refreshing gazpacho, a must in hot weather. The outdoor cafe here has been a longtime favorite of locals and tourists, but unfortunately the management appears to be overly confident in its continued success—prices have risen dramatically in recent years, and your check will reflect a charge for the bread served with your wine or soup. ♦ Spanish ♦ Daily lunch and dinner. Copenhague 26 (between Hamburgo and Paseo de la Reforma). 533.5306

84 Focolare ★★$$$ Although this restaurant tries too hard to combine an excellent menu of regional food with a forced ambience of Mexican folklore, it is still a good place for those who want a broader experience of traditional Mexican fare. Among the specialties are the 36-ingredient mole sauces from Puebla and Oaxaca, pork cooked in banana leaves from the Yucatán Peninsula, baby goat from the northern countryside, and corn tamales from Michoacán. The patio is a delightful place to dine during the day, though it's a bit nippy at night and you might want to opt for a table in the cavernous dining room. A leisurely tour of the breakfast buffet should keep you satisfied for hours. A *Fiesta Mexicana* is held on Friday and Saturday nights, when large tour groups pack the restaurant for the folkloric dance show and Mexican buffet. ♦ Mexican ♦ Daily breakfast, lunch, and dinner. Hamburgo 87 (between Niza and Copenhague). 207.8850

85 Daikoku ★★$$ This Japanese restaurant hidden off Génova in a tiny shopping mall has one of the most popular sushi bars in the city, offering grilled smoked salmon skins, *teppanyaki* (meats, shellfish, and vegetables prepared on a grill at your table), and the dark meat of the *hamachi* (yellowtail tuna). Although tables are available, sitting at the sushi bar or in front of the grill makes gratification all the more immediate. ♦ Japanese ♦ Daily lunch and dinner. Génova 44 (at Hamburgo). 533.4954

86 Café Konditori ★★★$$ In addition to the spacious dining room, this Danish-owned restaurant has tables set on the sidewalk, making it an excellent meeting place for any meal or occasion. The menu offers crepes, bagels with smoked salmon, and a variety of salads. ♦ International ♦ M-Sa breakfast, lunch, and dinner. Génova 61 (between Londres and Hamburgo). 525.6621

86 La Baguette A branch of the country's upscale bakery chain, this is a convenient spot to grab a quick coffee, juice, or tasty snack. ♦ M-Sa. Génova 65 (at Londres). 514.5484

87 El Chato Londres ★★★$$$ With more than 20 years in the Zona Rosa, this restaurant is something of a local institution. Businessmen come to unwind at the quiet, English-style bar (complete with a rifle rack), while patrons pack the red booths in the dining room for justly famous dishes such as enchiladas in plum mole and enchiladas *marineros* (stuffed with shrimp and smothered in a red chile sauce). A pianist plays nightly during dinner. ♦ Mexican ♦ M-Sa lunch and dinner. Reservations recommended. Londres 117 (between Génova and Amberes). 533.2854

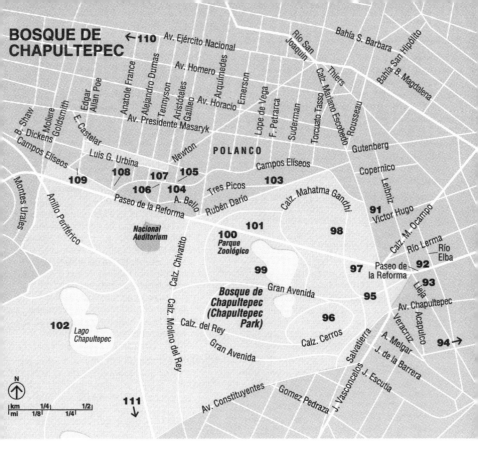

BOSQUE DE CHAPULTEPEC

←110 Av. Ejército Nacional

Río San Joaquín

Bahía S. Barbara

Bahía San Hipólito

Bahía B. Magdalena

Av. Homero

Calz. Thiers

Calz. Mariano Escobedo

Av. Arquímedes

Emerson

Anatole France

Av. Alejandro Dumas

Tennyson

Aristóteles

Galileo

Av. Horacio

Lope de Vega

F. Petrarca

Suderman

Torcuato Tasso

Rousseau

Edgar Allan Poe

E. Castelar

Av. Presidente Masaryk

B. Shaw

Molière

Goldsmith

B. Dickens

Campos Elíseos

Luis G. Urbina

Newton

POLANCO

Campos Elíseos

Gutenberg

Copernico

Leibniz

Montes Urales

Anillo Periférico

109

108

107

105

106

104

A. Bello

Tres Picos

103

Calz. Mahatma Gandhi

Victor Hugo

Calz. M. Ocampo

91

Río Lerma

Río Elba

Paseo de la Reforma

Rubén Darío

Nacional Auditorium

101

100
Parque Zoológico

98

Calz. Chivatito

99

97

Paseo de la Reforma

92

93

102
Lago Chapultepec

Bosque de Chapultepec (Chapultepec Park)

Gran Avenida

95

Lieja

Av. Chapultepec

Veracruz

Acapulco

Calz. Molino del Rey

Calz. del Rey

96

Calz. Cerros

A. Melgar

94→

Gran Avenida

J. de la Barrera

Salvatierra

J. Vasconcelos

J. Escutia

N

km 1/4 1/2
mi 1/8 1/4

111
↓

Av. Constituyentes

Gomez Pedraza

88 Mixup For recordings of Latin dance music—
cumbias, merengues, salsa, and *danzón*—
this shop has it all. The owner is from the US,
but has lived in Mexico most of his life. Music
from all over the world is also available—the
staff believes that there is no record, tape,
or CD that can't be found either immediately
or within seven days (maximum!). Tickets
for all kinds of musical performances
may be purchased here, and there's also
a good selection of international books
and magazines, some in English. ♦ Daily.
Génova 76 (between Liverpool and Londres).
511.0033, ticket reservations 325.9000

89 Bellinghausen ★★$$ Given a choice
between lunch or dinner here, choose the
former every time. Charming by day, when
businesspeople and tourists make the most
of the garden patio, in the evening it's much
more somber. The menu is Mexican and
ranges from the exotic *gusanos de maguey*
(cactus worms) to the restaurant's specialty,
la chemita (grilled steak with mashed
potatoes). Mexican wines are served,
as are draught beers, a rarity in this town.
♦ Mexican ♦ M-Sa lunch and dinner. Londres
95 (between Niza and Génova). 207.6149

90 Don Vasco de Quiroga $ Because this
family-run hotel is a bit east of the Zona Rosa,
both its pace and price are very desirable.
After a day you become a well-known guest,

and in a week you're one of the family. There
is a large lobby on the first floor, a decent
restaurant, and a variety of quirky rooms,
50 in all. While great for families and small
groups, it's not ideal for businesspeople, as
the telephones in the rooms don't have direct
dialing. ♦ Londres 15 (between Berlin and
Dinamarca). 566.1970; fax 566.2712

Bosque de Chapultepec (Chapultepec Park)

Commonly thought of as the lungs of polluted Mexico
City, **Bosque de Chapultepec** runs alongside **Paseo
de la Reforma** due west of the **Zona Rosa** and up into
the *lomas* (hills) that mark the westernmost extension
of the city. At the turn of the century former dictator/
president Porfirio Díaz added fountains, lakes, picnic
grounds, and access by street cars and trams to this
vast stretch of green, making it the most popular,
largest, and liveliest park in all of Mexico City.

Chapultepec—which underwent a $75-million
renovation in the early 1990s—is home to museums,
zoos, lakes, and restaurants, and is frequented by
families, schoolchildren, buskers, hawkers, and
lovers. In the 15th century, when the area was still
outside the city limits, Nezahualcóyotl, the king of the
Texcoco region (and also a famous poet), established
it as a park; it had already been used as a summer
retreat and zoo by previous Aztec emperors. The zoo
still exists and is now filled with exotic species, such

as giant pandas, that the Aztec never would have seen or perhaps even imagined. Numerous trees and sculpted rocks dating back to the early 16th century are also featured at the zoo, but the visitors are most interested in the park's modern additions, which include some of the city's most famous and best-run museums: the world-renowned **Museo Nacional de Antropología** (National Museum of Anthropology), with its pre-Hispanic treasures; several contemporary art museums; and Mexico's first children's museum.

The neighborhood just north of the park, called **Polanco,** has become one of the most fashionable areas in the city. Its tree-shaded streets are home to exclusive restaurants, while lavish, luxurious hotels rise at the edges of the park, offering their guests tree-top views of the city that residents seldom see.

91 Camino Real $$$$ Newer luxury hotels have been built in the neighborhood in recent years, but politicians, executives, and wealthy travelers have developed an unwavering loyalty to this eight-acre palace. The property was designed as a modern pyramid by one of Mexico's top modern architects, **Ricardo Legorreta.** Note his bold use of basic colors and sharp lines, and the fountain cascading in front of the main entrance; all provide a stark contrast to the anonymous, high-rise luxury towers of other deluxe hotels nearby. With 713 rooms and suites, three swimming pools, four lighted tennis courts, and 10 restaurants and bars, this is one of the most self-indulgent places to stay in Mexico City. The only drawbacks are the hotel's location—far from most tourist attractions and restaurants—and its layout, which makes you feel as if you're hiking through a maze to reach your room (although it does give you a chance to examine the artwork by Rufino Tamayo, Pedro Coronel, and Alexander Calder scattered throughout the public spaces). Still, it is a welcome escape from the noise of the city, and returning here after a hard day's touring is absolute bliss. ♦ Calzada Mariano Escobedo 700 (at Victor Hugo). 203.2121, 800/722.6466; fax 250.6897

Within the Camino Real:

Fouquet's de Paris ★★★$$$$ This very high-class dining room is a branch of the famous Parisian restaurant and often has the services of visiting French chefs. Specialties include salmon fillets with vanilla, quail *à la provençale,* several kinds of pâté, and passion-fruit sorbet. Imported wines are outrageously expensive. Reserve a window table overlooking the hotel's gardens. ♦ French ♦ M-F lunch and dinner; Sa dinner. Reservations recommended; jacket and tie required. 203.2121

Five million people ride the Mexico City metro every day.

92 Marquis Reforma $$$$ A member of the Small Luxury Hotels of the World group, this hostelry draws rave reviews from first-time guests who are never again satisfied with any other lodging place. The pink-stone and mirrored-glass Art Nouveau facade stands out on the sedate Paseo de la Reforma, and the 84 suites and 116 rooms follow through on the Art Deco theme, with furnishings of precious woods and silk and gorgeous lamps. High tea and cocktails are served in the **Caviar Bar** to the accompaniment of a string quartet, and the spa specializes in luxurious pampering. ♦ Paseo de la Reforma 465 (at Río Elba). 211.3600, 800/525.4800; fax 211.5561

Within the Marquis Reforma:

La Jolla ★★★$$$$ Sleek and minimalist in style, this has become one of the trendiest restaurants in the city. The original Belgian chef added Mexican touches to his native cuisine, creating nouvelle Mexican dishes with a Flemish twist, which the new chef has continued to prepare. Pheasant and duck are favorite entrées, and everyone saves room for the superb pastries. If the prices seem out of reach, try having breakfast here. It's less expensive but still wonderful, and the place is packed with professionals negotiating deals. ♦ Mexican/Continental ♦ Daily breakfast, lunch, and dinner. Reservations recommended; jacket and tie required. 211.3600

93 Four Seasons Hotel Mexico City $$$$ Though this hostelry opened in 1994, it blends in so well that it might always have stood on the historic Paseo de la Reforma. The building, designed by the Honolulu architectural firm of **Wimberly Allison Tong & Goo,** combines the city's historic Spanish and French influences in a building some say resembles the **Palacio de Iturbide** in the Centro Histórico. The colonial facade hides an elaborate central courtyard surrounded by 240 luxurious guest rooms and suites. The best seats for dining are along the courtyard terrace of the hotel's gourmet restaurant; other options include an indoor cafe, lobby lounge, and a library-style bar. An outdoor pool and indoor health club sit atop the eight-story building and are great spots for relaxing after a session in the well-equipped business center. ♦ Paseo de la Reforma 500 (at Lieja). 230.1818, 800/332.3442; fax 230.1817

94 La Casona $$$ Offering a pleasant escape from the larger properties, this early 20th-century apartment building has been converted into a special 30-room inn within walking distance of the Zona Rosa and **Chapultepec Park.** The individually designed rooms have antique furnishings (except for the thoroughy modern beds); breakfast is served in the patio dining area. The neighborhood of Colonia Roma is a good area for walking and offers visitors more of a view of Mexican life than the tourist areas. ♦ Durango 280 (at Cozumel). 286.3001, 800/223.5652; fax 211.0871

95 Monumento a los Niños Héroes (Monument to the Child Heroes) The tall columns that mark the park's entrance are a monument to six young cadets known as the *niños héroes,* the oldest of whom was only 16. In a very patriotic nation, these young men are almost deified for protecting the Mexican flag during the US invasion of 1847. Instead of giving themselves up to the more powerful north-of-the-border troops, the last six cadets defending **Castillo Chapultepec** jumped to their deaths from the high terrace, one supposedly wrapped in their country's flag to keep the pennant from being captured. ♦ Gran Avenida

96 Castillo Chapultepec (Chapultepec Castle) The castle takes its name from the Aztec word *chapulin* (grasshopper) and the hill on which the grasshoppers congregated. Although now in the heart of the city, the hill was used as a summer retreat by the Aztec emperors and Spanish viceroys, and only became incorporated into the city in the middle of the last century. The Aztec emperors had their likenesses (and those of the grasshoppers) carved into the side of the hill, and although the Spaniards destroyed most of these, there are some remains on the east slope, most dating from the reign of Montezuma II (1502-20). The castle was built on the top of the hill overlooking **Bosque de Chapultepec** in 1786 by the Catalonian architect **Agustín Mascaro** for the use of the viceroys. After the 1810 War of Independence, it passed into the hands of a military college and was home and school to the young cadets who died defending the flag.

The castle's next lodgers were Maximilian of Hapsburg and his Belgian wife, Carlota, who were invited to rule the country by Napoléon III (for more on the couple, see "Maximilian and Carlota: Mexico's Martyred Monarchs" on page 234). It then passed from one ruler to another, occasionally serving as the **Presidential Palace.** In 1939 the left-wing president Lázaro Cárdenas bequeathed it to the nation as the **Museo de la Historia Nacional** (Museum of National History). It's about a 10-minute walk up a steep hill to the castle; there is an elevator to the top, but it's rarely working. ♦ Calzada del Cerro (off Gran Avenida)

Within Castillo Chapultepec:

Museo de la Historia Nacional (Museum of National History) The history of Spanish influence on Mexico from the conquest to the eventual transformation into a distinct, bicultural nation unfolds in this museum. Covering two floors, the exhibits include examples of Spanish weapons, maps, and religious artifacts alongside portraits of Hernán Cortés and the viceroys, the Kings of Spain, heroes of the struggle for independence, and the subsequent presidents of the Republic of Mexico. Around the museum are murals by Siqueiros and Orozco, commemorating key acts in Mexican history. ♦ Admission. Tu-Su. 553.6246

97 Museo de Arte Moderno (Museum of Modern Art) On the edge of **Parque Chapultepec,** this museum is set in an elliptical, two-story building. Alongside the temporary exhibits are two halls showcasing the permanent collection, including Frida Kahlo's famous work *The Two Fridas* (1939). Along the walls hang paintings by Luis Nishizawa, Maria Izquierdo, and Abraham Angel. The upper floor's collection opens with Rufino Tamayo's *Hippy in White* (1972) and continues past the paintings of surrealists Remedios Varo from Spain and Leonora Carrington from England, both of whom spent many years in Mexico. The temporary exhibitions are always interesting, as are the large sculpture garden surrounding the museum and the small, well-stocked bookshop. ♦ Admission. Tu-Su. Paseo de la Reforma and Calzada Mahatma Gandhi. 211.8045

98 Museo Rufino Tamayo (Rufino Tamayo Museum) The Oaxacan-born muralist, painter, and collector Rufino Tamayo died in 1991 at the age of 92. His private collection of modern art is housed in this museum designed by architects **Teodoro González de León** and **Abraham Zabludowsky.** In addition to Tamayo's own work, including the famous slices of ripe, red watermelons, there are paintings by Francis Bacon, Mark Rothko, Pablo Picasso, Willem de Kooning, and the Mexican masters Luis Nishizawa, Alberto Gironella, and Tamayo's fellow Oaxacan Francisco Toledo. ♦ Admission. Tu-Su. Paseo de la Reforma and Calzada Mahatma Gandhi. 286.6519

99 Casa del Lago (Lake House) This pretty little building is often the setting for public events, political demonstrations, and open-air shows. Inside are temporary art exhibits and a small cafe. ♦ Daily. Gran Avenida. No phone

100 Parque Zoológico (Zoo) In the early 16th century, long before the current zoo existed, a menagerie of exotic animals from all over Mesoamerica was kept in the **Bosque de Chapultepec** area. Today the park is home to four giant pandas (the zoo was the first to breed them successfully in captivity), a white tiger, a pair of Mexican wolves (only 30 remain in the wild), and plenty of tamer animals, such as ponies, which children are allowed to ride. The 44-acre zoo was remodeled by architect **Ricardo Legorreta** in 1994, and now bears his signature bright yellow and purple walls, which mark exhibit entrances. The old-fashioned steel cages and cement floors have been replaced by landscaped areas designed to replicate the animals' native habitats as closely as possible. The aviary contains two golden eagles, the symbol of Mexico, and wonderful landscaping, including waterfalls, a tropical rainforest, and groves of bamboo. On Sunday this is one of the most visited spots in the city. ♦ Free. Tu-Su. Paseo de la Reforma (east of Calzada Chivatito). No phone

101 Museo Nacional de Antropología (National Museum of Anthropology) No journey to Mexico is complete without a visit to this outstanding anthropological museum. Here delicate sculptures rub shoulders with sacrificial altars, and gods with tongue-twisting names—Huitzilopochtli (War), Coatlicue (Earth Mother), Tlaloc (Rain), Chalchiuhtlicue (Corn), Huehueteotl (Fire), and Mictlantecuhtli (Death)—appear again

Museo Nacional de Antropología

J. DEL GAIZO

and again in many guises and under different appellations. A fascinating overview of the cultures that flourished in Mesoamerica before the arrival of the European conquerors, the museum features murals, wall maps, sculptures, jewels, weapons, masks, and reconstructed temples, altars, and tombs. The permanent collection is housed in 12 anthropological rooms on the ground floor and 11 ethnographical rooms on the upper floor. It covers every one of the great Mexican civilizations, from the Aztec in Mexico City to the Maya in the south, the Zapotec and Mixtec in Oaxaca, and the northernmost nomads. It is a beautiful museum, well deserving of its reputation as the best of its kind in the world.

After the destruction of the pre-Hispanic civilizations—due to time, war, and diseases brought by the Spanish—their ruins were covered over, tombs were lost, languages were scrambled, and gods were incorporated into the Catholic canon. However, they were never forgotten, and artifacts turned up in city squares, fields, and deep in the jungle. European and north-of-the-border explorers rediscovered some pyramids and temples, and many other sites were known by the locals, who continued to make offerings to their gods but refused to share their secrets with the Spanish. Many pre-Hispanic artifacts were taken out of the country by collectors, explorers, and archaeologists who felt, perhaps rightly at the time, that their finds would only be lost again if they were left in Mexico. As the centuries passed, the Spanish also became curious about the civilizations they had conquered; it was Viceroy Antonio Maria de Bucareli who returned the first artifacts to the Mexican government at the end of the 18th century. The collection grew as more artifacts were discovered by explorers and archaeologists, and, in 1865, Emperor Maximilian moved it to the **Museo de Culturas,** behind the **Palacio Nacional.** After the 1910 revolution, interest in preconquest Mexico increased, and President Adolfo López Mateos inaugurated this museum in 1964 to honor and preserve the country's heritage.

The museum's design, by architect **Pedro Ramírez Vázquez,** is remarkable. All the rooms open onto a central patio, allowing visitors to easily walk from one age of Mexican history to another according to their interests and whims. Alternatively, you can follow the rooms in chronological order, an approach that provides a sense of the development of the country in its different ages and geographical areas.

A few words of advice: **1)** Allow time for several short visits rather than a long, exhausting one; **2)** join up with a guided tour (given in English every 30 minutes); **3)** on Sunday admission is free, but the museum fills up with families and students; **4)** when museum fatigue sets in, spend a few minutes in the cool courtyard or escape to the restaurant; **5)** if possible, see the ruins at Teotihuacán (see page 246) before your visit to put the grandeur and splendor of this great civilization into context; **6)** if in a rush, skip the first three rooms on general world anthropology, which is of limited interest to non–Spanish-speakers, and begin with the exhibit on Teotihuacán; **7)** do not miss **Rooms IV** (Teotihuacán), **VII** (Aztec), and **X** (Maya). *Note:* At press time the museum was undergoing a multiyear renovation and upgrading: The project is scheduled for completion in the year 2000, so some exhibits may be shut down when you visit. As a result of this renovation, the Maya salon for the first time has important artifacts on display from sites in Chiapas and Campeche, such as Toniná, Calakmul, and the Rio Bec area. ◆ Admission; free Sunday. Tu-Su. Paseo de la Reforma (east of Calzada Chivatito). 553.1902

Within the Museo Nacional de Antropología:

Bookshop One of the best in the city for books on history, art, architecture, and pre-Hispanic Mexico, it has the latest titles in Spanish, English, German, and French. There are also good official guides to the museum and other sites around the country, posters, videos, tapes, and postcards. ◆ Tu-Su. 553.6226

Museum Restaurant $ Although the overpriced food isn't great, this is the only place to eat within acceptable walking distance of the exhibits. ◆ Mexican ◆ Tu-Su. 553.1902

Tlaloc At the entrance to the museum is a huge stone sculpture to Tlaloc, the god of rain. It dates from the first century and was rediscovered 30 miles from here. The enormous 23-foothigh, 167-metric-ton statue had to be transported on a 72-wheel trailer that was specially designed for the two-day journey. ◆ Outside the main museum entrance

102 Lago Chapultepec Restaurante
★★$$$$ Lago Chapultepec takes on an otherworldly appearance at night, when white lights illuminate streaming fountains and sparkle inside this lakeside restaurant. Formal to the point of pretentiousness, the dining spot is known more for its setting than its cuisine; stick to the lower-priced items, such as chicken, rather than splurging on a steak dinner. It's the most soothing place in the park for a leisurely lunch, though you may not wish to spend your day outdoors in clothing that

will pass muster with the haughty maître d'. ◆ Continental ◆ Daily lunch and dinner. Reservations recommended; jacket and tie required. West of Anillo Periférico. 515.9585

103 Museo-Casa Siqueiros (Siqueiros House Museum) Muralist, Stalinist, and political activist David Alfaro Siqueiros lived and painted in this house during the last years of his life, and he donated it to Mexico a month before he died. It combines his living space with an art gallery and an exhibit on his life. There are occasional screenings of European films here. ◆ Admission; free Sunday. Tu-Su. Tres Picos 29 (at Rubén Darío). 545.5952

104 Hotel Nikko México $$$$ This is generally considered to be one of the best business hotels in Mexico, receiving high marks for everything from the comfort of the 771 rooms and suites to the impeccable service. Japanese-style guest rooms with futon beds are available, and the regular accommodations vary in size. There are Japanese, French, and international restaurants, and British and Mexican bars; even the room service fare is top-notch. Tourists who can afford to stay here prefer it above all others, because it overlooks **Bosque de Chapultepec** and is within easy walking distance of the museums. ◆ Campos Elíseos 204 (between Arquímedes and Elliot). 280.1111, 800/645.5687; fax 280.9191

104 Presidente Inter-Continental $$$$ Almost brushing shoulders with the **Hotel Nikko,** this is another excellent high-rise hotel overlooking the park. With a huge lobby and 659 rooms and suites, it is a town within a town. To make the most of the views (smog permitting) get a room facing southwest and as high up the 42-story building as possible. The club floors have a private lounge with complimentary breakfast and evening appetizers; all rooms are large and comfortable, and the service is superb. The fitness center (no pool) is on the 11th floor, and there are seven restaurants. ◆ Campos Elíseos 218 (between Arquímedes and Elliot). 327.7700, 800/327.0200; fax 327.7750

Within the Presidente Inter-Continental:

Maxim's de Paris ★★★$$$ Operated under the auspices of the Paris original, this elegant French restaurant is an enduring favorite of Mexico City's elite gourmands. The chef is at his best with classic French dishes, including escargots, a hearty cassoulet, and *coquilles St-Jacques* (scallops in a cream sauce). The menu changes frequently to constantly offer the new choices to the loyal clientele. The refined decor is enhanced by a stained-glass ceiling and Art Deco furnishings. ◆ French ◆ M-F lunch and dinner; Sa dinner. Reservations recommended; jacket and tie required. 327.7700

105 LTG Antiguedades Situated right across from the **Hotel Nikko México,** this little shop boasts a wealth of Mexican antiques from the 18th and 19th centuries. The owners have spent a lifetime scouring Mexico for the collection, and the shop is crammed with several hundred paintings, sculptures, and all manner of odds and ends. Several pieces were originally made in Europe, but all made their way to Mexico by the turn of the century. Occupying pride of place in the center of the store is an ominous-looking black suit of armor from Japan. ♦ M-Sa. Campos Elíseos 215A (at Galileo). 280.5580

106 Centro Cultural Arte Contemporáneo (Center for Contemporary Art) Televisa, the largest and most important private TV company in Mexico, owns this four-story building, which houses the company's art, sculpture, and photographs. The permanent collection is always augmented with thought-provoking international exhibitions. ♦ Nominal admission. Tu-Su. Campos Elíseos and Elliot. 282.0355

Within the Centro Cultural Arte Contemporáneo:

Museum Shop A dangerously tempting store, this place is full of imaginative gifts ranging from blue blown-glass vases and the miniature boxes of craftsman Rafael Alvarez to witty T-shirts, posters, and books. ♦ Tu-Su. 282.0355

107 La Galvía ★★★$$$$ There are as many fierce defenders as detractors of this restaurant. Those in favor praise the high quality of the menu, which ranges from a soup of baby cactus leaves and pinto beans to main courses such as *pollo* (chicken) in phyllo. Critics find it overpriced, underspiced, and generally pretentious. Either way, it's always booked up. Try it and decide for yourself. ♦ Mexican ♦ Daily lunch and dinner. Reservations required. Campos Elíseos 247 (at Av Eugenio Sue). 281.0560

108 Galería Mexicana de Diseño This gallery has a small but attractive space dedicated to innovations in contemporary Mexican design, from plans for buildings to light fittings, telephones, and pens. Photographs and paintings are also on display. All items on exhibit are for sale. ♦ M-Sa. Anatole France 13 (at Campos Elíseos). 280.0080

109 La Bottiglia ★★$$$ This pretty and popular Italian restaurant with a Bolognese chef is always bustling—bear with the occasional air of Italian anarchy in the service. The menu ranges from pasta in pesto sauce to osso buco with white wine to the house specialty, carpaccio. The wine list is overpriced but does have some excellent Tuscan and Umbrian reds. ♦ Italian ♦ Daily breakfast, lunch, and dinner. Reservations recommended. Edgar Allan Poe 8 (between Campos Elíseos and Luis G. Urbina). 280.0609, 280.8441

109 Hotel Polanco $$ In a delightful area right around the corner from **La Bottiglia,** this pleasant hotel is the only affordable option in the neighborhood. It's one-third the price of the more deluxe hotels overlooking the park and a very acceptable alternative, with 77 simple rooms. There is no restaurant, but the neighborhood is filled with great eateries. ♦ Edgar Allan Poe 8 (between Campos Elíseos and Luis G. Urbina). 280.8082, 280.8066; fax 280.8082, 280.8066

110 Hacienda de los Morales ★★★★$$$ Named for the *morales* (mulberry trees) that were planted around the 16th-century hacienda when it was first built, this restaurant is a Mexico City institution. The museumlike building and grounds are worth seeing for their elegant colonial-style furnishings, formal gardens, and stone fountains, but it's the cuisine that keeps the city's elite coming back for more. Try the *crepas de huitlacoche;* thin crepes wrapped around a strip of *huitlacoche,* a dark, silky fungus spiced with *epazote* (a pungent herb) and covered with a cheese sauce. The abalone is spiced with chipotle chilies; beef fillets are topped with soft *machengo* cheese; and trout, sea bass, and snapper are served with imaginative sauces—it's hard to find a failure on the menu. The best time to dine here is on a weekend afternoon, when the bustling pace of weekday business lunches gives way to genteel tranquillity. The restaurant is located west of the Polanco neighborhood. ♦ Mexican/ International ♦ Daily lunch and dinner. Reservations recommended; jacket and tie recommended. Juan Vázquez de Mella 525 (between Av Homero and Ejército Nacional). 281.4554

111 Papalote Museo del Niño (Papalote Museum of the Child) Mexico's first interactive children's museum is an eye-catching, geometric-looking blue-tile building set on the western edge of

Bosque de Chapultepec on the Periferico highway. The privately owned **Papalote** (the word means "butterfly" in Nahuatl, the language of the Aztecs) opened in November 1993 and quickly became hugely popular with Mexico City residents. A total of 360 exhibits designed to teach scientific and technical principles are organized around five themes: the human body, communications, the arts, consciousness, and the physical world. Filled with mazes, dark tunnels, mock rain forests, computers, police cars, and fire engines, the museum delights both kids and adults and is almost always packed. ◆ Admission. Daily in two sessions, the first between 9AM and 1PM and the second between 2PM and 6PM, with a third night session on Thursday. Tickets allow admission to one session only, and sell out quickly on weekends. Anillo Periférico and Av Constituyentes. 237.1781

South of Mexico City

The city's southern portion stretches from the **Paseo de la Reforma** to the once-separate city of **Xochimilco,** Mexico City's last remnant of pre-Hispanic life, famous for its canals and nursery gardens. **Avenida Insurgentes Sur** is the central north-to-south street, running from Paseo de la Reforma to **Highway 95.** Some of Mexico City's loveliest neighborhoods are here, including colonial **San Angel,** with its stalwart Spanish mansions and its famous Saturday-morning **Bazar Sábado** handicrafts market, and nearby **Coyoacán,** where such diverse figures as Hernán Cortés, Frida Kahlo, Diego Rivera, Leon Trotsky, and various ex-

presidents have all lived. The south is a must for Rivera/Kahlo fans, since the couple spent most of their lives between Coyoacán and San Angel, and this is where their house and studios are located. During the week students from the nearby university congregate here to learn, dispute, and discuss. On weekends, the area is the provence of tourists and shoppers from all parts of the city. Make sure you budget enough time to stroll and browse; the south has plenty of interest for crafts' lovers and people watchers. The restaurants, bars, and theaters are geared for locals, with no special effects for tourists—and they're the better for it.

112 San Angel Inn ★★★★$$$ Certainly the most famous restaurant in the city, this is also one of the best. Many people come here just to enjoy the setting, an enchanting Spanish house with seating on the patio and inside. The menu is excellent, but with so much great dining in Mexico City, it can no longer claim superiority. Stick to what they do well—the duck in raspberry sauce or the *crepas huitlacoche,* for instance—and dinner will be superb. Or you can just drop in for margaritas in the early evening and enjoy the fabulous gardens and the opulence of this former hacienda. Weekend lunches are particularly popular, and a meal at the inn is a great capper after a tour of San Angel. But be forewarned, the unspoken dress code is firmly enforced: No one wearing shorts or jeans will be admitted, nor will women wearing casual walking shoes such as canvas slip-ons or huaraches. ◆ Mexican/International ◆ Daily lunch and dinner. Reservations recommended; jacket required except on weekends. Diego Rivera 50 (at Av Altavista). 616.1527

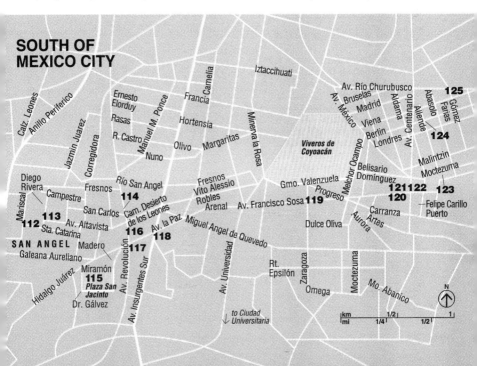

SOUTH OF MEXICO CITY

113 Museo Estudio Diego Rivera (Diego Rivera Studio Museum) Juan O'Gorman, a painter and architect friend of Diego Rivera and Frida Kahlo, designed these double studios for the artists in 1930. Much of Rivera's easel work was done in the studio on the top floor. There are still more than 500 of the artist's personal possessions here, including his paintbrushes, empty paint tubes, clothes, photographs, press clippings, and unusual art objects such as great papier-mâché Judas figures. ♦ Admission; free Sunday. Tu-Su. Diego Rivera and Av Altavista. 616.0996

114 Museo Alvar y Carmen T. de Carrillo Gil Méridan doctor Alvar Carrillo Gil (1899-1974) was a friend to many leading Mexican artists of his day. He started this fine collection when he was still a medical student and added to it throughout his life. Although it concentrates on national artists, there are also paintings from Japan, Europe, and other far-off places. Temporary exhibitions, special musical events, film screenings, and conferences also take place here. ♦ Admission. Tu-Su. Av Revolución 1608 (at Camino a Desierto de los Leones). 550.6289

115 Plaza San Jacinto This pretty plaza in the heart of the former village of San Angel is part of the great metropolis but still gives a strong flavor of small-town Spanish Mexico with its cobblestone streets, enchanting little church (one of the most sought-after in the city for weddings), and imposing Spanish mansions. The best day to visit is Saturday, when the neighborhood's famous market fills both the plaza and surrounding streets, though you're better off coming on a weekday if you want to sample San Angel's more relaxed ambience. ♦ Madero and Miramón

At Plaza San Jacinto:

Bazar del Sábado On Saturday mornings, artists and artisans set up their work in and around the square and the colonial house that held the original bazaar. Soon the square is filled with people buying, bartering, haggling, selling, and browsing. There are fantastic wooden animals from Oaxaca, textiles from Guatemala, glass and ceramics from Guadalajara, Otomí embroideries, brightly colored wooden fish, a rainbow of beads, and every imaginable Mexican craft. Although prices are generally more expensive than in other markets, the choice is more refined, with little glitz and a great deal of artistry. The market and surrounding streets get unbelievably crowded as the day progresses; arrive early for the best browsing. ♦ Sa

Bazar del Sábado Restaurant ★★★$$ Flowers fill the central fountain in the market's courtyard restaurant, where exhausted shoppers refuel themselves at the all-day buffet brunch featuring freshly squeezed fruit juices, eggs in spicy sauces, sweet breads, stuffed chilies, and tropical fruits. Marimbas play in the background, children frolic by the fountain, and the overall impression is one of a fanciful fiesta. ♦ Mexican ♦ Sa brunch. No phone

La Casona del Elefante ★★$$ On Saturday morning get one of the outside tables at this Northern Indian restaurant that overlooks the plaza, and while away the hours people watching. The menu includes hot curries and *lassi* (yogurt drinks), as well as an excellent vegetarian platter that has a little bit of everything and is more than enough for two people. ♦ Indian ♦ M-Sa lunch and dinner; Su lunch. No. 9. 616.1601, 616.2208

Fonda San Angel ★★$$ More of an evening spot, this attractive place offers seating in an indoor dining room and sidewalk tables facing the plaza. Dishes include chicken in pumpkin-seed sauce, shrimp stewed with roquefort, and chili peppers stuffed with Oaxacan cheese. ♦ Mexican ♦ M-Sa breakfast, lunch, and dinner; Su breakfast and lunch. No. 3. 548.7568

LE PETIT CLUNY

116 Le Petit Cluny ★★★$$ With not only the best baguettes and chocolate-filled croissants around, but the most delicious homemade pastas with pesto, carbonara, and *arrabiata* (spicy tomato) sauces, this small and busy restaurant is deservedly popular. The adjacent bakery keeps the same hours, so don't forget to buy the next morning's croissants after dinner. ♦ Italian/Bakery ♦ Tu-Su breakfast, lunch, and dinner. Av la Paz 58-14 (between Avs Insurgentes Sur and Revolución). 616.2288, 616.3043

117 Los Irabien ★★★$$$$ Supremely elegant, this is one of the most exclusive restaurants in the south of the city, catering to a yuppie crowd that gathers for power breakfasts, business lunches, or intimate dinners. The decor is seriously upmarket, with Mr. Irabien's superb art collection hanging on the dark blue walls. The menu ranges from prime rib to trout filled with salmon and served with a Champagne sauce, as well as such Mexican innovations as red snapper topped with squash flowers or nopal cactus filled with fish. Between courses, servings of lemon sorbet keep the palate fresh. ♦ International ♦ M-Sa breakfast, lunch, and dinner; Su breakfast and lunch. Reservations recommended; jacket and tie required. Av la Paz 45 (between Avs Insurgentes Sur and Revolución). 616.0014, 660.2382

118 La Carreta On one block, there are not only many great restaurants but also this cavernous shop. Alongside some junk, this pack rat's nest offers real jewels of Mexican work, including Pueblan ceramics, bark paintings, Oaxacan fantasy animals, and reproductions of pre-Hispanic sculptures in jade, onyx, and obsidian. ♦ M-Sa. Av la Paz 21 (at Av Insurgentes Sur). 616.2225

119 Avenida Francisco Sosa The most charming street in the city runs from Avenida Universidad, past several beautiful colonial houses, to Plaza de Santa Catarina and on down to Coyoacán's two main squares. Walk its length for an evocative sampling of the area's past and present glories. There are many *talleres* (workshops) here, where classes in dance, painting, and sculpture are taught all day. If it's open, stop in at **Viveros de Coyoacán**, a plant nursery and park—it's a pleasant place for a stroll. ♦ Between Avs Centenario and Universidad

119 Plaza de Santa Catarina A bust of writer Francisco Sosa, for whom the street is named, sits in this small park, one of the nicest in the city. ♦ Avs Francisco Sosa and Progreso

On Plaza de Santa Catarina:

Las Lupitas ★★$ *The* traditional neighborhood place serves good, cheap, homey food (try the excellent chili-and-cheese soup) plus the best breakfasts in Coyoacán. The setting may be low-key, but the atmosphere is fun and friendly; you'll stand out as a newcomer at first, but will be swiftly initiated. ♦ Mexican ♦ M-Sa breakfast, lunch, and dinner. 554.2875

120 Nalanda Libros Classical music plays in the background in this serene bookshop, where crystals and tarot cards are displayed among texts on mysticism, astrology, and religion. The clerks and customers are good sources for referrals to everything from vegetarian restaurants to acupuncturists. ♦ Daily. Av Centenario 16 (at Av Francisco Sosa). 554.7522

121 Los Geranios ★★$$ Ideally situated on Francisco Sosa as it meets the plaza, with tables both outdoors and in, this restaurant is perennially popular with the Coyoacán crowd of regulars. The owner spends his summers in Italy, and his menu ranges from fresh pastas or mozzarella and tomato salad to *carne à la tampiqueña* (a huge plate of grilled meat with guacamole, beans, and rice). Steak lovers must taste the specialty, the superb *puntas de filete* (beef tips in gravy). While it's packed all day Saturday and Sunday, you never have to wait long for a table. The only major drawback is sitting on the most uncomfortable seats in town. ♦ Mexican/Italian ♦ Daily breakfast, lunch, and dinner. Av Francisco Sosa 19 (at Av Centenario). 554.4745

122 Jardín Centenario The gathering spot for residents of Coyoacán, this small park is often the site of art fairs and impromptu musical performances. Street vendors display good quality folk art here, especially on weekends. Several small cafes with sidewalk tables front the park, and you can easily become absorbed in the street scene for hours. ♦ Av Centenario (between Ortega and Belisario Domínguez)

At Jardín Centenario:

El Hijo del Cuervo ★★$$ In Mexico City it isn't often that you find a good drinking place that isn't a male-only cantina, is lively and good-humored every night of the week, and knows how to serve drinks properly. This spot is all of the above and more. Often full to overflowing with the cool, the hip, and the trendy, it's a great place to meet, chat, drink, and eat *botanes* (appetizers) such as spiced peanuts, chunks of cheese, quesadillas, and other snacks. ♦ Daily lunch and dinner. Av Centenario 17. 658.5306

Café El Parnaso ★★★$ For many people, this is the heart and soul of Coyoacán. It's right in the middle of the twin plazas of **Jardín Centenario** and Plaza Hidalgo in front of the church, and has ringside seats for the weekend mayhem. Both a bookshop and a cafe, it is a gathering place for polemical, political discussions, posturings, posings, and good plain gossip. Sipping a cappuccino while reading the left-of-center newspaper *La Jornada* is de rigueur. The bookshop carries mostly Spanish-language titles by all the Latin American and Spanish publishing houses, as well as art books in English and Spanish, small-press magazines, posters, postcards, and attractive diaries. With an enormous range of titles crammed into one small room, you need time and patience to find what you want. ♦ Cafe ♦ Daily breakfast, lunch, and dinner. Felipe Carrillo Puerto 2 and 6. 554.2225

123 Museo de Culturas Populares (Museum of Popular Culture) Close to Coyoacán's main square, this museum concentrates on popular Mexican culture, with exhibits on such diverse topics as soap operas, the cult of *maíz* (corn), the Day of the Dead, *lucha libre*

(masked wrestling), and the history of radio in Mexico. The temporary exhibitions are always imaginative, well designed, fun, and thought-provoking, even though the museum itself is badly underfunded and constantly having to justify its existence to survive. ♦ Free. Tu-Su. Av Hidalgo 289 (between Abasolo and Caballocalco). 554.8968, 554.8848

124 Casa de Frida Kahlo (Frida Kahlo's House) The cornflower-blue house where Frida Kahlo was born and lived most of her life is on the quiet, residential side of Coyoacán. Filled with memorabilia of her life as a child, a young woman, wife of Diego Rivera, and artist, it includes family photographs, her own self-portraits, letters, and fragments of her journals. There is a small collection of paintings by friends and the Cubist group Rivera knew in Paris, as well as pre-Hispanic figurines and the fertility goddess figures that Kahlo collected (she was never able to have children and suffered several miscarriages trying). The couple's studio and library is on the upper floor, as is Kahlo's box bed, complete with the mirrored ceiling that helped her paint herself during the long months she spent bedridden. (For more on Kahlo, see "Frida Fervor" on page 221.) Note: Visitors are no longer allowed to take photographs inside the house, and the set admission hours are not always followed. ♦ Admission. Tu-Su. Londres 247 (at Allende). 554.5999

125 Museo Leon Trotsky (Leon Trotsky Museum) This biographical museum is in the house where the exiled Communist spent the last years of his life. Here Trotsky and his wife lived under constant fear of attack: Once the house was blasted with machine-gun bullets by the Stalinist painter David Alfaro Siqueiros (the holes still scar the walls of the bedroom), and Trotsky escaped only because he was feeding his pet rabbits in the garden. Then on 20 August 1945, a Catalan friend of his secretary asked for some help with a political piece, and, once in Trotsky's study, brutally stabbed him to death with an ice pick. The house, complete with gun turrets, high walls, thick metal-plated doors, and shuttered windows, has been kept much as it was (even the rabbit hutches are in place, but a tourist stole the infamous ice pick). There are photos and exhibits of every stage of Trotsky's life, including the short Mexican chapter in which he was a friend of the surrealist André Breton, muralist Diego Rivera, and supposedly a onetime lover of artist Frida Kahlo. In every photo he appears as a bespectacled, kind-looking man, certainly not the figure of terror he was to the Stalinists, who sent assassins all around the world to kill him and his political philosophies. The house is not always open during the hours posted outside; mornings seem to be the most opportune time to visit. ♦ Admission. Tu-Su. Av Río Churubusco 410 (between Morelos and Gómez Farias). 658.8732

Ruinas de San Juan Teotihuacán

Mystery surrounds the massive pyramids and palaces of Teotihuacán, spread over an eight-square-mile site north of Mexico City. No one knows who built or inhabited this city, which housed over 100,000 residents in AD 500 and was completely deserted 200 years later. The site is overwhelming, especially when viewed the first time around, and it's certainly worth a half-day's visit if you're a ruins buff.

Comfortable shoes, a hat, and drinking water are absolute necessities if you plan on climbing the ruins. The most impressive is the **Pirámide del Sol** (Pyramid of the Sun); with 248 steps to the top, it is the third-largest pyramid in the world (only the ones in Cholula, Mexico, and Cheops, Egypt are larger). The view from the summit is astounding and the climb breathtaking. The smaller **Pirámide de la Luna** (Pyramid of the Moon) is easier to climb and provides a good overview of the ruins lining the **Avenida de los Muertos** (Avenue of the Dead), a broad boulevard edged by smaller temples. Some buildings along the avenue still have touches of paint remaining from the frescoes that covered the buildings when Teotihuacán was a living city. The avenue leads from the **Pirámide de la Luna** to **La Ciudadela** (The Citadel), a large sunken square surrounded by thick walls.

The **Museum and Visitor's Center** is opposite the Pyramid of the Sun and contains a museum full of recently discovered artifacts from the site (although the really huge pieces are on display in Mexico City's **Museo Nacional de Antropología**). It also holds a giant scale model of the ruins that covers almost an entire room. The center has a coffee shop (there's a larger restaurant opposite The Citadel), rest rooms, a bookshop (with many publications in English), and souvenir stores. The site is open daily, the museum Tu-Su; there is an admission charge to the ruins and museum except on Sunday. Travel agencies in Mexico City offer tours to the ruins, or you can get here on your own by taking a bus from the **Central del Norte** (North Terminal; Eje Central, between Avs Instituto Politecnico and Fortuna, 587.5973). The trip takes about an hour each way.

126 Ciudad Universitaria (University City)
This is the 800-acre home of the **Universidad Nacional Autónoma de Mexico (UNAM)** (National Autonomous University of Mexico). The university, which dates back to 1551—making it the oldest in the Western Hemisphere—originally was located in the heart of the Centro Histórico. It moved to this specially designed campus in the 1950s. Several architects and artists worked on the project, trying to integrate the surrounding volcanic rock with the needs of a vast student population, now numbering roughly 300,000. The result is a flamboyant, dynamic collection of modern architecture that incorporates lively mosaics and murals by some of Mexico's top artists. ♦ Av Insurgentes Sur (between Anillo Periférico and Eje 10 Sur). For information on university events, call 658.1111, 525.9380

At Ciudad Universitaria:

Biblioteca (Library) Architect **Juan O'Gorman** used naturally colored tiles to create an amazing 10-story mosaic mural that wraps around the facade of the library, re-creating the course of Mexican history through depictions of many of its leading characters. ♦ Av Insurgentes Sur (between Circuito Escolar and Eje 10 Sur)

Rectoría (Rectory) Avant-garde artist David Alfaro Siqueiros played with colored glass on the exterior of this building and came up with extraordinary mosaic murals loosely dedicated to the importance of universities and education for the people of Mexico. ♦ Circuito Escolar (east of Av Insurgentes Sur)

Estadio Olímpico (Olympic Stadium)
Artist Diego Rivera contributed to the construction of the university by fashioning a mosaic mural (unfinished) of polychromatic stones above the entrance to one of the world's largest stadiums, which was the venue for the **1968 Summer Olympics.**

Centro Cultural Universitario (University Cultural Center) The campus's arts-and-performance complex provides culture-hungry students with inexpensive yet highly professional concert halls, art cinemas, exhibition spaces, a sculpture garden, and a cafe. To find out what's going on, check the weekly magazine *Tiempo Libre,* which comes out each Thursday and has listings in Spanish. ♦ Circuito Mario de la Cueva (between Av Insurgentes Sur and Circuito de la Investigación Científica)

127 Museo Anahuacalli As Diego Rivera's private stock of pre-Hispanic pieces grew, he decided to build a special museum that he could bequeath to Mexico to keep his collection intact. The result is this extraordinary volcanic-stone pyramid, which provides a somber background for the lively and ingenious pieces, most of which originate from the western states of Colima, Jalisco, and Nayarit. Rivera used part of the building as a studio, and his easel is still in place, holding the painting he was working on when he died. ♦ Admission. Tu-Su. Museo (between Diego Rivera and Av División del Norte). 617.4310

128 Xochimilco Back when the capital city was surrounded by lakes and swamps, waterways and canals crisscrossed the ancient Aztec city of Tenochtitlán. The Xochimilco peoples built islands of mud and reeds on the surface of these bodies of water, creating floating gardens. In the town of Xochimilco (pronounced So-chee-*meel*-co), these gardens, called *chinampas,* are still visible and in use today. Xochimilco (the name means "place of flowers" in the Nahuatl language) is the nursery garden of Mexico City, with flower and plant markets everywhere. But the big attractions here are the flower-bedecked boats that float through the waterways as mariachis serenade their passengers. Visitors may hire a boat captain for an hour's cruise through the canals (there's no need to bargain, since the prices are now fixed). The boats float in a languid parade, accompanied by cruising vendors offering snacks, drinks, and serapes. It's the ultimate Mexican Sunday outing.

Mexico City residents have long used Xochimilco as a weekend escape from urban pressures, and in years past the canals suffered from contamination. But a 1989 presidential decree made Xochimilco an ecological park, and subsequently the local council introduced a massive clean-up scheme. As a result, the boat dock has been refurbished; the long, narrow skiffs, called *trajineras,* are freshly painted; and the canals are well on their way to recovery. Note: Though you can get to Xochimilco by either public transportation or private car, it's easiest to take a tour (see "Tours" on page 216). ♦ Av Guadalupe I. Ramirez (east of Prolongación Division del Norte); take Metro *Line 2* south to Taxqueña and connect to a bus southbound on Calzada Tlalpan

Bests

Arq. Rodolfo Perez Alvarez
Director de Turismo Social Y Fronterizo-Sectur

If you like the colonial, visit **Coyoacán.**

You can take a walk through **Ciudad Universitaria** and its cultural center.

If you are a lover of ecology, visit the **Canals of Xochimilco** or **Bosque de Chalpultepec.**

If you are interested in history, you can visit the **Museo Nacional de Antropología (National Museum of Anthropology).**

If you visit the city in February or March, you can see the running of the bulls in the **Plaza Mexico.**

Take a walk in the **Zócalo** to see the national palace and cathedral.

History

1500 BC The Pre-Classic period, used to date the earliest archaeological sites, begins. The Olmec civilization, the most advanced in Mesoamerica during this period, is considered the Mother of Mexican culture and begins to spread throughout the land.

800-400 BC La Venta, a major Olmec worship center, is built near **Veracruz** on the gulf coast.

500 BC After the decline of the Olmec, the Zapotec emerge and begin to build great ceremonial centers in **Oaxaca.**

100 BC Teotihuacán, the first major city in the Americas, is established and reigns as Mexico's most powerful settlement for the next six centuries.

AD 300 The Classic Period begins. The Maya are at their cultural peak, as are other civilizations throughout Mexico; the Maya's work in art, astronomy, and architecture rivals similar projects around the world.

700 Teotihuacán is completely deserted.

900 The Post-Classic period begins. The Toltec, who are dominant in the region north of **Mexico City,** begin waging wars. They overtake other societies. War becomes commonplace, as does human sacrifice.

1100 The Maya culture, under Toltec influences, spreads throughout the **Yucatán Peninsula.**

1300-1400 The Aztec come to prominence and build **Tenochtitlán,** their grand capital city, on **Lake Texcoco** in the valley of Mexico.

1492 As Christopher Columbus enters the New World, the Aztec Empire continues to grow.

1519 On a quest for slaves, Hernán Cortés and 600 soldiers land on the coast of **Veracruz.** They begin exploring and conquering Mexico.

1521 Cortés defeats the Aztec. Emperor Cuauhtemoc is executed, and Tenochtitlán falls after three months of fighting. Construction begins on the Spanish capital of Mexico in Mexico City.

1535 Spain's first viceroy lands, establishing a basic form of government and the beginning of the viceregal period, which lasts until 1820.

1547 Cortés dies.

1549 Friar Diego de Landa arrives in Yucatán. To rid the land of evil, he burns what he doesn't understand, destroying the history of the Maya.

1810 Father Miguel Hidalgo y Costilla declares independence from Spain, initiating a war. Creoles, Indians, and mestizos rise up in revolt in response to Hidalgo's *Grito de Dolores* (cry for freedom), named after the town of **Dolores,** where he was a pastor.

1821 Spain recognizes the independence of Mexico with the Treaty of Córdoba.

1822 A new constitution is drawn up and an elderly revolutionary general, who adopts the name Guadalupe Victoria, becomes Mexico's first president.

1828 Slavery of the various Indian groups, which began under the conquistadores, is abolished by Mexico's independent government.

1833 General Antonio López de Santa Anna becomes the wily and unscrupulous president/dictator.

1835 In what is now Texas, a small group of North Americans tries to gain independence from Mexico. Santa Anna fights back by leading an attack on the Alamo mission in San Antonio, Texas, where 150 Northerners are killed. In the following months, Mexican troops overrun Texas.

1836 Sam Houston's army defeats Santa Anna's troops at the Battle of San Jacinto, and Santa Anna signs the treaty making Texas a republic. But the Mexican government refuses to recognize the treaty; the issue is left unsettled.

1844 Santa Anna is driven into exile in Havana.

1845 The United States agrees to annex Texas, and US troops under General Zachary Taylor enter disputed territory north of the **Río Grande.**

1846 The United States declares war on Mexico.

1848 The Treaty of Hidalgo is ratified by the US Senate. Mexico cedes more than half of its territory, including Texas, California, and New Mexico, to the US for $15 million.

1853 Santa Anna returns from exile to become Mexico's dictator ("His Most Serene Highness").

1855 During the War of Reform, Santa Anna is forced to leave Mexico. Moderate and liberal politicians control the government, passing a law redistributing the vast landholdings of the church and another abolishing special privileges of the church and army. Benito Juárez, the former governor of his native state of **Oaxaca,** assumes the presidency and becomes Mexico's first Indian head of state.

1857 The new constitution promises a democratic representative government; freedom of speech, press, and religion; free education; and separation of church and state. A violent conservative reaction throws the country into civil war, unseating President Juárez and driving the liberal government from the capital.

1860 The last conservative armies are defeated in the War of Reform.

1861 Juárez returns to the capital and declares a moratorium on government debts; conservatives again force the leader into exile.

1862 After half a century of political chaos, during which time Mexican conservatives had lobbied in Europe for a puppet monarchy, the French land in Veracruz. Napoléon III's invading French army is repulsed in **Puebla** on 5 May by a poorly armed but inspired corps of about 5,000 (the event is commemorated annually with the Cinco de Mayo celebration). In September a renewed assault by the French succeeds in driving Juárez from the capital.

1864 Archduke Ferdinand Maximilian Joseph, of Hapsburg, accepts the crown as Emperor Maximilian I, under the protection of Napoléon III, and arrives in Mexico with his wife, Carlota.

1867 Under international pressure to support an independent government in Mexico, Napoléon pulls his troops out of the country. Maximilian makes a stand at **Querétaro;** three months later he surrenders and is executed. Juárez returns as president.

1872 After uniting the people of Mexico and successfully implementing reforms stated in the Constitution of 1857, Juárez dies of a heart attack.

1876 Porfirio Díaz leads a rebellion and gains the presidency. He serves for 34 years (except for a four-year period beginning in 1880, when he allows a friend to take over). His term is essentially a dictatorship, since reelections aren't permitted. This period, called the Porfiriato, is characterized by economic stability and social oppression.

1911 Porfirio Díaz retires to Paris. Francisco I. Madero becomes president in Mexico's first public election. Emiliano Zapata, Francisco "Pancho" Villa, and others begin the second Mexican revolution.

1913 Conservatives plot to bring down the Madero government and install Victoriano Huerta as president.

Madero and his vice president are shot. During Huerta's violent, 17-month dictatorship, many of his opponents are murdered or jailed. Revolutionary leaders garner armies and begin to raid and occupy properties.

1914 Huerta flees to the United States as revolutionary forces led by Alvaro Obregón and Venustiano Carranza enter Mexico City.

1917 A new constitution is signed and reconstruction begins.

1920 The weak Carranza administration ends after three years. Carranza flees north and is murdered by one of his officers.

The subsequent presidency of Alvaro Obregón marks the beginning of Mexico's stabilization. A series of handpicked successors to Obregón slowly implement dicta of the Constitution of 1917.

Great advances are made in education and culture. Politics blends with art in the murals of Diego Rivera, José Clemente Orozco, David Alfaro Siqueiros, and other artists commissioned by the education minister, José Vasconcelos.

1923 Pancho Villa is assassinated.

1926 Obregón's successor, Plutarco Elías Calles, closes all religious schools. After a hundred priests and nuns are deported, the priests go on strike and stop conducting services for three years.

1934 President Lázaro Cárdenas, who was elected after Calles's term ended, begins a period of reform, including redistributing more land to peasants. Many public works are constructed, government-sponsored farming operations are initiated, and the oil industry is nationalized.

1940 Conservative Manuel Avila Camacho, a Cárdenas protégé, becomes president. An era of political stability continues.

1946 Miguel Alemán becomes president. Among his many achievements is the construction of **University City.**

1952 Adolfo Ruíz Cortines becomes president.

1955 Women gain the right to vote.

1958 Adolfo López Mateos becomes president.

1964 Gustavo Díaz Ordaz becomes president.

1968 The **Summer Olympics** are held in Mexico City. Shortly before the games begin, 6,000 university students and their supporters assemble to protest social conditions. More than 10,000 armed soldiers break up the demonstration; over 300 people are killed, 500 wounded, and 1,500 arrested.

1970 Luis Echeverría Alvarez becomes president.

1974 Baja California Sur and **Quintana Roo** achieve statehood. The federal government establishes the **National Foundation for Tourism Development (FONATUR),** an agency devoted to expanding Mexico's tourism industry.

1976 José López Portillo becomes president.

1982 Miguel de la Madrid becomes president. The peso is devalued and unemployment grows, creating an economic panic.

1985 On 19 and 20 September, an earthquake and several aftershocks destroy parts of Mexico City, killing thousands of people and causing an estimated $4 billion in property damage.

1988 In a bitterly debated election, Carlos Salinas de Gortari becomes president with the smallest margin of votes for the PRI (50.3 percent) ever recorded.

The systematic expansion of tourist facilities continues; *maquiladores* (foreign assembly plants) proliferate along the Mexico-US border; foreign investment is encouraged and solicited.

1993 NAFTA (North American Free Trade Agreement) is ratified by the US Congress, creating a new economic partnership between Mexico, the United States, and Canada. The currency changes with the introduction of the New Peso.

1994 The Zapatista Army for National Liberation invades the colonial city of **San Cristóbal de las Casas** in the southern state of **Chiapas.** The Mexican Army drives the rebels from San Cristóbal; negotiations begin between the Zapatistas and the federal government continue for more than two years.

Luis Donaldo Colosio, PRI presidential candidate, is assassinated at a political rally in **Tijuana.** Other political parties, including the Partido Acción Nacional (PAN) and the Partido Revolucionario Democrático (PRD) gain strength in local and national elections. Ernesto Zedillo Ponce de Leon becomes the PRI candidate and is elected. In December, the peso is devalued shortly after Zedillo takes office.

1995 The peso plunges in value over the first three months and continues to fluctuate for the rest of the year. Interest rates soar, people of all classes lose their businesses and homes, and demonstrations in Mexico City become a daily event.

1996 Devaluation continues to wreak havoc with the Mexican economy.

1997 Several governors and state repesentatives are elected from opposition parties, and the PRI continues losing power. Mexico City holds its first mayoral elections; the voters choose Cuauhtémoc Cardenas Solorzano of the PRD. The economy improves steadily, though individual citizens see little improvement in their standard of living.

1998 Octavio Paz, one of Mexico's literary giants, dies. Government officials deport travelers considered to be contributing to political unrest in Chiapas. The US State Department issues a travel advisory regarding crime in Mexico.

Index

Restaurant Ratings

Only restaurants with star ratings are listed in the restaurant indexes below. All restaurants are listed alphabetically in each area's main index. Always call in advance to ensure a restaurant has not closed, changed its hours, or booked its tables for a private party. The restaurant price ratings are based on the average cost of an entrée for one person, excluding tax and tip.

★★★★ An Extraordinary Experience
★★★ Excellent
★★ Very Good
★ Good
$$$$ Big Bucks ($15 and up)
$$$ Expensive ($12-$15)
$$ Reasonable ($6-$12)
$ The Price Is Right (less than $6)

Hotel Ratings

The hotels listed in the hotel indexes below are grouped according to their price ratings; they are also listed in each area's main index. The hotel price ratings reflect the base price of a standard room for two people for one night during the peak season.

$$$$ Big Bucks ($150 and up)
$$$ Expensive ($100-$150)
$$ Reasonable ($50-$100)
$ The Price Is Right (less than $50)

Acapulco

Acapulco Restaurants

Index

Mexico City Restaurants

Page **Entry#** **Notes**

Credits

Writer and Project Editor
Maribeth Mellin

Researchers
Jon Grimaud
Jane Onstott

ACCESS®PRESS

Editorial Director
Lois Spritzer

Managing Editor
Laura L. Brengelman

Senior Editors
Mary Callahan
Beth Schlau

Associate Editor
Beatrice Aranow

Map Coordinator
Jonathan Goodnough

Editorial Assistant
Susan Cutter Snyder

Contributing Editors
Jay Rhoderick
Susan Walton

Executive Art Director
C. Linda Dingler

Design Supervisor
Joy O'Meara

Designer
Elizabeth Paige Streit

Map Designers
Patricia Keelin
Mark Stein Studios

Associate Director
of Production
Dianne Pinkowitz

Director, Electronic
Publishing
John R. Day

Special Thanks
Lourdes Arrellano
Mollie Glasser
Gary L. Grimaud

The publisher and authors assume no legal responsibility for the completeness or accuracy of the contents of this book nor any legal responsibility for the appreciation or depreciation in the value of any premises, commercial or otherwise, by reason of inclusion in or exclusion from this book. All contents are based on information available at the time of publication. Some of the maps are diagrammatic and may be selective of street inclusion.

ACCESS®Press does not solicit individuals, organizations, or businesses for inclusion in our books, nor do we accept payment for inclusion. We welcome, however, information from our readers, including comments, criticisms, and suggestions for new listings. Send all correspondence to: **ACCESS®**PRESS, 10 East 53rd Street, 5th Floor, New York, NY 10022

*Catedral
Metropolitana,
Mexico City*

PRINTED IN CANADA

ACCESS® Guides

Order by phone, toll-free: 1-800-331-3761

Name _____ Phone _____

Address _____

City _____ State _____ Zip _____

Please send me the following ACCESS® Guides:

☐ **ATLANTA** ACCESS® $18.50
0-06-277156-6

☐ **BOSTON** ACCESS® $19.00
0-06-277197-3

☐ **BUDGET EUROPE** ACCESS® $18.50
0-06-277171-X

☐ **CAPE COD, MARTHA'S VINEYARD, & NANTUCKET** ACCESS® $19.00
0-06-277220-1

☐ **CARIBBEAN** ACCESS® $20.00
0-06-277165-5

☐ **CHICAGO** ACCESS® $19.00
0-06-277196-5

☐ **CRUISE** ACCESS® $20.00
0-06-277190-6

☐ **FLORENCE & VENICE** ACCESS® $19.00
0-06-277222-8

☐ **GAY USA** ACCESS® $19.95
0-06-277212-0

☐ **HAWAII** ACCESS® $19.00
0-06-277223-6

☐ **LAS VEGAS** ACCESS® $19.00
0-06-277224-4

☐ **LONDON** ACCESS® $19.00
0-06-277225-2

☐ **LOS ANGELES** ACCESS® $19.00
0-06-277167-1

☐ **MEXICO** ACCESS® $19.00
0-06-277251-1

☐ **MIAMI & SOUTH FLORIDA** ACCESS® $19.00
0-06-277226-0

☐ **MINNEAPOLIS/ST. PAUL** ACCESS® $19.00
0-06-277234-1

☐ **MONTREAL & QUEBEC CITY** ACCESS® $19.00
0-06-277160-4

☐ **NEW ORLEANS** ACCESS® $19.00
0-06-277227-9

☐ **NEW YORK CITY** ACCESS® $19.00
0-06-277162-0

☐ **NEW YORK RESTAURANTS** ACCESS®
$13.00 0-06-277218-X

☐ **ORLANDO & CENTRAL FLORIDA** ACCESS®
$19.00
0-06-277228-7

☐ **PARIS** ACCESS® $19.00
0-06-277229-5

☐ **PHILADELPHIA** ACCESS® $19.00
0-06-277230-9

☐ **ROME** ACCESS® $19.00
0-06-277195-7

☐ **SAN DIEGO** ACCESS® $19.00
0-06-277185-X

☐ **SAN FRANCISCO** ACCESS® $19.00
0-06-277169-8

☐ **SAN FRANCISCO RESTAURANTS** ACCESS®
$13.00
0-06-277219-8

☐ **SANTA FE/TAOS/ALBUQUERQUE** ACCESS®
$19.00
0-06-277194-9

☐ **SEATTLE** ACCESS® $19.00
0-06-277198-1

☐ **SKI COUNTRY** ACCESS®
Eastern United States $18.50
0-06-277189-2

☐ **SKI COUNTRY** ACCESS®
Western United States $19.00
0-06-277174-4

☐ **WASHINGTON DC** ACCESS® $19.00
0-06-277232-5

☐ **WINE COUNTRY** ACCESS® France $19.00
0-06-277193-0

☐ **WINE COUNTRY** ACCESS® California $19.00
0-06-277164-7

Prices subject to change without notice.

Total for **ACCESS®** Guides:	$
Please add applicable sales tax:	
Add $4.00 for first book S&H, $1.00 per additional book:	
Total payment:	$

☐ Check or Money Order enclosed. Offer valid in the United States only.
Please make payable to HarperCollins*Publishers*.

☐ Charge my credit card ☐ American Express ☐ Visa ☐ MasterCard

Card no. _____ Exp. date _____

Signature _____

Send orders to: HarperCollins*Publishers*
P.O. Box 588
Dunmore, PA 18512-0588

ACCESS®
Makes the World Your Neighborhood

Access Destinations

- Atlanta
- Boston
- Budget Europe
- Cape Cod, Martha's Vineyard, & Nantucket
- Caribbean
- Chicago
- Cruise
- Florence & Venice
- Gay USA
- Hawaii
- Las Vegas
- London
- Los Angeles
- Mexico
- Miami & South Florida
- Minneapolis/St. Paul
- Montreal & Quebec City
- New Orleans
- New York City
- New York Restaurants
- Orlando & Central Florida
- Paris
- Philadelphia
- Rome
- San Diego
- San Francisco
- San Francisco Restaurants
- Santa Fe/Taos/Albuquerque
- Seattle
- Ski Country Eastern US
- Ski Country Western US
- Washington DC
- Wine Country France
- Wine Country California

Pack lightly and carry the best travel guides going: ACCESS. Arranged by neighborhood and featuring color-coded entries keyed to easy-to-read maps, ACCESS guides are designed to help you explore a neighborhood or an entire city in depth. You'll never get lost with an ACCESS guide in hand, but you may well be lost without one. So whether you are visiting Miami or Montreal, you'll need a sturdy pair of walking shoes and plenty of ACCESS.

HarperReference
A Division of HarperCollins*Publishers*